London

timeout.com/london

Time Out Guides Ltd
Universal House
251 Tottenham Court Road
London W1T 7AB
United Kingdom
Tel: +44 (0)20 7813 3000
Fax: +44 (0)20 7813 6001
Email: guides@timeout.com
www.timeout.com

Published by Time Out Guides Ltd, a wholly owned subsidiary of Time Out Group Ltd.
Time Out and the Time Out logo are trademarks of Time Out Group Ltd.

© Time Out Group Ltd 2009
Previous editions 1989, 1990, 1992, 1994, 1995, 1997, 1998, 1999, 2000, 2001, 2002, 2003, 2004,
2005, 2006, 2007, 2008.

10 9 8 7 6 5 4 3 2 1

This edition first published in Great Britain in 2009 by Ebury Publishing.
A Random House Group Company
20 Vauxhall Bridge Road, London SW1V 2SA

Random House Australia Pty Ltd 20 Alfred Street, Milsons Point, Sydney, New South Wales 2061, Australia

Random House New Zealand Ltd 18 Poland Road, Glenfield, Auckland 10, New Zealand

Random House South Africa (Pty) Ltd Isle of Houghton, Corner Boundary Road & Carse O'Gowrie, Houghton
2198, South Africa

Random House UK Limited Reg. No. 954009

For further distribution details, see www.timeout.com.

ISBN: 978-1-84670-071-2

A CIP catalogue record for this book is available from the British Library.

Printed and bound by Firmengruppe APPL, aprinta druck, Wemding, Germany.

The Random House Group Limited supports The Forest Stewardship Council (FSC), the leading international
forest certification organisation. All our titles that are printed on Greenpeace approved FSC certified paper
carry the FSC logo. Our paper procurement policy can be found at http://www.rbooks.co.uk/environment.

Time Out carbon-offsets its flights with Trees for Cities (www.treesforcities.org).

Contents

In Context — 15

History — **16**
London Today — **31**
Architecture — **34**
Look of London — **40**

Sights — 43

The South Bank & Bankside — **44**
The City — **57**
Holborn & Clerkenwell — **72**
Bloomsbury & Fitzrovia — **75**
Covent Garden & the Strand — **81**
Soho & Leicester Square — **88**
Oxford Street & Marylebone — **94**
Paddington & Notting Hill — **100**
Piccadilly Circus & Mayfair — **102**
Westminster & St James's — **107**
Chelsea — **117**
Knightsbridge & South Kensington — **120**
North London — **125**
East London — **133**
South-east London — **142**
South-west London — **151**
West London — **159**

Consume — 165

Hotels — **166**
Restaurants & Cafés — **197**
Pubs & Bars — **226**
Shops & Services — **241**

Arts & Entertainment — 267

Calendar — **268**
Art Galleries — **276**
Children — **284**
Comedy — **290**
Dance — **293**
Film — **296**
Gay & Lesbian — **300**
Music — **307**
Nightlife — **319**
Sport & Fitness — **327**
Theatre & Dance — **335**

Escapes & Excursions — 345

Escapes & Excursions — **346**
  Map: Escapes & Excursions — **347**

Directory — 359

Getting Around — **360**
Resources A-Z — **366**
Further Reference — **377**
Index — **379**
Advertisers' Index — **388**

Maps — 389

Overview Maps — **390**
Street Maps — **394**
London Underground — **416**

Introduction

Perhaps it was the human tree applying the final touches to his green make-up in the toilet mirror under St Paul's Covent Garden. Maybe it was the cartoon punks sat postcard-cliché perfect under Big Ben. Either way, researching this book reminded us how much we love this big, old, smelly and decidedly mixed-up city. It's a chaotic place, contradictory layers of history creating a brilliantly fumbled street plan. It's cussed, too: half the residents seem intransigent in their desire to preserve the place in amber, while the other half are as stubbornly insistent that it should become a 'modern' city (translation: 'a bit more like New York'). It's also famously expensive, especially when it comes to hotels.

Yet the rewards of a visit to London are incalculable. Those who say this isn't a beautiful city should have stood beside us on the top floor of 30 St Mary Axe one hazy summer's evening, looking out on the Thames over the 2,000-year-old City and sucking in a view that new skyscrapers have already altered. And if you fear the cost of coming here, you can console yourself with the amazing museums that are free to all: both Tates, the National Gallery, South Kensington neighbours the Natural History Museum, V&A and Science Museum… even the British Museum, granddaddy of them all.

Of course, a visit isn't solely about sights. For sustenance, London has most of the country's finest exponents of modern British cooking, a surprisingly delightful mix of simplicity and seasonality, as well as any number of international cuisines. In the bars, our cocktails rival New York's and our real ale surpasses any beer in the world. You'll certainly hit the shops, everything from vital markets to whimsical fashion parlours. And then there's culture, especially the city's constantly mutating music, theatre and nightlife scenes.

This is a big city – no matter how long you have here, it won't be enough. Use this guide first to help you select a handful of musts, then to lead you to search out some of the eccentricities and particularities that give London its real flavour. Give yourself time even to get a little lost in the city's vastness. Us? We're still searching and still getting lost (every Londoner is, even the cabbies), but we're also smitten by the city that we – that's everyone involved in making this book – call home. We hope you will be too. *Simon Coppock, Editor*

London in Brief

IN CONTEXT

With 2,000 years of history, London tries to present a sober face to visitors. Don't be fooled: from the strange motifs that lurk amid the architectural grandeur of St Paul's Cathedral to the performance oddballs working the gap between art and fashion, this is a city that treasures irreverence. Which may explain, as we try to in this series of essays, how we ended up with Boris Johnson as mayor.
► *For more, see pp16-42.*

SIGHTS

Some of London's attractions write their own headlines: the world-renowned British Museum or the marvellous art at the riverside Tates. But such major sights come nowhere near accounting for the city's wealth of attractions: within these pages, you'll also find everything from brutal modern architecture to ancient palaces, quirky museums to expansive parks.
► *For more, see pp44-164.*

CONSUME

The British reputation for lousy cooking is no longer fair, as a visit to St John, Great Queen Street and Hereford Road will prove. Nor is drinking all about old-timers such as Ye Old Mitre: look no further than newcomers such as the comfortably sleek Coburg Bar. Also in this section, you'll find a survey of the capital's shopping scene, along with reviews of more than 80 hotels.
► *For more, see pp166-265.*

ARTS & ENTERTAINMENT

London's music scene is famously lively, with new venues such as Kings Place enhancing already stellar options. Head to Shoreditch for clubs and the best gay nights, and to pretty much anywhere in town for contemporary art. Add compelling theatre (both fringe and mainstream), viciously exciting comedy and uniquely hybrid dance shows, and you have a cultural scene that's second to none.
► *For more, see pp268-344.*

ESCAPES & EXCURSIONS

When a man tires of London… he can always take to his skulls for a row along the Thames in a century old rowing skiff. If that sounds like hard work, breezy Brighton is an easy train ride from the city and nothing but boho fun. Other escapes covered here include austere Dungeness, medieval Canterbury and the sweet village of Woodstock, handily close to mighty Blenheim Palace.
► *For more, see pp346-358.*

London in 48 Hours

Day 1 Trafalgar, Tradition and the Thames

10AM Start the day in **Trafalgar Square** (*see p107*). The centre of London is an impressive sight, especially when it's not too full of tourists snapping themselves with the lions. The masterpieces of the **National Gallery** (*see p107*) are on the square's pedestrianised northern side.

10.45AM Head south down Whitehall, keeping an eye out for the cavalryman on sentry duty. You should arrive in time to see Horse Guards with shiny swords and helmets go through the daily **Changing of the Guard** (*see p271*; it's an hour earlier on Sunday). The **Household Cavalry Museum** (*see p115*) is just off the parade ground if you want to learn more; otherwise, head into **St James's Park** (*see p114*) to feed the ducks and admire **Buckingham Palace** (*see p114*) at the end of the lake; **Inn the Park** (*see p216*) is a convenient early stop-off if you're already peckish or flagging.

NOON Just out of the park's southern corner is Parliament Square. Admire the tobacco-yellow stone of **Westminster Abbey**, **Parliament** and **Big Ben** (*see pp111-112*), then cross Westminster Bridge for County Hall and the **London Eye** (*see p47*). This walk is modern London's biggest tourist cliché, but it's wonderful to stroll along the South Bank even with the hoi polloi. Busy places to eat surround the **Southbank Centre** (*see p309*).

3PM Go with the flow past **BFI Southbank** (*see p299*) and the **National Theatre** (*see p336*) to **Tate Modern** (*see p52*) and **Shakespeare's Globe** (*see p51*), and finish your afternoon by crossing the Millennium Bridge for the slow climb up to **St Paul's Cathedral** (*see p61*), handily close to St Paul's tube station.

7PM Enough history and culture. Head to Clerkenwell for brilliant food: modern British at **St John** (*see p202*) or finest fusion at the **Modern Pantry** (*see pp323-325*). Committed hedonists can also try London's coolest superclub **Fabric** (*see p321*) at weekends.

NAVIGATING THE CITY

London is a wonderful place to visit, but its size can be overwhelming. Don't worry: with a little understanding of the geography and transport, not to mention a reliable set of maps (*see pp390-407*), it becomes much easier to navigate.

The tube is the most straightforward way to get around town – you're rarely far from a station in central London. Mix your tube journeys with bus rides to get a handle on London's topography; free bus maps are available at many tube stations and from the Britain & London Visitor Centre (*see p374*). And don't forget the river: commuter and tourist boats run all day on the Thames. For more on travel, and on guided tours, *see pp360-365*.

SEEING THE SIGHTS

To escape queues and overcrowding, try to avoid visiting major attractions at the weekend – and using any form of public transport during rush hour (roughly

Day 2 Culture and Clubbing from West to East

10AM Start at one of the world's finest museums – early enough to avoid the crowds. The **British Museum** (*see p77*) is so full of treasures you won't know where to begin, but turn left out of the spectacular central courtyard and the monumental antiquities won't disappoint.

NOON Wander south to the boutiques dotted around Seven Dials until lunch. **Great Queen Street** (*see p206*) is a good option if you didn't try St John last night; **Wahaca** (*see p208*) and **Food for Thought** (*see p206*) are handy on a budget. Covent Garden market is here, but the excellent **London Transport Museum** (*see p82*) and inspiringly opulent **Royal Opera House** (*see p311*) are the principal reasons to linger.

3PM Covent Garden station puts you on the right tube line for South Kensington's trio of superb museums: at this time of day, we recommend the quieter **V&A** (*see p122*), but parents should let themselves be bullied into the **Natural History Museum** (*see p121*) or **Science Museum** (*see p122*). If there's still some walking left in you after yesterday, head to the **Albert Memorial** (*see p121*) and the understated **Serpentine Gallery** (*see p124*).

7PM By now you need food. If you declined Exhibition Road, take on a sturdy refuel at **Tom's Place** (*see p217*); if you're in the park, keep north to **Le Café Anglais** (*see p218*).

9PM Those with energy left should head to the Central (red) underground line. Grown-ups turn west: **Notting Hill Gate** is the place for civilised – or, at least, sleek – cocktailing (*see p233*). Hip kids and the young at heart turn east: Liverpool Street station is the gateway to bleakly nondescript **Shoreditch**. Yes, the edgiest and artiest are migrating north and east, but you'll still find enough bars (*see p238*), clubs (*see pp323-325*) and rakishly hatted youths to give you a feel for what all the fuss has been about over the last decade. If it isn't as cutting-edge as it was, it's far easier to find a seat to watch the crazies and wannabes.

8-9.30am and 4.30-7pm, Monday to Friday). Many attractions, including all the big museums, offer free admission, so if you're on a budget you can tick off large numbers of places on your must-see list just for the price of getting there.

We've given last-entry times where they precede an attraction's official closing time by more than an hour. Some smaller venues may close early when they're quiet, and many places close all day on certain public holidays (notably Christmas and Easter). Always phone ahead before making a special trip.

PACKAGE DEALS
The **London Pass** (www.londonpass. com) gives pre-paid access to more than 50 sights and attractions. Unless you're prepared to visit several sights a day for four or five days, you're unlikely to get your money's worth. However, you will be able to jump the queues at such ultra-popular sights as the Tower of London.

London in Profile

THE SOUTH BANK & BANKSIDE
Running along the Thames from the London Eye to Gabriel's Wharf, the **South Bank** is the centre of the nation's arts scene. Directly east is **Bankside**, which has recently risen to prominence thanks to Tate Modern and Borough Market.
▶ *For more, see pp44-56.*

THE CITY
Reminders of London's long, ramshackle and occasionally great history jostle with latter-day citadels of high finance in the City, the fascinating 'square mile' (it's actually slightly over a mile) that essentially *was* London for centuries.
▶ *For more, see pp57-71.*

HOLBORN & CLERKENWELL
Just west of the City lie two different, distinct locales. Quietly historic **Clerkenwell** boasts some of London's best bars and restaurants. Adjacent **Holborn**, meanwhile, is the city's legal quarter, and sits on the fringes of London's West End.
▶ *For more, see pp72-74.*

BLOOMSBURY & FITZROVIA
North-west of Holborn, literary **Bloomsbury** draws millions to the British Museum, but the nearby, restaurant-packed area of **Fitzrovia** concerns itself only with its media-industry locals. North of Bloomsbury is fast-improving **King's Cross**.
▶ *For more, see pp75-80.*

COVENT GARDEN & THE STRAND
Covent Garden, just south of Bloomsbury, is a genuine visitor-magnet: tourists adore its open-plan piazza and wearingly cheery street entertainers. Between here and the Thames lies the traffic-choked, theatre-lined **Strand**.
▶ *For more, see pp81-87.*

SOHO & LEICESTER SQUARE
The hub of London's West End, **Soho** is London's most notorious district. These days, it's far more civilised than its naughty reputation suggests, but is still fun to wander. Just south sit bustling **Chinatown** and touristy **Leicester Square**.
▶ *For more, see pp88-93.*

OXFORD STREET & MARYLEBONE
London's shoppers get to choose from countless different shopping areas, but chain-heavy **Oxford Street** is where most of the money is spent. Oxford Street separates Soho and Mayfair from Fitzrovia and **Marylebone**, an agreeably villagey district dotted with boutiques and restaurants.
▶ *For more, see pp94-99.*

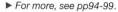

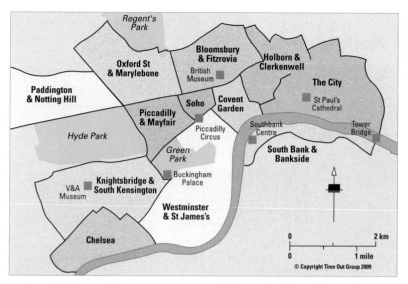

© Copyright Time Out Group 2009

PADDINGTON & NOTTING HILL

Millions have been spent on improving north-westerly **Paddington** in recent years, but it isn't there yet. Better to head further west into moneyed, cultured **Notting Hill**.
▶ *For more, see pp100-101.*

PICCADILLY & MAYFAIR

The flashing neon beguiles small-town tourists, but **Piccadilly Circus** is little more than a charmless traffic island nowadays. Instead of lingering there, stroll west into **Mayfair**, home to London's most upmarket shops and prestigious hotels.
▶ *For more, see pp102-106.*

WESTMINSTER & ST JAMES'S

With the northern edge pedestrianised, Trafalgar Square is as pleasant as it's ever been. Go south and you'll find yourself in historic **Westminster**, the home of government; go south-west and you'll reach immaculate, aristocratic **St James's**.
▶ *For more, see pp107-116.*

CHELSEA

Chelsea starts in earnest at Sloane Square, before stretching west and ebbing outwards off the shop-lined King's Road. Its southern border is the Thames.
▶ *For more, see pp117-119.*

KNIGHTSBRIDGE & SOUTH KENSINGTON

Knightsbridge draws devotees with a welter of high-class, high-priced shops. Adjoining **South Kensington** is where the throngs pile into London's three palatial Victorian museums.
▶ *For more, see pp120-124.*

Time Out
Travel Guides

Worldwide

All our guides are
written by a team of
local experts with
a unique and stylish
insider perspective.
We offer essential tips,
trusted advice and
honest reviews for
everything you need
to know in the city.

Over 50 destinations
available at all good
bookshops and at
timeout.com/shop

Time Out
Guides

Editorial

Editor Simon Coppock
Deputy Editor Charlie Godfrey-Faussett
Copy Editors Nicola Homer, Holly Pick
Listings Editors Shane Armstrong, Carol Baker,
  Alex Brown, Gemma Pritchard
Proofreader Mandy Martinez
Indexer Ismay Atkins

Managing Director Peter Fiennes
Editorial Director Ruth Jarvis
Series Editor Will Fulford-Jones
Business Manager Dan Allen
Editorial Manager Holly Pick
Assistant Management Accountant Ija Krasnikova

Design

Art Director Scott Moore
Art Editor Pinelope Kourmouzoglou
Senior Designer Henry Elphick
Graphic Designers Kei Ishimaru, Nicola Wilson
Advertising Designer Jodi Sher

Picture Desk

Picture Editor Jael Marschner
Deputy Picture Editor Lynn Chambers
Picture Researcher Gemma Walters
Picture Desk Assistant Marzena Zoladz
Picture Librarian Christina Theisen

Advertising

Commercial Director Mark Phillips
Advertising Sales Manager Alison Wallen
Sales Executives Ben Holt, Alex Matthews,
  Jason Trotman
Display Production Manager Sally Webb

Marketing

Marketing Manager Yvonne Poon
**Sales & Marketing Director, North America &
  Latin America** Lisa Levinson
Senior Publishing Brand Manager Luthfa Begum
Marketing Designer Anthony Huggins

Production

Group Production Director Mark Lamond
Production Manager Brendan McKeown
Production Controller Damian Bennett
Production Coordinator Julie Pallot

Time Out Group

Chairman Tony Elliott
Group General Manager/Director Nichola Coulthard
Time Out Communications Ltd MD David Pepper
Time Out International Ltd MD Cathy Runciman
Group IT Director Simon Chappell
Head of Marketing Catherine Demajo

Contributors

Introduction Simon Coppock. **History** Charlie Godfrey-Faussett. **London Today** Peter Watts. **Architecture** Simon Coppock. **Look of London** Jonathan Derbyshire (*Would You Look at Him?* Simone Baird). **Sights** Joe Bindloss, Simon Coppock, Charlie Godfrey-Faussett, Ronnie Haydon, Daniel Kramb, John Lewis (*Art with an Edge* Jonathan Derbyshire; *Born of Flames* Charlie Godfrey-Faussett; *The New City* Jessica Cargill-Thompson; *Spiv City* Peter Watts; *Back Streets* Helen Walasek; *Green Thought* Patrick Mulkern; *Renaissance Whitechapel* Martin Coomer; *House of Science, England's Galileo* Anna Faherty; additional reviews Patrick Welch). **Hotels** Simon Coppock, Helen Walasek (*No More Bed Bugs* Alice Malivoire; additional reviews Charlie Godfrey-Faussett, Ismay Atkins). **Restaurants & Cafés** contributors to *Time Out Eating & Drinking* (*Quality Fast Food, Eating In… and Eating Out, A Little of What You Fancy?* Charmaine Mok; *Profile* Charlie Godfrey-Faussett). **Pubs & Bars** contributors to *Time Out Bars, Pubs & Clubs* (*Profile, Good Mixers* Charlie Godfrey-Faussett). **Shops & Services** contributors to *Time Out Shopping & Services* (*Things Are What They Used to Be* Ismay Atkins; *Mount Street, Now You See Them* Jo Monk). **Calendar** Helen Walasek (*Standing on Ceremony* Charlie Godfrey-Faussett; *Christmas Markets* Jo Monk). **Art Galleries** Martin Coomer. **Children** Ronnie Haydon. **Comedy** Tim Arthur, Simon Coppock (*Profile* Charlie Godfrey-Faussett). **Dance** Tim Benzie. **Film** Helen Walasek (*Some Like It Short* David Jenkins). **Gay & Lesbian** Tim Benzie (*Reading Between the Lines* Paul Burston). **Music** John Lewis. **Nightlife** Kate Hutchinson (*What's the Matter?* John Lewis). **Sport & Fitness** Tom Davies. **Theatre** Caroline McGinn (*In the Pound Seats* Alice Malivoire, Caroline McGinn). **Escapes & Excursions** contributors to *Time Out Weekend Breaks* (*Dreamy Father Thames* Simon Coppock). **Directory** Shane Armstrong. The Editor would like to thank all contributors to previous editions of *Time Out London* and *Time Out* magazine, whose work forms the basis for parts of this book.

Maps john@jsgraphics.co.uk, except: page 416.

Photography Jonathan Perugia, except: page 3 David Axelbank; pages 4, 8 (Covent Garden), 56, 76, 103, 109, 122, 267, 296, 310 Andrew Brackenbury; pages 5 (St Paul's Cathedral), 36, 62 Peter Smith; pages 6, 8 (Bloomsbury), 9 (Mayfair), 36, 41, 52, 303, 138, 170, 171, 189, 197, 201, 203, 207, 220 222, 223, 246, 249, 257 Britta Jaschinski; pages 7, 9 (South Kensington) 58, 123, 211 Michael Franke; pages 9 (Notting Hill) 100, 319 Alys Tomlinson; page 16 akg-images; page 19 Museum of London; page 31 Getty Images; page 38 Andreas Schmidt; page 45 Abigail Lelliott; page 48 Stephen White; pages 49, 121 Simon Leigh; page 52 Belinda Lawley; page 55 Bridgeman Art Library; pages 71, 80, 82, 186, 208, 219, 290, 346, 348 Rob Greig; pages 82, 359 Ed Marshall; page 89 Paul Mattson; pages 89, 135 Simon Leigh; pages 99, 115 Martyn J Brooks; pages 125, 141 Nick Ballon; pages 142, 349 Scott Wishart; pages 143, 160 Tricia de Courcy Ling; pages 144, 151, 233 Anthony Webb; pages 145, 284 Tove K Breitstein; pages 152, 180, 307, 309 Olivia Rutherford; page 155 Mischa Haller; page 158 Jonas Rodin; pages 159, 285, 300, 301, 327, 334 Heloise Bergman; pages 166, 169, 173 Heike Bohnstengel; pages 209, 214, 226, 227, 240, 242 Ming-Tang Evans; pages 212, 262, 265 Michelle Grant; pages 229, 234 Hayley Harrison; pages 241, 252 Elisabeth Blanchet; pages 272 J McPhilimey; pages 268, 271 HQ Land Command Forces; page 275 Fiona Campbell; page 288 Susannah Stone; page 291 Kris Tunmore; page 293 Patrick Baldwin; page 313 Oliver Knight; page 320 Rogan Macdonald; page 329 Tim Motion; page 330 Pete Goding; page 353 Tim Stubbings. The following images were provided by the featured establishments/artists: pages 42, 312, 133, 286, 323, 152, 157, 176, 190, 277, 294, 336, 340, 232, 239, 348 354, 355, 260, 269, 270, 274.

About the Guide

GETTING AROUND

The back of the book contains street maps of London, as well as overview maps of the city and its surroundings. The maps start on page 389; on them are marked the locations of hotels (**❶**), restaurants and cafés (**❶**), and pubs and bars (**❶**). The majority of businesses listed in this guide are located in the areas we've mapped; the grid-square references in the listings refer to these maps.

THE ESSENTIALS

For practical information, including visas, disabled access, emergency numbers, lost property, useful websites and local transport, please see the Directory. It begins on page 360.

THE LISTINGS

Addresses, phone numbers, websites, transport information, hours and prices are all included in our listings, as are selected other facilities. All were checked and correct at press time. However, business owners can alter their arrangements at any time, and fluctuating economic conditions can cause prices to change rapidly.

The very best venues in the city, the must-sees and must-dos in every category, have been marked with a red star (★). In the Sights chapters, we've also marked venues with free admission with a **FREE** symbol.

PHONE NUMBERS

The area code for London is 020. You don't need to use the code when calling from within London: simply dial the eight-digit number as listed in this guide.

From outside the UK, dial your country's international access code (011 from the US) or a plus symbol, followed by the UK country code (44), 20 for London (dropping the initial zero) and the eight-digit number as listed in the guide. So, to reach the British Museum, dial +44 20 7323 8000. For more on phones, including information on calling abroad from the UK and details of local mobile-phone access, *see p374*.

FEEDBACK

We welcome feedback on this guide, both on the venues we've included and on any other locations that you'd like to see featured in future editions. Please email us at guides@timeout.com.

Time Out Guides

Founded in 1968, Time Out has grown from humble beginnings into the leading resource for anyone wanting to know what's happening in the world's greatest cities. Alongside our influential weeklies in London, New York and Chicago, we publish more than 20 magazines in cities as varied as Beijing and Beirut; a range of travel books, with the City Guides now joined by the newer Shortlist series; and an information-packed website. The company remains proudly independent, still owned by Tony Elliott four decades after he launched *Time Out London*.

Written by local experts and illustrated with original photography, our books also retain their independence. No business has been featured because it has advertised, and all restaurants and bars are visited and reviewed anonymously.

ABOUT THE EDITOR

Based in east London, **Simon Coppock** has edited a variety of books about London for Time Out, and has also written travel pieces on his favourite city for the *Sunday Times* and the *Sunday Telegraph*.

A full list of the book's contributors can be found opposite. However, we've also included details of our writers in selected chapters through the guide.

In Context

St Paul's Cathedral.
See p36.

History **16**
Roman London **19**
Tudor London **20**
Stuart London **25**
Victorian London **26**
Post-war London **29**
Key Events **30**

London Today **31**
Welcome to London? **33**

Architecture **34**
Profile St Paul's Cathedral **36**

Look of London **40**
Would You Look At Him? **42**

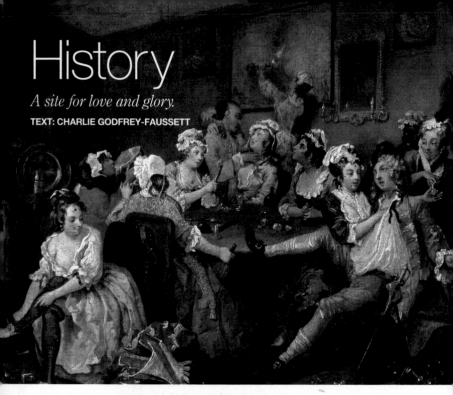

History

A site for love and glory.

TEXT: CHARLIE GODFREY-FAUSSETT

London is getting on for two millennia as a port, market, fort, seat of government and meeting place. Founded in AD 43 with the arrival of the Romans, Londinium became one of the most prosperous places in the empire. But, despite its long and rich history, the modern city is defined in no small part by three events that occurred in quick succession during the mid 17th century: in 1663, the first theatre opened on Drury Lane; two years later, the Great Plague killed 60,000, causing an exodus of the gentry to outlying districts; and in 1666, the Great Fire destroyed the medieval City of London. Together, these three events explain much of the character of latter-day London.

As a result of the Fire, the city was rebuilt in brick and stone, but dramatic expansion only occurred in the 19th century: along with Queen Victoria, the railways arrived, and the first underground line opened in 1863. Then, during World War II, the furious aerial bombardment of the Blitz again threatened London's survival. It wasn't until the start of the cultural revolution of the 1960s that the city recovered its exuberance. The seeds were sown of the extraordinary multicultural phenomenon that is the modern capital, its history still being rewritten with each new arrival.

LONDINIUM

While the capital's size and rapid expansion have long fascinated visitors, the city's origins are much less grand. Celtic tribes lived in scattered communities along the banks of the Thames before the Romans arrived in Britain, but no evidence suggests that there was a settlement on the site of the future metropolis before the invasion of the Emperor Claudius in AD 43. During the Roman conquest of the country, they forded the Thames at its shallowest point (near today's London Bridge) and, later, built a timber bridge here. A settlement developed on the north side of this crossing.

Over the next two centuries, the Romans constructed roads, towns and forts in the area. Progress was halted in AD 61 when Boudicca, the widow of an East Anglian chieftain, rebelled against the imperial forces who had seized her land, flogged her and raped her daughters. She led the Iceni in a savage revolt, destroying the Roman colony at Colchester before marching on London. The Romans were massacred and their settlement razed.

After order was restored, the town was rebuilt; around AD 200, a two-mile, 18-foot wall was put up around it. Chunks of the wall survive today; early names of the original gates – Ludgate, Newgate, Bishopsgate and Aldgate – are preserved on the map of the modern city. The street known as London Wall traces part of its original course. But by the fourth century, racked by barbarian invasions and internal strife, the Roman Empire was in decline. In 410, the last troops were withdrawn and London became a ghost town.

CHRISTIANITY ARRIVES IN LUNDENWIC

During the fifth and sixth centuries, history gives way to legend. The Saxons crossed the North Sea and settled in eastern and southern England. Pope Gregory then sent Augustine to convert the English to Christianity in 596; Mellitus, one of his missionaries, was appointed the first Bishop of London, and founded a wooden cathedral dedicated to St Paul inside the old city walls in 604.

London continued to expand; writing in 731, the Venerable Bede described 'Lundenwic' as 'the mart of many nations resorting to it by land and sea'. But during the ninth century, the city faced a new danger: the Vikings. The city was ransacked in 841 and 851, when the Danish raiders returned with 350 ships. It was not until 886 that King Alfred of Wessex – aka Alfred the Great – regained the city, re-establishing London as a major trading centre with a merchant navy and new wharfs at Billingsgate and Queenhithe.

Throughout the tenth century the city was prospering. Churches were built, parishes established and markets set up. However, the 11th century brought more harassment from the Vikings, and the English were forced to accept a Danish king, Cnut (Canute, 1016-35), during whose reign London replaced Winchester as the capital of England.

After a brief spell under Danish rule, the country's throne reverted to an Englishman in 1042: Edward the Confessor, by many accounts a saintly man who devoted himself to building England's grandest church two miles west of the City on an island in the river marshes at Thorney (meaning 'the isle of brambles'). Edward replaced the timber church of St Peter's with a huge abbey, 'the West Minster' (Westminster Abbey; consecrated in December 1065), and moved his court to the new Palace of Westminster. Just a week after the consecration, he died. But London now had two hubs: Westminster, the centre of the royal court, government and law, and the City of London, the commercial centre.

WILLIAM EARNS HIS NICKNAME

On Edward's death, William, Duke of Normandy, was crowned king on Christmas Day 1066, having defeated Edward's brother-in-law Harold at the Battle of Hastings. William immediately realised the need to win over the prosperous City merchants by negotiation rather than force, and granted the burgesses and the Bishop of London a charter – still kept at Guildhall – that acknowledged their rights and independence in return for taxes. But, 'against the fickleness of the vast and fierce population', he also ordered strongholds to be built at the city wall, including the White Tower (the tallest building in the Tower of London) and the now-lost Baynard's Castle at Blackfriars.

TIME TO VISIT GREENWICH
THREE MUSEUMS FOR FREE
ONE BREATHTAKING VIEW

Just 20 minutes from central London

Museums open daily

Cutty Sark Zone 2   Greenwich Zone 2   Greenwich Pier

Maritime GREENWICH
A WORLD HERITAGE SITE

'Relations between the monarch and the City were never easy.'

PARLIAMENT AND RIGHTS

The Model Parliament, which agreed the principles of government, was held at Westminster Hall in 1295, presided over by Edward I and attended by barons, clergy and representatives of knights and burgesses. The first step towards establishing personal rights and political liberty – not to mention curbing the power of the king – had already been taken in 1215 with the signing of the Magna Carta by King John. Then, in the 14th century, subsequent assemblies gave rise to the House of Lords (which met at the Palace of Westminster) and the House of Commons (which met in the Chapter House at Westminster Abbey). The king and his court had frequently travelled the kingdom during the 12th and 13th centuries, but now the Palace of Westminster was the seat of law and government; noblemen and bishops began to build themselves palatial houses along the Strand from the City to Westminster, with gardens that stretched down to the river.

Relations between the monarch and the City were never easy. Londoners closely guarded their privileges, and resisted attempts by kings to squeeze money out of them to finance wars and construction projects. Subsequent kings were forced to turn to Jewish and Lombard moneylenders, but the City merchants were as intolerant of foreigners as of the royals. Rioting, persecution and lynching were commonplace in medieval London.

The self-regulation privileges granted to the City merchants under Norman kings were extended by the monarchs who followed, in return for finance. In 1191, during the reign of Richard I, the City of London was formally recognised as a commune, or a self-governing

IN CONTEXT

Roman London

Where to see how London lived.

Although riverside settlements pre-date the arrival of the Romans, it was their bridging of the Thames and building of Londinium from AD 43 that marks the birth of the city proper. Physical traces of their time here are now rare, although the City does have the grubby, flat mess of stone that is all that remains of the **Temple of Mithras** (*see p65*).

The amphitheatre in the basement of the **Guildhall Art Gallery** (*see p67*) is more fun, with sound effects and quaint illuminated figures to feed the imagination. However, the key venues are the **British Museum** (*see pp76-77*) and the **Museum of London** (*see p63*), which both have great collections of artefacts, masonry and domestic objects. The latter is focused more tightly on London, with fabulous mosaics (*pictured*) and reconstructed rooms.

Tudor London

Where to see how London lived.

For the 500th anniversary of Henry VIII's accession, **Hampton Court Palace** (*see p157*) and the **Tower of London** (*see p71*) will both be hosting special events and grand exhibitions. But head also to Westminster and the church of **St Margaret** (*see p112*). Here, as well as memorials to Tudor luminaries like first British printer William Caxton and adventurer Sir Walter Raleigh, the east window (*pictured*) catches the eye: it commemorates the betrothal of Catherine of Aragon and… Arthur, Henry VIII's elder brother. Arthur's premature death meant Henry 'inherited' the throne, the first of his six brides and this window.

community; six years later, it won control of the Thames (which included lucrative fishing rights, retained by the City until 1857). In 1215, King John confirmed the city's right 'to elect every year a mayor', a position of great authority with power over the Sheriff and the Bishop of London. A month later, the mayor joined the rebel barons in signing the Magna Carta.

Over the next two centuries, the power and influence of the trade and craft guilds (later known as the City Livery Companies) increased as trade with Europe grew, and the wharfs by London Bridge were crowded with imported goods. The City's markets, already established, drew produce from miles around: livestock at Smithfield, fish at Billingsgate and poultry at Leadenhall. The street markets, or 'cheaps', around Westcheap (now Cheapside) and Eastcheap were crammed with a variety of goods. As commerce increased, foreign traders and craftsmen settled around the port; the population within the city wall grew from about 18,000 in 1100 to well over 50,000 in the 1340s.

THE PEASANTS ARE REVOLTING

Lack of hygiene became a serious problem. Water was provided in cisterns at Cheapside and elsewhere, but the supply, which came more or less direct from the Thames, was limited and polluted. Houndsditch was so named because Londoners threw their dead animals into the furrow that formed the City's eastern boundary; and in the streets around Smithfield (the Shambles), butchers dumped animal entrails in the gutters.

These appalling conditions provided the breeding ground for the greatest catastrophe of the Middle Ages: the Black Death of 1348 and 1349, which killed about 30 per cent of England's population. The plague came to London from Europe, carried by rats on ships, and was to recur in London several times during the next three centuries.

Disease left the harvests short-handed, causing unrest among the peasants whose labour was in such demand. The imposition of a poll tax of a shilling a head proved the final straw, leading to the Peasants' Revolt of 1381. Thousands marched on London, led by Jack Straw from Essex and Wat Tyler from Kent; the Archbishop of Canterbury was murdered and hundreds of prisoners were set free. When the 14-year-old Richard II rode out to face the rioters, Wat Tyler was fatally stabbed by the Lord Mayor; other ringleaders were subsequently rounded up and hanged. But no more poll taxes were imposed.

ROSES, WIVES AND BLOODY MARY

Spurred by the discovery of America and the ocean routes to Africa and the Orient, London became one of Europe's largest cities under the Tudors (1485-1603). But the growth was not without its hiccups under Henry VIII, the second Tudor monarch. Henry's first marriage to Catherine of Aragon failed to produce an heir, so in 1527 the King determined the union should be annulled. When the Pope refused to co-operate, Henry defied the Catholic Church, demanding to be recognised as Supreme Head of the Church in England and ordering the execution of anyone who opposed the plan (including his chancellor Sir Thomas More). England began the transition to Protestantism, and the subsequent dissolution of the monasteries transformed the face of the medieval city.

On a more positive note, Henry found time to develop a professional navy, founding the Royal Dockyards at Woolwich in 1512. He also established palaces at Hampton Court and Whitehall, and built a residence at St James's Palace. Much of the land he annexed for hunting became the Royal Parks, including Greenwich, Hyde and Regent's Parks.

RENAISSANCE REBIRTH

Elizabeth I's reign (1558-1603) saw the founding of the Royal Exchange by Sir Thomas Gresham in 1566, which allowed London to emerge as Europe's commercial hub. Merchant venturers and the first joint-stock companies established new trading enterprises, as adventuring seafarers Francis Drake, Walter Raleigh and Richard Hawkins sailed to the New World and beyond. As trade grew, so did London: it was home to some 200,000 people in 1600, many living in dirty, overcrowded conditions. The most complete picture of Tudor London is given in John Stow's *Survey of London* (1598), a fascinating first-hand account by a diligent Londoner whose monument stands in the church of St Andrew Undershaft.

These were the glory days of English drama. The Rose (1587) and the Globe (1599, now recreated; see p337), were erected at Bankside, providing homes for the works of popular playwrights Christopher Marlowe and William Shakespeare. Deemed officially 'a naughty place' by royal proclamation, 16th-century Bankside was a vibrant mix of entertainment and sport (bear-baiting, cock-fighting), drinking and whoring, all within easy reach of the City (which outlawed theatres in 1575).

In 1605, two years after the Tudor dynasty ended with Elizabeth's death, her Stuart successor, James I, narrowly escaped assassination on 5 November, when Guy Fawkes was discovered underneath the Palace of Westminster. The Gunpowder Plot was hatched in protest at the failure to improve conditions for the persecuted Catholics, but only resulted in an intensification of anti-papist sentiment. The non-event is commemorated as Bonfire Night even now, the burning of Guy in effigy celebrated with cheery fireworks.

IN CONTEXT

LET'S FILL THIS TOWN WITH ARTISTS

EASELS

£39.95
DALER-ROWNEY
COTSWOLD
STUDIO EASEL
RRP £113

LESS THAN HALF PRICE

£12.95
WINSOR & NEWTON
DART SKETCHING EASEL
RRP £39.99

70% OFF

PAINTS

WINSOR & NEWTON
14ML ARTISTS WATERCOLOUR

UP TO 40% OFF

DALER-ROWNEY
SYSTEM 3 250ML ACRYLIC
ALL HALF PRICE

HALF PRICE

WINSOR & NEWTON
ARTIST OIL 37ML

UP TO 40% OFF

BRUSHES

£12.95
CASS ART HOG BRUSH
PACK SET OF 6 RRP £18.95

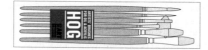

CANVAS

WINSOR & NEWTON
ARTIST QUALITY CANVAS
OVER 60 SIZES

HALF PRICE

SETS AND GIFTS

HALF PRICE

£9.95
WINSOR & NEWTON 8X14ML
DRAWING INKS SET RRP £19.95

A4 - £3.95
A5 - £2.95
DALER-ROWNEY EBONY
HARDBACK SKETCH PAD
RRP (A4) £8.95, (A5) £6.55

LESS THAN HALF PRICE

£5.25
FABER-CASTELL 9000 12 ART
PENCILS 8B-2H IN TIN RRP £10.50

HALF PRICE

£13.50
LETRASET MANGA PACK
RRP £31.86

LESS THAN HALF PRICE

CASS PROMISE – CREATIVITY AT THE LOWEST PRICES. WE'RE CONFIDENT OUR PRICES CAN'T BE BEATEN

FLAGSHIP STORE: 66-67 COLEBROOKE ROW
ISLINGTON N1 020 7354 2999

ALSO AT: 13 CHARING CROSS ROAD WC2 (NEXT TO THE NATIONAL GALLERY)
220 KENSINGTON HIGH STREET W8 AND 24 BERWICK STREET W1
ALL STORES OPEN 7 DAYS WWW.CASSART.CO.UK

CASS ART LONDON

PRICE SUBJECT TO CHANGE AND AVAILABILITY. PRICES VALID AT 01/11/08.

James I is also remembered for hiring Inigo Jones to design court masques (musical dramas) and the first beautiful and influential examples of classical Renaissance style in London. The Queen's House (1616; *see p147*), the Banqueting House (1619; *see p111*) and St Paul's, Covent Garden (1631; *see p83*) are all still standing today.

ROYALISTS AND ROUNDHEADS

Charles I succeeded his father in 1625, but gradually fell out of favour with the City of London and an increasingly independent-minded Parliament over taxation. The country slid into civil war (1642-49) between the supporters of Parliament (the Roundheads, led by Puritan Oliver Cromwell) and the supporters of the King (the Royalists).

Both sides knew that control of the country's major city and port was vital for victory, and London's sympathies were firmly with the Parliamentarians. In 1642, 24,000 citizens assembled at Turnham Green to face Charles's army, but the king withdrew. The move proved fatal: Charles never threatened the capital again, and was eventually was found guilty of treason. Taken to the Banqueting House in Whitehall on 30 January 1649, he declared himself a 'martyr of the people' and was beheaded. A commemorative wreath is still laid at the site of the execution on the last Sunday in January each year.

For the next 11 years, the country was ruled as a Commonwealth by Cromwell. But his son Richard's subsequent rule was brief: due to the Puritan closing of theatres, banning of Christmas (a Catholic superstition) and strictures on any sort of fun, the restoration of the exiled Charles II in 1660 was greeted with great rejoicing. The Stuart King had Cromwell exhumed from Westminster Abbey, and his body was hung in chains at Tyburn. His severed head was displayed on a pole outside the abbey until 1685.

PLAGUE, FIRE AND REVOLUTION

The year 1665 saw the most serious outbreak of bubonic plague since the Black Death, killing nearly 100,000 Londoners had died. Then, on 2 September 1666, a second disaster struck. The fire that spread from a carelessly tended oven in Thomas Farriner's baking shop on Pudding Lane raged for three days and consumed four-fifths of the City.

The Great Fire at least allowed planners the chance to rebuild London as a modern city. Many blueprints were considered, but Londoners were so impatient to get on with business that the City was reconstructed largely on its medieval street plan (albeit in brick and stone rather than wood). The prolific Sir Christopher Wren oversaw work on 51 of the 54 rebuilt churches. Among them was his masterpiece: the new St Paul's (*see p61*), completed in 1710 and effectively the world's first Protestant cathedral.

In the wake of the Great Fire, many well-to-do City dwellers moved to new residential developments west of the old quarters, an area subsequently known as the West End. In the City, the Royal Exchange was rebuilt, but merchants increasingly used the new coffeehouses to exchange news. With the expansion of the joint-stock companies and the chance to invest capital, the City emerged as a centre not of manufacturing, but of finance.

Anti-Catholic feeling still ran high. The accession in 1685 of Catholic James II aroused such fears of a return to papistry that a Dutch Protestant, William of Orange, was invited to take the throne with his wife, Mary Stuart (James's daughter). James fled to France in 1688 in what became known (by its beneficiaries) as the 'Glorious Revolution'. The Bank of England was founded during William's reign, initially to finance the King's wars with France.

CREATION OF THE PRIME MINISTER

In 1714, the throne passed to George, the Hanover-born great-grandson of James I. The German-speaking king – who never learned English – became the first of four long-reigning Georges in the Hanoverian line.

During George I's reign (1714-27), and for several years after, Sir Robert Walpole's Whig party monopolised Parliament. Their opponents, the Tories, supported the Stuarts and had opposed the exclusion of the Catholic James II. On the King's behalf, Walpole chaired a group of ministers (the forerunner of today's Cabinet), becoming, in effect, Britain's first

IN CONTEXT

prime minister. Walpole was presented with 10 Downing Street (constructed by Sir George Downing) as a residence; it remains the official home of all serving prime ministers.

During the 18th century, London grew with astonishing speed. New squares and terraced streets spread across Soho, Bloomsbury, Mayfair and Marylebone, as wealthy landowners and speculative developers cashed in on the new demand for leasehold properties. South London also became more accessible with the opening of the first new bridges for centuries: Westminster Bridge (1750) and Blackfriars Bridge (1769) joined London Bridge, long the only crossing.

GIN RUINS POOR, RICH MOCK MAD

But in the older districts, people were still living in terrible squalor. Some of the most notorious slums were located around Fleet Street and St Giles's (north of Covent Garden), only a short distance from streets of fashionable residences. To make matters worse, gin ('mother's ruin') was readily available at very low prices, and many poor Londoners drank excessive amounts in an attempt to escape the horrors of daily life. The well-off seemed complacent, amusing themselves at the popular Ranelagh and Vauxhall pleasure gardens or with organised trips to the Bedlam asylum to mock the patients. Public executions at Tyburn – near today's Marble Arch – were popular events in the social calendar.

The outrageous imbalance in the distribution of wealth encouraged crime, and there were daring daytime robberies in the West End. Reformers were few, though there were exceptions. Henry Fielding, author of the picaresque novel *Tom Jones*, was also an enlightened magistrate at Bow Street Court. In 1751, he and his blind half-brother John set up a volunteer force of 'thief-takers' to back up the often ineffective efforts of the parish constables and watchmen who were the only law-keepers in the city. This crime-busting group of early cops, known as the Bow Street Runners, were the forerunners of today's Metropolitan Police (established in 1829).

Meanwhile, five major new hospitals were founded by private philanthropists. St Thomas's and St Bartholomew's were long-established monastic institutions for the care of the sick, but Westminster (1720), Guy's (1725), St George's (1734), London (1740) and the Middlesex (1745) went on to become world-famous teaching hospitals. Thomas Coram's Foundling Hospital was another remarkable achievement of the time.

INDUSTRY AND CAPITAL-ISM

It wasn't just the indigenous population of London that was on the rise. Country people, whose common land had been replaced by sheep enclosures, were faced with starvation wages or unemployment, and drifted into the towns in large numbers. Just outside the old city walls, the East End drew many poor immigrant labourers to build the docks towards the end of the 18th century. London's total population had grown to one million by 1801, the largest of any city in Europe. By 1837, when Queen Victoria came to the throne, five more bridges and the capital's first passenger railway (running from Greenwich to London Bridge) gave hints that unprecedented expansion might be around the corner.

As well as being the administrative and financial capital of the British Empire, London was also its chief port and the world's largest manufacturing centre. On the one hand, it had splendid buildings, fine shops, theatres and museums; on the other, it was a city of poverty, pollution and disease. Residential areas were polarised into districts with fine terraces maintained by squads of servants, or overcrowded, insanitary slums.

The growth of the metropolis in the century before Victoria came to the throne had been spectacular, but during her reign (1837-1901), thousands more acres were covered with roads, houses and railway lines. If you visit a street within five miles of central London, its houses will be mostly Victorian. By the end of the 19th century, the city's population had swelled to more than six million, an incredible growth of five million in 100 years.

Despite social problems, memorably depicted in the writings of Charles Dickens, steps were being taken to improve conditions for the majority of Londoners by the turn of the century. The Metropolitan Board of Works installed an efficient sewerage system, street

Stuart London

Where to see how London lived.

Peter Paul Rubens' painted ceiling in the **Banqueting House** (*see p111*) is as fine a piece of Stuart propaganda as you could wish for, its chubby cherubs commissioned by Charles I to celebrate the magnificence of his father James I's rule under bombastic titles: 'The Union of the Crowns', 'The Apotheosis of James I', 'The Peaceful Reign of James I'. The building's architect, Inigo Jones, also built the **Queen's House** (*see p147*) and **St Paul's Covent Garden** (*see p83*).

lighting and better roads. The worst slums were replaced by low-cost building schemes funded by philanthropists such as the American George Peabody, who established the Peabody Donation Fund (which continues to provide subsidised housing to the working classes). The London County Council (created in 1888) also helped to house the poor.

The Victorian expansion would not have been possible without an efficient public transport network, with which to speed workers into and out of the city from the new suburbs. The horse-drawn bus appeared on London's streets in 1829, but it was the opening of the first passenger railway seven years later that heralded the commuters of the future. The first underground line, which ran between Paddington and Farringdon Road, opened in 1863 and proved an instant success, attracting more than 30,000 travellers on the first day. Soon after, the world's first electric track in a deep tunnel – the 'tube' – opened in 1890 between the City and Stockwell, later becoming part of the Northern Line.

THE CRYSTAL PALACE
If any one event crystallised the Victorian period of industry, science, discovery and invention, it was the Great Exhibition of 1851. Prince Albert, the Queen's Consort, helped organise this triumphant showcase, for which the Crystal Palace, a giant building of iron and glass was erected in Hyde Park. It looked like a giant greenhouse; hardly surprising as it was designed not by a professional architect but by the Duke of Devonshire's gardener, Joseph Paxton. Condemned by art critic John Ruskin as the model of dehumanisation in design, the Palace came to be presented as the prototype of modern architecture. During

the five months it was open, the Exhibition drew six million visitors. The profits were used by the Prince Consort to establish a permanent centre for the study of the applied arts and sciences; the enterprise survives today in the South Kensington museums of natural history, science, and decorative and applied arts, and in three colleges (of art, music and science). After the Exhibition, the Palace was moved to Sydenham and used as an exhibition centre until it burned down in 1936.

ZEPPELINS ATTACK FROM THE SKIES

London entered the 20th century as the capital of the largest empire in history. Its wealth and power were there for all to see in grandstanding monuments such as Tower Bridge and the Midland Grand Hotel at St Pancras Station, both of which married the retro stylings of High Gothic with modern iron and steel technology. During the brief reign of Edward VII (1901-10), London regained some of the gaiety and glamour it had lacked in the later years of Victoria's reign. Parisian chic came to London with the opening of the Ritz; Regent Street's Café Royal hit the heights as a meeting place for artists and writers; gentlemen's clubs proliferated; and 'luxury catering for the little man' was provided at the new Lyons Corner Houses (the Coventry Street branch held an incredible 4,500 people).

Victorian London

Where to see how London lived.

The legacy of Queen Victoria's reign is everywhere here – even buildings that preceded the Victorians (notably St Paul's and the Palace of Westminster) received 19th-century alterations to make them more 'historic' looking. But

South Kensington's palatial museums and monuments (*see pp121-123*) are the finest testament to the self-confidence and ingenuity of the Victorian era, with the strange detailing of the **Natural History Museum** (*pictured*) our favourite.

'German bombers dumped explosives on east London and the docks, destroying entire streets.'

Road transport, too, was revolutionised. By 1911, horse-drawn buses were abandoned, replaced by the motor cars, which put-putted around the city's streets, and the motor bus, introduced in 1904. Disruption came in the form of devastating air raids during World War I. Around 650 people lost their lives as a result of Zeppelin raids, but the greater impact was psychological – the mighty city had experienced helplessness.

ROARING BETWEEN THE WARS
Political change happened quickly after the war. David Lloyd George's government averted revolution in 1918-19 by promising (but not delivering) 'homes for heroes' – for the embittered returning soldiers. But the Liberal Party's days in power were numbered. In 1924, the Labour Party, led by Ramsay MacDonald, formed its first government.

A live-for-today attitude prevailed in the Roaring '20s among the young upper classes, who flitted from parties in Mayfair to dances at the Ritz. But this meant little to the mass of Londoners, who were suffering in the post-war slump. Civil disturbances, brought on by the high cost of living and rising unemployment, resulted in the nationwide General Strike of 1926, when the working classes downed tools en masse in support of striking miners. Prime Minister Baldwin encouraged volunteers to take over the public services and the streets teemed with army-escorted food convoys, aristocrats running soup kitchens and students driving buses. After nine days of chaos, the strike was called off.

The economic situation only worsened in the early 1930s following the New York Stock Exchange crash of 1929 – by 1931, more than three million Britons were jobless. During these years, the London County Council (LCC) began to have a greater impact on the city, clearing slums and building new houses, creating parks and taking control of public services. All the while, London's population increased, peaking at nearly 8.7 million in 1939. To accommodate the influx, the suburbs expanded, particularly to the north-west with the extension of the Metropolitan Line to an area that became known as 'Metroland'. Identical gabled houses sprang up in their thousands, from Golders Green to Surbiton.

At least Londoners were able to entertain themselves: film and radio had arrived. When London's first radio broadcast was beamed from the roof of Marconi House in the Strand in 1922, families were soon gathering around enormous Bakelite wireless sets to hear the BBC (the British Broadcasting Company; from 1927 the British Broadcasting Corporation). TV broadcasts started on 26 August 1936 when the first telecast went out live from Alexandra Palace, though very few could afford televisions until the 1950s.

THE BLITZ
Abroad, events had taken on a frightening impetus. Neville Chamberlain's policy of appeasement towards Hitler's aggressive Germany collapsed when the Germans invaded Poland, and Britain declared war on 3 September 1939. The government implemented precautionary measures against air raids, including the evacuation of 600,000 children and pregnant mothers, but the expected bombing raids didn't happen during the autumn and winter of 1939-40 (the so-called 'Phoney War'). Then, in September 1940, hundreds of German bombers dumped explosives on east London and the docks, destroying entire streets and killing or injuring more than 2,000 in this opening salvo. The Blitz had begun. The raids on London continued for 57 consecutive nights, then intermittently for a further six months. Londoners reacted with stoicism, famously asserting 'business as usual'. After a final raid on 10 May 1941, Germany had left a third of the City and the East End in ruins.

From 1942 onwards, the tide of the war began to turn, but Londoners had a new terror to face: the V1, or 'doodlebug'. Dozens of these deadly, explosive-packed, pilotless planes

IN CONTEXT

descended on the city in 1944, causing widespread destruction. Later in the year, the more powerful V2 rocket was launched. The last fell on 27 March 1945 in Orpington, Kent, around six weeks before Victory in Europe (VE Day) was declared on 8 May 1945.

YOU'VE NEVER HAD IT SO GOOD

World War II left Britain almost as shattered as Germany. Soon after VE Day, a general election was held and Winston Churchill was defeated by the Labour Party under Clement Attlee. The new government established the National Health Service in 1948, and began a massive nationalisation programme that included public transport, electricity, gas, postal and telephone services. For most people, however, life remained regimented and austere. In war-ravaged London, local authorities struggled with a critical shortage of housing. Prefabricated bungalows provided a temporary solution for some, but the huge new high-rise housing estates that the planners devised proved unpopular with their residents.

There were bright spots. London hosted the Olympics in 1948; three years later came the Festival of Britain, resulting in the first, full redevelopment of the riverside site into the South Bank Centre. As the 1950s progressed, life and prosperity returned, leading Prime Minister Harold Macmillan in 1957 to proclaim that 'most of our people have never had it so good'. However, many Londoners were leaving. The population dropped by half a million in the late 1950s, causing a labour shortage that prompted huge recruitment drives in Britain's former colonies. London Transport and the National Health Service were both particularly active in encouraging West Indians to emigrate to Britain. Unfortunately, as the Notting Hill race riots of 1958 illustrated, the welcome these new immigrants received was rarely friendly. Still, there were several areas of tolerance: Soho, for instance, which became famed for its mix of cultures, and the café and club life they brought with them.

THE SWINGING SIXTIES

By the mid 1960s, London had started to swing. The innovative fashions of Mary Quant and others broke Paris's stranglehold on couture: boutiques blossomed along the King's Road, while Biba set the pace in Kensington. Carnaby Street became a byword for hipness as the city basked in its new-found reputation as the music and fashion capital of the world – made official, it seemed, when *Time* magazine devoted its front cover to 'swinging London' in April 1966. The year of student unrest in Europe, 1968, saw the first issue of *Time Out* hit the streets in August; it was a fold-up sheet, sold for 5d. The decade ended with the Rolling Stones playing a free gig in Hyde Park that drew around 500,000 people.

Then the bubble burst. Many Londoners remember the 1970s as a decade of economic strife, the decade in which the IRA began its bombing campaign on mainland Britain. And after the Conservatives won the general election in 1979, Margaret Thatcher instituted a monetarist economic policy that depended on cuts to public services that widened the gap between rich and poor. Riots in Brixton (1981) and Tottenham (1985) were linked to unemployment and heavy-handed policing, keenly felt in London's black communities. The Greater London Council (GLC), led by Ken Livingstone, mounted opposition to the government with a series of populist measures. It was abolished in 1986.

The replacement of Thatcher by John Major in October 1990 signalled a short-lived upsurge of hope among Londoners. A riot in Trafalgar Square had helped to see off both Maggie and her inequitable Poll Tax. Yet the early 1990s were scarred by continuing recession and more IRA terrorist attacks.

THINGS CAN ONLY GET BETTER?

In May 1997, the British people ousted the Tories and gave Tony Blair's Labour Party the first of three election victories, but the initial enthusiasm didn't last. The government hoped the Millennium Dome would be a 21st-century rival to the 1851 Great Exhibition. It wasn't. Badly mismanaged, the Dome ate some £1 billion on the way to becoming a national joke.

Nobody was laughing when the government's plans to invade Iraq in 2003 generated the largest public demonstration in London's history: over one million participated – to

Post-war London

Where to see how London lived.

After the Blitz, vast tracts of land were left desolate and thousands of London residents needed rehousing. The city's saviour was surprising and divisive: concrete. Cheap, quick and strong enough to create extraordinary geometric buildings, it was loved by architects and hated by pretty much everyone else. The saw-tooth towers of the huge **Barbican** arts centre (*see p307*) are still the most frequently debated example, but we love the wonderfully angular **Hayward** gallery (*see p49*; *pictured*), right beside the Festival of Britain's Royal Festival Hall.

no avail. The new millennium saw Ken Livingstone, former leader of the GLC, become London's first directly elected mayor and head of the new Greater London Assembly (GLA). He was re-elected in 2004 for a second term, a thumbs up for his first term's policies, which included a congestion charge that sought to ease traffic gridlock by forcing drivers to pay £8 to enter the city centre.

The summer of 2005 was topsy-turvy. First came the city's elation at winning the bid to host the 2012 Olympics. Then a day later jubilation turned to shock, when bombs on tube trains and a bus killed 52 people and injured 700. These were followed two weeks later by similar, unsuccessful, attacks. In the immediate aftermath the number of people travelling on tubes and buses was fewer and more people took to cycling to work, but very quickly the first 'Not Afraid' T-shirts began to appear and London emerged with a revitalised sense of itself and bloody-minded determination to keep on with its ordinary life.

The run-up to the 2012 Olympics remains high on the agenda, but the City of London has gone into meltdown, the credit crunch is biting, recession looms, and thatch-headed former Conservative MP Boris Johnson is the new Mayor of London (*see pp31-33*). Things look like they might get worse before they can get better. But was it not ever thus?

Key Events

London in brief.

43 The Romans invade; a bridge is built on the Thames; Londinium is founded.
61 Boudicca burns Londinium; the city is rebuilt and made the provincial capital.
200 A city wall is built.
410 Roman troops evacuate Britain.
c600 Saxon London is built to the west.
841 The Norse raid for the first time.
c871 The Danes occupy London.
886 King Alfred of Wessex takes London.
1013 The Danes take back London.
1042 Edward the Confessor builds a palace and 'West Minster' upstream.
1066 William I is crowned in Westminster Abbey; London is granted a charter.
1078 The Tower of London begun.
1123 St Bart's Hospital is founded.
1197 Henry Fitzalwin is the first mayor.
1215 The mayor signs the Magna Carta.
1240 First Parliament sits at Westminster.
1290 Jews are expelled from London.
1348 The Black Death arrives.
1381 The Peasants' Revolt.
1397 Richard Whittington is Lord Mayor.
1476 William Caxton sets up the first printing press at Westminster.
1534 Henry VIII cuts off Catholic Church.
1555 Martyrs burned at Smithfield.
1565 Sir Thomas Gresham proposes the Royal Exchange.
1572 First known map of London printed.
1599 The Globe Theatre opens.
1605 Guy Fawkes's plot to blow up James I fails.
1642 The start of the Civil War.
1649 Charles I is executed; Cromwell establishes Commonwealth.
1664 Beginning of the Great Plague.
1666 The Great Fire.
1675 Building starts on the new St Paul's Cathedral.
1694 The Bank of England is established.
1710 St Paul's is completed.
1766 The city wall is demolished.
1769 Blackfriars Bridge opens.
1773 The Stock Exchange is founded.
1803 The first horse-drawn railway opens.
1820 The Regent's Canal opens.

1824 The National Gallery is founded.
1827 Regent's Park Zoo opens.
1829 Metropolitan Police Act is passed.
1833 The London Fire Brigade is set up.
1835 Madame Tussauds opens.
1836 The first passenger railway opens; Charles Dickens publishes *The Pickwick Papers*, his first novel.
1843 Trafalgar Square is laid out.
1851 The Great Exhibition takes place.
1853 Harrods opens its doors.
1858 The Great Stink: pollution in the Thames reaches hideous levels.
1863 The Metropolitan Line, the world's first underground railway, opens.
1866 London's last major cholera outbreak; the Sanitation Act is passed.
1868 The last public execution is held at Newgate prison.
1884 Greenwich Mean Time established.
1888 Jack the Ripper prowls the East End; London County Council is created.
1890 The Housing Act enables the LCC to clear the slums; the first electric underground railway opens.
1897 Motorised buses introduced.
1908 London hosts the Olympic Games.
1915 Zeppelins begin three years of bombing raids on London.
1940 The Blitz begins.
1948 London again hosts the Olympics.
1951 The Festival of Britain takes place.
1952 The last 'pea-souper' smog.
1953 Queen Elizabeth II is crowned.
1966 England's football team wins the World Cup at Wembley.
1975 Work starts on the Thames Barrier.
1981 Riots in Brixton.
1982 The last of London's docks close.
1986 The GLC is abolished.
1990 Poll Tax protesters riot.
1992 One Canada Square tower opens on Canary Wharf.
2000 Ken Livingstone is elected mayor; Tate Modern and the London Eye open.
2005 London wins bid to host the 2012 Olympics; suicide bombers kill 52.
2008 Boris Johnson becomes mayor.

London Today

What will life be like under the new mayor?

TEXT: PETER WATTS

When Conservative Boris Johnson defeated eight-year incumbent Ken Livingstone in London's 2008 mayoral elections, it signified any or all of three things. First, that voters were following a national urge to wake up a tired Labour administration. Second, that Londoners were being mischievous, replacing a left-wing, working-class, state-educated iconoclast with a right-wing, upper-class, Eton-educated iconoclast. And third, that this was the latest exchange in London's battle between the centre and the suburbs for control of the city – the 2008 version was dubbed the 'doughnut theory', with Johnson focusing on the Tory outer London boroughs' perceived neglect by Livingstone's inner-London-loving Greater London Assembly (GLA).

Whichever theory you choose, and all three have merits, the upshot was the same: the Conservatives were back in charge of London for the first time in decades. Their previous contribution to London's governance had been to abolish the Greater London Council (GLC) in 1985 and hand control back to the boroughs, leading to a period of stasis and torpor everywhere other in Docklands. So how will they fare this time? Breath of fresh air, or hurricane of incompetence?

Peter Watts is features writer for Time Out *magazine.*

'A journalist and politician, Johnson is a paradox. He's a riddle wrapped in a mystery, clad in a clown wig and a crumpled suit.'

TEETHING PROBLEMS

A journalist and politician, Johnson is a paradox. He is both a shambolic fool and an accomplished editor; a straight-talking, non-PC Tory who quotes Latin at press conferences yet rides to work on a bike; a caricature of an English gent who was born in New York and has Turkish, French and German ancestry. He's a riddle wrapped in a mystery, clad in a clown wig and a crumpled suit.

Naysayers – including Livingstone, who quickly pledged to run again in 2012 – expect the worst. Johnson's campaign had focused on battling a knife crime epidemic, and a populist promise to bring back the iconic but outdated Routemaster bus. Astute critics pointed to his poor grasp of detail and lack of vision. But this was lost in the white noise from other anti-Johnson commentators emphasising his poshness or perceived stupidity.

Johnson – not to mention Conservative Central Office (CCO), who are aware that he's seen as a potential party leader – began by appointing a series of deputies from both the private sector and Tory borough councils. But the two groups didn't gel and calamity ensued in August 2008 when Deputy Mayor Tim Parker, a businessman brought in to 'do detail', clashed with Deputy Mayor Sir Simon Milton, an experienced Tory councillor who baulked at Parker's cost-cutting and empire-building. Parker blinked first, and became the third Johnson appointee to stand down in as many months: advisor James McGrath had made thoughtless remarks about London's Caribbean community, and youth expert Ray Lewis had resigned after accusations of prior financial misconduct. City Hall was left in the hands of the astute Milton and assorted 'undistinguished Tory councillors', as one insider put it.

Londoners didn't quite know what to make of it. While Livingstone's City Hall had often clashed with local councils and central goverment, this sort of internecine warfare was unheard of among his staff of devoted left-wingers, whose fealty ensured that things got done. And amid the turmoil, commentators started to question whether Johnson had a 'vision for London' (*Economist*) or 'a narrative' (*Financial Times*), beyond a desire to reverse some of Livingstone's more ideological policies (raising the congestion charge to £25 for gas-guzzling 4x4s, aka 'Chelsea tractors'; subsidising cheap travel for the unemployed by importing cheap oil from socialist Hugo Chavez's Venezuela).

GROWING PAINS

What Johnson has promised is 'value-for-money', a nebulous phrase that essentially involves cutting costs and encouraging private firms to take more responsibility for things previously paid for by the GLA. So where Livingstone tried to run London as if it was Paris, with the state paying, Johnson wants to run it like New York, with private money replacing state funding; his admiration for New York mayor Michael Bloomberg is well known. British companies don't like footing the bill for the state, unless on seriously loaded terms – one such example is the Labour government's Private Finance Initiative, a deeply flawed scheme that funds the London Underground. Fortunately for Johnson, there are a couple of big schemes on the horizon. Years in the planning, Crossrail is a major high-speed east–west train line that will pass through Canary Wharf, Bond Street and Paddington and is due to open in 2017. But of more immediate concern are the 2012 Olympics. Planning for them will dominate the next few years, as London tries to come to terms with what it wants from the event. Johnson's enthusiasm could ensure that the Olympics get the public support that they badly need in order to succeed.

IN CONTEXT

Elsewhere, expect 2009 to witness the continued rise of west London. Tory-controlled Hammersmith and Fulham have submitted a number of regeneration proposals based around the little-known West London Line, linking Clapham Junction to Willesden Junction. An immense shopping centre opened at the end of 2008 in Shepherd's Bush, and there are plans for further developments at Earl's Court, White City and Wormwood Scrubs. The current economic climate means that redevelopments are ripe for revision (many of Livingstone's beloved skyscraper schemes have suddenly disappeared from the drawing board), and also that Johnson will have to cope with the other consequences of recession – crime and unemployment. Difficult, when the big drivers of the London economy in recent years, the housing market and the City, are in such serious trouble. In August 2008, shortly after Tim Parker's resignation, *The Times* asked whether London – sprawling, conflicted, inchoate – was 'ungovernable'. If the answer is 'no', 2009 could be the toughest and most important year yet of Boris Johnson's political career.

IN CONTEXT

Welcome to London?

We see how Heathrow's controversial new terminal is working.

'National embarrassment'. That's how the March 2008 opening of Heathrow's magnificent new Terminal 5 was described – not by one of the several thousand enraged travellers who lost luggage and had flights cancelled, but by the august MPs on a House of Commons Transport Committee six months later. Flagship infrastructure project thoroughly bungled? How very London.

Except that isn't the whole story. We visited Terminal 5 at about the same time the report came out and found that, in contrast to the cramped, chaotic hell of Terminal 2, the new terminal felt like being abroad. Passengers stroll into Paul Smith's Globe, sink into sofas at Gordon Ramsay's Plane Food or mount empty escalators beneath Troika's cloud sculpture. Richard Rogers's inside-out neo-industrialist style has created a building that looks intelligent and inspired. It's proof that Britain's airports don't have to resemble a run-down branch of a suburban DIY store, stuffed with low-grade retail.

From the sleek, Arup-designed control tower, a workspace of monkish tranquillity, our guide also pointed out the proposed site of the third runway. Vehemently opposed by local residents and environmentalists, just as fiercely supported by the government and the airport's administrators BAA, that's a whole new controversy to enjoy over the coming years.

Architecture

Pointing up, back and onward.

TEXT: SIMON COPPOCK

It long looked like it might never happen, but architecture in London has become fashionable. The populace is more engaged with the built environment than ever before. New projects become talking points, provoke fierce debate, and are applauded or vilified on completion. No doubt this is partly because London's architects have become much better at stimulating public interest: witness the success of the Open House festival (*see p273*). But it's also because the city has been going through another of its periodic stages of rapid change.

London is a European city, and everywhere in its architecture are signs of continental influence. In the 17th and 18th centuries, it was adapted with distinction by architects of genius: Palladians Inigo Jones and (later) Lord Burlington; baroque-builders Sir Christopher Wren and Nicholas Hawksmoor; and Greek Revivalist Sir John Soane. And the city's contemporary architects are no less global in their inspiration. The last time construction fuelled such ardour was when modern London sprang into being following the Great Fire.

'Much new architecture is to be found cunningly inserted into old buildings.'

AFTER THE BLAZE

In 1666, the Great Fire destroyed five-sixths of the City of London, burning some 13,200 houses and 89 churches. The devastation is commemorated by Sir Christopher Wren's 202-foot **Monument**, recently renovated and restored (see p66 **Born of Flames, Reborn in Gilt**); many of the finest buildings in the City still stand as testament to the talents of this man, the architect of the great remodelling, and his successors.

London was a densely populated place built largely of wood, and fire control was primitive. It was only after the inferno that the authorities insisted on a few basic building regulations. Brick and stone became the construction materials of choice, and key streets were widened to act as firebreaks. In spite of proposals from architects who hoped to reconfigure it along classical lines, London was reshaped around its old street pattern; buildings that had survived the Fire were allowed to stand as monuments to earlier ages.

Chief among these survivors was the Norman **Tower of London** (see p71), begun soon after William's 1066 conquest and extended over the next 300 years. The Navy cheated the advancing flames of the Great Fire by blowing up the surrounding houses before the inferno could get to it. Then there's **Westminster Abbey** (see p112), begun in 1245 when the site lay far outside London's walls and completed in 1745 by church architect Nicholas Hawksmoor's west towers. The abbey is the most French of England's Gothic churches, but the chapel added by Henry VII in 1512 is pure Tudor. Centuries later, Washington Irving gushed: 'Stone seems, by the winning labour of the chisel, to have been robbed of its weight and density, suspended aloft, as if by magic.'

THE CLASSICAL AGE

The European Renaissance came late, making its London debut with Inigo Jones's 1622 **Banqueting House** (see p111). The sumptuously decorated ceiling added in 1635 by Rubens celebrated the Stuart monarchy's Divine Right to rule; 14 years later, King Charles I provided an even greater spectacle when he was led from the room and beheaded on a stage outside. Tourists also have Jones to thank for **St Paul's Covent Garden** (see p83) and the immaculate **Queen's House** (see p147) at Greenwich, but these are not his only legacies. He also mastered the art of piazzas (notably Covent Garden), porticos and pilasters, changing British architecture forever.

Nothing cheers a builder like a natural disaster, and one can only guess at the relish with which Wren and co began rebuilding after the Fire. They brandished classicism like a new broom: the pointed arches of English Gothic were rounded off, Corinthian columns made an appearance and church spires became as multi-layered as a wedding cake.

Having warmed up with the spectacular **Old Royal Naval College** (see p147), Wren delivered daring plans for **St Paul's Cathedral** (see p36 **Profile**). He was soon joined by Nicholas Hawksmoor and James Gibbs, all three of them benefiting from a 1711 decree that 50 extra churches should be built in London. Gibbs became busy in and around Trafalgar Square with the steepled Roman temple of **St Martin-in-the-Fields** (see p110), as well as the baroque **St Mary-le-Strand** and the tower of **St Clement Danes** (for both, see p86). His work was well received, but the more prolific and experimental Hawksmoor had a rougher ride. Costing three times its £10,000 budget, **St George's Bloomsbury** (see p78), for example, aims to evoke the spirit of the ancients: rather than a spire, there's a stepped pyramid topped by a statue of George I in a toga.

Robert Adam, one of a large family of Scottish architects, suddenly found himself at the forefront of a movement that had come to see Italian baroque as a corruption of the real

Profile St Paul's Cathedral

Wren's masterpiece looks better now than even its creator intended.

Extraordinarily thorough restoration has left the façade of **St Paul's Cathedral** (*see p61*) looking as glorious today as it must have done when it opened in 1710. The interior might even look better than ever: the roof was the last part completed, meaning the inside had been exposed to the elements for three decades before St Paul's celebrated its first communion. Within, much of the decoration is Victorian. The lovely stained glass? The stunning mosaics? All added to satisfy Queen Victoria who had declared St Paul's 'dreary'.

Perhaps the cathedral's impish architect and the grumpy queen had reached an accord across the centuries. After all, Sir Christopher Wren had to fight to get his plans past the authorities – many politicians thought St Paul's too big and expensive. Even after spending the huge sum of £500 on an oak model

BAROQUE STARS
Three further masterworks, recently restored.

St Martin-in-the-Fields
See p110.

St George's Bloomsbury
See p78.

Christ Church Spitalfields
See p133.

of the scheme (which can still be seen on the Triforium tours, *see p62*), Wren's proposal – with a Catholic dome rather than a Protestant steeple – was considered to be too Roman for the Protestant establishment.

He duly incorporated a spire in his redesign, but – under the terms of the 'Warrant Design', which allowed him to make any necessary modifications during construction – set about a series of mischievous U-turns that gave us the building we know today: heavily suggestive of an ancient temple, a superb marriage of Greek and baroque. The massive dome is, in actual fact, three domes: inner and outer domes, which are separated by a hidden brick cone that supports the entire structure.

Accessible only on the paid tours, the Dean's Staircase is another St Paul's secret. A light, airy spiral (*pictured below*), it forms two circles of 66 steps each, its exquisite geometric balance ensuring each step is fully supported by the one below. The theory is impressive, and the effect – like the rest of St Paul's Cathedral – quite exquisite.

City Hall. *See p39*.

IN CONTEXT

thing. Architectural exuberance was dropped in favour of a simpler interpretation of the ancient forms. The best surviving work of Robert Adam, and his brothers James, John and William, can be found in London's great suburban houses Osterley Park, **Syon House** (*see p163*) and **Kenwood House** (*see p130*), but the project for which they are most famous no longer stands: the cripplingly dear Adelphi housing estate off the Strand. most of which was pulled down in the 1930s. Only a small part of the development remains in what is now the **Royal Society of Arts** (8 John Adam Street, Covent Garden, WC2).

Just as the first residents were moving into the Adelphi, a young unknown called John Soane was embarking on a domestic commission in Ireland. It was never completed, but Soane went on to build the **Bank of England** (*see p66*) and **Dulwich Picture Gallery** (*see p144*). The gallery remains; the bank, though, was demolished between the wars, leaving only the perimeter walls. A more authentic glimpse of what the bankers might have enjoyed can be gleaned from a visit to Soane's house: now the quirky **Sir John Soane's Museum** (*see p73*), it's an extraordinary and exquisite domestic architectural experiment.

A near-contemporary of Soane's, John Nash was arguably a less talented architect, but his contributions have proved comparable in importance to those of Wren. Among his buildings are the inner courtyard of **Buckingham Palace** (*see p114*), the **Theatre Royal Haymarket** (Haymarket, SW1) and **Regent Street** (Soho/Mayfair, W1). The latter began as a proposal to link the West End to the planned park further north, and simultaneously separate the toffs of Mayfair from Soho riff-raff; in Nash's words, a 'complete separation between the Streets occupied by the Nobility and Gentry, and the narrow Streets and meaner houses occupied by mechanics and the trading part of the community'.

ATTACK OF THE GOTHS

By the 1830s, the classical form of building had been established in England for 200 years, but this didn't prevent a handful of upstarts from pressing for change. In 1834, the **Houses of Parliament** (*see p111*) burned down, leading to the construction of Sir Charles Barry's Gothic masterpiece. This was the beginning of the Gothic Revival, a move to replace what was considered foreign and pagan with something that was native and Christian.

For the project, Barry sought out Augustus Welby Northmore Pugin to assist him in the building's design. Working alongside Barry, Pugin created a Victorian fantasy that would

Old Royal Naval College. *See p35.*

today be condemned as the Disneyfication of history. At the time, the two of them failed to agree on every detail: about Barry's symmetrical layout, Pugin famously remarked, 'All Grecian, sir. Tudor details on a classic body.'

Architects would now often decide that buildings weren't Gothic enough – as with the 15th-century Great Hall at the **Guildhall** (*see p67*), which gained its corner turrets and central spire only in 1862. This ongoing argument between classicists and Goths erupted in 1857, when the government hired Sir George Gilbert Scott, a leading light of the Gothic movement, to design a new HQ for the Foreign Office. Scott's design incensed anti-Goth Lord Palmerston, then prime minister, whose diktats prevailed. But Scott exacted his revenge by building an office in which everyone hated working, then constructing Gothic edifices all over town; among them are the **Albert Memorial** (*see p121*) and the frontage of **St Pancras International** (*see p79*), due to reopen as a hotel late this year.

St Pancras was completed in 1873, after the Midland Railway commissioned Scott to build a London terminus that would dwarf that of its rivals next door at King's Cross. Using the project as an opportunity to show his mastery of the Gothic form, Scott built an asymmetrical castle that obliterated views of the train shed behind, itself an engineering marvel completed earlier by William Barlow. Other charmingly imposing neo-Gothic buildings around the city include the **Royal Courts of Justice** (*see p59*), the **Natural History Museum** (*see p121*) and **Tower Bridge** (*see p71*). Under the influence of the Arts and Crafts movement, this medievalism easily morphed into mock-Tudor – the wonderful black-and-white **Liberty** department store (*see p242*) is a fine example.

MODERNISTS AND MORE

World War I and the coming of modernism led to a spirit of renewal and a starker aesthetic. **Freemason's Hall** (*see p83*) and the BBC's **Broadcasting House** (*see p95*) are good versions of the pared-down style of the 1920s and '30s, although the latter has been extended and modernised. Perhaps the finest example of between-the-wars modernism can be found at **London Zoo** (*see p99*). Built by Russian émigré Bertold Lubetkin and the Tecton group, the spiral ramps of the Penguin Pool (no longer used by penguins) explored the possibilities of concrete. The material was also put to good use on the Underground, enabling the quick, cheap building of cavernous spaces with sleek lines and curves.

There was nothing quick or cheap, however, about the art deco **Daily Express** (*see p58*) building (Fleet Street, the City, EC4). A black glass and chrome structure built in 1931, it's an early example of 'curtain wall' construction, in which the façade is literally hung on an internal frame. The building has been refurbished, but the original deco detailing – crazy flooring, snake handrails, funky lighting – remains intact. Public access is not guaranteed; still, it's what the *Architects' Journal* has called a 'defining monument of 1930s London'.

The aerial bombing of World War II left large areas of London ruined. Lamentably, the city was little improved by the rebuild; in many cases, it was worse off. The destruction left the capital with a dire housing shortage, so architects were given a chance to demonstrate the grim efficiency with which they could house large numbers of families in tower blocks. Nonetheless, there were post-war successes, the Royal Festival Hall (centrepiece of the **Southbank Centre**, *see p309*) among them. Sole survivor of the 1951 Festival of Britain, the RFH was built to celebrate the war's end and the centenary of the Great Exhibition. The neighbouring **Hayward Gallery** is an exemplar of the 1960s vogue for brutalism.

Moving forward, the 1970s and '80s offered up a pair of alternatives to brutalism: post-modernism and high-tech. The former is represented by Cesar Pelli's **One Canada Square** (*see p139*) at Canary Wharf in Docklands, an oversized obelisk that has become the archetypal expression of 1980s architecture and holds an ambiguous place in the city's affections. Richard Rogers' **Lloyd's of London** building (*see p67*) is London's best-known example of high-tech, in which commercial and industrial aesthetics cleverly combine to produce what is arguably one of the most significant British buildings since the war. Mocked on completion in 1986, the building still manages to outclass newer projects.

INTO THE FUTURE

The buildings that followed exhibit, if anything, even more invention. Take Future Systems' **NatWest Media Centre** at Lord's Cricket Ground (St John's Wood Road, St John's Wood, NW8): built from aluminium in a boatyard and perched high above the pitch, it's one of London's most daring constructions, especially given the traditional setting. Will Alsop's colourful **Peckham Library** (171 Peckham Hill Street, Peckham), which redefined community architecture and won the prestigious Stirling Prize in 2000, and the foyer of his **Palestra House** (197 Blackfriars Road, Waterloo) are as striking.

Thanks to the Heritage Lottery Fund, much new architecture has been cunningly inserted into old buildings. Herzog & de Meuron's fabulous transformation of a power station on Bankside into **Tate Modern** (*see p52*) is perhaps the most famous example, but it's not the only one. Lord Norman Foster's exercise in complexity at the **British Museum** (*see p76* **Profile**), where the £100 million Great Court created the largest covered square in Europe, is breathtaking: every one of its 3,300 triangular glass panels is unique. Indeed, discussion of the city's architecture is impossible without mention of Foster. His **City Hall** on the South Bank and the City's already iconic **30 St Mary Axe** (formerly the Swiss Re Tower aka 'The Gherkin') set new standards.

Modern London isn't all about the blockbuster commission, however. In dowdy Tower Hamlets, David Adjaye has designed new-build **Idea Stores** (www.ideastore.co.uk), libraries with a sleek and crisp aesthetic that is a world away from their traditional Victorian forebears. Confirming his status as a major player, he was responsible for the **Rivington Place** gallery (*see p137*), its design influenced by an African mask, and is arguably at his most modestly effective in the Mediatheque at **BFI Southbank** (*see p299*). What connects these latter two projects is an openess to the public, an insistence that his designs be *used*. A vaulting ambition that, you might hope, could even prove to be recession-proof.

IN CONTEXT

Look of London

To see the real London, look down and around, not up in awe.

Jonathan Derbyshire is a freelance arts journalist and editor of Time Out's 1,000 Books to Change Your Life.

L ondon has experienced a building boom over the past few years. The skyline has been thick with cranes, especially in the financial districts of the City and Canary Wharf. But while Lord Rogers and Sir Norman Foster, the superstar grey eminences of British architecture, collude with local politicians in Manhattan-ising the cityscape, throwing up statement public buildings and overbearing commercial edifices, a younger generation of architect-designers are ensuring that London's urban fabric remains gloriously, messily various.

For these newcomers, the interiors in which we live and play are of as much consequence as any grand City exterior, and the clothes we wear – and where we go to buy them – are as significant as any building. Much of their work is small-scale and invisible from the street. But if you know where to look, you'll find that the kind of PR boosterism that trumpets what writer and architecture critic Jonathan Meades has called the city's 'inexhaustible appetite for design innovation' is not entirely vacuous.

'Architects such as David Collins are now taking their cues from other disciplines.'

Young architect David Adjaye's willingness to use a wide palette of materials is typical of these successors to Foster and Rogers. Take, for example, his Idea Store in Whitechapel High Street, just a mile or so down the road from the City's gleaming temples to Mammon but a world away in socio-cultural terms. Behind its distinctive skin of green and blue glass, the Idea Store is ostensibly a public library, but the airy space also contains a café, a performance space and rooms set aside for complementary therapies. Although Adjaye has said that he wanted the Idea Store to be 'like a mall – clean and glass and glossy', the interior mixes impersonal concrete with the natural feel of rough wood; it's a nod towards the vernacular architecture of West Africa, from where Adjaye's family hails.

More recently, Adjaye has designed **Rivington Place** in Shoreditch, an arts centre devoted to the promotion of work from diverse cultures. As Adjaye pointed out at the autumn 2007 opening, the entrance has been deliberately placed down an alley to the side of the building; the floor-to-ceiling windows along Rivington Street work as a 'shop window', obliterating the division between inside and outside and engaging the curiosity of random passers-by to draw them into the photographic exhibitions within. The centre itself is also visually striking, its façade a geometrically complex series of charcoal grey blocks which cleverly combines deeply inset windows and flush tinted glazing.

The sculptural quality of some of Adjaye's work underlines the affinities between architecture and fine art. But, more unexpectedly, there are also connections between architecture and fashion. Heavily influenced by architectural theory in her clothing designs, Rei Kawakubo of Comme des Garçons was able to take her ideas a step further at **Dover Street Market** (*pictured left*), a store for which she and husband/business partner Adrian Joffe invited set designers such as Michael Howells to work; the aim, says Joffe, was to foster an 'interaction of creative ideas and diverse visions'. On the ground floor, for example, industrial chic collides with Eastern traditions: rough concrete flooring, exposed brickwork, display units fashioned from what looks like a grown-up's version of Meccano. In the centre is a corrugated tin shack, a kind of Japanese shanty dwelling that houses the tills and some storage. The changing room, meanwhile, is a reclaimed portable toilet.

IN CONTEXT

Connaught Bar.

Just as designers such as Kawakubo have been inspired by architectural theory, so some architects are taking their cues from other disciplines. David Collins' eponymous Studio began in the 1980s as a small architectural practice, but it's now a place where, as he puts it, 'interior architecture, furniture, lighting and graphic design could all interact and seamlessly produce a single strong vision'. That vision is much in evidence in a series of sumptuous interiors designed by Collins for some of London's most venerable institutions.

To commemorate the 300th anniversary of Piccadilly store **Fortnum & Mason**, Collins designed the 1707 Wine Bar in the shop's basement. A vaulted brick roof is supported by a series of very substantial wooden pillars; at ground level, tables are arranged around a large central bar made out of marble, behind which towers a glass case full of wine bottles. It's a quietly sumptuous shelter from the bustle of the food hall upstairs. Still, 1707 is less ostentatious than Collins' Connaught Bar at the **Connaught Hotel**, made up of three distinct but connected spaces. With armchairs that appear to be made from black snakeskin, the entrance lobby evokes the Roaring '20s. The area next door features a luxurious green carpet; marble lines the bar area, both on the floors and the bartop itself. The stainless steel and glass panelling, the art deco lamps and the beautiful cornicing all cement the sense that the visitor has stepped back into a more carefree age.

It's hard to discern unifying trends in the way London looks at the beginning of the 21st century. On the face of it, the stately opulence of a Collins interior couldn't be more distant from Adjaye's rigorously democratic way with concrete or the riotous stylistic collisions of Dover Street Market, but one thing these designers share is a commitment to innovation and a horror of the homogenous. Which is exactly the way London likes it.

Would You Look at Him?

Meet the 22-year-old who's at the extreme edge of performance art.

Scottee (*pictured*) shot to notoriety as one-half of self-proclaimed 'art terrorists' (basically, DJs and club promoters) Yr Mum Ya Dad, who ran cult Shoreditch night Antisocial through 2006. Full of the same folk who frequented also-defunct BoomBox down the road, Antisocial was where the worlds of fashion, music and clubbing collided, with edgy results.

After Yr Mum Ya Dad 'divorced' in 2007, Scottee pursued the ever-edgier end of the performance-art spectrum, providing short pieces for the influential

Bistrotheque restaurant's works-in-progress season UnderConstruction. More recently, a collaboration with DJ Warboy has resulted in a solo musical charting his damaged relationship with his mother and with food, and its impact on his self-confidence. 'Buy a Better You' will go to the Edinburgh Fringe in 2009; heaven knows what mainstream theatre types will make of it all.

Although Scottee considers any such comparison lazy, it's difficult not to draw comparisons with London's clubland of the 1980s: not so much Blitz, which spawned the new romantic movement, but the infamous Taboo club, founded by performance artist Leigh Bowery. As it was then, fashion is now extreme, but today's clubland is less self-destructively hedonistic. In magazines and fanzines, you'll see endless glossy photoshoots of east London's gender-busting performance artists. And club nights? There are dozens each week – just check *Time Out* magazine for details.

Sights

British
Library.
See p78.

The South Bank & Bankside **44**
Art with an Edge **48**
London Bridge Has Fallen
Down **55**

The City **57**
Born of Flames, Reborn in Gilt **66**
The New City **69**

Holborn & Clerkenwell **72**

Bloomsbury & Fitzrovia **75**
Profile British Museum **76**

Covent Garden & the Strand **81**
Plaques, Decay **85**

Soho & Leicester Square **88**
The Sordid Truth **91**
Walk Spiv City **92**

Oxford Street & Marylebone **94**
Walk Into the Back Streets **96**

Paddington & Notting Hill **100**

Piccadilly Circus & Mayfair **102**
Inside Science **104**

Westminster & St James's **107**
Boris and the Big Red Bus **108**

Chelsea **117**

Knightsbridge & South
Kensington **120**
Profile Natural History
Museum **123**

North London **125**
Walk A Green Thought in
a Green Shade **128**

East London **133**
Renaissance Whitechapel **136**

South-east London **142**
House of Science **148**

South-west London **151**
Profile Royal Botanic Gardens,
Kew **152**

West London **159**
England's Galileo **164**

The South Bank & Bankside

Show-stopper attractions linked by a brilliant riverside walk.

To describe the riverside walk along the south bank of the Thames as popular is an understatement; hardly a visitor arrives in the city without wanting to make this stroll. And for good reason. A walk from Lambeth Bridge to Tower Bridge has London's skyline for company on the left, from Big Ben to St Paul's and the Gherkin, with a wonderful parade of attractions on the right. Enjoying the buzz of the area today, it's hard to imagine that it was once a stretch of neglected factories and empty warehouses.

| Maps p401, p404, p405 | Restaurants & cafés p197 |
| Hotels p167 | Pubs & bars p226 |

It was the Festival of Britain that laid the foundation for a transformation in the 1950s, establishing the **Royal Festival Hall** (recently revamped) and, slightly later, the rest of the brutalist concrete complex that is the **Southbank Centre**. The inspired redevelopment of the **Oxo Tower Wharf** followed, as did the reconstruction of **Shakespeare's Globe**. But it wasn't until the millennium, nearly half a century later, that things kicked off properly, with the threefold arrival of the **London Eye**, **Tate Modern** and the **Millennium Bridge**. Further east, this year's spotlight is on historic **London Bridge**, reaching its 800th anniversary as a crossing point. Around **Tower Bridge**, meanwhile, where the old world of wharves and pull bridges sits next to a very modern **City Hall**, numerous construction sites indicate that the area's transformation is far from over.

THE SOUTH BANK

Lambeth Bridge to Hungerford Bridge

Embankment or Westminster tube/ Waterloo tube/rail.

Thanks to the sharp turn that the Thames makes around Waterloo, Lambeth Bridge, the westernmost crossing to the South Bank, in fact lands you east of the river, not south, opposite the Tudor gatehouse of Lambeth Palace. Since the 12th century, this has been the official residence of the Archbishops of Canterbury.

The palace is not normally open to the public, except on holidays, but the church next door, St Mary at Lambeth, serves as the pretty **Garden Museum** (*see p45*). The benches along the river here are great for viewing the Houses of Parliament opposite, before things get crowded after Westminster Bridge, where London's major riverside tourist zone begins. North of the bridge is **County Hall**, once the residence of London's city government, now home to the **London Aquarium**, the **Dalí Universe** (*see p45*) and newcomer attraction **Movieum** (*see p47*). The massive wheel of the **London Eye** (*see p47*) rotates in front of you.

London Eye. See p47.

Dalí Universe

County Hall Gallery, County Hall, Riverside Building, Queen's Walk, SE1 7PB (7620 2720/ www.daliuniverse.com). Westminster tube/Waterloo tube/rail. **Open** 9.30am-7pm Mon-Thur, Sat, Sun; 9.30am-8pm Fri. **Admission** £12; £10 reductions; £30 family. **Credit** AmEx, DC, MC, V. **Map** p401 M9.

At this curious wonderland of the famous surrealist's work, trademark attractions such as the Mae West Lips sofa and the Spellbound painting sit next to sculptures, watercolours (including his flamboyant tarot cards), rare etchings and lithographs, all exploring Dali's favourite themes: Dreams and Fantasy, Femininity and Sensuality, and Religion and Mythology. A new café serves organic fare amid large portraits of the mustachioed master.

Florence Nightingale Museum

St Thomas's Hospital, 2 Lambeth Palace Road, SE1 7EW (7620 0374/www.florence-nightingale.co.uk). Westminster tube/Waterloo tube/rail. **Open** 10am-5pm daily. **Admission** £5.80; £4.80 reductions; £16 family; free under-5s. **Credit** AmEx, MC, V. **Map** p401 M9.

The nursing skills and campaigning zeal that made Florence Nightingale's Crimean War work legendary are honoured here with a chronological tour through her remarkable life. On returning from the battlefields of Scutari she opened the Nightingale Nursing School in St Thomas's Hospital. Displays of period mementoes – clothing, furniture, books, letters and portraits – include her stuffed pet owl, Athena. Hands-on children's activities take place on most weekends.

★ Garden Museum

Lambeth Palace Road, SE1 7LB (7401 8865/www.gardenmuseum.org.uk). Lambeth North tube/Waterloo tube/rail. **Open** 10.30am-5pm Tue-Sun. **Admission** £6; £5 reductions; free under-16s. **Credit** AmEx, MC, V. **Map** p401 L10.

Fully refurbished, the world's first horticulture museum looks better than ever before. Topiaries, old roses, herbaceous perennials and bulbs give all-year interest in the small garden at the back, and most plants are labelled with their country of origin and year of introduction to these islands. The replica of a 17th-century knot garden was created in honour of John Tradescant, intrepid plant hunter and gardener to Charles I, who is buried here. A magnificent stone sarcophagus contains the remains of William Bligh, the captain of the mutinous HMS *Bounty*.

INSIDE TRACK
COME INTO THE GARDEN

The ancient, extensive and spectacular private gardens of **Lambeth Palace**, next door to the Garden Museum (*see above*), will be open to the public on at least three Saturday afternoons this year, on 30 May, 13 June and 27 June. Alternatively, you can apply for a guided tour by writing to Amy Wilson, Events Administrator, Lambeth Palace, SE1 7JU (for further details about visiting, see the website www.archbishopofcanterbury.org/1777).

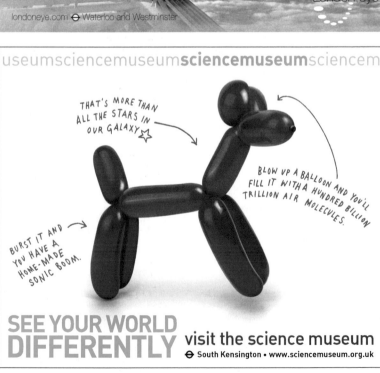

Displays of ancient tools and antique gnomes are now complemented by themed exhibitions about garden design and selections from the museum's collection of paintings.

▶ *The breadfruit that ruined Bligh's expedition can be seen at Kew Gardens; see p156.*

London Aquarium

County Hall, Riverside Building, Westminster Bridge Road, SE1 7PB (7967 8000/tours 7967 8007/www.londonaquarium.co.uk). Westminster tube/Waterloo tube/rail. **Open** 10am-6pm daily. **Admission** £13.25; £9.75-£11.50 reductions; £44 family; free under-3s. **Credit** MC, V. **Map** p401 M8.

The aquarium, one of Europe's largest, displays its inhabitants according to geographical origin. There are tanks of bright fish from the coral reefs and the Indian Ocean and temperate freshwater fish from the rivers of Europe and North America. Jellyfish, sharks, piranhas and octopuses join the fun and there's a touch pool with giant rays in it. If you're lucky, you'll catch one of the feeding sessions taking place throughout the day.

★ London Eye

Riverside Building, next to County Hall, Westminster Bridge Road, SE1 7PB (0870 500 0600/www.londoneye.com). Westminster tube/Waterloo tube/rail. **Open** *Oct-May* 10am-8pm daily. *June-Sept* 10am-9pm daily. **Admission** £15.50; £7.75-£12 reductions (only applicable Mon-Fri Sept-June); free under-5s. **Credit** AmEx, MC, V. **Map** p401 M8.

Hard to believe that this giant wheel was originally intended to turn beside the Thames for only five years: it has proved so popular that no one wants it to come down, and it's now scheduled to keep spinning for another 20 years. The 443ft frame, whose 32 glass capsules each hold 25 people, commands superb views over the heart of London and beyond. A 'flight' takes half an hour, allowing plenty of time to ogle the Queen's back garden and follow the snake of the Thames. Some people book in advance (taking a gamble with the weather), but it's possible to turn up and queue for a ticket on the day. There can be long queues in summer, and security is tight. *Photo p45.*

▶ *Book a ride after dark on one of the Eye's 'Night flights' for a twinkly view of London.*

Movieum

County Hall, Riverside Building, South Bank, SE1 7PB (7202 7040/www.themovieum.com). Westminster tube/Waterloo tube/rail. **Open** 10am-5pm Mon-Fri; 10am-6pm Sat, Sun. **Admission** £15; £9 reductions. **Credit** MC, V. **Map** p401 M8.

Dedicated to British film since the 1950s (films made in Britain, that is, so blockbusters like *Star Wars* can sneak in), the 30,000sq ft Movieum is focused more on fun than painstaking historical reconstruc-

tion – although the story of Pinewood Studios is told. Among thousands of artifacts, you can see the Rank gong and sets from *Star Wars*, while techniques from the Superman films allow visitors to take part in one of more than 200 films. The Balcony Terrace, outdoors, and Chamber at the Movieum, once County Hall's magnificent debating chamber, are performance spaces, while downstairs there's a Horror Promenade and animation education centre.

Topolski Century

Hungerford Bridge Arch 158, Concert Hall Approach, behind the Royal Festival Hall, South Bank, SE1 8XU (www.topolskicentury.org.uk). Waterloo tube/rail. **Open/admission** check website. **Map** p401 M8.

This extensive mural, underneath the arches at Waterloo station, depicts an extraordinary jumble of 20th-century events and faces, from Bob Dylan to Winston Churchill. It's the work of Feliks Topolski, a Polish-born artist who made his name as a war artist in World War II and then settled in the UK. Long closed for restoration work, the museum was due to reopen in late 2008.

Hungerford Bridge to Blackfriars Bridge

Embankment or Temple tube/Blackfriars or Waterloo tube/rail.

When the **Southbank Centre** was built in the 1950s, the big concrete boxes that form the Royal Festival Hall, Purcell Room and Queen Elizabeth Hall were hailed as a daring statement of modern architecture. Together with the National Theatre and the Hayward, they comprise one of the largest and most popular arts centres in the world. The centrepiece, Sir Leslie Martin's **Royal Festival Hall** (1951), has been given a £75 million overhaul: the main auditorium has had its acoustics enhanced and seating refurbished; the upper floors include an improved Poetry Library and event rooms in which readings are delivered against the backdrop of the Eye and, on the far side of the river, Big Ben.

SIGHTS

Art with an Edge

Hayward's director-curator explains why his exhibitions always surprise.

In the summer of 2008, the **Hayward** gallery (*see opposite*) celebrated its 40th birthday, and to mark the occasion it turned one of its sculpture courts into a miniature lake. Visitors puttered around the gallery's brutal reinforced concrete in a homemade boat, while water trickled down the walls into the street below. The boat and lake were the work of Viennese art collective Gelitin, who were part of last summer's lauded show 'Psycho Buildings', a show that encouraged its participating artists to 'take on architecture'. Elsewhere in the Hayward complex, Rachel Whiteread filled an exhibition space with empty dolls' houses, and Cuban art troupe Los Carpinteros dismembered a tangle of flat-pack furniture, suspending shards of plasterboard shrapnel on lengths of twine.

The man behind 'Psycho Buildings' was the Hayward's curator-director Ralph Rugoff, who arrived on the South Bank in 2006 having made his name at the helm of San Francisco's Wattis Institute. Rugoff says that key to the show was the element of surprise. 'Art tries to surprise us. It tries to make us look at things in a different way. And it has to find unexpected ways to think about familiar things.'

He says the Hayward, with its multiple gallery spaces, is the perfect place to pursue such a vision: 'It has always had a feeling of adventure. It allows exhibitions to take all kinds of forms and to be presented

in very different ways. There have definitely been moments in the Hayward's history when people had no idea what the gallery was going to look like next.'

That's certainly been true of Rugoff's tenure so far: the hugely popular 'Blind Light' showed newly commissioned installations by Antony Gormley (the title piece was a room of glass, filled with a fog of vapour in which visitors blundered around); then 'The Painting of Modern Life' explored painting and photography. Andy Warhol was preceded by Soviet-era photo artist Alexander Rodchenko.

Rodchenko was chosen because 'he was someone who was completely committed to art having a kind of multiple public role'. And Rugoff explains that he's always looking for 'exhibitions that reach beyond the art world, beyond art for art's sake.' This is his take on what he sees as the mission of the revivified **Southbank Centre** (*see p44*), of which the Hayward is an integral part. 'Artistically, the Southbank Centre is relaunching itself. Trying, on the one hand, to reclaim some of the heritage of the Festival of Britain, in terms of being very democratic. And, on the other hand, wanting to produce edgier things.' But blockbuster exhibitions are not a thing of the past: 2009 follows the Andy Warhol with Ed Ruscha and then a multi-artist installation show called 'Walking in My Mind', which Rugoff says will 'explore interior landscapes of thought and feeling'.

Next door, the **Hayward** (*see below*) is a landmark of brutalist architecture. The gallery's elliptical glass pavilion, Waterloo Sunset, was designed in collaboration with light artist Dan Graham. Tucked under Waterloo Bridge is **BFI Southbank** (*see p299*), the UK's premier arthouse cinema, run by the British Film Institute. Out front is a second-hand book market. **Waterloo Bridge** itself, designed by Sir Giles Gilbert Scott in 1942, provides some of the finest views of the City, especially at dusk.

East of the bridge is Denys Lasdun's terraced **Royal National Theatre** (*see p336*), which has popular free outdoor performances in the summer (*see p343*) and free chamber music within during winter. Shaded by LED-dotted trees, the river path then takes you past a rare sandy patch of the river bed (often busy with sand sculptors in the summer months) to **Gabriel's Wharf**, a collection of small independent shops, ranging from stylish to kitschy. Next door, the deco tower of the **Oxo Tower Wharf** was designed to circumvent advertising regulations for the stock cube company that used to own the building. Saved by local action group Coin Street Community Builders, it now provides affordable housing, interesting designer shops and galleries, and two restaurants on the second floor (our current favourite is Bincho; *see p199*) and a rooftop restaurant and bistro with more wonderful views. **Bernie Spain Gardens**, just behind, is great for a break from the crowds.

Hayward

Belvedere Road, SE1 8XX (information 7921 0813/box office 0870 169 1000/www.hayward. org.uk). Embankment tube/Waterloo tube/rail. **Open** 10am-6pm Mon-Thur, Sat, Sun; 10am-10pm Fri. **Admission** check website for details; £4.50 under-16s; free under-12s. **Credit** AmEx, MC, V. **Map** p401 M8.

Casual visitors to the Hayward can hang out in the new industrial-look café downstairs (which becomes a bar at night), aptly called Concrete, before visiting the free contemporary exhibitions at the inspired Hayward Project Space – take the stairs to the first floor from the glass foyer extension. Hot on the heels from celebrating its 40th birthday last year, the versatile gallery continues its excellent programme of contemporary exhibitions, loaned from around the world. *See also opposite* **Art with an Edge**.

Around Waterloo

Waterloo tube/rail.

Surprisingly perhaps, there's plenty of interest around the stone-meets-glass rail terminus of London Waterloo. The massive **BFI IMAX** (*see p299*) is in the middle of a roundabout at the end of Waterloo bridge. The £20 million cinema makes imaginative use of a desolate space that, as recently as the 1990s, had become notorious for its grim 'cardboard city'. Where the homeless once gathered to sleep is now a freerunning hotspot. Further south, on the corner of Waterloo Road and the street called

SIGHTS

Eating out in front of the **Royal Festival Hall**. *See p47.*

LONDON
AQUARIUM

Join us on a fascinating voyage through the rivers, lakes and oceans of the world
encountering wonderful creatures from sharks, stingrays and clownfish,
to moray eels, lionfish and amazing jellyfish!

SAVE 10% and get fast track entry when you book online
www.londonaquarium.co.uk

Opposite Westminster Underground Station, next to the London Eye
Operated by the London Aquarium (South Bank) Limited, a Merlin Entertainments Group Company

the Cut is the restored Victorian façade of the **Old Vic Theatre** (*see p337*). Further down the Cut is the **Young Vic** (*see p344*), a hotbed of theatrical talent, which has seen its home (inside a former butcher's shop) well renovated, with a stylish balcony bar. Both bring a touch of West End glamour across the river. To the north of the Cut, off Cornwall Road, are a number of atmospheric terraces of mid 19th-century artisans' houses.

BANKSIDE

Borough or Southwark tube/
London Bridge tube/rail.

In Shakespeare's day, the area that is known as Bankside was the centre of bawdy Southwark, neatly located just beyond the jurisdiction of the City fathers. As well as playhouses such as the Globe and the Rose, there were the famous 'stewes' (brothels) presided over by the Bishops of Winchester, making a tidy income from the fines they levied on 'Winchester Geese' – prostitutes. It's no longer 'Geese' that flock to Bankside but culture vultures, drawn in massive numbers to the **Tate Modern** (*see p52*), the former power station turned art gallery. Spanning the river in front of the Tate, the **Millennium Bridge** was the first new Thames crossing in London since Tower Bridge opened in 1894. The bridge opened on 10 June 2000 and promptly closed again two days later because of an excessive swaying motion (the 'wobble'). Engineers installed dampers under the deck, but it remains an extremely elegant structure – a 'ribbon of steel' in the words of its conceptualists, architect Sir Norman Foster and sculptor Anthony Caro. Cross it and you'll find yourself at the foot of the stairs leading up to St Paul's Cathedral (*see p61*).

Continuing east, the river walk passes **Shakespeare's Globe** (*see below*) and, beyond Southwark Bridge, the **Anchor Bankside** pub (34 Park Street, 7407 1577). Built in 1775 on the site of an even older inn, the Anchor has been a brothel, a chapel and a ship's chandlers. The outside terrace, across the pathway, offers fine river views. All that's left of the grand Palace of Winchester, home of successive bishops, is the ruined rose window of the Great Hall on Clink Street. It stands next to the site of the bishop's former Clink prison, now the **Clink Prison Museum** (1 Clink Street, SE1 9DG, 7403 0900, www.clink.co.uk), where thieves, prostitutes and debtors all served their sentences. Round the corner is the entrance to the wine showcase **Vinopolis** (*see p52*). At the other end of Clink Street, St Mary Overie's dock contains a terrific full-scale replica of Drake's ship, the **Golden Hinde** (*see below*).

FREE Bankside Gallery

48 Hopton Street, SE1 9JH (7928 7521/www. banksidegallery.com). Southwark or London Bridge tube/rail. **Open** 11am-6pm daily. **Admission** free; donations appreciated. **Credit** MC, V. **Map** p404 O7.
In the shadow of Tate Modern, this tiny gallery is the home of the Royal Watercolour Society and the Royal Society of Painter-Printmakers. It runs a frequently changing programme of delightful print and watercolour exhibitions throughout the year; many of the works on show are for sale. Both societies hold frequent events, including talks and demonstrations (check the website for details).

Golden Hinde

St Mary Overie Dock, Cathedral Street, SE1 9DE (0870 011 700/www.goldenhinde. org). Monument tube/London Bridge tube/rail. **Open** 10am-5.30pm daily. **Admission** £6; £4.50 reductions; £18 family. **Credit** MC, V. **Map** p404 P8.
This meticulously reconstructed replica of Sir Francis Drake's 16th-century flagship is thoroughly seaworthy: the ship has even reprised the privateer's circumnavigatory voyage. On weekends, it swarms with children dressed up as pirates for birthday dos, while 'Living History Experiences' (some overnight) allow participants to dress in period clothes, eat Tudor fare and learn the skills of the Elizabethan seafarer; be sure to book well in advance.

★ Shakespeare's Globe

21 New Globe Walk, SE1 9DT (7902 1400/ box office 7401 9919/www.shakespeares-globe. org). Mansion House or Southwark tube/London Bridge tube/rail. **Open** *Exhibition & tours* 10am-5pm daily. *Tours* every 15 mins. **Admission** £9; £6.50-£7.50 reductions; £20 family. **Credit** AmEx, MC, V. **Map** p404 O7.
The original Globe Theatre, where many of William Shakespeare's plays were first staged and which he co-owned, burned to the ground in 1613 during a

---

INSIDE TRACK
RAISING THE ROSE

The **Rose** (21 New Globe Walk, SE1 9DT, 7261 9565, www.rosetheatre.org.uk), built by Philip Henslowe in1587, was the first theatre on Bankside. Inside the building now standing on the site, red lights show the position of the original theatre. Funds are being sought to continue excavations and preserve the site. For now, access is possible for special shows and events (check the website for details) or, from April to October, as part of the tour of **Shakespeare's Globe** (*see above*).

SIGHTS

Tate Modern.

performance of *Henry VIII*. Nearly 400 years later, it was rebuilt not far from its original site, using construction methods and materials as close to the originals as possible. It's a fully operational theatre: historically authentic (and often very good) performances are staged from April to October. In the UnderGlobe beneath the theatre is a fine exhibition on the history of the reconstruction, Bankside and its Elizabethan theatres, and Shakespeare's London. Guided tours of the theatre run throughout the year – as well as around the Rose Theatre site (*see p51*). A tour and exhibition visit lasts around 90 minutes.

★ FREE Tate Modern

Bankside, SE1 9TG (7401 5120/7887 8888/www.tate.org.uk). Southwark tube or London Bridge tube/rail. **Open** 10am-6pm Mon-Thur, Sun; 10am-10pm Fri, Sat. *Tours* 11am, noon, 2pm, 3pm daily. **Admission** free. *Temporary exhibitions* vary. **Map** p404 O7.
This powerhouse of modern art is awe inspiring even before you enter, thanks to its industrial architecture. It was built as Bankside Power Station and designed by Sir Giles Gilbert Scott, architect of Battersea Power Station (*see p153*). Shut down in 1981, it opened as an art museum in 2000 and has enjoyed spectacular popularity ever since. The gallery now attracts five million visitors a year to a building intended for half that number and a projected £165 million addition, called TM2, a pyramid-like annexe, is now required. Work is scheduled to start in 2009.

Inside, the original cavernous turbine hall is used to jaw-dropping effect as the home of large-scale, temporary installations (the latest, by French artist Dominique Gonzalez-Foerster, will be on display until April 2009). The permanent collection draws

from the Tate organisation's collections of modern art (international works from 1900 and on) and features heavy-hitters such as Matisse, Rothko, Bacon, Twombly and Beuys. In 2006, the galleries were completely rehung, with the artworks grouped according to movement (Surrealism, Minimalism, Post-war abstraction) rather than theme. Temporary exhibitions in 2009 will include an exploration of Danish artist Per Kirkeby, a Roni Horn overview and a revision of the Futurist movement.

If you don't know where to start, take one of the guided tours (ask at the information desk). There are also various tour packages, some combined with Shakespeare's Globe (*see p51*) and others including lunch or dinner (the Level 2 café is recommended; *see p287*). The Tate-to-Tate boat service – decor courtesy of Damien Hirst, bar on board – links with Tate Britain (*see p113*) and runs every 20 minutes, stopping along the way at the Eye (*see p47*). Tickets are available from ticket desks at both Tates, on board, online or by phone (7887 8888, £4.30 adult).
▶ *The most impressive entrance is not on the riverside, but down the ramp at the west end.*

Vinopolis

1 Bank End, SE1 9BU (0870 241 4040/www. vinopolis.co.uk). London Bridge tube/rail. **Open** *Jan-Nov* noon-10pm Mon, Thur, Fri; 11am-9pm Sat; noon-6pm Sun. *Dec* noon-6pm daily. Last entry 2hrs before closing. **Admission** £19.50-£32.50; free under-16s. **Credit** AmEx, MC, V. **Map** p404 P8.
Glossy Vinopolis is more of an introduction to wine-tasting than a resource for cognoscenti, but you do need to have some prior interest to get a kick out of it. Participants are furnished with a wine glass and an audio guide. Exhibits are set out by country, with

five opportunities to taste wine or champagne from different regions. Gin crashes the party courtesy of a Bombay Sapphire cocktail, and you can also sample Caribbean rum, beer from the venue's micro-brewery and even different types of absinthe.

BOROUGH

Borough or Southwark tube/London Bridge tube/rail.

At Clink Street, the route cuts inland, skirting the edge of the district of Borough. The landmark here is the Anglican **Southwark Cathedral** (*see below*), formerly St Saviour's and before that the monastic church of St Mary Overie. Shakespeare's brother Edmund was buried in the graveyard and there's a monument to the playwright inside. Just south of the cathedral you'll find the roof of **Borough Market**, a busy food market dating back to the 13th century. It's wholesale only for most of the week but hosts London's best food market (*see p258*) on Thursdays, Fridays and Saturdays – understandably crowded, especially on a Saturday – and surrounded by good places to eat and drink. Not far away, at 77 Borough High Street, is the quaint **George** (7407 2056), London's last surviving galleried coaching inn.

Around London Bridge Station tourist attractions clamour for attention. One of the grisliest, with its displays of body parts and surgical implements, is the **Old Operating Theatre, Museum & Herb Garret** although it's the really less scary **London Dungeon** (for both, *see below*) that draws the biggest queues. Competing with the blood-curdling shrieks emanating from its entrance are the dulcet tones of Vera Lynn, broadcast in an attempt to lure visitors into **Winston Churchill's Britain at War Experience** (*see below*). Underneath the arches, there's the history-meets-kitsch **London Bridge Experience** (*see below*).

London Dungeon

28-34 Tooley Street, SE1 2SZ (7403 7221/ www.thedungeons.com). London Bridge tube/rail. **Open** *Jan* 10.30am-5pm daily. *Feb, Mar* 9.30am-6.30pm daily. *Apr, Aug* 9.30am-7pm daily. *May-July, Sept, Oct* 10am-5.30pm daily. *Nov, Dec* 10am-5pm daily. **Admission** £20.95; £15.95-£18.95 reductions. **Credit** AmEx, MC, V. **Map** p405 Q8.
Enter the Victorian railway arches of London Bridge for this jokey celebration of torture, death and disease. Visitors are led through a dry-ice fog past gravestones and hideously rotting corpses to experience nasty symptoms from the Great Plague exhibition: an actor-led medley of corpses, boils, projectile vomiting, worm-filled skulls and scuttling rats. The Great Fire and Judgement Day also get the treatment.

London Bridge Experience

2-4 Tooley Street, Bankside, SE1 2PF (0800 043 4666/www.thelondonbridgeexperience.com). London Bridge tube/rail. **Open** 10am-6pm daily. **Admission** £19.95; £14.95-£15.95 reductions. **Credit** MC, V. **Map** p405 Q8.
See p55 **London Bridge Has Fallen Down**.

★ Old Operating Theatre, Museum & Herb Garret

9A St Thomas's Street, SE1 9RY (7188 2679/ www.thegarret.org.uk). London Bridge tube/rail. **Open** 10.30am-5pm daily. **Admission** £5.45; £3-£4.45 reductions; £13.25 family; free under-6s. **No credit cards**. **Map** p405 Q8.
The tower that houses this salutary reminder of antique surgical practice used to be part of the chapel of St Thomas's Hospital. Visitors enter via a vertiginous wooden spiral staircase to view a pre-anaesthetic operating theatre dating from 1822, with tiered viewing seats for students. Just as gruesome are the operating tools that look like torture implements.

FREE Southwark Cathedral

London Bridge, SE1 9DA (7367 6700/tours 7367 6734/www.dswark.org/cathedral). London Bridge tube/rail. **Open** 8am-6pm daily (closing times vary on religious holidays). *Services* 8am, 8.15am, 12.30pm, 12.45pm, 5.30pm Mon-Fri; 9am, 9.15am, 4pm Sat; 8.45am, 9am, 11am, 3pm, 6.30pm Sun. *Choral Evensong* 5.30pm Tue (boys & men), Fri (men only); 5.30pm Mon, Thur (girls). **Admission** Suggested donation £4. **Credit** AmEx, MC, V. **Map** p404 P8.
The oldest bits of this building date back more than 800 years. The retro-choir was the setting for several Protestant martyr trials during the reign of Mary Tudor. The courtyard is one of the area's prettiest places for a rest, especially during the summer. Inside, there are memorials to Shakespeare, John Harvard (benefactor of the American university) and Sam Wanamaker (the force behind Shakespeare's Globe, *see p51*), while Chaucer features in the stained glass.

Winston Churchill's Britain at War Experience

64-66 Tooley Street, SE1 2TF (7403 3171/ www.britainatwar.co.uk). London Bridge tube/ rail. **Open** *Apr-Oct* 10am-6pm daily. *Nov-Mar* 10am-5pm daily. **Admission** £10.45; £4.95-£5.95 reductions; £26 family; free under-5s. **Credit** AmEx, MC, V. **Map** p405 Q8.
This old-fashioned exhibition recalls the privations endured by the British during World War II. Visitors descend from street level in an ancient lift to a reconstructed tube station shelter. The experience continues with displays about London during the Blitz, including real bombs, rare documents, photos and reconstructed shopfronts. The displays on rationing, food production and Land Girls are fascinating, and the set-piece walk-through bombsite quite disturbing.

SIGHTS

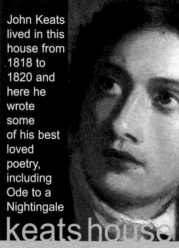
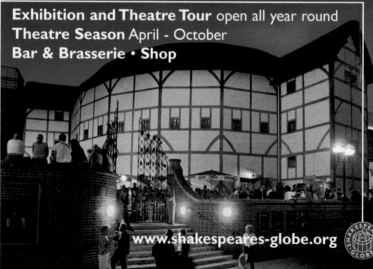

LONDON BRIDGE TO TOWER BRIDGE

Bermondsey tube/London Bridge tube/rail.

Across the street from the Dungeon is Hay's Galleria. Once an enclosed dock, these days it's dominated by a peculiar kinetic sculpture called the *Navigators* and several unremarkable craft stalls. Exiting on the riverside, you can walk east past the great grey hulk of **HMS Belfast** (*see p56*) to Tower Bridge.

Beyond the battleship you pass the pristine, but rather soulless environs of **City Hall**, home of London's current government. Designed by Lord Norman Foster, the eco-friendly rotund glass structure leans squiffily away from the river (to prevent it casting shade on the walkers below – very thoughtful). There's a pleasant outside 'amphitheatre' called the Scoop, used for lunch breaks, sunbathing and outdoor events in summer.

Near **Tower Bridge**, a board announces when the bridge is next due to be raised (which

London Bridge Has Fallen Down

Happy 800th birthday, London Bridge… only, which bridge exactly?

Ever since the Romans first constructed a crossing here for their Londinium about 2,000 years ago, there have been many London Bridges. The one being celebrated this year is that which, to date, lasted longest. Old London Bridge, finished in 1209, after 33 years of building work, was the first Thames crossing made of stone – and London's only bridge over the river until 1750, when Westminster Bridge was finished. Old London Bridge, cluttered with houses to the extent that it almost became a tunnel, linked the City with Southwark for some 600 years.

All that remains of it today are three stone alcoves, originally installed on the bridge in the 18th century to prevent pedestrians from being trampled by traffic. Two of the original 14 are in Hackney's Victoria Park, but another stayed close to the current bridge – in the courtyard of Guy's Hospital. Old London Bridge was demolished in 1831, after the climate and continuous underfunding by the spendthrift queen had taken their toll

(sparking the angry folk song 'London Bridge is falling down, my fair lady'). A new museum celebrating the life and times of the old bridge is to be built in the vaults beneath its offspring, but it is not scheduled to open until 2012 (for details, see www.oldlondonbridge.com).

In the meantime, there's the splendidly kitsch **London Bridge Experience** (*see p53*). Spread over two levels, this costumed whistle-stop tour comprises a family-friendly lesson on the crossing's past, as well as a scary adventure into the haunted foundations of the bridge. As you pass through heavy doors, the sacking of London by Boudicca is described by a bloodied Roman soldier. There's a Russell Crowe-like Viking warrior, the ghost of William Wallace and a chamber of gore hosted by the chap in charge of putting chopped-off heads on poles. Then it's down to the catacombs, dank, pestilential corridors peopled by crazed zombies and animatronic torture victims.

It was Sir John Rennie (you'll meet him in a cobwebbed replica of his Victorian study) who designed the 1831 follow-up to the old bridge. Built 180 feet upriver, it was made out of granite; you can still see one of its original vaults where the western end of Tooley Street passes beneath today's bridge. Rennie's bridge lasted until the 1960s, when it was put up for sale. American Robert McCulloch spent $2,460,000 dismantling and rebuilding it – in Lake Havasu City, Arizona, where it still carries traffic today. The current London Bridge, made of rather unimpressive grey concrete, replaced Rennie's. Standing on it now, it is hard to imagine the bustling old London Bridge just downstream. But do give it a try: it is the old thing's birthday.

SIGHTS

happens about 900 times a year). It's one of the lowest bridges over the Thames – hence the twin lifting sections or bascules. Their original steam-driven hydraulic machinery can still be seen at the **Tower Bridge Exhibition** (*see p71*), with its fantastic views from the top.

Further east, the former warehouses of **Butler's Wharf** are now mainly given over to expensive riverside dining; one of them also now houses the **Design Museum** (*see below*).

On Bermondsey Street, many of the historic houses now host hip design studios. It's also the address of the **London Fashion & Textile Museum** (*see below*). The redevelopment of Bermondsey Square has thankfully spared the traditional eel and pie shop M Manze (*see p199*) and the Friday antiques market (4am-2pm) is still great for browsing, even though the bargains are usually gone before breakfast.

Design Museum

Shad Thames, SE1 2YD (7403 6933/www. designmuseum.org). Tower Hill tube/London Bridge tube/rail. **Open** *10am-5.45pm daily.* **Admission** £8.50; £5-£6.50 reductions; free under-12s. **Credit** AmEx, MC, V. **Map** p405 S9.
Exhibitions in this white 1930s building (once a banana warehouse) focus on modern and contemporary design. The smart Blueprint Café has a fine balcony overlooking the Thames. You can buy designer books in the museum's shop, as well as items related to the exhibitions, which in 2009 include shows on fashion designer Hussein Chalayan (Jan-May) and architect David Chipperfield (from Sept 2009).
▶ *Fine exhibitions of contemporary design are also held at the V&A; see p122.*

Fashion & Textile Museum

83 Bermondsey Street, Borough, SE1 3XF (7407 8664/www.ftmlondon.org). London Bridge tube/rail. **Open** 11am-6pm Wed-Sun. **Admission** £5; free-£3 reductions. **Map** p405 Q9.
Flamboyant as its founder, fashion designer Zandra Rhodes, this pink and orange museum reopened in 2008. It holds 3,000 of Rhodes' garments, some on permanent display, along with her archive of paper designs, sketchbooks, silk screens and show videos. A quirky shop sells ware by new designers. Exhibitions in 2009 include Swedish Fashion, and Undercover: the Evolution of Underwear.

★ HMS Belfast

Morgan's Lane, Tooley Street, SE1 2JH (7940 6300/www.iwm.org.uk). London Bridge tube/rail. **Open** *Mar-Oct* 10am-6pm daily. *Nov-Feb* 10am-5pm daily. **Admission** £9.95; £6.15 reductions; free under-16s (must be accompanied by an adult). **Credit** MC, V. **Map** p405 R8.
This 11,500-ton 'Edinburgh' class large light cruiser is the last surviving big gun World War II warship in Europe. A floating branch of the Imperial War Museum (*see p142*), it makes an unlikely playground for children, who tear easily around its cramped complex of gun turrets, bridge, decks, and engine room. The *Belfast* was built in 1938, provided cover for convoys to Russia, and was instrumental in the Normandy Landings. She also supported United Nations forces in Korea, before being decommissioned in 1965. Running until autumn 2010, a new interactive exhibition explores British shipbuilding techniques through the ages, from the days of sail to modern prefabrication.

City Hall. See p55.

The City

The centre of the financial world and the historic heart of London.

The City means business. Less than 10,000 souls actually reside within the Square Mile (in fact, it measures 1.21 square miles). This precinct of land is bounded by the 2nd-century walls of Roman *Londinium*, a city that contained six times the current number of residents. Every working day, though, the population increases tenfold here as bankers, brokers, lawyers and traders storm into their towering office blocks to mash up billions of other people's money. Apart from the two big crowd-pullers – **St Paul's** and the **Tower of London**

| Map p402, p404, p405 | Restaurants & cafés p199 |
| Hotels p169 | Pubs & bars p227 |

– the City might not immediately appear to have much to offer casual visitors, but dive into the throng of office workers and you'll find that the streets are paved with historical treasures.

ABOUT THE CITY

From the start London has been divided in two, with Westminster the centre of politics and the City the capital of commerce. Many of the City's administrative affairs are still run on a feudal basis, under the auspices of the arcane borough council once known as the Corporation of London. Now rebranded the City of London, it is the richest local authority in Britain. The sheer wealth of this part of London has always been hard for ordinary mortals to conceive – the City was able to bounce back after losing half its population to the Black Death and half its buildings first to the Great Fire and much later to Nazi bombing during the Blitz. To really understand the City, visit on a weekday when the great economic machine is running at full tilt; at weekends, many of the streets fall eerily quiet, although key sightseeing areas – especially around **St Paul's** (*see p59*) – are busy all week. Having recognised the value of tourism, the City is pursuing plans to draw more people here at the weekends (*see p69* **The New City**).

City of London Information Centre
St Paul's Churchyard, EC4M 8BX (7332 1456/ www.cityoflondon.gov.uk). St Paul's tube. **Open** 9.30am-5.30pm Mon-Sat; 10am-4pm Sun. **No credit cards. Map** p404 O6.

Run by the City of London, the striking new tourist office on the Thames side of St Paul's opened in 2008. As well as information and brochures on sights, events, walks and talks, it offers tours with specialist City of London-trained guides.

FLEET STREET
Temple tube/Blackfriars tube/rail.

Without Fleet Street, the daily newspaper might never have been invented. Marking the route of the vanished River Fleet, which still gurgles somewhere below street level, Fleet Street was a major artery for the delivery of goods into the City, including the first printing press, which was installed behind **St Bride's**

INSIDE TRACK
BRILLIANT BUILDINGS

During the annual **Open House** in September (*see p273*), several of the City's iconic buildings usually open to the public. Last year these included Lloyd's of London and the Bank of England. For the big-hitters, get there early or expect to face a big queue.

Temple Church.

Church (*see p59*) in 1500 by William Caxton's assistant, Wynkyn de Worde, who also set up a bookstall in the churchyard of St Paul's. In 1702, London's first daily newspaper, the *Daily Courant*, rolled off the presses and, in 1712, Fleet Street saw the first of many libel cases when the *Courant* leaked the details of a private parliamentary debate. By the end of World War II, half a dozen newspaper offices were churning out scoops and scandals between the Strand and Farringdon Road. Most of the newspapers moved away after Rupert Murdoch won his war with the print unions in the 1980s; the last of the news agencies, Reuters, finally followed suit in 2005. Today the only periodical published on Fleet Street is a comic – the much-loved *Beano*. You can see some interesting relics from the media days, though, including the Portland-stone **Reuters building** (no.85), the Egyptian-influenced **Daily Telegraph building** (no.135) and the sleek, black **Daily Express building** (nos.121-128), designed by Owen Williams in the 1930s and arguably the only art deco building of note in London (stand across the road for a glimpse into the magnificent chrome-lined lobby).

Tucked away on an alley behind St Bride's Church is the **St Bride Foundation Institute** (7353 3331, www.stbridefoundation.org) with a library (7353 4660, www.stbride.org; noon-5.30pm Tue, Thur; noon-9pm Wed) dedicated to printing and typography. Recently refurbished, the library mounts a series of temporary exhibitions showing off its collections, which include rare works by Eric Gill, woodblocks from the Chiswick Press, and maquettes for Kinnear and Calvert's distinctive road signs, blue for the motorways and green for main roads.

Back on Fleet Street is **St Dunstan-in-the-West** (7405 1929, www.stdunstaninthewest.org; free tours 11am-3pm Tue), where the poet John Donne was rector in the 17th century. The church was rebuilt in the 1830s, but the eye-catching clock with chimes beaten by clockwork giants dates to 1671. It is now designated the Diocese of London's Church for Europe.

Next door, no.186 is the house where Sweeney Todd, the 'demon barber of Fleet Street', allegedly murdered his customers before selling their bodies to a local pie shop. The legend itself is in fact a porky pie – Todd was invented by the editors of a Victorian penny dreadful in 1846 and propelled to fame by a stage play and Stephen Sondheim musical.

Fleet Street has always been known for its alehouses. Half the newspaper editorials in London were once composed over liquid lunches at pubs like the Old Bell Tavern (no.95, 7583 0216) and the Punch Tavern (no.99, 7353 6658), where the satirical magazine *Punch* was launched in 1841; both pubs are closed at weekends. On the other side of the road, **Ye Olde Cheshire Cheese** (no.145, 7353 6170) was a favourite watering hole of Dickens, and later Yeats, and in its heyday hosted the bibulous literary salons of Dr Samuel Johnson, who lived around the corner at 17 Gough Square (*see below*). At no.66, the **Tipperary** (7583 6470) is the oldest Irish pub outside Ireland – it opened in the 1700s and sold the first pint of Guinness on the British mainland shortly after.

Dr Johnson's House

17 Gough Square, off Fleet Street, EC4A 3DE (7353 3745/www.drjohnsonshouse.org). Chancery Lane or Temple tube/Blackfriars tube/rail. **Open** *May-Sept* 11am-5.30pm Mon-Sat. *Oct-Apr* 11am-5pm Mon-Sat. *Tours* by arrangement, groups of 10 or more only. **Admission** £4.50; £1.50-£3.50 reductions; £10 family; free under-5s. *Tours* free. **No credit cards. Map** p404 N6.

Famed as the author of one of the first – as well as being surely the most significant and certainly the wittiest – dictionary of the English language, Dr Samuel Johnson (1709-84) also wrote poems, a novel and one of the earliest travelogues, an acerbic account of a tour of the Western Isles with his indefatigable biographer James Boswell. You can tour the stately Georgian town house off Fleet Street where Johnson came up with his inspired definitions – 'to make dictionaries is dull work,' was his definition of the word 'dull'. In 2009 the museum will be celebrating the 300th anniversary of the great man's birth, with a series of special events and exhibitions.

FREE St Bride's Church

Fleet Street, EC4Y 8AU (7427 0133/www.st brides.com). Temple tube/Blackfriars tube/rail. **Open** 8am-6pm Mon-Fri; 11am-3pm Sat; 10am-1pm, 5-7.30pm Sun. Times vary Mon-Sat, so phone ahead to check. **Admission** free. **Map** p404 N6.

Hidden away down an alley south of Fleet Street, St Bride's is still popularly known as the journalists' church. In the north aisle is a shrine dedicated to journos killed in action. Down in the crypt a very fine museum displays a number of fragments of the churches that have existed on this site since the sixth century. According to local legend, the Wren-designed spire was the inspiration behind the traditional tiered wedding cake.

TEMPLE

Temple tube/Blackfriars tube/rail.

At its western end, Fleet Street becomes the Strand at **Temple Bar**, the City's ancient western boundary and once the site of Wren's great gateway, now relocated beside St Paul's (*see p61*). This area has long been linked to the law and here on the edge of Holborn (*see p72*) stand the splendid neo-Gothic **Royal Courts of Justice** (7947 6000, www.hmcourts-service.gov.uk). Two of the highest civil courts in the land sit here, the High Court and Appeals

Court – justice at its most bewigged and ermine-robed – and visitors are welcome to observe the process of law in any of the 88 courtrooms. Across the road are the interconnected courtyards of the **Middle Temple** (7427 4800, www.middletemple.org.uk) and **Inner Temple** (7797 8183, www.inner temple.org.uk), two of the Inns of Court that provided training and lodging for London's medieval lawyers. Access is usually reserved for lawyers and barristers, but tours of the Inner Temple can be arranged for £10 per person (minimum five people, call 7797 8241 to book).

The site was formerly the headquarters of the Knights Templar, an order of warrior monks founded in the 12th century to protect pilgrims travelling to the Holy Land. The Templars built the original **Temple Church** (*see below*) in 1185, but they fell foul of Catholic orthodoxy during the Crusades and the order was disbanded for heresy. Dan Brown used the Temple Church as a setting for his bestselling conspiracy novel *The Da Vinci Code* (2003). Robin Griffith-Jones, the master of Temple Church, has produced a robust response to his claims at www.beliefnet.com/templechurch.

FREE Temple Church

King's Bench Walk, EC4Y 7BB (7353 8559/www.templechurch.com). Temple tube. **Open** 1-4pm Mon-Wed; phone or check website for details Thur-Sun. *Services* 1.15pm Thur; 8.30am, 11.15am Sun. **Admission** free. **Map** p404 N6.

Inspired by Jerusalem's Church of the Holy Sepulchre, the Temple Church was the private chapel of the mystical Knights Templar. The rounded apse contains the worn gravestones of several Crusader knights, but the church was refurbished by Wren and the Victorians, and few original features survived the Blitz bombing. Not that it puts off the wild speculations of all those avid *Da Vinci Code* fans. There are organ recitals most Wednesdays (phone for details). ▶ *There is a Crusader altar in All Hallows by the Tower; see p70. For the Hospitallers, try the Museum of the Order of St John; see p74.*

ST PAUL'S & AROUND

St Paul's tube.

After Big Ben, the towering dome of **St Paul's Cathedral** (*see p61*) is probably the definitive symbol of London, an architectural two fingers up to the Great Fire and later, in a famous photograph, to the German bombers that tried to destroy the city. The first cathedral to St Paul was built on the Ludgate Hill site in 604, but it fell to Viking marauders and its Norman replacement – a magnificent Gothic structure with a 490-foot spire, taller than any London building until the 1960s – burned to the ground

SIGHTS

in the Great Fire. The new St Paul's was commissioned from Sir Christopher Wren in 1673 as the centrepiece of London's resurgence from the ashes. Wren had won a royal commission to build 53 churches, of which more than 20 still survive intact; St Paul's was his magnum opus. Modern buildings now encroach on the cathedral from all sides but the open-air gallery at the top of the dome still provides the finest viewpoint in the City.

Immediately north of the cathedral is the redeveloped **Paternoster Square**, a modern plaza incorporating a sundial that only very rarely tells the time. The name harks back to the days when priests from St Paul's walked the streets chanting the Lord's Prayer (the opening line being *Pater noster*, 'Our Father'). Also of interest here is Wren's statue-covered **Temple Bar**, which previously stood at the intersection of Fleet Street and the Strand, marking the boundary between the City of London and neighbouring Westminster. During the Middle Ages, the monarch was only allowed to pass through the Temple Bar into the City with the approval of the Lord Mayor of London. The archway was dismantled as part of a Victorian road-widening programme in 1878 and became a garden ornament for a country estate in Hertfordshire, before being installed in its current location, as the gateway between St Paul's and Paternoster Square, in 2004.

South of St Paul's, a cascade of steps runs down to the **Millennium Bridge**, which spans the river to **Tate Modern** (*see p52*). The stairs take you close to the 17th-century **College of Arms** (*see below*), the official seat of heraldry in Great Britain. East of the cathedral is narrow Bow Lane, lined with bijou shops, bistros and champagne bars. The lane is bookended by St **Mary-le-Bow** (7248 5139, www.stmarylebow.co.uk, 7am-6pm Tue-Thur, 7am-4pm Fri), constructed by Wren between 1671 and 1680, its peals once defined anyone born within earshot as a true Cockney; and St **Mary Aldermary** (7248 9902, www.stmaryaldermary.co.uk, 11am-3pm Mon, Wed, Thur), with its pin-straight spire, designed by Wren's office; the only Gothic church by Wren to survive World War II. Inside, there's a fabulous moulded plaster ceiling and original wooden sword rest (London parishioners carried arms up until the late 19th century). Roman coins are sold here to fund the renovation of the church.

There are more Wren creations south of St Paul's. On Garlick Hill, named after the medieval garlic market, is St **James Garlickhythe** (7236 1719, www.stjames garlickhythe.org.uk, 10.30am-4pm Mon-Fri), the official church of London's vintners and joiners, built by Wren in 1682. The church was hit by bombs in World War I and World War II and partly ruined by a falling crane in 1991, but the interior has been convincingly restored. Off Victoria Street is St **Nicholas Cole Abbey**, the first church to be rebuilt after the Great Fire.

To the north-west of the cathedral is the **Old Bailey** (*see below*).

FREE Old Bailey (Central Criminal Court)

Corner of Newgate Street & Old Bailey, EC4M 7EH (7248 3277). St Paul's tube. **Open** *Public gallery* 10am-1pm, 2-4.30pm Mon-Fri. **Admission** free. No under-14s; 14-16s only if accompanied by adults. **Map** p404 O6.

A gilded statue of blind (meaning impartial) justice stands atop London's most famous criminal court. Although the current building was only completed in 1907, the site has hosted some of the most controversial trials in British history, including that of Oscar Wilde. More recently, the Kray brothers and IRA bombers have been put in the dock here. The public is welcome to attend trials but bags, cameras, dictaphones, mobile phones and food are prohibited (and no storage facilities are provided).

FREE College of Arms

130 Queen Victoria Street, EC4V 4BT (7248 2762/www.college-of-arms.gov.uk). St Paul's tube/Blackfriars tube/rail. **Open** 10am-4pm Mon-Fri. *Tours* by arrangement. **Admission** free. **Map** p404 O7.

Originally created to identify competing knights at medieval jousting tournaments, coats of arms soon became an integral part of family identity for the landed gentry of Britain. Visitors interested in tracking down their family history can arrange tours.

★ St Paul's Cathedral

Ludgate Hill, EC4M 8AD (7236 4128/www. stpauls.co.uk). St Paul's tube. **Open** 8.30am-4pm Mon-Sat. *Galleries, crypt & ambulatory* 8.30am-3.45pm Mon-Sat. Special events may cause closure; check before visiting. *Tours of cathedral & crypt* 11am, 11.30am, 1.30pm, 2pm Mon-Sat. **Admission** *Cathedral, crypt & gallery* £10; £3.50-£8.50 reductions; £23.50 family; free under-6s. *Tours* £3; £1-£2.50 reductions. **Credit** (shop) AmEx, MC, V. **Map** p404 O6.

The passing of three centuries has done nothing to diminish the magnificence of London's most famous cathedral. In the last decade, a £40m restoration project has painstakingly removed most of the Victorian grime from the walls and the extravagant main façade looks as brilliant today as it must have when the last stone was placed in 1708 (for more on Wren and the architecture here, *see p36* **Profile**). On the south side of the cathedral, an austere new park has been laid out, tracing the outline of the medieval chapter house whose remains lie 4ft beneath the park.

SIGHTS

Millennium Bridge and St Paul's Cathedral. *See p61.*

The vast open spaces of the interior contain memorials to national heroes such as Wellington, Lawrence of Arabia and General Gordon of Khartoum. The statue of John Donne – metaphysical poet and former Dean of St Paul's – is frequently overlooked, but it's the only monument to have been saved from Old St Paul's. The Whispering Gallery, inside the dome, is reached by 259 shallow steps from the main hall (the acoustics here are so good that a whisper can be bounced clearly to the other side of the dome). Steps continue up to first the Stone Gallery (119 tighter, steeper steps), with its high external balustrades, then outside to the Golden Gallery (152 steps), with its giddying views – come here to orient yourself before setting off in search of other City monuments.

Before leaving St Paul's, head down to the maze-like crypt (through a door whose frame is decorated with skull and crossbones), which contains a shop and café and memorials to such dignitaries as Alexander Fleming, William Blake and Admiral Lord Nelson, whose grand tomb (purloined from Wolsey by Henry VIII but never used by him) is right beneath the centre of the dome. To one side is the small, plain tombstone of Christopher Wren himself, inscribed by his son with the epitaph, 'Reader, if you seek a monument, look around you'; Millais and Turner were buried near him at their request.

As well as tours of the main cathedral and self-guided audio tours (£3.50, £3 reductions), you can join special tours of the Triforium – visiting the library and Wren's 'Great Model' – at 11.30am and 2pm on Monday and Tuesday and at 2pm on Friday (pre-book on 7246 8357, £14.50 incl admission).

NORTH TO SMITHFIELD

Barbican or St Paul's tube.

North of St Paul's on Foster Lane is **St Vedast-alias-Foster** (7606 3998, www.vedast.net, 8am-6pm Mon-Fri), another finely proportioned Wren church, restored after World War II using spare trim from other churches in the area. Nearby, off Aldersgate Street, peaceful, fern-filled **Postman's Park** contains the Watts Memorial to Heroic Sacrifice: a wall of Victorian ceramic plaques, each of which commemorates an heroic but fatal act of bravery, such as the sad story of Sarah Smith, a pantomime artiste at the Prince's Theatre, who received 'terrible injuries when attempting in her inflammable dress to extinguish the flames which had engulfed her companion (1863)'.

Further west on Little Britain (named after the Duke of Brittany, not the TV show) is **St Bartholomew-the-Great** (*see p63*) founded along with St Bartholomew's Hospital in the 12th century. Popularly known as St Bart's, the hospital treated air-raid casualties throughout World War II – shrapnel damage from German bombs is still clearly visible on the outside walls. Scottish nationalists now come here to lay flowers at the monument to William Wallace, who was executed in front of the church on the orders of Edward I in 1305. Just beyond St Bart's is bustling Smithfield Market (*see p74*).

St Bartholomew-the-Great

West Smithfield, EC1A 9DS (7606 5171/www.
greatsbarts.com). Barbican tube/Farringdon
tube/rail. **Open** 8.30am-5pm Mon-Fri (until 4pm
Nov-Feb); 10.30am-4pm Sat; 2.30-6.30pm Sun.
Services 9am, 11am, 6.30pm Sun; 12.30pm Tue;
8.30am Thur. **Admission** £4; £3 reductions;
£10 family. **Map** p402 O5.

This atmospheric medieval church was built over
the remains of the 12th-century priory hospital of
St Bartholomew, founded by Prior Rahere, a former
courtier of Henry I. The church was chopped about
during Henry VIII's reign and the interior is
now firmly Elizabethan, although it also contains
donated works of modern art. You may recognise
the main hall from the movies *Shakespeare in Love*
and *Four Weddings & a Funeral. Photos p64.*

FREE Museum of
St Bartholomew's Hospital

North Win, West Smithfield, EC1A 7BE (7601
8152/www.bartsandthelondon.nhs.uk/museums).
Barbican or Farringdon tube/rail. **Open** 10am-
4pm Tue-Fri. **Admission** free; donations
welcome. **Map** p402 O5.

Be glad you are living in the 21st century. Many of
the displays in this small museum inside St Bart's
Hospital relate to the days before anaesthetics, when
surgery and carpentry were kindred occupations.
Every Friday at 2pm visitors can take a guided tour
of the museum (£5, book ahead on 7837 0546) that
takes in the Hogarth paintings in the Great Hall, the
little church of St Bartholomew-the-Less, neighbouring St Bartholomew-the-Great and Smithfield.

NORTH OF LONDON WALL

Barbican tube/Moorgate tube/rail.

From St Bart's, the road known as London
Wall runs east to Bishopsgate, following the
approximate route of the old Roman walls.
Tower blocks have sprung up here like daisies,
but the odd lump of weathered stonework
can still be seen poking up between the office
blocks, marking the path of the old City wall.
You can patrol the remaining stretches of the
wall, with panels (some barely legible) pointing
out the highlights along a route of almost two
miles. The walk starts near the **Museum
of London** (*see right*) and continues to the
Tower of London.

The area north of London Wall was reduced
to rubble by German bombs in World War II.
In 1958, the City of London and London County
Council clubbed together to buy the land for
the construction of 'a genuine residential
neighbourhood, with schools, shops, open
spaces and amenities'. What Londoners got
was the **Barbican**, a vast concrete estate of
2,000 flats that feels a bit like a university

campus after the students have all gone home.
Casual visitors may get the eerie feeling they
have been miniaturised and transported into a
giant architect's model, but design enthusiasts
will recognise the Barbican as a prime example
of 1970s brutalism, softened a little by time and
rectangular ponds of friendly resident ducks.

The main attraction here is the Barbican arts
complex, with its library, cinema, theatre and
concert hall – each reviewed in the appropriate
chapters – plus an art gallery (*see below*) and
the **Barbican Conservatory** (noon-5pm Sun),
a giant greenhouse full of exotic ferns and
palms. Unfortunately, pedestrian access was
not high on the architects' list of priorities – the
Barbican is a maze of blank passages and dead-
end walkways, not much improved by a recent
injection of millions of pounds into renewal and
refurbishment. Marooned amid the concrete
towers is the only pre-war building in the
vicinity: the heavily restored 16th-century
church of **St Giles Cripplegate** (7638 1997,
www.stgilescripplegate.com, 11am-4pm Mon-
Fri), where Oliver Cromwell was married and
John Milton buried.

North-east of the Barbican on City Road
are **John Wesley's House** (*see p64*) and
Bunhill Fields, the nonconformist cemetery
where William Blake, the preacher John Bunyan
and novelist Daniel Defoe are buried.

Barbican Art Gallery

Barbican Centre, Silk Street, EC2Y 8DS (7638
8891/7382 7006/www.barbican.org.uk). Barbican
tube/Moorgate tube/rail. **Open** 11am-8pm Mon,
Fri-Sun; 11am-6pm Tue, Wed,; 11am-10pm Thur.
Admission £8; £4-£6 reductions; under-12s
free. **Credit** (shop) AmEx, MC, V. **Map** p402 P5.

The art gallery at the Barbican Centre on the third
floor isn't quite as 'out there' as it would like you to
think, but the exhibitions on design, architecture and
pop culture are usually pretty diverting, as are their
often attention-grabbing titles.

▶ *On the ground floor, the Curve is a free
exhibition space (yes, it's curved) for specially
commissioned works and contemporary art.*

★ FREE Museum of London

150 London Wall, EC2Y 5HN (0870 444 3851/
www.museumoflondon.org.uk). Barbican or St
Paul's tube. **Open** 10am-5.50pm Mon-Sat; noon-
5.50pm Sun. **Admission** free; suggested
donation £2. **Credit** (shop) AmEx, MC, V.
Map p402 P5.

Opened in 1976, this expansive museum, which is
set in the middle of a decidedly unpromising roundabout on London Wall, these days shares the job of
recreating London's history with the Museum of
London Docklands (*see p140*). The chronological
displays begin with 'London Before London': flint
axes from 300,000 BC found in Glasshouse Street,

SIGHTS

St Bartholomew-the-Great.
See p63.

Piccadilly; bones from an aurochs and hippopotami; and the Bronze Age Dagenham idol, a fertility image carved from a single piece of Scots pine. 'Roman London' includes an impressive reconstructed dining room complete with mosaic floor. Windows overlook a sizeable fragment of the City wall, whose Roman foundations have clearly been built upon many times over the centuries. Sound effects and audio-visual displays illustrate the medieval city, with clothes, shoes and armour on display. From Elizabethan and Jacobean London, heyday of the Globe Theatre, comes the Cheapside Hoard, an astonishing cache of jewellery unearthed in 1912. The downstairs galleries (Victorian London, 'World City' and Lord Mayor's coach) are closed for remodelling until spring 2010. The website has details of temporary exhibitions and activities for children.

FREE John Wesley's House & Museum of Methodism

Wesley's Chapel, 49 City Road, EC1Y 1AU (7253 2262/www.wesleyschapel.org.uk). Moorgate or Old Street tube/rail. **Open** 10am-4pm Mon-Sat; after the service until 1.45pm Sun. *Tours* arrangements on arrival; groups of 10 or more phone ahead. **Admission** free; donations welcome. **Map** p403 Q4.

The founder of Methodism, John Wesley (1703-91), was a man of legendary self-discipline. You can see the minister's nightcap, preaching gown and personal experimental electric-shock machine on a

tour of his austere home on City Road. The adjacent chapel has a small museum on the history of Methodism and fine memorials of dour, sideburn-sporting preachers. A full refurbishment is on the cards for 2009, so phone ahead before visiting. Downstairs (to the right) are some of the finest public toilets in London, built in 1899 with original fittings by Sir Thomas Crapper.

BANK & AROUND

Mansion House tube/Bank tube/DLR.

Few places in London have quite the same sense of pomp and circumstance as Bank. Above Bank Station, seven streets come together to mark the symbolic heart of the Square Mile, ringed by some of the most important buildings in the City. Constructed from steely Portland stone, the Bank of England, the Royal Exchange and Mansion House form a stirring monument to the importance of money: most decisions concerning the British economy are still made within this small precinct.

Easily the most dramatic building here is the **Bank of England**, founded in 1694 to fund William III's war against the French. It's a veritable fortress, with no accessible windows and just one public entrance, leading to the **Bank of England Museum** (*see p66*). The outer walls were constructed in 1788 by Sir

John Soane, whose personal museum can still be seen in Holborn (*see p73*). Although millions have been stolen from its depots elsewhere in London, the bank itself has never been robbed. Today it is responsible for printing the nation's banknotes and setting the base rates for borrowing and lending.

On the south side of the square is the Lord Mayor of London's official residence, **Mansion House** (7626 2500, group visits by written application two months in advance to the Diary Office, Mansion House, Walbrook, EC4N 8BH), an imposing neoclassical building constructed by George Dance in 1753. It's the only private residence in the UK to have its own court and prison cells for unruly guests. Just behind Mansion House is the superbly elegant church of **St Stephen Walbrook** (7626 9000, www. ststephenwalbrook.net, 11am-4pm Mon-Fri), built by Wren in 1672, with its gleaming domed, coffered ceiling borrowed from Wren's original design for St Paul's and an incongruous altar – dubbed 'the camembert' – sculpted by Sir Henry Moore.

To the east of Mansion House is the **Royal Exchange**, the Parthenon-like former home of the London Stock Exchange, which was founded way back in 1565 to facilitate the newly invented trade in stocks and shares with Antwerp. In 1972, the exchange shifted to offices on Threadneedle Street, thence to Paternoster Square, and today the Royal Exchange houses a posh champagne bar and the staggeringly expensive emporiums of Tiffany's, de Beers and Chanel. Flanking the Royal Exchange are statues of James Henry Greathead, who invented the machine that cut the tunnels for the London Underground, and Paul Reuter, who founded the Reuters news agency here in 1851.

The period grandeur is undermined somewhat by the monstrosity on the west side of the square, **No.1 Poultry**; the name fits – it's a total turkey, especially as it replaced the beautiful 1870s Mappin & Webb building. A short walk down Queen Victoria Street will lead you to the eroded foundations of the **Temple of Mithras**, constructed by Roman soldiers in AD 240-250. Beliefs from the cult of Mithras were incorporated into Christianity when Rome abandoned paganism in the fourth century, but what remains of the site is rather unimpressive.

Further south, on Cannon Street, you can observe the **London Stone**, thought to mark the Roman's measuring point for distances across Britain or a druidic altar, depending who you talk to – some even have the effrontery to claim it's just a lump of rock. Either way, it's a small thing preserved behind a grille in the wall. Nearby on College Hill is the late Wren church of **St Michael Paternoster Royal** (7248 5202, 9am-5pm Mon-Fri), the final resting

place of London's first Lord Mayor, Richard 'Dick' Whittington. Later transformed into a rags-to-riches pantomime hero, the real Dick Whittington was a wealthy merchant who was elected Lord Mayor four times between 1397 and 1420. The role of Dick Whittington's cat is less clear – many now believe that the cat was actually a ship, but an excavation to find Whittington's tomb in 1949 did uncover the body of a mummified medieval moggy. The happy pair are depicted in the stained-glass windows.

Returning to Bank, stroll north along Prince's Street, beside the Bank of England's blind wall. Look right along Lothbury to find **St Margaret Lothbury** (7606 8330, www.stml. org.uk, 7am-6pm Mon-Fri). The grand screen dividing the choir from the nave was designed by Wren himself, while other works here by his favourite woodcarver, Grinling Gibbons, were recovered from various churches damaged in World War II.

South-east of Bank on Lombard Street is Hawksmoor's striking **St Mary Woolnoth**, squeezed in between the 17th-century banking houses with their gilded signboards. The gilded grasshopper at 68 Lombard Street is the heraldic emblem of Sir Thomas Gresham, who founded the Royal Exchange. Further east on Lombard Street is Wren's **St Edmund the King** (7626 5031, www.spiritualitycentre.org, 10am-6pm Mon-Fri), which now houses a centre for modern spirituality. Other significant churches in the area include Wren's handsome red-brick **St Mary Abchurch**, off Abchurch Lane, and **St Clement**, on Clement's Lane, immortalised in the nursery rhyme 'Oranges and Lemons'. Over on Cornhill are two more Wren churches; **St Peter-upon-Cornhill** was mentioned by Dickens in *Our Mutual Friend*, while **St Michael Cornhill** contains a bizarre statue of a pelican feeding its young with pieces of its own body – a medieval symbol for the Eucharist – sculpted by someone who had plainly never seen a pelican.

North-west of the Bank of England is the **Guildhall**, City of London headquarters. 'Guildhall' can either describe the original banqueting hall (*see p67*) or cluster of buildings around it, of which the **Guildhall Art Gallery** (*see p67*), **Clockmakers' Museum & Library** (*see p66*) and church of **St Lawrence Jewry** (7600 9478, 8am-1pm Mon-Fri), opposite the hall, are also open to the public. St Lawrence is another restored Wren, with an impressive gilt ceiling. Within, you can hear the renowned Klais organ for lunchtime organ recitals from 1pm on Tuesdays.

Glance north along Wood Street to see the isolated tower of **St Alban**, built by Wren in 1685 but ruined in World War II and now an eccentric private home. At the end of the street

SIGHTS

is **St Anne & St Agnes** (7606 4986, 10.30am-5pm Mon-Fri, Sun), laid out in the form of a Greek cross. Recitals take place here also on weekday lunchtimes.

FREE **Bank of England Museum**

Entrance on Bartholomew Lane, EC2R 8AH (7601 5545/www.bankofengland.co.uk/museum). Bank tube/DLR. **Open** *10am-5pm Mon-Fri.* **Tours** by arrangement. **Admission** free. *Tours* free. **Map** p405 Q6.

Housed inside the former Stock Offices of the Bank of England, this engaging museum explores the history of the national bank. As well as ancient coins and original artwork for British banknotes, the museum offers a rare chance to manhandle a real 13kg gold bar (closely monitored, more's the pity, by CCTV). A new permanent exhibit looks at the life of Kenneth Grahame – author of *The Wind in the Willows* and a long-term employee of the bank. Child-friendly temporary exhibitions take place in the museum lobby.

FREE **Clockmakers' Museum & Guildhall Library**

Aldermanbury, EC2V 7HH (Guildhall Library 7332 1868/www.clockmakers.org). Mansion House or St Paul's tube/Bank tube/DLR/

Born of Flames, Reborn in Gilt

Wren's Monument has been dramatically reconditioned.

One of 17th-century London's most important landmarks, the **Monument** (*see opposite*) is due to reopen this spring after an 18-month refurbishment costing £4.5 million. It was designed by Sir Christopher Wren and his (often overlooked) associate Robert Hooke as a memorial to the Great Fire of London, and is the world's tallest free-standing stone column: it measures 202 feet from the ground to the tip of the golden flame licking around the orb at its top, exactly the distance east to Farriner's bakery in Pudding Lane, where the fire is supposed to have begun on 2 September

1666. Plaques around its base record the mayors that oversaw its construction (east), the munificence of King Charles II in restoring the smoking ruins (south) and the story of the city's destruction (north). For much of the Monument's history, this last panel also blamed the blaze on papist insurgents: 'On the third day… the fatal fire stayed its course and everywhere died out,' it currently concludes, but in 1681, as a result of the 'Popish Plot' fabricated by Titus Oates, it was seen fit to add: 'But Popish frenzy, which wrought such horrors, is not yet quenched.' In 1830, following Catholic Emancipation, the inflammatory slur was removed.

The recent refurbishment has gone considerably further: the column's magnificent Portland stone has been completely cleaned and repaired, the golden orb at the top has been re-gilded with more than 30,000 leaves of gold, new lighting has been installed, and cumbersome old iron bars of the viewing platform have been replaced with a new, lightweight mesh cage. For those reluctant or unable to climb the Monument's 311 steps up the internal spiral staircase, a live feed beams views from the top to visitors on the ground floor. The surrounding area has also been spruced up as part of the renewal, with the addition of a stone and glass pavilion specially designed by Bere architects to reflect the Monument's gleaming orb and gilded flames from its roof. All in all, the thing has been given the loving care and attention that it deserves as a memorial to the resurrection of London after the most cataclysmic event in its history.

SIGHTS

Moorgate tube/rail. **Open** 9.30am-5pm Mon-Sat. **Admission** free. **Map** p404 P6.

Hundreds of ticking, chiming clocks and watches are displayed in this single-room museum, from the egg-sized Elizabethan pocket watches to marine chronometers, via a 'fuse for a nuclear device'. Highlights are Marine Chronometer H5, built by John Harrison (1693-1776) to solve the problem of longitude, and the plain Smith's Imperial wrist-watch worn by Sir Edmund Hillary on the first – Rolex-sponsored – ascent of Everest. Just down the corridor, the library has books, manuscripts and prints relating to the history of London – original historic works can be requested for browsing (bring ID). The bookshop stocks loads of London books and maps.

▶ *The National Maritime Museum has more on the problem of longitude; see p147.*

FREE Guildhall

Gresham Street, EC2P 2EJ (7606 3030/tours ext 1463/www.corpoflondon.gov.uk). St Paul's tube/ Bank tube/DLR. **Open** *May-Sept* 10am-5pm daily. *Oct-Apr* 10am-5pm Mon-Sat. *Tours* by arrangement; groups of 10 or more only. **Admission** free. **Map** p404 P6.

The City of London and its progenitors have been holding grand ceremonial dinners in this hall for eight centuries. Memorials to national heroes line the walls, shields of the 100 livery companies grace the ceiling, and every Lord Mayor since 1189 gets a namecheck on the windows. Many famous trials have taken place here, including the treason trial of Lady Jane Grey, 'the nine days queen', in 1553.

Guildhall Art Gallery

Guildhall Yard, off Gresham Street, EC2P 2EJ (7332 3700/www.guildhall-art-gallery.org.uk). Mansion House or St Paul's tube/Bank tube/ DLR/Moorgate tube/rail. **Open** 10am-5pm Mon-Sat; noon-4pm Sun. **Admission** £2.50; £1 reductions; free under-16s. Free to all from 3.30pm daily, all day Fri. **Credit** (over £5) MC, V. **Map** p404 P6.

The City of London's gallery contains numerous dull or unimpressive portraits of royalty and long-gone mayors, but also some wonderful surprises, including a brilliant Constable, some wonderfully camp Pre-Raphaelite works (Clytemnestra looks mighty riled) and a number of absorbing paintings of London through the ages – from moving depictions of war or melancholy working streets to the likes of the grandiloquent (and sadly never enacted) George Dance plan for a new London Bridge. The collection's centrepiece is the massive *Siege of Gibraltar* by John Copley, which spans two entire stories of the purpose-built gallery. A sub-basement contains the scant remains of London's 6,000-seater Roman amphitheatre, built around AD 70; *Tron*-like figures and crowd sound effects give an quaint inkling of scale.

MONUMENT & AROUND

Monument tube.

From Bank, King William Street runs south-east towards London Bridge, passing the small square containing the **Monument** (*see below*). South of the Monument on Lower Thames Street is the moody-looking church of **St Magnus the Martyr** (*see below*), and nearby are several relics from the days when this part of the City was a busy port, including the old Customs House and Billingsgate Market, London's main fish market until 1982. North of the Monument along Gracechurch Street is the atmospheric **Leadenhall Market**, constructed in 1881 by Horace Jones (who also built the market at Smithfield; *see p74*). The vaulted roof was restored to its original Victorian finery in 1991 and city workers come here in droves to lunch at the pubs, cafés and restaurants, including the historic Lamb Tavern. Fantasy fans may recognise the market as Diagon Alley from *Harry Potter & the Philosopher's Stone*.

Behind the market is Sir Richard Rogers' high-tech **Lloyd's of London** building, constructed in 1986, with all its ducts, vents, stairwells and lift shafts on the outside, like an oil rig dumped in the heart of the City – we still think it's brilliant. The original Lloyd's Register of Shipping, decorated with evocative bas-reliefs of sea monsters and nautical scenes, is on Fenchurch Street. Just south on Eastcheap (derived from the Old English 'ceap' meaning 'barter') is Wren's **St Margaret Pattens**, with an original 17th-century interior.

Monument

Monument Street, EC3R 8AH (7626 2717/ www.themonument.info). Monument tube. **Open** 9.30am-5pm daily. **Admission** £2; £1 reductions; free under-5s. **No credit cards. Map** p407 Q7.

See opposite **Born of Flames, Reborn in Gilt.**

FREE St Magnus the Martyr

Lower Thames Street, EC3R 6DN (7626 4481/ www.stmagnusmartyr.org.uk). Monument tube.

INSIDE TRACK
GOG AND MAGOG

Above the entrance to the **Guildhall** (*see above*) are statues of Gog and Magog. Born of the union of demons and exiled Roman princesses, these two mythical giants are said to protect the City of London. The current statues replaced 18th-century forebears that had been destroyed in the Blitz.

Open 10am-4pm Tue-Fri; 10am-1pm Sun. *Mass* 11am Sun; 12.30pm Tue, Thur, Fri. **Admission** free; donations appreciated. **Map** p405 Q7. Downhill from the Monument, this looming Wren church marked the entrance to the original London Bridge. A cute scale model of the old bridge is displayed inside the church, along with a statue of axe-wielding St Magnus, the 12th-century Earl of Orkney. The church is mentioned at one of the climaxes of TS Eliot's *The Waste Land*: 'Where the walls/Of Magnus Martyr hold/Inexplicable splendour of Ionian white and gold.'

▶ *Old London Bridge is celebrating its birthday this year; see p55.*

TOWER OF LONDON

Tower Hill tube/Tower Gateway DLR.

Marking the eastern edge of the City, the **Tower of London** (*see p71*) was the palace of the medieval kings and queens of England. Home to the Crown Jewels and the Royal Armoury, it's one of Britain's best-loved tourist attractions and, accordingly, is mobbed by visitors seven days a week. Inside, you can see famous treasures of state, reconstructed royal chambers, the spot where two of Henry VIII's wives were beheaded and the Bloody Tower, where Sir Walter Raleigh was imprisoned and the princes Edward V and Richard brutally murdered, allegedly on the orders of Richard III.

At the south-east corner of the Tower is **Tower Bridge** (*see p71*), built in 1894. It is still London's most distinctive bridge. Used as a navigation aid by German bombers, it escaped the firestorm of the Blitz. East across Bridge Approach is **St Katharine's Docks**, the first London docks to be formally closed when the River Thames silted up in the 1960s. The restaurants around the marina offer more dignified dining than those around the Tower.

Immediately north of the Tower, **Trinity Square Gardens** are a humbling memorial to the tens of thousands of merchant seamen killed in the two World Wars. Just beyond is one of the City's finest Edwardian buildings, the former Port of London HQ at 10 Trinity Square, with a towering neoclassical façade and gigantic statues symbolising Commerce, Navigation, Export, Produce and Father Thames. Next door is **Trinity House**, the headquarters of the General Lighthouse Authority, founded by Henry VIII for the upkeep of shipping beacons along the river.

The surrounding streets and alleys have evocative names: Crutched Friars, Savage Gardens and Pepys Street. The famous diarist lived in nearby Seething Lane and observed the Great Fire of London from **All Hallows by the Tower** (*see p70*). Pepys is buried in the church of St Olave on Hart Street, nicknamed 'St Ghastly Grim' by Dickens for the leering skulls at the entrance.

North of the Tower are **St Botolph's-without-Aldgate** (*see p70*) and the tiny stone church of **St Katharine Cree** (7283 5733, 10.30am-4pm Mon-Thur, 10.30am-1pm Fri) on Leadenhall Street, one of only eight churches to survive the Great Fire. Inside is a memorial to Sir Nicholas Throckmorton, Queen Elizabeth I's ambassador to France, who was imprisoned for treason on numerous occasions, despite – or perhaps because of – his friendship with the temperamental queen. Just north of St Katharine is **Mitre Square**, site of the fourth Jack the Ripper murder. Nearby on Bevis Marks, the superbly preserved **Bevis Marks Synagogue** (7626 1274, 11am-1pm Mon-Fri, 10.30am-12.30pm Sun) was founded in 1701 by Sephardic Jews fleeing the Spanish Inquisition. Services are still held in Portuguese as well as Hebrew. On neighbouring Heneage Lane is the classy kosher Bevis Marks Restaurant (no.4, 7283 2220, www.bevismarkstherestaurant.com).

Bevis Marks connects with St Mary Axe, named after a vanished church that is said to have contained an axe used by Attila the Hun to behead English virgins. Here you'll find Lord Norman Foster's **30 St Mary Axe**, arguably London's finest modern building. It's known as 'the Gherkin' (even 'the Erotic Gherkin') for reasons that are obvious once you see it. Nearby are two more medieval churches that survived the Great Fire – **St Helen's Bishopsgate** (*see p70*) and **St Andrew Undershaft**. To the west of St Mary Axe is the ugly and rather dated **Tower 42** (25 Old Broad Street). It was the tallest building in Britain until the construction of 1 Canada Square (*see p139*) in Docklands in 1990. Behind, on Bishopsgate, is Gibson Hall, the ostentatious former offices of the National Provincial Bank of England.

One block north, St Mary Axe intersects with **Houndsditch**, where Londoners threw dead dogs and other rubbish in medieval times. The ditch ran outside the London Wall (*see p63*), dividing the City from the East End (*see p133*).

INSIDE TRACK
TOWER BRIDGE

A three-year, £4 million programme of restoration to **Tower Bridge** (*see p71*) began in summer 2008. The work is being phased, so that only part of the bridge is covered at any one time. The exhibition remains open throughout the repainting – and the views from the upper walkways will be unaffected.

30 St Mary Axe.

The New City

The most ancient part of London is suddenly solicitous.

When the Millennium Bridge connected the City to the burgeoning cultural quarter of Bankside, it brought a new type of tourist and reinvented the stuffy Square Mile as a place with something for everyone.

The City is no longer a ghost town out of working hours. It's now encouraging visitors to look beyond the historic monuments to cultural gems such as the **Barbican** (*see p307*) and the **City of London Festival** (*see p310*), or intriguing nooks like **Postman's Park** (*see p62*) and Broadgate ice rink. Bars and cafés stay open in the evenings and at weekends, with **Paternoster Square** (*see p61*) now heaving all week. Hotels have increased from two to ten this decade. The City of London Corporation, who look after the affairs of the Square Mile, even hope to introduce weekend free parking to attract more people.

Lord Norman Foster's **30 St Mary Axe** (aka the Gherkin) helped people fall in love with office buildings and now architectural tourism is on the rise, with Blue Badge and City of London guides giving tailored tours. At ground level, 40,000 square metres of public space has been created or improved: the route from the Millennium Bridge to St Pauls; a new public square at the base of the Monument; and fountains at the Old Bailey.

The most extensive changes are taking place along Cheapside, perfectly positioned (next to St Paul's) to take advantage of visitors arriving across the bridge. By 2012, a collection of separate projects will have created 167 new shops – not just sandwich bars and shirt makers but high-end fashion, design, homeware and groceries.

Biggest is **One New Change** where international starchitect Jean Nouvel is creating a shopping mall along the historic route of Watling Street, framing dramatic views of St Paul's. Opening in 2010, it will provide leisure facilities, three floors of retail, roof gardens and a rooftop restaurant.

Many other landmark buildings will soon be vying for attention. Dutch maestro Rem Koolhaas is expanding Rothschild's offices at Mansion House, also to be completed in 2010. The following year, Richard Rogers will complement his 1986 rule-breaking **Lloyd's of London** building with 122 Leadenhall Street, known as the 'cheesegrater'. It will be joined by Rafael Vignoly's 'walkie talkie' at 20 Fenchurch Street, and two towers by architects Kohn Pedersen Fox – Heron Tower and Bishopsgate Tower (aka the 'pinnacle' or 'helter skelter'), the latter one of Europe's tallest at 302 metres. A collaboration between Nouvel and Foster at Walbrook Square ('Darth Vader's helmet'), due to be completed in 2012, will provide more offices and shopping, a new entrance for Bank station and a new home for the Roman **Temple of Mithras** (*see p65*). Already in place are Foster & Partners' Willis Building (51 Lime Street) and SOM's Broadgate Tower, both completed in 2008.

For more information, check out www.cityoflondon.gov.uk or go to the new **visitor centre** beside St Paul's (*see p57*).

FREE All Hallows by the Tower

Byward Street, EC3R 5BJ (7481 2928/www.all hallowsbythetower.org.uk). Tower Hill tube/Tower Gateway DLR. **Open** 9am-5.30pm Mon-Fri; 10am-5pm Sat, Sun. *Tours* phone for details, donation requested. *Services* 11am Sun; 12.30pm Mon, Wed, Fri; 8.30am Tue, Thur. **Admission** free; donations appreciated. **Map** p405 R7.

Often described as London's oldest church, All Hallows is built on the foundations of a seventh-century Saxon church. Much of what survives today was reconstructed after World War II, but several Saxon details can be seen in the main hall, where the Knights Templar were tried by Edward II in 1314. The undercroft contains a museum with Roman and Saxon relics and a Crusader altar. William Penn, founder of Pennsylvania, was baptised here in 1644.

FREE St Botolph's-without-Aldgate

Aldgate High Street, EC3N 1AB (7283 1670/ www.stbotolphs.org.uk). Aldgate tube. **Open**

10am-3pm Mon-Thur; 10am-12.30pm Sun. *Eucharist* 10.30am Sun; 1.05pm Mon (during school term), Thur. **Admission** free; donations appreciated. **Map** p405 R6.

The oldest of three churches of St Botolph in the City, this handsome monument was built at the gates of Roman London as a homage to the patron saint of travellers. The building was reconstructed by George Dance in 1744 and a beautiful ornamental ceiling was added in the 19th century by John Francis Bentley, who also created Westminster Cathedral.

FREE St Ethelburga Centre for Reconciliation & Peace

78 Bishopsgate, EC2N 4AG (7496 1610/www. stethelburgas.org). Bank tube/DLR/Liverpool Street tube/rail. **Open** 11am-3pm Wed, Fri. **Admission** free; donations appreciated. **Map** p405 R6.

Built around 1390, the tiny church of St Ethelburga was reduced to rubble by an IRA bomb in 1993 and rebuilt as a centre for peace and reconciliation. Behind the chapel is a Bedouin tent where events are held to promote dialogue between the faiths (phone or check the website for details), an increasingly heated issue in modern Britain. Meditation classes are held here on Tuesdays and Thursdays.

FREE St Helen's Bishopsgate

Great St Helen's, off Bishopsgate, EC3A 6AT (7283 2231/www.st-helens.org.uk). Bank tube/ DLR/Liverpool Street tube/rail. **Open** 9.30am-12.30pm Mon-Fri. *Services* 10.30am, 6pm Sun.

INSIDE TRACK
ARCADIAN DREAM GARDEN

On curved stone benches either side of **30 St Mary Axe** (*see p68*) are separately inscribed the 20 lines of Scottish poet Ian Hamilton Finlay's 'Arcadian Dream Garden', a curious counterpart to Lord Norman Foster's hugely popular building.

Tower of London.

Mon, Sun; 9am-6pm Tue-Sat. *Nov-Feb* 10am-5pm Mon, Sun; 9am-5pm Tue-Sat. **Admission** £16.50; £9.50-£14 reductions; £46 family; free under-5s. **Credit** AmEx, MC, V. **Map** p405 R8.

If you haven't been to the Tower of London before, go now. Despite exhausting crowds and long climbs up inaccessible stairways, this is one of Britain's finest historical attractions. Who would not be fascinated by a close-up look at the crown of Queen Victoria or the armour (and prodigious codpiece) of King Henry VIII? The buildings of the Tower span 900 years of history and the bastions and battlements house a series of interactive displays on the lives of British monarchs – and the often excruciatingly painful deaths of traitors. There's plenty here to fill a whole day, and it's worth joining one of the highly recommended and entertaining free tours led by the Yeoman Warders (or Beefeaters).

Make the Crown Jewels your first stop – and as early in the day as possible; if you wait until you've pottered around other things, the queues will already be prodigious. Beyond satisfyingly solid 2,000kg vault doors, you get to glide along travelators (branded with the Queen's 'EIIR' badge) past such treasures of state as the Monarch's Sceptre, mounted with the Cullinan I diamond, and the Imperial State Crown, worn by the Queen each year for the opening of Parliament.

The other big draw to the tower is the Royal Armoury in the central White Tower, with its swords, armour, poleaxes, halberds, morning stars (spiky maces) and other gruesome tools for separating human beings from their body parts. Kids are entertained by swordsmanship games, coinminting activities and even a child-sized long bow. The garderobes (medieval toilets) also seem to appeal. This year, in commemoration of the 500th anniversary of Henry VIII's accession to the throne, 'Henry VIII: Dressed to Kill' will use each floor of the White Tower to display a different aspect of the monarch, using the largest collection of artefacts related to the famously hearty king ever assembled.

Back outside, Tower Green – where executions of prisoners of noble birth were carried out, continuing until 1941 – is marked by a glass pillow, sculpted by poet and artist Brian Catling. Overlooking the green, Beauchamp Tower, dating to 1280, has an upper floor full of intriguing graffiti by the prisoners that were held here (including Anne Boleyn, Rudolf Hess and the Krays). Back towards the entrance, the 13th-century Bloody Tower is another must-see that gets overwhelmed by numbers later in the day. The ground floor is a reconstruction of Sir Walter Raleigh's study, the upper floor details the fate of the Princes in the Tower. In the riverside wall is the unexpectedly beautiful Medieval Palace, with its reconstructed bedroom and throne room, and spectacularly complex stained glass in the private chapel. The whole palace is deliciously cool if you've been struggling round the site on a hot summer's day.

Lunchtime meetings 1-2pm Tue, Thur. **Admission** free. **Map** p405 R6.

Founded in 1210, St Helen's Bishopsgate is actually two churches knocked into one, which explains its unusual shape. The church survived the Great Fire and the Blitz, but was partly wrecked by IRA bombs in 1992 and 1993. The hugely impressive 16th- and 17th-century memorials inside include the grave of Thomas Gresham, founder of the Royal Exchange (*see p65*).

Tower Bridge Exhibition

Tower Bridge, SE1 2UP (7403 3761/www. towerbridge.org.uk). Tower Hill tube/Tower Gateway DLR. **Open** *Apr-Sept* 10am-6.30pm daily. *Oct-Mar* 9.30am-6pm daily. **Admission** £6; £3-£4.50 reductions; £14 family; free under-5s. **Credit** AmEx, MC, V. **Map** p405 R8.

Opened in 1894, this is the 'London Bridge' that wasn't sold to America. Originally powered by steam, the drawbridge is now opened by electric rams when big ships need to venture this far upstream (you can check when the bridge is next due to be raised on the website). An entertaining exhibition on the history of the bridge is displayed in the old steamrooms and the west walkway, which provides a crow's-nest view along the Thames. *See also p68* **Inside Track**.

★ Tower of London

Tower Hill, EC3N 4AB (0870 950 4466/www.hrp. org.uk). Tower Hill tube//Tower Gateway DLR/ Fenchurch Street rail. **Open** *Mar-Oct* 10am-6pm

SIGHTS

Holborn &
Clerkenwell

Judicial wigs and pubs remain, but all the newspapermen have gone.

The City of London collides with the West End in Holborn and Clerkenwell. Be-wigged barristers inhabit the picturesque **Inns of Court**, while left-leaning City boys pull on their tracks to journey from loft conversion to the latest gastropub. Butchers still haul fresh and frozen meat around **Smithfield Market** at the crack of dawn – to the consternation of bug-eyed clubbers weaving their way unsteadily home from Fabric – although the future of the splendid Victorian wrought-iron structure remains at issue.

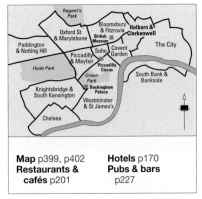

Map p399, p402	**Hotels** p170
Restaurants &	**Pubs & bars**
cafés p201	p227

Map p399, p402 · **Hotels** p170 · **Restaurants & cafés** p201 · **Pubs & bars** p227

HOLBORN

Holborn tube.

A sharp left out of Holborn tube and left again leads into the unexpectedly lovely **Lincoln's Inn Fields**. What is surely London's largest square – more park than square, in fact – comes complete with gnarled oaks casting dappled shade over a tired bandstand and tennis courts. On the south side of the park, the neoclassical façade of the Royal College of Surgeons houses the **Hunterian Museum** (*see p73*); facing it from the north side is the **Sir John Soane's Museum** (*see p73*), a magic box of architectural oddities and one of the most unusual attractions in the city. To the east of the square lies **Lincoln's Inn** (7405 1393, www.lincolnsinn.org.uk) itself, one of the capital's four Inns of Court, its grounds open to pottering members of the public hoping to ogle an odd mix of Gothic, Tudor and Palladian architecture. On nearby Portsmouth Street lies the **Old Curiosity Shop** – now an upmarket shoe store – its creaking 16th-century timbers known to Dickens, once a resident a little to the north in Bloomsbury (*see p77*).

Another of London's few timber buildings to survive the Great Fire can be found at Chancery Lane tube. This is the wooden frontispiece of **Staple Inn** (7632 2127) – try to ignore the ground-level mobile phone ads. Opposite, Gray's Inn Road runs north beside the second Inn of Court. The sculpted gardens at **Gray's Inn** (7458 7800, www.graysinn.org.uk), dating back to 1606, are open to the public between 10am and 2.30pm on weekdays. The **London Silver Vaults** (7242 3844, www.thesilvervaults.com), opened in 1876 on Chancery Lane as a series of strong rooms for the upper classes to secure their valuables, are now a hive of dealers buying, selling and repairing silverware. Equally liable to turn brown eyes green with envy are the glittering window displays of **Hatton Market**, London's jewellery and diamond centre since medieval times; it's a short walk – but a million miles aesthetically speaking – from the Cockney fruit stalls and sock merchants of the market on **Leather Lane** (10am-2.30pm Mon-Fri).

Further on is enigmatic **Ely Place**, its postcode notably absent from the street sign as a result of it falling technically under the jurisdiction of Cambridgeshire. The street has a rich literary history: the church garden of ancient **St Etheldreda** (*see p73*) produced

SIGHTS

strawberries so delicious that they made the pages of Shakespeare's *Richard III* (a celebratory Strawberrie Fayre is still held on the street each June). The 16th-century **Ye Old Mitre** (*see p228*) was reputedly a favourite of Dr Johnson; it remains an atmospheric pub rather than a mere museum piece.

FREE Hunterian Museum
Royal College of Surgeons, 35-43 Lincoln's Inn Fields, WC2A 3PE (7869 6560/www.rcseng.ac.uk/ museums). Holborn tube. **Open** 10am-5pm Tue-Sat. **Admission** free. **Map** p399 M6.
John Hunter (1728-93) was a pioneering surgeon and anatomist, appointed physician to King George III. His huge collection of medical specimens can be viewed in this two-floor museum upstairs. The sparkling glass cabinets of the main room offset the goriness of many of the exhibits – these include the brain of 19th-century mathematician Charles Babbage and Winston Churchill's dentures, as well as shelf after shelf of diligently classified pickled body parts and animals. Even harder hitting is the upper floor's account of surgical techniques. Kids' activities include occasional demonstrations by a scary 'barber surgeon' (book on 7869 6560).
▶ *Surgical history also comes alive at the Old Operating Theatre & Herb Garret; see p53.*

FREE St Etheldreda
14 Ely Place, EC1N 6RY (7405 1061/www.st etheldreda.com). Chancery Lane tube/Farringdon tube/rail. **Open** 8.30am-7pm daily. **Admission** free; donations appreciated. **Map** p402 N5.
St Etheldreda, dedicated to the saintly seventh-century Queen of Northumbria, is Britain's oldest Catholic church and London's only surviving example of 13th-century Gothic architecture. Saved from the Great Fire by a change in the wind, it is all that remains of the Bishop of Ely's palace. The crypt is darkly atmospheric, untouched by traffic noise, and the stained glass (actually from the 1960s) stunning.

★ FREE Sir John Soane's Museum
13 Lincoln's Inn Fields, WC2A 3BP (7405 2107/ www.soane.org). Holborn tube. **Open** 10am-5pm Tue-Sat; 10am-5pm, 6-9pm 1st Tue of mth. *Tours* 11am Sat. **Admission** free; donations appreciated. *Tours* £5; free reductions. **Credit** (shop) AmEx, MC, V. **Map** p399 M5.
A leading architect of his day – responsible for the building that housed the Bank of England (only the perimeter walls remain) – Sir John Soane (1753-1837) obsessively collected art, furniture and architectural ornamentation, partly for enjoyment and partly for research. In the early 19th century, he turned his house into a museum to which 'amateurs and students' should have access. Much of the museum's appeal derives from the domestic setting. Rooms are modestly sized but have been modified by Soane with ingenious devices to channel and direct natural

Sir John Soane's Museum.

daylight and to expand available space, including walls that open out like cabinets to display some of his many paintings (works by Canaletto, Turner and Hogarth). The Breakfast Room has a beautiful and much-imitated domed ceiling, inset with convex mirrors, but the real wow is the Monument Court. At its lowest level is a sarcophagus of alabaster so fine that it's almost translucent. It was carved for the pharaoh Seti I (1291-78 BC) and discovered in his tomb in Egypt's Valley of the Kings, before being removed by 19th-century treasure hunters. There are also numerous examples of Soane's eccentricity – not least the cell set aside for his imaginary monk 'Padre Giovanni'. The museum has launched an appeal that will open up Soane's top-floor 'private apartments', recreated from contemporary watercolours.
▶ *Another Soane masterpiece is the Dulwich Picture Gallery; see p144. Soane's family tomb is at St Pancras Old Church; see p79.*

INSIDE TRACK
ALFRESCO EATS

In summer, book an outside seat for Caribbean-accented modern European food at the **Terrace** (7430 1234, www. theterrace.info). It's the airy, wood-heavy, eco-friendly building by the tennis courts in **Lincoln's Inn Fields** (*see opposite*).

SIGHTS

CLERKENWELL & FARRINGDON

Farringdon tube/rail.

Few places encapsulate London's capacity for reinvention quite like Clerkenwell, an erstwhile religious centre that takes its name from the parish clerks who once performed Biblical mystery plays on its streets. The nuns of St Mary's, meanwhile, occupied what is now **St James Church** (Clerkenwell Close, 7251 1190, www.jc-church.org), home to a memorial to Protestants burned at the stake by Mary Tudor. The most lasting holy legacy is that of the 11th-century knights of the Order of St John: the remains of their priory can still be seen at **St John's Gate**, a crenellated gatehouse which dates from 1504 and is home to the **Museum & Library of the Order of St John** (*see below*).

By the 17th century, Clerkenwell was a rather fashionable locale, but the Industrial Revolution soon buried it under warehouses and factories. Numerous printing houses were established and the district gained a reputation as a safe haven for radicals, whether 16th-century Lollards or 19th-century Chartists. In 1903 Lenin is believed to have met Stalin for a drink in what is now the **Crown Tavern** (43 Clerkenwell Green, 7253 4973), one year after moving publication of *Iskra* to neighbouring 37A, now the **Marx Memorial Library** (7253 1485, www.marx-memorial-library.org). The left-leaning *Guardian* newspaper moved to the locale in 1964, but last year it relocated to brand new offices in King's Cross (Kings Place; *see p308*).

Industrial dereliction and decay were the theme until property development in the 1980s and '90s turned this into a desirable residential area. The slew of artfully distressed gastropubs that followed Farringdon Road's pioneering **Eagle** (*see p202*), and the associated artisan food shops, fashion boutiques, restaurants and

INSIDE TRACK
LOST RIVER

The **Fleet River** runs right through Clerkenwell and into the Thames – you just can't see it any more. Threatening to overwhelm the neighbourhood with effluent and illness, its filthy waters choked with canine corpses, the river was boarded over in 1733. It is now a sewer beneath Farringdon Road, visible only as the name of a street from which even the muckraking hacks have been swept away.

bohemian bars strung along the colourful strip of **Exmouth Market,** may well begin to feel the pinch now that the *Guardian*'s staff epicures have moved on.

FREE **Museum & Library of the Order of St John**
St John's Gate, St John's Lane, EC1M 4DA (7324 4005/www.sja.org.uk/museum). Farringdon tube/rail. **Open** 10am-5pm Mon-Fri; 10am-4pm Sat. *Tours* 11am, 2.30pm Tue, Fri, Sat. **Admission** free. *Tours* free. Suggested donation £5; £4 reductions. **Credit** MC, V. **Map** p402 O4.
Today, the Order of St John is best known in London for its ambulance service, but its roots lie in the Christian medical practices of the Crusades between the 11th and 13th centuries. A collection of artifacts (illuminated manuscripts, armour, Islamic items) related to the Order of Hospitaller Knights, from Jerusalem, Malta and the Ottoman Empire, is displayed here. A separate collection relates specifically to the evolution of the modern ambulance service. The museum closes for major refurbishments in autumn 2009, but it's unlikely to affect the archive and tours; phone for details nearer the time.

SMITHFIELD
Farringdon tube/rail.

In a city increasingly dependent on tasteless supermarket produce, **Smithfield Market** provides a colourful link to an age when the quality of British beef was a symbol of national virility and good humour. Yet the market of today is a sometime squat often used as little more than wall space for fly posters. Only the meat market remains of what was once the largest food market in the capital. Designed by Horace Jones, Smithfield opened for business in 1868 but was shattered by World War II bombs. Early risers will find traders setting up their stalls at first light inside the metal structure – its ornate arched ceiling and bizarre colour scheme (white, purple, blue and green) meeting with a row of traditional red phone boxes in the photogenic Central Avenue. The **Cock Tavern** (7248 2918) is licensed from 6am to serve beer and breakfast to famished meat handlers; the **Fox & Anchor** (*see p171*) offers a more civilised 8am breakfast to a City clientele.

Nowadays Smithfield is most notable for its swanky eateries, odd neighbours for **Fabric** (*see p321*), the chaotic and cavernous superclub that is still drawing queues of Bambi-eyed bass addicts. For a little peace and quiet, stroll by the **Charterhouse**. This Carthusian monastery, founded in 1370, is now Anglican almshouses that retain the original 14th-century chapel and a 17th-century library.

Bloomsbury & Fitzrovia

Books, trains and boy wizards.

Bloomsbury is a name to conjure with in bookish circles: it is the headquarters of London University and the home of the sternly brilliant **British Museum**. The name was famously attached to the progressive group of early 20th-century artists and intellectuals that included Virginia Woolf and John Maynard Keynes, and more recently to the publishing company that gave us Harry Potter – the Hogwart's Express leaves from King's Cross station. Indeed, the once-insalubrious King's Cross area is undergoing massive redevelopment around the new **St Pancras International** and now well-established 'new' **British Library**. To the west of Bloomsbury, the bars of Fitzrovia retain enough subtle traces of bohemianism to appeal to the media types that now frequent them.

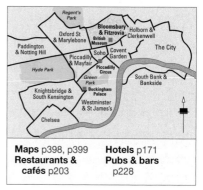

Maps p398, p399	**Hotels** p171
Restaurants &	**Pubs & bars**
cafés p203	p228

BLOOMSBURY

Holborn, Euston Square, Russell Square or Tottenham Court Road tube.

Though most often associated with the group of academics, writers and artists who once colonised its townhouses, Bloomsbury's florid name in fact has more prosaic origins: it's taken from 'Blemondisberi', the manor (or 'bury') of William Blemond, who acquired the area in the early 13th century. It remained rural until the 1660s, when the fourth Earl of Southampton built Bloomsbury Square around his house. The Southamptons intermarried with the Russells, the Dukes of Bedford, and together they developed the area as one of London's first planned suburbs. Over the next two centuries, they built a series of grand squares: charming **Bedford Square** (1775-80) is London's only complete Georgian square, while huge **Russell Square**, for years a run-down haunt of drunks, has been restored as an attractive public park with a popular café with outdoor terrace.

The area's charm is the sum of its parts, best experienced as an idle afternoon's meander, browsing Great Russell Street's **bookshops** and relaxing in historic pubs. The blue plaques here are a 'who's who' of English literature: William Butler Yeats lived at 5 Upper Woburn Place, Edgar Allan Poe at 83 Southampton Row and TS Eliot at 28 Bedford Place; 6 Store Street was the birthplace of Anthony Trollope. The house of Charles Dickens at 48 Doughty Street is now the **Charles Dickens Museum** (*see p77*). As for the famous Bloomsbury Group (denounced by DH Lawrence as 'this horror of little swarming selves'), its headquarters was at 50 Gordon Square, where EM Forster, Lytton Strachey, John Maynard Keynes, Clive and Vanessa Bell, and Duncan Grant would discuss literature, art, politics and, above all, each other. Virginia and Leonard Woolf lived at 52 Tavistock Square, and Wyndham Lewis's Rebel Art Centre occupied 38 Great Ormond Street. On Bloomsbury's western border, Malet Street, Gordon Street and Gower Street are dominated by the University of London.

Profile British Museum

A world of human history in a single, extraordinary collection.

SIGHTS

Officially the country's most popular tourist attraction, the **British Museum** (*see right*) is a neoclassical marvel that was built in 1847 by Robert Smirke, one of the pioneers of the Greek Revival style. Equally impressive is Lord Norman Foster's glass-roofed Great Court, opened in 2000 and now claimed to be 'the largest covered public square in Europe'. This £100m landmark surrounds the domed Reading Room (used by the British Library until its move to King's Cross; *see p78*), where Marx, Lenin, Dickens, Darwin, Hardy and Yeats once worked.

Star exhibits include ancient Egyptian artefacts – the Rosetta Stone on the ground floor (with a barely noticed, perfect replica in the King's Library), mummies upstairs – and Greek antiquities including the marble friezes from the Parthenon known as the Elgin Marbles. The Celts gallery upstairs has Lindow Man, killed in 300 BC and preserved in peat, while the Wellcome Gallery of Ethnography holds an Easter Island statue and regalia from Captain Cook's travels.

The King's Library, which opened in 2004, is a calming home to a permanent exhibition, 'Enlightenment: Discovering the World in the 18th Century', a 5,000-piece collection devoted to the extraordinary formative period of the museum. The remit covers archaeology, science and the natural world; the objects displayed range from Indonesian puppets to a beautiful orrery.

You won't be able to see everything in one day, so buy a souvenir guide and pick out the showstoppers, or plan several visits. Highlights tours focus on specific aspects of the huge collection; Eye Opener tours offer specific introductions to world cultures.

THREE TO SEE
Room 18
The amazing Parthenon sculptures.

Room 1
Enlighten yourself in the King's Library.

Rooms 62-63
Mummies, dearest.

The most notable building is Gower Street's **University College**, founded in 1826. Inside is the 'Autoicon' of utilitarian philosopher and founder of the university Jeremy Bentham – his preserved cadaver, fully clothed, sitting in a glass-fronted cabinet. The university's main library is housed in towering Gotham City-like **Senate House**, over on Malet Street. It is one of London's most imposing, bulky examples of monumental art deco. Monolithic and brooding, it was the model for Orwell's Ministry of Truth in his dystopic novel *1984*.

South of the university sprawls the **British Museum** (*see below*), with its vast collection of archaeological and artistic treasures. Running off Great Russell Street, which is where you'll find the museum's main entrance, are three attractive parallel streets (Coptic, Museum and Bury), with the **Cartoon Museum** (*see below*), while Bloomsbury Way has Hawksmoor's newly restored **St George's Bloomsbury** (*see p78*). Nearby **Sicilian Avenue** is an Italianate, pedestrian precinct of colonnaded shops that links with Southampton Row.

North-east of here is **Lamb's Conduit Street**, a convivial neighbourhood with interesting shops, one of London's finest old pubs (the **Lamb**; *see p229*) and, at the top of the street, **Coram's Fields** (*see p289*), a delightful children's park on the grounds of the former Thomas Coram's Foundling Hospital. The legacy of the great Coram family is commemorated in the beautiful **Foundling Museum** (*see below*).

★ FREE British Museum

Great Russell Street, WC1B 3DG (7323 8000/ recorded information 7323 8783/www.british museum.org). Russell Square or Tottenham Court Road tube. **Open** *Galleries* 10am-5.30pm Mon-Wed, Sat, Sun; 10am-8.30pm Thur, Fri. *Great Court* 9am-6pm Mon-Wed, Sun; 9am-11pm Thur-Sat. *Highlights tours* (90mins) 10.30am, 1pm, 3pm daily. *Eye opener tours* (50mins) phone for details. **Admission** free; donations appreciated. *Temporary exhibitions* prices vary. *Highlights tours* £8; £5 reductions. *Eye opener tours* free. **Credit** (shop) AmEx, DC, MC, V. **Map** p399 K/L5. *See left* **Profile**.

▶ *The historic Museum Tavern (49 Great Russell Street, 7242 8987), by the front gate, is no mere tourist trap – it serves fine guest ales.*

Cartoon Museum

35 Little Russell Street, WC1A 2HH (7580 8155/ www.cartoonmuseum.org). Tottenham Court Road tube. **Open** 10.30am-5.30pm Tue-Sat; noon-5.30pm Sun. **Admission** £4; free-£3 reductions. **Credit** (shop) MC, V. **Map** p407 Y1.

On the ground floor of this former dairy, the best in British cartoon art is displayed in chronological order, starting with the early 18th century, when high-society types back from the Grand Tour introduced the Italian practice of *caricatura* to polite company. From Hogarth it moves through Britain's cartooning 'golden age' (1770-1830) to examples of wartime cartoons, ending up with modern satirists such as Gerald Scarfe, the wonderfully loopy Ralph Steadman and the *Guardian*'s Steve Bell. Upstairs is a celebration of UK comic art, with original 1921 *Rupert the Bear* artwork by Mary Tourtel, Frank Hampson's *Dan Dare*, Leo Baxendale's *Bash Street Kids* and a painted *Asterix* cover by that well-known Brit Albert Uderzo.

▶ *The museum shop isn't half as good as Gosh! (39 Great Russell Street, 7636 1011, www.gosh london.com), just round the corner.*

Charles Dickens Museum

48 Doughty Street, WC1N 2LX (7405 2127/ www.dickensmuseum.com). Chancery Lane or Russell Square tube. **Open** 10am-5pm Mon-Sat; 11am-5pm Sun. *Tours* by arrangement. **Admission** £5; £3-£4 reductions; £14 family. **Credit** (shop) AmEx, DC, MC, V. **Map** p399 M4.

London is scattered with plaques marking the addresses where the peripatetic Charles Dickens lived, but this is the only one still standing. He lived here from 1837 to 1840, writing *Nicholas Nickleby* and *Oliver Twist*. Ring the doorbell to gain access to four floors of Dickensiana, collected over the years from various former residences. Some rooms are arranged as they might have been when he lived here; others deal with different aspects of his life, whether struggling hack writer or world-famous performer of his stories. The top floor has a new exhibit about vicious Victorian country schooling.

▶ *Dickens was keenly interested in the Foundling Hospital, now another museum; see below.*

Foundling Museum

40 Brunswick Square, WC1N 1AZ (7841 3600/ www.foundlingmuseum.org.uk). Russell Square tube. **Open** 10am-5pm Tue-Sat; 11am-5pm Sun. **Admission** £5; £4 reductions; free under-16s. **Credit** MC, V. **Map** p399 L4.

This museum recalls the social history of the Foundling Hospital, set up in 1739 by a compassionate shipwright and sailor, Captain Thomas Coram. Returning to England from America in 1720, he was appalled by the number of abandoned children on the streets. Securing royal patronage, he persuaded the artist William Hogarth and the composer GF Handel to become governors; Hogarth decreed the building should become the first public art gallery, and artists including Gainsborough and Reynolds Wilson are on display upstairs. Among the pictures, manuscripts and objects on display, the most heart-rending is a tiny case of mementoes that were all mothers could leave the children they abandoned here. There's also a monthly programme of concerts.

SIGHTS

SIGHTS

FREE Petrie Museum of Egyptian Archaeology

University College London, Malet Place, WC1E 6BT (7679 2884/www.petrie.ucl.ac.uk). Euston Square, Goodge Street or Warren Street tube. **Open** 1-5pm Tue-Fri; 10am-1pm Sat. **Admission** free; donations appreciated. **Map** p399 K4.

The museum, set up in 1892 by eccentric traveller and diaryist Amelia Edwards, is named after Flinders Petrie, tireless excavator of ancient Egypt. Where the British Museum's Egyptology collection is strong on the big stuff, the Petrie is dim case after dim case of minutiae. Its aged wooden cabinets are full of pottery shards, grooming accessories, jewellery and primitive tools. Highlights include artefacts from the heretic pharaoh Akhenaten's short-lived capital Tell el Amarna. Among the oddities are a 4,000-year-old skeleton of a man who was buried in an earthenware pot. Wind-up torches help you peer into the gloomy corners.

▶ *The British Museum's Egyptian holdings are divided between Rooms 4 (sculpture) and 62-66 (including the all-important mummies).*

FREE St George's Bloomsbury

Bloomsbury Way, WC1A 2HR (7405 3044/ www.stgeorgesbloomsbury.org.uk). Holborn or Tottenham Court Road tube. **Open** 11am-4pm Mon-Fri; 11.30am-5pm Sat; 10.30am-5pm Sun. *Services* 1.10pm Wed, Fri; 10.30am Sun. **Admission** free. **Map** p399 L5.

Consecrated in 1730, St George's is a grand and typically disturbing work by Nicholas Hawksmoor, with an offset, stepped spire inspired by Pliny's account of the Mausoleum at Halicarnassus, one of the Seven Wonders. The church reopened in 2006 following major renovations: highlights include the mahogany reredos, and 10ft-high sculptures of lions and unicorns clawing at the base of the steeple. In the cool, pale undercroft, you can learn about the building and restoration of the church. On Sundays, the church remains open for visitors after the regular service is over; indeed, the cited opening hours can be a little erratic. As well as guided tours, there are regular concerts.

▶ *Hawksmoor's Christ Church Spitalfields is another recently restored masterpiece; see p133.*

INSIDE TRACK
SCARY SKELETONS

Just down the alley from the entrance to the **Petrie** (*see above*), past the security guards and right into University College London itself, the **Grant Museum** (7679 2647) is another eccentric joy. This time you get Victorian animal skeletons, crammed into an atmospheric single room. It is open weekday afternoons.

★ FREE Wellcome Collection

183 Euston Road, NW1 2BE (7611 2222/www. wellcomecollection.org). Euston Square tube/ Euston tube/rail. **Open** 10am-6pm Tue, Wed, Fri, Sat; 10am-10pm Thur; 11am-6pm Sun. *Library* 10am-6pm Mon, Wed, Fri; 10am-8pm Tue, Thur; 10am-4pm Sat. **Admission** free. **Map** p399 K4.

Founder Sir Henry Wellcome, a pioneering 19th-century pharmacist and entrepreneur, amassed a vast and idiosyncratic collection of implements and curios relating to the medical trade, now displayed in this swanky little new museum. In addition to these fascinating and often grisly items – delicate ivory carvings of pregnant women, used guillotine blades, a viciously bladed torture chair, Napoleon's toothbrush – there are several serious (and sometimes disturbing) works of modern art, most of them on display in a smaller room to one side of the main chamber of curiosities. The temporary exhibitions are usually wonderfully interesting.

▶ *The ground-floor Peyton & Byrne café is a handy stop, whatever you're exploring hereabouts.*

KING'S CROSS & ST PANCRAS

King's Cross or Euston tube/rail.

North-east of Bloomsbury, King's Cross is well on the way to becoming a major European transport hub, thanks to a £500m makeover of the area and the opening of its glorious centrepiece, the renovated and restored **St Pancras Station** (*see p79*). The gaping badlands to the north are being transformed into a mixed-use nucleus called King's Cross Central. Until then, there are still a few places to explore: the **London Canal Museum** (*see below*), secreted north of King's Cross Station right by the new **Kings Place** (*see p308*) arts complex on York Way; kids' favourite **Camley Street Natural Park** (*see p288*); and the delightful churchyard of **St Pancras Old Church** (*see p79*).

★ FREE British Library

96 Euston Road, Somers Town, NW1 2DB (7412 7332/www.bl.uk). Euston Square tube/ Euston or King's Cross tube/rail. **Open** 9.30am-6pm Mon, Wed-Fri; 9.30am-8pm Tue; 9.30am-5pm Sat; 11am-5pm Sun. **Admission** free; donations appreciated. **Map** p399 K/L3.

'One of the ugliest buildings in the world,' opined a Parliamentary committee on the opening of the new British Library in 1997. But don't judge a book by its cover: the interior is a model of cool, spacious functionality, and the reading rooms (closed Sundays and only open to card holders) became so popular the only complaint now is that they're too busy. This is one of the greatest libraries in the world, holding over 150 million items. It receives a copy of every

British Library.

new publication produced in the UK and Ireland, from the daily papers to the most obscure academic treatises. In the John Ritblat Gallery, the library's main treasures are displayed: the Magna Carta, the Lindisfarne Gospels and original manuscripts from Chaucer, as well as Beatles lyrics. The focal point of the building is the King's Library, a six-storey glass-walled tower housing George III's collection. The temporary exhibitions are often superb.

London Canal Museum

12-13 New Wharf Road, off Wharfdale Road, King's Cross, N1 9RT (7713 0836/www.canal museum.org.uk). King's Cross tube/rail. **Open** 10am-4.30pm Tue-Sun. **Admission** £3; £2 reductions; £1.50 children; free under-8s. **Map** p399 M2.

The museum is housed in a former 19th-century ice warehouse, used by Carlo Gatti for his ice-cream, and includes an exhibit on the history of the ice trade. This is perhaps the most interesting part of the exhibition; the collection looking at the history of the waterways and those who worked on them is rather sparse by comparison. The canalside walk from here to Camden Town is most enjoyable.

FREE St Pancras International

Pancras Road, King's Cross, Somers Town, NW1 2QP (7843 4250/www.stpancras.com). King's Cross tube/rail. **Open** 3.45am-12.30am Mon-Fri; 5am-12.30am Sat; 6am-12.30am Sun. **Admission** free. **Map** p399 L3.

Welcoming the high-speed Eurostar train from Paris is William Barlow's gorgeous Victorian glass-and-iron train shed, which for many years had the largest clear-span in the world. Unthinkable a year or so ago, the redeveloped station has become somewhere where you can linger, but – for all the public artworks,

'the longest champagne bar in Europe', high-end boutiques, the gastropub, a destination restaurant and various chain eateries it now contains – St Pancras is only really worth a diversion because of the beauty of the original structure. Sir George Gilbert Scott's magnificent neo-Gothic hotel building, which fronts the station, is due to reopen at the end of 2009.

FREE St Pancras Old Church & St Pancras Gardens

St Pancras Road, King's Cross, NW1 1UL (7387 4193). Mornington Crescent tube/King's Cross tube/rail. **Open** *Gardens* 7am-dusk daily. *Services* 9am Mon-Fri; 7pm Tue; 9.30am Sun. **Admission** free. **Map** p399 K2.

The Old Church, whose site may date back to the fourth century, has been ruined and rebuilt many times. The current structure is handsome, but it's the restored churchyard that delights. Among those buried here are writer William Godwin and his wife, Mary Wollstonecraft; over this grave, their daughter Mary Godwin (author of *Frankenstein*) declared her love for poet Percy Bysshe Shelley. The grave of Sir John Soane is one of only two Grade I-listed tombs (the other is Karl Marx's, in Highgate Cemetery; *see p131*); designed for his wife, its dome influenced Gilbert Scott's design for the red British phone box.
► *Soane's life and work can be explored at Sir John Soane's Museum; see p73.*

FITZROVIA

Tottenham Court Road or Goodge Street tube.

Squeezed in between Tottenham Court Road, Oxford Street, Great Portland Street and Euston Road, Fitzrovia is not as famous as Bloomsbury but its history is just as rich. The origins of the

St Pancras International. *See p79.*

SIGHTS

name are hazy: some believe it comes from
Fitzroy Square, which was named after Henry
Fitzroy, son of Charles II; others insist it is due
to the famous **Fitzroy Tavern** (16 Charlotte
Street, 7580 3714), ground zero for London
bohemia of the 1930s and '40s, a favourite
with such regulars as Dylan Thomas and
George Orwell. Fitzrovia had its share of
artists too: James McNeill Whistler lived at
8 Fitzroy Square, a number later taken over
by British Impressionist Walter Sickert, while
Roger Fry's Omega Workshops, blurring the
old distinction between fine and decorative
arts, had its studio at no.33.

Fitzrovia's raffish image is almost entirely
a thing of the past. It's better known now as
a high-powered media centre. ITN started
broadcasting from 48 Wells Street, and Channel
4's first office was at 60 Charlotte Street from
1982. The district's icon is the **BT Tower**,
completed in 1964 as the Post Office Tower.
Its revolving restaurant and observation deck
were open to the public and featured in almost
any film that wanted to prove how prodigiously
London was swinging (*Bedazzled* is just one
example). Until, that is, the IRA exploded a
bomb in the toilets; the restaurant now revolves
for the benefit of corporate functions. **Charlotte
Street** and neighbouring byways remain a
good destination for dining and drinking.

FREE All Saints

*7 Margaret Street, W1W 8JG (7636 1788/www.all
saintsmargaretstreet.org.uk). Oxford Circus tube.*

Open 7am-7pm daily. *Services* 7.30am, 8am,
1.10pm, 6pm, 6.30pm Mon-Fri; 7.30am, 8am,
6pm, 6.30pm Sat; 8am, 10.20am, 11am, 5.15pm,
6pm Sun. **Admission** free. **Map** p406 U1.
A quiet respite from the tumult of nearby Oxford
Street, this 1850s church was designed by William
Butterfield, one of the great Gothic Revivalists. The
church is squeezed into a tiny site, but its soaring
architecture and a lofty spire – the second-highest
in London – disguise the fact. Behind the polychro-
matic brick façade, the shadowy, lavish interior is
one of the capital's most impressive ecclesiastical
triumphs, with luxurious marble, flamboyant tile
work and glittering stones built into its pillars.
Architectural critic Ian Nairn called it an 'orgasm'.

Pollock's Toy Museum

*1 Scala Street (entrance on Whitfield Street),
W1T 2HL (7636 3452/www.pollockstoymuseum.
com). Goodge Street tube.* **Open** 10am-5pm
Mon-Sat. **Admission** £5; £2-£4 reductions;
free under-3s. **Credit** (shop) AmEx, MC, V.
Map p398 J5.
Housed in a wonderfully creaky Georgian townhouse, Pollock's is named after Benjamin Pollock,
the last of the Victorian toy theatre printers. By turns
beguiling and creepy, the museum is a nostalgia-fest
of old board games, tin trains, porcelain dolls and
Robertson's gollies. It's fascinating for adults but
less so for children, for whom the displays may
seem a bit static – describing a pile of painted woodblocks stuffed in a cardboard box as a 'Build a
skyscraper' kit may only make them feel lucky to be
going home to a PlayStation.

Covent Garden & the Strand

Opera on the piazza, fine art on the river, and street fashion in the shops.

Covent Garden is quite understandably popular with visitors. A traffic-free oasis in the heart of the city, replete with shops, cafés and bars, it centres on a restored 19th-century covered market and the revamped **London Transport Museum** is great fun. On the west side of the square, laid out in the early 17th century, Inigo Jones's neoclassical **St Paul's Covent Garden** still easily upstages the jugglers and escapologists that now regularly entertain crowds in front of its portico. If you're looking for great performances rather than street performances, the **Royal Opera House** is just on the far side of the market, and the superb **Courtauld** collection of fine art and **Somerset House** are only a short walk away, by the river on the Strand.

Map p405, p407	**Hotels** p177
Restaurants &	**Pubs & bars**
cafés p206	p230

COVENT GARDEN

Covent Garden or Leicester Square tube.

Once the property of the medieval Abbey (or 'convent') of Westminster, on Henry VIII's dissolution of the monasteries this land passed to John Russell, first Earl of Bedford, in 1552; his family still owns land hereabouts. During the following century, his descendants extensively developed the area: the fourth Earl of Bedford employed sought-after architect Inigo Jones, who created the Italianate open square that remains the centrepiece of today's Covent Garden.

The first recorded market in Covent Garden appeared on the south side of the square in 1640, selling fruit and vegetables. It attracted coffee-houses and theatres, as well as gambling dens and brothels. The market grew until it had become London's pre-eminent fruit and vegetable wholesaler, employing over 1,000 porters. A flower market was added (where the Transport Museum now stands) and the market building itself was redesigned in the early 19th century by the architect Charles Fowler.

In the second half of the 20th century, it was obvious that the congested streets of central London were unsuitable for market traffic and the decision was taken to move the traders out (for a last look at the market shortly before it closed, watch Alfred Hitchcock's 1972 thriller *Frenzy*). In 1974, with the market gone, the threat of property development loomed for the empty stalls and offices. It was only through mass squats and demonstrations that the area was saved. It's now a pleasant place to stroll – wonderfully so if you catch it early enough on a fine morning.

Coven Garden Piazza

Visitors flock here for a combination of rather gentrified shopping, outdoor restaurant and café seating, street artists and classical music renditions in the lower courtyard. The majority of the street entertainment takes place under the portico of **St Paul's** (*see p83*). It was here that Samuel Pepys observed what is thought to be Britain's first Punch & Judy show ('an Italian puppet play', as he described it), on 9 May 1662.

London Transport Museum.

Tourists favour the **old covered market** (7836 9136, www.coventgardenlondon.uk.com), which combines a collection of small, and sometimes quirky shops, many of them rather twee, alongside upmarket chain stores such as Hobbs, Whistles and Crabtree & Evelyn. The **Apple Market**, in the North Hall, has arts and crafts stalls every Tuesday to Sunday, and antiques on Monday. Across the road, the tackier **Jubilee Market** deals mostly in novelty T-shirts and other tat.

The Piazza and market is best viewed from the Amphitheatre Café Bar's terrace loggia at the **Royal Opera House** (*see p83*).

★ London Transport Museum

The Piazza, WC2E 7BB (7379 6344/www.lt museum.co.uk). Covent Garden tube. **Open** 10am-6pm Mon-Thur, Sat; 11am-9pm Fri. **Admission** £8; £6.50 reductions; free under-16s. **Credit** AmEx, DC, MC, V. **Map** p407 Z3.

Re-opened in 2007 after the most thorough refurbishment since its move to Covent Garden in 1980, London's Transport Museum traces the city's transport history from the horse age to the present day. As well as remodelling the interior of the magnificent old flower market building, with its great arched windows and soaring iron columns, the museum has emerged with a much more confident focus on social history and design, illustrated by a superb array of preserved buses, trams and trains. Appropriately, it's now also much easier to get around. The collections are in broadly chronological order, beginning with the Victorian gallery, where a replica of Shillibeer's first horse-drawn bus service in 1829 takes pride of place. Another gallery is dedicated to the museum's truly impressive collection of poster art. Under the inspirational leadership of Frank Pick, in the early 20th century London Transport developed one of the most coherent and accessible brand identities in the world. The new museum also raises some interesting and important questions about the future of public transport in the capital, with a display on ideas that are 'coming soon'.

▶ *Boys who like machines will also adore the Kew Bridge Steam Museum; see p162.*

Royal Opera House

Bow Street, WC2E 9DD (7304 4000/www.royal operahouse.org). Covent Garden tube. **Open** 10am-3pm Mon-Sat. **Admission** free. *Stage tours* £9; £7-£8 reductions. **Credit** AmEx, DC, MC, V. **Map** p407 Y3.

The Royal Opera House was founded in 1732 by John Rich on the profits of his production of John Gay's *Beggar's Opera*. The current building is the third on the site. Between 1735 and 1759 Handel premièred, among many other works, *Samson*, *Judas Maccabaeus* and *Solomon* here. Frenzied opera-lovers twice rioted against ticket price rises, for 61 nights in 1809, while the 1763 fracas came within an iron pillar of bringing down the galleries. It's possible to explore the massive eight-floor building as part of an organised tour, including the main auditorium, nosing into the costume workshops and sometimes even a rehearsal. Certain parts of the building are also open to the general public, including the glass-roofed Floral Hall, the Crush Bar (so named because in Victorian times the only thing served during intermissions was orange and lemon crush) and the Amphitheatre Café Bar, with its terrace overlooking the Piazza.

▶ *For the Royal Opera House's primary function as a music venue, see p311.*

FREE St Paul's Covent Garden

Bedford Street, WC2E 9ED (7836 5221/www. actorschurch.org). Covent Garden or Leicester Square tube. **Open** 9am-4.30pm Mon-Fri; 9am-12.30pm Sun. *Services* 1.10pm Wed; 11am Sun. *Choral Evensong* 4pm 2nd Sun of mth. **Admission** free; donations appreciated. **Map** p407 Y3.

Known as the Actors' Church for its long association with Covent Garden's theatres (and resplendent with some of the best memorials in London, *see p85* **Plaques, Decay**), this magnificently spare building was designed by Inigo Jones for the Earl of Bedford in 1631. A beautiful limewood wreath carved by the 17th-century master Grinling Gibbons hangs inside the front door as a reminder that he and his wife are interred in the crypt. George Bernard Shaw set the first scene of *Pygmalion* under the church's rear portico, and the first known victim of the plague, Margaret Ponteous, is buried in the pleasant churchyard. *Photos p85.*

Elsewhere in Covent Garden

The area offers a mixed bag of entertainment, eateries and shops. On the area's western border, at opposite ends of St Martin's Lane – and the social spectrum – are celebrated lap-dancing establishment **Stringfellows** (16-19 Upper St Martin's Lane, 7240 5534) and the **Coliseum** (*see p310*), home of English National Opera.

Closer to the Piazza, most of the older, more unusual shops have been superseded by a homogeneous mass of cafés. High-profile fashion designers have all but domesticated main shopping street **Long Acre**. More interesting shopping experiences lie in the streets north of Long Acre, notably on the attractive trio of **Neal Street**, **Monmouth Street** and **Earlham Street**. In Earlham is the **Donmar Warehouse** (*see p343*), a former banana-ripening depot that is now an intimate and ground-breaking theatre. On tiny Shorts Gardens next door is pungent and wonderful **Neal's Yard Dairy** (*see p258*), purveyor of exceptional UK cheeses, while down a little passageway one door along is **Neal's Yard** itself, known for its co-operative cafés, herbalists and head shops.

Where Monmouth and Earlham Streets meet Shorts Gardens is **Seven Dials**, named after the number of sundials incorporated into the central monument (the seventh being formed by the pillar itself). The original pillar, an infamous criminal rendezvous, was torn down in 1773 by a mob who believed that there was treasure buried at its base. There wasn't.

South of Long Acre and east of the Piazza, historical depravity is called to account at the former **Bow Street Magistrates Court**. Once home to the Bow Street Runners, the precursors of the Metropolitan Police, this was also where Oscar Wilde entered his plea when arrested for 'indecent acts' in 1895. To the south, Wellington and Catherine Streets mix restaurants and theatres – including, notably, the grand **Theatre Royal**.

Freemasons' Hall (7831 9811, www. freemasonry.london.museum; call for details of guided tours) – the impressive stone building where Long Acre becomes Great Queen Street – has a museum, open to the public on weekdays.

THE STRAND & EMBANKMENT

Embankment tube or Charing Cross tube/rail.

Until as recently as the 1860s, the bustling street known as the Strand ran beside the Thames – in fact, it was originally the river's bridlepath. In the 14th century, it was lined with grand residences whose gardens ran down

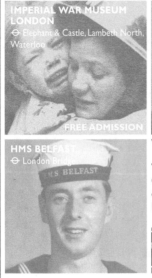

to the water. It wasn't until the 1870s that the Thames was pushed back with the creation of the Embankment and its adjacent gardens. By the time George Newnes's famed *Strand* magazine was introducing its readership to Sherlock Holmes (1891), the street after which the magazine was named boasted the **Savoy** (due to reopen after massive refurbishment in spring this year) and its theatre, the Cecil Hotel (long since demolished), Simpson's, King's College and **Somerset House** (*see p87*). Prime Minister Benjamin Disraeli described it as 'perhaps the finest street in Europe'.

Nobody would make such a claim today – there are too many overbearing office blocks and underwhelming restaurants – but there's still plenty to interest visitors. In 1292, the body of Eleanor of Castile, consort to King Edward I, completed its funerary procession from Lincoln in the small hamlet of Charing, which was at the western end of what is now the Strand. The occasion was marked by the erection of the last of 12 elaborate crosses. A replica of the Eleanor Cross was placed in 1865 on the forecourt of **Charing Cross Station**, where it remains today, looking like the spire of a sunken cathedral. Across the road, behind St Martin-in-the-Fields (*see p110*) is Maggie Hambling's eccentric memorial to a more recent queen: *A Conversation with Oscar Wilde*.

Plaques, Decay

London's lost actors and their testaments to mortality.

St Paul's Covent Garden (*see p83*) is justly known as the Actors' Church. Thespians commemorated on its walls range from those lost in obscurity – step forward Percy Press the Punch and Judy man – to those destined for immortality – Charlie Chaplin. Perhaps most charming are the numerous sublunary figures. Hello, William Henry Pratt, his birth name forgotten to all but devotees, yet – as Boris Karloff – universally famous as the real flesh behind unforgettable monsters. Take a bow too, Hattie Jacques, archetypal matron in the interminable series of *Carry On…* films. The Jacques memorial is so very plain you wonder if the inscriber felt that any embellishment would seem impertinence in the face of such a big comic persona.

There are plenty of inadvertently comic and inescapably tragic memorials across London, not least in the tranquil, lovely **Postman's Park** (*see p62*), but surely no more romantic tribute is paid anywhere in the city than from here to Vivien Leigh. Her plaque is simply inscribed with words from Shakespeare's *Antony & Cleopatra*: 'Now boast thee, death, in thy possession lies a lass unparallel'd.'

When we visit this church, however, our first homage is always paid to the memory of the mysterious 'Pantopuck the Puppetman', one AR Philpott. Who was he? Why is he here? We choose to imagine him wooing Edna Best, who is remembered not far away as 'The Constant Nymph'. Was ever name so charming as Edna? How could our Mr Philpott have resisted?

St Paul's Covent Garden. *See p83*.

SIGHTS

Hidden away downstairs in the **Courtauld** (*see below*), the sweet little gallery café is frequently forgotten. Its little sub-level courtyard can't compete with the main caff's grand Thameside terrace, but it feels delightfully separate from the rest of **Somerset House**. Make a free Monday morning visit to the amazing art collection and finish it off with a relaxed lunch.

The Embankment itself can be approached down **Villiers Street**. Pass through the tube station to where **boat tours** with on-board entertainment embark. Just to the east stands **Cleopatra's Needle**, an obelisk presented to the British nation by the viceroy of Egypt, Mohammed Ali, in 1820 (it was to be another 59 years before it was finally set in place beside the Thames). It was originally erected in around 1500 BC by the pharaoh Tuthmosis III at a site near modern-day Cairo, before being moved to Alexandria, Cleopatra's capital, in 10 BC; by this time, however, the great queen was 20 years dead.

Back on the Strand, the majestic **Savoy Hotel** is currently undergoing extensive re-furbishment, due to reopen in spring 2009. It first opened in 1889, financed by the profits made from Richard D'Oyly Carte's productions of Gilbert and Sullivan's light operas at the neighbouring Savoy Theatre (which pre-dates the hotel by eight years, becoming the first theatre to use electric lights, and has remained open during the refurbishment).

Benjamin Franklin House

36 Craven Street, WC2N 5NF (7925 1405/ www.benjaminfranklinhouse.org). Charing Cross tube/rail. **Open** pre-book tours by phone or online. **Box office** 10.30am-5pm Wed-Sun. **Admission** £7; £5 reductions; free under-16s. **Credit** AmEx, MC, V. **Map** p407 Y5.

Restoration of the house where Franklin – scientist, diplomat, philosopher, inventor and Founding Father of the United States – lived between 1757 and 1775 was completed in 2006. The house is not a museum in the conventional sense, but it can be explored on well-run, pre-booked 'experiences' lasting a short but intense 45 minutes (at noon, 1pm, 2pm, 3.15pm, and 4.15pm on Wednesday to Sunday). These are led by an actress in character as Franklin's landlady Margaret Stevenson, using projections and sound to conjure up the world and times in which Franklin lived. More straightforward, 20-minute tours are given by house interns from noon on Mondays, costing £3.50.

THE ALDWYCH

Temple tube.

At the eastern end of the Strand is the Aldwych, a grand crescent that dates back only to 1905, although the name 'ald wic' (old settlement) has its origins in the 14th century. To the south is regal **Somerset House** (*see p87*); even if you aren't interested in the galleries, it's worth visiting the fountain courtyard. Almost in front of it is **St Mary-le-Strand** (7836 3126, open 11am-4pm daily), James Gibbs's first public building, built from 1714-17. The church was intended to have a statue of Queen Anne on a column beside it, but she died before it could be built and the plan was scrapped. On Strand Lane, reached via Surrey Street, is the so-called **'Roman' bath** where Dickens took the waters.

On a traffic island just east of the Aldwych is **St Clement Danes** (7242 8282). It's believed that a church was first built here by the Danish in the ninth century, but the current building is mainly Wren's handiwork. It is the principal church of the RAF. Just beyond the church are the **Royal Courts of Justice** (*see below*) and the original site of Temple Bar, which once marked the boundary between Westminster and the City of London; Temple Bar is now next to St Paul's Cathedral (*see p61*).

★ Courtauld Gallery

Strand, WC2R 1LA (7848 2526/www.courtauld. ac.uk/gallery). Temple or Embankment tube/ Charing Cross tube/rail. **Open** 10am-6pm (last entry 5.15pm) daily. *Tours* phone for details. **Admission** £5; £4 reductions. Free 10am-2pm Mon; students & under-18s daily. **Credit** *Shop* MC, V. **Map** p401 M7.

Located just off the Strand in the north wing of Somerset House (*see p87*), the Courtauld has one of Britain's greatest collections of paintings, and contains several works of world importance. Although there are some outstanding works from earlier periods (be sure you don't miss the wonderful *Adam & Eve* by Lucas Cranach), the collection's strongest suit is its holdings of Impressionist and post-Impressionist paintings. There are some popular masterpieces: Manet's astonishing *A Bar at the Folies-Bergère* is undoubtedly the centrepiece, alongside plenty of superb Monets and Cézannes, important Gauguins (including *Nevermore*), and some excellent Van Goghs and Seurats. On the top floor, we get to the 20th century with a selection of gorgeous Fauvist works, a lovely room of Kandinskys and plenty more besides. An essential stop if you have any interest in art. Bulky backpacks must be carried, not worn, through the collection – there are a few coin-operated lockers downstairs.

▶ *The Courtauld Gallery was the first home of the Royal Academy; see p106.*

FREE Royal Courts of Justice

Strand, WC2A 2LL (7947 6000/www.hmcourts-service.gov.uk). Temple tube. **Open** 9am-5pm Mon-Fri. **Admission** free. **Map** p399 M6.

The magnificent Royal Courts preside over the most serious civil cases in British law. Members of the public can attend these trials (with exceptions made for sensitive cases), but there are few trials in August and September. Cameras and children under 14 are not allowed in. Tours of the building are given on the first and third Tuesday of each month (though not in late July and early August) from 11am to 1pm and from 2pm to 4pm. They cost £6 per person and can be booked by phoning 7947 7684.

Somerset House & the Embankment Galleries

Strand, WC2R 1LA (7845 4600/www.somerset house.org.uk). Temple or Embankment tube/ Charing Cross tube/rail. **Open** 10am-6pm (last entry 5.15pm) daily. *Tours* phone for details. **Admission** *Courtyard & terrace* free. *Embankment Galleries* £8; £6 reductions. Free students & under-18s daily. *Tours* phone for details. **Credit** *Shop* MC, V. **Map** p401 M7.

The original Somerset House was a Tudor palace commissioned by the Duke of Somerset. In 1775, it was demolished to make way for an entirely new building, effectively the first purpose-built office block in the world. The architect Sir William Chambers spent the last 20 years of his life working on the neoclassical edifice overlooking the Thames. It was built to accommodate learned societies such as the Royal Academy, but various governmental offices also took up residence, including the Inland Revenue. The taxmen are still here, but the rest of the building is open to the public. It houses a formidable art gallery (the wonderful Courtauld, *see p86*), the beautiful fountain court, a terraced café and a classy restaurant. Having replaced the Hermitage Rooms and Gilbert Collection on the river side of the building in April 2008, the new Embankment Galleries explore connections between art, architecture and design with a series of temporary exhibitions; downstairs a ceremonial Thames barge and information boards explain the place's history, to the accompaniment of Handel's *Water Music*. In summer, children never tire of running through the choreographed fountains.

▶ *The Gilbert Collection is due to reopen in the V&A in autumn 2009; see p122.*

Somerset House.

Soho & Leicester Square

The centre of the city is a 24-hour merry-go-round of activity.

Fenced in by Oxford and Regent Streets, Charing Cross Road and Shaftesbury Avenue, **Soho** is central London's louche and libertine party zone. Forever unconventional, packed tight with a huge range of restaurants, clubs and bars, it remains London at its most game. Shoppers and visitors mingle with the musos, gays, boozers and perverts who have colonised the area since the late 1800s. Nearby **Leicester Square** is pleasant by day, but by night becomes a hellish sinkhole of semi-undressed inebriates out on a big night 'up west'.

Map p406, p407	**Hotels** p177
Restaurants &	**Pubs & bars**
cafés p208	p231

SOHO SQUARE

Tottenham Court Road tube.

Soho Square forms the neighbourhood's northern gateway. This tree-lined quadrangle was laid out in 1681 and initially called King's Square – a weather-beaten statue of Charles II stands just north of centre. By day, its grassy spaces are filled with canoodling couples, while snacking workers occupy its benches; one of them bears a plaque dedicated to singer Kirsty MacColl in honour of her song of the same name. The denominations of the two churches on the square testify to the area's long-standing European credentials: as well as the French Protestant church, you'll find St Patrick's, one of the first Catholic churches built in England after the Reformation.

Two classic Soho streets run south from the square. Greek Street, named after the church that once stood here, is lined with an eclectic range of restaurants and drinkeries; first up is the **Gay Hussar** (no.2, 7437 0973), more than 50 years old and London's only Hungarian restaurant. The nearby **Pillars of Hercules** pub (no.7, 7437 1179), former haunt of the all-round Aussie man of letters Clive James, supports an arch leading to Manette Street

(named after the doctor in Dickens' *A Tale of Two Cities*, which mentions the pub) and the Charing Cross Road. There you'll find an entrance to **Foyles** (*see p262*).

Two corners south of here, at the junction with Romilly Street, stands the **Coach & Horses** (no.29, 7437 5920), legendarily louche hangout that's been tamer since the 2006 retirement of famously rude landlord Norman Balon. Nearby pâtisserie **Maison Bertaux** (*see p211*) and champagne bar **Kettners** (29 Romilly Street, 7734 6112) add a touch of class.

Parallel to Greek Street is Frith Street, once home to Mozart (1764-65, no.20) and John Constable (1810-11, no.49). Humanist essayist

INSIDE TRACK
SOHO, SO LONG

While new ventures keep springing up in Soho, a surprising number of shops and businesses in the area remain virtually unchanged since the 1960s or even earlier. For a glimpse of Soho past, visit **Bar Italia** (*see p88*), the **Star Café** (22 Great Chapel Street, 7437 8778) and the **Algerian Coffee Stores** (*see p256*).

SIGHTS

William Hazlitt died in 1830 at no.6, now a discreet hotel named in his memory (*see p179*).

A little further down is **Ronnie Scott's** (*see p318*), Britain's best-known jazz club. Across from Ronnie's is the also mythologised **Bar Italia** (no.22, 7437 4520), an authentically Italian café and restaurant. A large portrait of Rocky Marciano dominates the narrow, chrome bar, but it is the place's 24-hour opening that dominates the thinking of many of its patrons.

OLD COMPTON STREET & AROUND

Leicester Square or Tottenham Court Road tube.

Linking the Charing Cross Road to Wardour Street and crossed by Greek, Frith and Dean Streets, Old Compton Street is gay central. Tight T-shirts congregate around **Balans** (*see p300*), **Compton's** (nos.51-53) and the **Admiral Duncan** (no.54). Another gay-friendly spot, the **Boulevard Bar & Dining Room** (no.59), was formerly the 2i's Coffee Bar, birthplace of rock 'n' roll in London, where stars and svengalis would mingle in the late 1950s and early 1960s.

Visit the street in the morning for a sense of the immigrant Soho of old. Cheeses and cooked meats from **Camisa** (no.61, 7437 7610) and roasting beans from the **Algerian Coffee Stores** (*see p256*) combine to scent the air, while **Pâtisserie Valerie** (no.44, 7437 3466,

INSIDE TRACK JUST JESSIE

Egalitarian chatter in the finest Soho tradition still reigns at the **Blue Posts** pub (*see p91*), where builders, post-production editors, restaurateurs and market traders gabble and glug as one. Overseeing proceedings is a portrait of Jessie Matthews, star of stage and radio (1907-81). Berwick Street born and bred, she's also the only personality to have a plaque on this road. Marx? Mozart? Pah!

www.patisserie-valerie.co.uk) does a brisk trade in buttery croissants and cakes.

Around the corner, the **French House** (*see p231*) was De Gaulle's London base for French resistance in World War II and later became a favourite of painters Francis Bacon and Lucian Freud. Crowds of smokers gather outside. Dean Street is also the address of the members-only **Groucho Club** (no.45), one of the first of its type, founded in the mid '80s. A few doors along, something closer to the Groucho's original character is emerging at **Quo Vadis** (*see p211*), a costly, sophisticated grill room with a members' only bar upstairs. Karl Marx, who lived here in the garret at no.28 from 1850 to 1856, would probably not have approved. To the north is the **Soho Theatre** (*see p343*), which programmes new plays and comedy.

SIGHTS

Soho Square.

City of Westminster
Soho Square
Tel: (020) 7641 5271
www.westminster.gov.uk
Email: parks@westminster.gov.uk

Parallel to Dean Street, **Wardour Street** today provides offices for an assortment of film and TV production companies, but is also known for its rock history. What's now upscale tapas joint **Meza** (no.100, 7314 4002, www. mezabar.co.uk) was, for nearly three decades, the Marquee club, where Led Zeppelin played their first London gig and Hendrix appeared four times. The latter's favourite Soho haunt was the nearby **Ship** pub (no.116, 7437 8446), still with a sprinkling of music-themed knick-knacks. Punk band the Jam played a secret gig at the venue a year after releasing their top-ten hit 'A-Bomb in Wardour Street'. Nearby **St Anne's Court** is home of Trident Studios, where Lou Reed's *Transformer* and David Bowie's *Hunky Dory* and *Ziggy Stardust* were recorded. (The *Ziggy* album cover was, however, shot in Mayfair; *see p102*.) Adjoining Brewer Street was where a young Bowie, as David Jones, played a gig in 1964 at the Jack of Clubs (no.10, now Madame JoJo's; *see p321*).

One street west again, **Berwick Street** is making a sturdy last stand. While the rest of London's sassiest square mile succumbs to chains and clean-up campaigns, this amiable thoroughfare offers authenticity by the pound. A few fruit and veg stalls, along with sweets, nuts and even a fishmonger, can still be found here (9am-6pm Mon-Sat). Berwick Street was also once best known for its music shops, but many have gone or are selling stock off fast.

If you a (no.90, 743 you'll be d (no.17, 773 same block the French 4606) and c (no.18, 7437 over the roa teahouse an eaterie **Yau** by Richard l Liagre could with the illu ...y.c anu genuine retro feel of the **Blue Posts** pub (no.22, 7437 5008) on the other side of the street. Unceasingly popular, this corner boozer is set in a gabled house with 'Watney's Ales' still stencilled on the windows.

WEST SOHO

Piccadilly Circus tube.

West of Berwick Street, Soho has been branded 'West Soho' in a misplaced bid to give some kind of upmarket identity to its shops. Brewer Street does have a handful of interesting places, among them the **Vintage Magazine Store** (nos.39-43, 7439 8525) for everything from retro robots to pre-war issues of *Vogue*. On Great Windmill Street is the **Windmill Theatre**

The Sordid Truth

The best of times and worst of times – to see Leicester Square.

Unless numbed by alcohol, Londoners avoid the cheap fast food, expensive cinemas and tacky pavement artists of **Leicester Square** (*see p93*). Apart from the excellent **tkts** booth (*see p339*), selling cut-price, same-day theatre tickets, and Leicester Place's unlikely neighbours the **Prince Charles Cinema** (*see p299*) and the French Catholic church of **Notre Dame de France** (no.5, 7437 9363, www.notredamechurch.co.uk), with its Jean Cocteau murals, there's no reason to spend time here. The green patch in the centre of the square is bearable on a sunny day, but don't venture here after dark unless you enjoy being jostled by throngs of drunken idiots. Plans are afoot for redevelopment: the north-east corner will be home to a swanky new W Hotel... but unless you're happy hanging here until 2010, we suggest you turn to any other page of this guide and get some real joy.

...ootsteps of London chancers and ne'er-do-wells.

...ly Street
...rench House on Dean Street
...40mins.

Soho has been London's playground for more than two centuries, where poseurs, spivs, chancers, bohemians, cynics, drunks and wide boys have come to spend their money. It's a bit calmer these days, but some illicit corners remain.

Start at Soho's west end, on **Kingly Street**, a narrowly oppressive alley that runs parallel to Carnaby Street. No.7 was once a brothel owned by the Messini brothers, five Maltese siblings who ran Soho's vice trade from the 1930s until their empire was finally cracked by a crusading journalist in the 1950s. Two doors down at no.9 was Soho's other face. This used to be the Bag O Nails, the trendy nightclub where Paul met Linda and where Jimi Hendrix played his official introduction to the press in 1966. Kingly Street still has fashionable bars such as Two Floors (at no.3; *see p233*), secreted

in Kingly Court, popular boho drinks club Tatty Bogles (no.11, 7734 4475).

Turn left down **Beak Street**. At the corner with Carnaby Street is a plaque to John Stephen, who opened His Clothes in 1956, instantly making Carnaby Street the fashion mecca it remained for more than a decade. Walk along Beak Street, up Lexington Street and right into Broadwick Street until you reach **Berwick Street**. Turn right and walk through the market, past pubs, bistros, adverts for 'models' and fly-by-night fashion outlets, to get a flavour of the old Soho. The neon alleyway of **Walker's Court** is where the Raymond Revue Bar opened in 1958, swiftly becoming London's most famous strip club. The area remains the centre of Soho's dwindling sex trade. Raymond's is now the Soho Revue Bar (*see p321*), staging an eclectic range of burlesque and pop – much like its Brewer Street neighbour, Madame JoJo's (*see p321*).

Walk left along Brewer Street until it becomes **Old Compton Street**, London's

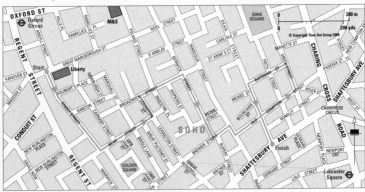

(nos.17-19), which gained fame in the 1930s and 1940s for its 'revuedeville' shows with erotic 'tableaux' – naked girls who remained stationary in order to stay within the law. The story of the theatre was retold in the 2005 film *Mrs Henderson Presents*. The place is now a lap-dancing joint.

North of Brewer Street is **Golden Square**. Developed in the 1670s, it became the political and ambassadorial district of the late 17th and early 18th centuries, and remains home to some

of the area's grandest residential buildings – many of which are now filled by media companies. And just north of the square is **Carnaby Street**. After serving as the hub of swinging '60s London, it became a rather seamy commercialised backwater. But along with **Newburgh Street** and **Kingly Court** nearby, it's recently undergone a revival. Interesting independents now sit alongside tourist traps doing no more than trade happily off the history of the area.

gay superhighway. No.59 used to be the 2i's, the skiffle venue where a young Cliff Richard strutted his stuff in the 1950s. Further along, at the corner of Frith Street, is the scene of a legendary gangland battle between two Soho crime bosses, Jack Spot and Albert Dimes, in August 1955. At no.20, there used to be a cheap Italian restaurant called Pollo, in which Pink Floyd's Syd Barrett whiled away his time. These days, your best bet for cheap food is the hardy Stockpot (no.18, 7287 1066).

Head left up **Greek Street**, away from the Coach & Horses (no.29, 7437 5920), where Soho flâneur Jeffrey Bernard held court for decades, and past Soho House (no.40, 7734 5188), where the current crop of wannabes hope to channel the same vibe. No.49 was once Les Cousins, a folk venue (note the heldover mosaic featuring a musical note), while no.46 was a house in which Casanova briefly lived.

Turn left again on Bateman Street and cross Frith Street. Next you reach **Dean Street**, the centre of Soho's private clubland. You have the Groucho at no.45, favoured by writers and drunks; Gerry's at no.52, favoured by actors and drunks; and, at no.41, the Colony Room, favoured by artists and drunks for 60 years but threatened with closure in 2008. Gerry's was once owned by actor Gerry Campion, who played Billy Bunter through the 1950s and 1960s. In 1963, membership included Tony Hancock, Stanley Baker, Galton & Simpson, Graham Hill, Ron Grainer and Wilfred Bramble. Non-members should head to the French House (no.49; *see p231*), where you can buy half pints of lager or decent wine and watch the cool kids and bad lads walk past, on their way to prior engagements at drinking dens and with the spirit of the past.

CHINATOWN & LEICESTER SQUARE

Leicester Square tube.

Shaftesbury Avenue is the very heart of Theatreland. The Victorians built seven grand theatres here; six of which still stand. The most impressive is the gorgeous **Palace Theatre** on Cambridge Circus. It opened in 1891 as the Royal English Opera House, but grand opera

flopped here and the theatre reopened as a music hall two years later. It has been home mostly to musicals: *The Sound of Music* in 1961, *Jesus Christ Superstar* in 1972, and *Les Misérables*, which racked up 7,602 performances between 1985 and 2004. Just opposite the theatre, what's now the Med Kitchen occupies premises that were once home to Marks & Co, the shop that was immortalised in Helene Hanff's *84 Charing Cross Road*. Second-hand bookshops still line the road to the south.

Behind, south of Shaftesbury Avenue and west of Charing Cross Road, is **Chinatown**. The Chinese are relative latecomers to the area. London's original Chinatown was set around Limehouse in east London, but hysteria about Chinese opium dens and criminality led to 'slum clearances' in 1934 (interestingly, the surrounding slums were deemed to be in considerably less urgent need of clearance). It wasn't until the 1950s that the Chinese put down roots here, attracted by the cheap rents along Gerrard and Lisle Streets.

The ersatz oriental gates, stone lions and pagoda-topped phone boxes around **Gerrard Street** suggest a Chinese theme park, but this remains a close-knit residential and working enclave, a genuine focal point for the Chinese community in London. The area is crammed with restaurants, Asian grocery stores and a host of small shops selling iced-grass jelly, speciality teas and cheap air tickets to Beijing.

South of Chinatown, **Leicester Square** was one of London's most exclusive addresses in the 17th century; in the 18th, it became home to the royal court of Prince George (later George II). How different it all is now (*see p91* **The Sordid Truth**). Satirical painter William Hogarth had a studio here (1733-64), as did 18th-century artist Sir Joshua Reynolds; both are commemorated by busts in the small gardens that lie at the heart of the square, although it's the statue of a tottering Charlie Chaplin that gets all the attention.

There's no particular reason for Chaplin to be here, other than that Leicester Square is considered the home of British film thanks to its numerous cinemas. The monolithic **Odeon Leicester Square** (*see p297*) once boasted the UK's largest screen, and probably still has the UK's highest ticket prices. Like the neighbouring Empire, it's regularly used for movie premières.

The **Hippodrome**, on the corner beside the tube station, is an impressive red-brick edifice designed by the prolific theatre architect Frank Matcham. It became famous as the 'Talk of the Town' cabaret venue in the 1960s, featuring the likes of Shirley Bassey and Judy Garland. Currently being refurbished, it is scheduled to become a posh casino in 2010.

SIGHTS

Oxford Street & Marylebone

Turn off the busy shopping street for the zoo and a village of boutiques.

The mile or so of **Oxford Street** continues to rule supreme in the city's shopping stakes. Plans are afoot to ease the congested pavements in time for the London Olympics, but for now it still remains somewhere locals visit only to shop. North of Oxford Street, things are much more pleasant. Londoners drift around Marylebone's leafy squares and streets lined with luxury cafés and boutiques. In **Regent's Park**, you can soak up the sun rather than splash out the cash, although **London Zoo** gives you the opportunity to do both.

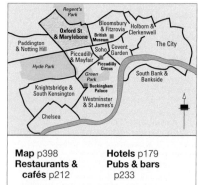

Map p398	Hotels p179
Restaurants &	**Pubs & bars**
cafés p212	p233

Map p398
Restaurants &
cafés p212
Hotels p179
Pubs & bars
p233

OXFORD STREET

Bond Street, Marble Arch, Oxford Circus or Tottenham Court Road tube.

The relentless trade here accounts for ten per cent of all spending in the capital. Impressive, yes, but few Londoners esteem historic Oxford Street. In existence since the 12th century, the road gained notoriety as the route by which condemned men were conveyed from Newgate Prison to the old Tyburn gallows (*see p95*), stopping only for a last pint at the **Angel** pub (61 St Giles High Street, 7240 2876) near its eastern end. It was during the 19th century that the street became primarily a shopping district and its more salubrious western stretch is still punctuated with large department stores: **John Lewis** (nos.278-306, 7629 7711), **Debenhams** (nos.334-348, 08445 616161) and **Selfridges** (no.400; *see p243*). The latter, opened in 1909, is especially grand, with much of the building completed in the art deco heyday of the 1920s.

Elsewhere, major architectural interest is limited to Oxford Circus's four identical convex corners, constructed between 1913 and 1928. Here the overwhelming crush of the crowds and rush of the traffic hampers investigations – a problem being addressed by controversial plans to pedestrianise Oxford Street, banning cars – perhaps as early as this year – and installing a tram by 2013, or to institute the less radical solution of widening pavements, removing street clutter and creating Tokyo Shibuya-style diagonal crossings. For a more entertaining traverse of the Oxford Street area, with plenty of shopping options, *see p96* **Walk**.

At the western end of Oxford Street, **Marble Arch** stands forlorn on a hectic traffic island. You can still admire its Carrara marble and sculptures, which celebrate the victories of Nelson and Wellington.

North of Oxford Circus

Great Portland Street, Oxford Circus or Regent's Park tube.

Immediately north of Oxford Circus runs Langham Place, notable for the Bath stone façade of John Nash's **All Souls Church** (Langham Place, 2 All Souls Place, 7580 3522, www.allsouls.org). Its bold combination of a Gothic spire and classical rotunda wasn't always popular: in 1824, a year after it was officially opened, the church was condemned in the House of Commons as a 'deplorable and horrible object'.

SIGHTS

Opposite the church you'll find the BBC headquarters in **Broadcasting House**, an oddly asymmetrical art deco building that is shipshape in more ways than one. Prominent among the building's carvings is a statue of Shakespeare's Prospero and Ariel, his spirit of the air – or, in this case, the airwaves. The statue caused controversy when it was unveiled due to the flattering size of the manhood of the airy sprite; artist Eric Gill was summoned back to make it more modest. Major renovation work is under way, due for completion in 2011. Over the road is the **Langham Hotel** (1C Portland Place, Regent Street, W1B 1JA, 7636 1000, http:// london.langhamhotels.co.uk). Opened in 1865 as Britain's first grand hotel, its history is peppered with notable guests, from Mark Twain and Napoleon III to Oscar Wilde (who was commissioned to write *The Picture of Dorian Gray* during a dinner here).

North, Langham Place turns into **Portland Place**, designed by Robert and James Adam as the glory of 18th-century London. Its Georgian terraced houses are now mostly occupied by embassies and swanky offices. At no.66 is the **Royal Institute of British Architects** (*see p283*). Running parallel to Portland Place is **Harley Street**, famous for its high-cost dentists and doctors, and **Wimpole Street**, erstwhile home to the poet Elizabeth Barrett Browning (no.50) and Sir Arthur Conan Doyle (2 Upper Wimpole Street). More recently, a young Paul McCartney woke up at no.57, the house of then-girlfriend Jane Asher's parents, and dashed to the piano to transcribe a tune that had been playing in his dream: it became 'Yesterday'.

MARYLEBONE

Baker Street, Bond Street, Marble Arch, Oxford Circus or Regent's Park tube.

North of Oxford Street, the fashionable district known as 'Marylebone Village' has become a magnet for moneyed Londoners. It wasn't always so idyllic: the area once offered the morbid attraction of Tyburn gallows, with crowds of thousands gathering to watch the

Oxford Street.

countless executions over a period of some 600 years (the last execution took place here in 1783). **St Marylebone Church** stands in its fourth incarnation at the northern end of the high street: the name of this district is a contraction of the church's earlier name, St Mary by the Bourne. The 'bourne', Tyburn stream, still filters into the Thames near Pimlico – but its entire length is now covered over.

Many visitors to Marylebone head directly for the waxworks of **Madame Tussauds**, although there's also a small and often over-looked museum at the neighbouring **Royal Academy of Music** (7873 7300, www.ram. ac.uk). The area's beating heart, however, is **Marylebone High Street**, teeming with interesting shops. More lovely boutiques can be found on quaint, winding Marylebone Lane, as well as an atmospheric corner pub, the **Golden Eagle** (no.59, 7935 3228), which often hosts regular old-style Cockney piano singalongs. Marylebone is also a popular foodie destination, with upmarket eateries snuggling up alongside tempting delicatessens like **La Fromagerie** (*see p213*) and the century-old lunchroom **Paul Rothe & Son** (35 Marylebone Lane, 7935 6783). Marylebone Farmers' Market takes place in the Cramer Street car park every Sunday.

Further south, 19th-century **St James's Roman Catholic Church** (22 George Street)

Walk Back to the Back Streets

Avoid Oxford Street's horrors with a trail through the side streets.

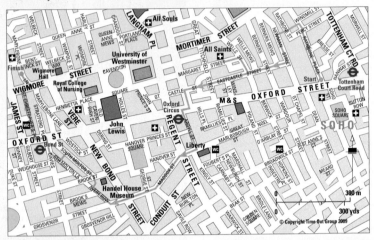

SIGHTS

Start Rathbone Place, W1
Finish St Christopher's Place
or Marylebone Lane
Time 2 hours (allowing about
an hour for browsing)

When it comes to shopping on Oxford
Street the average Londoner doesn't. But
when a trip is unavoidable, they know how
to escape the crowds by diving into the
streets and alleys that fringe the street,
relaxing at a café not devoted to feeding
battalions of tourists, visiting a quirky
boutique, taking in a gallery. This walk
introduces you to hinterlands of Oxford
Street, prized by locals. Start it, drop it,
linger at any point you fancy… you'll find
you're never very far from transport,
refreshment – or shops.

Rathbone Place marks the lower
reaches of Fitzrovia, where the worlds
of media and design collide with the rag
trade in handsome streets. Once past
the unprepossessing Post Office sorting
office, the fun begins at Hobgoblin Music
(no.24, 7323 9040), which often has an
impromptu concert in progress as
musicians test-drive zithers and exotic
percussion. Peek around the corner to
the right, along Percy Street, where
Contemporary Applied Arts (*see p259*)
sells outstanding British crafts from
jewellery to furniture. Keep north up

restaurant-lined **Charlotte Street**, buzzing
with media types, then turn left beside the
comfortably suave Charlotte Street Hotel
(*see p171*) through Percy Passage. Cross
the dog-leg of Rathbone Street, and head
on via Dickensian **Newman Passage**
(watch out for film crews) to emerge in
Newman Street. Pause for a perfect snap
of the iconic BT Tower. Next, turn left
and then right on to Eastcastle Street,
detouring north up **Margaret Street** to
take in the truly sensational interior of
All Saints Church (*see p80*).

Back on **Eastcastle Street** is cutting-
edge gallery Stuart Shave/Modern Art (*see
p279*). Over the road Fever (no.52, 7636
6326) mixes cute retro-inspired clothing
and accessories with vintage, while Getty
Images Gallery (no.46, 7291 5380) holds
great photography exhibitions and sells
prints from the famous photo archive.
Market Place opens ahead – a tranquil
oasis of sidewalk cafés just yards from
the frenzy of Oxford Street. Plunge across
Oxford Street, down Argyll Street, aiming
for the half-timbered **Liberty** building
(*see p242*) and its spectacular galleried
hall – think William Morris meets William
Shakespeare. One of London's legendary
stores, the shopping here is sumptuous.

Next, cross Regent Street, continue
along **Maddox Street**, over New Bond
Street into Grosvenor Street, then right,

up **Avery Row**. This is the land of Victorian London's great aristocratic estates, where narrow service alleys brought tradesmen to the rear entrances of the grand residences. The alleys still offer services to the gentry – but now they're exclusive little boutiques and restaurants hidden from the dazed tourists wandering nearby. Top marks on Avery Row go to French cobblers Hardrige (no.4, 7355 1504) and also the Paul Smith Sale Shop (no.23, 7493 1287). Adjoining **Lancashire Court** is home to a clutch of restaurants and the Handel House Museum (see p105).

Handel's house faces **Brook Street**, right beside the home of another musical legend: Jimi Hendrix. Check out their blue plaques, then cross the road to Alessi (no.22, 7518 9091), full of goodies from the Italian design legend. Tucked in the yard further left is the Haunch of Venison gallery (see p276). Move on then to pedestrianised **South Molton Street** with its strong mix of chain stores, cafés and independents, among them glittery Butler & Wilson (no.20, 7409 2955). Take the passage to the left of fashion queen Browns (see p249) and pop out by the imposing terracotta structure of **Grays Antique Markets** (see p263).

Cross Oxford Street again, battling your way just for a short distance left to the freestanding clock signposting the narrow entrance to **St Christopher's Place**. This warren of little streets houses an appealing traffic-free complex of outdoor cafés and specialist shops, complete with fountain and a flower-decked Victorian WC. There's loads of shopping to choose from here, including Ollie & Nic (no.5, 7935 2160) for their trademark tweed handbags and the Finnish designers Marimekko (nos.16-17, 7486 6454) for cutting-edge clothing, houseware and textiles.

Can't stop shopping? Continue north to **Wigmore Street**: turn right for Robert Clergerie Shoes (no.67, 7935 3601), then nip across the road for the coolly eclectic home furnishings at Mint (see p263). Now you've reached **Marylebone Lane** with its array of distinctive shops, like the long-established and always wonderful Button Queen (no.19, 7935 1505). And this is where we'll leave you to start making your own discoveries.

boasts a soaring neo-Gothic interior dramatically lit by stained-glass windows – Vivien Leigh (née Hartley) married barrister Herbert Leigh Hunt here in 1932 – and, on Manchester Square, don't miss the wonderful art and armour at the **Wallace Collection** (see below). The fine auditorium of nearby **Wigmore Hall** (see p309) is a jewel in London's classical music crown.

Madame Tussauds

Marylebone Road, NW1 5LR (0870 400 3000/ www.madame-tussauds.co.uk). Baker Street tube. **Open** 9.30am-6pm (last entry 5.30pm) daily. **Admission** £25; £21 reductions; £85 family (internet booking only, only available 24hrs in advance). **Credit** MC, V. **Map** p398 G4.
Streams of humanity jostle excitedly here for the chance to take pictures of each other planting a smacker on the waxen visage of fame and fortune. Founded in Paris in 1770, Madame Tussaud brought her show to London in 1802. It has been expanding ever since. There are 300 figures in the collection now, among them a suspiciously clear-complexioned Amy Winehouse. Kylie, who's always being recast, currently sits in a large sequinned crescent moon. Angelina, Brad and Keira receive all the attention their A-lister status affords them. If you're not already overheating, your palms will be sweating by the time you descend to the alarming Chamber of Horrors – the 'Live!' element of which only teens claim to enjoy. Much more pleasant is the wonderfully kitsch Spirit of London ride, whisking you through 400 years of London life in a taxi pod. Be here before 10am to avoid the queues, or come after 5.30pm and take advantage of the reduced admission charge (£18; £12.50-£15 reductions).

★ FREE Wallace Collection

Hertford House, Manchester Square, W1U 3BN (7935 0687/www.wallacecollection.org). Bond Street tube. **Open** 10am-5pm daily. **Admission** free. **Credit** (shop) AmEx, MC, V. **Map** p398 G5.
This handsome house, built in 1776, contains an exceptional collection of 18th-century French furniture, painting and objets d'art, as well as an amazing array of medieval armour and weaponry. It all belonged to Sir Richard Wallace, who, as the illegitimate offspring of the fourth Marquess of Hertford, inherited in 1870 the treasures that his father had amassed in the last 30 years of his life. Open to the public since 1900, room after grand room contains Louis XIV and XV furnishings and Sèvres porcelain, while the galleries are hung with paintings by Titian, Velázquez, Fragonard, Gainsborough and Reynolds; Franz Hals's *Laughing Cavalier* (neither laughing, nor a Cavalier) is one of the best known, along with Fragonard's *The Swing*. There are also regular temporary exhibitions.
▶ *Oliver Peyton (see p219 Profile) runs the museum restaurant: it isn't cheap, but it is beautifully set in a glass-roofed courtyard.*

SIGHTS

REGENT'S PARK

Baker Street or Regent's Park tube.

Regent's Park (open 5am-dusk daily) is one of London's most popular open spaces. Originally a hunting ground for Henry VIII, it remained a royals-only retreat long after it was formally designed by John Nash in 1811; only in 1845 did it open to the public as a spectacular shared space. Attractions run from the animal noises and odours of **London Zoo** (*see below*) to enchanting **Open Air Theatre** (*see p337*) performances of *A Midsummer Night's Dream* that are an integral part of the London summer. Rowing boat hire, spectacular rose gardens, ice-cream stands and the **Garden Café** (7935 5729, www.thegardencafe.co.uk) complete the picture.

West of Regent's Park looms the golden dome of the **London Central Mosque** (www.iccuk.org) and the northern end of **Baker Street**, which is, unsurprisingly, heavy on nods to the world's favourite freelance detective. Not least among them is the **Sherlock Holmes Museum** (7935 8866, www.sherlock-holmes.co.uk) at, of course, no.221B. Here the Holmes stories are earnestly re-enacted: there's a bobby guarding the front door and Victorian maids man the tills at the shop. Serious fans will probably find more of interest among the books and photos of the Sherlock Holmes Collection at **Marylebone Library** (7641 1206, by appointment only). They could also make a pilgrimage to Conan Doyle's former home on Upper Wimpole Street or the Langham Hotel (for both, *see p95*), which features in several of the stories.

From crime fiction to music fact, another true story of Baker Street involves the Beatles having painted no.94 with a mind-boggling psychedelic mural before opening it in December 1967 as the Apple Boutique, a clothing store run on such whimsical hippie principles that it quickly began losing money and had to close within six months. Fab Four pilgrims head to the **London Beatles Store** (no.231, 7935 4464, www.beatles storelondon.co.uk), where the ground-floor shop offers a predictable array of Beatles-branded accessories alongside genuine collectibles. The gallery above (admission £1) has original album

Regent's Park.

artwork, photographs and a few of Paul's sketches. Next door, the Presley store **Elvisly Yours** (7486 2005) caters comprehensively to the blue suede shoes fraternity.

London Zoo

Regent's Park, NW1 4RY (7722 3333/www.zsl. org/london-zoo). Baker Street or Camden Town tube then 274, C2 bus. **Open** *Late Oct-mid Mar* 10am-4pm daily. *Mid Mar-late Oct* 10am-5.30pm daily. **Admission** £15.40; £11.90-£13.90 reductions; £49.10 family; free under-3s. **Credit** AmEx, MC, V. **Map** p398 G2.

London Zoo has been open in one form or another since 1826. Spread over 36 acres and containing more than 600 species, it cares for many of the endangered variety – part of the entry price (pretty steep at £17, if you include the voluntary donation) goes towards the ZSL's projects around the world. The emphasis is firmly on upbeat education. Regular events include 'animals in action' and keeper talks; explanations are simple, short and lively. Exhibits are entertaining (we especially like the recreation of a kitchen overrun with large cockroaches). The 'Meet the Monkeys' attraction allows visitors to walk through an enclosure that recreates the natural habitat of black-capped Bolivian squirrel monkeys, while personal encounters of the avian kind can be had in the Blackburn Pavilion. The reptile house, as always, delights and horrifies in equal measure; likewise the Komodo dragons. In Easter 2009, a terrific-sounding children's zoo will open. Bring a picnic and you can spend a day here.
▶ *The children's zoo in Battersea Park is a winner, and half the price; see p153.*

SIGHTS

Paddington & Notting Hill

The Middle East in the West End and a whole hill of have-beans.

At first sight, Paddington is just a big railway station with a hospital attached. But the area has its attractions: the time-warp **Alexander Fleming Laboratory Museum**; the sleek Paddington Central development on the canal; and, on the Marylebone side, the wondrous trove at Alfie's Antique Market. Notting Hill, however, remains a major tick on many tourist itineraries, not least because of the indefatigable **Portobello Market**. While you're there, pop in on the quirky **Museum of Brands, Packaging & Advertising**.

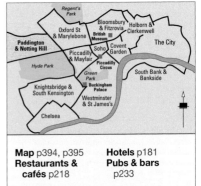

Map p394, p395	**Hotels** p181
Restaurants &	**Pubs & bars**
cafés p218	p233

SIGHTS

EDGWARE ROAD & PADDINGTON

Edgware Road, Lancaster Gate, Marble Arch or Paddington tube/rail.

Edgware Road rules a definite north–south line marking where the central West End stops and central west London begins. It's best known these days as the heart of the city's Middle East end. If you want to pick up your copy of *Al Hayat*, cash a cheque at the Bank of Kuwait or catch Egyptian football, this is the place to come. North of the Marylebone Road flyover, **Church Street** has a local food market, and wonderous **Alfie's Antique Market** (*see p263*).

The fact that the name Paddington has been immortalised by a certain small, ursine Peruvian émigré is appropriate, given that the area has long been home to refugees and immigrants. It was a country village until the Grand Junction Canal arrived in 1801, linking London to the Midlands, and followed in the 1830s by the railway. The current **Paddington Station**, with its fine triple roof of iron and glass, was built in 1851 to the specifications of the great engineer Isambard Kingdom Brunel.

Despite its reputation for poverty and over-crowding, the area's proximity to central

London eventually drew in the developers. The gleaming **Paddington Central** development east of the station is the most significant result, a million square feet of office space, canalside apartments and restaurants – among them, the beautifully designed Chinese Pearl Liang (8 Sheldon Square, 7289 7000, www.pearl liang.co.uk). East of the station, in St Mary's Hospital, the old-fashioned **Alexander Fleming Laboratory Museum** gives a sense of what the district used to be like.

Alexander Fleming Laboratory Museum

St Mary's Hospital, Praed Street, W2 1NY (7886 6528/www.imperial.nhs.uk/aboutus/ museumsandarchives/index.htm). Paddington tube/rail. **Open** 10am-1pm Mon-Thur. *By appointment* 2-5pm Mon-Thur; 10am-5pm Fri. **Admission** £2; £1 reductions; free under-5s. **No credit cards. Map** p395 D5.
Buzz in at the tatty entrance to your left to find this tiny, dusty, instrument-cluttered laboratory room. The enthusiastic guide conjures up the professor, smoking 60 a day but insisting his two colleagues keep the windows shut for fear of contamination. Even so, in 1928 it was Fleming's noticing that mould contamination had destroyed some staphylococcus bacteria on a set-aside culture plate that

handed humanity a powerful weapon against bacterial enemies – penicillin. The pub across the street subsequently advertised its own healthful properties, claiming the miracle fungus had blown into the lab from them.

NOTTING HILL

Notting Hill Gate, Ladbroke Grove or Westbourne Park tube.

Head north up Queensway from Kensington Gardens (*see p124*) and turn west along **Westbourne Grove**. It starts humble but gets posher the further west you go. Once you cross Chepstow Road you're really into Notting Hill, where the shopping is stellar. A host of fashionable restaurants and bars still exploit the lingering street cred of the fast-disappearing black and working-class residents. **Notting Hill Gate** is not itself an attractive street, but the leafy avenues south are; so is Pembridge Road, to the north, leading to the boutique-filled streets of Westbourne Grove and Ledbury Road, and more notably to **Portobello Road** and its renowned market (*see p243*).

Half way down, Blenheim Crescent boasts three notable independent booksellers. The **Travel Bookshop** (nos.13-15, 7229 5260, www.thetravelbookshop.com) is the store on which Hugh Grant's bookshop was based in the movie *Notting Hill* – a film that did more to undermine the area's bohemian credentials than a fleet of Starbucks. Under the Westway, that elevated section of the M40 motorway linking London with Oxford, is the small but busy **Portobello Green Market** (*see below*).

North of the Westway, Portobello's vitality fizzles out. It sparks back to life at Golborne Road, the heartland of London's North African community and the address of the excellent, no-frills **Moroccan Tagine** café (no.95, 8968 8055). Here too are the rival Portuguese café-delis **Lisboa Pâtisserie** (no.57, 8968 5242) and **Café Oporto** (no.62A, 8968 8839). **Trellick Tower**, the concrete building at the north-eastern end of Golborne Road, is one of London's most divisive bits of architecture – a significant like-it-or-loathe-it piece of modernism by Ernö Goldfinger. At its western end, Golborne Road connects with Ladbroke Grove, which can be followed north to spooky **Kensal Green Cemetery**.

FREE Kensal Green Cemetery

Harrow Road, Kensal Green, W10 4RA (8969 0152/www.kensalgreen.co.uk). Kensal Green tube. **Open** *Apr-Sept* 9am-6pm Mon-Sat; 10am-6pm Sun. *Oct-Mar* 9am-5pm Mon-Sat; 10am-5pm Sun. *Tours* 2pm Sun; (incl catacombs) 2pm 1st & 3rd Sun of mth. **Admission** free. *Tours* £5 (£4 reductions) donation. **No credit cards**.

Portobello Market.

Behind the neoclassical gate is a green oasis of the dead. The resting place of both the Duke of Sussex, sixth son of George III, and his sister, Princess Sophia, also buried here are Wilkie Collins, Anthony Trollope and William Makepeace Thackeray.

Museum of Brands, Packaging & Advertising

Colville Mews, Lonsdale Road, W11 2AR (7908 0880/www.museumofbrands.com). Notting Hill Gate tube. **Open** 10am-6pm Tue-Sat; 11am-5pm Sun. **Admission** £5.80; £2-£3.50 reductions; free under-7s. **Credit** MC, V. **Map** p394 A6. Robert Opie began collecting the things most of us throw away when he was 16. Over the years the collection has grown to include everything from milk bottles to vacuum cleaners and cereal packets. The emphasis is on British consumerism through the last century, though there are items as old as an ancient Egyptian doll. One for Brit-brand nostalgists.

INSIDE TRACK
PORTOBELLO GREEN MARKET

This is where you'll find Portobello's best vintage fashion stalls. Look out for the excellent second-hand boot and shoe stall and brilliant vintage handbag stall (usually outside the Falafel King), along with vintage clothing stall Sage Femme, often outside the Antique Clothing Shop.

Brigh~... ...spenders.

Mayfair means money. And these days that doesn't necessarily translate into stuffy exclusivity. Even the tailors of **Savile Row**, low be it spoken, have loosened their ties a little; the **Royal Institution** has been given a fantastic, user-friendly makeover; and the galleries of **Cork Street** have been given a shaking by the East End. Even so, there's enough old-world decorum here to satisfy the most fastidious of visitors, for a price, from elegant shopping arcades to five-star hotels. **Piccadilly Circus** remains its impossible self.

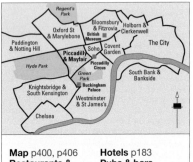

Map p400, p406	**Hotels** p183
Restaurants &	**Pubs & bars**
cafés p213	p234

SIGHTS

PICCADILLY CIRCUS & REGENT STREET

Oxford Circus or Piccadilly Circus tube.

Bustling, hectic **Piccadilly Circus** is an uneasy mix of tawdry and grand. It certainly has little to do with the original vision of its architect John Nash. His 1820s design for the intersection of two of the West End's most elegant streets, Regent Street and Piccadilly, was a harmonious circle of curved frontages. But 60 years later Shaftesbury Avenue muscled in, creating the present lopsided and usually pandemonious traffic junction. Alfred Gilbert's memorial fountain in honour of child-labour abolitionist Earl Shaftesbury was erected in 1893. It is properly known as the Shaftesbury Memorial, with the statue on top intended to show the Angel of Christian Charity, but critics and public alike recognised the likeness of **Eros** and their judgement has stuck. The illuminated advertising panels first appeared late in the 19th century and have been present ever since.

Just opposite, the **Trocadero** (www.london trocadero.com) has seen several ventures come and go, most of them driven out by a combination of high rents and low footfall in this prime, but increasingly tired location. Tween magnet Funland (www.funland.co.uk) seems to be a

fixture; and the US crowd-puller Ripley's Believe It or Not! (www.ripleyslondon.com, 3238 0022) – having reportedly taken a 25-year lease at £1.75 million a year – is the newest arrival. A planned £100 million revamp of the entire site, to include a hotel complex and smart new retail space, may yet make this a shrewd investment.

Connecting Piccadilly Circus to Oxford Circus to the north and Pall Mall to the south, the broad curve of **Regent Street** was designed by Nash in the early 1800s, with the aims of improving access to Regent's Park and bumping up property values in Haymarket and Pall Mall. The grandeur of the street remains impressive – even though much of Nash's architecture, including the original covered colonnade, was destroyed in the early 20th century. Halfway up, on the left side, **Heddon Street** is where the iconic photo was taken that graces the cover of David Bowie's *Ziggy Stardust* album – the building that he is posed in front of is now the Moroccan-flavoured Mô Tea Room, next door to famed North African eaterie **Momo** (*see p214*); the cover's bright 'K West' sign was long since stolen by a Bowie fan. Further north on Regent Street are the mammoth children's emporium **Hamleys** (nos.188-196, 0870 333 2455, www. hamleys.com) and the landmark department store **Liberty** (*see p242*).

MAYFAIR

Bond Street or Green Park tube.

The gaiety suggested by this area's name – derived from a long-departed spring fair – is belied by its atmosphere today. Even on Mayfair's busy shopping streets you may feel out of place without the reassuring heft of a platinum card. Nonetheless, there are many pleasures to enjoy if you fancy a stroll – not least the concentration of blue-chip commercial galleries (*see pp276-279*).

The Grosvenor and Berkeley families bought the rolling green fields that would become Mayfair in the mid 17th century. In the 1700s, they developed the pastures into a posh new neighbourhood. In particular they built a series of squares surrounded by elegant houses. The most famous of these, **Grosvenor Square**, built 1725-31, is now dominated by the supremely inelegant US Embassy, its only decorative touches a fierce eagle and a mass of post-9/11 protective barricades. Out front, a statue of President Dwight Eisenhower has pride of place (Roosevelt is in the park nearby). Plans are afoot to move everything south of the river to Vauxhall, but not anytime soon.

When in London, Eisenhower stayed at the exclusive hotel **Claridge's** (*see p183*). **Brook Street** has impressive music credentials: GF Handel lived and died (1759) at no.25, and Jimi Hendrix roomed briefly next door at no.23.

These adjacent buildings have been combined into the **Handel House Museum** (*see p105*). For most visitors, however, this part of Mayfair is all about shopping. **South Molton Street**, connecting Brook Street with Oxford Street to the north, is no longer as hip as it once was, but is still home to the fabulous boutique-emporium **Browns** (*see p249*), while **New Bond Street** is an A-Z of every top-end, mainstream fashion house you can name.

Beyond New Bond Street, **Hanover Square** is another of the area's big squares, now a busy traffic chicane. Just south is **St George's Church**, built in the 1720s and once everybody's favourite place to get married. Handel, who married nobody, attended services here. South of St George's, salubrious **Conduit Street** is where fashion shocker Vivienne Westwood (no.44) faces staid Rigby & Peller (no.22A), corsetière to the Queen.

Running south off Conduit Street is the most famous Mayfair shopping street of all, **Savile Row**. Gieves & Hawkes (no.1) should be a compulsory address for anyone interested in the history of British menswear, having operated a bespoke tailoring service for more than two centuries, while at no.15 the estimable Henry Poole & Co has cut suits for clients including Napoleon III, Charles Dickens and 'Buffalo Bill' Cody. No.3 was the home of Apple Records, the Beatles' recording studio.

Two streets west, **Cork Street** is known as the heart of the West End art scene – more than

SIGHTS

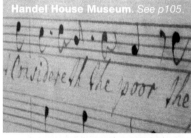

Handel House Museum. *See p105.*

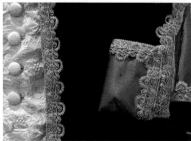

SIGHTS

Inside Science

The Royal Institution reopens after a magnificent refurbishment.

Behind the grand, neoclassical façade of the **Royal Institution** (*see p105*), a revolution has been taking place. It began ten years ago, when Baroness Susan Greenfield became the RI's first female director, a move that signalled it was time for serious changes. The scientific body was founded in 1799 for 'diffusing the knowledge... and application of science to the common purposes of life' and has been at the forefront of London's scientific achievements for more than 200 years. As Greenfield puts it, 'The RI was a charming but fusty old institution and it needed to change... We hope it will become the premier London venue for scientists, people who want to learn about science and for the general public.'

Architect Sir Terry Farrell was appointed to design a complete rebuild, inside and out; the project took two years and cost £22 million. Accessibility is the key word. 'One of the problems is that our absolutely stunning Grade I-listed façade is very intimidating, especially given the location. It feels like a private gentlemen's club, and that's the absolute opposite of what it is,' says Claire Gardner, the premises manager. The new idea was to lure people inside, so they can learn more about the RI's history. It's quite a history too: 14 RI scientists have been awarded the Nobel

Prize and ten chemical elements were discovered here (four by its first lecturer, the English chemist Sir Humphry Davy). The RI's greatest achievements, however, came when Michael Faraday worked here in the early 19th century. The Michael Faraday Laboratory – a complete replica of Faraday's former workspace – is in the basement, alongside a working laboratory in which RI scientists can be observed researching their current project on nanotechnology. Some 1,000 of the RI's 7,000-odd scientific objects are now on display, including the world's first electric transformer, a prototype Davy lamp and a print-out of the first transatlantic telegraph signal, sent in 1858.

Another exciting development is a new events programme, on which light-hearted Family Fun Days (at which you can make your own slime) are counterbalanced by serious and compelling events such as a discussion entitled 'Use and Abuse: Science Under the Nazi Regime' or a debate focused on which US presidential candidate is likely to be the best for the global scientific community. Such thorny issues can be thrashed out post-event at the brand new Time & Space restaurant-café – which is open also, you may be relieved to learn, to those entirely uninterested in science.

half a dozen galleries, at last count, are strung along its few hundred feet of shopfront. A couple of streets over again is Albemarle Street, where you'll find the handsomely rejuvenated **Royal Institution**, home to the **Faraday Museum** (*see below*).

★ FREE Royal Institution & Faraday Museum

21 Albemarle Street, W1S 4BS (7409 2992/ www.rigb.org). Green Park tube. **Open** 9am-5pm Mon-Fri. **Admission** free. **No credit cards.** **Map** p406 U4.
See opposite **Inside Science**.

Shepherd Market

In **Berkeley Square**, just west of Albemarle Street, no.44 is one of the square's original houses, built in the 1740s, and described by architectural historian Nikolaus Pevsner 'the finest terrace house of London'. **Curzon Street**, which runs off the south-west corner of Berkeley Square, was home to MI5, Britain's secret service, from 1945 until the 1990s; it's also the northern boundary of **Shepherd Market**, which is named after a food market set up here by architect Edward Shepherd in the early 18th century. From 1686, this was where the raucous May Fair was held, until it was shut down in the late 18th century due to 'drunkenness, fornication, gaming and lewdness'. You'll still manage the drunkenness easily enough in what is now a pleasant, upscale area with a couple of good pubs (Ye Grapes at 16 Shepherd Market and the Shepherd's Tavern at 50 Hertford Street) and some of London's most agreeable pavement dining. The cobbler on adjoining White Horse Street ('Don't throw away old shoes, they can be restored!') and an ironmongers on Shepherd Street keep things from becoming too genteel.

★ Handel House Museum

25 Brook Street (entrance in Lancashire Court), W1K 4HB (7399 1953/www.handelhouse.org). Bond Street tube. **Open** 10am-6pm Tue, Wed, Fri, Sat; 10am-8pm Thur; noon-6pm Sun. **Admission** £5; £2-£4.50 reductions; free under-5s. **Credit** MC, V. **Map** p398 H6.
George Frideric Handel moved to Britain from his native Germany aged 25 and settled in this Mayfair house 12 years later, remaining here until his death in 1759. The house has been beautifully restored with original and recreated furnishings, paintings and a welter of the composer's scores (in the same room as photos of Jimi Hendrix, who lived next door). The regular programme of events includes recitals every Thursday. *Photo p103.*
▶ *Handel is also honoured at the Foundling Museum, see p77; for 250th anniversary events, see p308 London Can Handel It.*

PICCADILLY & GREEN PARK

Green Park, Hyde Park Corner or Piccadilly Circus tube.

Piccadilly's name is derived from a type of suit collar (the 'picadil') that was in vogue during the 18th century; the first of the area's main buildings was built by tailor Robert Baker and, indicating the source of his wealth, nicknamed 'Piccadilly Hall'. A stroll through the handful of Regency shopping arcades confirms that the rag trade is still flourishing in the area, and you are mere minutes away from **Savile Row** and **Jermyn Street**. The renovated **Burlington Arcade** (*see p241*) is the oldest and most famous of these. Resplendent in top hats and livery, its security staff (known as 'beadles') are on hand to ensure that there is no singing, whistling or hurrying in the arcade: such uncouth behaviour is prohibited by archaic bylaws. Formerly Burlington House (1665), the **Royal Academy of Arts** (*see p106*) is next door to the arcade's entrance. It hosts several lavish, crowd-pleasing exhibitions each year and has a pleasant courtyard café.

On Piccadilly itself are further representatives of high-end retail. **Fortnum & Mason** (*see p242*), London's most prestigious food store, was founded in 1707 by a former footman to Queen Anne and was splendidly refurbished to celebrate its third century. A couple of doors away at no.187, **Hatchard's the Bookseller** (7439 9921, www.hatchards.co.uk) dates back to

Royal Academy of Arts. *See p106.*

SIGHTS

1797. The simple-looking church at no.197 is St James's (see below), a personal favourite of its architect Sir Christopher Wren. William Blake was baptised in the font here in 1757.

West down Piccadilly, smartly uniformed doormen mark the **Wolseley** (*see p215*), a former car showroom reopened in 2004 as an instant classic of a restaurant, and the **Ritz** (*see p187*). The green expanse just beyond the Ritz is Green Park (*see p105*). Work your way further along Piccadilly, following the northern edge of Green Park on past the queue outside the Hard Rock Café to the Duke of Wellington's old home, **Apsley House**, opposite **Wellington Arch** (for both, *see below*), the best reasons to visit hectic Hyde Park Corner.

To the south-east, Buckingham Palace (*see p114*) is just a short walk away, while Hyde Park (*see p124*) and the upper-crust enclave of Belgravia (*see p120*) are to the west.

Apsley House

149 Piccadilly, W1J 7NT (7499 5676/www. english-heritage.org.uk). Hyde Park Corner tube. **Open** *Nov-Mar* 10am-4pm Wed-Sun. *Apr-Oct* 10am-5pm Wed-Sun. *Tours* by arrangement. **Admission** £5.50; £4.40 reductions. *Tours* phone in advance. *Joint ticket with Wellington Arch* £6.90; £5.50 reductions; £17.30 family. **Credit** MC, V. **Map** p400 G8.

Called No.1 London because it was the first London building encountered on the road to the city from the village of Kensington, Apsley House was built by Robert Adam in the 1770s. The Duke of Wellington kept it as his London residence for 35 years. Although his descendants still live here, several rooms are open to the public providing a superb feel for the man and his era. Admire the extravagant porcelain dinnerware and plates or ask for a demonstration of the crafty mirrors in the scarlet and gilt picture gallery, where a fine Velázquez and a Correggio hang near Goya's portrait of the Iron Duke after he defeated the French in 1812. (This was a last-minute edit: X-rays have revealed that Wellington's head was brushed on over that of Joseph Bonaparte, Napoleon's brother.)
▶ *There's a model of the battle of Waterloo at the National Army Museum; see p119.*

INSIDE TRACK
ACHILLES LAID BARE

The towering statue in Hyde Park behind **Apsley House** (*see above*) of a naked Achilles wielding his sword and buckler was given to the Duke of Wellington 'by the women of England' in 1822. Achilles' fig leaf has been removed by curious admirers – twice, most recently in 1961.

FREE Royal Academy of Arts

Burlington House, Piccadilly, W1J 0BD (7300 8000/www.royalacademy.org.uk). Green Park or Piccadilly Circus tube. **Open** 10am-6pm Mon-Thur, Sat, Sun; 10am-10pm Fri. **Admission** free. *Special exhibitions* varies. **Credit** AmEx, DC, MC, V. **Map** p406 U4.

Britain's first art school was founded in 1768 and moved to the extravagantly Palladian Burlington House a century later. It is now best known for the galleries. Expect to pay for blockbusters (like 2008's popular *From Russia* show) in the Sackler Wing or main galleries, while shows in the John Madejski Fine Rooms are drawn from the RA's holdings – ranging from Constable to Hockney – and are free. The Academy's biggest event is the Summer Exhibition, which for more than two centuries has drawn from works entered by the public, but we're excited about its new annual arts programme 'Contemporary', launched in 2008 with exhibitions, live events and film screenings. *Photo p105.*

FREE St James's Piccadilly

197 Piccadilly, W1J 9LL (7734 4511/www.st-james-piccadilly.org). Piccadilly Circus tube. **Open** 8am-6.30pm daily. *Evening events* times vary. **Admission** free. **Map** p406 V4.

Consecrated in 1684, St James's is the only church Sir Christopher Wren built on an entirely new site. A calming building, with few architectural airs or graces, it was bombed to within an inch of its life in World War II but painstakingly reconstructed. Grinling Gibbons's delicate limewood garlanding around the sanctuary survived and is one of the few real frills. This is a busy church, staging regular classical concerts, providing a home for the William Blake Society, and hosting markets in the churchyard: antiques on Tuesday, arts and crafts from Wednesday to Saturday. There's also a handy café tucked into a corner by the quiet garden.
▶ *Gibbons also carved the superb choir stalls and organ case of St Paul's Cathedral; see p61.*

Wellington Arch

Hyde Park Corner, W1J 7JZ (7930 2726/ www.english-heritage.org.uk). Hyde Park Corner tube. **Open** *Apr-Oct* 10am-5pm Wed-Sun. *Nov-Mar* 10am-4pm Wed-Sun. **Admission** £3.30; £1.70-£2.60 reductions; free under-5s. *Joint ticket with Apsley House* £6.90; £5.50 reductions; £17.30 family. **Credit** MC, V. **Map** p400 G8.

Built in the late 1820s to mark Britain's triumph over Napoleonic France, Decimus Burton's Wellington Arch was initially topped by an out-of-proportion equestrian statue of Wellington, but since 1912 Captain Adrian Jones's 38-ton bronze *Peace Descending on the Quadriga of War* has finished it with a flourish. It has three floors of displays, covering the history of the arch and the Blue Plaques scheme, and great views in winter from the balcony.

Westminster & St James's

Pomp, ceremony and politics at the seat of English power.

As the official seat of government and the home of the monarchy, Westminster packs some serious historical punch. It dates to the 11th century, when Edward the Confessor shifted the royal palace west from the City. Now the **Houses of Parliament**, **St Margaret's Church** and **Westminster Abbey** are a UNESCO World Heritage Site. **Trafalgar Square** is the popular pivot of Whitehall (for government) and the Mall (for royalty – coming from **Buckingham Palace**). The square is overlooked by the **National Gallery**, while **Tate Britain** peers at the river.

Map p400, p401, p406, p407 Hotels p187	Restaurants & cafés p216 Pubs & bars p235

TRAFALGAR SQUARE

Leicester Square tube or Charing Cross tube/rail.

Laid out through the 1820s by John Nash, the architectural genius behind Regent Street, Trafalgar Square is the heart of modern London. Tourists come in their thousands to pose for photographs in front of **Nelson's Column**. It was erected in 1840 to honour Vice Admiral Horatio Nelson, who died at the point of victory at the Battle of Trafalgar in 1805. The statue atop the 150-foot-high Corinthian column is foreshortened to appear in perfect proportion from the ground. The granite fountains were added in 1845 and Sir Edwin Landseer's bronze lions joined them in 1867.

Today, Trafalgar Square is a frequent venue for concerts and festivals. Once isolated by busy roads, it was improved markedly by pedestrianisation in 2003 of the North Terrace, right in front of the **National Gallery** (*see below*). Another positive step was the mayor's ban on feeding pigeons – visitors miss the ritual but the square looks better without an inch-thick layer of guano. Around the perimeter of the square are three plinths bearing statues of

George IV and Victorian military heroes, Henry Havelock and Sir Charles James Napier. The **fourth plinth** was never filled – since 1999, it has displayed temporary, contemporary art. The next installation, by Antony Gormley, will feature several thousand volunteers, each standing on the plinth for an hour; however, calls instead for a permanent statue of another hero or a royal seem to be finding a sympathetic ear with the new mayor. Other points of interest around the square include an equestrian **statue of Charles I**, dating from the 1630s, with a plaque behind it that marks the original site of Edward I's Eleanor Cross, the official centre of London. At the north-east corner of the square is **St Martin-in-the-Fields** (*see p110*).

★ FREE National Gallery

Trafalgar Square, WC2N 5DN (7747 2885/ www.nationalgallery.org.uk). Leicester Square tube/Charing Cross tube/rail. **Open** 10am-6pm Mon, Tue, Thur-Sun; 10am-9pm Wed. *Tours* 11.30am, 2.30pm daily. **Admission** free. *Special exhibitions* vary. **Credit** (shop) MC, V. **Map** p407 X5.

Founded in 1824 to display a collection of just 36 paintings, today the National Gallery is home to more than 2,000 works. There are masterpieces from

Boris and the Big Red Bus

How long will we wait for the next Routemaster?

SIGHTS

Ask most Londoners about Routemaster buses, and a faraway look will come into their eyes. Some will talk wistfully about the charm of London's original red double-deckers, the convenience of a proper bus conductor with a pocket full of change, instead of an Oyster card and an army of jobsworths issuing fixed penalty notices. Others will reminisce about the ease of getting on and off open-backed buses between stops, the giddy thrill of hanging off the back handrail looking out over the traffic. The Routemaster permeated popular culture, with generations of schoolchildren taking home a model Routemaster (typically made in Taiwan) as a souvenir of London.

The history of the Routemaster dates back to 1956, when the new London Transport Commission introduced a fleet of buses to replace the obsolete wartime trolley-buses. The last Routemaster rolled off the production line in 1968, but the distinctive double-deckers survived 50 years of service. It all came to an end in December 2005, when then mayor Ken Livingstone ditched the entire fleet in favour of 18-metre-long, single-decker 'bendy buses'. Despite earlier pointing out that 'only a ghastly dehumanised moron would want to get rid of the Routemaster'.

The 2008 mayoral election suggested that many Londoners agreed with Ken's statement. Boris Johnson waltzed into City Hall with a healthy majority and a manifesto commitment to return the Routemaster to London's streets. In July 2008, he launched a public competition to design a new, eco-friendly Routemaster, with a commitment to reinstating the hop-on, hop-off principle of the original. This crowd-pleasing was not without its critics, including (of course) Ken Livingstone, who pointed out some rather large holes in Boris's accounting for the project. Ken also claimed that the new Routemasters would increase the death toll on London's roads with passengers falling out the back – neatly overlooking the fact that the number of pedestrians and cyclists killed by London buses doubled after the bendy bus appeared.

Until the new Routemasters come into service, you can experience the joy of the old on two 'heritage routes'. Lovingly refurbished buses from the 1960-1964 fleet run on Route 9 (from Aldwych via the Strand, Trafalgar Square and Piccadilly Circus to the Royal Albert Hall) and 15 (from Trafalgar Square to Tower Hill, with glimpses of the Strand, Fleet Street and St Paul's Cathedral); head to Stops B or S in the south-west corner of Trafalgar Square. Buses run every 15 minutes from 9.30am. Fares match the rest of the bus network (see p363), and you must buy a ticket before boarding (or use Oyster; see p361).

virtually every European school of art, from austere 13th-century religious paintings to the sensual delights of Caravaggio and Van Gogh.

Furthest to the left of the main entrance, the modern Sainsbury Wing extension contains the gallery's earliest works: Italian paintings by early masters like Giotto and Piero della Francesca, as well as the *Wilton Diptych*, the finest medieval English picture in the collection, showing Richard II with the Virgin and Child. The basement of the Sainsbury Wing is also the setting for temporary exhibitions – in 2009, 'Picasso: Challenging the Past' (25 Feb-7 June) and a major exhibition of 17th-century sacred Spanish painting and sculpture (from 21 Oct).

In the West Wing (left of the main entrance) are Italian Renaissance masterpieces by Correggio, Titian and Raphael. Straight ahead on entry, in the North Wing, are 17th-century Dutch, Flemish, Italian and Spanish Old Masters, including works such as Rembrandt's *A Woman Bathing in a Stream* and Caravaggio's *Supper at Emmaus*. Velasquez's *Rokeby Venus* is one of the artist's most famous paintings, a reclining nude asking herself – and us – 'How do we look?' Also in this wing are works by the great landscape artists Claude and Poussin. Turner insisted that his *Dido Building Carthage* and *Sun Rising through Vapour* should hang alongside two Claudes here that particularly inspired him.

In the East Wing (to the right of the main entrance, and most easily reached via the new street-level entrance on Trafalgar Square) are some of the gallery's most popular paintings: works by French Impressionists and Post-Impressionists, including Monet's *Water-Lilies*, one of Van Gogh's *Sunflowers* and Seurat's *Bathers at Asnières*. Don't miss Renoir's astonishingly lovely *Les Parapluies*.

You can't see everything in one visit, but the free guided tours and audio guides will help you make the best of your time.

▶ *In the gallery, Oliver Peyton's National Dining Rooms are a destination in themselves; see p216.*

FREE National Portrait Gallery

2 St Martin's Place, WC2H 0HE (7306 0055/ www.npg.org.uk). Leicester Square tube/Charing Cross tube/rail. **Open** 10am-6pm Mon-Wed, Sat, Sun; 10am-9pm Thur, Fri. **Admission** free. *Special exhibitions vary.* **Credit** AmEx, MC, V. **Map** p407 X4.

Portraits don't have to be stuffy. The National Portrait Gallery has everything from oil paintings of stiff-backed royals to photos of soccer stars and gloriously unflattering political caricatures. The portraits of musicians, scientists, artists, philanthropists and celebrities are arranged in chronological order from the top to the bottom of the building.

At the top of the escalator up from the main foyer, on the second floor, are the earliest works, portraits of Tudor and Stuart royals and notables, most notably the 'Chandos' Shakespeare, Holbein's 'cartoon' of Henry VIII and the 'Ditchley Portrait' of his daughter, Elizabeth I, her pearly slippers placed firmly on a colourful map of England. On the same floor, the 18th-century collection features Georgian writers and artists, with one room devoted to the influential Kit-Cat Club of be-wigged Whig (leftish) intellectuals, Congreve and Dryden among them. More famous names here include Wren and Swift.

SIGHTS

National Gallery.

St Martin-in-the-Fields.

The Duveen Extension contains Regency greats, military men such as Wellington and Nelson, as well as Byron, Wordsworth and other Romantics.

The first floor is devoted to the Victorians (Dickens, Brunel, Darwin) and, in the Duveen Extension, the 20th century.

▶ *Each September, the NPG exhibits the best entrants for the prestigious BP Portrait Award.*

FREE St Martin-in-the-Fields

Trafalgar Square, WC2N 4JJ (7766 1100/ Brass Rubbing Centre 7766 1122/www.smitf. org). Leicester Square tube/Charing Cross tube/ rail. **Open** 8am-6pm daily. *Services* 8am, 1.15pm, 6pm Mon, Tue, Thur, Fri; 8am, 1.15pm, 5.30pm, 6pm Wed; 8am, 10am, 1.15pm (Mandarin), 2.15pm (Cantonese), 5pm, 6.30pm Sun. *Brass Rubbing Centre* 10am-7pm Mon-Wed; 10am-10pm Thur-Sat; noon-7pm Sun. *Tours* 11.30am Thur, free. **Admission** free. *Brass rubbing* £4.50. **Credit** MC, V. **Map** p407 X4.

There has been a church 'in the fields' between Westminster and the City since the 13th century, but the current church was built in 1726 by James Gibbs, using a fusion of neoclassical and baroque styles. The parish church for Buckingham Palace (note the royal box to the left of the gallery), St Martin's benefited from a £36m Lottery-funded refurbishment, completed in 2008. The bright interior has been fully restored, with Victorian furbelows removed and the addition of a controversial altar window that shows the Cross, stylised as if rippling on water. The crypt, its fine café and the London Brass Rubbing Centre have all been modernised.

▶ *For lunchtime and evening concerts, see p309.*

WHITEHALL TO PARLIAMENT SQUARE

Westminster tube or Charing Cross tube/rail.

The offices of the British government are lined up along Whitehall, named after Henry VIII's magnificent palace, which burned to the ground in 1698. Walking south from Trafalgar Square, you pass the old Admiralty Offices and War Office, the Ministry of Defence, the Foreign Office and the Treasury, as well as the **Banqueting House** (*see below*), one of the few buildings to survive the blaze. Also here is Horse Guards, headquarters of the Household Cavalry, the elite army unit that protects the Queen. The millions who died in the service of the nation in World War I and World War II are commemorated by Sir Edwin Lutyens's dignified Cenotaph, focal point of Remembrance Day (*see p275*). Nearby, a separate memorial to the women of World War II, by sculptor John Mills, recalls the seven million women who contributed to the war effort. Churchill planned his war campaigns in the claustrophobic **Cabinet War Rooms** (*see below*), hidden beneath government offices at the west end of King Charles Street. Downing Street, home to the prime minister (no.10) and chancellor (no.11), is closed to the public.

The broad sweep of Whitehall is an apt introduction to the grand monuments of **Parliament Square**. Laid out in 1868, this tiny green space is flanked by the extravagant **Houses of Parliament** (*see below*), the neo-Gothic Middlesex Guildhall (1906-13) and the twin spires of **Westminster Abbey** (*see p112*). Dotted around the square are statues of British politicians, including Disraeli and Churchill, and foreign dignitaries, such as Abraham Lincoln and Nelson Mandela. In the middle of the green, facing Parliament, you'll see the banners and placards of Brian Haw's one-man, seven-year protest against the wars in Iraq and Afghanistan, which continues despite a government ban designed specifically to shift him from the square.

Parliament itself simply dazzles. An outrageous neo-Gothic fantasy, the seat of the British government is still formally known as the Palace of Westminster, though the only remaining parts of the medieval palace are Westminster Hall and the **Jewel Tower** (*see below*). At the north end of the palace is the clocktower housing the huge 'Big Ben' bell – more than seven feet tall, it weighs over 13 tons.

Banqueting House

Whitehall, SW1A 2ER (0844 482 7777/www. hrp.org.uk). Westminster tube/Charing Cross tube/rail. **Open** 10am-5pm Mon-Sat. **Admission** £4.50; £2.25-£3.50 reductions; free under-5s. **Credit** MC, V. **Map** p401 L8.

This handsome Italianate mansion, designed by Inigo Jones, was constructed in 1620. It was the first true Renaissance building in London. The sole surviving part of the Tudor and Stuart kings' Whitehall Palace, the Banqueting House features a lavish painted ceiling by Rubens, glorifying James I, 'the wisest fool in Christendom'. Regrettably, James' successor, Charles I, did not rule wisely. After losing the English Civil War to Cromwell's Roundheads, he was executed in front of Banqueting House in 1649 (the event is marked every 31 January). Lunchtime concerts are held on the first Monday of every month except August. Call before you visit – the mansion sometimes closes for corporate functions.

▶ *For the small but perfectly formed Queen's House, also by Inigo Jones, see p147.*

Cabinet War Rooms & Churchill Museum

Clive Steps, King Charles Street, SW1A 2AQ (7930 6961/www.iwm.org.uk). St James's Park or Westminster tube. **Open** 9.30am-6pm daily. **Admission** £12; £9.50 reductions; free under-16s. **Credit** MC, V. **Map** p401 K9.

Well out of harm's way beneath Whitehall, this cramped and spartan bunker was where Winston Churchill planned the Allied victory in World War II. Now open to the public, the rooms powerfully bring to life the reality of a nation at war. The cabinet rooms were sealed on 16 August 1945, keeping the complex in a state of suspended animation: every pin stuck into the vast charts was placed there in the final days of the conflict. The humble quarters occupied by Churchill and his deputies give a tangible sense of wartime hardship, an effect reinforced by the wailing sirens and wartime speeches on the audio guide (free with admission). Adjoining the War Rooms is the engaging Churchill Museum, devoted to the great man and his famous speeches.

FREE Houses of Parliament

Parliament Square, SW1A 0AA (Commons information 7219 4272/Lords information 7219 3107/tours information 0870 906 3773/www. parliament.uk). Westminster tube. **Open** (when in session) *House of Commons Visitors' Gallery* 2.30-10.30pm Mon, Tue; 11.30am-7.30pm Wed; 10.30am-6.30pm Thur; 9.30am-3pm Fri. *House of Lords Visitors' Gallery* 2.30-10.30pm Mon, Tue; 3-10pm Wed; 11am-7.30pm Thur; from 10am Fri. *Tours* summer recess only; phone for details. **Admission** *Visitors' Gallery* free. *Tours* £12; £5-£8 reductions; free under-5s. **Credit** MC, V. **Map** p401 L9.

After strict security checks at St Stephen's Gate (the only public access to Parliament), visitors are welcome to observe the debates at the House of Lords and House of Commons, though the experience can be soporific. An exception is Prime Minister's Question Time at noon on Wednesday, when the incumbent PM fields a barrage of hostile questions from the opposition and planted questions, designed to present the government in a good light, from loyal back-benchers. Tickets must be arranged in advance through your embassy or MP, who can also arrange tours. The best time to visit Parliament is during the summer recess, when the main ceremonial rooms, including Westminster Hall and the two houses, are thrown open to the general public as part of an organised tour (book in advance by phone).

The first parliamentary session was held in St Stephen's Chapel in 1275, but Westminster only became the permanent seat of parliament in 1532, when Henry VIII decided to move to a new des-res in Whitehall. Designed by Charles Barry, the Palace of Westminster is now a wonderful mish-mash of styles, dominated by Gothic buttresses, towers and arches. It looks much older than it is – the Parliament buildings were created in 1860 to replace the original Houses of Parliament, destroyed by fire in 1834. The compound contains a staggering 1,000 rooms, 11 courtyards, eight bars and six restaurants, plus a small cafeteria for visitors. Of the original palace, only the Jewel Tower (*see below*) and the ancient Westminster Hall remain.

Jewel Tower

Abingdon Street, SW1P 3JY (7222 2219/www. english-heritage.org.uk). Westminster tube. **Open** *Mar-Oct* 10am-5pm daily. *Nov-Mar* 10am-4pm daily. **Admission** £3; £1.50-£2.40 reductions; free under-5s. **Credit** MC, V. **Map** p401 L9.

This easy-to-overlook little stone tower opposite Parliament was built in 1365 to house Edward III's treasure. It is, with Westminster Hall, all that

SIGHTS

comprising some of the most expensive real estate in London. Antiques stores and upscale restaurants line Pimlico Road.

North of Victoria Street towards Parliament Square is **Christchurch Gardens**, burial site of Thomas ('Colonel') Blood, who stole the Crown Jewels – he was apprehended while making his getaway in 1671 and, amazingly, managed to talk his way into a full pardon. Also in the area are **New Scotland Yard**, with its famous revolving sign, and the art deco headquarters of **London Underground** at 55 Broadway – public outrage about the graphic nudes on the façade almost led to the resignation of the managing director in 1929.

FREE **Westminster Cathedral**

42 Francis Street, SW1P 1QW (7798 9055/www. westminstercathedral.org.uk). Victoria tube/rail. **Open** 7am-6pm Mon-Fri; 8am-6.30pm Sat; 8am-7pm Sun. *Bell tower* 9.30am-5pm Mon-Fri; 10am-4.30pm Sat, Sun. *Services* see p374. **Admission** free; donations appreciated. *Bell tower* £5; £2.50 reductions. **Credit** MC, V. **Map** p400 J10.

With its domes, arches and soaring tower, the most important Catholic church in England looks more Islamic than Christian. There's a reason for this – architect John Francis Bentley, who built the cathedral between 1895 and 1903, was heavily influenced by Istanbul's Hagia Sophia mosque. Compared to the candy-cane exterior, the interior of the cathedral is surprisingly restrained (in fact, it is unfinished), but there are still some impressive marble columns and mosaics. Eric Gill's sculptures of the Stations of the Cross (1914-18) were dismissed as crude and 'Babylonian' when they were first installed, but worshippers have come to love them. A lift runs to the top of the 273ft bell tower for dizzying views over Victoria, Westminster and St James's. *Photo p113.*

AROUND ST JAMES'S PARK

St James's Park tube.

St James's Park was founded as a deer park for the royal occupants of St James's Palace, and remodelled by John Nash on the orders of George IV. The central lake is home to numerous species of wildfowl, including pelicans that have been kept here since the 17th century, when the Russian ambassador donated several of the bag-jawed birds to Charles II. The pelicans are fed at 3pm daily, though they have been known to supplement their diet at other times of the day with the occasional pigeon. The bridge over the lake offers very snappable views of **Buckingham Palace** (*see below*).

Along the north side of the park, the Mall connects Buckingham Palace with Trafalgar Square (*see p107*). It looks like a classic processional route, but the Mall was actually laid out as a pitch for Charles II to play 'pallemaille' (an early version of croquet imported from France) after the pitch at Pall Mall became too crowded. On the south side of the park, Wellington Barracks contains the **Guards Museum**; to the east, Horse Guards contains the **Household Cavalry Museum** (for both, *see below*). A debate is currently raging over the guard's bearskin hats, traditionally made from Canadian black bear skin, with Stella McCartney and Vivienne Westwood weighing in with new designs made from artificial fur. (For the Changing of the Guard, *see p271* **Standing on Ceremony**.)

Along the north side of the Mall, **Carlton House Terrace** was the last project completed by John Nash before his death in 1835, built over the site of Carlton House, the first residence of George IV. Part of the terrace now houses the **ICA** (*see below*), and just behind is the **Duke of York column**, commemorating Prince Frederick, Duke of York, who led the British Army against the French. He's the nursery rhyme's 'Grand old Duke of York', who marched his 10,000 men neither up nor down Cassel hill in Flanders.

Buckingham Palace & Royal Mews

The Mall, SW1A 1AA (Palace 7766 7300/ Queen's Gallery 7766 7301/Royal Mews 7766 7302/www.royalcollection.org.uk). Green Park or St James's Park tube/Victoria tube/rail. **Open** *State Rooms* mid July-Sept 9.45am-6pm (last entry 3.45pm) daily. *Queen's Gallery* 10am-5.30pm daily. *Royal Mews* Mar-July, Oct 11am-4pm Mon-Thur, Sat, Sun; Aug, Sept 10am-5pm daily. **Admission** *Palace* £15.50; £8.75-£14 reductions; £39.75 family; free under-5s. *Queen's Gallery* £8.50; £4.25-£7.50 reductions; £21.50 family; free under-5s. *Royal Mews* £7.50; £4.80-£6.75 reductions; £19.80 family; free under-5s. **Credit** AmEx, MC, V. **Map** p400 H9.

Although every monarch since Queen Victoria has taken Buckingham Palace as their primary home, nearby St James's Palace (*see p116*) remains the official seat of the British court. Originally known as Buckingham House, the present home of the British royals was constructed as a private house for the Duke of Buckingham in 1703, but George III liked it so much he purchased it for his German bride Charlotte in 1761. George IV decided to occupy the mansion himself after taking the throne in 1820 and John Nash was hired to convert it into a palace befitting a king. Construction was beset with problems, and Nash – whose expensive plans had always been disliked by Parliament – was dismissed in 1830. When Victoria came to the throne in 1837, the building was barely habitable. The job of finishing the palace fell to the reliable but unimaginative Edward Blore ('Blore the Bore'). The neoclassical frontage now in place was the work of Aston Webb in 1913.

Buckingham Palace & Royal Mews.

As the home of the Queen, the palace is usually closed to visitors, but you can view the interior for a brief period each year while the family Windsor are away on their summer holidays; you'll be able to see the State Apartments, which are still used to entertain dignitaries and guests of state. At other times of year, you can still visit the Queen's Gallery to see the Queen's personal collection of treasures, including paintings by Rubens and Rembrandt, Sèvres porcelain and the Diamond Diadem crown (familiar from millions of Commonwealth postage stamps). Further along Buckingham Palace Road, the Royal Mews is the grand garage for the royal fleet of Rolls-Royces and the home of the splendid royal carriages and the horses (individually named by the Queen herself) that pull them.

Guards Museum
Wellington Barracks, Birdcage Walk, SW1E 6HQ (7414 3428/www.theguardsmuseum.com). St James's Park tube. **Open** 10am-4pm daily. **Admission** £3; £2 reductions; free under-16s. **Credit** (shop) AmEx, MC, V. **Map** p400 J9.
Just down the road from Horse Guards, this small museum tells the 350-year story of the Foot Guards, using flamboyant uniforms, medals, period paintings and intriguing memorabilia, such as the stuffed body of Jacob the Goose, the Guard's Victorian mascot, who was regrettably run over by a van in barracks. Appropriately, the museum shop is well stocked with toy soldiers of the British regiments.
► *The Guards form up on the parade ground here before the Changing of the Guard; see p271.*

Household Cavalry Museum
Horse Guards, Whitehall, SW1A 2AX (7930 3070/www.householdcavalry.co.uk). Embankment tube/Charing Cross tube/rail. **Open** *Mar-Sept* 10am-6pm daily. *Oct-Feb* 10am-5pm daily. **Admission** £6; £4 reductions; £15 family ticket; free under-5s. **Credit** MC, V. **Map** p401 K8.
Household Cavalry is a fairly workaday name for the military peacocks who make up the Queen's official guard. They get to tell their stories through video diaries at this small but entertaining museum, which also offers the chance to see medals, uniforms and shiny cuirasses (breastplates) up close. You'll also get a peek – and sniff – of the magnificent horses that parade just outside every day: the stables are separated from the main museum by no more than a screen of glass.

FREE ICA (Institute of Contemporary Arts)
The Mall, SW1Y 5AH (7930 0493/box office 7930 3647/www.ica.org.uk). Piccadilly Circus tube/Charing Cross tube/rail. **Open** *Galleries* (during exhibitions) noon-7pm Mon-Wed, Fri-Sun; noon-9pm Thur. **Admission** free. **Credit** AmEx, DC, MC, V. **Map** p401 K8.
Founded in 1947 by a collective of poets, artists and critics, the ICA continues to drive the London arts scene forward into brave new territory. The institute moved to the Mall in 1968 and set itself up as a venue for arthouse cinema, performance art, philosophical debates, art-themed club nights and anything else that might challenge accepted notions.

Not that this stopped former ICA chairman Ivan Massow dismissing conceptual art as 'pretentious, self-indulgent, craftless tat' in 2002; current artistic director Ekow Eshun made a more valuable contribution to artistic debate by announcing in summer 2008 that admission would henceforth be free.

▶ *For the ICA's cinema, see p297.*

ST JAMES'S

Green Park or Piccadilly Circus tube.

One of London's most refined residential districts, St James's was laid out in the 1660s for the benefit of royal and aristocratic families, some whom still live here today. Bordered by Piccadilly, Haymarket, the Mall and Green Park, the district is centred on **St James's Square**, which counted seven dukes and seven earls as local residents in the 1720s. It's now home to the members-only **London Library**, founded by Thomas Carlyle in 1841 in disgust at the inefficiency of the British Library.

Just south of the square, **Pall Mall** is lined with exclusive, members-only gentlemen's clubs (in the old-fashioned sense of the word – we don't mean Spearmint Rhino). Polished brass nameplates reveal such prestigious establishments as the Institute of Directors (no.116) and the Reform Club (nos.104-105), site of Phileas Fogg's famous bet in *Around the World in Eighty Days*. Around the corner on St James's Street, the Carlton Club (no.69) is the official club of the Conservative Party; Lady Thatcher remains the only woman to be granted full membership on a par with male Carlton members. Nearby on King Street is **Christie's** (7839 9060, www.christies.com), the world's oldest fine art auctioneers.

At the south end of St James's Street, **St James's Palace** was originally built for Henry VIII in the 1530s. Extensively remodelled over the centuries, the red-brick palace is still the official address of the Royal Court, even though every monarch since 1837 has actually lived at Buckingham Palace (*see p114*). From here, Mary Tudor surrendered Calais and

Elizabeth I led the campaign against the Spanish Armada. This is also where Charles I was confined before his 1649 execution. Today the palace is home to the Princess Royal (the title given to the monarch's eldest daughter, currently Princess Anne). Although the palace is closed to the public, you can attend Sunday services at its historic Chapel Royal (1st Sun of mth, Oct-Easter Sunday; 8.30am, 11.15am).

Adjacent to St James's Palace is the former residence of the Queen Mother, **Clarence House** and a few streets north is the delightful **Spencer House** (for both, *see below*), the ancestral home of the family of the late Princess Diana. Across Marlborough Road lies the pocket-sized **Queen's Chapel**, designed by Inigo Jones in the 1620s for Charles I's Catholic Queen Henrietta Maria, at a time when Catholic places of worship were officially banned. The Queen's Chapel can only be visited for Sunday services (Easter-July; 8.30am, 11.15am).

Clarence House

The Mall, SW1A 1AA (7766 7303/www.royal collection.org.uk). Green Park tube. **Open** *Aug, Sept* 10am-5.30pm daily. **Admission** £7.50; £4 under-17s; free under-5s. *Tours* pre-booked tickets only. **Credit** AmEx, MC, V. **Map** p400 J8. Currently the official residence of Prince Charles and the Duchess of Cornwall, this somewhat austere royal mansion was built between 1825 and 1827 for Prince William Henry, Duke of Clarence, who stayed on in the house after his coronation as King William IV. Originally designed by John Nash, the house has been much altered by its many royal inhabitants, including the late Queen Mother. Despite being a functioning royal residence, five receiving rooms and the small British art collection accumulated by the Queen Mother are open to the public in summer. Tickets usually sell out by the end of August.

Spencer House

27 St James's Place, SW1A 1NR (7514 1958/ recorded information 7499 8620/www.spencer house.co.uk). Green Park tube. **Open** *Feb-July, Sept-Dec* 10.30am-5.45pm Sun. Last tour 4.45pm. *Gardens* phone or check the website for details. **Admission** £9; £7 reductions. Under-10s not allowed. **Credit** MC, V. **Map** p400 J8. One of the last surviving private residences in St James's, this handsome mansion was designed for John Spencer by John Vardy, but completed in 1766 by Hellenophile architect James Stuart, which explains all the mock-Greek flourishes. Lady Georgiana, subject of last year's bodice-ripping film *The Duchess*, lived here all her life. The Spencers left the property generations before Diana married into the Windsor family, but the palatial building is worth visiting for its lavish and painstakingly restored interior decor. It's now mainly used for corporate entertaining, hence the limited access.

**INSIDE TRACK
SPENCER HOUSE GARDEN**

The lovely garden of **Spencer House** (*see right*) has been beautifully restored, planted with flowers and shrubs typical of the late 18th century. And it enjoys a wonderful position on the edge of Green Park. It's open on selected days in spring and summer; check www.spencerhouse. co.uk for details.

Chelsea

Village life continues beside the river.

Chelsea started life as a fishing hamlet, but by the 16th century had become a 'village of palaces', thanks to residences inhabited by the likes of Henry VIII's ill-fated advisor Sir Thomas More. Fast forward 400 years and the artists and poets have arrived in force – George and TS Eliot, Whistler, Carlyle, Oscar Wilde. Then it's the turn of fashion: Mary Quant's Bazaar opens on the **King's Road** in 1955 and, not happy with sending the mini skirt and hot pants global, she gives Charlotte Rampling's classic *Georgy Girl* outfits to the world.

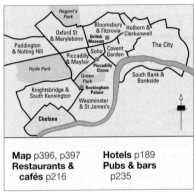

Map p396, p397	Hotels p189
Restaurants &	Pubs & bars
cafés p216	p235

SLOANE SQUARE & THE KING'S ROAD

Sloane Square tube then various buses.

Synonymous with the Swinging Sixties, made immortal by Vivienne Westwood and punk, the dissipated phase of the King's Road is now as much a matter for the historians as those Tudor palaces. The street teems with perma-tanned

Sloane Square.

yuppies, New Sloanes, pricey fashion houses and air-conditioned poodle parlours. Yet, given a sunny day, it does make a vivid stroll: you don't have to take yourself as seriously as the locals, for one thing; for another, the area is figuratively rich with historical associations and literally so with the expensive red-brick houses that slumber down leafy mews and charming, cobbled side streets.

At the top of the King's Road is **Sloane Square**, named after Sir Hans Sloane, who provided the land for the **Chelsea Physic Garden** (*see p119*) and invented milk chocolate in the early 18th century; his inventiveness is celebrated at the Botanist (*see p216*), our pick of the square's eateries. In the middle of the square sits a fountain erected in 1953, a gift to the borough from the Royal Academy of Arts. Sculpted by local man Gilbert Ledward, it depicts Venus, an allusion to King Charles II's mistress Nell Gwynne, who lived nearby – hence the road's name. The shaded benches in the middle of the square provide a lovely counterpoint to the looming façades of Tiffany & Co and the enormous Peter Jones department store, the latter in a refurbished 1930s building with excellent views from its top-floor café. Come summer, the terraces of the brasseries teem with stereotypical blonde Sloane Rangers sipping rosé, the air thick with cigar smoke and conversations about ski chalets. A certain edginess is lent to proceedings by the **Royal Court Theatre** (*see p337*), which shocked the nation with its 1956 première of John Osborne's

Look Back in Anger; expect a crop of whatever replaces the Agyness Deyn platinum bob to be resident outside the café-bar for summer 2009.

To escape the bustle and fumes head to the **Duke of York Square**, a pedestrianised enclave of glass-fronted boutiques and various restaurants, presided over by a statue of Hans Sloane. In the summer, the cooling fountains attract hordes of children, their parents sitting to watch from the outdoor areas of the cafés or taking advantage of the Saturday food market. The square also hosts the mercilessly modern art of the **Saatchi Gallery** (*see below*), housed in vast former military barracks.

The once-adventurous shops along the King's Road are now an insipid mix of trendier-than-thou fashion houses and tawdry high street chains, enlivened by a few gems: **John Sandoe Books** (*see p245*) and **Antiquarius** (*see p263*) represent a glorious past, **Shop at Bluebird** (*see p250*) suggests future directions. Wander Cale Street for the likes of jewellery boutique **Felt** (7349 8829, www.felt-london. com) or **Traditional Toys** (7352 1718, www.traditionaltoy.com), or head for **Chelsea Farmers' Market**, on adjoining Sydney Street, to find a clutter of artfully distressed rustic sheds housing restaurants and shops selling a myriad of goods from Cheeky Boo's photography books and cigars to the Chelsea Gardener's extensive range of garden products. Sydney Street also leads to **St Luke's Church**, where Charles Dickens married Catherine Hogarth in 1836.

Towards the western end of the King's Road is **Bluebird**, a dramatic art deco former motor garage housing a café and restaurant (*see p216*). It's worth a peek even if you can't afford Chelsea rates to eat here. A little further up the road, the World's End store at no.430 occupies what was once Vivienne Westwood's notorious leather and fetish wear boutique SEX; a green-haired Johnny Rotten auditioned for the Sex Pistols here in 1975 by singing along to an Alice Cooper record on the shop's jukebox.

FREE Saatchi Gallery

Duke of York's HQ, off King's Road, SW3 4SQ (7823 2363/www.saatchi-gallery.co.uk). Sloane Square tube. **Open** 10am-6pm daily. **Admission** free. **Map** p397 F11.

Charles Saatchi's new gallery, which opened after numerous delays in October 2008, has three floors, providing more than 50,000sq ft of space for temporary exhibitions. Given his fame as a promoter in the 1990s of what became known as the Young British Artists – Damien Hirst, Tracey Emin, Gavin Turk, Sarah Lucas et al – it will surprise many that the opening exhibition was of new Chinese art. This will be followed by exhibitions in 2009 featuring US and Indian artists.

CHEYNE WALK & CHELSEA EMBANKMENT

Sloane Square tube then various buses.

Chelsea's riverside has long been noted for its nurseries and gardens, first introduced in the 17th century. The borough's horticultural curiosity is still very much alive, lending a village air that befits a place of retirement for the Chelsea Pensioners, former British soldiers living in the splendour of the **Royal Hospital Chelsea** (*see p119*). In summer, they regularly don red coats and tricorn hats when venturing beyond the gates. The Royal Hospital's lovely gardens host the Chelsea Flower Show in May each year. Next door is the **National Army Museum** (*see p119*).

West from the river end of Royal Hospital Road is **Cheyne Walk**, less peaceful than it once was due to embankment traffic. Its river-view benches remain good spots for a sit-down, but the tranquillity of **Chelsea Physic Garden** (*see p119*) is the real treat around here.

Further west on Cheyne Walk, the park benches of **Chelsea Embankment Gardens** face Albert Bridge, where signs still order troops to 'Break step when marching over this bridge'. In the small gardens you'll find a statue of the great historian Thomas Carlyle – the 'sage of Chelsea', whose home is preserved (**Carlyle's House**; *see p119*). Nearby, a gold-faced statue of Sir Thomas looks out over the river from the garden of **Chelsea Old Church** (*see p119*), where he once sang in the choir and may well be (partially) buried. Follow adjoining Old Church Street north and you'll find the **Chelsea Arts Club** (no.143), founded in 1871 by Whistler.

A short way north of the western extremity of Cheyne Walk are **Brompton Cemetery** (*see p160*) and Chelsea FC's home ground, **Stamford Bridge** (*see p329*). Football fans might be interested in the Chelsea Centenary Museum (www.chelseafc.com, 10.30am-4.30pm daily, except match days; £6, £4 reductions), which has just opened here – only three years after the titular 1905 anniversary.

Royal Hospital Chelsea.

Carlyle's House

*24 Cheyne Row, SW3 5HL (7352 7087/www.
nationaltrust.org.uk). Sloane Square tube/11,
19, 22, 49, 211, 239, 319 bus.* **Open** *Apr-Oct*
2-5pm Wed-Fri; 11am-5pm Sat, Sun. **Admission**
£4.75; £2.40 reductions; £11.90 family. **Credit**
MC, V. **Map** p397 E12.

Thomas Carlyle and his wife Jane, both towering
intellects, moved to this four-storey, Queen Anne
house in 1834. In 1896, 15 years after Carlyle's death,
the house was preserved as a museum, offering an
intriguing snapshot of Victorian life. The writer's
quest for quiet (details of his valiant attempts to
soundproof the attic) strikes a chord today – he was
plagued by the sound of revelry from Cremorne
Pleasure Gardens.

FREE Chelsea Old Church

*Cheyne Walk, Old Church Street, SW3 5DQ
(7795 1019/www.chelseaoldchurch.org.uk).
Sloane Square tube/11, 19, 22, 49, 319 bus.*
Open 2-4pm Tue-Thur. *Services*
8am, 10am, 11am, 12.15pm Sun. *Evensong* 6pm
Sun. **Admission** free; donations appreciated.

Legend has it that the Thomas More Chapel, which
remains on the south side, has his headless body
buried somewhere under the walls (his head, after
being spiked on London Bridge, was 'rescued' and
buried in a family vault in St Dunstan's Church,
Canterbury). Guides are on hand on Sundays.

★ Chelsea Physic Garden

*66 Royal Hospital Road (entrance on Swan
Walk), SW3 4HS (7352 5646/www.chelsea
physicgarden.co.uk). Sloane Square tube/11,
19, 239 bus.* **Open** *Apr-Oct* noon-5pm Wed-
Fri; noon-6pm Sun. *Tours* times vary; phone
to check. **Admission** £7; £4 reductions; free
under-5s. *Tours* free. **Credit** (shop) AmEx,
MC, V. **Map** p397 F12.

The 165,000sq ft grounds of this gorgeous botanic
garden are filled with healing herbs and vegetables,
rare trees and dye plants. The garden was founded
in 1673 by Sir Hans Sloane with the purpose of culti-
vating and studying plants for medical purposes. The
first plant specimens were brought to England and
planted here in 1676, with the famous Cedars of
Lebanon (the first to be grown in England) arriving
a little later. The garden opened to the public in 1893.
► *Sir Hans Sloane's 'cabinet of curiosities' can
be seen at the British Museum; see p77.*

FREE National Army Museum

*Royal Hospital Road, SW3 4HT (7730 0717/
www.national-army-museum.ac.uk). Sloane
Square tube/11, 137, 239 bus.* **Open** 10am-
5.30pm daily. **Admission** free. **Credit** (shop)
AmEx, MC, V. **Map** p397 F12.

More entertaining than its modern exterior suggests,
this museum dedicated to the history of the British
Army kicks off with 'Redcoats', a gallery that starts
at Agincourt in 1415 and ends with the American
War of Independence. Upstairs, 'The Road to
Waterloo' marches through 20 years of struggle
against the French, featuring 70,000 model soldiers.
Also on display is the kit of Olympic medal winner
Dame Kelly Holmes (an ex-army athlete), while
Major Michael 'Bronco' Lane, conqueror of Everest,
has donated his frostbitten fingertips.
► *Military buffs will also not want to miss
the Imperial War Museum; see p142.*

FREE Royal Hospital Chelsea

*Royal Hospital Road, SW3 4SR (7881 5200/
www.chelsea-pensioners.org.uk). Sloane Square
tube/11, 19, 22, 137, 211, 239 bus.* **Open** *Oct-
Apr* 10am-noon, 2-4pm Mon-Sat. *May-Sept* 10am-
noon, 2-4pm Mon-Sat; 2-4pm Sun. **Admission**
free. **Map** p397 F12.

About 350 Chelsea Pensioners (retired soldiers) live
here. Their quarters, the Royal Hospital, was founded in 1682 by Charles II and the building was
designed by Sir Christopher Wren, with later adjustments by Robert Adam and Sir John Soane. Retired
soldiers are still eligible to apply for a final posting
here if they are over 65 and in receipt of an Army or
War Disability Pension for Army Service. They
have their own club room, bowling green and
gardens. The museum (open at the same times as
the Hospital) has more about their life.
► *The Royal Hospital's naval cousin was the
Old Royal Naval College; see p147.*

SIGHTS

Knightsbridge & South Kensington

Flash, brash, and an amazing stash in the free 'big three' museums.

Knightsbridge is where the real cash gets splashed. Rows of designer shops, world-famous department stores and crowded, fashionable restaurants attract a global clientele. For all that, the area is neither hip nor particularly stylish. South Kensington is a little less stuffy, and boasts a world-beating complement of cultural landmarks, each within minutes of the other: three of London's finest museums; three internationally respected colleges; a renowned concert hall; and, in **Kensington Gardens**, excellently curated contemporary art at the **Serpentine Gallery**.

| Map p394, p395, p397 | Restaurants & cafés p217 |
| Hotels p190 | Pubs & bars p236 |

KNIGHTSBRIDGE

Knightsbridge tube.

Knightsbridge in the 11th century was a village celebrated for its taverns, highwaymen and the legend that two knights once fought to the death on the bridge that spanned the Westbourne River (dammed to form Hyde Park's Serpentine lake). In modern Knightsbridge, urban princesses would be far too busy unsheathing the credit card to notice duelling knights. Voguish **Harvey Nichols** (*see p242*) holds court at the top of **Sloane Street**, which leads down to Sloane Square (*see p117*). Expensive brands – Gucci, Prada, Chanel, Christian Dior – predominate here.

East of Sloane Street is Belgravia, characterised by a cluster of embassies around **Belgrave Square**. Hidden behind the stucco-clad parades fronting the square are numerous tiny mews well worth exploring if only for the great pubs they conceal, notably the nostalgic **Nag's Head** (*see p236*).

For many tourists, Knightsbridge means one thing: **Harrods** (*see p242*). From its tan bricks and olive green awning to its green-coated doormen, it's an instantly recognisable retail legend – all the more so at night when lit up like a Vegas casino. Owner Mohammed Al Fayed continues to add to the richness of eccentricity here, notably with his mawkish memorial to son Dodi and Princess Diana.

The western end of Knightsbridge is dominated by the imposing mass of the **Brompton Oratory** (*see below*), a church of suitably lavish proportions for an area long associated with extravagant displays of wealth.

FREE Brompton Oratory

Thurloe Place, Brompton Road, SW7 2RP (7808 0900/www.bromptonoratory.com). South Kensington tube. **Open** 6.30am-8pm daily. **Admission** free; donations appreciated. **Map** p397 E10.

The second-biggest Catholic church in the country (after Westminster Cathedral) is formally known as the Church of the Immaculate Heart of Mary, but is almost universally known as the 'Brompton Oratory'. Completed in 1884, it feels older – partly because of the baroque Italianate style, but also because much of the decoration pre-dates the structure: Mazzuoli's late 17th-century apostle statues, for example, are from Siena cathedral. The 11am Solemn Mass sung in Latin on Sundays is enchanting, as are Vespers, sung at 3.30pm; the website has details.

Hyde Park. *See p124.*

SOUTH KENSINGTON

Gloucester Road or South Kensington tube.

This is the land of plenty as far as cultural and academic institutions are concerned: the area was once known as 'Albertopolis' in honour of the prince who oversaw the inception of its world-class museums, colleges and concert hall, using the profits of the 1851 Great Exhibition. Hence the **Natural History Museum** (*see below*), the **Science Museum** and the **Victoria & Albert** (for both, *see p122*), **Imperial College**, the **Royal College of Art** and the **Royal College of Music** (Prince Consort Road, 7589 3643; call for details of Wednesday openings of the musical instrument museum) which forms a unity with the **Royal Albert Hall** (*see p309*). This great performance space, inaugurated in 1871, has since been used for boxing, motor shows, marathons (524 circuits of the arena equal 26 miles), the Eurovision Song Contest, Miss World and rock concerts. Opposite is the **Albert Memorial** (*see below*).

Albert Memorial
Kensington Gardens (opposite Royal Albert Hall), SW7 (tours 7495 0916). South Kensington tube. **Tours** 2pm, 3pm 1st Sun of mth. **Admission** *Tours* £5; £4.50 reductions. **No credit cards**. **Map** p395 D8.
'I would rather not be made the prominent feature of such a monument,' was Prince Albert's reported response when the subject of his commemoration

arose – hard then to imagine what he would have made of this extraordinary thing, unveiled 15 years after his death. Created by Sir George Gilbert Scott, it centres around a gilded Prince Albert holding a catalogue of the 1851 Great Exhibition. He's guarded on four corners by the continents of Africa, America, Asia and Europe; pillars are crowned with bronze statues of the sciences; and the freize at the base of the monument depicts major artists, architects and musicians. The dramatic 180ft spire is inlaid with semi-precious stones.

★ FREE Natural History Museum
Cromwell Road, SW7 5BD (information 7942 5725/switchboard 7942 5000/www.nhm.ac.uk). South Kensington tube. **Open** 10am-5.50pm daily. **Admission** free; charges apply for special exhibitions. *Tours* free. **Credit** (shop) MC, V. **Map** p397 D10.
The Natural History Museum opened in Alfred Waterhouse's purpose-built, Romanesque palazzo on the Cromwell Road in 1881. From the beginning it has been both a research institution and a fabulous museum, and the building still looks quite magnificent. *See p123* **Profile**. *Photos p123*.

INSIDE TRACK
SECRETS AND SPIES

During the Cold War, KGB agents used the **Brompton Oratory** (*see opposite*) as a dead-letter box.

SIGHTS

SIGHTS

★ FREE Science Museum

Exhibition Road, SW7 2DD (7942 4000/booking & information 0870 870 4868/www.science museum.org.uk). South Kensington tube. **Open** 10am-5.45pm daily. **Admission** free; charges apply for special exhibitions. **Credit** MC, V. **Map** p397 D9.

Only marginally less popular with the kids than its natural historical neighbour, the Science Museum is a celebration of the wonders of technology in the service of our daily lives. On the ground floor, the shop – selling wacky toys – is part of the revamped Energy Hall, which introduces the museum's collections with impressive 18th-century steam engines. In Exploring Space, rocket science and the lunar landings are illustrated by dramatically lit mock-ups and models, before the museum gears up for its core collection in Making the Modern World. Introduced by *Puffing Billy*, the world's oldest steam locomotive (built in 1815), the gallery also contains Stephenson's *Rocket* and the first purpose-built, mass-production system ever: the Portsmouth Block-Making Machines designed by Marc Isambard Brunel, the father of Isambard Kingdom, in 1803. Also here are the Apollo 10 command module, classic cars, and wall cabinets displaying an absorbing collection of everyday technological marvels from 1750 to the present.

Beyond is the Wellcome Wing, bathed in an eerie blue light, occupying three floors and celebrating the latest discoveries in the biomedical sciences. The Who Am I? gallery on the first floor explores discoveries in genetics, brain science and psychology. Back in the main body of the museum, the second floor holds displays on computing, marine engineering and mathematics; the third floor is dedicated to

Victoria & Albert Museum.

flight, among other things, including the hands-on Launchpad gallery which features levers, pulleys, explosions and all manner of experiments for children (and their associated grown-ups). On the fifth floor is an intriguing display on the science and art of medicine. Tickets to the museum's in-house IMAX 3D cinema cost extra.

▶ *The Wellcome Collection makes further connections between art and medicine; see p78.*

★ FREE Victoria & Albert Museum

Cromwell Road, SW7 2RL (7942 2000/www.vam. ac.uk). South Kensington tube. **Open** 10am-5.45pm Mon-Thur, Sat, Sun; 10am-10pm Fri. *Tours* hourly, 10.30am-3.30pm daily. **Admission** free; charges apply for special exhibitions. **Credit** (shop) MC, V. **Map** p397 E10.

The V&A – its foundation stone laid on this site by Queen Victoria herself in her last official public engagement in 1899 – is one of the world's most magnificent museums. It is a superb showcase for applied arts from around the world, and appreciably calmer than its tearaway cousins on the other side of Exhibition Road. Some 150 grand galleries on seven floors contain around four million pieces of furniture, ceramics, sculpture, paintings, posters, jewellery, metalwork, glass, textiles and dress, spanning several centuries. Items are grouped by theme, origin or age, but any attempt to comprehend the whole collection in a single visit is doomed. For advice, tap the admirably patient information desk staff who field a formidable combination of leaflets, floorplans, general knowledge and polite concern.

Unmissable highlights include the seven Raphael Cartoons painted in 1515 as tapestry designs for the Sistine Chapel; the finest collection of Italian Renaissance sculpture outside Italy; the Gloucester Candlestick; the Great Bed of Ware; Canova's *Three Graces* (returning to the V&A in 2009); the Ardabil carpet, the world's oldest and arguably most splendid floor covering, in the Jameel Gallery of Islamic Art; Medici porcelain; and the Luck of Edenhall, a 13th-century glass beaker from Syria. The Fashion galleries run from 18th-century court dress right up to contemporary chiffon numbers. The Architecture gallery has videos, models, plans and descriptions of various styles, and the famous Photography collection holds over 500,000 images.

The latest instalment in the V&A's FuturePlan is the newly opened William & Judith Bollinger Gallery, dedicated to the history of European jewellery over the past 800 years. Among the 3,500 items on display are diamonds worn by Catherine the Great of Russia and the Beauharnais Emeralds, a gift from Napoleon to his adopted daughter. In 2009 the completely refurbished Medieval & Renaissance Galleries will open, and the Gilbert Collection of silver, gold and gemmed ornaments arrives here in autumn from Somerset House (*see p87*). We're also looking forward to the new Theatre & Performance Galleries, with exhibits from Covent Garden's defunct Theatre Museum.

Profile Natural History Museum

From the dinosaurs to Darwin, planet Earth gets investigated here.

The pale blue and terracotta façade of the **Natural History Museum** (*see p121*) just about prepares you for the natural wonders within. Taking up the full length of the vast entrance hall is the cast of a *Diplodocus* skeleton. A left turn leads into the west wing or Blue Zone, where long queues form to see the animatronic dinosaurs. Like many of the displays, they're pitched squarely at ten-year-olds. A display on Human Biology features an illuminated, man-sized model of a foetus in the womb along with graphic diagrams of how it might have got there. A right turn from the central hall leads past the horribly intriguing Creepy Crawlies exhibition to the Green Zone. Star exhibits include a cross-section through a Giant Sequoia tree and an amazing array of stuffed birds, including the chance to compare the egg of a hummingbird – smaller than a little finger nail – with that of an elephant bird (now extinct) – almost football-sized.

Beyond is the Red Zone, formerly the Earth Galleries and once the entirely separate Geological Museum: Earth's Treasury is a veritable mine of information on a variety of precious metals, gems and crystals; From the Beginning is a brave attempt to give the expanse of geological time a human perspective. Outside, the delightful Wildlife Garden (open Apr-Oct only) showcases a range of British lowland habitats, including a Bee Tree, a hollow tree trunk that opens to reveal a busy hive.

Many of the museum's 22 million insect and plant specimens are housed in the new Darwin Centre, where they take up nearly 17 miles of shelving; with its brand-new eight-storey 'cocoon', this is

also home to the museum's research scientists, who can be watched at work. But a great deal of this amazing institution is hidden from public view, given over to labs and specialised storage (*pictured above*).

In 2009 the museum will celebrate two Charles Darwin anniversaries – the 150th since the publication of his *Origin of the Species* and the 200th since the great scientist's birth: on 12 February, Tania Kovats's specially commissioned artwork *Tree* will be put on permanent show. For details of Darwin's Downe home, *see p148* **House of Science**.

SIGHTS

THREE TO SEE

Blue Whale
It's 90ft long and hanging above you!

Fossils
Including an ichthyosaur, within which you can see remains of ichthyosaur babies.

Humming-birds
A 200-year-old collection of all known species, with their eggs.

HYDE PARK & KENSINGTON GARDENS

Hyde Park Corner, Knightsbridge, Lancaster Gate or Queensway tube.

At 1.5 miles long and about a mile wide, Hyde Park (7298 2000, www.royalparks.gov.uk) is one of the largest of London's Royal Parks. The land was appropriated in 1536 from the monks of Westminster Abbey by Henry VIII for hunting deer. Despite opening to the public in the early 1600s, the parks were only frequented by the upper echelons of society. At the end of the 17th century, William III – averse to the dank air of Whitehall Palace – relocated to **Kensington Palace** (*see below*). A corner of Hyde Park was sectioned off to make grounds for the palace and closed to the public, until King George II opened it on Sundays to those wearing formal dress. Nowadays, **Kensington Gardens** is only delineated from Hyde Park by the line of the Serpentine and the Long Water. Beside the Long Water is a bronze statue of **Peter Pan**, erected in 1912: it was in Kensington Gardens beside the Round Pond eight years earlier that playwright JM Barrie met Jack Lewellyn Davies, the boy who was the inspiration for Peter. Princess Diana's presence here is also strong: **Diana, Princess of Wales Memorial Playground** (*see p289*) is a favourite for children, whereas the ring-shaped **Princess Diana Memorial Fountain**, created by US architect Kathryn Gustafson and set up beside the Serpentine, was for a while nobody's idea of a good time – would-be paddlers slipped over on the granite almost as soon as it was unveiled in 2004. Nearby is the **Serpentine Gallery** (*see below*).

The **Serpentine** itself, London's oldest boating lake and home to ducks, coots, swans and tufty-headed grebes, is at the bottom of **Hyde Park**, which isn't especially beautiful, but is of great historic interest. It was a hotspot for mass demonstrations in the 19th century and remains so today – a march against war in Iraq in 2003 was (according to police) the largest in British history. The legalisation of public assembly in the park led to the establishment of **Speakers' Corner** in 1872 (close to Marble Arch tube), where political and religious ranters – sane and otherwise – still have the floor. Marx, Lenin, Orwell and the Pankhursts have all spoken here.

The park perimeter is popular with skaters, as well as with bike- and horse-riders (for the riding school, *see p333*). If you're exploring on foot and the vast expanses defeat you, look out for the Liberty Drives (May-Oct). Driven by volunteers (there's no fare, but offer a donation if you can), these electric buggies pick up groups of sightseers and ferry them around.

On 7 July 2009, a new monument is to be unveiled in the south-east corner of Hyde Park, between the Lover's Walk and busy Park Lane. Commemorating the victims of the four bombs detonated in the city on 7 July 2005, it will consist of 52 10-foot-tall square columns of individually treated stainless steel – one for each of the dead. It promises to be an austerely beautiful, human-scale memorial.

Kensington Palace

Kensington Gardens, W8 4PX (0844 482 7777/ booking line 0844 482 7799/www.hrp.org.uk). Bayswater, High Street Kensington or Queensway tube. **Open** *Mar-Oct* 10am-5pm daily. *Nov-Feb* 10am-4pm daily. **Admission** £12.30; £6.15-£10.75 reductions; £34 family; free under-5s. **Credit** MC, V. **Map** p394 B8.

Sir Christopher Wren extended this Jacobean mansion to palatial proportions on the instructions of William III. The sections of the palace the public are allowed to see give the impression of intimacy, though the King's Apartments (which you enter via Wren's lofty staircase) are pretty grand. It appears from the Queen's Apartments, however, that William and his wife Mary II lived quite simply in these smaller rooms. The Royal Ceremonial Dress Collection is a display of lavish ensembles worn for state occasions, including a permanent collection of dresses worn by Diana, Princess of Wales, the palace's most famous resident. Make time for tea in Queen Anne's Orangery and admire the Sunken Garden.

★ FREE Serpentine Gallery

Kensington Gardens (near Albert Memorial), W2 3XA (7402 6075/www.serpentinegallery.org). Lancaster Gate or South Kensington tube. **Open** 10am-6pm daily. **Admission** free; donations appreciated. **Credit** AmEx, MC, V. **Map** p395 D8.

The secluded location to the west of the Long Water makes this small and airy gallery for contemporary art an attractive destination. A rolling two-monthly programme of exhibitions featuring up-to-the-minute artists keeps the Serpentine in the arts news, as does the annual Serpentine Pavilion: every spring an internationally renowned architect, who has never before built in the UK, is commissioned to build a new pavilion that opens to the public between June and September. Good little art bookshop too.

INSIDE TRACK
MORNING MANOEUVRES

You can watch the Household Cavalry emerge from their South Carriage Drive barracks in **Hyde Park** (*see above*) at 10.30am daily (9.30am on Sundays). They then ride to Horse Guards Parade for the **Changing of the Guard** (*see p271*).

SIGHTS

North London

Where indie mayhem gives way to the leafy land of the middle classes.

North London has spawned some of the city's most progressive thinkers and many seminal rock bands. Daniel Defoe, John Wesley and Karl Marx were all local residents, and the Clash, Blur and Madness got their first big breaks in Camden Town pubs. **Camden**, with its markets, music and general craziness, is the first port of call for most visitors, but venture out also to the restaurants of **Islington** – and, further afield, **Stoke Newington** and **Dalston**. Further to the north, **Hampstead** and **Highgate** offer genteel village life and a glorious public space: **Hampstead Heath**.

Map p402	Hotels p192
Restaurants &	Pubs & bars
cafés p221	p236

Map p402 Restaurants & cafés p221 Hotels p192 Pubs & bars p236

CAMDEN

Camden Town or Chalk Farm tube.

Despite the pressures of modernisation and gentrification, Camden has steadfastly refused to leave behind its grungy history as the cradle of British rock music. Against a backdrop of social deprivation in Thatcher's Britain, venues such as the Electric Ballroom and Dingwalls provided a platform for a generation of musical rebels. More musicians were launched in the 1990s by the Creation label, based in nearby Primrose Hill (*see p127*), among them My Bloody Valentine and the Jesus & Mary Chain. Creation were also responsible for the meteoric rise of Oasis, often seen trading insults with Blur at the **Good Mixer** (30 Inverness Street, 7916 7929). The music still plays at revitalised Camden icon the **Roundhouse** and at **KOKO** (for both, *see p313*), which blazed through the 1970s and '80s first as the Music Machine and then as the Camden Palace.

Being outside the mainstream is nothing new for Camden. Before the Victorian expansion of London, Camden was a watering stop on the highway to Hampstead (*see p127*), with two notorious taverns – the Mother Black Cap and Mother Red Cap (now the **World's End** pub, opposite the tube) – frequented by highwaymen and brigands. After the gaps were filled in with terraced houses, the borough became a magnet for Irish and Greek railway workers, many of them working in the engine turning-house that is now the Roundhouse. The squalor of the area had a powerful influence on the young Charles Dickens, who lived briefly on Bayham Street. He described it as 'shabby, dingy, damp, and as mean a neighbourhood as one would desire not to see'. From the 1960s, things started to pick up for Camden, helped by an influx of students, lured by low rents and the growing arts scene that gave birth first to punk rock, then indie and the tragically over-hyped Britpop, and nowadays any number of short-lived indie-electro and alt-folk hybrids.

Camden still has a rough quality – dealers and junkies loiter like ghosts around Camden Town tube station – but the hardcore rebellion of the rock 'n' roll years has been replaced by a more laid-back carnival vibe, as goths, indie kids, emos and the last punk rockers vie for attention around the canal. Tourists travel here in their thousands for the sprawling mayhem of **Camden Market** (*see p126*), which stretches north from the tube along boutique-lined Camden High Street and Chalk Farm Road. A dozen different countercultures depend on the market for thigh-length Frankenstein boots, studded collars and new leather jackets emblazoned with the mispunctuated mantra 'Punks not Dead'. The market narrowly escaped disaster in February 2008, when fire swept through the Canal Market, destroying the Hawley Arms, a onetime hangout of Amy Winehouse and Pete Doherty. The rest of the

SIGHTS

Camden Market.

market is still one of London's biggest tourist attractions and the weekend crowds can be impossible; best visit on a weekday.

Cutting through the market is **Regent's Canal**, which opened in 1820 to provide a link between east and west London for horse-drawn narrowboats loaded with coal. Today, the canal is used by the jolly tour-boats of the London Waterbus Company (7482 2550, www.london waterbus.com), Jason's Trip (7286 3428, www. jasons.co.uk) and Walker's Quay (7485 4433, www.walkersquay.com), which run between Camden Lock and picturesque **Little Venice** (Warwick Avenue tube) in summer and on winter weekends. Locals use the canal towpath as a convenient walking route to west Regent's Park and **London Zoo** (*see p99*), or east to Islington (*see p131*) and through Hackney (*see p140*) all the way to the Thames. Another popular walk is the stroll up to genteel Primrose Hill (*see p127*), with its bijou cafés and upscale restaurants and gastropubs. West of Camden Town tube on Albert Street, the consolidated **Jewish Museum** (8371 7373, www.jewish museum.org.uk) is due to reopen after a major refurb in late autumn 2009.

Camden is still one of the best places in London to catch a gig. As well as big venues like Koko and the Roundhouse, there are plenty of small pub stages where next year's headliners can be spotted before they make it big. Top spots to catch these up-and-comers include **Barfly** (*see p314*), the **Underworld** (*see p317*), the **Jazz Café** (*see p315*) and the stalwart **Dublin Castle** (*see p315*), where Madness and later Blur were first launched into the limelight in the 1970s and '90s.

Camden Market

Camden Lock *Camden Lock Place, off Chalk Farm Road, NW1 8AF (www.camdenlockmarket. com).* **Open** 10am-6pm daily.
Camden Market *Camden High Street, at Buck Street, NW1 (www.camdenmarkets.org).* **Open** 9.30am-6pm daily.
Inverness Street Market *Inverness Street, NW1 (www.camdenlock.net).* **Open** 8.30am-5pm daily.
Stables Market *off Chalk Farm Road, opposite Hartland Road, NW1 8AH (7485 5511/ www.stablesmarket.com).* **Open** 10.30am-6pm Mon-Fri (reduced stalls); 10am-6pm Sat, Sun.
All *Camden Town or Chalk Farm tube.*
Camden Market is actually a series of markets spread out around Chalk Farm Road and the Regent's Canal. Camden Market (formerly Buck Street Market) is the place for fake sunglasses and cut-price interpretations of urban fashion. Similar stalls, along with fruit and veg stands, are found across the road in the Inverness Street Market. Records, CDs and fashion are sold at weekends in the Electric Ballroom, though the future of the venue is threatened by the redevelopment of the tube station. Further north, along the canal, Camden Lock Market has some good world food stands and vendors selling crafts and ethnic imports. North of the courtyard that contains Gilgamesh (*see p236*), the gentrified Stables Market offers more food stands, as well as vintage clothing and clubwear shops tucked into the rail arches. Antiques and contempo-

rary designer furniture are sold at the north end of the market in the Horse Hospital area (which once cared for horses injured while pulling barges). This is also where you'll find the appealing Proud club-bar-gallery (*see p323*).

Around Camden

Primrose Hill, to the west of Camden, is just as attractive as the actors and pop stars who frequent the gastropubs and quaint cafés along **Regent's Park Road** and **Gloucester Avenue**. On sunny Sunday mornings, there's no better spot to read the papers than the pavement tables in front of Ukrainian café, **Trojka** (101 Regent's Park Road, 7483 3765). Other favourite hangouts include the long-established **Primrose Pâtisserie** (no.136, 7722 7848) and upmarket Greek bistro **Lemonia** (no.89, 7586 7454). For a gastropub feed, head to Gloucester Avenue: both the **Engineer** (no.65, 7722 0950) and **Lansdowne** (no.90, 7483 0409) are here. On any clear day, taking a walk up the hill itself is a delight.

ST JOHN'S WOOD

St John's Wood or Swiss Cottage tube.

The woodland that gives St John's Wood its name was part of the great Middlesex Forest, before the land was claimed by the Knights of St John of Jerusalem. Areas of forest were cleared for private villas in the mid-19th century, but the district has retained its green and pleasant glow. Some uncharacteristically sensitive redevelopment during the 1950s has left the area smart and eminently desirable: even a modest semi can cost £2 million. The expensive tastes of locals are reflected in the posh boutiques along the High Street. The main tourist attraction is **Lord's** cricket ground (*see below*), but a steady stream of music fans pay tribute to the Beatles by crossing the zebra crossing in front of **Abbey Road Studios** (3 Abbey Road). The studio, founded in 1931

by Sir Edward Elgar, is ʃ albums and film scores, in to the *Lord of the Rings* tril prequels and *Harry Potter* fi for a photo on the famous cros: you to copy the Red Hot Chili Pe wore nothing but socks to preserve modesty. Up the Finchley Road fron. Wood is **Swiss Cottage**, worth a vis modernist library designed by Sir Basil in the early '60s.

Lord's Tour & MCC Museum

St John's Wood Road, NW8 8QN (7616 8595/ www.lords.org). St John's Wood tube. **Tours** *Nov-Mar* noon, 2pm daily. *Apr-Oct* 10am, noon, 2pm daily. **Admission** £12; £6-£7 reductions; £31 family; free under-5s. **Credit** AmEx, MC, V.
Lord's is more than just a famous cricket ground – as the headquarters of the Marylebone Cricket Club (MCC), it is official guardian of the rules of cricket. As well as staging test matches and internationals, the ground is also home to the Middlesex County Cricket Club (MCCC). Visitors can take an organised tour round the futuristic, pod-like NatWest Media Centre and august, portrait-bedecked Long Room. Highlights include the tiny urn containing the Ashes and memorabilia celebrating the achievements of WG Grace, winner of the 1883 Best British Beard Award (not really, but it is an impressive beard).

HAMPSTEAD

Hampstead or Golders Green tube/ Gospel Oak or Hampstead Heath rail.

It may have been absorbed into London during the city's great Victorian expansion, but hilltop Hampstead still feels like a Home Counties' village. It has long been a favoured roost for literary and artistic types: Keats and Constable lived here in the 19th century, and sculptors Barbara Hepworth and Henry Moore took up residence in the 1930s.

The undisputed highlight of the district is **Hampstead Heath**, the relatively vast and in places wonderfully overgrown tract of countryside between Hampstead village and Highgate. The heath covers 791 acres of woodland, playing fields, swimming ponds (the source of the lost River Fleet, *see p74* **Inside Track**) and meadows of tall grass that attract picnickers and couples in search of privacy (*see p128* **Walk**).

At the south east end of the heath is dinky Hampstead village, with genteel shops and cafés, restaurants and pubs. While you are here, you can tour the gorgeous sunken gardens and antique collection at **Fenton House** (*see p129*), or gaze at the stars from the **Hampstead Scientific Society Observatory** (Lower

---

INSIDE TRACK
CHEAP EATS IN CAMDEN

For a long time it was relatively difficult to find quality cheap eats around Camden. Not any more. Try the local branches of **Wagamama** (11 Jamestown Road, 7428 0800) and **Masala Zone** (*see p221*), get dim sum and Chinese snacks at **Teachi** (29-31 Parkway, 7485 9933), or tuck in to one of the delicious deluxe burgers at **Haché** (*see p221*).

...ll used to record
including soundtracks
...ry, *Star Wars*
...ns. If you pose
...ing, we dare
...pers, who
... their
... St John's
...t for the
Spence

North London

...ght in a Green Shade

...ws beckon the wanderer here.

...ll

...nd
...permitting –
...it.

..., turn left on to
High Street where, if you're
...ng a picnic (highly recommended),
you can stock up at some excellent food
shops and bakeries. Gail's and Paul both
have mouth-watering displays. Turn left
down narrow Flask Walk and descend into
Hampstead village through its delightful
terraces of tightly packed cottages; note
the Narnia-style Victorian street lamps.

Passing a red-brick former washhouse,
carry on along **Well Walk** by the swanky
gastropub Wells Tavern. Look out for
no.40, once home to landscape painter
John Constable. He loved the Heath and
spent his final years here. Cross over East
Heath Road with the Pryors mansion block
on your right. You are now on the Heath.

Follow the wide path between lime
trees for five minutes until you reach a
crossroads, with a playing field opening
to the right. Check out the engraved slab
commemorating the 1987 hurricane that
felled many of the Heath's ancient trees.

Take the left path and you'll soon be
crossing **Viaduct Pond**. It's worth looping
round the water below, lily-strewn in
summer, to gaze back at the picturesque
arches (built 1845). From the top of the

SIGHTS

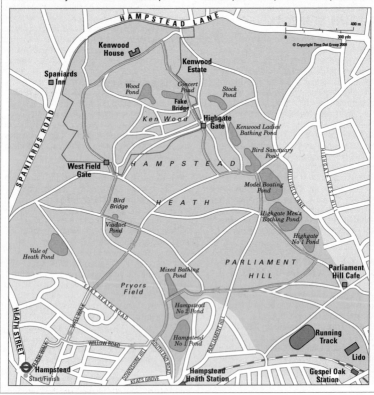

HAMPSTEAD LANE

Kenwood House

Kenwood Estate

Spaniards Inn

Wood Pond

Concert Pond

Stock Pond

Fake Bridge

Ken Wood

Highgate Gate

Kenwood Ladies' Bathing Pond

Bird Sanctuary Pond

West Field Gate

HAMPSTEAD

SPANIARDS ROAD

Model Boating Pond

Bird Bridge

HEATH

Highgate Men's Bathing Pond

Viaduct Pond

Highgate No 1 Pond

Vale of Heath Pond

PARLIAMENT HILL

Mixed Bathing Pond

Parliament Hill Cafe

EAST HEATH ROAD

Pryors Field

Hampstead No 2 Pond

HEATH STREET

WILLOW ROAD

Hampstead No 1 Pond

Running Track

SOUTH END ROAD

DOWNSHIRE HILL

Lido

FLASK WALK

Hampstead
Start/Finish

KEATS GROVE

Hampstead Heath Station

PARLIAMENT HILL

Gospel Oak Station

HIGHGATE WEST HILL

MILLFIELD LANE

© Copyright Time Out Group 2009

0   400 m
0   300 yds

viaduct, continue roughly 60 paces and take a smaller path right over tiny **Bird Bridge**. Follow the path uphill and, at the top, circle left around a large oak, its roots protected by a barrage of logs. Now take the main path straight ahead, leading to West Field Gate.

The black railings enclose the more landscaped Kenwood estate that adjoins the Heath. Follow the path arcing round West Meadow and fork right. Through the next gate, you'll see a Henry Moore sculpture ahead. Make for the gleaming stucco of **Kenwood House** (*see p130*).

The sloping lawns are an idyllic spot for a picnic but there are other food options – and toilets – within the grounds. The Brew House offers substantial fare (9am-5pm daily; closes an hour earlier in winter) and has a shaded and inviting terrace.

Walk around the lawn down towards the lake with its faux bridge (up close, you can see it's just a white-painted panel). Keep to the main path up through Ken Wood and emerge via Highgate Gate back on to the Heath. There's a tantalising view across the treetops of the City skyline.

Go straight ahead, keeping to the winding tarmac path towards **Highgate Ponds**, which are formed from natural springs. Two are open all year round for a refreshing dip: peel left for the secluded ladies' bathing pond (women only, of course) or stroll alongside the others to the penultimate men-only pond. In summer, the grass bank on the far side is a magnet for gay sunbathers.

At the southernmost pond take the path sharp right to the summit of **Parliament Hill** (98 metres). Legend has it the name derives from Guy Fawkes' confederates gathering here to watch the Houses of Parliament blow up in 1605. Popular for flying kites, the hill offers a superb panorama of central London and, back over the ponds, woody Highgate village.

Keeping on the same path, descend towards the trees, pass between two **Hampstead Ponds** (the right one is designated for mixed bathing). Veer left across the last scrubby patch of heathland towards East Heath Road and perhaps grab a pint at the Devonshire Arms. Take Willow Road back up to Flask Walk and you're back where you began.

Terrace, 8346 1056, www.hampsteadscience.ac.uk/astro), open on clear Friday and Saturday evenings and Sunday lunchtimes from mid September to mid April. A stroll along nearby Judges Walk reveals a line of horse chestnuts and limes virtually unchanged since they appeared in a Constable painting in 1820. Constable was buried nearby at **St John-at-Hampstead Church** (7794 5808), as was Peter Cook. At the top of Hampstead, North End Way divides the main heath from the wooded West Heath, one of London's oldest gay cruising areas (but perfectly family-friendly by day) – it was here, in September 2008, that George Michael was arrested and cautioned for possession of drugs. Just off North End Way is Hampstead's best kept secret, the secluded and charmingly overgrown **Hill Garden & Pergola** (open 8.30am-dusk daily), built by Lord Leverhulme using soil from the excavation of the tunnels for the Northern Line.

East of Hampstead tube, a maze of postcard-pretty residential streets shelters **Burgh House** on New End Square (7431 0144, www.burgh house.org.uk), a Queen Anne house with a small local history museum and gallery. Also in the area are **2 Willow Road** (*see p131*), architect Ernö Goldfinger's residence in the 1930s, and 40 Well Walk, Constable's home for the last ten years of his life. Downhill towards Hampstead Heath train station is **Keats House** (*see p130*).

Further west, and marginally closer to Finchley Road tube, is the **Freud Museum** (*see below*) and, almost opposite the station, is the innovative **Camden Arts Centre** (Arkwright Road, corner of Finchley Road, 7472 5500, www.camdenartscentre.org). It hosts edgy art shows, as well as film screenings and performances in the terrace café.

Fenton House

3 Hampstead Grove, NW3 6RT (7435 3471/ www.nationaltrust.org.uk). Hampstead tube. **Open** *Mar* 2-5pm Sat, Sun. *Apr-Oct* 2-5pm Wed-Fri; 11am-5pm Sat, Sun. **Admission** *House & gardens* £5.40; £2.70 under-18s; free under-5s. *Gardens* £1. *Joint ticket with 2 Willow Road* £7.30. **Credit** MC, V.
Set in a gorgeous garden, with a 300-year-old apple orchard, this manor house is notable for its 17th- and 18th-century harpsichords, virginals and spinets, which are still played at lunchtime and evening concerts (phone for details). Also on display are European and China porcelain, Chippendale furniture and some artful 17th-century needlework.

Freud Museum

20 Maresfield Gardens, NW3 5SX (7435 2002/ www.freud.org.uk). Finchley Road tube. **Open** noon-5pm Wed-Sun. **Admission** £5; £3 reductions; free under-12s. **Credit** AmEx, MC, V.

SIGHTS

Hampstead Heath. See p127.

SIGHTS

Driven from Vienna by the Nazi occupation, the great psychoanalyst Sigmund Freud was resident in this quiet suburban house in north London with his wife Martha and daughter Anna until his death in 1939. Now a museum, the house displays Freud's antiques, art and therapy tools, including his famous couch. The building is one of the few in London to have two blue plaques, one for Sigmund and another for Anna, a pioneer in child psychiatry.

Keats House
Keats Grove, NW3 2RR (7332 2820/www.city oflondon.gov.uk). Hampstead tube/Hampstead Heath rail/24, 46, 168 bus. **Open/Admission** phone for details. **Credit** MC, V.

INSIDE TRACK
PARKLAND WALK

This strange, leafy trail leads from Shepherd's Hill near Highgate tube along the line of a former railway through comfortable, middle-class Crouch End – densely populated by the acting fraternity – passing neat back gardens and beneath bridges all the way to Finsbury Park.

Due to reopen in early 2009, this was the home of the Romantic poet from 1818 to 1820, when he left for Rome in hope of alleviating his tuberculosis (he died of the disease the next year, aged 25). As well as mooching through the rooms, you can attend events and talks in the poetry reading room and see a display on Keats's sweetheart, Fanny Brawne, who lived next door. The garden, in which Keats wrote 'Ode to a Nightingale', is a particularly pleasant spot.

★ FREE Kenwood House/ Iveagh Bequest
Hampstead Lane, NW3 7JR (8348 1286/www. english-heritage.org.uk). Hampstead tube/Golders Green tube then 210 bus. **Open** 11.30am-4pm daily. *Tours* (for groups by appointment only) £5. **Admission** free; donations appreciated. **Credit** MC, V.

Set in lovely grounds at the top of Hampstead Heath, Kenwood House is every inch the country manor house. Built in 1616, the mansion was remodelled in the 18th century for William Murray, who made the pivotal court ruling in 1772 that made it illegal to own slaves in England. The house was purchased by brewing magnate Edward Guinness, who was kind enough to donate his art collection to the nation in 1927. Highlights include Vermeer's *The Guitar Player*, a panoramic view of old London Bridge by

Claude de Jongh (1630), Gainsborough's *Countess Howe*, and one of Rembrandt's finest self-portraits (c1663). *See also p128* **Walk**.

▶ *The house and its interiors were redesigned by the Adam brothers, Robert and James. Their designs are kept at the Soane Museum; see p73.*

2 Willow Road

2 Willow Road, NW3 1TH (7435 6166/www. nationaltrust.org.uk). Hampstead tube/Hampstead Heath rail. **Open** *Mar-Nov* 11am-5pm Sat. *Late Mar-Oct* noon-5pm Thur, Fri; 11am-5pm Sat. *Tours* noon, 1pm, 2pm Thur, Fri; 11am, noon, 1pm, 2pm Sat. **Admission** £5.10; £2.60 children; £12.80 family; free under-5s. *Joint ticket with Fenton House* £7.30. **No credit cards**.

A surprising addition to the National Trust's collection of historic houses, this modernist building was designed by Hungarian-born architect, Ernö Goldfinger. The house was designed to be flexible, with movable partitions and folding doors. Home to the architect and his wife until their deaths, it contains the likes of Max Ernst and Henry Moore.

▶ *Goldfinger also designed Notting Hill's brutalist Trellick Tower; see p101.*

HIGHGATE

Archway or Highgate tube.

Taking its name from the tollgate that once stood on the High Street, Highgate is inexorably linked with London's medieval mayor, Richard 'Dick' Whittington. As the story goes, the disheartened Whittington fled the City as far as Highgate Hill, but turned back when he heard the Bow Bells peal out 'Turn again, Whittington, thrice Mayor of London'. Today, the area is best known for the atmospheric grounds of **Highgate Cemetery** (*see below*), last resting place of Karl Marx. Adjoining the cemetery is pretty **Waterlow Park**, created by low-cost housing pioneer Sir Sydney Waterlow in 1889, with ponds, a mini-aviary, tennis courts and a cute garden café in 16th-century **Lauderdale House** (8348 8716, www. lauderdalehouse.co.uk), former home of Charles II's mistress, Nell Gwynn. North of Highgate tube, shady **Highgate Woods** are preserved as a conservation area, with a nature trail, adventure playground and café that hosts live jazz during the summer.

★ Highgate Cemetery

Swains Lane, N6 6PJ (8340 1834/www.highgate-cemetery.org). Archway tube. **Open** *East Cemetery* Apr-Oct 10am 4.30pm Mon-Fri; 11am-4.30pm Sat, Sun; Nov-Mar 10am-3.30pm Mon-Fri; 11am-3.30pm Sat, Sun. *West Cemetery* by tour only. **Tours** *Nov-Mar* hourly 11am-3pm Sat, Sun.

Apr-Oct 2pm Mon-Fri; hourly 11am-4pm Sat, Sun. No under-8s. **Admission** £3. *Tours* £5. **No credit cards**.

The final resting place of some very famous Londoners, Highgate Cemetery is a wonderfully overgrown maze of ivy-cloaked Victorian tombs and time-shattered urns. Visitors are free to wander through the East Cemetery, with its memorials to Karl Marx, George Eliot and Douglas Adams, but the most atmospheric part of the cemetery is the foliage-shrouded West Cemetery, laid out in 1839. Only accessible on an organised tour (book ahead, dress respectfully and arrive 30mins early), the shady paths wind past gloomy catacombs, grand Victorian pharaonic tombs, and the graves of notables such as poet Christina Rossetti, scientist Michael Faraday and poisoned Russian dissident Alexander Litvinenko. The cemetery closes during burials, so call ahead.

▶ *Michael Faraday's laboratory can be seen at the refurbished Royal Institution; see pp104-105.*

ISLINGTON

Angel tube/Highbury & Islington tube/rail.

The suburban bower of the *Guardian*-reading middle classes, Islington started life as a small country village beside one of Henry VIII's expansive hunting reserves. It soon became an important livestock market supplying the Smithfield meat yards, before being enveloped into Greater London. During the 19th century, the Regent's Canal brought industry and later industrial decay, but locals kept their spirits up at the local music halls, which launched such working-class heroes as Marie Lloyd, George Formby and Norman Wisdom. From the 1960s, the borough attracted a massive influx of arts and media types, who gentrified the Georgian squares and Victorian terraces and opened cafés, restaurants and boutiques around Upper Street and Essex Road.

Close to the station on Upper Street, the popular **Camden Passage** antiques market (*see p263*) bustles with browsing activity on Wednesdays and Saturdays. The music halls have long gone, but local residents take full advantage of the cultural offerings at the charming **Screen on the Green** cinema (*see p298*), the **Almeida Theatre** (*see p341*) and the often-raucous **King's Head** theatre pub (*see p343*).

East of Angel, Regency-era **Canonbury Square** was once home to George Orwell (no.27) and Evelyn Waugh (no.17A). One of the handsome town houses now contains the **Estorick Collection of Modern Italian Art** (*see below*). Just beyond the end of Upper Street is **Highbury Fields**, where 200,000 Londoners fled in 1666 to escape the Great Fire. The surrounding district is best known as the home of Arsenal Football Club, who abandoned the charming Highbury Stadium in 2006 for the 60,000-seater behemoth that is the **Emirates Stadium** (*see p329*). Fans can tour the ground or just visit the **Arsenal Museum** (7619 5000, www.arsenal.com). If you fancy a stroll, the Regent's Canal towpath runs east from just south of Angel tube past Hackney's Broadway Market and as far as the Thames, which it joins at **Limehouse Basin** (*see p139*).

Estorick Collection of Modern Italian Art

39A Canonbury Square, N1 2AN (7704 9522/ www.estorickcollection.com). Highbury & Islington tube/rail/271 bus. **Open** 11am-6pm Wed, Fri, Sat;

Highgate Cemetery, *See p131.*

11am-8pm Thur; noon-5pm Sun. **Admission** £3.50; £2.50 reductions; free under-16s, students. **Credit** AmEx, MC, V.

Eric Estorick was a US political scientist, writer and art collector who formed an intense attachment to modern Italian art on tours through Europe after World War II. His personal collection of 20th-century Italian paintings has been here since 1998 – highlights include Balla's *Hand of the Violinist* and Boccioni's *Modern Idol*. The museum also has a library, shop and café.

FREE Islington Museum

245 St John Street, Finsbury, EC1V 4NB (7527 3235/www.islington.gov.uk). Angel tube. **Open** 10am-5pm Mon, Tue, Thur-Sat. **Admission** free. **No credit cards**. **Map** p402 O3.

Following in the footsteps of the borough museum in Hackney, Islington Museum opened its doors in May 2008, so all the displays are gleaming and new. Most deal with local history and the political and ethical credentials of the borough, exemplified by local heroes like reformist preacher John Wesley, playwright Joe Orton, women's health pioneer Marie Stopes and eminent feminist pioneer Mary Wollstonecraft.

DALSTON & STOKE NEWINGTON

Dalston Kingsland rail or Stoke Newington rail.

Although scruffy, Dalston scores points for the vibrant African-flavoured market on Ridley Road, and the Turkish ocakbasis (grill restaurants) along Stoke Newington Road, including excellent **Mangal II** (no.4, 7254 7888). Low property prices have attracted a growing contingent of student types, who congregate at the appealingly urban **Dalston Jazz Bar** (4 Bradbury Street, 7254 9728) and the brilliant **Vortex Jazz Club** (*see p318*).

Neighbouring **Stoke Newington** is the richer cousin of Dalston and poorer cousin of Islington, home to a disproportionate number of journalists and TV news presenters. At weekends, pretty **Clissold Park** (7923 3660) is overrun with picnickers, mums pushing prams and twenty-somethings practising capoeira and slacklining. Most visitors head to bijou **Church Street** for its second-hand bookshops, cute boutiques and kids' stores, and superior cafés and restaurants – Keralan vegetarian restaurant **Rasa** (no.55, 7249 0344) is our pick. Another local highlight is the simply wonderful **Abney Park Cemetery** (7275 7557, www.abney-park.org.uk), a wild and overgrown Victorian boneyard that looks like a set from a Sam Raimi zombie movie; it is also a nature reserve, with rare butterflies, woodpeckers and bats.

SIGHTS

East London

The artists and night owls remain – and athletes are on their way.

From fashion markets to street art, in east London sightseeing comes with plenty of distractions. Once London's industrial sector, based around the docks and their warehouses, living conditions here were hopelessly overcrowded and deprived, with tight-knit communities suffered grinding poverty and the worst of the Blitz. Nowadays, the East End is an extraordinary hotchpotch of cultures, religions and lifestyles – more than four centuries of immigration have made the character of this area as surely as the influx of artists and clubbers since the

Map p403, p405	Hotels p193
Restaurants &	Pubs & bars
cafés p223	p238

'80s has made it fashionable. Now the neighbouring City draws ever nearer. Tough housing estates and tatty tower blocks stand cheek-by-jowl with glitzy new office skyscrapers, while Cockney mythology persists in lending a patina – and a bit of patter – to the area's unstoppable bars and nightlife.

SIGHTS

SPITALFIELDS

Aldgate East tube/Liverpool Street tube/rail.

Approach this area from Liverpool Street Station, up Brushfield Street, and you'll know you're on the right track when the magnificent spike spire of **Christ Church Spitalfields** (*see below*) comes into sight. The area's other signature sight, **Spitalfields Market** (*see p243*), has emerged from protracted redevelopment and the market stalls have moved back underneath the vaulted Victorian roof of the original building.

Outside, along Brushfield Street, the shops might look as if they're from Dickens's day, but most are recent inventions: the charming grocery shop **A Gold** (no.42; *see p258*) was lovingly restored in the noughties; the owners of the **Market Coffee House** (nos.50-52, 7247 4110) put reclaimed wood panelling and creaky furniture into an empty shell; and the deli **Verde & Co** (no.40, 7247 1924) was opened by its owner, author Jeanette Winterson, inspired by the local food shops she found in – whisper it – France. It's a nice enough stroll, but for another perspective on Spitalfields head a few streets south

on a Sunday to find the famously salt-of-the-earth **Petticoat Lane Market**, hawking knickers and cheap electronics around Middlesex Street. At the foot of Goulston Street, **Tubby Isaacs** seafood stall has sold whelks and cockles since 1919.

A block north of Spitalfields Market is **Dennis Severs' House** (*see p134*), across from the market, on the east side of Commercial Street and in the shadow of Christ Church, the **Ten Bells** (84 Commercial Street, 7366 1721) is where one of Jack the Ripper's prostitute victims drank her last gin. The streets between here and Brick Lane to the east are dourly impressive, lined with tall, shuttered Huguenot houses; **19 Princelet Street** (www.19princeletstreet.org.uk) is opened to the public a few times a year. This unrestored 18th-century house was home first to French silk merchants and later Polish Jews who built a synagogue in the garden.

FREE Christ Church Spitalfields

Commercial Street, E1 6QE (7859 3035/www. christchurchspitalfields.org). Liverpool Street tube/rail. **Open** 11am-4pm Tue; 1-4pm Sun. **Admission** free. **Map** p403 S5.

Spitalfields Market. *See p133.*

Built in 1729 by architect Nicholas Hawksmoor, this splendid church has in recent years been restored to its original state (tasteless alterations had followed a 19th-century lightning strike). Most tourists get no further than cowering before the wonderfully over-bearing spire, but the revived interior is impressive, its pristine whiteness in marked contrast to its architect's dark reputation. The formidable 1735 Richard Bridge organ is almost as old as the church. Regular concerts are held here, often from the resident Gabrieli Consort & Players.

▶ *The East End's other Hawksmoor churches are St Anne's Limehouse (on Commercial Road, between Limehouse and Westferry DLRs, www. stanneslimehouse.org) and St George-in-the-East (on the Highway, near Shadwell DLR).*

Dennis Severs' House

18 Folgate Street, E1 6BX (7247 4013/www. dennissevershouse.co.uk). Liverpool Street tube/ rail. **Open** noon-4pm 1st & 3rd Sun of mth; noon-2pm Mon following 1st & 3rd Sun of mth; times vary Mon evenings. **Admission** £8 Sun; £5 noon-2pm Mon; £12 Mon evenings. **Credit** V. **Map** p403 R5.

The ten rooms of this original Huguenot house have been decked out to recreate snapshots of life in Spitalfields between 1724 and 1914. A tour through the compelling 'still-life drama', as American creator Dennis Severs dubbed it, takes you through the cellar, kitchen, dining room, smoking room and upstairs to the bedrooms. With hearth and candles burning, smells lingering and objects scattered apparently haphazardly, it feels as though the inhabitants had deserted the rooms only moments before.

BRICK LANE

Aldgate East tube.

Join the crowds flowing east from Spitalfields Market (*see p243*) along Hanbury Street during the weekend, and the direction you turn at the end determines which Brick Lane you see. Turn right and you'll know you're in 'Banglatown', the name adopted by the ward back in 2002: until you hit the bland modern offices beside the kitsch Banglatown arch, it's almost all Bangladeshi cafés, curry houses, grocery stores, money transfer services and sari shops – plus the **Pride of Spitalfields** (3 Heneage Street, 7247 8933), a down-at-heel, old-style East End boozer serving up fine real ale to all-comers. Despite the street's global reputation for curries (there's a Brick Lane restaurant in Manhattan, you know), we continue to be disappointed by the quality of food on offer (*see p221* **Inside Track**). Opt instead for some Bengali sweets from the **Madhubon Sweet Centre** at no.42. **Jamme Masjid Mosque**, between Fournier Street and Princelet Street, is a key symbol of Brick Lane's hybridity. It began as a Huguenot chapel, became a synagogue and was converted, in 1976, into a mosque – in other words, immigrant communities have been layering their experiences on this street at least since 1572, when the St Bartholomew's Day Massacre forced many French Huguenots into exile.

The newest layer is gentrification: turn left from Hanbury Street, and it's all about young urban bohemians. On a Sunday there's the lively street market, complemented by the trendier UpMarket (*see p243* **Inside Track**) and Backyard Market (for arts and crafts), both held in the **Old Truman Brewery** (nos.91-95). Pedestrianised Dray Walk is crowded every day. It's full of hip independent businesses like **Rootmaster** (www.root-master.co.uk), a vegetarian café in an old red bus. Heading north on Brick Lane, you'll find the **Vibe Bar** (7377 2899, www.vibe-bar.co.uk) and shops such as second-hand clothes store **Rokit** (nos.101 & 107, 7375 3864, 7247 3777). Further north, Cheshire Street is vintage fashion heaven.

WHITECHAPEL

Aldgate East or Whitechapel tube.

Not one of the prettier London thoroughfares, busy but anonymous Whitechapel Road sets the tone for this area. One bright spot is

INSIDE TRACK
CELL OUT

Behind the Royal London Hospital, the brand new, high-tech **Centre of the Cell** (64 Turner Street, 7882 2562, www. centreofthecell.org), is due to open after many delays in June 2009. It promises to give visitors a lively, interactive and occasionally grisly insight into cell biology in a purpose-built pod, suspended over labs that are engaged in investigating cancer and tuberculosis.

Whitechapel Art Gallery (*see p136* **Renaissance Whitechapel**), at the foot of Brick Lane (*see below*), while a little to the east, the **Whitechapel Bell Foundry** (nos.32 & 34, 7247 2599, www.whitechapelbellfoundry. co.uk) continues to manufacture bells, as it has since 1570. It famously produced Philadelphia's Liberty Bell and Big Ben. To join one of the fascinating Saturday tours you'll have to reserve a place (usually well in advance).

At Whitechapel's foremost place of worship, it isn't bells but a muezzin that summons the faithful each Friday: the **East London Mosque**, focal point for the largest Muslim community in Britain, can accommodate 10,000 worshippers. Behind is Fieldgate Street and the dark mass of **Tower House**, a former doss house whose 700 rooms have, inevitably, been redeveloped

into flats. This 'sought after converted warehouse building' was a rather dismal – but decidedly cheaper – proposition when Joseph Stalin and George Orwell (researching his book *Down and Out in Paris and London*) kipped here for pennies. The red-brick alleys give a flavour of Victorian Whitechapel, but this street has also been home to the cheap seekh kebabs of **New Tayyabs** (nos.83-89, 7247 9543) for over three decades.

East again is the Royal London Hospital and, in a small crypt on Newark Street, the **Royal London Hospital Archives & Museum** (7377 7608, closed Sat, Sun). Inside are reproduction letters from Jack the Ripper (including the notorious missive 'From Hell', delivered with an enclosed portion of human kidney) and information on Joseph Merrick, the 'Elephant Man', so named for his fearsome congenital deformities. Rescued by surgeon Sir Frederick Treves, Merrick was given his own room in the Royal London Hospital.

FREE **Whitechapel Art Gallery**
80-82 Whitechapel High Street, E1 7QX (7522 7888/www.whitechapel.org). Aldgate East tube. **Open** *phone for details. Whitechapel Laboratory* 11am-6pm Wed-Sun. **Admission** free. **Map** p405 S6.

Until the gallery fully reopens in spring 2009 (*see p136* **Renaissance Whitechapel**), a programme of events and exhibitions is being run in the Whitechapel Laboratory, accessed down the alley to the left of the main façade. *Photo p136.*

Brick Lane.

SIGHTS

Renaissance Whitechapel

The arty East End finally gets the public space it deserves.

Nikolaus Pevsner described it as a 'wonderfully original and epoch-making building', but a century or so after it was built, the **Whitechapel Art Gallery** (*see p135*) – designed in an art nouveau style by Charles Harrison Townsend, also responsible for the Horniman Museum (*see p144*) – clearly needed to expand if it was to meet the needs of a flagship gallery in the heart of London's contemporary art quarter. The answer appeared when the adjacent Passmore Edwards library became vacant (bibliophiles needn't despair: the library has been transferred to the David Adjaye-designed Idea Store along the road).

Spilling into a neighbouring building sounds easy enough, yet the expansion has been a lengthy process, the key obstacle being how to sympathetically unite two roughly contemporary but stylistically different buildings. From April 2009, we'll have a chance to see what the Belgian architects Robbrecht en Daem, working in association with London practice Witherford Watson Mann, have achieved. Expect a sensitive blending of spaces – the architects were chosen for their low-key, intelligent approach to the project. We also know that gallery space will have grown by a whopping 78 per cent and that, in addition to the original galleries, auditorium, bookshop and café, there'll be new Collections & Commissions galleries, an Archive Collection Gallery and a three-storey Education & Research Tower.

How the gallery's rich history – Picasso's *Guernica* was shown here in 1939, and in 1958 the Whitechapel gave Jackson Pollock his first major show in the UK – intertwines with that of the local area is illustrated by the first show in the Archive Collection Gallery. The story of early 20th-century British modernism is told through the work of the Whitechapel Boys – a group of London-based Jewish writers and artists including David Bomberg and Mark Gertler who, in around 1910, would meet at the gallery and the library next door.

The Commissions Gallery, meanwhile, opens with a work by the 2008 Turner Prize nominee Goshka Macuga whose quizzical responses to various collections, libraries and archives makes her ideal for baptising the space. Since the Whitechapel has no permanent collection,

the Collections Gallery allows for lengthy loans to be accommodated from British or international collections, public or private; first up is an 18-month, changing display of works drawn from the British Council collection. Known for her architectural assemblages, German sculptor Isa Genzken is an artist we haven't had the fortune to see at full tilt in this country: she inaugurates the reopened main galleries.

Following Genzken's show is East End Academy (9 July-20 Sept 2009). This open-submission exhibition for East London artists was first held in 1932 and resurrected by Whitechapel director Iwona Blazwick in 2004, strengthening ties with the local artistic community, even if that community now finds itself on the fringes of Essex in the hunt for affordable studio space. All the more reason for such a revamp of the Whitechapel mothership. It now shares the Whitechapel/Hoxton/Shoreditch triangle with socially minded cultural centres including inIVA's **Rivington Place** hub (*see p137*), the multiculti **Rich Mix** (35-47 Bethnal Green Road, 7613 7498, www.richmix.org.uk) and **Calvert 22**, a space with a bias towards Russian and Eastern European art, due to open in 2009. It will become a key part of a Hoxditch scene that's looking livelier than it has in years.

SHOREDITCH & HOXTON

Old Street tube/rail.

The story has become familiar: impecunious artists moved into the area's derelict warehouses in the '80s, taking advantage of cheap rent, and quickly turned the triangle formed by Old Street, Shoreditch High Street and Great Eastern Street into the place to be. These days, most the artists have moved further east, as City workers happy to pay serious money for street cred have driven rents through the roof. Yet this small patch of real estate is clinging on to its reputation as the city's most exciting arts and clubbing centre.

Nightlife permeates the whole area, with centres on Curtain Road, the lower end of Kingsland Road and around Hoxton Square. Nostalgists have to pencil in a visit to **333** (*see p325*) – no longer cutting-edge, but certainly some kind of visually unremarkable landmark – but for the best idea of the non-conformist early days, duck into the **Foundry** (84-86 Great Eastern Street, 7739 6900), a resilient madhouse of impromptu art work, relatively cheap beer and dogs off the leash.

Apart from Hoxton Square galleries **White Cube** (*see p279*) and newcomer **Yvon Lambert** (*see p282*), the area's sole bona fide tourist attraction is the exquisite **Geffrye Museum** (*see below*), a short walk north up Kingsland Road. The surrounding area is dense with Vietnamese restaurants, notably **Sông Quê** (*see p224*).

★ FREE Geffrye Museum

136 Kingsland Road, E2 8EA (7739 9893/ recorded information 7739 8543/www.geffrye-museum.org.uk). Liverpool Street tube/rail then 149, 242 bus/Old Street tube/rail then 243 bus. **Open** 10am-5pm Tue-Sat; noon-5pm Sun. *Almshouse tours* 1st Sat, 1st & 3rd Wed of mth. **Admission** free; donations appreciated. *Almshouse tours* £2; free under-16s. **Credit** (shop) MC, V. **Map** p403 R3.

Housed in a set of 18th-century almshouses, the Geffrye Museum offers a vivid physical history of the English interior. Displaying original furniture, paintings, textiles and decorative arts, the museum recreates a sequence of typical middle-class living rooms from 1600 to the present. It is a fascinating way to take in domestic history, with any number of intriguing details to catch your eye – from a bell jar of stuffed birds to a particular decorative flourish on a chair. There's an airy restaurant overlooking the lovely gardens, which include a walled plot for herbs and a chronological series in different historical styles.

▶ *Charmed by the greenery? Seek out the Chelsea Physic Garden; see p119.*

INSIDE
SHAKE
SHORE

East London

Remains
built the
and alm
premièr
Juliet, i
Road (
london.org.
when building work beg..
theatre for the Tower Theatre Compa...,
(www.towertheatre.org.uk), date to 1576.

FREE Rivington Place

Rivington Place, EC2A 3BA (7729 9616/www. rivingtonplace.org). Old Street tube/rail. **Open** 11am-6pm Tue, Wed, Fri; 11am-8.30pm Thur; noon-6pm Sat. **Admission** free. **Credit** (shop) MC, V. **Map** p403 R4.

One of Shoreditch's more exciting recent additions, this public space designed by David Adjaye champions culturally diverse visual arts. Two project spaces provide a platform for British and international work, including exhibitions, screenings, installations and site-specific commissions. The site has a ground-floor café. *Photo p139.*

▶ *This is the first new-build public gallery since the opening of the Hayward in 1968; see p49.*

BETHNAL GREEN

Bethnal Green tube/rail/Cambridge Heath rail/ Mile End tube.

Once a suburb of spacious townhouses, by the mid 19th century Bethnal Green was one of the city's poorest neighbourhoods. As in neighbouring Hoxton, a recent upturn in fortunes has in part been occasioned by Bethnal Green's adoption as home by a new generation of artists. The long-standing **Maureen Paley** gallery (*see p281*) remains the key venue, but the new Bethnal Green is typified by places like **Herald Street** (*see p280*) just down the road. The old Bethnal Green is best experienced by taking a seat at **E Pellicci** (*see p223*), the exemplary traditional London caff.

The **Museum of Childhood** (*see p138*) is handily positioned close to Bethnal Green tube station, whereas the area's other main attraction is a bit of a walk away to the west. Nonetheless, a visit to the weekly **Columbia Road flower market** (*see p243*) is a lovely way to fritter away a Sunday morning. A microcosmic retail community has grown up around the market: **Treacle** (nos.110-112, 7729 5657) for groovy

SIGHTS

crockery and cup cakes; **Angela Flanders** (no.96, 7739 7555) for perfume; **Marcos & Trump** (no.146, 7739 9008) for vintage fashion.

🆓 Ragged School Museum
46-50 Copperfield Road, E3 4RR (8980 6405/ www.raggedschoolmuseum.org.uk). Mile End tube. **Open** 10am-5pm Wed, Thur; 2-5pm 1st Sun of mth. *Tours* by arrangement; phone for details. **Admission** free; donations appreciated.
Ragged schools were an early experiment in public education: they provided tuition, food and clothes for destitute children. This one was the largest in London, and Dr Barnardo himself taught here. It's now a sweet local museum that contains a complete mock-up of a ragged classroom, as well as an Edwardian kitchen.

★ 🆓 V&A Museum of Childhood
Cambridge Heath Road, E2 9PA (8983 5200/ recorded information 8983 5235/www.museum ofchildhood.org.uk). Bethnal Green tube/rail/ Cambridge Heath rail. **Open** 10am-5.45pm daily. **Admission** free; donations appreciated. **Credit** MC, V.
Home to one of the world's finest collections of children's toys, dolls' houses, games and costumes, the Museum of Childhood shines brighter than ever after extensive refurbishment, which has given it an impressive entrance. Part of the Victoria & Albert Museum (*see p122*), the museum has been amassing childhood-related objects since 1872 and continues to do so, with *Incredibles* figures complementing bonkers 1970s puppets, Barbie Dolls and Victorian praxinoscopes. There are regular exhibitions upstairs; 2009's highlight will be 'Snozzcumbers and Frobscuttle', a celebration of the work of Roald Dahl and his illustrator Quentin Blake (May-Sept). The museum has lots of hands-on stuff for kids, while the café helps revive flagging grown-ups.

DOCKLANDS

London's docks were fundamental to the prosperity of the British Empire. Between 1802 and 1921, ten separate docks were built between Tower Bridge in the west and Woolwich in the east. These employed tens of thousands of people. Yet by the 1960s the shipping industry was changing irrevocably. The new 'container' system of cargo demanded larger, deep-draught ships, as a result of which the work moved out to Tilbury, from where lorries would ship the containers into the city. By 1980, the London docks had closed.

The London Docklands Development Corporation (LDDC), founded in 1981, spent £790 million of public money on redevelopment during the following decade, only for a country-wide property slump in the early 1990s to leave the shiny new high-rise offices and luxury flats

V&A Museum of Childhood.

The origin of the name 'Isle of Dogs' remains
uncertain, but the first recorded use is on a
map of 1588; one theory claims Henry VIII
kept his hunting dogs here. One thing is clear:
it certainly isn't an island, but rather a
peninsula, extending into the Thames to create
the prominent loop that features in the title
sequence of the BBC soap opera *EastEnders*.
In the 19th century, a huge system of docks
and locks completely transformed what had
been no more than drained marshland; in
fact, the West India Docks cut right across
the peninsula, so the Isle did become
some sort of island.

Almost all the interest for visitors is to be
found in the vicinity of Cesar Pelli's dramatic
One Canada Square, the country's tallest
habitable building since 1991. The only slightly
shorter HSBC and Citygroup towers joined it in
the noughties, and clones are springing up thick
and fast. Shopping options are limited to the
mall beneath the towers (www.mycanarywharf.
com), but you'll find a soothing if rather crisp
Japanese garden beside Canary Wharf tube
station. Across a floating bridge over the dock
to the north, there's the **Museum of London
Docklands** (*see p140*).

It's also well worth hopping on the DLR
and heading to Island Gardens station at the
southerly tip of the Isle of Dogs. Nearby, at
Mudchute Park & Farm (Pier Street, Isle
of Dogs, E14 3HP, 7515 5901, www.mudchute.
org; see also p275) farmyard animals graze in

unoccupied. Nowadays, though, as a financial
hub, Docklands is a booming rival to the City
of London, with an estimated 90,000 workers
commuting to the area each day. For visitors,
regular **Thames Clippers** (0870 781 5049,
www.thamesclippers.com) boat connections
with central London and the **Docklands Light
Railway** (DLR) make the area easily accessible.

Wapping & Limehouse

Limehouse DLR/rail.

In 1598, John Stowe described Wapping High
Street as 'a filthy strait passage, with alleys of
small tenements or cottages, inhabited by sailors'
victuallers'. This can still just about be imagined
as you walk along it now, flanked by tall
Victorian warehouses. The historic **Town of
Ramsgate** (no.62, 7481 8000), dating to 1545,
helps. Here 'hanging judge' George Jeffreys was
captured in 1688, trying to escape to Europe in
disguise as a woman. Privateer Captain William
Kidd was executed in 1701 at Execution Dock,
near Wapping New Stairs; the bodies of pirates
were hanged from a gibbet until seven tides had
washed over them. Further east, the **Prospect
of Whitby** (57 Wapping Wall, 7481 1095) dates
from 1520 and has counted Samuel Pepys and
Charles Dickens among its regulars. It has good
riverside terraces and a fine pewter bar counter.
Opposite sits a rather more modern 'victualler':
Wapping Food (*see p224*) occupies an ivy-clad
Victorian hydraulic power station.

Isle of Dogs

*West India Quay, Mudchute or Island Gardens
DLR/Canary Wharf tube/DLR.*

Rivington Place. See p137.

SIGHTS

front of the ultramodern skyscrapers. From **Island Gardens** themselves, there are famous views of Greenwich – and the entrance to the Victorian pedestrian tunnel (*see p145*).

★ Museum of London Docklands

No.1 Warehouse, West India Quay, Hertsmere Road, E14 4AL (recorded information 0870 444 3856/box office 0870 444 3857/www. museumindocklands.org.uk). West India Quay DLR/Canary Wharf tube. **Open** 10am-6pm daily. Last entry 5.30pm. **Admission** £5; £3 reductions; free under-16s. **Credit** MC, V.
Housed in a 19th-century warehouse (itself a Grade I-listed building), this huge museum explores the complex history of London's docklands and the river over two millennia. Displays spreading over three storeys take you from the arrival of the Romans all the way to the docks' 1980s closure and the area's subsequent redevelopment. The Docklands at War section is very moving, while a haunting new per-manent exhibition sheds light on the dark side of London's rise as a centre for finance and commerce, exploring the city's heavy involvement in the transatlantic slave trade. You can also walk through full-scale mock-ups of a quayside and a dingy river-front alley. Temporary exhibitions are frequently set up on the ground floor, where you'll also find a café and a docks-themed play area for kids. Bring plenty of time to this fascinating storehouse, or return later – your ticket is valid for a year.

Further east

Pontoon Dock to King George V DLR.

Pontoon Dock is the stop for the beautiful **Thames Barrier Park** (www.thamesbarrier park.org.uk). Opened in 2001, this was London's first new park in half a century. It has a lush

---

INSIDE TRACK
VILLAGE LIFE

Walthamstow Village is a surprising delight: on Orford Road stands an ancient timber-framed cottage, deliberately given a slump by Victorian restorers who felt it would look older that way. Just opposite is St Mary's Church, parts of which date back to the 16th century. Across Vinegar Alley are the Monoux Almshouses. Further almshouses lead back along Church End to the modest **Vestry House Museum** (Vestry Road, 8509 1917, closed Sun & bank holidays), with its quiet garden and the reconstructed Bremer Car, London's – perhaps Britain's – first petrol-driven vehicle.

---

sunken garden of waggly hedges and offers perhaps the best views from land of the fabulously sculptural **Thames Barrier** (*see p149*). Head to the current terminus of this branch of the DLR at King George V for ready access to the jolly little **North Woolwich Old Station Museum** (Pier Road, 7474 7244, open 1-5pm Sat, Sun; 1-5pm Mon-Fri during school hols, closed Dec) and the free ferry (every 15mins daily, 8921 5786) that chugs pedestrians and cars across the river; a DLR extension under the river to **Woolwich Arsenal** (*see p149*) should be operational from early 2009.

HACKNEY

London Fields or Hackney Central rail.

Few tourists ever make it out to this tube-less, north-eastern district – after all, there are no blockbuster sights – but the area is a good example of lived-in London. Its centre is the refurbished 1901 **Hackney Empire** (291 Mare Street, 8985 2424, www.hackneyempire. co.uk), beside the art deco town hall and the impressive little **Hackney Museum** (1 Reading Lane, 8356 3500, www.hackney. gov.uk/museum). Just to the east, **Sutton House** (*see below*) is the oldest house in east London. The area of London Fields demonstrates the borough's ongoing gentrification. Once a lacklustre fruit and veg market, **Broadway Market** is now brimming with young urbanites browsing gourmet food stalls and the surrounding shops. There's a wonderful deli, an inspiring independent bookshop and a fine pub – the **Dove** (nos.24-28, 7275 7617, www.belgian bars.com), with its immense selection of Belgian beers. The old days are respectably represented by **F Cooke** (no.9, 7254 6458), a pie and mash place that's been here since the early 1900s.

Sutton House

2-4 Homerton High Street, E9 6JQ (8986 2264/www.nationaltrust.org.uk). Bethnal Green tube then 254, 106, D6 bus/Hackney Central rail. **Open** 12.30-4.30pm Thur-Sun. *Café, gallery & shop* noon-4.30pm Thur-Sun. *Tours* phone for details; free tours on 1st Sun of mth. **Admission** £2.80; 70p 5-16s; £6.30 family; free under-5s, National Trust members. **Credit** MC, V.
Built in 1535 for Henry VIII's first secretary of state, Sir Ralph Sadleir, this red-brick Tudor mansion is east London's oldest home. Now beautifully restored in authentic original decor, with a real Tudor kitchen to boot, it makes no secret of its history of neglect: even some 1980s squatter graffiti has been pre-served. The house closes for January each year.

THREE MILLS & STRATFORD

Bromley-by-Bow tube/Stratford tube/DLR/rail.

Ignore the thundering roads and gasworks surrounding it and **Three Mills Island** (*see below*) is a delight. A short walk north-east up the canal-like tributary brings you to **Stratford**, nucleus of the transformation for the **2012 Olympics** (*see p327*). Feverish construction work is already under way. After wriggling through the grassland of Hackney Marshes, the river passes the **WaterWorks Nature Reserve** (Lammas Road, 8988 7566, open 8am-9pm or dusk daily). A touchingly odd combination of golf course and nature reserve, these water-filter beds were built in 1849 to purify water during a cholera epidemic.

Three Mills Island

Three Mill Lane, E3 3DU (8980 4626/www. housemill.org.uk). Bromley-by-Bow tube. **Tours** *May-Dec* 1-4pm Sun. **Admission** £3; £1.50 reductions; free under-16s. **No credit cards.** This pretty island in the River Lea takes its name from the three mills that, until the 18th century, ground flour and gunpowder here. The House Mill, built in 1776, is the oldest and largest tidal mill in Britain and, though out of service, it is occasionally opened to the public. The island offers pleasant walks that can feel surprisingly rural once you're among the undergrowth. There's also a small café and, to puncture the idyll, one of the other mills is a TV studio.

WALTHAMSTOW

Walthamstow Central tube/rail.

Last year's sad news that **Walthamstow Stadium** greyhound track had been sold to developers (the 'Save Our Stow' campaign group were busy trying to buy it back to continue the racing as we went to press) puts the spotlight firmly on this area's other asset: quaint Walthamstow Village (*see p140* **Inside Track**), just a few minutes' walk east of the tube station. Further north, near the junction of Hoe Street and Forest Road, is peaceful Lloyd Park; the grand Georgian house at its entrance is home to the **William Morris Gallery** (*see below*) – the Arts and Crafts pioneer was a Walthamstow boy.

FREE William Morris Gallery

Lloyd Park, Forest Road, E17 4PP (8527 3782/ www.lbwf.gov.uk/wmg). Walthamstow Central tube/rail/34, 97, 215, 275 bus. **Open** 10am-5pm Thur-Sun. *Tours* phone for details. **Admission** free; donations appreciated. **Credit** (shop) MC, V. Artist, socialist and source of all that flowery wallpaper, William Morris lived here between 1848 and 1856. There are plenty of wonderful designs in fabric, stained glass and ceramic on show, produced by Morris and his acolytes. The gallery features the medieval-style helmet and sword the designer used as props for some of his murals, but we prefer the humbler domestic objects: Morris' coffee cup and the satchel he used to distribute his radical pamphlets. ▶ *You can also visit the Red House; see p150.*

Museum of London Docklands.

SIGHTS

South-east London

A proud maritime history meets the grubbiness of the inner city.

Most visitors are wary of venturing off the tube system, meaning they overlook the charms of the city's south-east. Don't be among them: there are frequent overground trains from London Bridge, extensive bus routes and a DLR network that keeps adding useful extensions.

And the rewards? Perhaps start with the immense view from the Wolfe monument in **Greenwich Park** across the river to the Docklands monoliths. After that, there are few free museums outside South Kensington that hold the amazing range of treasures displayed by **National Maritime Museum** or the **Horniman**, while the **Dulwich Picture Gallery** is an architectural, historic and artistic marvel. It's also worth exploring more widely to discover **Woolwich Arsenal**, with its soon-to-open DLR station and Thames Clipper connection to Canary Wharf, art deco **Eltham Palace** and Darwin's home **Down House**.

All over the south-east, gargantuan regeneration projects are kicking off with the demolition of infamous 1960s housing estates. Take note, fans of *A Clockwork Orange*, and pop down to SE28 before that brutalist backdrop is eradicated.

Map p404	Hotels p194
Restaurants &	Pubs & bars
bars p224	p239

KENNINGTON & THE ELEPHANT

Kennington tube/Elephant & Castle tube/rail.

Even back in the 17th century, the Elephant & Castle (named perhaps after the ivory-dealing Cutlers Company, or perhaps after Charles I's once-intended the Infanta of Castille) was a busy place. A junction for roads to Kennington, Walworth and Lambeth, it became a place to meet, trade and change carriages. By the early 20th century, it was a tram terminus and south London's West End. It then lost its looks to World War II bombing and a grisly 1960s makeover, becoming a famously ugly shopping centre that covered a forbidding warren of stench-ridden subways.

All this is now to change. One of the biggest regeneration programmes ever seen in Europe (£1.5 billion, 170 acres) is due for completion in 2014, with the shopping centre vanishing as early as next year. The arrival, in May 2008, of gaudy **St Mary's Churchyard Park**, with its new playground, benches and bizarre collection of orange and red molehills is just the start. Even so, some aspects of the ill-favoured Elephant will be missed, and the prospect of aspirational glass and chrome apartment blocks hardly inspires. It's also hard to imagine as you elbow through the still-salty area en route to the **Imperial War Museum** (*see below*).

Behind the museum, Kennington Road leads through an area once blighted by factory stink (young resident Charlie Chaplin's abiding memory). Today, the area's smarter houses are favoured by medics and lawyers requiring easy access to the city. For many, Kennington means cricket – especially in the beery atmosphere of a Test Match at the **Brit Oval** (*see p328*), home of Surrey County Cricket Club.

★ FREE Imperial War Museum
Lambeth Road, SE1 6HZ (7416 5320/www. iwm.org.uk). Lambeth North tube/Elephant & Castle tube/rail. **Open** 10am-6pm daily. **Admission** free. Special exhibitions prices vary. **Credit** MC, V. **Map** p404 N10.

Antique guns, tanks, aircraft and artillery are parked up in the main hall of this imposing edifice, built in 1814 as the Bethlehem Royal Hospital (Bedlam) – a lunatic asylum. The inmates were moved out in 1930 and the central block became the war museum, only to be damaged by World War II air raids. Today, the museum gives the history of armed conflict, especially involving Britain and the Commonwealth, from World War I to the present day.

Moving on from the more gung-ho exhibits on the ground floor, there are extensive galleries devoted to the two World Wars – on the Home Front, in Europe and further afield. The tone of the museum darkens as you ascend. On the third floor, the Holocaust Exhibition traces the history of European anti-Semitism and its nadir in the concentration camps – not recommended for under-14s. Upstairs, Crimes Against Humanity is a minimalist space in which a film exploring contemporary genocide and ethnic violence rolls relentlessly; this is unsuitable for under-16s. 'In Memoriam: Remembering the Great War,' which marks the 90th anniversary of the Armistice by concentrating on the lives of World War I combatants, continues until September; other special exhibitions include 'Unspeakable: The Artist as Witness to the Holocaust' (until August). The long-running Children's War exhibition ends its popular run in January 2010.

CAMBERWELL & PECKHAM

Denmark Hill, Nunhead or Peckham Rye rail.

The Camberwell Beauty still makes rare forays into Britain from Scandinavia, but the butterfly is hardly likely to ever again be found in the area where it was first identified. Camberwell is now more notable for the red buses that belch out fumes on their way to Dulwich, Peckham and the Elephant. Keep going down Church Street, though, past areas where old '60s blocks have been razed for yet more apartments to reach the town hall and **Camberwell College of Arts** (Peckham Road, 7514 6300), London's oldest art college, and the **South London Gallery** (*see p282*). Social life revolves around pubs such as the Bear (296A Camberwell New Road, SE5 0RP 7274 7037).

Moving east to Peckham, an area still associated with teenage gangs and down-at-heel traders from telly comedy fame, huge injections of cash from regeneration schemes continue to spruce up the streets. **Rye Lane**, however, looks like old Peckham, whereas Will Alsop's RIBA award-winning and frankly odd-looking library represents the new. It's in an area now known as **Peckham Square** that has a weekly farmers' market. Due south up Rye Lane is **Peckham Rye** – where Blake saw his angels – now a prettily laid-out park with well-kept gardens (Japanese, American, an arboretum).

Imperial War Museum.

SIGHTS

Keep walking south from Peckham Rye (or take a P4 or P12 bus) to enjoy views over London and Kent from Honor Oak and One Tree Hill, where Elizabeth I picnicked with Richard Bukeley of Beaumaris in 1602.

Travelling east from Peckham brings you to newly trendy **Nunhead**. Nunhead Lane has a traditional butchers, bakers, florist and fishmongers, but visitors should head along Linden Grove to **Nunhead Cemetery** – a mysterious Victorian maze of commemorative statuary half-buried by undergrowth.

DULWICH & CRYSTAL PALACE

Crystal Palace, East Dulwich, Herne Hill, North Dulwich or West Dulwich rail.

'The Village' of Dulwich is a little piece of rural England that guards its bucolic prosperity fiercely. The houses are big and detached; there's a village school and various posh delis.

> **INSIDE TRACK**
> **SIGN OF THE TIMES**
>
> So named because it was built on the site of a convent whose mother superior was beheaded, the once shabby **Old Nun's Head** (17 Nunhead Green, SE15 3QQ, 7639 4007) is now a fine gastropub.

Dulwich Picture Gallery.

It has an attractive park (once a favourite duelling spot), a historic boys' public school, founded by actor Edward Alleyn in 1616, and the **Dulwich Picture Gallery** (*see below*).

East and west of the village, East Dulwich and Herne Hill represent the middle(-class) way: smart, but not as expensive as Dulwich and less challenging than the relentless pace of Brixton (*see p151*). It's a pleasant, brisk half-hour's walk from Dulwich Picture Gallery across the park and up Lordship Lane to the **Horniman Museum** (*see below*) in Forest Hill.

Crystal Palace is so called because Joseph Paxton's famous structure, built for the Great Exhibition in Hyde Park in 1851, was moved here. It sat regally in parkland until a fire destroyed it in 1936. **Crystal Palace Park** still contains some arches and the sphinx from the Exhibition's Egyptian-themed display, as well as the Dinosaur Park, a lake surrounded by Benjamin Waterhouse-Hawkins's life-sized dinosaur statues. The park also has a maze, twisty paths and the **National Sports Centre** (*see p327*). Built in 1964 as a showpiece for the nation's sporting prowess, it might reach the end of a £4 million refurbishment some time in 2009. The **Crystal Palace Museum** (Anerley Hill, SE19 2BA, 8676 0700, www.crystalpalace museum.org.uk), opened by volunteers each weekend, has an 'exhibition of the Exhibition'.

★ Dulwich Picture Gallery
Gallery Road, SE21 7AD (8693 5254/www. dulwichpicturegallery.org.uk). North Dulwich or West Dulwich rail. **Open** 10am-5pm Tue-Fri; 11am-5pm Sat, Sun. **Admission** £5; £4 reductions; free under-16s, students, unemployed, disabled. **Credit** MC, V.

Lending weight to the idea that the best things come in small packages, this bijou gallery – the first to be purpose-built in the UK – was designed by Sir John Soane in 1811. (Soane also designed the mausoleum of the gallery's founders, Sir Francis Bourgeois, Noel Desanfans and his wife, Margaret.) It's a beautiful space that shows off Soane's ingenuity with and interest in lighting effects. The gallery displays a small but outstanding collection of work by Old Masters, offering a fine introduction to the baroque era through works by Rembrandt, Rubens, Poussin and Gainsborough. It also has a fine programme of temporary exhibitions and live events.

► *For Sir John Soane's Museum, see p73.*

★ FREE Horniman Museum
100 London Road, SE23 3PQ (8699 1872/www.horniman.ac.uk). Forest Hill rail/363, 122, 176, 185, 312, P4, P13 bus. **Open** 10.30am-5.30pm daily. **Admission** free; donations appreciated. **Credit** MC, V.

Justifiably cited as south-east London's premier free family attraction, the Horniman is a museum of many parts. Once the home of Frederick J Horniman, a tea trader and prodigious collector, it consists of an eccentric-looking art nouveau building whose main entrance gives out on to extensive gardens. Indoors, the oldest part of the museum is the Natural History gallery, dominated by an ancient walrus, mistakenly overstuffed by Victorian taxidermists, and now surrounded by lovely old glass cabinets containing pickled animals, stuffed birds and insect models. Other galleries include the Environment Room with its observation beehive, African Worlds, and the Centenary Gallery, which focuses on world cultures. Downstairs, the Music Room contains hundreds of instruments in glass cabinets: their sounds can be unleashed via touch-screen tables, while

SIGHTS

hardier instruments (flip-flop drums, thumb pianos) can be bashed with impunity. The most popular part of the museum is its showpiece Aquarium, where a series of tanks and rockpools cover seven distinct aquatic ecosystems. There are mesmerising moon jellyfish, strangely large British seahorses, starfish, tropical fish and creatures from the mangroves. Temporary exhibitions for 2009 will include the art installation 'China: Symbols in Silk'.

▶ *There's an excellent collection of automatic instruments at the Musical Museum; see p163.*

ROTHERHITHE

Rotherhithe tube.

Apart from the busy Surrey Quays retail park and ever-popular **Surrey Docks City Farm** (www.surreydocksfarm.org.uk) on the eastern side of the Rotherhithe Peninsula, this is a ghostly locale. A cobbled conservation area is flanked by a mish-mash of swanky riverside apartments, the capital's largest working marina (South Dock) and deserted ecoparks. Once a shipbuilding village and a centre for London's whaling trade in the 17th and 18th centuries, Rotherhithe's docks have long since been filled in. Take a glimpse at the old days in the **Brunel Engine House & Tunnel Exhibition** (*see below*) or peek at the mariners' church of **St Mary's Rotherhithe** (St Mary Church Street, SE16 4JE, 7967 0518, www.st maryrotherhithe.org). Completed in 1715, this community church was built by sailors and watermen. It contains many maritime oddities, not least a communion table and Bishop's chair in the Lady Chapel that were made from timber salvaged from warship the HMS *Temeraire*,

immortalised by Turner's famous painting (which can be seen in the National Gallery, *see p107*). Unless you fancy attending a service, these treasures have to be viewed through a glass door. Captain Christopher Jones was buried here in 1622; his ship was the *Mayflower*, which set sail from Rotherhithe in 1620, and a waterside pub of the same name marks the spot from which the pilgrims embarked.

Rotherhithe's road tunnel takes cars across to Limehouse (*see p139*). At the mouth of the tunnel stands the **Norwegian Church & Seaman's Mission**, one of a number of Scandinavian churches in the area. There's also a Finnish church – with a sauna – at 33 Albion Street (7237 1261). Across Jamaica Road, **Southwark Park**, London's oldest municipal park, has a community art gallery (7237 1230, www.cafegalleryprojects.com), an old bandstand, a lake and playgrounds.

Brunel Engine House & Tunnel Exhibition
Brunel Engine House, Railway Avenue, SE16 4LF (7231 3840/www.brunelenginehouse.org.uk). Rotherhithe tube. **Open** 10am-5pm daily. *Tours*

Horniman Museum.

by appointment only. **Admission** £2; £1 reductions; £5 family; free under-5s. **No credit cards**.

This little museum occupies the original engine house where the father and son team – Sir Marc and Isambard Kingdom Brunel – worked to create the world's first tunnel beneath a navigable river. It took them nearly two decades from 1825. The story of their achievement is told most entertainingly during guided tours (see the website for details). There's a pleasant riverside café and attractive gardens.

▶ *For a model of Brunel's monster steamship, SS Great Eastern, which was launched just across the Thames from here, visit the Museum of London Docklands; see p140.*

GREENWICH

Cutty Sark DLR for Maritime Greenwich.

A tourist showcase, riverside Greenwich is an irresistible mixture of maritime, royal and horological history, all of which have earned it recognition as a UNESCO World Heritage Site. Even better, the permanent attractions are gathered around **Greenwich Park**, a handsome green space with exceptional views. Royalty has stalked the area since 1300, when Edward I stayed here. Greenwich Palace, a favourite Tudor residence that was built in 1437, was the birthplace of Henry VIII. It survived until 1652, when the Parliamentarians made free with its treasures and turned it into a biscuit factory. Its remains were eventually demolished to make way for Christopher Wren's Royal Naval Hospital – later the **Royal Naval College** (*see right*). The **Greenwich Gateway Visitor Centre** (0870 608 2000, www.greenwich.gov.uk), based in the College, is a useful first port of call. A short walk away, shoppers swarm to **Greenwich Market**.

Keeping the river to your left, you reach the Thames-lapped **Trafalgar Tavern** (6 Park Row, 8858 2909), haunt of Thackeray, Dickens and Wilkie Collins, and the **Cutty Sark Tavern** (4-6 Ballast Quay, 8858 3146), which dates to 1695. Near the DLR stop, now with a Novotel hotel and cocktail bar on the forecourt, is Greenwich Pier. Every quarter of an hour at peak times the **Thames Clipper** commuter boat (0870 781 5049, www.thamesclippers.com) shuttles to and from central London. The pier is beside the tarp-covered work-in-progress that is the **Cutty Sark** (www.cuttysark.org.uk). This historic vessel, the fastest ever sailing tea clipper, was halfway through a comprehensive conservation project when it was devastated by fire – apparently caused by a vacuum cleaner overheating. The restored vessel will be ship-shape, 90% original and, for the first time, raised above curious visitors for early 2010.

From the riverside it's a ten-minute walk (or you can take the shuttle bus) up the steep slopes of Greenwich Park to the **Royal Observatory** (*see p149*). This building looks even more stunning at night, when the bright green Meridian Line Laser illuminates the path of the Prime Meridian across the London sky.

The riverside Thames Path leads past rusting piers and boarded-up factories, and rather unsatisfactorily over the Blackwall Tunnel approach, to the **Greenwich Peninsula**. It's dominated by the **O2** (*see p313*), formerly known as the Millennium Dome. Designed by the Richard Rogers Partnership for a millennial knees-up, this once-maligned structure's fortunes have changed considerably since its change of use. It boasts of being the world's 'best concert venue' – who judges such things? – but was certainly London's *first* purpose-built concert venue since the Royal Albert Hall opened in 1871. Last year's Tutankhamun exhibition at the O2 brought more than one million visitors; Dr Gunther van Hagens 'Bodyworlds' (until March 2009) may well repeat the trick. More wholesome culture can be found in **Greenwich Peninsula Ecology Park** (*see p288*) or on riverside walks that afford broad, flat, bracing views and various artworks – look out for *Slice of Reality*, a rusting ship cut in half by Richard Wilson and plonked to the west of the O2.

Fan Museum

12 Crooms Hill, SE10 8ER (8305 1441/8293 1889/www.fan-museum.org). Cutty Sark DLR/ Greenwich DLR/rail. **Open** 11am-5pm Tue-Sat; noon-5pm Sun (last admission 4.30pm). **Admission** £4; £3 reductions; £10 family; free under-7s; OAPs, disabled free 2-5pm Tue. **Credit** MC, V.

The world's most important collection of hand-held fans is displayed in a pair of restored Georgian town-houses. There are about 3,500 fans here, including some beauties in the Hélène Alexander collection,

---

INSIDE TRACK (UNDER)WATER WALKING

Close to the *Cutty Sark* is the entrance to a Victorian pedestrian tunnel right under the Thames. A little dank and full of echoes, especially whenever children are walking through, it's an entertaining way to get across to the Isle of Dogs (*see pp139-140*). There's a lift (7am-7pm Mon-Sat; 10am-5.30pm Sun) at either end and, from Island Gardens on the far side, Wren's favourite view of the **Old Royal Naval Hospital** (*see right*).

Royal Observatory & Planetarium. *See p149.*

but only a proportion is on display at any one time, rotated every four months or so. If you come on a Tuesday or Sunday afternoon you can also take an elegant tea in the Orangery. For fan-making workshops and temporary exhibitions, see the website.

★ FREE National Maritime Museum

Romney Road, SE10 9NF (8858 4422/ information 8312 6565/tours 8312 6608/ www.nmm.ac.uk). Cutty Sark DLR/Greenwich DLR/rail. **Open** 10am-5pm daily. *Tours* phone for details. **Admission** free; donations appreciated. **Credit** (shop) MC, V.

This, the world's largest maritime museum, opened in 1937. It contains a huge store of creatively organised maritime art, cartography, models and regalia. Ground-level galleries include Passengers, a delightful exploration of the 20th-century fashion for cruise travel, as well as the story of mass emigration by sea. Explorers covers great sea expeditions all the way back to medieval times. Maritime London concentrates on the city as a port.

Upstairs, Your Ocean reveals our dependence on the health of the world's oceans. Also on this level, in Gallery 15, is Nelson's Navy, exhibiting more than 250 objects drawn from the museum's collection of naval memorabilia from this period, including the undress coat worn by Nelson at the Battle of Trafalgar. Up on Level 2 are the interactives: The Bridge has a ship simulator and All Hands lets children load cargo and practise Morse Code. The Ship of War is the museum's collection of models and Oceans of Discovery commemorates the history of world exploration.

► *From the museum a colonnaded walkway leads to the Queen's House; see right. Up the hill in the park, the Observatory and Planetarium are also part of the museum; see p149.*

FREE Old Royal Naval College

Greenwich, SE10 9LW (8269 4747/group tours 8269 4791/www.oldroyalnavalcollege.org.uk). Cutty Sark DLR/Greenwich DLR/rail. **Open** 10am-5pm daily. *Tours* by arrangement. **Admission** free. **Credit** (shop) MC, V.

Designed by Wren in 1694, with Hawksmoor and Vanbrugh helping to complete the project, this superb collection of buildings was originally a hospital for the relief and support of seamen and their dependants. Pensioners lived here from 1705 to 1869, supplementing their pocket money with work as caddies at Blackheath Golf Club or as tourist guides. The complex became the Royal Naval College in 1873.

The Navy left in 1998, and the neoclassical buildings now house part of the University of Greenwich and Trinity College of Music. The public are allowed into the rococo chapel, where there are free organ recitals, and the Painted Hall, a tribute to William and Mary that took Sir James Thornhill 19 years to complete. Nelson lay in state in the Painted Hall for three days in 1806, before being taken to St Paul's Cathedral for his funeral. The Pepys building, currently the visitor centre, will become the £5.8-million Discover Greenwich education centre in winter 2009, when it will contain a permanent exhibition on Greenwich's history and a revived brewery (*see p232* **Profile**).

► *Nelson's tomb can be visited in the crypt of St Paul's Cathedral; see p61.*

FREE Queen's House

Romney Road, SE10 9NF (8312 6565/www. nmm.ac.uk). Cutty Sark DLR/Greenwich DLR/ rail. **Open** 10am-5pm daily. *Tours* noon, 2.30pm. **Admission** free; occasional charge for temporary exhibitions. *Tours* free. **Credit** (over £5) MC, V.

SIGHTS

SIGHTS

Charles Darwin had noted his preliminary thoughts about evolution a few years prior to his move from London to Kent in 1842. But it was the years of experimentation, correspondence and thinking at **Down House** (*see p150*), his home for 40 years, that gave Darwin enough evidence for him to contemplate publishing *On the Origin of the Species by Means of Natural Selection*, the book that revolutionised biology. Despite the less-than-catchy title, his book was an instant and controversial bestseller when it published in 1859.

To celebrate 150 years since the book's appearance, and 200 years since Darwin was born, Down House is reopening after extensive refurbishment. In the scientist's day, the house overflowed with playful children, piles of post and jars of exotic specimens. Even in the eerie stillness of the vacant rooms today, it's obvious that Darwin was constantly working: a jar of earthworms sits on Emma's cherished rosewood piano; a skeleton lies on the billiard table; trailing plants and bees take over the greenhouses.

The restored rooms downstairs use as much original furniture as possible, including Darwin's study chair, the board he laid across his lap to handwrite *Origin*, the backgammon set used for twice-daily games with Emma, and the signed copy of *Das Kapital* on his bookcase. Sir David Attenborough describes Darwin's life and work in a free hand-held multimedia tour.

Upstairs, displays explore Darwin's early years, his life-changing voyage on HMS *Beagle* (including a recreation of his ship study), and the development of and controversy surrounding the *Origin*. A handful of interactive exhibits illuminate the concepts of adaption and evolutionary theory, and plenty of Darwin paraphernalia is on display. Look out for the panama hat that shaded Darwin's balding pate during his *Beagle* adventures, his compass and pistol, his beetle collections and a browsable digital version of his pocket notebooks. There's even a clinical diary of the debilitating illness that cursed his life at Down House, through the course of which Darwin noted daily changes in symptoms with characteristic fastidiousness.

The immaculately tended grounds served as Darwin's own personal outdoor laboratory. You can walk in his footsteps, following the 'thinking' sandwalk that he himself constructed and walked around three times a day like clockwork, whatever the weather. With views across open countryside, it's hard to believe you're so close to London, but it's also easy to see how the routine cleared Darwin's head.

When Darwin died at Down House, aged 73, a little local funeral was planned. However, the science establishment had bigger ideas: the father of evolutionary theory was buried in **Westminster Abbey** (*see p112*), close to fellow science superstar Isaac Newton.

The art collection of the National Maritime Museum (*see p147*) is displayed in what was formerly the summer villa of Charles I's queen, Henrietta Maria. Completed in 1638 by Inigo Jones, the house has an interior as impressive as the paintings on the walls. As well as the stunning 1635 marble floor, look for Britain's first centrally unsupported spiral stair, and the fine painted woodwork and ceilings. The art collection includes portraits of famous maritime figures and works by Hogarth and Gainsborough.
► *Inigo Jones also designed Banqueting House (see p111) and St Paul's Covent Garden (see p83).*

Ranger's House

Chesterfield Walk, SE10 8QX (8853 0035/ www.english-heritage.org.uk). Blackheath rail/ Cutty Sark DLR/53 bus. **Open** *Apr-Sept* 10am-5pm Mon-Wed, Sun. *Oct-Dec* group bookings only. **Admission** £5.50; £2.80-£4.40 reductions; free under-5s. **Credit** MC, V.

The house of the 'Ranger of Greenwich Park', a post held by George III's niece, Princess Sophia Matilda, from 1815, now contains the collection of treasure amassed by millionaire Julius Wernher. A German, who made his fortune in the South African diamond trade, Wernher collected medieval and Renaissance art, including jewellery, bronzes, tapestries, furniture, porcelain and paintings. It's all displayed in 12 lovely rooms in this Georgian villa, whose back garden is the fragrant Greenwich Park rose collection.

★ FREE Royal Observatory & Planetarium

Greenwich Park, SE10 9NF (8312 6565/www. rog.nmm.ac.uk). Cutty Sark DLR/Greenwich DLR/ rail. **Open** 10am-5pm daily. *Tours* phone for details. **Admission** *Observatory* free. *Planetarium* £6; £4 reductions; £16 family. **Credit** MC, V.

This is an attraction of two halves. The north site chronicles Greenwich's horological connection. Flamsteed House (the Observatory originally built on the orders of Charles II, designed in 1675 by Sir Christopher Wren) contains the apartments of Sir John Flamsteed and other Astronomers Royal, as well as instruments used in timekeeping since the 14th century. The observatory on this site has a striking onion dome that houses the country's largest refracting telescope. In the courtyard is the Prime Meridian Line – star of a billion snaps of happy tourists with a foot in each hemisphere.

The south site is the Astronomy Centre, home to the Peter Harrison Planetarium and Weller Astronomy Galleries. The 120-seater planetarium's architecture cleverly reflects its astrological position: the semi-submerged cone tilts at 51.5 degrees, the latitude of Greenwich, pointing to the north star, and its reflective disc is aligned with the celestial equator. Daily and weekend shows include 'Black Holes: The Other Side of Infinity', narrated by Liam Neeson, and 'Starlife', a show describing the birth and death of stars. *Photo p147.*

WOOLWICH ARSENAL & THE THAMES BARRIER

Woolwich Arsenal or Woolwich Dockyard rail/Woolwich Arsenal DLR.

Established in Tudor times as the country's main source of munitions, Woolwich Arsenal stretched 32 miles along the river by World War I. It had its own internal railway system and employed 72,000 people. Much of the land was sold off during the '60s, but the main section has been preserved and is now home to **Firepower** (*see below*). To the south, the Royal Artillery Barracks has the longest Georgian façade in the country. The river here is spanned by a rather different architectural triumph: the impressively sculptural **Thames Barrier** (*see below*).

In other respects, this is a pretty grim bit of London. Regeneration can't come soon enough, and civilisation is indeed due to pull in later this year in the form of an extension of the DLR from King George V station under the river to Woolwich Arsenal. Until then, hop on the ramshackle **Woolwich Ferry** (8921 5786). These diesel-driven boats take pedestrians (for free) and cars across the river every ten minutes daily. The ferry to the north shore lands you by **North Woolwich Old Station Museum** (*see p140*).

Firepower

Royal Arsenal, SE18 6ST (8855 7755/www. firepower.org.uk). Woolwich Arsenal rail. **Open** 10.30am-5pm Wed-Sun. **Admission** £5; £2.50-£4.50 reductions; free under-5s; £12 family. **Credit** MC, V.

Firepower occupies a series of converted Woolwich Arsenal buildings beside the river, and fairly bristles with preserved artillery pieces, some of them many centuries old. An introductory presentation in the Breech Cinema tells the story of the Royal Artillery, leading on to 'Field of Fire', where four massive screens relay archive film and documentary footage of desert and jungle warfare. Smoke fills the air, searchlights pick out the ordnance that surrounds you and the sound of exploding bombs shakes the floor. Across the courtyard another building contains a huge collection of trophy guns and the Cold War gallery, focused on the 'monster bits' (tanks and guns used from 1945 to the present). Here too is the Command Post, where a Rolling Rocks climbing wall, an Anderson shelter and a paintball range provide entertainment. There are special events throughout the year: the website has details.

Thames Barrier Information & Learning Centre

1 Unity Way, SE18 5NJ (8305 4188/www. environment-agency.gov.uk/thamesbarrier). North Greenwich tube/Charlton rail/180 bus.

SIGHTS

Open *Apr-Sept* 10.30am-4.30pm daily. *Oct-Mar* 11am-3.30pm daily. **Admission** £2; £1-£1.50 reductions; free under-5s. **Credit** MC, V.
This adjustable dam has been variously called a triumph of modern engineering and the eighth wonder of the world. The shiny silver fins, lined up across Woolwich Reach, are indeed an impressive sight. Built in 1982 at a cost of £535m, the barrier has already saved London from flooding some 80 times. The barrier is regularly in action for maintenance purposes – the website has a current timetable.

To learn more, pay £2 for a look around the learning centre, where you'll find an account of the 1953 flood that led to the barrier's construction, as well displays on wildlife in the Thames and how a flood would actually affect London. The learning centre is on the south side of the Thames, along with a pleasant café with riverside picnic benches. The north end of the Barrier, meanwhile, sits adjacent to lovely Thames Barrier Park (*see p140*).

FURTHER SOUTH-EAST

Watling Street, the old pilgrims' way out of London to Canterbury, is now the A207 and the villages it once passed through are suburbs. South of the pilgrims' way, Eltham was well known to Londoners, particularly to Geoffrey Chaucer. He served as the clerk of works during improvements to **Eltham Palace** (*see below*) in the reign of Richard II – and was once mugged on his way to work here. When the Courtaulds bought Eltham Palace in the early 1930s, it was in deepest Kent. As the suburbs encroached, they acquired more land to keep the great unwashed at bay, an acquisitiveness that has meant Eltham's present-day unwashed have been blessed with a delightful green oasis.

Paths around the area link up with the **Green Chain Walk** (www.greenchain.com), a 40-mile network starting near the Thames Barrier (*see above*) and ending at Crystal Palace (*see p144*), having taken in ancient woodland along the way. Further south into Kent, the village of **Chislehurst** has some impressive Druids' caves (8467 3264, www.chislehurstcaves.co.uk).

**INSIDE TRACK
BARRIER VIEWS**

For a waterborne view of the Thames Barrier feat of engineering, take the **Woolwich Ferry** (*see p149*) or, from Greenwich, hop on a **Thames River Services** boat (7930 4097, www.thames riverservices.co.uk; Mar-Oct only). Another fine vantage, on the north bank, is **Thames Barrier Park** (*see p140*).

★ **Down House**
Downe, Bromley, Kent BR6 7JT (01689 859119/www.english-heritage.org.uk). Bromley North or Bromley South rail then 146 bus/ Orpington rail then R8 bus. **Open** *Sept-June* 11am-5pm Wed-Sun. *July-Aug* 11am-5pm daily. **Admission** £9; £4.50-£7.70 reductions; £22.50 family. **Credit** (house only) MC, V.
See p148 **House of Science**. *Photos p148.*
▶ *The Herbarium at Kew contains specimens that were brought back to Britain by Darwin on HMS Beagle; see p156.*

★ **Eltham Palace**
Court Yard, SE9 5QE (8294 2548/www.english-heritage.org.uk). Eltham rail. **Open** *Feb, Mar, Nov, Dec* 11am-4pm Mon-Wed, Sun. *Apr-Oct* 10am-5pm Mon-Wed, Sun. **Admission** *House & grounds* (incl audio tour) £8.20; £4.10-£6.60 reductions; free under-5s; £20.50 family. *Grounds only* £5.10; £2.60-£4.10 reductions; free under-5s. **Credit** MC, V.
When the minted society couple Stephen and Virginia Courtauld bought this ancient palace in 1931, it had been out of favour as a sovereign residence for centuries. Originally acquired by Edward II in 1305, and enjoyed by Henry VIII as a child, Eltham was abandoned in favour of Greenwich and fell into disrepair. What remains of the royal residence is the Great Hall, used as a barn for decades, but repaired by the Courtaulds in the style they thought fitting. Other medieval remains include the stone bridge over the moat (now filled with carp as big as otters) over which you enter the grounds. The Courtaulds lived, briefly, a charmed life here and Stephen, with a sure designer's eye, transformed the house into a paean to art deco glamour.

Red House
13 Red House Lane, Bexleyheath, Kent DA6 8JF (bookings 8304 9878/information 01494 559799/www.nationaltrust.org.uk). Bexleyheath rail then 15min walk or taxi from station. **Open** (pre-booked tour only) *Mar-Nov* 11am-4.45pm Wed-Sun. *Dec* 11am-4.45pm Fri-Sun. **Admission** £6.90; £3.45 reductions; £17.25 family. *Gardens only* 50p. **Credit** MC, V.
This handsome red-brick house down in deepest Bexleyheath was built in 1859 for William Morris, whose Society for the Protection of Ancient Buildings gave rise to the National Trust itself. In furnishing Red House, Morris sought to combine his taste for Gothic romanticism with the need for practical domesticity. Beautifully detailed stained glass, tiling, paintings and items of furniture remain in the house, and plenty is being uncovered in the continuing restoration work. The new 50p ticket gives access to the garden, tearoom and shop.
▶ *For fans of Morris, the William Morris Gallery in Walthamstow may be a bit more accessible; see p141.*

South-west London

The river runs through it.

South-west London is a strange mixture of gentrifying urban and pure urban gentry. The former covers a range of areas, from the nightlife and streetlife of Brixton and Vauxhall to the family-friendly charms of Clapham, with its wide common, and Battersea, with its riverside park. The latter is represented by semi-rural suburbs like Richmond, Putney and Wimbledon, which have some of the highest house prices outside central London. Here, the same things that appeal to the self-congratulatory locals draw in casual visitors: proximity to the Thames, the wide expanse of **Richmond Park** with its herds of deer and world-class attractions such as **Kew Gardens** and **Hampton Court Palace**.

| Restaurants & cafés p225 | Hotels p194 |
| Pubs & bars p239 | |

Restaurants & cafés p225 Hotels p194 Pubs & bars p239

SIGHTS

VAUXHALL, STOCKWELL & BRIXTON

Brixton or Vauxhall tube/rail, Stockwell tube.

The area now known as Vauxhall was, in the 13th century, home to a big house owned by one Falkes de Bréauté, a soldier rewarded for carrying out King John's dirtier military deeds. Over time Falkes' Hall became Fox Hall and finally Vauxhall. Vauxhall's heyday was in the 18th century when the infamous Pleasure Gardens, built back in 1661, reached the height of their popularity. As described in William Thackeray's *Vanity Fair*, the wealthy mingled here with the not-so-wealthy, getting into all kinds of trouble on 'lovers' walks'.

INSIDE TRACK
ART COMES OF AGE

Close to the chaos of Brixton station is the excellent 21-year-old **Brixton Art Gallery** (35 Brixton Station Road, www.brixtonartgallery.co.uk), with changing displays of contemporary art. Turn the corner and you're in the extended, colourful and noisy mess of **Brixton Market**.

The Gardens closed in 1859 and the area became reasonably respectable – all that remains is Spring Garden, behind popular gay haunt the Royal Vauxhall Tavern (**RVT**, *see p302*). For a glimpse of old Vauxhall head to lovely, leafy **Bonnington Square**, a bohemian enclave thanks to its squatter heritage. Down on the river is the cream and emerald ziggurat designed by Terry Farrell for the Secret Intelligence Service. On the other side of the south end of Vauxhall Bridge stands St George's Wharf, a glitzy apartment complex justifiably nicknamed the 'five ugly sisters'.

At the top end of the South Lambeth Road, **Little Portugal** – a cluster of Portuguese cafés, shops and tapas bars – is an enticing oasis. At the other end, **Stockwell** is prime commuter territory, with little to lure visitors except some charming Victorian backstreets: Albert Square, Durand Gardens and Stockwell Park Crescent. Hackford Road was briefly home to Van Gogh (at no.87), while at no.100 the **Type Museum** (7735 0055, www.typemuseum.org) is currently working towards opening its premises, a former veterinary hospital, to the public.

South of Stockwell is **Brixton**, a lively hub of clubs and music, with a long-established Afro-Caribbean community – indeed, the Black Cultural Archives are developing a Centre for Black Heritage that should open (most likely in

Profile Royal Botanic Gardens, Kew

London's green wonder reaches its 250th anniversary.

Kew's lush, landscaped beauty represents the pinnacle of our national gardening obsession. From the early 1700s until 1840, when the gardens were given to the nation, these were the grounds for two fine royal residences – the White House and Richmond Lodge. Early resident Queen Caroline, wife of George II, was very fond of exotic plants brought back by voyaging botanists. In 1759, the renowned 'Capability' Brown was employed by George III to improve on the work here of his predecessors, William Kent and Charles Bridgeman. Thus began the shape of the extraordinary garden that today attracts hundreds of thousands of visitors every year.

Covering half a square mile, Kew feels surprisingly big – pick up a map at the ticket office and follow the handy signs. For the anniversary, TV celebrity gardener Diarmuid Gavin is creating a new garden by the main gate; there will also be new plantings of British orchids and a Thames Valley native,

wild clary. But head straight for the 19th-century greenhouses, filled to the roof with plants – some of which have been here as long as the huge glass structures themselves. The sultry **Palm House** holds tropical plants: palms, bamboo, tamarind, mango and fig trees, not to mention fragrant hibiscus and frangipani. (Downstairs, the Marine Display isn't always open – but it has seahorses.) The **Temperate House** features *Pendiculata sanderina*, the Holy Grail for orchid hunters, with petals some three feet long. Also of note is the **Princess of Wales Conservatory**, divided into ten climate zones. There's a 'Tropical Extravaganza' this year: orchids and bug-eating plants.

For an interesting perspective on 18th-century life, head to **Kew Palace** (www.hrp.org.uk/KewPalace; £5, free-£4.50 reductions) – Britain's smallest royal palace. Little more than an addition to the now-gone White House, the building opens from March to September. On the opposite side of the gardens is a 163-foot Japanese **pagoda**, completed in 1762, with a formal rock garden just nearby. But wherever you wander here, lovely planned vistas open up.

THREE TO SEE

Waterlily House
Closed in winter, the quiet, round indoor pond is just lovely.

Rhododendron Dell
Capabilty Brown's finest idea. Visit in May.

Xstrata Treetop Walkway
Get in among the leaves, almost 60ft above the ground.

Raleigh Hall) by 2010. An interesting, often unpredictable area, Brixton has a big, chaotic street market. Its main streets are modern and filled with chain stores, but there is also some attractive architecture – check out the 1911 **Ritzy Cinema** (Brixton Oval, Coldharbour Lane, 0871 704 2065, www.picturehouses.co.uk). Brixton's best-known street, **Electric Avenue**, was immortalised during the 1980s by Eddy Grant's eponymous song – it got its name when, in 1880, it became one of the first shopping streets to get electric lights. The Clash's 'Guns of Brixton' famously deals with the tensions felt here in the 1980s, but the rage of the persecuted black community, still finding themselves isolated and under suspicion decades after arriving from the West Indies, is expressed by dub poet Linton Kwesi Johnson – try 'Sonny's Lettah (Anti-Sus Poem)' and 'Five Nights of Bleeding' for starters. The riots of 1981 and 1985 around Railton Road and Coldharbour Lane left the district scarred for years.

BATTERSEA

Battersea Park or Clapham Junction rail.

Battersea started life as an island in the Thames, but it was reclaimed when the surrounding marshes were drained. Huguenots settled here from the 16th century and, prior to the Industrial Revolution, the area was mostly farmland. The river is dominated by Sir Giles Gilbert Scott's magnificent four-chimneyed **Battersea Power Station** (www.batterseapowerstation.org.uk), which can be seen close up from all trains leaving Victoria station. Images of this iconic building have graced album covers (notably Pink Floyd's *Animals*) and films (among them Ian McKellen's *Richard III*, Michael Radford's *1984*), and its instantly recognisable silhouette pops up repeatedly as you move around the capital. Work started on what was to become the largest brick-built structure in Europe in 1929 and the power station was in operation through to the early 1980s. Too impressive to be destroyed, the power station's future continues to be the subject of intense public debate – who knows if the latest ambitious, modishly 'green' plan hatched by Real Estate Opportunities will survive current economic woes. Meanwhile, the roofless power station continues to suffer weather damage.

Overlooking the river a little further west, **Battersea Park** (www.batterseapark.org) has beautiful lakes (one with a fine Barbara Hepworth sculpture) and gardens. Much of the park was relandscaped in 2004 according to the original 19th-century plans, albeit with some modern additions left in place: the Russell Page Garden, designed for the 1951 Festival of

Britain; a Peace Pagoda, built by a Buddhist sect in 1985 to commemorate Hiroshima Day; a small petting zoo (7924 5826; *see p288*); and an art gallery within a Grade II-listed brick building (the Pumphouse, 7350 0523, www.wandsworth.gov.uk/gallery). The park extends to the Thames; from the wide and lovely riverside walk you can see both the elaborate **Albert Bridge** and the simpler **Battersea Bridge**, rebuilt between 1886 and 1890 by the sewer engineer, Joseph Bazalgette.

Keep on west of the bridges to find the beautiful church of **St Mary's Battersea** (Battersea Church Road); this was where poet William Blake was married and Benedict Arnold, who contrived to fight on both sides during the American War of Independence, is buried. From here, JMW Turner used to paint the river.

CLAPHAM & WANDSWORTH

Clapham Common tube, Wandsworth Common rail or Wandsworth Town rail.

In the 18th and 19th centuries Clapham was colonised by the wealthy upper classes and social reformers, notably abolitionist William Wilberforce's Clapham Sect. But the coming of the railways meant that the posh folk upped sticks, and from 1900 the area fell into decline. Nowadays the area is once again one of the capital's more desirable addresses. **Clapham Common** provides an oasis of peace amid busy traffic, with Holy Trinity Church, which dates from 1776, at its perimeter. During the summer, the common switches into music festival mode, attracting thousands to a series of high-profile events. From Clapham Common station, turn north into the street called **The Pavement** – it leads to the pubs and shops of Clapham Old Town. Alternatively, head south to the smart shops and cafés of **Abbeville Road**. The area to the west of the common is known as 'Nappy Valley', because of the many young middle-class families who reside there. They're out in force at weekends. If you can fight your way between the baby carriages, head straight for **Northcote Road** – especially on weekends, when a lovely little market sets up. Rocketing rents have meant closures and the loss of some character, but it still bustles. Is the future here now Starbucks (no.33) or the Hive Honey Shop (no.93)?

PUTNEY & BARNES

East Putney or Putney Bridge tube, Barnes or Putney rail.

If you want proof of an area's well-to-do credentials, count the rowing clubs: Putney has a couple of dozen. Putney Bridge is partly

SIGHTS

responsible, as its buttresses made it difficult for large boats to continue upstream, creating a stretch of water conducive to rowing. The **Oxford & Cambridge Boat Race** (*see p270*) has started in Putney since 1845. The river has good paths in either direction; heading west along the Putney side of the river will take you past the **WWT Wetland Centre** (*below*), which lies alongside **Barnes Common**. The main road across the expanse, Queen's Ride, humpbacks over the railway line below. It was here, on 16 September 1977, that singer Gloria Jones's Mini drove off the road, killing her passenger (and boyfriend) T-Rex singer Marc Bolan. The slim trunk of the sycamore tree hit by the car is covered with notes, poems and declarations of love; steps lead to a bronze bust.

★ WWT Wetland Centre

Queen Elizabeth's Walk, SW13 9WT (8409 4400/www.wwt.org.uk). Hammersmith tube then 283 bus/Barnes rail/33, 72 209 bus. **Open** *Mar-Oct 9.30am-6pm daily. Nov-Feb 9.30am-5pm daily.* **Admission** £8.95; £4.95-£6.70 reductions; £25 family; free under-4s. **Credit** MC, V.
The 43-acre Wildfowl & Wetlands Trust Wetland Centre may be a mere four miles from central London, but it feels like a world away. Quiet ponds, rushes, rustling reeds and wildflower gardens all teem with bird life – some 150 species – as well as the now very rare water vole (think Ratty from *The*

Electric Avenue. See p153.

Wind in the Willows). Naturalists ponder its 27,000 trees and 300,000 aquatic plants, swoon over 300 varieties of butterfly, 20 types of dragonfly, and four species of bat. Until 1989, the site consisted of four huge concrete reservoirs owned by the local water company. Then Sir Peter Scott transformed the marshy space into a unique wildlife habitat. The visitors' centre has a café with an outdoor terrace. If you forget your binoculars, hire them on site.

KEW & RICHMOND

*Kew Gardens or Richmond tube/rail,
Kew Bridge rail.*

Kew's big appeal is its vast and glorious **Royal Botanic Gardens** (*see p156*). The **National Archives** – formerly the Public Records Office – are housed here too, a repository for everything from the Domesday Book to recently released government documents. The place is always full of people researching their family trees. Overlooking the gardens is the **Watermans Arts Centre** (40 High Street, TW8 0DS, 8232 1010, www.watermans.org.uk), which contains a gallery, independent cinema, 239-seater theatre, bar and restaurant. The centre focuses on Brit-Asian and South Asian arts in particular. Much of Kew has a rarified air, with leafy streets that lead you into a quaint world of teashops, tiny bookstores and gift shops, a sweet village green, ancient pubs and pleasant riverpaths.

Originally known as the Shene, the wealthy area of **Richmond**, about 15 minutes' walk west down Kew Road, has been linked with royalty for centuries: Edward III had a palace here in the 1300s and Henry VII loved the area so much that in 1501 he built another (naming it Richmond after his favourite earldom); this was where Elizabeth I spent her last summers. Ultimately, the whole neighbourhood took the palace's name, although the building itself is long gone – pretty much all that's left is a small gateway on **Richmond Green**. On the east side of the Green, medieval alleys (such as Brewer's Lane) replete with ancient pubs lead to the traffic-choked high street. The **Church of St Mary Magdalene**, on Paradise Road, blends architectural styles from 1507 to 1904. A short walk away in Richmond's Old Town Hall, you'll find the small **Museum of Richmond** (Whittaker Avenue, 8332 1141, www.museumofrichmond.com, closed Mon & Sun). Nearby, the riverside promenade is eminently strollable and dotted with pubs; the **White Cross** (Water Lane, 8940 6844), which has been here since 1835, has a special 'entrance at high tide' – the river floods regularly. The 13 arches of Richmond Bridge date from 1774 – this is the oldest surviving crossing over the Thames and offers fine sweeping views.

SIGHTS

Richmond Park is the largest of the Royal Parks, occupying some 2,500 acres. There are hundreds of red and fallow deer roaming free across it – presumably much happier without having to listen out for the 'View halloo!' of one of Henry VIII's hunting parties. Within the park's bounds are the Palladian splendour of White Lodge and Pembroke Lodge, childhood home to philosopher Bertrand Russell but now a café. From the park's highest point, there are unobstructed views of St Paul's Cathedral (*see p61*) more than twelve miles in the distance.

Royal Botanic Gardens (Kew Gardens)

Kew, Richmond, Surrey TW9 3AB (8332 5655/ information 8940 1171/www.kew.org). Kew Gardens tube/rail/Kew Bridge rail/riverboat to Kew Pier. **Open** *Apr-Aug* 9.30am-6.30pm Mon-Fri; 9.30am-7.30pm Sat, Sun. *Sept, Oct* 9.30am-6pm daily. *Late Oct-early Feb* 9.30am-4.15pm daily. *Early Feb-late Mar* 9.30am-5.30pm daily. **Admission** £13; £12 reductions; free under-17s. **Credit** AmEx, MC, V.
See p152 **Profile**. *Photos p152.*

WIMBLEDON

Wimbledon tube/rail.

Beyond the world-famous tennis tournament, Wimbledon is little but a wealthy and genteel suburb. Turn left out of the station on to the uninspiring **Broadway**, and you'll wonder why you bothered. So turn right instead, climbing a steep hill lined with huge houses. At the top is **Wimbledon Village**, a trendy little enclave of posh shops, eateries and some decent pubs.

From here you can hardly miss Wimbledon Common, a huge, wild, partly wooded park, criss-crossed by paths and horse tracks (*see below* **Inside Track**). East of the common lies Wimbledon Park, with its boating lake, and the All England Lawn Tennis Club and **Wimbledon Lawn Tennis Museum** (*see below*). Two other attractions are worth seeking out – lovely, Grade II-listed **Cannizaro Park** (www.cannizaropark.org.uk) and the gorgeous **Buddhapadipa Temple** (14 Calonne Road, Wimbledon Parkside, 8946 1357, www.buddha padipa.org). When it was built in the early 1980s, this was the only Thai temple in Europe. The warm and sweet-smelling Shrine Room contains a golden statue of Buddha, a copy of the Buddhashing in Bangkok's National Museum. Visitors are welcome, but shoes must be removed before entering the temple, you are not permitted to touch the monks and the soles of your feet must never face the Buddha.

156 Time Out London

INSIDE TRACK WIMBLEDON WINDMILL

An eccentric touch, and certainly worth seeking out: Wimbledon Common has a **windmill** (Windmill Road, 8947 2825, www.wimbledonwindmillmuseum.org.uk). Here Baden-Powell wrote *Scouting for Boys* (1910), but it is now home to a tearoom and hands-on milling museum.

Wimbledon Lawn Tennis Museum

Museum Building, All England Lawn Tennis Club, Church Road, SW19 5AE (8946 6131/ www.wimbledon.org/museum). Southfields tube/39, 493 bus. **Open** 10.30am-5pm daily; ticket holders only during championships. **Admission** (incl tour) £15.50; £11-£13.75 reductions; free under-5s. **Credit** MC, V.
Highlights at this popular museum on the history of tennis include a 200° cinema screen that allows you to find out what it's like to play on Centre Court and a re-creation of a 1980s men's dressing room, complete with a 'ghost' of John McEnroe. Visitors can also enjoy a behind-the-scenes tour.

FURTHER SOUTH-WEST

Richmond tube/rail, Hampton Court or St Margaret's rail.

If the water level allows, follow the river from Richmond on a pastoral walk west. You could stop at **Petersham**, home to the Petersham Nurseries with its garden café (Church Lane, off Petersham Road, 8605 3627, www.petersham nurseries.com), or take in a grand country mansion, perhaps **Ham House** (*see below*) or **Marble Hill House** (*see p158*). Next door is **Orleans House Gallery** (*see p158*).

Further along, the river meanders past Twickenham, home to rugby's **Twickenham Stadium** (*see p158*), to the evocatively named **Strawberry Hill** (0870 626 0402, www.friends ofstrawberryhill.org), home of Horace Walpole, who pretty much invented the Gothic novel with *The Castle of Otranto* (1764) and filled the place with Gothic curios. Several miles further along the Thames, after a leisurely trip through suburban Kingston, the river passes beside the magnificent **Hampton Court Palace** (*see p157*). Few visitors will want to walk this far, of course – instead take a train from Waterloo or, for that extra fillip of adventure, a boat.

★ Ham House

Ham, Richmond, Surrey TW10 7RS (8940 1950/www.nationaltrust.org.uk/hamhouse). Richmond tube/rail then 371 bus. **Open**

Gardens 11am-6pm or dusk if earlier Mon-Wed, Sat, Sun. *House* Late Mar-Oct noon-4pm Mon-Wed, Sat, Sun. **Admission** *House & gardens* £9.90; £5.50 reductions; £25.30 family; free under-5s. *Gardens only* £3.30; £2.20 reductions; £8.80 family; free under-5s. **Credit** MC, V.

Built in 1610 for one of James I's courtiers, Thomas Vavasour, this lavish red-brick mansion is full of period furnishings, rococo mirrors and ornate tapestries. Detailing is exquisite, down to a table in the dairy with sculpted cows' legs. The restored formal grounds also attract attention: there's a lovely trellised Cherry Garden and some lavender parterres. The tearoom in the old orangery turns out historic dishes (lavender syllabub, for instance) using ingredients from the Kitchen Gardens.

▶ *A ferry crosses the river (Feb-Oct, weekends only in winter) to Marble Hill House; see p158.*

★ Hampton Court Palace

East Molesey, Surrey KT8 9AU (0870 751 5175/ 0870 752 7777/0870 753 7777/information 0844 482 7777/www.hrp.org.uk). Hampton Court rail/ riverboat from Westminster or Richmond to Hampton Court Pier (Apr-Oct). **Open** *Palace* Apr-Oct 10am-6pm daily. Nov-Mar 10am-4.30pm daily. *Park* dawn-dusk daily. **Admission** *Palace, courtyard, cloister & maze* £13.30; £6.65-£11.30 reductions; £37 family; free under-5s. *Maze only* £3.50; £2.50 reductions. *Gardens only* Apr-Oct £4.60; £4 reductions. Nov-Feb free. **Credit** AmEx, MC, V.

It may be a half-hour train ride from central London, but this spectacular palace, once owned by Henry VIII, is well worth the trek. It was built in 1514 by Cardinal Wolsey, the high-flying Lord Chancellor, but Henry liked it so much he seized it for himself in 1528. For the next 200 years it was a focal point of English history: Elizabeth I was imprisoned in a tower by her jealous and fearful elder sister Mary I; Shakespeare gave his first performance to James I in 1604; and, after the Civil War, Oliver Cromwell was so besotted by the building he ditched his puritanical principles and moved in to enjoy its luxuries.

Centuries later, the rosy walls of the palace still dazzle. Its vast size can be daunting, so it's a good idea to take advantage of the costumed guided tours – or to get involved with the plethora of special events to mark the 500th anniversary of Henry's accession in 1509, including recreated wedding parties for his nuptials with Catherine Parr. If you do decide to go it alone, start with King Henry VIII's State Apartments, which include the Great Hall, noted for its splendid hammer-beam roof, beautiful stained-glass windows and elaborate religious tapestries; in the Haunted Gallery, the ghost of Catherine Howard – Henry's fifth wife, executed for adultery in 1542 – can reputedly be heard shrieking. The King's Apartments, added in 1689 by Sir Christopher Wren, are notable for a splendid mural of Alexander the Great, painted by Antonio Verrio. The Queen's Apartments and Georgian Rooms feature similarly elaborate paintings, chandeliers and tapestries, and the Council Chamber will be displaying together for the first time this year contemporaneous portraits of all six of Henry VIII's wives – and a book of music written for Anne Boleyn by one of her possible lovers. The Tudor Kitchens are great fun, with their giant cauldrons, fake pies and blood-spattered walls.

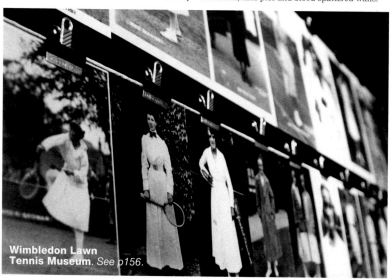

Wimbledon Lawn Tennis Museum. *See p156.*

SIGHTS

More spectacular sights await outside, where the exquisitely landscaped gardens contain superb topiary, peaceful Thames views, a new reconstruction of a 16th-century heraldic garden and the famous Hampton Court maze. In summer there's a music festival and a flower show that rivals that at Chelsea; in winter check out the ice-skating rink.

Marble Hill House

Richmond Road, Twickenham, Middx TW1 2NL (8892 5115/www.english-heritage.org.uk). Richmond tube/rail/St Margaret's rail/33, 90, 490, H22, R70 bus. **Open** *Apr-Oct* 10am-2pm Sat; 10am-5pm Sun; group visits Mon-Fri by request. *Nov-Mar* by request. **Admission** £4.20; £3.40 reductions; free under-5s. **Credit** MC, V.

King George II spared no expense to win the favour of his mistress, Henrietta Howard. Not only did he build this perfect Palladian house (1724) for his lover, he almost dragged Britain into a war while doing so: by using Honduran mahogany to construct the grand staircase, he managed to spark off a major diplomatic row with Spain. Frankly, it was worth it. Picnic parties are welcome to the grounds here, as are sporty types (there are tennis, putting and cricket facilities). A programme of concerts and events keeps things busy in the summer, and ferries regularly cross the Thames to neighbouring Ham House (*see p156*).

FREE Orleans House Gallery

Riverside, Twickenham, Middx TW1 3DJ (8831 6000/www.richmond.gov.uk/orleans_house_gallery). Richmond tube then 33, 490, H22, R68, R70 bus/St Margaret's or Twickenham rail. **Open** *Apr-Sept* 1-5.30pm Tue-Sat; 2-5.30pm Sun. *Oct-Mar* 1-4.30pm Tue-Sat; 2-4.30pm Sun. **Admission** free.

Secluded in pretty gardens, this Grade I-listed riverside house was constructed in 1710 for James Johnson, Secretary of State for Scotland. It was later named after the Duke of Orleans, Louis-Philippe, who lived in exile here from 1800 until 1817 before returning to France to claim his throne. Though the house was partially demolished in 1926, the building retains James Gibbs's neoclassical Octagon Room, which houses a soothing collection of paintings of the local countryside dating back to the early 1700s. A display shows off recreated Chinese wallpaper, just like that which Henrietta Howard hung in the dining room in 1751. Each sheet of this fine replica is, like the original, different, having been hand-painted by Chinese artists.

World Rugby Museum/ Twickenham Stadium

Twickenham Rugby Stadium, Rugby Road, Twickenham, Middx TW1 1DZ (8892 8877/ www.rfu.com). Hounslow East tube then 281 bus/ Twickenham rail. **Open** *Museum* 10am-5pm Tue-Sat; 11am-5pm Sun. *Tours* 10.30am, noon, 1.30pm, 3pm Tue-Sat; 1pm, 3pm Sun. **Admission** £10; £7 reductions; £34 family. **Credit** AmEx, MC, V.

The impressive Twickenham Stadium is the home of English rugby union. Tickets for international matches are extremely hard to come by, but the Museum of Rugby offers some compensation. Tours take in the England dressing room, the players' tunnel and the Royal Box. Memorabilia, selected from some 10,000 pieces, charts the game's development.

RVT. *See p151.*

West London

Great wealth and wondrous places of easter

West London is a quadrant of the city's compass that's somehow turned inside-out. London's other cardinal compass points have posh suburbs near the M25, with hard-bitten estates closer to the centre. But the smartest parts of the West – Fulham, Kensington, Notting Hill – are near the centre of town, with working-class districts such as **Southall** and **Wembley** pushed out beyond. That's largely because west London was the first of the city's frontiers to be developed: those elegant Georgian townhouses in **Holland Park** and **Kensington** were once the fringe of the City of Westminster, and have retained their high status. The Victorians continued the trend – partly because the prevailing winds blew the coal smogs eastwards, providing a model for urban expansion across the capital.

| Maps p394, p396 | Hotels p194 |
| Restaurants & cafés p225 | Pubs & bars p240 |

KENSINGTON & HOLLAND PARK

High Street Kensington or Holland Park tube.

There are more millionaires per square mile in this corner of London than in any other part of Europe, a hangover from the days when Kensington was a semi-rural retreat for aristocrats. Just off **Kensington High Street**, one of London's classiest shopping stretches, handsome squares are lined with grand 19th-century houses, many of them still homes.

Linking with Notting Hill (*see p101*) to the north, **Kensington Church Street** has many antiques shops selling furniture so fine you would probably never dare use it. **St Mary Abbots** (7937 6032, www.stmaryabbotschurch.org), at the junction of Church Street and High Street, is a wonderful Victorian neo-Gothic church, built on the site of the 12th-century original by Sir George Gilbert Scott in 1869-72. Past worshippers include Newton and William Wilberforce. As well as beautiful stained-glass windows, it has London's tallest spire (278 feet).

Across the road is a striking art deco building, once the department store Barkers but now taken over by Texan organic food giant **Whole Foods Market** (nos.63-97,

7368 4500, www.wholefoodsmarket.co.uk). South down Derry Street, past the entrance to the **Roof Gardens** (*see below* **Inside Track**), is Kensington Square, which boasts one of London's highest concentrations of blue plaques. The writer William Thackeray lived at no.16 and the painter Edward Burne-Jones at no.41; at no.18, John Stuart Mill's maid made her bid for 'man from Porlock' status by using Carlyle's sole manuscript of *The French Revolution* to start the fire. The houses, though

<aside>

INSIDE TRACK
UP ON THE ROOF

Now more than 70 years old, the **Roof Gardens** (99 Kensington High Street, 7937 7994, www.virgin.com/roofgardens) remain largely unknown outside the world of corporate entertaining. But as long as they haven't been booked for an event (phone to check), they're open to all. Take the lift up six floors and emerge to the sound of water gurgling between trees rooted 100 feet above the ground. There are even a pair of flamingos dabbling among the ducks.

</aside>

velopment of
ard to believe now –
ds until 1840.
t is one of London's finest
and Park. Along its eastern
alk is one of the most pleasant
ral London, but the heart of the
e Jacobean **Holland House**. Left
t after World War II, it was bought by
London County Council in 1952; the east
wing now houses the city's best-sited youth
hostel (*see p196*). In summer, open-air theatre
and opera are staged on the front terrace. Three
lovely formal gardens are laid out near the
house. A little further west, the Japanese-style
Kyoto Garden has huge koi carp and a bridge
at the foot of a waterfall. Elsewhere, rabbits hop
about and peacocks stroll with the confidence
of all beautiful creatures. To the south of
the park are two more fine historic houses:
Linley Sambourne House and, closed for
refurbishment through 2009, **Leighton House**
(12 Holland Park Road, W14 8LZ, 7602 3316,
www.rbkc.gov.uk/leightonhousemuseum)
with its sternly Victorian red-brick façade.

Linley Sambourne House

*18 Stafford Terrace, W8 7BH (Mon-Fri 7471
9160/Sat, Sun 7938 1295/www.rbkc.gov.uk/
linleysambournehouse). High Street Kensington
tube.* **Open** *Mar-Dec* by appointment only.
Admission £6; £4 reductions; £1 children.
Credit MC, V. **Map** p396 A9.
The home of cartoonist Edward Linley Sambourne
was built in the 1870s and has almost all of its original fittings and furniture. Tours must be booked in
advance; they last 90mins, with weekend tours led
by an actor in period costume.
▶ *If you enjoy the re-enactment tours here,
note that they do something similar at Benjamin
Franklin House; see p86.*

EARL'S COURT & FULHAM

*Earl's Court, Fulham Broadway or West
Brompton tube.*

Earl's Court sells itself short, grammatically
speaking, since it was once the site of the
courthouse of two earls: both the Earl of
Warwick and the Earl of Holland. The 1860s
saw Earl's Court move from rural hamlet to
investment opportunity as the Metropolitan
Railway arrived. Some 20 years later it was
already much as we see it today, bar the fast
food joints. The terraces of grand old houses
are mostly subdivided into bedsits and cheap
hotels, once inhabited by so many Australians
the area was nicknamed Kangaroo Valley.
These days, the transient population tends
to be Eastern European or South American.

Fulham Palace & Museum.

In 1937, the **Earl's Court Exhibition
Centre** was built, and in its day was the
largest reinforced concrete building in Europe –
a phrase that truly makes the heart sing.
The centre hosts a year-round calendar of
events, from trade shows and pop concerts
(Pink Floyd built and tore down *The Wall* here)
to the Ideal Home Show. Two minutes south
down Warwick Road is a tiny venue, with an
equally impressive pedigree: the **Troubadour**
(263-267 Old Brompton Road, 7370 1434,
www.troubadour.co.uk), a 1950s coffeehouse
with a downstairs club that hosted Jimi
Hendrix, Joni Mitchell, Bob Dylan and Paul
Simon in the 1960s. While it's no longer at the
cutting edge, it still delivers a full programme
of music, poetry and comedy.

West along Warwick Road are the gates of
Brompton Cemetery. It's full of magnificent
monuments commemorating the famous and
infamous, including suffragette Emmeline
Pankhurst, and his grave marked by a lion,
boxer 'Gentleman' John Jackson – 'Gentleman'
John taught Lord Byron to box. The peace and
quiet of the cemetery is regularly disturbed at
its southern end by neighbouring **Stamford
Bridge** (*see p329*), home of Chelsea FC.
Craven Cottage (*see p329*), the home of west
London's other Premiership team, Fulham FC,
is west of here, at the northern end of the park
that surrounds **Fulham Palace**.

★ FREE Fulham Palace & Museum

Bishop's Avenue, off Fulham Palace Road,
SW6 6EA (7736 3233/www.fulhampalace.org).
Putney Bridge tube/14, 74, 220, 414, 430 bus.
Open *Museum & gallery* noon-4pm Mon, Tue;
11am-2pm Sat; 11.30am-3.30pm Sun. *Gardens*
dawn-dusk daily. *Tours* 2pm 2nd & 4th Sun
of mth. **Admission** free; under-16s must be
accompanied by an adult. *Tours* £5; free under-
16s. **No credit cards.**
Fulham Palace was the episcopal retreat of the
Bishops of London. The present building was built
in Tudor times, with later significant Georgian and
Victorian additions. It would be more accurate to call
it a manor house than a palace, but it gives a fine
glimpse into the changing lifestyles and architecture
of nearly 500 years, from the Tudor hall to the
Victorian chapel; try out the echo in the courtyard.
There's also access to a glorious stretch of riverside
walk. Best of all, these delights still seem largely
undiscovered by the majority of Londoners.
▶ *Lawn, the café here, is the latest Oliver Peyton*
outfit; see p219 Profile.

SHEPHERD'S BUSH

Goldhawk Road or Shepherd's Bush Market
tube/Shepherd's Bush tube/rail.

Shepherd's Bush was once west London's
impoverished backwater, the setting for
junkyard sitcom *Steptoe & Son*. Now, a couple
of decades after house prices started going
through the roof, there's visible evidence of
gentrification. **Queens Park Rangers** (*see*
p329), the underperforming local football team,
has benefited from a huge cash injection from
three of the world's richest businessmen, while
Shepherd's Bush got a similar boost from the
Westfield London shopping mall (*see p241*).
The **Shepherd's Bush Empire** (*see p314*)
and the **Bush Hall** (310 Uxbridge Road, W12
7LJ, 8222 6955, www.bushhallmusic.co.uk)
have become essential destinations in the
music scene, the **Bush Theatre** (*see p341*)
stages excellent leftfield drama, and the bar at
the **K West** hotel (Richmond Way, W14 0AX,
8008 6600, www.k-west.co.uk) is the place to
spot trendy young American bands.

BBC Television Centre

TV Centre, Wood Lane, W12 7RJ (0370
603 0304/www.bbc.co.uk/tours). **Tours**
by appointment only Mon-Sat. **Admission**
£9.50; £8.50 reductions; £7 10-16s, students;
£27 family. No under-9s. **Credit** MC, V.
Half a mile north of Shepherd's Bush Green is the
BBC TV Centre where, if you book in advance, you
can catch a fascinating tour around the temple of
British televisual history. Tours include visits to the
news desk, the TV studios and the Weather Centre.

HAMMERSMITH

Hammersmith tube.

Dominated by the grey concrete of its
flyover, the centre point of Hammersmith is
Hammersmith Broadway, once a grotty bus
garage, now a shiny new shopping mall. Make
it over the road and you'll find one of London's
most notable rock venues, the **Hammersmith
Apollo** (*see p313*). Opened in 1932 as the
Gaumont Palace, it entered rock legend as the
Hammersmith Odeon, hosting pivotal gigs by
the Beatles, Motörhead and Public Enemy.
   Hammersmith Bridge, the city's oldest
suspension bridge, is a green and gold hymn
to the strength of Victorian ironwork. There's
a lovely walk west along the Thames Path from
here that takes in a clutch of historic pubs
including the **Blue Anchor** (13 Lower Mall,
8748 5774); head in the opposite direction for
Riverside Studios arts centre (*see p299*).

CHISWICK

Turnham Green tube/Chiswick rail.

Once a sleepy, semi-rural suburb, Chiswick
is now one of London's swankiest postcodes,
its residents including broadcasters, directors,
actors, advertising bods and a smattering of
rock 'n' roll royalty. In recent years, **Chiswick
High Road**, its main thoroughfare, has
developed a gastronomic reputation, with
dozens of high-end eateries.
   Chiswick also has a surprising number of
sightseeing attractions. **Chiswick Mall** is a
beautiful residential path that runs alongside
the river from Hammersmith, and includes
Kelmscott House (26 Upper Mall, 8741
3735, www.morrissociety.org), once home to
pioneering socialist William Morris but now a
private house that opens to the public 2-5pm on
Thursdays and Saturdays. From here, it's a
short walk to **Fuller's Brewery** and
Hogarth's House, while the **Kew Bridge
Steam Museum** and the **Musical Museum**
are only a bus ride away; for all, *see pp162-163*.
It's possible to return to the river path after
visiting **Chiswick House** (*see p162*), and the
wonderful **Royal Botanic Gardens** at Kew

SIGHTS

Hogarth's House

(*see p156*) are just over the bridge. Further upstream is **Syon House** (*see p163*), with enough attractions to fill most of a day – among them the **Tropical Forest** animal sanctuary (8847 4730, www.tropicalforest.co.uk, £4-£5).

Chiswick House
Burlington Lane, W4 2RP (8995 0508/www.chgt.org.uk). Turnham Green tube then E3 bus to Edensor Road/Hammersmith tube/rail then 190 bus/Chiswick rail. **Open** *Apr-Oct* 10am-5pm Mon-Wed, Sun. **Admission** £4.20; £3.40 reductions; £2.10 5-16s; free under-5s. **Credit** MC, V.
Richard Boyle, third Earl of Burlington, designed this lovely Palladian villa in 1725 as a place to entertain the artistic and philosophical luminaries of his day. The Chiswick House & Gardens Trust aims to restore the gardens to Burlington's original design. The restoration will be helped by details from the newly acquired painting *A View of Chiswick House from the South-west* by Dutch landscape artist Pieter Andreas Rysbrack (c1685-1748).

Fuller's Brewery
Griffin Brewery, Chiswick Lane South, W4 2QB (8996 2063/www.fullers.co.uk). Turnham Green tube. **Tours** hourly 11am-3pm, by appointment only. **Admission** (incl tasting session) £10; £8 reductions. **Credit** MC, V.
Fuller's – or Fuller Smith & Turner PLC, to give them their official title – are London's last family-run brewery. Most of this current building dates

back to 1845 but there's been a brewery on this site since Elizabethan times. The two-hour tours need to be booked in advance.
▶ *London Pride and ESB are the most popular Fuller's brews, available in pubs across London.*

FREE Hogarth's House
Hogarth Lane, Great West Road, W4 2QN (8994 6757). Turnham Green tube/Chiswick rail. **Open** *Apr-Oct* 1-5pm Tue-Fri; 1-6pm Sat, Sun. *Nov, Dec, Feb, Mar* 1-4pm Tue-Fri; 1-5pm Sat, Sun. **Admission** free; donations appreciated. **No credit cards.**
Closed for refurbishment until May 2009, this is the country retreat of the 18th-century painter, engraver and social commentator William Hogarth. On display are most of his engravings, including *Gin Lane*, *Marriage à la Mode* and a copy of *Rake's Progress*.

★ Kew Bridge Steam Museum
Green Dragon Lane, Brentford, Middx TW8 0EN (8568 4757/www.kbsm.org). Gunnersbury tube/Kew Bridge rail/65, 237, 267, 391 bus. **Open** 11am-4pm Tue-Sun. **Admission** *Tue-Fri* £5; £4 reductions; free under-15s. *Sat, Sun* £7.50 reductions; free under-15s. Under-15s must be accompanied by an adult. **Credit** MC, V.
One of London's most engaging small museums, this impressive old Victorian pumping station is a reminder that steam wasn't just used for powering trains but also for supplying enough water to the citizens of an expanding London. It's now home to

SIGHTS

Kew Bridge Steam Museum.

Syon House
Syon Park, Brentford, Middx TW8 8JF (8560
0883/www.syonpark.co.uk). Gunnersbury tube/
rail then 237, 267 bus. Open House (mid Mar-
Oct only) 11am-5pm Wed, Thur, Sun. Gardens
(all year) 10.30am-dusk daily. Tours by
arrangement. Admission House & gardens
£8; £4-£7 reductions; £18 family. Gardens
only £4; £2.50 reductions; £9 family. Tours
free. Credit MC, V.
The Percys, Dukes of Northumberland, were once
known as 'the Kings of the North'. Their old house
is on the site of a Bridgettine convent, suppressed by
Henry VIII in 1534. The building was converted into
a house in 1547 for the Duke of Northumberland, its
neoclassical interior created by Robert Adam in 1761;
there's an outstanding range of Regency portraits
by the likes of Gainsborough. The gardens, by
Capability Brown, are enhanced by the splendid
Great Conservatory and in winter you can take an
evening walk through illuminated woodland. This
was also where the first astronomical study of the
moon was made; see p164 England's Galileo.

SOUTHALL

Southall rail.

Immigrants used to enter London via the docks
and settle in the East End. Now, though, they
come via Heathrow and settle here: thus a huge
arc of suburban west London – Hounslow,
Hayes, Southall, Harrow, Wembley,
Neasden – has become home to Europe's
biggest South Asian population.

Southall is Britain's best-established
immigrant community. From the 1950s
onwards, Punjabi Sikhs flocked to the area
to work at the Wolf Rubber Factory and in
London Transport; the area soon developed a
thriving Asian infrastructure of restaurants,
shops and wholesalers that attracted Hindus,
Muslims, Tamils, Indian Christians and, more
recently, Somalis and Afghans. Take a 607 bus
from Shepherd's Bush or a Great Western train
from Paddington and, on arrival in Southall,
you'll think you're in downtown Delhi – all
pounding Bollywood hits, sari fabrics, pungent
spices and freshly fried samosas.

Southall Broadway is well worth a visit if
only to gawp at Southall Market. Located
on the east of the town, near Southall Park,
it's a unique mix of rural India and cockney
London. What's on sale varies daily, from
squawking poultry on Tuesday, to horses
(honestly) on Wednesday, general bric-a-brac
on Friday and then, on Saturday, pretty much
everything else. Equally unmissable is a show
at the three-screen Himalaya Palace (14
South Road, 8813 8844), a beautifully restored
old movie house dedicated to Bollywood epics.

an extraordinary collection of different engines.
There are lots of hands-on exhibits for kids, a great
dressing-up box and even a miniature steam train.

Musical Museum
399 High Street, Brentford, Middx TW8 0DU
(8560 8108/www.musicalmuseum.co.uk). Kew
Bridge rail/65, 237, 267 bus. Open 11am-
5.30pm (last admission 4.30pm) Tue-Sun.
Admission £7; £5.50 reductions, accompanied
under-16s free. Credit (over £10) MC, V.
This recently refurbished museum, a converted
church, contains one of the world's foremost collections of automatic instruments. From tiny Swiss
musical boxes to the self-playing Mighty Wurlitzer,
the collection embraces an impressive array of
sophisticated pianolas, cranky barrel organs, spooky
orchestrions, residence organs and violin players.

INSIDE TRACK
STEAMED UP

Each weekend, an awesome display of
steam power can be seen at the Kew
Bridge Steam Museum (see opposite).
Particularly impressive are the Cornish
Beam engines, which are fired up once a
month, while the beautifully engineered
rotative engines purr away every other
weekend (the website has details).

SIGHTS

But it's the food that makes Southall really special: for our recommendations, *see p221* **Inside Track**. There's even a Punjabi pub, the **Glassy Junction** (97 South Road, 8574 1626): all the trappings of a white working men's club – patterned carpet, keg beer – plus the considerable boon of hot parathas. It's said to be the only pub in the UK that accepts payment in rupees.

A short walk south of Southall railway station, the **Gurdwara Sri Guru Singh Sabha Southall** (Havelock Road, 8574 4311, www.sgsss.org) is the largest Sikh place of worship outside India. Its golden dome is visible from the London Eye in the east and Windsor Castle to the west; it also provides vegetarian food free to all visitors from the *langar*, or communal kitchen. Non-Sikh visitors are welcome but must take off their shoes before entering, and women must wear a headscarf (they're provided, should you not have one to hand). Enthroned within is the Guru Granth Sahib, the Sikh scripture and supreme spiritual authority of Sikhism.

The suburb of Neasden, six miles north-east of Southall, has its own claim to British Asian fame: the **Shri Swaminarayan Mandir** (105-119 Brentfield Road, 8965 2651, www.mandir.org), the largest Hindu temple outside India to have been built using traditional methods. To this end, nearly 5,000 tons of stone and marble were shipped out to India, where craftsmen carved it into the intricate designs that make up the temple. Then the temple was shipped, piece by piece, to England, where it was assembled on site. The shining marble temple stands incongruously close to one of IKEA's giant blue boxes.

England's Galileo

Meet London's great lost astronomer.

On a clear summer's evening in 1609, Thomas Harriot (c1560-1621) climbed the stairs to his garret room overlooking the Thames at **Syon House** (*see p163*) and became the first man to study the moon through a telescope. Already an accomplished ethnographer and experimental scientist, Harriot spent the next decade drawing detailed lunar maps, following Jupiter's satellites, tracking comets and cataloguing nearly 500 sunspot observations.

After studying at Oxford, Harriot befriended the young Walter Raleigh in London, lodging in Raleigh's rooms in the Strand. As Raleigh's accountant and navigational advisor, Harriot travelled to the New World in 1586, spending a year mapping modern-day North Carolina, cataloguing local plants and observing indigenous customs. He was the first Englishman to learn the local Algonquin language, even inventing an alphabet to record its distinctive sounds, and his account of the voyage eventually became the first English-language publication on the Americas.

Harriot later fell under the patronage of the 'Wizard' Earl of Northumberland, Sir Henry Percy, known for his free-thinking interest in science. Supported by spacious rooms and servants at Syon, a talented technical assistant and a sizeable annual pension, Harriot devoted the rest of his life to determining nature's mathematical laws. He developed a symbolic notation for algebra that's still taught in schools, constructed a binary number system similar to that used in all digital devices today, studied rainbows and worked on the timely problem of calculating longitude at sea. Despite corresponding openly with other scientists, Harriot failed to publish any of his work, leaving the glory for his pioneering efforts to be claimed by others – notably Galileo, who is usually credited with the earliest telescopic moon observations.

On 4 November 1605, Harriot had the misfortune to dine at Syon with Northumberland and his cousin, Thomas Percy. Three days later, Percy, a key conspirator in the Gunpowder Plot, was dead. His dining companions were arrested and Harriot spent weeks in Westminster's Gatehouse Prison. The unlucky Northumberland was imprisoned for life in the Tower of London, where Harriot continued to visit him and the now-disgraced Raleigh.

Syon House and National Astronomy Week will celebrate the 400th anniversary of the first lunar observations with a day of family astronomical activities, culminating in the unveiling of a commemorative plaque on the site of Harriot's lodgings, on 26 July 2009. In Greenwich, the **Royal Observatory** (*see p149*) is also running a programme of events to mark the International Year of Astronomy.

SIGHTS

Consume

Rookery.
See p170.

Hotels **166**
No More Bed Bugs **176**
Profile Terence Conran **186**
Swimming in Heaven **193**

Restaurants & Cafés **197**
Quality Fast Food **207**
Eating Out... **208**
...and Eating In **209**
Profile Oliver Peyton **219**
A Little of What You Fancy?
207

Pubs & Bars **226**
Profile Real Ale **232**
Good Mixers **237**

Shops & Services **241**
Where to Shop **246**
Things Are What They Used
to Be **251**
The Rise of Mount Street **254**
Now You See Them **259**
Foyled Again? **262**

Hotels

Quality and imagination aplenty – but bargains are hard to find.

Bijou luxury has been the most exciting recent development among London's hotels. The **Fox & Anchor** turned 'a room above a pub' into something romantic, luxurious and fun, while Gordon Ramsay's first hotel, the **York & Albany**, did a great deal towards rekindling our interest in his portfolio. At the top end of the market, services are becoming key in the battle for custom, with more and more being included in the room price, notably at the **Lanesborough** and **Andaz**. While Kit Kemp, doyenne of London's boutique hotels, still sets the standard with the 'modern English' style of her Firmdale group (**Covent Garden Hotel** remains our pick), we're also excited about the rebirth of formal British elegance at the **Connaught** and enjoyed the calm discretion of long-stay specialists **No.5 Maddox**.

　　Disappointingly, there's little new to recommend in the moderate price bracket since the appearance of the still funky **Hoxton Hotel**. The city's small cadre of stylish budget options (the **Hoxton**, the **Mayflower** group, **Base2Stay**, **Stylotel**) continues to impress and the well-run **Apex**, friendly **City Inn Westminster** and enthusiastic **Park Plaza County Hall** are all good if you can get a decent rate.

CONSUME

THE LOWDOWN

We're not going to lie to you: room rates in London are scary. The week we went to press, there was good news: a 10% drop in prices. In effect, the average room rate dropped from just over £130 to just under £120. It still means there are few options under £100, unless you're happy with a hostel, pokey B&B or somewhere out in the sticks. Our **Inside Track** boxes might help you out: for cautionary tales, *see right*; for some good news, *see p169 & p171*.

　　Always try to book ahead. If you can't, the obliging staff at **Visit London** (1 Lower Regent Street, Piccadilly Circus, 0870 156 6366, www.visitlondon.com) will look for a place within your selected area and price range for free. You can also check availability and reserve rooms on its website.

> ❶ Red numbers given in this chapter correspond to the location of each hotel on the street maps. *See pp394-407.*

The geography of London gives some guidance as to the price and type of lodging you're likely to find. Many of the swankier hotels are found in Mayfair (W1), for example, whereas Bloomsbury (WC1) is good for mid-priced hotels and B&Bs. If you're looking for a cheap hotel, try Ebury Street in Victoria (SW1) or Gower Street in Bloomsbury (WC1), as well as Earl's Court (SW5), Bayswater (W2), Paddington (W2) and South Kensington (SW7).

PRICES AND CLASSIFICATION

We don't list official star ratings, which reflect facilities rather than quality; instead, we've classified hotels within each area heading by the price of a double room per night. Given average room rates that hover around the £120 mark, we've roughly followed categories of £100 or less for cheap, £100-£200 moderate, £200-£300 expensive, £300 and above for deluxe. Room rates change frequently though, so confirm them before you book. B&Bs excepted, breakfast isn't usually included.

Check discount hotel websites – such as **www.alpharooms.com** or **www.london-discount-hotel.com** – for prices that can fall well below the rack rates we list.

FACILITIES AND ACCESSIBILITY

In this chapter, we list the main services offered by each hotel but concierges can often arrange far more, including theatre tickets and meal reservations. We have also tried to indicate which hotels offer rooms adapted for disabled customers, but it's always best to confirm the precise facilities with each place before you travel. **Tourism For All** (0845 124 9971, www.tourismforall.org.uk) has details of wheelchair-accessible places. We've also stated which hotels offer parking facilities, but again enquire in advance rather than just pitching up in your car: spaces are sometimes limited.

THE SOUTH BANK & BANKSIDE

Moderate

Park Plaza County Hall

1 Addington Street, Waterloo, SE1 7RY (7021 1800/www.parkplaza.com). Lambeth North tube. **Rates** £116-£211 double. **Rooms** 398. **Credit** MC, V. **Map** p401 M9 ❶

Approach along the grubby streets from Lambeth North and you'll wonder why we've brought you here, but this is an enthusiastically – if somewhat haphazardly – run new-build. Each room has its own kitchenette with microwave and sink, room sizes aren't bad across the price range (the floor-to-ceiling windows help them feel bigger). There's a handsomely vertiginous atrium, enabling you to peer down into the central restaurant from the frustratingly infrequent glass lifts, and the ground-floor bar is buzzy with business types after work. But it is the views from the expansive penthouses that are the real knock-out.
Bars (2). Disabled-adapted rooms. Gym. Internet (wireless, £7.95/day). Restaurant. TV.
Other locations Park Plaza Riverside, 18 Albert Embankment, SE1 7TJ (7034 4829); Park Plaza Victoria, 239 Vauxhall Bridge Road, SW1V 1EQ (7034 4820).

Premier Inn London County Hall

County Hall, Belvedere Road, South Bank, SE1 7PB (0870 238 3300/www.premiertravelinn.com). Waterloo tube/rail. **Rates** £104-£149 double. **Rooms** 316. **Credit** AmEx, DC, MC, V. **Map** p401 M8 ❷

Location, location, location is the selling point of this budget chain hotel housed in the back of London's old County Hall, slap bang next to the London Eye.

There may be queue-control barriers in the too-small lobby, but the rooms are as spacious (and as acceptably kitted out) as many a more upmarket gaff and the restaurant/bar area is a cosy surprise. A rolling refurbishment is planned over 2009, but Premier assures us it won't affect the running of the hotel.
Bar. Disabled-adapted rooms. Internet (wireless, £10/day). Restaurant. TV.
Other locations throughout the city.

Southwark Rose

47 Southwark Bridge Road, South Bank, SE1 9HH (7015 1480/www.southwarkrose hotel.co.uk). London Bridge tube/rail. **Rates** £180 double. **Rooms** 84. **Credit** AmEx, MC, V. **Map** p404 P8 ❸

Perfectly positioned for sampling the South Bank's many delights, the five-year-old Rose declares itself as sleekly modern with giant domed brushed aluminium lampshades and smart metal-framed cube chairs in a lobby hung with the work of Japanese photographer Mayumi. The rooms feature the dark woods, panelled headboards and crisp white linens of many of London's 'contemporary' hotels – but hey, who's knocking it? Fully wired up, there are even electric blackout blinds. Guests can use the next-door Novotel's gym.
Bar. Disabled-adapted rooms. Internet (wireless, £10/day). Parking (£16/day). Restaurant. Smoking rooms. TV (pay movies).

INSIDE TRACK
BUYER BEWARE!

They're not being naughty, as it happens, they're just catering to their core clientele: businessmen. Unlike this chapter, most luxury hotels quote prices exclusive of VAT – all very well, but if you're already splurging on a suite for a special occasion, that extra 15 per cent is going to hurt. Also remember that many of the high-end places charge extra for services – notably internet use, although wireless access has made this less common. So it could cost £25 to send that boasting email to your mates about where you're staying, another £40 for breakfast... and with no teamaking facilities in the room, any pre-breakfast straightener is going on that already engorged room service bill. Suddenly your once-in-a-lifetime treat has become a plastic-battering ordeal.

At the other end of the market, be wary of websites that offer unusually brilliant bargains. Check a map before you congratulate yourself: one site offered us a £25 a night double in 'London' that was, in fact, an hour's drive into Kent.

CONSUME

Andaz.

THE CITY

Deluxe

Andaz Liverpool Street
40 Liverpool Street, EC2M 7QN (7961 1234/www.london.liverpoolstreet.andaz.com). Liverpool Street tube/rail. **Rates** £329-£605 double. **Rooms** 267. **Credit** AmEx, DC, MC, V. **Map** p405 R6 ❹

A faded railway hotel until its £70m Conran over-haul in 2000, the Great Eastern became in 2007 the first of Hyatt's new Andaz portfolio. The new approach means out with gimmicky menus, closet-sized minibars and even the lobby reception desk, and in with down-to-earth, well-informed service and eco-friendliness. The bedrooms still wear style-mag uniform – Eames chairs, Frette linens – and are minimalist at a point close to underfurnished, but free services (breakfast, local calls, movies, internet, healthy minibar, laundry) and the management's savvy efforts to connect with the vibey local area are appreciated: witness Silent Cinema events at the base of the breathtaking atrium, or the comedy nights in the hotel's magnificent old Freemasons' Temple.
Bar. Business centre. Concierge. Disabled-adapted rooms. Gym. Internet (broadband/wireless, free). Restaurants (4). Room service. Smoking rooms. TV (free movies).

INSIDE TRACK YOTEL

Awkward check-in time? Book four hours in a **Yotel** 'pod' hotel (www.yotel.com) at Heathrow or Gatwick for around £80.

Expensive

Threadneedles
5 Threadneedle Street, EC2R 8AY (7657 8080/www.theetoncollection.com). Bank tube/DLR. **Rates** £206-£394 double. **Rooms** 69. **Credit** AmEx, MC, V. **Map** p405 Q6 ❺

Occupying a Victorian banking hall, the former headquarters of the Midland Bank, Threadneedles successfully integrates modern design with a monumental space, its lobby and bar area centrepieced by a magnificent atrium. The obvious constraints of redeveloping a listed building mean that rooms aren't uniform shapes, but there are advantages: many of them still have their original 19th-century windows. The decor throughout is kept soothingly neutral, and you'll find Korres natural toiletries in the serene limestone bathrooms. The provision of little stress-busting comforts reflects the hotel's business-friendly location: there are fleecy throws, a scented candle lit at turndown, and a 'movie treats' menu of popcorn, ice-cream and Coke.
Bar. Concierge. Disabled-adapted rooms. Internet (wireless, £20/day). Restaurant. Room service. TV (pay movies).
▶ *Threadneedles' in-house bar Bonds (7657 8088) offers carefully made cocktails, a well-pitched wine list and exemplary tapas.*

Moderate

Apex City of London Hotel
1 Seething Lane, EC3N 4AX (7702 2020/www.apexhotels.co.uk). Tower Hill tube. **Rates** £130-£311 double. **Rooms** 130. **Credit** AmEx, MC, V. **Map** p405 R7 ❻

CONSUME

Rookery.

Part of a small chain, this sleek, modern business hotel has built a sturdy reputation – so much so, they were planning to have opened 49 new rooms by the end of 2008. The public areas, including a ground-floor restaurant off the reception area at the front, are nothing special, but staff members are accommodating, room details are obliging (free Wi-Fi, pillow menu, rubber duck in the bathroom), rates are impressive (especially at weekends) and the location – right by the Tower of London – is terrific. A new, smaller Apex is due to open near the Bank of England this summer.

Bar. Disabled-adapted rooms. Gym. Internet (wireless, free). Restaurant. Room service (24hr). Smoking rooms. TV (DVD).

HOLBORN & CLERKENWELL

Expensive

Malmaison

Charterhouse Square, Clerkenwell, EC1M 6AH (7012 3700/www.malmaison.com). Barbican tube/Farringdon tube/rail. **Rates** £241-£294 double. **Rooms** 97. **Credit** AmEx, DC, MC, V. **Map** p402 O5 **7**

For all that it's part of a chain, the Malmaison is a charming hotel. Location is key: it's set in a lovely cobblestone square, near the lively restaurants and bars of Smithfield Market. The reception is stylishly kitted out with a lilac and cream chequered floor, exotic plants and a petite champagne bar, while purples, dove-grey and black wood dominate the rooms and two suites. Nice extra touches in the rooms include free broadband and creative lighting; for something more luxurious, the hotel's newest suite – the Square – has a four-poster bed, Bose sound sys-

tem and original artworks. The gym and a subterranean brasserie complete the picture.

Bar. Disabled-adapted rooms. Gym. Internet (broadband, free). Restaurant. Room service. TV.

★ Rookery

12 Peter's Lane, Cowcross Street, Clerkenwell, EC1M 6DS (7336 0931/www.rookeryhotel.com). Farringdon tube/rail. **Rates** £247-£347 double. **Rooms** 33. **Credit** AmEx, DC, MC, V. **Map** p402 O5 **8**

Sister hotel to Hazlitt's (*see p179*), the Rookery has long been something of a celebrity hideaway. Deep in Clerkenwell, the front door is satisfyingly hard to find, especially when the streets around are teeming with Fabric (*see p321*) devotees; the front rooms can be noisy on these nights. Once inside, guests enjoy an atmospheric warren of creaky rooms, each individually decorated in the style of a Georgian town house: huge clawfoot baths, elegant four-posters and an honesty bar in the drawing room. The ground-floor suite has its own hallway, a cosy boudoir and a subterranean bathroom. Topping it all is the huge split-level Rook's Nest suite, which has views of St Paul's Cathedral (*see p61*).

Bar. Concierge. Internet (dataport/wireless, free). Room service. TV.

Zetter

86-88 Clerkenwell Road, Clerkenwell, EC1M 5RJ (7324 4444/www.thezetter.com). Farringdon tube/rail. **Rates** £160-£399 double. **Rooms** 59. **Credit** AmEx, MC, V. **Map** p402 O4 **9**

Zetter is a fun, laid-back, modern hotel with some interesting design notes. There's a refreshing lack of attitude – the polyglot staff clearly enjoy their job. The rooms, stacked up on five galleried storeys over-

looking the intimate bar area, are sleek and functional, but cosied up with choice home comforts like hot-water bottles and old Penguin paperbacks, while the walk-in Raindance showers are stocked with Elemis products. The picture windows in the restaurant make for amusing people-watching over breakfast, and top-floor suites have great rooftop views. Rooms on the St John's Square side are quietest.

Bar. Concierge. Disabled-adapted rooms. Internet (dataport/wireless, free). Restaurant. Room service. Smoking rooms. TV (pay movies/music/DVD).

Moderate

★ Fox & Anchor

115 Charterhouse Street, Clerkenwell, EC1M 6AA (0845 347 0100/www.foxandanchor.com). Barbican tube/Farringdon tube/rail. **Rates** £112-£217 double. **Rooms** 6. **Credit** AmEx, DC, MC, V. **Map** p402 O5 ⑩

This handful of well-appointed, atmospheric and surprisingly luxurious rooms above a bustling and historic Smithfield pub was one of our most enjoyable stays this year. Each en suite room differs, but the high-spec facilities (big flatscreen TV, clawfoot bath and drench shower) and quirky attention to detail (bottles of ale in the minibar, the 'Nursing hangover' signs to hang out for privacy) are common throughout. Expect some clanking market noise in the early mornings, but proximity to the historic meat market also means a feisty fry-up in the morning in the handsome dark wood and pewter tankards pub below. The pub is where you check in, but you do have a key to the separate entrance door, with its lovely floor mosaic. *Photos p173.*

Bar. Internet (dataport, free). Restaurant. TV.

BLOOMSBURY & FITZROVIA

Deluxe

Charlotte Street Hotel

15-17 Charlotte Street, Fitzrovia, W1T 1RJ (7806 2000/www.firmdale.com). Goodge Street or Tottenham Court Road tube. **Rates** £294-£364 double. **Rooms** 52. **Credit** AmEx, DC, MC, V. **Map** p399 K5 ⑪

This gorgeous hotel is a fine exponent of Kit Kemp's much imitated fusion of traditional English and avant-garde; it's hard to believe it was once a dental hospital. Public rooms are adorned with genuine Bloomsbury Set paintings, by the likes of Duncan Grant and Vanessa Bell, while bedrooms mix English understatement with bold flourishes: soft beiges and greys spiced up with plaid-floral combinations. The huge, comfortable beds and trademark polished granite and oak bathrooms are suitably indulgent, and some rooms have unbelievably high ceilings. The Oscar restaurant and bar are

---

INSIDE TRACK
BARGAIN BASEMENT

Hotels that rely on business custom often offer fabulous rates for weekend stays. **Myhotel Bloomsbury** (see p173), for example, sometimes has rooms for as low as £125, and for the same price you might get a riverview suite at **City Inn Westminster** (see p187). Our deal of the year? A weekend room at the **Fox & Anchor** (see p171) for £95.

classy and always busy with a smart crowd from the area's media and ad offices. On Sundays, you can combine a three-course set meal with a classic film screened in the mini-cinema.

Bar. Concierge. Gym. Internet (broadband/ wireless, from 30p/min to £20/day). Restaurant. Room service. Smoking rooms. TV (DVD).

Sanderson

50 Berners Street, Fitzrovia, W1T 3NG (7300 1400/www.morganshotelgroup.com). Oxford Circus tube. **Rates** £235-£470 double. **Rooms** 150. **Credit** AmEx, DC, MC, V. **Map** p406 V1 ⓬

No designer flash in the pan, the Sanderson remains a statement hotel, a Schrager/Starck creation that takes clinical chic in the bedrooms to new heights. The only touch of colour in our room was a naïve landscape painting nailed to the ceiling directly above the silver sleigh bed. Otherwise, it's all flowing white net drapes, gleaming glass cabinets and retractable screens. The residents-only Purple Bar sports a button-backed purple leather ceiling and fabulous cocktails: we recommend the Vesper. The 'billiard room' has a purple-topped pool table, surrounded by strange tribal adaptations of classic dining room furniture. Smashing.

Bars (2). Business services. Concierge. Disabled-adapted rooms. Gym. Internet (dataport/wireless, £15/day). Restaurant. Room service. Spa. TV (DVD).

Fox & Anchor. See p171.

Expensive

Academy Hotel

21 Gower Street, Bloomsbury, WC1E 6HG (7631 4115/www.theetoncollection.com). Goodge Street tube. **Rates** £205 double. **Rooms** 49. **Credit** AmEx, DC, MC, V. **Map** p399 K5 ⓭

Comprising five Georgian town houses, the Academy has a restrained country-house style – decor in most rooms is soft, summery florals and checks, although eight suites have more sophisticated colour schemes. Guests are cocooned from the busy streets and those in the split-level doubles get plenty of breathing space at decent rates. The library and conservatory open on to fragrant walled gardens where drinks and breakfast are served in summer.

Bar. Internet (dataport/wireless, £6.50/hr). Room service. TV.

Myhotel Bloomsbury

11-13 Bayley Street, Bloomsbury, WC1B 3HD (7667 6000/www.myhotels.co.uk). Goodge Street or Tottenham Court Road tube. **Rates** £210-£246 double. **Rooms** 78. **Credit** AmEx, DC, MC, V. **Map** p399 K5 ⓮

Back in 1999, this Conran-designed hotel combined Asian fusion decor and feng shui principles – and launched a mini-chain (*see also p189*). The essential features remain: an aquarium and floral arrangements in the calming lobby, strategically placed

CONSUME

crystals and scented candles, a wonderfully chill library in the cellared basement. Rooms are minimalist, but exoticised (buddha heads, south-east Asian furnishings) and fully accessorised (plasma screens, wireless internet). The top-floor myspace is a fabulous self-contained apartment and studio – retrofuturist to a tee, and with a rooftop terrace. *Bar. Concierge. Gym. Internet (dataport/wireless, free). Restaurant. Room service. Smoking rooms. TV (pay movies/DVD).*

Moderate

Harlingford Hotel

61-63 Cartwright Gardens, Bloomsbury, WC1H 9EL (7387 1551/www.harlingfordhotel.com). Russell Square tube/Euston tube/rail. **Rates** £129 double. **Rooms** 43. **Credit** AmEx, MC, V. **Map** p399 L4 ⓰

It's very leafy, very Bloomsbury, in Cartwright Gardens, a graceful Georgian crescent lined with B&Bs. Despite the reasonable room rates, the Harlingford has boutique hotel aspirations and leaves other contenders on the block far behind. A stylish redesign has fitted it out with light airy rooms accented with splashes of vibrant turquoise and purple – there's even a Harlingford logo. You can lob a tennis ball in the crescent's private garden or just dream under the trees on a summer's night. *TV.*

Cheap

Arosfa

83 Gower Street, Bloomsbury, WC1E 6HJ (7636 2115/www.arosfalondon.com). Goodge Street tube. **Rates** £90 double. **Rooms** 16. **Credit** MC, V. **Map** p399 K4 ⓰

A change of owner and the Arosfa's gone from spartan to Manhattan. Yes, those are Phillippe Starck Ghost chairs in the lounge, alongside the mirrored chests and black-and-white blow-up of the New York skyline. The rest of the hotel is more restrained: cappuccino-tinted walls hung with architectural engravings in the halls, neutrally-decorated bedrooms decked out with the ubiquitous white linens draped with a silky throw. Those who like elbow room in the shower might find the bathroom units a tad cramped. *Internet (wireless, free; shared terminal, free). TV.*

Ashlee House

261-265 Gray's Inn Road, Bloomsbury, WC1X 8QT (7833 9400/www.ashleehouse. co.uk). King's Cross tube/rail. **Rates** £27-£28 double; £17-£22 dorm bed. **Beds** 172. **Credit** MC, V. **Map** p399 L3 ⓱

The older sister of the Clink Hostel is a smaller-scale cosier establishment than the new kid, but it's still design-led: funky sheepskin-backed swoosh-shaped seating and bleached out digitally-printed London

---

THE BEST BARGAIN BEDS

For cheap chic
Hoxton Hotel. *See p193.*

For a lushly located B&B
Vicarage Hotel. *See p192.*

For a super new studio
Stylotel. *See p183.*

For a weekend treat
Fox & Anchor. *See p171.*

---

scenes on the lobby walls, where a huge blackboard lists tips for cracking the big city. There's a quirky comfy lounge filled with squashy Chesterfields and a cheerful kitchen/dining area. The rooms (all with sinks) are rather more ordinary, ranging from singles to 16-bed dorms. *Internet (shared terminals, £1/hr). TV (lounge).*

★ Clink Hostel

78 King's Cross Road, Bloomsbury, WC1X 9QG (7183 9400/www.clinkhostel.com). King's Cross tube/rail. **Rates** £80 double; £15 dorm bed. **Beds** 600. **Credit** MC, V. **Map** p399 M3 ⓲

Located in a former courthouse, the awesome Clink sets the bar high for hosteldom. There's the setting: the superb original wood-panelled lobby and court-room where the Clash once stood before the beak (now filled with backpackers surfing the web). Then there's the urban chic ethos that permeates the whole enterprise, from the streamlined red reception counter to the Japanese-style 'pod' beds and the dining area's chunky wooden tables. The promised bar should be opened this year – but laundry facilities had yet to materialise by time of press. *Photo p176. Bar. Internet (shared terminals, £1/hr). TV (lounge).*

Jenkins Hotel

45 Cartwright Gardens, Bloomsbury, WC1H 9EH (7387 2067/www.jenkinshotel.demon. co.uk). Russell Square tube/Euston tube/rail. **Rates** £89 double. **Rooms** 14. **Credit** MC, V. **Map** p399 K3 ⓳

Not much has changed at this Bloomsbury favourite since one Miss Maggie Jenkins converted the Georgian house into a hotel back in the 1920s. There may be TVs and mini-fridges in the rooms, but the decor unselfconsciously replicates the B&Bs of pre-World War II England – so much so that an episode of Agatha Christie's *Poirot* was filmed here. It's not overly chintzy – just cream walls, generous floral curtains and pretty bedspreads in the bedrooms, Nottingham lace tablecloths and Windsor chairs in the breakfast room. *TV.*

No More Bed Bugs

A new wave of London hostels means backpacking here is no longer a gamble.

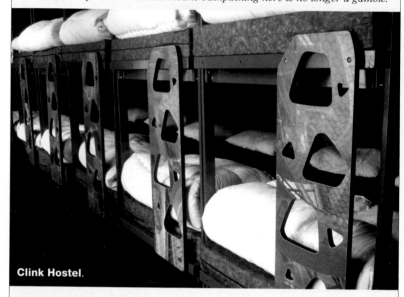

Clink Hostel.

If you're looking for a cheap and easy stay in London, hostels are no longer the worst possible alternative. No longer unhygienic digs that only hardened backpackers would deign to chance, the new breed of hostels are well furnished and carefully designed places that welcome as many families as indigent students.

Opened in 2007, the **Clink Hostel** (*see p175*) is a glimpse of the future that also happens to be packed to the brim with history. Set in a 300-year-old court-house, it has created a funky modern feel by combining stylish 21st-century design elements with the original architecture, which includes a couple of wood-panelled courtrooms where Charles Dickens once worked as a crime reporter. Location is another key attraction: the Clink is close to St Pancras International, with the British Library and the British Museum both in easy – and pleasant – walking distance. The Clink's nearby sister-hostel, **Ashlee House** (*see p175*) is smaller, but shares many of the design features – without the historic setting. They share a version of the popular Japanese 'pod' bed concept, which means that beds are sectioned-off

from each other for privacy, with a reading light and little safety box above each.

The third floor of the **Piccadilly Backpackers** (*see p179*) also has neat 'pod' beds, but even if you don't secure a place on that floor you'll benefit from the brilliantly central location near Piccadilly Circus. The **Oxford Street YHA** (*see p196*) is also wonderfully central: it sits just to the south of London's most famous shopping street, as near to Soho Square as it is to Oxford Circus.

Hostels are becoming a far more popular option for families and older travellers nowadays. If you are travelling with kids, the **Meininger** (*see p192*) is a few minutes' walk from Hyde Park, providing a clean and safe environment with helpful staff and a strict no alcohol policy to keep out the riff-raff. Families will also find the Youth Hostel Association properties at **St Paul's** and **Holland Park** (for both, *see p196*) perfect for the sights. The former could hardly be closer to the Wren cathedral and is a fun walk over the Millennium Bridge to the South Bank, while the latter is actually inside one of London's most beautiful parks.

Morgan

*24 Bloomsbury Street, Bloomsbury, WC1B 3QJ
(7636 3735/www.morganhotel.co.uk). Tottenham
Court Road tube.* **Rates** £100 double. **Rooms** 21.
Credit MC, V. **Map** p399 K5 ②
Run by the same family since 1978, the guestrooms
of this comfortable budget hotel have a distinctly
Seventies air – those nifty headboards with the built-
in bedside tables and reading lamps, the gathered
floral bedspreads. But they're well-equipped and all
geared for the electronic age with wireless and voice-
mail. And the cosy room where the slap-up English
breakfast is served is a charmer with its wood panelling, London prints and blue and white china
plates. Their spacious flats are excellent value.
Internet (wireless, free). TV.

COVENT GARDEN & THE STRAND

Deluxe

The **Savoy** (www.savoy2009.com) is due to
reopen in 2009 after a huge refurbishment.

★ Covent Garden Hotel

*10 Monmouth Street, Covent Garden, WC2H
9LF (7806 1000/www.firmdale.com). Covent
Garden or Leicester Square tube.* **Rates** £276-
£388 double. **Rooms** 58. **Credit** AmEx, MC, V.
Map p407 X2 ②
On the ground floor of the Covent Garden Hotel, the
1920s Paris-style Brasserie Max and its retro zinc
bar have been cunningly expanded – testament to
the continuing popularity of Kit Kemp's snug and
stylish 1996 establishment. Its location and tucked-
away screening room ensure it continues to attract
starry customers, with anyone needing a bit of privacy able to retreat upstairs to the lovely panelled
private library and drawing room. In the guest
rooms, Kemp's distinctive style mixes pinstriped
wallpaper, pristine white quilts, floral upholstery
with bold, contemporary elements; each room is
unique, but each has the Kemp trademark upholstered mannequin and granite and oak bathroom.
*Bar. Business centre. Concierge. Gym. Internet
(dataport/wireless, £20/day). Parking (£37/day).
Restaurant. Room service. Smoking rooms.
TV (DVD).*

★ One Aldwych

*1 Aldwych, the Strand, WC2B 4RH (7300 1000/
www.onealdwych.com). Covent Garden/Temple
tube/Charing Cross tube/rail.* **Rates** £230-£550
double. **Rooms** 105. **Credit** AmEx, DC, MC, V.
Map p407 Z3 ②
You only have to push through the front door and
enter the breathtaking Lobby Bar (*see p230*) to know
you're in for a treat. Despite weighty history – the
1907 building was designed by the men behind
the Ritz (*see p187*) – One Aldwych is thoroughly

modern, from Frette linen through bathroom mini-
TVs to the environmentally friendly loo-flushing
system. Flowers and fruit are replenished daily and
a card with the next day's weather forecast appears
at turndown. The location is perfect for Theatreland,
but the cosy little screening room and downstairs
swimming pool where soothing classical music is
played may keep you indoors. If you can, book one
of the three round corner suites – very romantic.
*Bar. Business services. Coffeeshop. Concierge.
Disabled-adapted rooms. Gym. Internet (dataport,
£15.50/day; wireless, free). Parking (£35/day).
Pool (1, indoor). Restaurants (2). Room service.
Smoking rooms. Spa. TV (pay movies/DVD).*

St Martins Lane Hotel

*45 St Martin's Lane, Covent Garden, WC2N
4HX (7300 5500/www.stmartinslane.com).
Leicester Square tube/Charing Cross tube/rail.*
Rates £395-£558 double. **Rooms** 204. **Credit**
AmEx, DC, MC, V. **Map** p407 X4 ②
When it opened as a Schrager property a decade ago,
the St Martins was the toast of the town. The flamboyant lobby was constantly buzzing, and guests
giggled like schoolgirls at Philippe Starck's playful
decor. The Starck objects – such as the gold tooth
stools in the lobby – remain, but the space lacks the
impact of its heyday. The all-white bedrooms have
comfortable minimalism down to a T, with floor-to-
ceiling windows, gadgetry secreted in sculptural
cabinets and sleek limestone bathrooms with toiletries from the spa at sister property Sanderson (*see
p173*). Asia de Cuba Chino-Latino restaurant is still
good-looking, and the Light Bar remains dramatic.
*Bar. Business services. Concierge. Disabled-
adapted rooms. Gym. Internet (dataport/high-
speed, £15/day). Parking (£40/day). Restaurant.
Room service. TV (pay movies/DVD).*

SOHO & LEICESTER SQUARE

Deluxe

Soho Hotel

*4 Richmond Mews (off Dean Street), Soho,
W1D 3DH (7559 3000/www.firmdale.com).
Tottenham Court Road tube.* **Rates** £329-£411
double. **Rooms** 91. **Credit** AmEx, DC, MC, V.
Map p406 W2 ②
Kit Kemp's 2004 shot at urban hip is still her most
edgy creation. Located in the heart of Soho – not that
you'd know it once you're inside, the place is
wonderfully quiet – the former carpark resembles a
converted loft building. The big bedrooms exhibit
a contemporary edge, with modern furniture,
industrial-style windows and nicely planned mod
cons (digital radios as well as flatscreen TVs),
although they're also classically Kemp with bold
stripes, traditional florals, plump sofas, oversized
bedheads and upholstered tailor's dummies. The

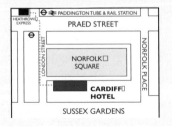

quiet drawing room and other public spaces feature groovy colours – shocking pinks and acid greens – while Refuel, the loungey bar and restaurant, has an open kitchen and, yes, a car-themed mural.
Bar. Business services. Concierge. Disabled-adapted rooms. Gym. Internet (dataport/wireless, £20/day). Restaurant. Room service. Smoking rooms. TV (DVD).

Expensive

Hazlitt's

6 Frith Street, Soho, W1D 3JA (7434 1771/ www.hazlittshotel.com). Tottenham Court Road tube. **Rates** £247-£258 double. **Rooms** 30. **Credit** AmEx, DC, MC, V. **Map** p406 W2 ㉕
Three Georgian town houses comprise this charming place, named after William Hazlitt, the spirited 18th-century essayist who lodged (and died in abject poverty) here. Quieter standard doubles are at the back of the house, while from the superior double front rooms it's easy to imagine the child prodigy Mozart strolling home with his dad after a recital: they lodged on this street in 1765. The rooms have fireplaces, superb carved wooden four-posters and half-testers, free-standing bathtubs and handsome cast-iron Shanks toilet cisterns. It gets creakier and more crooked the higher you go, culminating in enchanting garret single rooms with rooftop views. Air-conditioning, TVs in antique cupboards and triple-glazed windows are standard. Seven new bedrooms should have been added by early 2009.
Business services. Concierge. Internet (dataport/ web TV/wireless, free). Room service. Smoking rooms. TV (DVD).
▶ *Hazlitt was buried at St Anne's, Soho (www.st annes-soho.org.uk); his memorial can be seen in the Churchyard Gardens, just off Wardour Street.*

Cheap

Piccadilly Backpackers

12 Sherwood Street, Soho, W1F 7BR (7434 9009/www.piccadillybackpackers.com). Piccadilly Circus tube. **Rates** £55-£62 double; £12-£22 dorm bed. **Beds** 700. **Credit** AmEx, MC, V. **Map** p406 V4 ㉖
Want to be at the centre of things? You couldn't be more so than at this enormous hostel plunked right behind Piccadilly Circus. The almost invisible entrance gives way to several floors of accommodation and facilities like a travel shop, laundry, internet cafe and TV lounge. Sure, it's basic, but it's bright and airy and there's a relaxed, friendly vibe. Try for the third floor – here's where you'll find dorms of pod beds (with individual reading lights) quirkily decorated by graphic art students.
Internet (shared terminals/wireless, £1.50/hr). TV (lounge).
▶ *There's a travel shop and backpackers' bar nearby at 4 Golden Square (7287 9241).*

OXFORD STREET & MARYLEBONE

Deluxe

Cumberland

Great Cumberland Place, off Oxford Street, W1H 7DL (0870 333 9280/www.guoman.com). Marble Arch tube. **Rates** £351-£363 double. **Rooms** 900 (1,019 incl annexe). **Credit** AmEx, DC, MC, V. **Map** p395 F6 ㉗
Perfectly located by Marble Arch tube (turn the right way and you're there in seconds), the Cumberland is a bit of a monster. There are 900 rooms, plus another 119 in an annexe just down the road, and an echoing, rather chaotic lobby with dramatic modern art and a somewhat severe waterfall sculpture. The rooms are minimalist, with acid-etched headboards, neatly modern bathrooms and plasma TVs – nicely designed, but rather small. The hotel's excellent dining room is the exclusive Rhodes W1 (*see p213*), but there are also a bar-brasserie and boisterous, trash-industrial style, late-night DJ bar. Weekend breakfasts feel like the feeding of the 5,000.
Bars & restaurants (3). Concierge. Gym. Internet (dataport/high-speed, £10/day). Room service. TV.

Expensive

★ Montagu Place

2 Montagu Place, Marylebone, W1H 2ER (7467 2777/www.montagu-place.co.uk). Baker Street tube. **Rates** £198-£276 double. **Rooms** 16. **Credit** AmEx, DC, MC, V. **Map** p398 G5 ㉘
The Montagu is a stylish, small hotel in a pair of Grade II-listed Georgian town houses. Catering primarily for the midweek business traveller, its 16 rooms are divided into categories by size – Swanky are the largest, with enormous bathrooms, while Comfy are the smallest and, being at the back, have no street views. All rooms have deluxe pocket-sprung beds, as well as cafetières with freshly ground coffee and flatscreen TVs (DVD players are available from reception). The look is boutique-hotel sharp, except the uneasy overlap of bar and reception – though that means you can get a drink at any time and retire to the graciously modern lounge.
Bar. TV (widescreen/DVD).

Sherlock Holmes Hotel

108 Baker Street, Marylebone, W1U 6LJ (7486 6161/www.sherlockholmeshotel.com). Baker Street tube. **Rates** (incl breakfast at weekends) £139-£317 double. **Rooms** 119. **Credit** AmEx, DC, MC, V. **Map** p398 G5 ㉙
Park Plaza transformed a dreary, chintz-filled Hilton into this hip boutique hotel a few years back. Guests now mingle with local office workers in the casually chic bar, which extends to a lounge in the style of a glossed-up gentlemen's club, and the organic restau-

CONSUME

Portobello Hotel.

rant. The rooms, meanwhile, resemble hip bachelor pads: beige and brown colour scheme, leather headboards, pinstripe scatter cushions and spiffy bathrooms. Split-level 'loft' suites take advantage of the first floor's double-height ceilings. There's a gym with sauna and treatments, and the inevitable memorabilia ranges from expressionist paintings of Holmes and Watson to magnifying glasses.
Bar. Business centre. Concierge. Disabled-adapted rooms. Gym. Internet (broadband/dataport/ wireless). Restaurant. Room service. TV (pay movies).

Moderate

Sumner

54 Upper Berkeley Street, Marylebone, W1H 7QR (7723 2244/www.thesumner.com). Marble Arch tube. **Rates** (incl breakfast) £150-£200 double. **Rooms** 20. **Credit** AmEx, DC, MC, V. **Map** p395 F6 **⓷⓪**
Sitting on the fringes of newly-branded Portman Village, this coolly chic boutique hotel set in a Georgian town house is run by the award-winning team behind Five Sumner Place. It's all shades of grey in the lounge and halls, and the decor of the custom-designed deluxe rooms may be too hard-edged for some (though they've terrific walk-in showers). Other rooms are softer-toned and the buttercup-strewn wall and multi-coloured Arne Jacobsen chairs in the breakfast room make for a cheerily elegant start to the day.
Disabled access. Internet (wireless). TV (widescreen).

★ 22 York Street

22 York Street, Marylebone, W1U 6PX (7224 2990/www.22yorkstreet.co.uk). Baker Street tube. **Rates** £100-£120 double. **Rooms** 10. **Credit** AmEx, MC, V. **Map** p398 G5 **⓷⓵**
Imagine one of those bohemian French country houses featured in *Elle Décoration* – all pale pink lime-washed walls, wooden floors, sprinklings of quirky antiques and subtly-faded textiles – and you'll have the feel of this graceful, unpretentious bed and breakfast in the heart of Marylebone. There's no sign on the door and the sense of staying in a hospitable home continues when you're offered coffee in the spacious breakfast room-cum-kitchen with its huge curved communal table. Many of the predominantly good-sized rooms have en suite baths – a rarity in this price range.
Internet (wireless). TV.

Cheap

Weardowney Guesthouse

9 Ashbridge Street, Marylebone, NW8 8DH (7725 9694/www.weardowney.com). Marylebone tube/rail. **Rates** £79-£94 double. **Rooms** 7. **Credit** AmEx, DC, MC, V. **Map** p395 E4 **⓷⓶**
This 'artisan guesthouse' (thus named by its owners, knitwear designers Amy Wear and Gail Downey) is a charming place in a quiet backwater. It's just seven rooms above their corner boutique in an early Victorian house-turned-pub-turned-shop. Only three are en suite – but there are two bathrooms for the others to share. The guesthouse is done up in pale muted tones: an appealing mix of handknitted

bedspreads, antiques, art and photos. There's also a pretty roof terrace, and guests can use the kitchen. *Internet (wireless, free). TV.*

PADDINGTON & NOTTING HILL

Deluxe

Hempel
31-35 Craven Hill Gardens, Paddington, W2 3EA (7298 9000/www.the-hempel.co.uk). Lancaster Gate or Queensway tube/Paddington tube/rail. **Rates** £347-£370 double. **Rooms** 51. **Credit** AmEx, DC, MC, V. **Map** p394 C6 ③

Suave in low-lit creams and soft beiges, this bastion of minimalism was formerly an Anouska Hempel. The new owners have kept the wildly luxurious fittings (Pour rugs at £10,000 a pop, Zents bathroom products, canned oxygen in the minibars) and such features as the bed suspended from the ceiling by iron bars, but are refurbishing the rooms and restaurant – the work should be complete by mid 2009. The rooms may seem a little formal for slouchers, but the quality of the package shines through. Don't miss the hotel's austerely pristine garden square. *Bar. Business services. Concierge. Disabled-adapted rooms. Restaurant. Room service. TV (pay movies/music/DVD).*

Expensive

Guesthouse West
163-165 Westbourne Grove, Notting Hill, W11 2RS (7792 9800/www.guesthousewest.com). Notting Hill Gate tube. **Rates** (incl continental breakfast) £182-£217 double. **Rooms** 20. **Credit** AmEx, MC, V. **Map** p394 B6 ③

Set in an impressive three-floor, cream-coloured building, Guesthouse West is a stylish, affordable antidote to exorbitant hotels. It keeps prices down by cutting out room service and offering instead a handy list of local businesses. The look is Notting Hillbilly hip: the retro lobby bar (only licensed to serve until 10pm) has a changing art display and the front terrace is perfect

---

THE BEST PURE CLASS

For luxury you can live in
Covent Garden Hotel. *See p177.*

For old-school service
Connaught. *See p184.*

For period drama
Hazlitt's. *See p179.*

For somewhere discreet
No.5 Maddox. *See p185.*

---

for posing. Minimalist bedrooms have enough extras to keep hip young things happy: wireless internet, flatscreen TVs, Molton Brown toiletries. *Bar. Internet (high-speed/wireless). Restaurant. TV (pay movies/music/DVD).*

★ Miller's Residence
111A Westbourne Grove, Bayswater, W2 4UW (7243 1024/www.millershotel.com). Bayswater or Notting Hill Gate tube. **Rates** (incl continental breakfast) £176-£270 double. **Rooms** 8. **Credit** AmEx, MC, V. **Map** p394 B6 ③

This gloriously atmospheric pad, hidden behind an unmarked door in an unprepossessing side street, is a cross between a baronial family pile and a Portobello arcade. Owned by antiques expert Martin Miller, it is furnished at every turn with chandeliers, antique vases and cabinets of curios. Rooms, some featuring four-poster beds, may be named after 19th-century poets, but they come with 21st-century amenities (air-con, CD and DVD players). The drawing room, where a generous breakfast buffet is laid out, is an Aladdin's cave of artefacts; it's even more atmospheric at night, when you can relax by the elaborate fireplace with a whisky from the free bar. *Internet (wireless). TV.*

Portobello Hotel
22 Stanley Gardens, Notting Hill, W11 2NG (7727 2777/www.portobello-hotel.co.uk). Holland Park or Notting Hill Gate tube. **Rates** (incl breakfast) £195-£350 double. **Rooms** 23. **Credit** AmEx, MC, V. **Map** p394 A6 ③

The lift in the Portobello has a mind of its own. Perhaps it's weighing up the celebrity status of guests before taking them through the five floors of this Notting Hill mansion. If so, it's been calibrated by the likes of Johnny Depp, Kate Moss, Van Morrison and Alice Cooper, who used his tub to house a boa constrictor. This is a pleasingly unpretentious place that still feels like many hotels once did: hard to pinpoint in time and place. The rooms are themed – the basement Japanese Water Garden, for example, has an elaborate spa bath, its own private grotto and a small private garden. *Bar. Internet (wireless). Room service (24hr). TV (movies, free).*

Moderate

New Linden
59 Leinster Square, Bayswater, W2 4PS (7221 4321/www.newlinden.co.uk). Bayswater tube. **Rates** £116-£211 double. **Rooms** 51. **Credit** AmEx, MC, V. **Map** p394 B6 ③

The Mayflower Group have done it again: transforming an indifferent Bayswater hotel into an affordable showstopper. Following a refit, the lobby and lounge are all black and gold glamour with those nods to Asian opulence the group's design team like – here it's a spectacular teak arch. The

rooms are tranquil havens: creamy walls, low key colours, gleaming woods, the occasional richly coloured accent. Bathrooms are marble and showers are all walk-ins, some with deluge shower heads. *Concierge. Internet (wireless). TV.*

Vancouver Studios

30 Prince's Square, Bayswater, W2 4NJ (7243 1270/www.vancouverstudios.co.uk). Bayswater or Queensway tube. **Rates** £108-£125 double. **Rooms** 48. **Credit** AmEx, DC, MC, V. **Map** p394 B6 ❸

You'll think you've arrived at an Edwardian bachelor's town house when you turn up at this welcoming all-studios hotel in lodging-dense Bayswater – the boots by the stairs, the kilim-effect upholstery in the cosy sitting-room, the resident feline. But just when you think you've got the Vancouver pegged, you're shown into one of their well-equipped studios that are mainly unfussy contemporary, but could equally be drop-dead glamorous, or prettily old-fashioned. With their sleek kitchenettes, flatscreen TVs and DVD players, they're superb value. *Internet (dataport/shared terminal/wireless). TV (DVD).*

Cheap

Garden Court Hotel

30-31 Kensington Gardens Square, Bayswater, W2 4BG (7229 2553/www.gardencourthotel. co.uk). Bayswater or Queensway tube. **Rates** (incl breakfast) £77-£120 double. **Rooms** 32. **Credit** MC, V. **Map** p394 B6 ❸

Long-established and family-owned, this friendly well-run hotel in a grand Victorian terrace has a traditional feel that's been brought up to date with lots of white and fresh contemporary colours. The comfortable rooms are papered in light patterns above the dado rail and the lounge with its wood floor, leather covered furniture, sprightly floral wallpaper and elegant mantelpiece is charming. A big plus in Bayswater's tall cream canyons is the recently installed lift. *Internet (shared terminal, £1/30mins). TV.*

Pavilion

34-36 Sussex Gardens, Paddington, W2 1UL (7262 0905/www.pavilionhoteluk.com). Edgware Road tube/Marylebone or Paddington tube/rail. **Rates** £85-£100 double. **Rooms** 29. **Credit** AmEx, MC, V. **Map** p395 E5 ❹

Behind a deceptively modest façade at the unprepossessing end of Sussex Gardens is what could just be London's funkiest, most original hotel – and all at budget prices. A voluptuously exotic paean to excess and paint effects, the Pavilion's assortment of madly colourful individually-themed rooms ('Highland Fling', 'Afro Honky Tonk' or 'Casablanca Nights' anyone?) has become a celeb-magnet and it's often used for fashion shoots. Not for those looking

for minimalism and 'facilities' – though it's got most of the usual. Absolutely fabulous! *Internet (wireless, £10/day). Parking (£10/day). Room service (24hr). TV.*

Stylotel

160-162 Sussex Gardens, Paddington, W2 1UD (7723 1026/www.stylotel.com). **Rates** £90 double. **Rooms** 39. **Credit** AmEx, MC, V. **Map** p395 E6 ❹

Do we love it or loathe it? We're listing it, so it must be love – or perhaps it's just the enthusiastic young manager. It's a retro-futurist dream: metal floors and panelling, lots of royal blue surfaces (the hall walls, the padded headboards) and pod bathrooms. But the real deal at Stylotel is its new bargain-priced studio and apartment (respectively, £120-£150 and £150-£200, including breakfast). Designed – like the hotel – by the owner's son, he's calmed down with age. Here's real minimalist chic: sleek brushed steel or white glass walls panels, simply-styled contemporary furniture upholstered in black or white. *Concierge. Internet (wireless, £2/hr). Smoking rooms. TV.*

PICCADILLY CIRCUS & MAYFAIR

Deluxe

Brown's

Albemarle Street, Mayfair, W1S 4BP (7493 6020/www.roccofortecollection.com). Green Park tube. **Rates** £529-£734 double. **Rooms** 117. **Credit** AmEx, DC, MC, V. **Map** p406 U5 ❹

Brown's was opened in 1837 by Lord Byron's butler, James Brown. The first British telephone call was made from here in 1876, five years after Napoleon III and Empress Eugenie took refuge in one of the suites after fleeing the Third Republic. Haile Selassie and Rudyard Kipling have both been guests. The public spaces resonate history – non-residents can visit the English Tea Room, with its wood panelling, fireplaces and Jacobean ceilings for afternoon tea (3-6pm, £35.50), or sup in the classy Donovan Bar. All 117 bedrooms, super-large and extremely comfortable, were reconfigured in a major 2003 refit, but keep their character with original art, book collections and, in the suites, fireplaces. *Bar. Business centre. Concierge. Disabled-adapted rooms. Gym. Internet (high-speed/wireless). Restaurants. Room service (24hr). Spa. Tearoom. TV (music/pay movies).*

★ Claridge's

55 Brook Street, Mayfair, W1K 4HR (7629 8860/www.claridges.co.uk). Bond Street tube. **Rates** £700-£830 double. **Rooms** 203. **Credit** AmEx, DC, MC, V. **Map** p398 H6 ❹

Claridge's is sheer class and pure atmosphere, with its signature art deco redesign still simply dazzling.

CONSUME

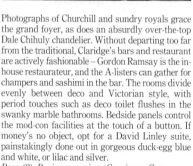

Photographs of Churchill and sundry royals grace the grand foyer, as does an absurdly over-the-top Dale Chihuly chandelier. Without departing too far from the traditional, Claridge's bars and restaurant are actively fashionable – Gordon Ramsay is the in-house restaurateur, and the A-listers can gather for champers and sashimi in the bar. The rooms divide evenly between deco and Victorian style, with period touches such as deco toilet flushes in the swanky marble bathrooms. Bedside panels control the mod-con facilities at the touch of a button. If money's no object, opt for a David Linley suite, painstakingly done out in gorgeous duck-egg blue and white, or lilac and silver.

Bars (2). Business services. Concierge. Gym. Internet (wireless, free). Restaurants (3). Room service (24hr). Smoking rooms. TV (DVD/pay movies).

INSIDE TRACK
SKY-HIGH CEILINGS

You have Britain's class-system to thank, but we can guide you to the biggest rooms in almost every renovated town house hotel. The rule is simple: servants' quarters were at the top of the house, so those rooms have lower ceilings than the rooms for the family. Opt for the first floor if you can, sometimes the ground floor is as good. And since there is rarely a lift that might be wise anyway…

★ Connaught

Carlos Place, Mayfair, W1K 2AL (7499 7070/ www.the-connaught.co.uk). Bond Street tube. **Rates** £410-£717 double. **Rooms** 68. **Credit** AmEx, DC, MC, V. **Map** p400 H7 ⓮

This isn't the only hotel in London to provide butlers, but there can't be many that offer 'a secured gun cabinet room' for hunting season. This is traditional British hospitality for those who love 23-carat gold leaf trimmings and stern portraits in the halls, but all mod cons in their room. Too lazy to polish your own shoes? The butlers are trained in shoe care by the expert cobblers at John Lobb. Both bars – the gentleman's club cosy Coburg (*see p234*) and cruise-ship deco, David Collins-designed Connaught – are impressive; a new restaurant and more modern wing (increasing the number of rooms to 123, as well as adding a gym and spa) are on the way this year.

Bars (2). Concierge. Internet (wireless, free). Restaurants (2). Room service (24hr). Smoking rooms. TV (DVD).

Dorchester

53 Park Lane, Mayfair, W1K 1QA (7629 8888/ www.thedorchester.com). Hyde Park Corner tube. **Rates** £664-£734 double. **Rooms** 249. **Credit** AmEx, DC, MC, V. **Map** p400 G7 ⓯

The Dorchester has been a Park Lane fixture since 1931; the view over Hyde Park from the expansive terrace is the same one Elizabeth Taylor would have seen when she took the call about taking a part in *Cleopatra*. And the 49 other suites? Eisenhower planned the D-Day landings in one and Prince Philip held his stag in another. This opulence is reflected

Connaught.

in the grandest lobby in town, complete with Liberace's piano. The hotel continually upgrades older rooms to the same high standard as the rest, with floral decor, antiques and lavish marble bathrooms. The Dorchester also employs 90 full-time chefs – the Grill Room is excellent, while the Alain Ducasse team of Nicola Canuti and Bruno Riou launched the master's first London restaurant here in 2007. After a revamp, the spa should be back for spring this year; non-residents can use it too.
Bar. Concierge. Disabled-adapted rooms. Gym. Internet (dataport/high-speed/web TV, £19.50/day). Parking (£30-£40/day). Restaurants (3). Room service (24hr). Smoking rooms. Spa. TV (pay movies/music/DVD).

Haymarket Hotel
1 Suffolk Place, off Piccadilly Circus, SW1Y 4BP (7470 4000/www.firmdale.com). Piccadilly Circus tube. **Rates** *£294-£535 double.* **Rooms** 50. **Credit** AmEx, DC, MC, V. **Map** p406 W5
This is the latest opening from Kit Kemp's Firmdale group. The block-size building was designed by John Nash, the architect of Regency London, and it is a pleasure simply to inhabit spaces he created, one that Kemp's decor, with sinuous sculptures, fuschia paint and shiny sofas, somewhat against the odds, manages to enhance. Wow-factors are the surprisingly bling basement swimming pool and bar (shiny sofas, twinkly roof) and the couldn't-be-more central location with accompanying street views. Rooms are generously sized (as are bathrooms), individually decorated and discreetly stuffed with facilities, and there's plenty of attention from the switched-on staff.

Bar. Concierge. Disabled-adapted rooms. Gym. Internet (wireless, £20/day). Pool (1, indoor). Restaurant. Room service. Smoking rooms. Spa. TV (DVD/pay movies).
▶ *For more on architect John Nash, see p37.*

Metropolitan
19 Old Park Lane, Mayfair, W1K 1LB (7447 1000/www.metropolitan.como.bz). Hyde Park Corner tube. **Rates** *£499-£793 double.* **Rooms** 150. **Credit** AmEx, DC, MC, V. **Map** p400 H8
Christina Ong's chic, contemporary Metropolitan – the sassier, younger sister of the Halkin (*see p191*) – forms part of the celeb-friendly COMO group of hotels and resorts in Bali, Bangkok and the Turks and Caicos. Ong's background in retail and interior design stands out in the relaxed lobby bar area and throughout the spacious rooms, soundproofed from the hum of Mayfair traffic, their creamy furnishings now brought out by plum carpets. With its park-view rooms, destination dining spot Nobu and famously papped Met Bar, this is still a hotel with credentials, even a decade after opening.
Bar. Business centre. Concierge. Gym. Internet (dataport/high-speed/wireless). Parking (£40/day). Restaurant. Room service (24hr). Smoking rooms. Spa. TV (pay movies/DVD).

★ No.5 Maddox Street
5 Maddox Street, Mayfair, W1S 2QD (7647 0200/www.living-rooms.co.uk). Oxford Circus tube. **Rates** *£300-£752 double.* **Rooms** 12. **Credit** AmEx, DC, MC, V. **Map** p406 U2
This bolthole just off Regent Street is perfect for visiting film directors looking to be accommodated in a chic apartment at a reasonable long-term rate. Here they can shut the discreet brown front door, climb the stairs and flop into a home from home with all contemporary cons, including new flatscreen TVs. The East-meets-West decor is classic 1990s minimalist, but very bright and clean after a gentle refurbishment. Each apartment has a fully equipped kitchen, but room service will shop for you as well as providing the usual hotel services. There's no bar, but breakfasts and snacks are served, the Thai restaurant Patara is on the ground floor and all the bars of Soho lie just across the road.
Business centre. Concierge. Internet (dataport/high-speed/wireless, £15/day, £60/week). Private kitchen. Room service. TV (DVD/music).

THE BEST
CULTURE CONNECTIONS

For edgy art and events
Andaz Liverpool Street. *See p169.*

For a medialand location
Soho Hotel. *See p177.*

CONSUME

Profile Terence Conran

The design mogul re-enters the hotel trade this year – and we're excited.

The influence of Terence Conran (www.conran.co.uk) on British design can't be underestimated. His first venture was the **Soup Kitchen** in Chandos Place, near Trafalgar Square, which brought notions from shop display into a café, allying exotic innovations like London's second Gaggia espresso machine to the simple notion of serving soup at a shilling (5p) a bowl. But it was the opening on 11 May 1964 of the **Habitat** store – seeking to bring high-end design to the masses – that guaranteed his fame. With staff dressed by Mary Quant and sporting sleek haircuts by Vidal Sassoon, the clean, functional aesthetic of Conran's shop proved hugely popular with middle-class shoppers, who had read all about it in the new colour supplements that were folded into their weekend papers.

Nowadays, a feel for the excitement generated by that first Habitat can still be gleaned from a visit to the flagship **Conran Shop** (*see p263*) on the Fulham Road. The original opened opposite here in 1973, but since 1987 the shop has occupied this appropriately gorgeous Michelin building. The **Design Museum** (*see p56*), another Conran initiative that opened on Butlers Wharf in summer 1989, continues to promote design from a typically unapologetic, modernist warehouse conversion.

Having designed interiors for hotels (including Myhotel Bloomsbury, *see p173*), Conran launched his own in 2000: the **Great Eastern**. The Grade II-listed, Victorian station hotel was transformed with a modern extension

Boundary Street.

that enabled Conran to keep original features like a masonic temple intact, but also introduce a stunning new atrium.

The Great Eastern was bought by Hyatt in 2006, becoming **Andaz**, but it turns out Conran hadn't given up on hotels. Due to open early this year, **Boundary** (2-4 Boundary Street, Bethnal Green, E2 7JE, www.theboundary.co.uk) is his latest project, four individual businesses in, yes, a converted warehouse. The hotel part is 17 bedrooms (£200-£350 double), each with wet room and hand-made bed, but otherwise all individually designed. Next come the Rooftop terrace bar and grill, the Albion bakery-café for all-day breakfasts and classic Brit snacks (pork pies and the like), and a restaurant with a menu of mostly French, seasonal classics, a substantial wine list and uniformed staff. We're already in the queue for the grand opening.

THREE TO SEE

Andaz
See p169.
Sneak up in the lift of the former Great Eastern for a peak down the amazing atrium.

Shop at Bluebird
See p250.
A deco garage brilliantly converted into a shop and eaterie.

Boundary
www.the boundary. co.uk.
Conran's excellent new venture.

Ritz

150 Piccadilly, W1J 9BR (7493 8181/www.theritz london.com). Green Park tube. **Rates** *£586-£646 double.* **Rooms** *136.* **Credit** *AmEx, DC, MC, V.* **Map** p400 J8 ⓭

Class or snobbishness? If you like the idea of a world where jeans and trainers are banned and jackets must be worn by gentlemen when dining (the requirement is waived for breakfast), the Ritz is for you. Founded by hotelier extraordinaire César Ritz, the hotel is deluxe in excelsis. The show-stopper is the ridiculously ornate, vaulted Long Gallery, an orgy of chandeliers, rococo mirrors and marble columns, but all the high-ceilinged, Louis XVI-style bedrooms have been painstakingly renovated to their former glory in restrained pastel colours. Amid the old-world luxury, mod cons include wireless internet, large TVs and a gym. With hotel tours no longer offered, an elegant afternoon tea in the Palm Court is the only way in for interlopers.

Bar. Concierge. Gym. Internet (dataport/high-speed, £25/day). Restaurant. Room service. TV (DVD/VCR).

▶ *The wonderful One Aldwych hotel was also designed by Ritz's architects Charles Mewes and Arthur Davis; see p177.*

WESTMINSTER & ST JAMES'S

Deluxe

St James's Hotel & Club

7-8 Park Place, St James's, SW1A 1LP (7316 1600/www.stjameshotelandclub.com). Green Park tube. **Rates** *£318-£405 double.* **Rooms** *60.* **Credit** *AmEx, DC, MC, V.* **Map** p400 J8 ⓯

Secreted in blissful exclusivity in a 19th-century town house on one of London's stuffiest streets, the St James's Hotel & Club opened in late 2008 after a lavish 18-month makeover. In tune with the Mayfair surrounds, the bedrooms are a picture of sober understatement, sporting neutral colours and expensive raw materials (silk wallpaper, cashmere throws, polished stone bathrooms). The rooms come up short on space, but they do buy you proximity to one of London's most extravagant new restaurants: as you might expect from a hotel chain in possession of nine Michelin stars (between just six hotels), the house restaurant – Andaman – is the very model of gastronomic artistry and accuracy.

Bar. Disabled-adapted rooms. Internet (wireless, free). Restaurant. Room service (24hr). TV.

Expensive

City Inn Westminster

30 John Islip Street, Westminster, SW1P 4DD (7630 1000/www.cityinn.com). Pimlico tube. **Rates** *£159-£394 double.* **Rooms** *420.* **Credit** *AmEx, DC, MC, V.* **Map** p401 K10 ⓱

There's nothing particularly flashy about this new-build hotel, but it is well run, neatly designed and obliging: the rooms have all the added extras you'd want (iMacs, CD/DVD library for your in-room player, free broadband, flatscreen TVs) and the floor-to-ceiling windows mean that river-facing suites on the 12th and 13th floors have superb night views – when the businessmen go home for the weekend you might grab one for £125. With half an eye on near neighbour Tate Britain (*see p113*), the owners have collaborated with the Chelsea College of Art to provide changing art through the lobbies and meeting rooms; outside the rather unconvincing City Café you can sit on a Ron Arad chair.

Bars (2). Business centre. Concierge. Disabled-adapted rooms. Gym. Parking (£30/day). Restaurant. Room service (24hr). Smoking rooms. TV (CD/DVD/pay movies).

★ Trafalgar

2 Spring Gardens, off Trafalgar Square, SW1A 2TS (7870 2900/www.thetrafalgar.com). Charing Cross tube/rail. **Rates** *£235-£294 double.* **Rooms** *129.* **Credit** *AmEx, DC, MC, V.* **Map** p407 X5 ⓲

The Trafalgar is a Hilton – but you'd hardly notice. The mood is young and dynamic at the chain's first 'concept' hotel, for all that it's housed in an imposing edifice. To the right of the open reception is the Rockwell Bar, which serves good cocktails with a DJ soundtrack most nights, while breakfast downstairs is accompanied by a gentle live music. Yet it is the none-more-central location that's the biggest draw – the few corner suites look directly into Trafalgar Square (prices reflect location), but those without a room view can, in season, avail themselves of the small rooftop bar. The good-sized rooms have a masculine feel, with white walls and walnut furniture.

Bars (2). Concierge. Disabled-adapted rooms. Gym. Internet (dataport, £15/day). Restaurant. Room service (24hr). Smoking floor. TV (CD/DVD/pay movies/games).

▶ *Formerly the headquarters of Cunard, it was in this building that the Titanic was conceived.*

Moderate

B+B Belgravia

64-66 Ebury Street, Belgravia, SW1W 9QD (7823 4928/www.bb-belgravia.com). Victoria tube/rail. **Rates** *(incl breakfast) £120 double.* **Rooms** *17.* **Credit** *AmEx, MC, V.* **Map** p400 H10 ⓳

How do you make a lounge full of white and black contemporary furnishings seem cosy and welcoming? Hard to achieve, but they've succeeded at B+B Belgravia who've taken the B&B experience to a new level. It's fresh and sophisticated without being hard-edged: there's nothing to make the most design-conscious of you wince (you know who you are), nor is it overly precious. And there are all kinds of goodies to make you feel at home: a gleaming

CONSUME

B+B Belgravia. *See p187.*

espresso machine for 24/7 caffeine, an open fireplace, newspapers and DVDs.
Disabled-adapted rooms. Internet (high-speed). TV.

Windermere Hotel
142-144 Warwick Way, Pimlico, SW1V 4JE (7834 5163/www.windermere-hotel.co.uk). Victoria tube/rail. **Rates** (incl breakfast) £119-£144 double. **Rooms** 20. **Credit** AmEx, MC, V. **Map** p400 H11
Heading the procession of small hotels strung along Warwick Way, the Windermere is a comfortable, traditionally decked-out London hotel with no aspirations to boutique status. The decor may be showing its age a bit in the hall, but you'll receive a warm welcome and excellent service – there are over a dozen staff for just 20 rooms. There's a cosy basement restaurant-bar (breakfasts are top-notch) and guests get a discount at the neighbouring car park.
Bar. Business services. Internet (dataport). Restaurant. Room service. TV.

Cheap

Morgan House
120 Ebury Street, Belgravia, SW1W 9QQ (7730 2384/www.morganhouse.co.uk). Pimlico tube/Victoria tube/rail. **Rates** (incl breakfast) £72-£92 double. **Rooms** 11. **Credit** MC, V. **Map** p400 G10
The Morgan has the understated charm of the old family home of a posh but unpretentious English friend: a pleasing mix of nice old wooden or traditional iron beds, pretty floral curtains and coverlets in subtle hues, the odd chandelier or big gilt mirror over original mantelpieces, padded wicker chairs

and sinks in every bedroom. Though there's no guest lounge, guests can sit in the little patio garden. And for Belgravia, it's a steal.
Internet (shared terminal, wireless). TV.

CHELSEA
Deluxe

Cadogan
75 Sloane Street, SW1X 9SG (7235 7141/ www.cadogan.com). Sloane Square tube. **Rates** £347-£464 double. **Rooms** 65. **Credit** AmEx, DC, MC, V. **Map** p397 F10
Time has rather caught up with this terribly British hotel. Wood panels and pretty mosaic flooring at both entrances, plus an old-fashioned cage lift, remind you of naughtier times: Edward VII visited his mistress Lillie Langtry here and Oscar Wilde was arrested in room 118. The signature suites are fun for history buffs, but the other bedrooms are a mixed bag – some are rather dowdy, others (like a verdant junior suite with central arch) genuinely romantic. On a misty morning, though, the private gardens opposite – only guests and residents of the grand square are allowed in – are truly enchanting.
Bar. Business centre. Concierge. Gym. Internet (wireless, £10/day). Restaurant. Room service. TV (DVD).

Expensive

★ Myhotel Chelsea
35 Ixworth Place, SW3 3QX (7225 7500/www. myhotels.com). South Kensington tube. **Rates** £276-£311 double. **Rooms** 45. **Credit** AmEx, DC, MC, V. **Map** p397 E11

CONSUME

Myhotel Chelsea. *See p189.*

CONSUME

The Chelsea Myhotel feels a world away from its sleekly modern Bloomsbury sister (*see p173*), its aesthetic softer and more feminine – precious certainly, perhaps in both senses. Pink walls, a floral sofa and a plate of scones in the lobby offer a posh English foil to the mini-chain's signature feng shui touches and aquarium, continued through the rooms with dusky pink wallpaper, white wicker headboards and velvet cushions. The modernised country farmhouse feel of the bar-restaurant works better for breakfast than it does for a boozy cocktail, but the conservatory-style library in a central courtyard is wonderful. Just sink into one of the ample comfy chairs and listen to the tinkling water feature or your own choice of CD.
Bar. Business centre. Concierge. Gym. Internet (dataport/wireless). Restaurant. Room service. Spa. TV (DVD).

KNIGHTSBRIDGE & SOUTH KENSINGTON

Deluxe

Baglioni
60 Hyde Park Gate, Kensington, SW7 5BB (7368 5700/www.baglionihotellondon.com). High Street Kensington or Gloucester Road tube. **Rates** £341-£482 double. **Rooms** 68. **Credit** AmEx, DC, MC, V. **Map** p394 C9 ⑤⑧
Occupying a mansion opposite Kensington Palace and offering a butler on each floor and a chauffeur-driven Maserati, the Baglioni is certainly luxurious,

yet it has none of the snooty formality of some of its deluxe English counterparts. The ground-floor Italian restaurant and bar are part baroque, part Donatella Versace: spidery black chandeliers, burnished gold ceilings, gigantic vases and a truly magnificent mirror from Venice. The chic bedrooms are more subdued: black floorboards, taupe and gold-leaf walls, dark wood furniture enlivened by jewel-coloured cushions and soft throws. Instead of the usual marble, the swanky black-panelled bathrooms have hammered iron sinks imported from Morocco.
Bar. Business centre. Concierge. Disabled-adapted rooms. Gym. Internet (dataport/high-speed/web TV/wireless). Parking (£38/day). Restaurant. Room service (24hr). Spa. TV (DVD/movies/music).

Bentley
27-33 Harrington Gardens, South Kensington, SW7 4JX (7244 5555/www.thebentley-hotel.com). Gloucester Road tube. **Rates** £352-£470 double. **Rooms** 64. **Credit** AmEx, DC, MC, V. **Map** p396 C10 ⑤⑨
Although it isn't large, the Bentley's style is on a grand scale: Louis XV-style furniture, gilt mirrors, gleaming marble – 600 tons of it, all imported – and a sweeping circular staircase perfect for making an entrance. Chandeliers are everywhere, in the bedrooms as well as the lobby, and the former also have plush carpets, satin bedspreads and dark marble bathrooms with gold fittings and jacuzzi tubs. Glitzy restaurant 1880 gets its name from the date the building was opened on this quiet Kensington street.

The Malachite Bar is a dimly lit, decadent hideaway in deep red, green and leopard-print, but the showpiece is the classical spa, with gold-laced mosaics and a full-size Turkish hammam.

Bar. Business centre. Concierge. Disabled-adapted rooms. Gym. Internet (dataport/high-speed, £5.99/hr). Restaurants (2). Room service (24hr). Smoking rooms. Spa. TV (pay movies/music/DVD).

Blakes

33 Roland Gardens, South Kensington, SW7 3PF (7370 6701/www.blakeshotels.com). South Kensington tube. **Rates** £311-£440 double. **Rooms** 48. **Credit** AmEx, DC, MC, V. **Map** p397 D11 ⑩

As original as when Anouska Hempel opened it in 1983 – the scent of oranges and the twittering of a pair of lovebirds fill the dark, oriental lobby – Blakes and its maximalist decor have stood the test of time, a living casebook for interior design students. Each room is in a different style, with influences from Italy, India, Turkey and China. Exotic antiques picked up on the designer's travels – intricately carved beds, Chinese birdcages, ancient trunks – are complemented with sweeping drapery and piles of plump cushions. Downstairs is the eclectic, Eastern-influenced restaurant, complemented by a gym and wireless internet for a celebrity clientele enticed by the discreet, residential location.

Bar. Business services. Concierge. Internet (dataport/wireless, £12/day). Restaurant. Room service (24hr). TV (pay movies/DVD).

Gore

190 Queen's Gate, South Kensington, SW7 5EX (7584 6601/www.gorehotel.com). South Kensington tube. **Rates** £341-£458 double. **Rooms** 50. **Credit** AmEx, DC, MC, V. **Map** p397 D9 ⑪

This fin-de-siècle period piece was founded by descendants of Captain Cook in two grand Victorian town houses. The lobby and staircase are close hung with old paintings, and the bedrooms all have fantastic 19th-century carved oak beds, sumptuous drapes and shelves of old books. The suites are spectacular: the Tudor Room has a huge stone-faced fireplace and a minstrels' gallery, while tragedy queens

should plump for the Venus room and Judy Garland's old bed (and replica ruby slippers). Bistrot 190 provides a casually elegant setting for great breakfasts, while the warm, wood-panelled 190 bar (*see p236*) is a charming setting for cocktails.

Bar. Concierge. Internet (dataport/wireless). Restaurant. Room service. TV.

Halkin

Halkin Street, Belgravia, SW1X 7DJ (7333 1000/www.halkin.como.bz). Hyde Park Corner tube. **Rates** £458 double. **Rooms** 41. **Credit** AmEx, DC, MC, V. **Map** p400 G9 ⑫

Gracious and discreet behind a Georgian-style façade, the first hotel of Singaporean fashion magnate Christina Ong (whose COMO group also includes the more famous Metropolitan, *see p185*) was ahead of the East-meets-West design trend when it opened in 1991 and its subtle design – a marriage of European luxury and oriental serenity – looks more current than hotels half its age. The rooms, located off curving black corridors, combine stylish classical sofas with black lacquer tables and Asian artefacts. A high-tech touchscreen bedside console controls everything from the 'do not disturb' sign to the air-conditioning.

Bar. Concierge. Disabled-adapted rooms. Internet (high-speed/wireless). Parking (£45/day). Restaurant. Room service (24hr). TV (pay movies/DVD).

▶ *Halkin is renowned for its Michelin-starred Thai restaurant, Nahm; see p217.*

★ Lanesborough

1 Lanesborough Place, Hyde Park Corner, SW1X 7TA (7259 5599/www.lanesborough. com). Hyde Park Corner tube. **Rates** £581-£699 double. **Rooms** 95. **Credit** AmEx, DC, MC, V. **Map** p400 G8 ⑬

Considered one of London's more historic luxury hotels, the Lanesborough was in fact redeveloped – impressively – only in 1991. Occupying an 1820s Greek Revival building, originally a hospital, its luxurious guest rooms are traditionally decorated with thick fabrics, antique furniture and lavish Carrera-marble bathrooms. Electronic keypads control everything from the air-conditioning to the superb 24hr room service at the touch of a button. As luxury hotels go, the Lanesborough's rates are unusually inclusive: high-speed internet access, movies and calls within the EU and to the USA are complimentary, as are personalised business cards stating your residence. The Library Bar (*see p236*) and new modern Italian restaurant, Apsleys, are excellent.

Bar. Business centre. Concierge. Disabled-adapted rooms. Gym. Internet (dataport/wireless). Parking (£40/day). Restaurant. Room service (24hr). Spa. TV (DVD/movies).

▶ *The Lanesborough's original hospital building was designed by William Wilkins, the man behind the National Gallery; see p107.*

THE BEST HOTEL BARS

For a gentleman's club vibe
Coburg at the **Connaught**. *See p184.*

For a cool, calm cocktail
Lobby Bar at **One Aldwych**. *See p177.*

For the new thing in an old place
190 at the **Gore**. *See above.*

Milestone Hotel & Apartments
*1 Kensington Court, Kensington, W8 5DL
(7917 1000/www.milestonehotel.com). High
Street Kensington tube.* **Rates** £311-£370
double. **Rooms** 57. **Credit** AmEx, DC, MC, V.
Map p394 C8 ⓺④

Wealthy American visitors make annual pilgrim-
ages here, their arrival greeted by the comforting,
gravel tones of their regular concierge, as English
as roast beef, and the glass of sherry in the room.
Yet amid old-school luxury (butlers on 24hr call)
thrives inventive modernity (the resistance pool in
the spa). Rooms overlooking Kensington Gardens
feature the inspired decor of South African owner
Beatrice Tillman: the Safari suite contains tent-like
draperies and leopard-print upholstery; the Tudor
Suite has an elaborate inglenook fireplace, minstrels'
gallery and a pouffe concealing a pop-up TV.
*Bar. Business services. Concierge. Disabled-
adapted rooms. Gym. Internet (dataport/wireless).
Pool (1, indoor). Restaurant. Room service (24hr).
Smoking floor. TV (DVD/pay movies).*

Expensive

★ Number Sixteen
*16 Sumner Place, South Kensington, SW7
3EG (7589 5232/www.firmdale.com). South
Kensington tube.* **Rates** £217-£311 double.
Rooms 42. **Credit** AmEx, DC, MC, V.
Map p397 D10 ⓺⑤

This may be Kit Kemp's most affordable hotel but
there's no slacking in style or comforts – witness the
fresh flowers and origami-ed birdbook decorations
in the ultra-comfy drawing room. Bedrooms are
generously sized, bright and very light, and carry
the Kemp trademark mix of bold and traditional.
The whole place has an appealing freshness about
it, enhanced by a delicious, large back garden with
its central water feature. By the time you finish
breakfast in the sweet conservatory you'll have
forgotten you're in the city.
*Bar. Business centre. Concierge. Internet (dataport/
wireless, £20/day). Parking (£39/day). Room
service (24hr). TV (DVD).*
▶ *If your budget can stretch, the Knightsbridge
(10 Beaufort Gardens, SW3 1PT, 7584 6300)
is another excellent Firmdale hotel just nearby.*

Moderate

Aster House
*3 Sumner Place, South Kensington, SW7 3EE
(7581 5888/www.asterhouse.com). South
Kensington tube.* **Rates** (incl breakfast) £146-
£185 double. **Rooms** 13. **Credit** MC, V. **Map**
p397 D10 ⓺⑥

You'll not find many hotels along this swish archetypal white-terraced South Kensington street. One
of the favoured few, the Aster's become an award-
winner through attention to detail (like impeccable

housekeeping and the mobile phone guests can
borrow) and the warmth of its managers, Leona and
Simon Tan. It's all low-key, comfortably soothing
creams with touches of dusty rose and muted green.
Star of the show is the plant-filled conservatory that
serves as a breakfast room and guest lounge – after
Ollie and Cordelia, the resident ducks, that is.
Internet (dataport/wireless). TV.

Cheap

Meininger
*Baden-Powell House, 65-67 Queen's Gate,
South Kensington, SW7 5JS (7590 6910/
www.meininger-hostels.com). Gloucester Road
or South Kensington tube.* **Rates** £98 double;
£13-£25 dorm bed. **Rooms** 46. **Credit** MC, V.
Map p397 D10 ⓺⑦

This German hostel chain now runs the accommodation part of the Scout Association's London HQ,
a classy early 1960s building beside the Natural
History Museum. It benefits from the building's
good design: all the public spaces, bedrooms and
dorms are spacious and light-filled, moving this a
cut above many other hostels, as do the en suite
bathing facilities, individual reading lights, free
wireless internet and flatscreen TVs in all rooms. A
roof terrace hosts barbecues. Traffic noise might be
a problem in some rooms.
Internet (shared terminal, £2/hr). TV.

★ Vicarage Hotel
*10 Vicarage Gate, Kensington, W8 4AG (7229
4030/www.londonvicaragehotel.com). High Street
Kensington or Notting Hill Gate tube.* **Rates** (incl
breakfast) £88-£114 double. **Rooms** 17. **Credit**
AmEx, MC, V. **Map** p394 B8 ⓺⑧

There are scores of devotees who return regularly
to this tall Victorian town house tucked in a quiet
leafy square just off High Street Ken, hard by
Kensington Gardens. It's a comfortable, resolutely
old-fashioned establishment – and that's what the
punters come for. There's a wonderfully grand
entrance hall with red and gold striped wallpaper,
huge gilt mirror and chandelier, with a sweeping
staircase that ascends to an assortment of good-
sized rooms furnished in pale florals and nice old
pieces of furniture.
TV.

NORTH LONDON

Expensive

★ York & Albany
*127-129 Parkway, Camden, NW1 7PS (7387
5700/www.gordonramsay.com). Camden Town
tube.* **Rates** £182-£241 double. **Rooms** 10.
Credit AmEx, MC, V.

The most recent horse to bolt from the Gordon
Ramsay stables, the York & Albany is housed in a

CONSUME

grand old John Nash building that was designed as a coaching house but spent the recent past as a pub. Downstairs is a restaurant (split over two levels), a bar and a delicatessen; above them sit ten hand-some rooms, designed by Russell Sage in some pleasingly mellow shades. The decor is an effective mix of ancient and modern, sturdy and quietly charismatic furniture married to modern technology; if you're lucky, you'll have views of Regent's Park from your bedroom window.

Bar. Disabled-adapted room. Internet (wireless, free). Restaurant. Room service (24hr). TV (DVD).
▶ *For more on architect John Nash, see p37.*

Moderate

Colonnade

2 Warrington Crescent, Little Venice, W9 1ER (7286 1052/www.theetoncollection.com/colonnade). Warwick Avenue tube. **Rates** £147-£213 double. **Rooms** 43. **Credit** AmEx, MC, V.

Housed in an imposingly-sited white Maida Vale mansion, the Colonnade has been lushly done up in interior-designer traditional – lots of swagged curtains, deep opulent colours, luxurious fabrics and careful arrangements of smoothly upholstered furniture. Some of the larger high-ceilinged rooms have had mezzanine floors added. Guests breakfast in a subterranean tapas bar. The bar is beneath a front-of-hotel terrace that makes a good spot for lingering with a glass of wine on warm evenings.

Bar. Internet (wireless, £15/day). Parking (£20/day). Restaurant. Room service (24hr). TV.

Cheap

Hampstead Village Guesthouse

2 Kemplay Road, Hampstead, NW3 1SY (7435 8679/www.hampsteadguesthouse. com). Hampstead tube/Hampstead Heath rail. **Rates** £80-£95 double. **Rooms** 9. **Credit** AmEx, MC, V.

Owner Annemarie van der Meer loves to point out all the quirky space-saving surprises as she shows you round the rooms of her wonderful and idiosyn-cratic bed and breakfast. There's the folding sink, the bed that pops out of an antique wardrobe… The special atmosphere at this spacious double-fronted Victorian house, set on a quiet Hampstead street, means that guests return year after year. Each room is uniquely decorated with an eclectic collection of furnishings – like the French steel bathtub contained in one room. The guesthouse has all the home com-forts you might want as well, from hot water bottles to a laptop and mobile phones.

Internet (wireless). TV.

EAST LONDON
Moderate

★ Hoxton Hotel

81 Great Eastern Street, Shoreditch, EC2A 3HU (7550 1000/www.hoxtonhotels.com). Old Street tube/rail. **Rates** (incl breakfast) £59-£199 double. **Rooms** 205. **Credit** AmEx, MC, V. **Map** p403 Q4 ❻❾

Swimming in Heaven

Legal highs don't come much better than swimming in a rooftop pool.

The **Savoy** (www.savoy2009.com) is due to reopen in spring after a thoroughly going £100m, 18-month refurbishment. Even the iconic cul-de-sac entryway is to get a fancy new garden of topiary and Lalique crystal fountain, but – of the things they chose to leave alone – the foremost are the American Bar, the Savoy Grill… and the rooftop swimming pool.

Until that grand reopening, your best dip in the high-life is at the **Berkeley** (Wilton Place, Knightsbridge, SW1X 7RL, 7235 6000, www.the-berkeley.co.uk), the only other hotel in London for a rooftop swim. The shimmering water here is open to the heavens (but with a sliding roof in case the weather turns ugly) and has great views of Hyde Park. Day-membership needs to be booked in advance and costs £65 – really rather frugal compared to double room rates of nearly ten times that a night.

Berkeley.

CONSUME

Ah, the Hoxton… you must have heard about it: winner of this, winner of that, best hotel in London, best deal in London. Well, everything you've heard is true. First, there's the hip Shoreditch location. Then there are the great design values (the foyer is a sort of postmodern country lodge, complete with stag's head) and rooms that are well thought out with lots of nice touches (like Frette bed linens and free fresh milk placed in the mini-fridge). Above all, it's the budget-airline style pricing system, by which the early bird catches a very cheap worm – perhaps even one of those publicity-garnering £1 a night rooms, still released in very small numbers every few months. The downside? If you don't book ahead and miss the good rates, you could end up paying rather more money.

Bars. Business centre. Disabled-adapted rooms. Internet (dataport/wireless, free). Restaurant. Room service. TV (pay movies).

SOUTH-EAST LONDON

Moderate

Church Street Hotel
29-33 Camberwell Church Street, Camberwell, SE5 8TR (7703 5984/www.churchstreethotel. com). Denmark Hill rail/36, 436 bus. **Rates** (incl breakfast) £120-£180 double. **Rooms** 31. **Credit** AmEx, MC, V.

Craftsman José Raido is behind this attractive and original family-run hotel, opened in 2007 near the busy bus junction of Camberwell Green. Funky bathroom tiles in the bright, high-ceilinged bedrooms, for example, come from Guadalajara, a perfect match for Mexicana such as imported film posters, while the bed frames were forged by José himself. Bathroom products are organic, as are the pastries and cereals served for breakfast in an icon-filled dining room that also operates as a 24-hour honesty bar. You pay £70-£90 for a shared-bathroom 'Poblito' room. A downstairs restaurant is planned for this year.

Bar. Business centre. Internet (wireless). Parking (£5/day). Restaurant. Room service (24hr). TV.

**INSIDE TRACK
COMING SOON**

The biggest opening of the year will be the relaunch after a £100m refurbishment of the **Savoy** (www.savoy2009.com), scheduled for spring. We're also watching with interest the smaller scale arrivals of Terence Conran's **Boundary** (due early 2009; *see p186* **Profile**) in the East End and, in the West End, **Dean Street House** (due mid 2009; www.sohohouse.com) from private members' club Soho House.

SOUTH-WEST LONDON

Moderate

Windmill on the Common
Windmill Drive, Clapham Common Southside, Clapham, SW4 9DE (8673 4578/www.windmill clapham.co.uk). Clapham Common or Clapham South tube. **Rates** (incl breakfast) £125-£140 double. **Rooms** 29. **Credit** AmEx, MC, V.

Perched on the edge of Clapham Common, the Windmill is a pleasant neighbourhood pub in a building dating from 1729. Comfortable and reasonably priced, it is a lovely short stroll from Clapham Common or Clapham South tube stops. The tidy bedrooms are being redecorated, ten at a time, and ten are designated 'premium', coming with stocked fridge and fluffy towels. A full English breakfast is provided for all guests and a three-night non-premium weekend rate of £270 per room is appealing.

Bar. Disabled-adapted room. Internet (dataport/ wireless). Parking. Restaurant. Room service. TV.

WEST LONDON

Moderate

Base2Stay
25 Courtfield Gardens, Earl's Court, SW5 0PG (0845 262 8000/www.base2stay.com). Earl's Court tube. **Rates** £105-£205 double. **Rooms** 67. **Credit** AmEx, MC, V. **Map** p396 B10 ⑦

Base2Stay looks good, with its modernist limestone and taupe tones, and keeps prices low by removing inessentials: no bar, no restaurant. Instead, there's the increasingly popular solution of a 'kitchenette' (microwave, sink, silent mini-fridge, kettle), but here with all details attended to (not just token cutlery, but sufficient kitchenware with corkscrew and can opener). The rooms, en suite (with power showers) and air-conditioned, are as carefully thought out, with desks, modem points and flatscreens, but the single/bunkbed rooms are small. Discount vouchers for nearby chain eateries are supplied by the friendly duo on 24hr reception duty, and free wireless internet should be available from April.

Disabled-adapted rooms. Internet (dataport, £2.95/hr; from Apr: wireless, free). TV (flatscreen/pay movies).

High Road House
162 Chiswick High Road, Chiswick, W4 1PR (8742 1717/www.highroadhouse.co.uk). Turnham Green tube. **Rates** £140-£160 double. **Rooms** 14. **Credit** AmEx, DC, MC, V.

This west London outpost of Nick Jones's Soho House stable features guestrooms designed by Ilse Crawford, and a members' bar and restaurant above the buzzing ground-floor brasserie. Serving a modern British menu, this has a retro sophisticated-Parisian-bistro-meets-Bloomsbury feel and, as you might expect, the food and service are excellent. Guestrooms are soothing, unadorned, white Shaker Modern with little fizzes of colour (and little hidden treats), the bathrooms well-stocked with Cowshed products. There's a basement games room too.

Bars (2). Concierge. Disabled-adapted rooms. Internet (wireless). Restaurants (2). Room service. TV (pay movies/DVD).

Hotel 55

55 Hanger Lane, Ealing, W5 3HL (8991 4450/ www.hotel55-london.com). North Ealing tube. **Rates** (incl breakfast) £130 double. **Rooms** 25. **Credit** AmEx, MC, V.

Turn the corner past the pleasant Greystoke pub and up to Hanger Lane and a surprise awaits. At this junction of bucolic west London and traffic-choked North Circular, where once the prosaic Glencairn Hotel was a popular stop for lonely truck drivers, is now a contemporary, design-led hotel. True, it ticks the boxes of many of London's other contemporary, design-led hotels – Molton Brown bath products, sheets of Egyptian cotton, 24hr lounge bar – but considering the price and location, this is no bad thing at all. Individuality is provided by the modern canvases of Indian artist Sudhir Deshpande, the natural woods that are integral to the design of Babettli Azzone, and a lovely landscaped garden.

Bar. Disabled-adapted rooms. Internet (wireless). TV.

★ Mayflower Hotel

26-28 Trebovir Road, Earl's Court, SW5 9NJ (7370 0991/www.mayflower-group.co.uk). Earl's Court tube. **Rates** (incl continental breakfast) £92-£115 double. **Rooms** 46. **Credit** AmEx, MC, V. **Map** p396 B11 ⓲

After fighting on the frontlines of the Earl's Court budget-hotel style revolution, the Mayflower's taken the struggle to other parts of London (New Linden, *see p181*). But here's where the lushly contemporary house style evolved, proving affordability can be opulently chic. Cream walls and sleek dark woods are an understated background for richly coloured fabrics, and the intricate wooden architectural fragments from Asia, like the lobby's imposing Jaipuri arch. And then there are the marble bathrooms, Egyptian cotton sheets, CD players…

Business centre. Internet (wireless). Parking (£25/day, booking essential). TV.

Rockwell

181-183 Cromwell Road, Earl's Court, SW5 0SF (7244 2000/www.therockwell.com). Earl's Court tube. **Rates** £160-£180 double. **Rooms** 40. **Credit** AmEx, MC, V. **Map** p396 B10 ⓲

The Rockwell aims for relaxed contemporary elegance – and succeeds magnificently. There are no identikit rooms here: they're all individually designed with gleaming woods and muted glowing colours alongside creams and neutrals. Each has a

power shower, Starck fittings and bespoke cabinets in the bathrooms. Garden rooms have tiny patios, complete with garden furniture, and the lounge and bar-restaurant are welcoming. Triple glazing ensures you'll never know you're on a noisy road.

Bar. Internet (broadband). Restaurant. TV (pay movies/DVD).

Twenty Nevern Square

20 Nevern Square, Earl's Court, SW5 9PD (7565 9555/www.twentynevernsquare.co.uk). Earl's Court tube. **Rates** (incl breakfast) £90-£150 double. **Rooms** 20. **Credit** AmEx, DC, MC, V. **Map** p396 A11 ⓲

Only the less-than-posh location of this immaculate boutique hotel keeps the rates reasonable. Tucked away in a private garden square, it feels far from its locale. The modern-colonial style was created by its well-travelled owner, who personally sourced many of the exotic and antique furnishings (as well as those in sister hotel the Mayflower; *see above*). In the sleek marble bathrooms, toiletries are tidied away in decorative caskets, but the beds are the real stars: from elaborately carved four-posters to Egyptian sleigh styles, all with luxurious mattresses. The Far East feel extends into the lounge and the airy conservatory, with its dark wicker furniture.

Bar. Internet (dataport/wireless). Parking (£25/day). Room service (24hr). TV (DVD).

Cheap

EasyHotel

14 Lexham Gardens, Earl's Court, W8 5JE (www.easyhotel.com). Earl's Court tube. **Rates** from £25 double. **Rooms** 34. **Credit** MC, V. **Map** p396 B10 ⓲

The budget airline no-frills approach has been applied to this mini-chain of hotels, which makes it unlikely to appeal to anyone but a stop-out. Rooms come in three sizes – small, really small and tiny – the last of which is the precise width of the bed. Rooms come with a bed and pre-fab bathroom unit (toilet, sink and showerhead almost on top of the sink), with no wardrobe, lift or breakfast. Want a window? Pay extra. TV? Housekeeping? Ditto. The rooms, bookable online only, start low – but book well in advance or expect to pay around £40-£50. The check-in (3pm) and check-out (10am) times and the chain's cancellation policy are hardly generous.

Housekeeping (£10). TV (£5).

Other locations 36-40 Belgrave Road, Victoria, SW1V 1RG; 44-48 West Cromwell Road, Kensington, SW5 9QL; 10 Norfolk Place, Paddington, W2 1QL.

APARTMENT RENTAL

The companies we have listed below specialise in holiday lets, although some of them have minimum stay requirements (making this an

CONSUME

affordable option only if you're planning a relatively protracted visit to the city). Typical daily rates on a reasonably central property are around £70-£90 for a studio or one-bed, up to £100 for a two-bed, although, as with any aspect of staying in London, the sky's the limit if you want to pay it. Respected all-rounders with properties around the city include **Holiday Serviced Apartments** (0845 060 4477, www.holidayapartments.co.uk) and **Palace Court Holiday Apartments** (7727 3467, www.palacecourt.co.uk). **Accommodation Outlet** (7287 4244, www.outlet4holidays.com) is a recommended lesbian and gay agency that has some excellent properties in Soho, in particular.

CAMPING & CARAVANNING

If putting yourself at the mercy of English weather in a far-flung suburban field doesn't put you off, transport links into central London might do the job instead. Good prices, though.

Crystal Palace Caravan Club *Crystal Palace Parade, SE19 1UF (8778 7155). Crystal Palace rail/3 bus.* **Open** *Mar-Oct* 8.30am-6pm Mon-Thur, Sat, Sun; 8.30am-8pm Fri. *Nov-Feb* 9am-6pm Mon-Thur, Sat, Sun; 9am-8pm Fri. **Rates** *Caravan* £5-£8. *Tent* £5-£15. **Credit** MC, V.

Lee Valley Campsite *Sewardstone Road, Chingford, E4 7RA (8529 5689/www.leevalley park.org.uk). Walthamstow Central tube/rail then 215 bus.* **Open** *Apr-Oct* 8am-9pm daily. **Rates** £6.80; £3 under-16s; free under-2s. *Electricity* £3/day. **Credit** MC, V.

Lee Valley Leisure Centre Camping & Caravan Park *Meridian Way, Pickett's Lock, Edmonton, N9 0AR (8803 6900/www.leevalley park.org.uk). Edmonton Green rail/W8 bus.* **Open** 8am-10pm daily. **Rates** £6.80; £3 reductions; free under-5s. **Credit** MC, V.

STAYING WITH THE LOCALS

Several agencies can arrange for individuals and families to stay in Londoners' homes. Prices for a stay are around £20-£85 for a single and £45-£105 for a double, including breakfast, and depending on the location and degree of comfort. Agencies include **At Home in London** (8748 1943, www.athomeinlondon.co.uk), **Bulldog Club** (0870 803 4414, www.bulldogclub.com), **Host & Guest Service** (7385 9922, www. host-guest.co.uk), **London Bed & Breakfast Agency** (7586 2768, www.londonbb.com) and **London Homestead Services** (7286 5115, www.lhslondon.com). There may be a minimum stay. Alternatively, you can browse around noticeboard-style 'online community' websites such as **Gumtree** (www.gumtree.com).

UNIVERSITY RESIDENCES

During the university vacations much of London's dedicated student accommodation is opened up to visitors, providing them with a source of basic but cheap digs.

International Students House *229 Great Portland Street, Marylebone, W1W 5PN (7631 8300/www.ish.org.uk). Great Portland Street tube.* **Rates** (per person) £12-£21 dormitory; £34 single; £26.50 (per person) twin. **Available** all year. **Map** p398 H4 ⑦⑤

King's College Conference & Vacation Bureau *Strand Bridge House, 138-142 Strand, Covent Garden, WC2R 1HH (7848 1700/www.kcl. ac.uk/kcvb). Temple tube.* **Rates** £20-£40 single; £54-£59 twin. **Available** end of June-mid Sept. **Map** p407 Z3 ⑦⑥

LSE *Bankside House, 24 Sumner Street, South Bank, SE1 9JA (7107 5773/www.lsevacations. co.uk). London Bridge tube.* **Rates** £39-£48 single; £70 twin/double. **Available** July-Sept. **Map** p404 O8 ⑦⑦

The London School of Economics has vacation rentals across town, but Bankside House (tucked just behind Tate Modern) is the best located.

YOUTH HOSTELS

If you're not already a member of the IYHF (International Youth Hostel Federation), you'll have to pay an extra £3 a night. Avoid this by joining for £13 (£6.50 for under-18s) at your hostel on arrival, or through www.yha.org.uk prior to departure. All under-18s receive a 25 per cent discount in any case. The hostels below include breakfast in the price. Youth hostel beds are arranged either in dormitories or in twin rooms. *See also p176* **No More Bed Bugs**.

Earl's Court *38 Bolton Gardens, SW5 0AQ (7373 7083/www.yha.org.uk). Earl's Court tube.* **Open** 24hrs daily. **Rates** £17.95-£60. **Map** p396 B11 ⑦⑧

Holland Park *Holland Walk, Kensington, W8 7QU (7937 0748/www.yha.org.uk). High Street Kensington tube.* **Open** 24hrs daily. **Rates** £14.95-£100. **Map** p394 A8 ⑦⑨

Oxford Street *14 Noel Street, Soho, W1F 8GJ (7734 1618/www.yha.org.uk). Oxford Circus tube.* **Open** 24hrs daily. *Reception* 7am-11pm daily. **Rates** £16.50-£60.95. **Map** p406 V2 ⑧⓪

St Pancras *79-81 Euston Road, King's Cross, NW1 2QE (0870 770 6044/www.yha.org.uk). King's Cross tube/rail.* **Open** 24hrs daily. **Rates** £16.50-£31.95. **Map** p399 L3 ⑧①

St Paul's *36 Carter Lane, the City, EC4V 5AB (7236 4965/www.yha.org.uk). St Paul's tube/ Blackfriars tube/rail.* **Open** 24hrs daily. **Rates** £14.95-£60. **Map** p404 O6 ⑧②

CONSUME

Restaurants & Cafés

By embracing the globe, London's restaurants are topping the world.

You'll find Bangladeshi, Burmese, Iranian, Moroccan, Lebanese, Polish, Turkish and Vietnamese food represented in the following chapter, as well as fine exponents of the familiar French, Italian, Japanese, Spanish, Chinese and Thai arts. Oh, and British cuisine that no longer has to hang its head in shame when standing in company with the world's finest, served at places like **St John** or its brilliant disciples **Great Queen Street** and the **Anchor & Hope**. There are plenty of old-school options too, perhaps fish and chips (**Rock & Sole Plaice**, **Golden Hind**), a classic café (**E Pellicci**) or even an old-as-the-hills joint serving that Cockney staple, stewed eels and mash (**M Manze**). Armed with this guide, it's going to be hard to have a bad meal.

DOS AND DON'TS

It's always best to book in advance. At many places it's essential and at a select few (notably Nobu and anything to do with Gordon Ramsay) you're going to have to book a month ahead. Since the summer of 2007 smoking has been banned inside cafés and restaurants. Tipping is standard practice: ten to 15 per cent is usual. Many restaurants add this automatically to your bill, some do so but still present the credit card slip 'open' – check to avoid tipping twice.

We've listed a range of meal prices for each place. However, restaurants often change their menus, so treat these prices only as guidelines. Budget venues are marked **£**.

For a selection of the best places to eat with children, *see pp286-288*.

THE SOUTH BANK & BANKSIDE

Borough Market (*see p258*), full of stalls selling all kinds of wonderful food, is a superb forage for gourmet snackers. **Tate Modern Café: Level 2** (*see p287*) is superb for those with children, and under the Royal Festival

About the reviews

This chapter is compiled from our annual London Eating & Drinking Guide *(£11.99) and* Cheap Eats in London *(£7.99), both of which are available from www.timeout.com.*

Hall the neighbouring outposts of **Wagamama** (*see p205*) and **Giraffe** (*see p286*) can be life-savers. Our most recent meal at **Skylon** (*see p226*), the huge, handsome modern European bar-restaurant in the Royal Festival Hall, was a disappointment for the price – but sipping a bellini by the floor-to-ceiling windows over the Thames is an essential London experience.

Anchor & Hope
36 The Cut, Waterloo, SE1 8LP (7928 9898). Southwark or Waterloo tube/rail. **Open** 5-11pm Mon; 11am-11pm Tue-Sat; 12.30-5pm Sun. **Main courses** £11-£16. **Credit** MC, V. **Map** p404 N8
❶ Gastropub
Around half the room was devoted to tables laid for lunch on our weekday visit, and several were free even after 1pm; you're unlikely to be as lucky post-work. Also surprising was the number of pension-ers enjoying this favourite destination for food and style mavens. But such folk know the pleasures of dishes like cold roast beef on dripping toast, and brawn – both of which were on the appealing menu.
▶ *If it is too busy, head south down Waterloo Road for no-frills fish and chips at Masters Super Fish (no.191, 7928 6924, closed Sun).*

---

❶ Blue numbers given in this chapter correspond to the location of each restaurant or café on the street maps. *See pp394-407.*

SAGAR

VEGETARIAN RESTAURANT

www.gosagar.com

'One of the Best South Indian Vegetarian Restaurants in Londo
-Time (

Baltic

74 Blackfriars Road, Waterloo, SE1 8HA (7928 1111/www.balticrestaurant.co.uk). Southwark tube/rail. **Open** noon-3pm daily; 6-11pm Mon-Sat; 6-10.30pm Sun. **Main courses** £10-£17. **Credit** AmEx, MC, V. **Map** p404 N8 ❷ **East European**
London's only East European 'destination' restaurant, Baltic has wow factor. Make your way through the lively bar to the high-ceilinged main room, its stark whiteness punctuated by exposed beams, bare red brickwork and a chandelier of gleaming amber shards. Add a great cocktail list, a wide choice of vodkas, an eclectic wine list and proper, friendly service, and you have Baltic bliss.

★ Bincho

2nd floor, Oxo Tower Wharf, Barge House Street, South Bank, SE1 9PH (7803 0858/www. bincho.co.uk). Waterloo tube/rail/Blackfriars rail. **Open** noon-3pm, 5-11.30pm Mon-Fri; 12.30-3.30pm, 5.30-11.30pm Sat; 12.30-3.30pm, 5.30-10.30pm Sun. **Yakitori** £1-£11. **Credit** AmEx, DC, MC, V. **Map** p404 N7 ❸ **Japanese grill**
Many London restaurants boast impressive views, but Bincho, with its glorious Thames-side vista, has one of the best. They serve excellent yakitori (grilled meat, fish and veg) and sake (hot or cold) amid the beautiful scent of the barbecue. Music keeps the energy of the chic young crowd high. *Photos p201.* **Other locations** 16 Old Compton Street, Soho, W1D 4TL (7287 9111).

Magdalen

152 Tooley Street, Bankside, SE1 2TU (7403 1342/www.magdalenrestaurant.co.uk). London Bridge tube/rail. **Open** noon-2.30pm, 6.30-10.30pm Mon-Fri; 6.30-10.30pm Sat. **Main courses** £12-£21. **Credit** AmEx, MC, V. **Map** p405 Q8 ❹ **British**
The Magdalen is extremely comfortable, with discreetly elegant, understated decor and a slightly hushed atmosphere in its ground- and first-floor dining rooms. The frequently changing seasonal menus are imaginative and notably refined, and show admirable ambition. Service is charming, and presentation very pretty. All quite a surprise in an area riddled with tacky tourist attractions.

£ M Manze

87 Tower Bridge Road, Southwark, SE1 4TW (7407 2985/www.manze.co.uk). Bus 1, 42, 188. **Open** 11am-2pm Mon; 10.30am-2pm Tue-Thur; 10am-2.15pm Fri; 10am-2.45pm Sat. **No credit cards. Map** p405 Q10 ❺ **Pie & mash**
Manze's is the finest remaining purveyor of the dirt-cheap traditional foodstuff of London's working classes. It is not only the oldest pie shop, established in 1902, but the most beautiful, with tiles, marble-topped tables and worn wood benches. Expect mashed potato, minced beef pies and liquor (a parsley sauce); braver souls should try the stewed eels.

Roast

Floral Hall, Borough Market, Stoney Street, Bankside, SE1 1TL (7940 1300/www.roast-restaurant.com). London Bridge tube/rail. **Open** 7-9.30am, noon-2.30pm, 5.30-10.30pm Mon-Fri; 8-10.30am, 11.30am-3.30pm, 6-10.30pm Sat; noon-3.30pm Sun. **Main courses** £12-£20. **Credit** AmEx, MC, V. **Map** p404 P8 ❻ **British**
Perched above Borough Market, Roast celebrates its marvellous location with a menu inspired by British produce, much of it sourced from the stall-holders below. Seasonality and freshness are the buzz words and there's no doubting the quality of the ingredients. *See p208 Eating In.*
▶ *Borough Market is also home to the excellent, busy Brindisa Tapas (18-20 Southwark Street, 7357 8880, www.brindisa.com).*

£ Tsuru

4 Canvey Street, Bankside, SE1 8AN (7928 2228/www.tsuru-sushi.co.uk). Southwark tube/ London Bridge tube/rail. **Open** 11am-6pm Mon-Wed; 11am-9pm Thur, Fri. **Main courses** £5-£8. **Credit** MC, V. **Map** p404 O8 ❼ **Japanese**
A tiny yet remarkable canteen, to which media honeys from the Blue Fin Building slip away every lunch hour to deplete the supply of silky, umami-rich katsu curries. On Thursdays and Fridays, the welcoming space becomes a trendy nightspot where *ippin ryori* (Japanese 'tapas') can be enjoyed along with sake and shochu cocktails. *See also p207* **Quality Fast Food.**

THE CITY

£ Bodean's

16 Byward Street, EC3R 5BA (7488 3883/www. bodeansbbq.com). Tower Hill tube. **Open** noon-11pm Mon-Fri; 6-10.30pm Sat. **Main courses** £8-£16. **Credit** AmEx, MC, V. **Map** p405 R7 ❽ **North American**
Bodean's now has five branches: Soho, Westbourne Grove, Fulham, Clapham and, handily, here. The schtick remains unchanged: Kansas City barbecue, with a small informal upstairs and bigger, smarter downstairs with US sport on TV. The food is decent, generous and very, very meaty – bring an appetite. **Other locations** throughout the city.

THE BEST BRITISH FOOD

For a modern British pioneer
St John. *See p202.*

For proper fish and chips
Fish Central. *See p201.*

For a taste of disappearing London
M Manze. *See left.*

CONSUME

Bincho. *See p199.*

★ £ Fish Central
149-155 Central Street, EC1V 8AP (7253 4970).
Old Street tube/rail/55 bus. **Open** 11am-2.30pm
Mon-Sat; 5-10.30pm Mon-Thur; 5-11pm Fri, Sat.
Main courses £8-£15. **Credit** MC, V. **Map**
p402 P3 ❾ **Fish & chips**
This area was hardly residential in 1968, when Fish
Central took a unit in the shopping precinct. Now it
spans four units – rather stylishly, with etched glass
and pale white and mint tones – but still serves
simple fish to enthusiastic locals. *Photos p203.*

Northbank
One Paul's Walk, EC4V 3QH (7329 9299/
www.northbankrestaurant.com). *St Paul's tube/*
Blackfriars tube/rail. **Open** noon-3pm, 6-11pm
Mon-Sat; 11am-5pm, 6-11pm Sun. **Main courses**
£12-£23. **Credit** AmEx, MC, V. **Map** p404 O7 ❿
British
On the brink of the Thames, Northbank feels like
a place for a special occasion. There's a terrace outside where you can sip cocktails, and picture windows in the dining room frame the South Bank. The
menu is short, straightforward and mainly modern
British. And we like the wallpaper: 19th-century
toile de jouy at a glance; on closer inspection filled
with grim vignettes of contemporary London life.
▶ *Just over the bridge is Tate Modern; see p52.*

Sauterelle
Royal Exchange, EC3V 3LR (7618 2483/www.
danddlondon.com). *Bank tube/DLR.* **Open** noon-
2.30pm, 6-10pm Mon-Fri. **Main courses** £16-
£19. **Credit** AmEx, DC, MC, V. **Map** p405 Q6 ⓫
French
Situated on the mezzanine level of the Royal
Exchange, Sauterelle has a fantastic vantage point
over the buzzing Grand Café below. It is set up for
City power lunches and after-work dinners, with
comfortable blue club chairs and a simple chic look.
The owners describe their style as 'bourgeois'
French cooking, but they also do more rustic fare.

Sweetings
39 Queen Victoria Street, EC4N 4SA (7248 3062).
Mansion House tube. **Open** 11.30am-3pm Mon-Fri.
Main courses £11-£28. **Credit** AmEx, MC, V.
Map p404 P6 ⓬ **Fish**
In these days of makeovers and global menus,
Sweetings is that rare thing – a traditional British
restaurant that clings to its traditions as if the
Empire depended on it. It opens only for lunch, takes
no bookings, and is full soon after noon, so order a
silver pewter mug of Guinness and enjoy the wait.

HOLBORN & CLERKENWELL

★ £ Clerkenwell Kitchen
27-31 Clerkenwell Close, EC1R 0AT (7101 9959/
www.theclerkenwellkitchen.co.uk). *Angel tube/*
Farringdon tube/rail. **Open** 8am-5pm Mon-Fri.
Main courses £4-£14. **Credit** MC, V. **Map**
p402 N4 ⓭ **Eco-restaurant**

THE BEST TREAT EATS

For Mittel Europe chic
Wolseley. *See p215.*

For drop-dead style
Hakkasan. *See p205.*

For wow factor
Landau. *See p205.*

First winner of Best Sustainable Restaurant in our Eating & Drinking Awards, this new restaurant serves delicious, fresh, seasonal food at fair prices. The furnishings are simple: plenty of wood, windows and white walls with architectural seating and an open kitchen. See p209 **Eating Out**.

Le Comptoir Gascon

61-63 Charterhouse Street, EC1M 6HJ (7608 0851/www.comptoirgascon.com). Farringdon tube/rail. **Open** noon-2pm Tue-Fri; 10.30am-2.30pm Sat; 7-10pm Tue, Wed, Sat; 7-10.30pm Thur, Fri. **Main courses** £7-£14. **Credit** AmEx, MC, V. **Map** p402 O5 ⓮ **French**
Le Comptoir Gascon is the modern rustic cousin (dainty velour chairs, exposed pipes, open brickwork and pottery dishes) of the more famous and high-falutin' Club Gascon (57 West Smithfield, 7796 0600, www.clubgascon.com), but it still exudes class and confidence in its presentation of delectable regional specialities of Gascony. The posh café vibe is enhanced by the capable and amiable French staff.

Eagle

159 Farringdon Road, Clerkenwell, EC1R 3AL (7837 1353). Farringdon tube/rail. **Open** noon-11pm Mon-Sat; noon-5pm Sun. **Main courses** £5-£15. **Credit** MC, V. **Map** p402 N4 ⓯ **Gastropub**
Widely credited with being the first London gastropub (opened in 1991), this is still recognisably a pub with quality food: noisy, often crowded, with no-frills service and dominated by a giant open range where T-shirted cooks toss earthy grills in theatrical bursts of flame. The Iberian/Med-influenced menu (chalked-up, of course) has stayed true to its original idea of 'big flavours'. A convivial spot.
▶ *If the Eagle's too busy, try the Peasant (240 St John Street, EC1V 4PH, 7336 7726, www.thepeasant.co.uk).*

Hix Oyster & Chop House

36-37 Greenhill Rents, off Cowcross Street, EC1M 6BN (7017 1930/www.restaurantsetcltd. co.uk). Farringdon tube/rail. **Open** noon-3pm Mon-Fri; 6-11pm Mon-Sat; noon-5pm Sun (single seating at 2pm). **Main courses** £11-£55. **Credit** AmEx, MC, V. **Map** p402 O5 ⓰ **British**

Renowned for innovative updates of British food, Mark Hix's menu is a roll-call for local, seasonal produce, the farmers and growers duly name-checked. His food is set against a simple, pared-down decor that recalls postwar village halls. Service, though willing, can be a bit clumsy, giving a sense of amateurishness to an otherwise professional operation.

★ Modern Pantry

47-48 St John's Square, Clerkenwell, EC1V 4JJ (7250 0833/www.themodernpantry.co.uk). Farringdon tube/rail. **Open** 11am-11pm daily. **Main courses** £10-£16. **Credit** AmEx, MC, V. **Map** p402 O4 ⓱ **Brasserie**
Immediately on opening, the Modern Pantry was full of Clerkenwell's many self-consciously creative types. Inside a handsome, Grade II-listed Georgian building that used to be townhouse and steel foundry, the good-looking café space has lots of natural light, silvery-grey walls and beautiful detailing. The style of cooking is a genre-bending fusion of ingredients and styles from around the world. A deli and fancier dining room should now have opened upstairs. See also p207 **Quality Fast Food**.

Moro

34-36 Exmouth Market, Clerkenwell, EC1R 4QE (7833 8336/www.moro.co.uk). Farringdon tube/ rail/19, 38 bus. **Open** 12.30-11.45pm Mon-Sat (last entry 10.30pm). **Tapas** £3-£15. **Main courses** £14-£20. **Credit** AmEx, DC, MC, V. **Map** p402 N4 ⓲ **Spanish-North African**
Now a plucky 11 years old, Moro has an enduring popularity that seems unassailable. It's fully booked night after night, so phone at least 48 hours ahead if you want to sample the secret of its success: high-quality cooking and a convivial dining space on fashionable Exmouth Market. The inventive menu is Moorish – in other words it adds Spanish accents to essentially North African food.
▶ *Opposite, all-day French café Ambassador (no.55, 7837 0009, www.theambassadorcafe.co. uk) serves classy food all day, without the wait.*

★ St John

26 St John Street, Clerkenwell, EC1M 4AY (7251 0848/4998/www.stjohnrestaurant.com). Barbican tube/Farringdon tube/rail. **Open** noon-5pm, 6pm-midnight Mon-Fri; 6pm-midnight Sat. **Main courses** £13-£23. **Credit** AmEx, DC, MC, V. **Map** p402 O5 ⓳ **British**
A leading light of the British revival, St John is a remarkably austere-looking and modest place, opened in the shell of a former Smithfield smokehouse by architect and chef-patron Fergus Henderson in 1995. Its spirit hasn't changed since then. The focus is entirely on seasonal and unusual British ingredients, simply cooked and presented. If you find the dining room too formal (or expensive), try eating in the no-reservations bar, which pares down the menu and is more convivial (aka noisier).

THE BEST CHEAP EATS

For café cu^lure
F⸱⸱⸱ **Wells**. *See p211.*

⸱⸱⸱ haute cuisine
⸱⸱⸱ *08.*

⸱⸱⸱out
⸱⸱⸱ *08.*

Smiths of Smithfield

*67-77 Charterhouse Street, Clerkenwell, EC1M
6HJ (7251 7950/www.smithsofsmithfield.co.uk).
Barbican tube/Farringdon tube/rail.* **Open** *Café*
7am-4.30pm Mon-Fri; 9.30am-5.30pm Sat, Sun.
Dining Room noon-2.45pm, 6-10.45pm Mon-Fri;
6-10.45pm Sat. *Bar* 11am-11pm Mon-Sat; noon-
10.30pm Sun. **Main courses** *Café £4-£8. Dining
Room* £10-£28. **Credit** AmEx, DC, MC, V. **Map**
p402 O5 ❷⓿ **Modern European/bar/brasserie**
John Torode's eating and drinking emporium inhabits a former warehouse, with brick walls, iron pillars, huge windows and bags of noisy atmosphere.
The ground floor is an expansive sofa bar; next up
is a wine bar with snacky mod-Brit food and more
global mains. Segregated from the masses, Top
Floor is Torode's svelter fine-dining operation. In
between is the main dining room, where an open
kitchen dispenses a simple menu of grills (eating
here à deux is fun, but hardly intimate).

BLOOMSBURY & FITZROVIA

Camino

*3 Varnishers Yard, Regents Quarter, King's
Cross, N1 9AF (7841 7331/www.camino.uk.
com). King's Cross tube/rail.* **Open** *Restaurant*
8am-3pm, 6.30-11pm Mon-Fri; 7-11pm Sat. *Bar*
noon-midnight Mon-Wed; noon-1am Thur-Sat.
Main courses £10-£20. **Credit** AmEx, MC, V.
Map p399 L3 ❷❶ **Spanish**

INSIDE TRACK BURRITOS

Goodge Street isn't likely to put you in
mind of San Francisco's Mission District,
but it is suddenly home to London's best
burritos: both **Benito's Hat** (no.56, 7637
3732, www.benitos-hat.com) and **El
Burrito** (5 Charlotte Place, off Goodge
Street, 7580 5048) serve cheap, fat,
satisfying tortilla wraps.

A huge, Spanish-themed bar-restaurant in the heart
of the King's Cross construction zone, Camino is a
shining beacon of things to come. In the bar you can
order good tapas, but it's worth sitting down for a
proper meal in the restaurant, where the cooking
conveys the central principle of traditional Spanish
food: the finest ingredients, simply cooked.

★ Giaconda Dining Room

*9 Denmark Street, Bloomsbury, WC2H
8LS (7240 3334/www.giacondadining.com).
Tottenham Court Road tube.* **Open** noon-
2.15pm, 6-9.45pm Mon-Fri. **Main courses**
£9-£13. **Credit** AmEx, MC, V. **Map** p407 X2
❷❷ **Modern European**
The simple black-and-white dining room belies the
esteem in which chef Paul Merrony is held in his
native Australia. This is a generous, egalitarian spot

Fish Central. See p201.

wagamama

delicious noodles ı **rice dishes**
freshly squeezed juices ı **salads**
wine ı **sake** ı **asian beers**

for locations visit wagamama.com

where the unpretentious food is the star. We loved the hot pillow of ham hock hash with fried egg and lightly dressed mixed leaves.

★ Hakkasan

8 Hanway Place, Fitzrovia, W1T 1HD (7907 1888). Tottenham Court Road tube. **Open** noon-12.30am Mon-Wed; noon-1.30am Thur-Sat; noon-midnight Sun. **Dim sum** £3-£20. **Main courses** £9-£58. **Credit** AmEx, MC, V. **Map** p406 W1 ㉓ **Chinese**

When Alan Yau opened this glamtastic take on the Shanghai teahouse in 2001, he redefined Chinese dining in the UK. Its moody, nightclub feel, lounge music and high-ticket dining still pull one of the liveliest, monied crowds in town. *See p208* **Eating In.**

▶ *To enjoy the Hakkasan experience for less, visit for the brilliant lunchtime dim sum.*

Konstam at the Prince Albert

2 Acton Street, Bloomsbury, WC1X 9NA (7833 5040/www.konstam.co.uk). King's Cross tube/rail. **Open** 12.30-3pm, 6.30-10.30pm Mon-Fri; 6.30-10.30pm Sat. **Main courses** £10-£16. **Credit** AmEx, MC, V. **Map** p399 M3 ㉔ **Eco-restaurant**

The USP at this eco-conscious restaurant is that 'over 85% of the produce used… is grown or reared within the area covered by the London Underground network'. Which is not to say that owner/chef Oliver Rowe's menu is limited or unimaginative. Try the unusual ice-creams, such as quince, for dessert. The cutely designed room is attractive, but it's pretty small and tables are snug.

▶ *On parallel Swinton Street, Acorn House (no.69, 7812 1842, www.acornhouserestaurant. com) is another sassy eco-restaurant.*

★ Landau

Langham, Portland Place, Fitzrovia, W1B 1JA (7965 0165/www.thelandau.com). Oxford Circus tube. **Open** 7am-11pm Mon-Sat, 7am-10pm Sun. **Main courses** £19-£30. **Credit** AmEx, DC, MC, V. **Map** p398 H5 ㉕ **Modern European**

David Collins' interior, with its otherworldly brass fittings and olde worlde wood panelling, smacks of an HG Wells novel. It perfectly suits a restaurant where chef Andrew Turner presents British ingredients with molecular gastronomy touches, while customers enjoy a view of Nash's All Souls Church and the BBC's Broadcasting House through regal windows curved around one end of the oval room.

£ Meals

1st floor, Heal's, 196 Tottenham Court Road, Bloomsbury, W1T 7LQ (7580 2522/www.heals. co.uk). Goodge Street or Warren Street tube. **Open** 10am-6pm Mon-Wed, Fri; 10am-7.30pm Thur; 9.30am-6.30pm Sat; noon-6pm Sun. **Main courses** £9-£11. **Credit** AmEx, DC, MC, V. **Map** p399 K5 ㉖ **Café**

Cross an alpine lodge with a toddler's bedroom, add cut-out cupboards that suggest a fairytale landscape, and marshmallow pink chairs on the ironic side of twee – and you've got runner-up for Best Design in our 2007 awards. The food doesn't quite taste as well as it reads, but it's enjoyable, cultured and surprisingly generous. 'Squillionaire's shortbread' isn't far short of sensational.

▶ *This is one of several restaurants run by Oliver Peyton; for more, see p219 Profile.*

£ Ooze

62 Goodge Street, Fitzrovia, W1T 4NE (7436 9444/www.ooze.biz). Goodge Street tube. **Open** noon-11pm Mon-Sat. **Main courses** £5-£10. **Credit** AmEx, MC, V. **Map** p398 J5 ㉗ **Risotto café**

Risotto is the selling point, though there are plenty of alternatives. Most of the risottos come in two sizes: small isn't very small and costs £6.50-£7.95; large is £8.50-£13.95. Service is smiley, and there's a nicely priced wine list. The pared-down, gently modern decor looks briskly efficient at lunchtimes, while clever lighting makes it seem cosier by night.

Salt Yard

54 Goodge Street, Fitzrovia, W1T 4NA (7637 0657/www.saltyard.co.uk). Goodge Street tube. **Open** noon-11pm Mon-Fri; 5-11pm Sat. **Tapas** £3-£9. **Credit** AmEx, DC, MC, V. **Map** p398 J5 ㉘ **Spanish-Italian tapas**

After four years of popularity, Salt Yard spawned a second branch (Dehesa, *see p209*) in 2008. This is tapas, but not as we knew it, bringing Spanish and Italian ideas and ingredients together with brilliant results. The setting is sophisticated, yet relaxed. Fine selections of charcuterie and cheese front the menu. Confit of Gloucester Old Spot with cannellini beans is always a sensation, and one of the only perennials on the alluring, frequently changing menu. Book ahead, and try to get a table upstairs.

Snazz Sichuan

New China Club, 37 Chalton Street, King's Cross, NW1 1JD (7388 0808). Euston tube/rail. **Open** noon-midnight daily. **Main courses** £6-£27. **Credit** MC, V. **Map** p399 K3 ㉙ **Sichuanese**

The bizarre decor (flimsy magenta curtains, Cultural Revolution poster), the enthusiasm of the staff, the skill of the chef and the wonderful aromas are all testament to authenticity. This is ma-la (hot and numbing) fare, so don't expect familiar Cantonese dishes – instead try the likes of spicy pigs' ears.

£ Wagamama

4A Streatham Street, Bloomsbury, WC1A 1JB (7323 9223/www.wagamama.com). Holborn or Tottenham Court Road tube. **Open** noon-11pm Mon-Sat; noon-10pm Sun. **Main courses** £6-£10. **Credit** AmEx, DC, MC, V. **Map** p407 X1 ㉚ **Oriental canteen**

CONSUME

Since starting life in the basement here in 1992, this chain of noodle bars has become an international phenomenon, with branches as far afield as Cyprus, Boston and New Zealand. The British Wagamamas all serve the same menu: rice plate meals and Japanese ramen, soba and udon noodles, cooked teppanyaki-style on a flat griddle or simmered in huge bowls of spicy soup, all served in double-quick time. The use of high-quality ingredients raises the chain above many of its imitators, but how much you enjoy the food will depend on how much you like canteen-style dining.
Other locations throughout the city.

COVENT GARDEN

The Covent Garden **Masala Zone** (48 Floral Street, 7379 0101, www.masalazone.com; *see also p221*) is located near the Opera House.

£ Abeno Too
17-18 Great Newport Street, WC2H 7JE (7379 1160/www.abeno.co.uk). Leicester Square tube. **Open** noon-11pm Mon-Sat; noon-10.30pm Sun. **Main courses** £7-£20. **Credit** AmEx, DC, MC, V. **Map** p407 X3 ❸ **Japanese**
Okonomiyaki (hearty pancakes with nuggets of vegetables, seafood, pork and other titbits added to a disc of noodles) are cooked to order on hot-plates set into Abeno's tables and counter. Don't dismiss the desserts: own-made matcha ice-cream, a rice dumpling pancake, whipped cream, aduki beans and maple syrup make a sensational combination.
Other locations Abeno, 47 Museum Street, Bloomsbury, WC1A 1LY (7405 3211).

L'Atelier de Joël Robuchon
13-15 West Street, WC2H 9NE (7010 8600/ www.joel-robuchon.com). Leicester Square tube. **Open** *Restaurant* noon-2.30pm, 5.30-11.30pm Mon-Sat; noon-2.30pm, 5.30-10.30pm Sun. *Bar* 2.30pm-2am Mon-Sat; 2.30-11pm Sun. **Main courses** £15-£55. **Credit** AmEx, MC, V. **Map** p407 X3 ❸ **Modern European**
The locations in Joël Robuchon's restaurant empire sound like 007 stopovers – Macau, Hong Kong, Monaco – but Robuchon is no Bond baddie, he's a

French super-chef. The Japanese-inspired ground-floor L'Atelier is dimly lit, but the open kitchen makes an impressive focal point. The small tasting dishes are the best way to explore the work of this fine chef, though a European-style menu format is available both on the ground floor and in the first-floor dining room, La Cuisine (a brighter, more traditional-looking space).

£ Food for Thought
31 Neal Street, WC2H 9PR (7836 0239). Covent Garden tube. **Open** noon-8.30pm Mon-Sat; noon-5pm Sun. **Main courses** £4-£8. **No credit cards. Map** p407 Y2 ❸ **Vegetarian café**
The menu of this very much-loved Covent Garden stalwart changes daily, though you can expect three or four main courses, a selection of salads and a few desserts. The laid-back restaurant is down a steep, narrow stairway that, during the lunchtime rush, is usually filled with a patient queue. The ground floor offers the same cut-above vegetarian menu to take away for busy office folk on the move.
▶ *Just after organic coffee and a cake? On the third floor of nearby extreme-sports shop Snow & Rock (4 Mercer Street, WC2H 9QA, 7836 4922, www.bullet-coffee.com), Bullet is a little gem.*

★ Great Queen Street
32 Great Queen Street, WC2B 5AA (7242 0622). Covent Garden or Holborn tube. **Open** 6-10.30pm Mon; noon-2.30pm, 6-10.30pm Tue-Sat; noon-3pm Sun. **Main courses** £9-£18. **Credit** MC, V. **Map** p407 Z2 ❸ **British**
The pub-style room here thrumms with bonhomie. Ranging from snacks to shared mains, the menu is designed to tempt and satisfy rather than educate or impress. Booking is essential, and the robust food is worth it. New this year: a Sunday lunch session, just like at sister establishment Anchor & Hope (*see p197*), where diners sit and are served together, and the Dive bar which has opened in the basement, serving snacks as well as drinks.

★ J Sheekey
28-32 St Martin's Court, WC2N 4AL (7240 2565/www.j-sheekey.co.uk). Leicester Square tube. **Open** noon-3pm, 5.30pm-midnight Mon-Sat; noon-3.30pm, 6-11pm Sun. **Main courses** £13-£40. **Credit** AmEx, DC, MC, V. **Map** p407 X4 ❸ **Fish**
Unlike many of London's period pieces (which this certainly is, it was first chartered in the mid 19th century), Sheekey's buzzes with fashionable folk and famous faces. Your party of four may be crammed on to a table that other restaurants would allocate to two, but best consider this part of the fun. The menu stretches from comforting favourites (fish pie, dense salmon fish cakes) to accomplished modern British and European cooking.
▶ *Sheekey's new, no-bookings Oyster Bar should open early this year.*

INSIDE TRACK CHINATOWN

For atmosphere, drop in for a 'bubble tea' (sweet, icy, full of balls of jelly and slurped up with a straw) at the bustling **Jen Café** (4-8 Newport Place, no phone) or late-night fave **HK Diner** (22 Wardour Street, 7434 9544). If you need to eat especially late, Cantonese old-stager the **New Mayflower** (68-70 Shaftesbury Avenue, 7734 9207) is open daily until 4am.

Quality Fast Food

There's no need to settle for rubbish just because you're in a rush.

The meaning of fast food has changed in London. Cheery eat-and-leave joints have continued to gain popularity with their winning combination of quality food, casual surroundings and, natch, affordable prices. More than 15 years on from restaurateur Alan Yau's groundbreaking concept of rubbing elbows with strangers at the communal tables of **Wagamama** (*see p205*), bolstered by the subsequent success of his **Busaba Eathai** (*see p209*), the number of canteen-style eateries has skyrocketed. The legacy continued with the arrival of **Cha Cha Moon** (*see p209*) in last year. Based on Yau's native Chinese roots, Cha Cha Moon serves trad noodle dishes whipped up by hand-plucked chefs from around Asia in a trendily plain interior.

The Chinese revolution continues with newcomer **Baozi Inn** (*see p208*), where diners settled in retro *hutong*-inspired digs chow down on snappy fresh noodle dishes, wontons and China's (healthier) answer to the burger – thick, comforting *baozi* (steamed buns). Other Asian cuisines are proving just as popular: behind Tate Modern, **Tsuru** (*see p199*) is just another example of Londoners' all-encompassing love affair with Japanese food, while fans of *pho* (Vietnamese noodle soup) are getting ever more opportunities to enjoy it (**Sông Quê**, *see p224*, remains the stand-out exponent).

There's plenty of snack action beyond the Asian cuisines. **Hummus Bros** (*see p211*) – self-proclaimed 'first hummus bar in London' – woos harried office workers with creative houmous-based lunches and Med-inspired sides. Choose your toppings from moreish, gravy-rich braised chunks of beef to smokey chargrilled veg and mop the lot up with warm pitta, washed down with refreshing ginger and mint lemonade. **Ottolenghi** (*see p222*) also follows the Mediterranean route to light luncheons –

Cha Cha Moon.

it's a top-notch dining destination that contrasts a minimalist décor with exquisitely made and boldly flavoured dishes. The vegetarian and vegan creations show real culinary verve.

One of this year's most exciting openings has been Anna Hansen's **Modern Pantry** (*see p202*), which serves the kind of fusion-tinted dishes she was known for at Providores (*see p213*). The handsome space combines top-quality food with amicable service and wallet-friendly prices. Perfect, but perhaps not for unreconstructed fast-fooders? Time, then, for the juicy, meaty joyfulness of biting into a speciality burger at **Haché** (*see p221*).

CONSUME

£ Rock & Sole Plaice
47 Endell Street, WC2H 9AJ (7836 3785/www. rockandsoleplaice.com). Covent Garden tube.
Open 11.30am-11pm Mon-Sat; noon-10pm Sun. **Main courses** £8-£14. **Credit** MC, V. **Map** p407 Y2 ㊱ **Fish & chips**
A chippie since 1874, this establishment has walls covered in theatre posters and a busy vibe. The ground-floor tables are often all taken (check

whether there's space in the basement dining room), and the outside seats are never empty in summer.

★ £ Scoop
40 Shorts Gardens, WC2H 9AB (7240 7086/ www.scoopgelato.com). Covent Garden tube.
Open 11.30am-11.30pm daily. **Main courses** £2-£8. **Credit** AmEx, DC, MC, V. **Map** p407 Y2 ㊲ **Ice-cream**

Eating In...

Our pick of the best winter dining.

Hakkasan
See p205.
In this glamorous dining den, hidden deep underground, it couldn't matter less what the weather is doing outside. Descend the stairs to a warm, incense-filled space where you can choose from impeccable, hearty Chinese braises or superior Imperial-style soups.

Little Lamb
See p211.
The concept behind this Chinatown restaurant (*pictured*) is the Mongolian hotpot. Diners order raw ingredients (slices of lamb, beef, pork; fresh veg; tofu and noodles) and dip them into a pot of bubbling spicy (or mild and herbal) broth to cook before gobbling morsels down. A surefire winter warmer.

Nordic Bakery
See p211.
The cool, wintery blue hues and severe design at this Finnish café might not seem the most coddling, but just try a fresh-out-of-the-oven cinnamon bun. Thick and fluffy and oozing with spicy sweetness – these are the real deal, the best buffer against a frosty morning.

Roast
See p199.
It can get too hot for comfort here in the summer but for winter dining it's perfect. Plenty of natural light streams over tables of happy diners enjoying scrumptious breakfasts and the eponymous blood-warming roasts.

Long queues are a testament to the quality of the ice-creams, even dairy-free health versions, at this Italian artisan's shop. Flavours include ricotta and fig, and a very superior Piedmont hazelnut type.

£ Wahaca
66 Chandos Place, WC2N 4HG (7240 1883/ www.wahaca.co.uk). Covent Garden or Leicester Square tube. **Open** noon-11pm Mon-Sat; noon-10.30pm Sun. **Main courses** £6-£10. **Credit** AmEx, MC, V. **Map** p407 Y4 ❸ **Mexican canteen**
Queues snake into this colourful canteen daily, and Wahaca has a look as cheery as its staff, created from lamps made out of tomatillo cans dotted with bottle tops, wooden crates packed with fruit, and tubs of chilli plants. Choose one of the large plato fuertes (enchiladas, burritos or grilled dishes) if you don't feel like sharing, or go for the selection of kindly priced tacos, tostadas and quesadillas.

SOHO & CHINATOWN

Chinatown stalwarts like **Mr Kong** (21 Lisle Street, 7437 7341) and **Wong Kei** (41-43 Wardour Street, 0871 332 8296) still ply their trade, but we're more excited by newcomers **Baozi Inn** and **Bar Shu** (for both, *see below*).

★ Arbutus
63-64 Frith Street, Soho, W1D 3JW (7734 4545/www.arbutusrestaurant.co.uk). Tottenham Court Road tube. **Open** noon-2.30pm, 5-11pm Mon-Sat; 12.30-3.30pm, 5.30-9.30pm Sun. **Main courses** £12-£16. **Credit** AmEx, MC, V. **Map** p406 W2 ❸ **Modern European**
The menu here is strong on hearty British fare, accented with continental flavours, and seasonality matters. Arbutus is very popular, and its renown is likely to spread further with the publication of chef-owner Anthony Demetre's first book. Book ahead, and expect the place to be full to bursting at dinner. The lunchtime set menus are a bargain.

★ £ Baozi Inn
25 Newport Court, Chinatown, WC2H 7JS (7287 6877). Leicester Square tube. **Open** 11am-10pm daily. **Main courses** £6-£7. **No credit cards**. **Map** p407 X3 ❹ **Beijing noodles**
The decor, inspired by Beijing's hutongs circa 1952, signals kitsch rather than culture, and the backless wooden pews are far from conducive to a lingering lunch, yet these Beijing- and Chengdu-style street snacks (including dan dan noodles, handmade daily) are 100% authentic. No wonder this was a runner-up for our Best Cheap Eats award last year. *See also p207* **Quality Fast Food**.

Bar Shu
28 Frith Street, Soho, W1D 5LF (7287 6688). Leicester Square or Tottenham Court Road tube.

Open noon-11.30pm Mon-Sat; noon-11pm Sun.
Main courses £7-£28. **Credit** AmEx, MC, V.
Map p406 W3 ❸ **Sichuanese**
A shining example of a regional Chinese restaurant
(in this case the chilli- and pepper-laced cuisine of
Sichuan) that hasn't compromised on authenticity,
Bar Shu serves up fiery food for the brave, with
great rewards.

★ £ Busaba Eathai
*106-110 Wardour Street, Soho, W1F 0TR (7255
8686). Oxford Circus, Tottenham Court Road or
Leicester Square tube.* **Open** noon-11pm Mon-
Thur; noon-11.30pm Fri, Sat; noon-10pm Sun.
Main courses £5-£9. **Credit** AmEx, MC, V.
Map p406 W2 ❷ **Thai**
This is probably the handiest branch of Thai fast
food canteen – although there's frequently a queue
outside. It combines shared tables and bench seats
with a touch of oriental mystique (dark wood, incense,
low lighting). The dishes are always intriguing, as
you'd expect of a menu developed by David
Thompson of Nahm (*see p217*).
Other locations 8-13 Bird Street, Marylebone,
W1U 1BU (7518 8080); 22 Store Street,
Bloomsbury, WC1E 7DS (7299 7900).

£ Cha Cha Moon
*15-21 Ganton Street, Soho, W1F 9BN (7297
9800). Oxford Circus tube.* **Open** noon-11pm
Mon-Thur; noon-11.30pm Fri, Sat; noon-10pm
Sun. **Main courses** £3.50. **Credit** AmEx, MC,
V. **Map** p406 U3 ❸ **Hong Kong noodles**
Still attracting queues of diners, Alan Yau's latest
venture offers accessible prices, communal tables and
a no-booking policy to on-the-go Soho-ites after a quick
pit-stop. Noodles are the order of the day, inspired by
Hong Kong mein dong (noodle stalls) but with influences from across China, Malaysia and Singapore. *See
p207* **Quality Fast Food**. *Photo p207.*
▶ *For Japanese, Donzoko (15 Kingly Street,
7734 1974) is just round the corner. On Ganton
Street, also try Diner (nos.16-18, 7287 8962,
www.thedinersoho.com) or Mother Mash (no.26,
7494 9644, www.mothermash.co.uk).*

★ Dehesa
*25 Ganton Street, Soho, W1F 9BP (7494 4170).
Oxford Circus tube.* **Open** noon-11pm Mon-Sat;
noon-5pm Sun. **Tapas** £3-£7. **Credit** AmEx,
MC, V. **Map** p406 U3 ❹ **Spanish-Italian tapas**
A bijou place serving top-rank Spanish-Italian tapas
and a runner-up for our best new restaurant award
in 2008. Expect bicultural bites such as jamón iberi-
co, hand-sliced from a leg on display and intensely
flavoured wild boar salami, plus a range of cheeses
from the bar snacks and charcuterie. Reservations
aren't taken, so expect to wait a while. *Photo p211.*
▶ *You also won't regret queuing for the exquisite
tapas at Barrafina (54 Frith Street, 7813 8016,
www.barrafina.co.uk), on the other side of Soho.*

…and Eating Out
Our pick of the best summer dining.

Barrafina
See left.
For people-watchers, a handful of tiny
tables are dotted out front, but it's best
to watch the cooking action from a seat
at the marble-topped counter. Modelled
after Barcelona's famous Cal Pep, it is
hard not to imagine, while tucking into
the perfect tapas (*pictured*), that you're
in sunny Spain rather than grimy Soho.

Clerkenwell Kitchen
See p201.
Stake out a seat in the ace courtyard,
which has umbrellas for rain or shine.
Eating here is a virtue in more ways than
one: the superb, British-accented dishes
are made with fresh, locally sourced
produce and the restaurant's carbon
footprint is carefully monitored.

Lawn
See p219 **Profile**.
Oliver Peyton's latest offering is a
stunner of a restaurant and café set in
the regal setting of Fulham Palace (*see
p161*). Quintessentially British dishes
include spatchcocked chicken with
Jersey royals and watercress.

River Café
See p225.
Such a shame this iconic Italian was
closed for most of summer 2008 due
to a fire; newly reopened, there is no
better place for an alfresco lunch by
the waters. The kitchen is dedicated to
fresh and seasonal ingredients whipped
up to the highest standards. A real treat.

CONSUME

★ £ Fernandez & Wells

73 Beak Street, Soho, W1F 9SR (7287 8124/ www.fernandezandwells.com). Oxford Circus or Piccadilly Circus tube. **Open** 7.30am-7pm Mon-Fri; 9am-7pm Sat, Sun. **Main courses** £3-£5. **Credit** (over £5) MC, V. **Map** p406 V3 ⑮ **Café**
If only there were more coffee bars like this in central London. Its sandwiches aren't cheap, but they are special. Drop by in the morning for, say, a cheese toastie made with sourdough bread, or a breakfast pastry. At lunchtime, seats are at a premium but worth the wait. F&W also run a takeaway/deli in Lexington Street, specialising in Spanish products.

★ £ Hummus Bros

88 Wardour Street, Soho, W1F 0TJ (7734 1311/ www.hbros.co.uk). Oxford Circus or Tottenham Court Road tube. **Open** 11am-10pm Mon-Wed; 11am-11pm Thur, Fri; noon-11pm Sat; noon-10pm Sun. **Main courses** £2-£6. **Credit** AmEx, MC, V. **Map** p406 W3 ⑯ **Café**
The simple and hugely successful formula at this café/takeaway is to serve houmous as a base for a selection of toppings, which you scoop up with excellent pitta bread. The food is nutritious and good value – although there's a price hike at peak times. *See also p207* **Quality Fast Food**.
Other locations 37-63 Southampton Row, Bloomsbury, WC1B 4DA (7404 7079).

£ Little Lamb

72 Shaftesbury Avenue, Chinatown, W1D 6NA (7287 8078). Leicester Square or Piccadilly Circus tube. **Open** noon-11.30pm Mon-Sat; noon-10.30pm Sun. **Main courses** £10-£20. **Credit** MC, V. **Map** p406 W3 ⑰ **Oriental hot-pot**
Little Lamb suffers from a common Chinatown malaise – the urge to dumb down flavours beyond the mild Cantonese norm. So despite the Genghis Khan schtick, don't expect Mongolian specialities. Still, the hot-pot set meals are great. *See p208* **Eating In**.

£ Maison Bertaux

28 Greek Street, Soho, W1D 5DQ (7437 6007). Leicester Square, Piccadilly Circus or Tottenham Court Road tube. **Open** 8.30am-11pm Mon-Sat; 8am-7pm Sun. **Main courses** £1-£5. **No credit cards**. **Map** p407 X3 ⑱ **Café**
Oozing arty, bohemian charm, this café dates back to 1871 when Soho was London's little piece of the Continent. Battered old bentwood tables and chairs add to the feeling of being in a pâtisserie in rural France. The provisions (cream cakes, greasy pastries, pots of tea) really aren't the point.

£ Nordic Bakery

14 Golden Square, Soho, W1F 9JF (3230 1077/ www.nordicbakery.com). Oxford Circus or Piccadilly Circus tube. **Open** 8am-8pm Mon-Fri; noon-7pm Sat. **Main courses** £3-£4. **Credit** MC, V. **Map** p406 V3 ⑲ **Café**

Dehesa. *See p209.*

A haven of über-stylish Scandinavian cool warmed up with baskets, tea towels, denim aprons and a nature-inspired wall rug. *See p208* **Eating In**.

Quo Vadis

26-29 Dean Street, Soho, W1D 3LL (7437 9585/www.quovadissoho.co.uk). Leicester Square, Piccadilly Circus or Tottenham Court Road tube. **Open** noon-2.30pm, 5.30-10.30pm Mon-Sat. **Main courses** £12-£27. **Credit** AmEx, DC, MC, V. **Map** p404 W2 ⑳ **Modern European**
This Soho stalwart (in situ since 1926) has enjoyed an agreeably slick reinvention under brothers Eddie and Sam Hart, the pair responsible for top-quality Spanish eateries Fino and Barrafina. The dishes here have a British/modern European bent – a couple of flavours nodding towards Spain excepted (garlic and chilli razor clams). Dover sole and Colchester oysters vie for space with grill-restaurant classics including steaks, rack of lamb and ethically sound rose veal.

Red Fort

77 Dean Street, Soho, W1D 3SH (7437 2115/ www.redfort.co.uk). Leicester Square or Tottenham Court Road tube. **Open** noon-2pm, 5.45-11pm Mon-Fri; 5.45-11pm Sat; 5.30-10pm Sun. **Main courses** £12-£20. **Credit** AmEx, MC, V. **Map** p406 W2 ㉑ **Indian**
The epitome of elegance, the Red Fort has a calming, restrained demeanour. Food is classic Moghul (especially from regal Lucknow), rather than innovative,

CONSUME

Yauatcha.

so don't expect surprises – save, perhaps, for the size of the bill. The wine list, like the rest of this faultless operation, can't fail to impress business clients.

£ Spiga

84-86 Wardour Street, Soho, W1V 3LF (7734 3444/www.vpmg.net). Leicester Square, Piccadilly Circus or Tottenham Court Road tube. **Open** noon-11pm Mon, Tue; noon-midnight Wed-Sat. **Main courses** £8-£18. **Credit** AmEx, MC, V. **Map** p406 W3 ⑫ Pizza

Spiga makes a refreshing change from common or garden pizza chains, distinguished by interesting dishes created from super-fresh ingredients. Decorated with mirrored walls and Italian movie posters, it's packed most nights. The vibe is buzzy (even noisy), but the staff keep on top of things.

▶ *As we went to press, historic Soho pizza and champagne joint Kettners (29 Romilly Street, 7734 6112, www.kettners.com) was closed for a promising refurbishment by Ilse Crawford.*

Yauatcha

15 Broadwick Street, Soho, W1F 0DL (7494 8888). Oxford Circus, Piccadilly Circus or Tottenham Court Road tube. **Open** 11am-11.30pm Mon-Sat; 11am-10.30pm Sun. **Dim sum** £3-£27. **Credit** AmEx, MC, V. **Map** p406 V2 ⑬ Dim sum/teahouse

This ground-breaking dim sum destination is a sultry lounge-like basement den, with glowing fish tanks and starry ceiling lights, where young profes-

sionals, Chinese families and suited businessmen enjoy a succession of freshly prepared, highly impressive, perennial favourites such as har gau; chicken congee (rice porridge); and sticky rice encased in lotus leaf wrappers.

OXFORD STREET & MARYLEBONE

★ L'Autre Pied

5-7 Blandford Street, Marylebone, W1U 3DB (7486 9696/www.lautrepied.co.uk). Baker Street tube. **Open** noon-2.45pm, 6-10.30pm Mon-Sat; noon-3pm, 6.30-9.30pm Sun. **Main courses** £20-£23. **Credit** AmEx, MC, V. **Map** p398 G5 ⑭ French

This sister restaurant to the fabled Pied à Terre made its debut in autumn 2007 with talented chef Marcus Eaves at the helm. The cooking is accomplished and precise, with imaginative yet well-considered flavour combinations, and the food looks stunning too. We think it's one of the best places to dine in the capital: it won our Best New Restaurant award in 2008 and was a runner-up for Best Design.

Fairuz

3 Blandford Street, Marylebone, W1U 3DA (7486 8108/8182/www.fairuz.uk.com). Baker Street or Bond Street tube. **Open** noon-11.30pm Mon-Sat; noon-11pm Sun. **Main courses** £11-£19. **Credit** AmEx, MC, V. **Map** p398 G5 ⑮ Middle Eastern

Fairuz is a rough-hewn one-off. A youngish crowd are attracted by the relatively low prices at this singularly rustic and well-regarded Lebanese. Check out the makloobeh, a terrific stew of aubergine, rice, lamb and almonds.

£ La Fromagerie
2-6 Moxon Street, Marylebone, W1U 4EW (7935 0341/www.lafromagerie.co.uk). Baker Street or Bond Street tube. **Open** 10.30am-7.30pm Mon; 8am-7.30pm Tue-Fri; 9am-7pm Sat; 10am-6pm Sun. **Main courses** £6-£12. **Credit** AmEx, MC, V. **Map** p398 G5 ⑤ **Café/delicatessen**
Famed with foodies for its dedicated cheese room, Patricia Michelson's high-end deli also dishes out freshly cooked café food. Its communal tables are often packed with devotees. Fromage-o-philes are spoilt with plates of artisan cheese served with great bread, and a daily changing kitchen menu.
Other locations 30 Highbury Park, Highbury, N5 2AA (7359 7440).

Galvin Bistrot de Luxe
66 Baker Street, Marylebone, W1U 7DJ (7935 4007/www.galvinuk.com). Baker Street tube. **Open** noon-2.30pm, 6-11pm Mon-Sat; noon-5pm, 6-9.30pm Sun. **Main courses** £10-£21. **Credit** AmEx, MC, V. **Map** p398 G5 ⑤ **French**
On a rather impersonal stretch of Baker Street, the comforting 1930s decor and friendly, efficient staff here are most welcoming. A cheerful buzz accompanies the delightful food, which is consistently better than you might expect at these upper mid-range prices. Fresh ingredients and contrasting textures dominate the menu. Long may it flourish.

£ Golden Hind
73 Marylebone Lane, Marylebone, W1U 2PN (7486 3644). Bond Street tube. **Open** noon-3pm Mon-Fri; 6-10pm Mon-Sat. **Main courses** £5-£11. **Credit** AmEx, MC, V. **Map** p398 G5 ⑤ **Fish & chips**
The pastel-hued art deco fryer at this marvellous chip shop is sadly only used to store menus these days (the cooking's done in a kitchen at the back), but the Golden Hind still oozes local character, entirely in keeping with its mazy Marylebone Lane location. Their fish and chips really hit the spot.

★ Providores & Tapa Room
109 Marylebone High Street, Marylebone, W1U 4RX (7935 6175/www.theprovidores.co.uk). Baker Street or Bond Street tube. **Open** *Providores* noon-2.45pm, 6-10.30pm Mon-Sat; noon-2.45pm, 6-10pm Sun. *Tapa Room* 9-10.30am, noon-10.30pm Mon-Fri; 10am-3pm, 4-10.30pm Sat; 4-10pm Sun. **Mains** £18-£25. *Tapas* £2-£14. **Credit** AmEx, MC, V. **Map** p398 G5 ⑤ **Global tapas**
Chef Peter Gordon dazzles with such epicurean obscurities as barrel-aged Banyuls vinegar, and

produce from his native New Zealand like kumara (a uniquely flavoured sweet potato). The flavours of his complex dishes work in blissful harmony. The ground-floor Tapa Room is tailored to extravagant breakfasts and exuberant evening drinks. *Photo p214.*

Rhodes W1
Cumberland, Great Cumberland Place, Marble Arch, W1A 4RF (7616 5930/www.rhodesw1. com). Marble Arch tube. **Open** noon-2.30pm Tue-Fri; 7-10.30pm Tue-Sat. **Main courses** £15-£21. *Set menus* £55 2 courses; £65 3 courses. **Credit** AmEx, MC, V. **Map** p395 F6 ⑥ **Modern European**
A smallish, windowless den beautifully designed by Kelly Hoppen in her signature black and taupe colours, brought to glittering life by contemporary chandeliers (dripping thousands of crystals), Gary Rhodes' restaurant is one for an occasion. The menu sparkles too, dotted with gutsy French, Italian and British specialities.
Other locations Rhodes Twenty Four, Tower 42, Old Broad Street, the City, EC2N 1HQ (7877 7703/www.rhodes24.co.uk).

Royal China Club
40-42 Baker Street, Marylebone, W1U 7AJ (7486 3898/www.royalchinagroup.co.uk). Baker Street or Marble Arch tube. **Open** noon-11pm Mon-Thur; noon-11.30pm Fri, Sat; noon-10.30pm Sun. **Main courses** £8-£35. **Credit** AmEx, MC, V. **Map** p398 G5 ⑥ **Dim sum**
This sleek establishment, part of the popular Royal China chain, is a temple of Cantonese fine dining. Attention to quality and detail is apparent from the first sip of fragrant, premium jasmine tea. Here, the dim sum (which translates as 'touch the heart') touches the soul. Traditional and unusual combinations are executed with sublime grace, and service is swift, professional and knowledgeable.
▶ *The Docklands branch (30 Westferry Circus, 7719 0888) has a fine riverside terrace.*

PICCADILLY & MAYFAIR
★ Bentley's Oyster Bar & Grill
11-15 Swallow Street, Piccadilly, W1B 4DG (7734 4756/www.bentleysoysterbarandgrill.co.uk). Piccadilly Circus tube. **Open** *Oyster Bar* noon-midnight Mon-Sat; noon-10pm Sun. *Restaurant* noon-3pm, 6-11pm Mon-Sat; noon-3pm, 6-10pm Sun. **Main courses** £8-£38. **Credit** AmEx, MC, V. **Map** p406 V4 ⑥ **Fish**
Ever since Irish-born Richard Corrigan and his partners took over this 92-year-old veteran a couple of years ago, Bentley's has been one of the capital's most charming and consistent performers. While the first-floor dining rooms are more sedate and well-mannered, the downstairs oyster bar is where the action is – yes, it's expensive, but you can't help feeling that your boat has come in.

CONSUME

Providores & Tapa Room. *See p213.*

Chisou

*4 Princes Street, Mayfair, W1B 2LE (7629
3931/www.chisou.co.uk). Oxford Circus tube.*
Open noon-2.30pm, 6-10.15pm Mon-Sat. **Main
courses** £12-£20. **Credit** AmEx, MC, V. **Map**
p406 U2 🚳 **Japanese**
In spite of the black-clad staff, plain wooden tables,
smart blond chairs and black slate floor, Chisou has
a friendly *izakaya* tavern-style atmosphere that lures
regulars back time and again. It looks like a restaurant that means business, and that business is putting
a bright contemporary spin on Japanese classics.

Gaucho Piccadilly

*25 Swallow Street, Piccadilly, W1B 4DJ (7734
4040/www.gauchorestaurants.co.uk). Piccadilly
Circus tube.* **Open** noon-midnight Mon-Sat;
noon-10.30pm Sun. **Main courses** £8-£32.
Credit AmEx, DC, MC, V. **Map** p406 V5 🚳
Steakhouse
Steakhouse chic is what the Gaucho flagship branch
is all about – from its well-stocked Cavas wine shop
to a pitch-dark cocktail bar and penchant for cowskin
wallpaper and pouffes. The steaks? Good, with the *bife
de lomo* (fillet) often outstanding. Service is a touch too
slick, but that's the nature of smart chains.
Other locations throughout the city.

★ Hibiscus

*29 Maddox Street, Mayfair, W1S 2PA (7629
2999/www.hibiscusrestaurant.co.uk). Oxford
Circus tube.* **Open** noon-2.30pm, 6.30-10pm
Mon-Fri. **Set meals** £25 3-course lunch; £60
3-course dinner. **Credit** AmEx, MC, V. **Map**
p406 U3 🚳 **Modern European**
Small and intimate, Hibiscus is one of the most exciting places to eat in the capital and was a runner-up

for our Best New Restaurant gong in 2008. Chef-
patron Claude Bosi is a kitchen magician, playing
with texture and flavour in ways that challenge and
excite, but stop short of making diners feel they're
taking part in a weird experiment. Inevitably, not
every flavour combination works, and a meal here
doesn't come cheap, but it's bound to be memorable.

Maze

*10-13 Grosvenor Square, Mayfair, W1K 6JP
(7107 0000/www.gordonramsay.com). Bond
Street tube.* **Open** noon-midnight daily. **Main
courses** £16-£30. **Credit** AmEx, DC, MC, V.
Map p400 G6 🚳 **Modern European**
Although part of Gordon Ramsay's stable, Maze
owes its success to star chef Jason Atherton. He has
earned accolades for a line-up of sophisticated tapas,
miniature main courses and awe-inspiring desserts.
This is a modern, spacious set-up, with a glamorous
cocktail bar by the entrance, buff-hued banquettes
and groovy coloured glass panels in the dining area.

Momo

*25 Heddon Street, Mayfair, W1B 4BH (7434
4040/www.momoresto.com). Piccadilly Circus
tube.* **Open** noon-2.30pm, 6.30-11pm Mon-Sat;
6.30-10.30pm Sun. **Main courses** £13-£23.
Credit AmEx, DC, MC, V. **Map** p406 U3 🚳
North African
A high reputation, great Maghrebi soundtrack, cool
Marrakech-style decor and some of the best North
African food in London keep punters pouring in to
Momo for an experience to savour.

Parlour

*1st floor, Fortnum & Mason, 181 Piccadilly, W1A
1ER (7734 8040/www.fortnumandmason.co.uk).*

CONSUME

Green Park or Piccadilly Circus tube. **Open** 10am-7.30pm Mon-Sat; noon-4.30pm Sun. **Main courses** £6-£10. **Credit** AmEx, MC, V. **Map** p406 V5 🟢
Ice-cream parlour
The Parlour's warm, silky Amedei chocolate sauce is superior to the chocolate ice-cream here, so order an ice-cream flight – three scoops of, say, marmalade and bergamot, strawberry and balsamic, and lemon curd – with the sauce to pour on top. Prices are on the high side, but coffees come with a tiny sample cone, and the David Collins interior is a stunner.

La Petite Maison
54 Brooks Mews, Mayfair, W1K 4EG (7495 4774/www.lpmlondon.co.uk). Bond Street tube. **Open** noon-3pm, 6-11pm Mon-Sat; 12.30-4pm Sun. **Main courses** £9-£35. **Credit** AmEx, MC, V. **Map** p400 H6 🟢 **French**
Part of the buzz around this place is that it's based on a namesake in Nice and co-owned by Arjun Waney, one of the owners of Roka and Zuma (*see p218*). It's usually full of locals, financiers, couples and socialites, audibly excited by the high standard of the food (the likes of anchovies sandwiched between sage leaves or turbot on the bone with chorizo). Dishes are served to be shared, though you may have to wait longer than desired for them.

★ Scott's
20 Mount Street, Mayfair, W1K 2HE (7495 7309/www.caprice-holdings.co.uk). Bond Street or Green Park tube. **Open** noon-midnight Mon-Sat; noon-10pm Sun. **Main courses** £16-£40. **Cover** £2. **Credit** AmEx, DC, MC, V. **Map** p400 G7 🟢
Fish
Of the celebrity hangouts in the capital, Scott's is the one that most justifies the hype: from the greeting by doorman Sean to the look-at-me contemporary British art on the walls and the glossy Rich List crowd. Yes, tables are like hen's teeth, so snare a perch at the slow curve of onyx bar, where you'll be rewarded by superior, elevated views of the action. The food – perhaps tiny boar sausages with chilled rock oysters – gets better and better. *Photos p217.*

Sketch
9 Conduit Street, Mayfair, W1S 2XZ (0870 777 4488/www.sketch.uk.com). Oxford Circus tube. **Open** noon-2.30pm, 7-10.30pm Tue-Fri; 7-10.30pm Sat. **Main courses** £12-£59. **Credit** AmEx, DC, MC, V. **Map** p406 U3 🟢 **Modern European**
Of the three bits of Pierre Gagnaire's legendarily expensive Sketch – including destination dining at the Gallery and the Lecture Room's haute-beyond-haute cuisine – the Glade is the most egalitarian. The lunchtime brasserie (in which, horrors, staff wear jeans) threatens to jar with Sketch's finely honed sensibilities, but the menus are appropriately artful and not unreasonably priced for the quality. But nothing can prepare you for the loos, each of them housed in a gleaming white egg.

Tamarind
20-22 Queen Street, Mayfair, W1J 5PR (7629 3561/www.tamarindrestaurant.com). Green Park tube. **Open** noon-2.45pm, 6-11.30pm Mon-Fri; 6-11.30pm Sat; noon-2.45pm, 6-10.30pm Sun. **Main courses** £16-£28. **Credit** AmEx, DC, MC, V. **Map** p400 H7 🟢 **Indian**
Chef Alfred Prasad has maintained Tamarind in the top rank of Indian restaurants. This capacious basement has a grandiose demeanour, helped by burnished gold pillars and walls, polished wooden flooring and equally polished (if a little overbearing) service. Prasad relies on innovative spicing, expert presentation and a lightness of touch to make his mark; most dishes are classic North Indian.

★ Wild Honey
12 St George Street, Mayfair, W1S 2FB (7758 9160/www.wildhoneyrestaurant.co.uk). Oxford Circus or Bond Street tube. **Open** noon-2.30pm, 6-10.30pm Mon-Sat; noon-3pm, 6-10.30pm Sun. **Set meals** £16.95-£18.95. **Credit** AmEx, MC, V. **Map** p398 H6 🟢 **Modern European**
This sister of Arbutus (*see p208*) has both charm and professionalism in spades. The oak-panelled walls could be stifling, but modern artworks banish thoughts of the old world order, and a happy buzz predominates. The reasonably priced menu ranges across the best of the UK and mainland Europe.
▶ *Don't get lost! Wild Honey is on* St *George Street, not nearby George Street in Marylebone.*

★ Wolseley
160 Piccadilly, W1J 9EB (7499 6996/www.thewolseley.com). Green Park tube. **Open** 7am-midnight Mon-Fri; 8am-midnight Sat; 8am-11pm Sun. **Main courses** £7-£30. **Credit** AmEx, DC, MC, V. **Map** p406 U5 🟢 **Modern European/brasserie**
The Wolseley shimmers with glamour and excitement, and the dining room is filled with a lively social energy. It's a sought-after venue at any time of day: breakfast, brunch, lunch, tea or dinner. Waiting staff are warm and professional, and the tables are laid out with good linen and silverware.
▶ *The newer venture from the Wolseley's Chris Corbin and Jeremy King is the equally classy but thoroughly modern St Alban (4-12 Regent Street, 7499 8558, www.stalban.net).*

Yoshino
3 Piccadilly Place, Piccadilly, W1J 0DB (7287 6622/www.yoshino.net). Piccadilly Circus tube. **Open** noon-9pm Mon-Sat. **Set meals** £5.80-£19.80. **Credit** AmEx, MC, V. **Map** p406 V4 🟢 **Japanese**
Yoshino used to be the preserve of Japanese diners on expense accounts, but things have changed. Service is now smiling, the menu's fully bilingual, and the prices, once prohibitive, have come down. This is now a mid-range venue with great sashimi.

CONSUME

WESTMINSTER & ST JAMES'S

Cinnamon Club

Old Westminster Library, 30-32 Great Smith Street, Westminster, SW1P 3BU (7222 2555/ www.cinnamonclub.com). St James's Park or Westminster tube. **Open** 7.30-9.30am, noon-12.30pm, 6-10.45pm Mon-Sat. **Main courses** £11-£29. **Credit** AmEx, DC, MC, V. **Map** p401 K9 ⑯ **Indian**

Housed in a former Victorian library, the Cinnamon Club is a grand affair with high ceilings, a gallery of bookshelves and elegant leather chairs. The food is exemplary: chef Vivek Singh opts for Western-style presentation, but with classic Indian spicing.

▶ *Cinnamon Kitchen, a new, less formal branch, was due to open in the City late last year.*

Inn The Park

St James's Park, St James's, SW1A 2BJ (7451 9999/www.innthepark.com). St James's Park tube. **Open** 8am-9pm Mon-Fri; 9am-9pm Sat, Sun. **Main courses** £14-£23. **Credit** AmEx, MC, V. **Map** p401 K8 ⑰ **British**

The English class system is alive and well here: self-service customers fight over tables at the back, while the front terrace overlooking the lake is reserved for the fatter of wallet. The restaurant is open from (build your own) breakfast to dinner, with the accent on in-season ingredients. But the food struggles to match a spectacular setting. *See also p219* **Profile**.

★ National Dining Rooms

Sainsbury Wing, National Gallery, Trafalgar Square, WC2N 5DN (7747 2525/www.the nationaldiningrooms.co.uk). Charing Cross tube/rail. **Open** 10am-5.30pm Mon, Tue, Thur-Sun; 10am-8.30pm Wed. **Set meals** £17.50 1 course; £24.50 2 courses; £29.50 3 courses. **Credit** AmEx, MC, V. **Map** p407 X5 ⑱ **British**

Oliver Peyton's winner of our 2007 Best British Restaurant gong is still in fine shape. Choose from a bar menu, sample an array of tempting baked goods or even take a cultured, cheeky afternoon tea. But the real attraction remains the main menu of British staples, delivered with skill and efficiency – far more impressive than the institutional location might suggest. *See also p219* **Profile**.

▶ *The East Wing's darkly romantic National Café bar-restaurant (7747 2525, www.the nationalcafe.com) opens until 11pm daily.*

Sake No Hana

23 St James's Street, St James's, SW1A 1HA (7925 8988). Green Park tube. **Open** noon-3pm, 6pm-midnight Mon-Sat; noon-3pm, 6-11pm Sun. **Main courses** £4-£40. **Credit** AmEx, DC, MC, V. **Map** p400 J8 ⑲ **Japanese**

With a glittering track record (Wagamama, Busaba, Hakkasan, Yauatcha), Alan Yau had much to live

up to with this, his first Japanese fine-dining restaurant. Sake No Hana is discreet and coolly designed, winning our 2008 Award for Best Restaurant Design. Cedar tables with foot-wells sit amid acres of tatami (there's Western-style seating too), while narrow tilted screens add elegance to wraparound, ceiling-high windows. Some dishes are modern and playful, but many are orthodox and simple.

CHELSEA

Bluebird

350 King's Road, SW3 5UU (7559 1000/www. danddlondon.com). Sloane Square tube then 11, 19, 22, 49, 319 bus. **Open** *Restaurant* 12.30-2.30pm, 6-10.30pm Mon-Fri; noon-3.30pm, 6-10.30pm Sat; noon-3.30pm, 6-9.30pm Sun. *Bar* noon-midnight Mon-Thur; noon-1am Fri, Sat; noon-11.30pm Sun. **Main courses** £13-£25. **Credit** AmEx, DC, MC, V. **Map** p397 D12 ㉚ **Modern European**

A cunning conversion of an amazing art-deco garage, complete with café and expensive épicerie, Bluebird remains a relatively popular meeting place for Chelsea residents. The menu is eclectic and please-all, with French accents. Prices reflect the swanky location.

Botanist

7 Sloane Square, SW1W 8EE (7730 0077/ www.thebotanistonsloanesquare.com). Sloane Square tube. **Open** 8am-10.30pm Mon-Sat; noon-10.30pm Sun. **Main courses** £14-£19. **Credit** AmEx, MC, V. **Map** p400 G10 ㉛ **British bar-restaurant**

Tom and Ed Martin, well-known for their gastropub group which includes favourites such as the Gun (*see p224*), appropriately first opened this rather beautiful dining room and bar during the Chelsea Flower Show. Food (including afternoon tea) is served most of the day and there are majestic roasts on Sundays. Breakfast comprises all the usual cooked and continental options, perfectly presented, so wonderful, in fact, that Botanist became the first to win in our new category for Best Breakfast at the 2008 *Time Out* Eating & Drinking Awards.

Scott's. *See p215.*

Chutney Mary

*535 King's Road, SW10 0SZ (7351 3113/www.
realindianfood.com). Fulham Broadway tube/11,
22 bus.* **Open** 6.30-11pm Mon-Fri; 12.30-2.30pm,
6.30-11pm Sat; 12.30-3pm, 6.30-10.30pm Sun.
Main courses £14-£31. **Credit** AmEx, DC, MC,
V. **Map** p396 C13 ❸ **Indian**
When it opened in 1991, this was Britain's smartest
and most ambitious Indian restaurant. Serving fine
regional cooking, it continues to introduce new and
innovative dishes. The premises look fresh, and a
memorable meal is pretty much guaranteed.

★ Tom's Kitchen

*27 Cale Street, SW3 3QP (7349 0202/www.
tomskitchen.co.uk). South Kensington or Sloane
Square tube.* **Open** 7-10am, noon-3pm, 6pm-
midnight Mon-Fri; 10am-3pm, 6pm-midnight
Sat, Sun. **Main courses** £14-£27. **Credit**
AmEx, MC, V. **Map** p397 E11 ❸ **Brasserie**
This is home from home for Chelsea's super-rich, but
don't let that put you off. The warm, welcoming
room, framed in gleaming white tiles and homespun
prints, feels as if it was set up just to make you
happy. The menu is superb, covering much of what
you'd want to eat from early morning until night.

KNIGHTSBRIDGE &
SOUTH KENSINGTON

Amaya

*19 Motcomb Street, Halkin Arcade, Knightsbridge,
SW1X 8JT (7823 1166/www.realindianfood.com).*

Knightsbridge tube. **Open** 12.30-2.15pm, 6.30-
11.15pm Mon-Sat; 12.45-2.30pm, 6.30-10.15pm
Sun. **Main courses** £8-£25. **Credit** AmEx, DC,
MC, V. **Map** p400 G9 ❸ **Indian**
Glamorous, stylish and seductive, Amaya is sleekly appointed with sparkly chandeliers, splashes of
modern art and a groovy bar. This restaurant's calling card is its imaginative Indian creations from a
menu that cleverly links dressed-up street food with
regal specialities. It's a magnet for deep-pocketed
Knightsbridge suits as well as romancing couples.

£ Hummingbird Bakery

*47 Old Brompton Road, South Kensington, SW7
3JP (7584 0055/www.hummingbirdbakery.com).
South Kensington tube.* **Open** 10.30am-7pm daily.
Main courses £2-£4. **Credit** AmEx, MC, V.
Map p397 D10 ❸ **Café**
This NY-style bakery-cum-café, done out in pink,
black and brown, and with ruby-red velvet chairs
and stools, is a popular spot for a slice of home-
baked Americana: thickly frosted cupcakes, zingy
key lime pie and proper American brownies.

Nahm

*Halkin, Halkin Street, Belgravia, SW1X 7DJ
(7333 1234/www.nahm.como.bz). Hyde Park
Corner tube.* **Open** noon-2.30pm, 7-10.45pm Mon-
Fri, 7-10.45pm Sat; 7-9.45pm Sun. **Main courses**
£11-£17. **Set meals** £26-£55. **Credit** AmEx,
DC, MC, V. **Map** p400 G9 ❸ **Thai**
Truly exceptional food is produced in the chic din-
ing room of the Halkin (*see p191*) – at seriously high

prices. The menu features traditional Thai dishes as well as updated versions using British ingredients. Sleek, subtle and cool, this is the best Thai restaurant in London. The website offers discount menus.

Olivomare
10 Lower Belgrave Street, Belgravia, SW1W 0LJ (7730 9022). Victoria tube/rail. **Open** noon-2.30pm, 7-11pm Mon-Sat. **Main courses** £14-£27. **Credit** AmEx, DC, MC, V. **Map** p400 H10 **⑰ Fish**
Olivomare's stark minimalist monochrome fish-patterned decor is as single-minded as the fish-only menu of impeccably fresh, intelligently cooked seafood. Even the (Italian) waiters are fresh, in a good way.

Racine
239 Brompton Road, Knightsbridge, SW3 2EP (7584 4477). Knightsbridge or South Kensington tube/14, 74 bus. **Open** noon-3pm, 6-10.30pm Mon-Sat; 6-10pm Sun. **Main courses** £12-£21. **Credit** AmEx, MC, V. **Map** p397 E10 **⑱ French**
Heavy curtains inside the door allow diners to make a grand entrance into the warm, vibrant 1930s retro atmosphere here. The food, though not cutting edge, has character. Get a window table. *Photos p222.*

★ Zuma
5 Raphael Street, Knightsbridge, SW7 1DL (7584 1010/www.zumarestaurant.com). Knightsbridge tube. **Open** *Restaurant* noon-2.15pm, 6-10.45pm Mon-Fri; 12.30-2.45pm, 6-10.45pm Sat; 12.30-2.45pm, 6-10.15pm Sun. *Bar* noon-11pm Mon-Fri; 12.30-11pm Sat; noon-10pm Sun. **Main courses** £15-£70. **Credit** AmEx, DC, MC, V. **Map** p397 F9 **⑲ Japanese fusion**
The bar crammed with beautiful people testifies to Zuma's staying power among London's smartest top restaurants. But there's more to this 'contemporary izakaya' than a striking wood-and-stone interior and a stylish wine and sake list. The surprise is that the mix of Japanese and fusion food on the long menu fully justifies the high prices.
▶ *For Zuma's younger sibling Roka and Shochu Lounge, see p230.*

PADDINGTON & NOTTING HILL

Assaggi
1st floor, 39 Chepstow Place, Bayswater, W2 4TS (7792 5501). Bayswater, Queensway or Notting Hill Gate tube. **Open** 12.30-2.30pm, 7.30-11pm Mon-Sat. **Main courses** £18-£24. **Credit** MC, V. **Map** p394 B6 **⑳ Italian**
Despite the informal, pared-down dining room with scrubbed wooden floorboards and paper table mats, this is one of those rare places in London where prime ingredients are married with culinary artistry at reasonable prices. Booking is imperative. *Photo p225.*

★ Le Café Anglais
8 Porchester Gardens, Bayswater, W2 4DB (7221 1415/www.lecafeanglais.co.uk). Bayswater tube. **Open** noon-3pm, 6.30-11.30pm Mon-Sat; noon-3pm, 6.30-10pm Sun. **Main courses** £8-£28. **Credit** AmEx, MC, V. **Map** p394 B6 **㉛ Modern European**
Chef-proprietor Rowley Leigh's new restaurant opened to great acclaim at the end of 2007. The white, art deco-style room is very big, with floor-to-ceiling leaded windows on one side, the open kitchen, rotisserie grill and bar opposite. It's a see-and-be-seen kind of place with a long menu that's a mix-and-match delight, divided into first courses, fish, roasts, vegetables and desserts. Professional service, a lengthy wine list divided by region and a buzzy vibe add to the satisfaction. *Photo p220.*

Cow
89 Westbourne Park Road, Westbourne Grove, W2 5QH (7221 0021/www.thecowlondon.co.uk). Royal Oak or Westbourne Park tube. **Open** noon-11pm Mon-Thur; noon-midnight Fri, Sat; noon-10.30pm Sun. **Main courses** £9-£19. **Credit** MC, V. **Map** p394 B5 **㉜ Gastropub**
Tom Conran's highly popular Cow has a ramshackle retro-Irish vibe. Downstairs, punters cram in, happily standing by the bar to drink. In the first-floor restaurant, long-haired bambis with it-bags eat with doe-eyed boyfriends in tight sweaters. Wherever you sit, the smart order is seafood. Service ranges from sweet to smart-arse: the Cow knows it's cool.

Geales
2 Farmer Street, Notting Hill, W8 7SN (7727 7528/www.geales.com). Notting Hill Gate tube. **Open** 6-10.30pm Mon; noon-2.30pm, 6-11pm Tue-Fri; noon-2.30pm, 6-10.30pm Sat, Sun. **Main courses** £9-£14. **Credit** AmEx, MC, V. **Map** p394 A7 **㉝ Fish & chips**
Geales opened as a chippie in 1939, but since its 2006 takeover it has become the habitat of Notting Hill's casually dressed middle-class. Fish remains the focus of the menu, which states plainly that the restaurant is 'dedicated to using sustainable fisheries only', and the likes of cod, hake and haddock arrive beautifully battered and fresh as the new tide.

★ Hereford Road
3 Hereford Road, Bayswater, W2 4AB (7727 1144/www.herefordroad.org). Bayswater tube. **Open** noon-3pm daily; 6-11pm Mon-Sat, 6-10pm Sun. **Main courses** £8-£16. **Credit** AmEx, MC, V. **Map** p394 B6 **㉞ British**
Chef Tom Pemberton is a graduate of St John (*see p202*), and the influence behind his forthright cooking is clear, from the deep-fried calf's brain to the laverbread and piccalilli – you could only be dining in Britain. The room is sparse and there's no music; just the chatter of happy diners. It was one of the runners-up for our Best New Restaurant Award in 2008.

Profile Oliver Peyton

The Irish restaurateur who is everywhere in London.

Oliver Peyton has been artfully catering to the culinary whims of the capital for more than a decade. Born in County Mayo, he made a splash here in 1994 with the Atlantic Bar & Grill, right in the heart of Soho. For a few months, the Atlantic was the bar to be seen in, with huge queues, an unpredictable door policy and heavenly cocktails (*see p237* **Good Mixers**).

Although he enjoyed success in the 1990s with other ventures (the futuristic Coast, ambitious micro-brewery Mash), it's only been in recent years, after the formerly wild restaurateur had calmed down, that Peyton's really hit the big time. He opened **Inn The Park** (*see p216*) in 2004. Designed to blend with St James's Park (*see p114*), it became a lakeside family favourite. The link between tourist attractions and Peyton's catering had been made.

During 2006, Peyton opened a new eaterie as often as the rest of us open a newspaper. Pick of the bunch was the **National Dining Rooms** (*see p216*) – not for its tricky location in the National Gallery, but for chef Jess Dunford Wood's use of British ingredients. He won the contract for the **Wallace Collection** (*see p97*), turning its splendid atrium into a fine French restaurant, and his **Meals** (*see p205*) proved that department store eateries can do a lot more than sarnies and scones. The Peyton & Byrne

ICA Café.

bakery-shop – downstairs from Meals, in a former florist's stall – was such a success it led to café versions in the **Wellcome Collection** (*see p78*) and **St Pancras International** (*see p79*). By October, Peyton was evidently bored: to fill the idle hours he returned to the National Gallery to open the handsome **National Café** (*see p216*).

In 2008, he not only took over the café at the **ICA** (*see p115*), presenting the contemporary arts centre with an appetisingly contemporary menu in an funky little dining room, but also opened the **Lawn** in Fulham Palace (*see p161*), where – like all Peyton venues – thought and money were devoted to providing a stylish setting, both inside and outside on the grass. Even that isn't enough for him: this year he is planning to open **Petit Oiseau** (1 Queens Gardens, 7689 9056) in Nest, a new GuestInvest hotel in Bayswater.

We asked Peyton what the capital means to him. 'The thing about London is the amount of arts culture that is here. It's enormous, you're spoiled for choice. The galleries are much more reactive to people's needs. They are pulling on shows that people are interested in.' As, indeed, is Peyton himself.

THREE TO VISIT

National Dining Rooms
The best British seasonal ingredients, served up to fine artistic appreciation.

Lawn
Expert grilling and an elegant menu, in a classic English setting with an expansive terrace.

ICA Café
Simple, fresh, seasonal dishes in a colourful little dining den right on the Mall.

CONSUME

Le Café Anglais

A Little of What You Fancy?

We take a stand against the fashion for teeny-tiny eats.

Only in a pre-crunch world could diners and restaurateurs have become obsessed with the mini portion, from über-slick bars serving munchkin versions of English classics (that's you Hoxton Pony, with your Shoreditch take on 'East End Grub') to New Age eateries latching on to the tapas phenomenon. Jason Atherton's **Maze** (see p214), for example, serves perfectly executed British dishes – in tapas formation. So how can you ever get enough of that exquisite Berkshire pork loin and belly, short of ordering six portions of the same dish? Similarly, the **Providores & Tapa Room** (see p213), long-term dish downsizer, never followed the 'starter, main, pud' format but, inspired by Japanese *ippin ryori* ('small dishes', offers a series of petite plates.

All very well for those who crave variety above all else (Providores chef-proprietor

Peter Gordon is unquestionably inventive), but whatever happened to hearty British grub on a moon-sized plate? Tom Pemberton's solemn tribute to great English produce, **Hereford Road** (see p218), will set your mind at rest. Pemberton's signature whole braised oxtail is a formidable hulk of a dish that wouldn't look out of place in a medieval banquet. The 'nose-to-tail eating' at Fergus Henderson's **St John** (see p202) is another source of no-nonsense British food. As well as rabbit with mustard and roasted bone marrow, a special 'feasting menu' provides whole roast suckling pig.

Even better, Rowley Leigh's star newcomer, **Le Café Anglais** (see p218), combines both tendencies: fleets of exquisite hors d'oeuvres for grazers, and trad favourites – rotisserie chicken, trifle, fine cheese – for anyone with a belly.

£ Kiasu

48 Queensway, Bayswater, W2 3RY (7727 8810). Bayswater or Queensway tube. **Open** noon-11pm daily. **Main courses** £5-£8. **Credit** (min £10) MC, V. **Map** p394 C6 ⑨⑤ **Malaysian**
A cheerful, cheap, all-day restaurant frequented by South-east Asians. Glass mugs of sweet teh tarik, Malaysia's favourite blend of tea and condensed milk, help to soothe the chilli heat of dishes such as soft-shell crab, served in the Singapore chilli crab style. Portions are generous.

Ledbury

127 Ledbury Road, Westbourne Grove, W11 2AQ (7792 9090/www.theledbury.com). Westbourne Park tube. **Open** noon-2pm, 6.30-10.15pm Mon-Fri; noon-3pm, 6.30-10.15pm Sat, Sun. **Set meals** £19-£50. **Credit** AmEx, MC, V. **Map** p394 A6 ⑨⑥ **French**
Notting Hillites flock to this elegant gastronomic gem, where the food is as adventurous and accomplished as any, but less expensive. Aimed squarely at the palate, flavours are intense and delicate, and

often powerfully earthy. Spending £20-£30 on wine is possible, but it's also worth pushing the boat out to complement this world-class cooking.

£ Taqueria
139-143 Westbourne Grove, Notting Hill, W11 2RS (7229 4734/www.coolchiletaqueria.co.uk). Notting Hill Gate tube. **Open** noon-11pm Mon-Thur; noon-11.30pm Fri; 10am-11.30pm Sat; noon-10.30pm Sun. **Main courses** £3-£8. **Credit** MC, V. **Map** p394 A6 ❻ **Mexican**
With its real-deal tortilla-making machine from Guadalajara, this place shows what Mexican street food is about: masa (maize dough) is flattened into soft tortillas for tacos, fried crisp for tostadas and shaped into thick patties for griddled sopes. Masks, movie posters and gorgeous staff make Taqueria easy on the eye, as well as the taste buds.
▶ *Nearby García (246 Portobello Rd, 7221 6119, www.cafegarcia.co.uk) is a trad Spanish café.*

£ Urban Turban
98 Westbourne Grove, Notting Hill, W2 5RU (7243 4200/www.urbanturban.uk.com). Bayswater or Notting Hill Gate tube. **Open** 6-11pm Mon-Fri; noon-4pm, 6-11pm Sat, Sun. **Main courses** £6-£12. **Credit** AmEx, MC, V. **Map** p394 B6 ❾ **Indian tapas**
Younger sister to the fine-dining Rasoi Vineet Bhatia, this is a trendy lounge bar themed around stylised Indian tapas and cool cocktails. There isn't much by way of innovation in the cooking, but the seared 'gunpowder' prawns were truly noteworthy.

NORTH LONDON

For Oriental food, try **Gilgamesh** (*see p236*), which serves assured and sometimes inspired pan Asian food with its extraordinary cocktails.

Duke of Cambridge
30 St Peter's Street, Islington, N1 8JT (7359 3066/www.dukeorganic.co.uk). Angel tube. **Open** noon-11pm Mon-Sat; noon-10.30pm Sun. **Main courses** £10-£18. **Credit** MC, V. **Map** p402 O2 ❻❾ **Gastropub**
The UK's first certified organic gastropub ticks every box on sustainability, but it's also a very appealing pub, with great organic beers from Pitfield Brewery, an attractive open room, and a friendly mix of green-thinking folk (from dread-locked cyclists to City suits). As a purely culinary destination, though, it still has some way to go: you need more than ethics to run a really good kitchen.
▶ *Fellow Islington gastro the Marquess Tavern (32 Canonbury Street, 7354 2975, www.the marquesstavern.co.uk) is also attentive to sourcing.*

Haché
24 Inverness Street, Camden, NW1 7HJ (7485 9100/www.hacheburgers.com). Camden Town

tube. **Open** noon-10.30pm Mon-Sat; noon-10pm Sun. **Main courses** £6-£12. **Credit** AmEx, MC, V. **Burgers**
Haché is a cosy bistro-style restaurant specialising in superior burgers: good-quality Ayrshire steaks, chopped, grilled and served in ciabatta-like buns; the superiority of the meat compared to most rivals is undeniable. Sides are a cut above, and the smooth-ies delicious. *See also p207* **Quality Fast Food**.
Other locations 329 Fulham Road, Chelsea, SW10 9QL (7823 3515).

Manna
4 Erskine Road, Primrose Hill, NW3 3AJ (7722 8028/www.mannav.com). Chalk Farm tube/31, 168 bus. **Open** 6.30am-10.30pm Mon; 10am-3pm, 6.30-10.30pm Tue-Sun. **Main courses** £10-£13. **Credit** MC, V. **Vegetarian**
Following a refurb, Manna seems keen to shed any old-fashioned notions of what vegetarianism entails and shift the emphasis to its gourmet credentials. The menu picks and chooses from global cuisines, and as a special-occasion venue, Manna remains a cut above most other meat-free contenders.

£ Masala Zone
25 Parkway, Camden, NW1 7PG (7267 4422/ www.masalazone.com). Camden Town tube.

INSIDE TRACK
CURRY IN FAVOUR?

We recommend visiting **Brick Lane** (*see p134*), just not for the curries. Repeated visits have uncovered nothing better than the standard Anglo-Indian fare you'd find on any British high street. But there are signs of improvement. The formula curry houses are being joined by a few caffs offering proper Bangladeshi dishes, especially around the south end of Brick Lane: try point-and-order dishes in **Sabuj Bangla** (102 Brick Lane, 7247 6222) or **Ruchi** (303 Whitechapel Road, 7247 6666). In Whitechapel, try **Kolapata**, **Tayyabs** or the **Lahore Kebab House** (for all, *see p224*). But real curry pilgrims do far better in Southall: **Brilliant** (72-76 Western Road, 8574 1928, www.brilliant restaurant.com) and **Madhu's** (39 South Road, 8574 1897) offer boldly spiced and excellently char-grilled Indo-Kenyan food, while the best kebabs and yoghurt-based snacks can be had at the **New Asian Tandoori Centre** (114-118 The Green, 8574 2597). The less intrepid can enjoy great Indian food at compellingly cheap prices at **Imli** (167-169 Wardour Street, 7287 4243, www.imli.co.uk) in Soho.

CONSUME

Open 12.30-3pm, 5.30-11pm Mon-Fri; 12.30-11pm Sat; 12.30-10.30pm Sun. **Main courses** £7-£15. **Credit** MC, V. **Indian**
This recent addition to the Masala Zone chain is especially popular with hip youngsters who come for the buzzy vibe, reasonable prices and decent pan-Indian food. The eye-catching decor is themed round colourful 1930s-style posters, retro artefacts and bright lampshades. The menu is notable for its earthy curries, thalis and zesty street snacks.
Other locations throughout the city.

Morgan M

489 Liverpool Road, Islington, N7 8NS (7609 3560/www.morganm.com). Highbury & Islington tube/rail. **Open** 7-10pm Tue, Sat; noon-2.30pm, 7-10pm Wed-Fri; noon-2.30pm Sun. **Set meals** £39-£48. **Credit** MC, V. **French**
After so many overhyped but essentially ordinary restaurants, it's a delight to find one that delivers. Morgan Meunier's cooking is supremely skilful; painstakingly intricate but without just-to-impress gestures, producing multiple layers of subtle flavours. Meunier is also known for his vegetarian creations: there's an all-vegetarian menu. The wine list is on a par with the food, the service utterly charming.

Osteria Stecca

1 Blenheim Terrace, St John's Wood, NW8 0EH (7328 5014/www.osteriastecca.com). St John's Wood tube. **Open** noon-2.30pm, 6.30-10.30pm Tue-Thur; noon-3pm, 6.30-11pm Fri, Sat; noon-3pm, 7-10pm Sun. **Main courses** £12-£21. **Credit** AmEx, MC, V. **Italian**
Osteria Stecca's large front terrace, with its big black umbrellas and smart box hedging, is the choice spot for a balmy summer night. The menu offers classic dishes from the north and south of Italy, often with a modern slant. It was a runner-up for Best Local Restaurant in our 2008 Eating & Drinking Awards.

★ £ Ottolenghi

287 Upper Street, Islington, N1 2TZ (7288 1454/ www.ottolenghi.co.uk). Angel tube/Highbury & Islington tube/rail. **Open** 8am-10.30pm Mon-Sat; 9am-7pm Sun. **Main courses** £8-£14. **Credit** AmEx, MC, V. **Map** p402 O1 **100 Bakery café**
This is more than an inviting bakery. Behind the pastries piled in the window is a comparatively prim deli counter with lush salads, available day and evening, eat-in or take away. As a stylish daytime café, Ottolenghi is undeniably brilliant, but the long canteen-style central table, slow-footed service and bright white decor are not for special occasions. *See also p207* **Quality Fast Food**.

£ S&M Café

4-6 Essex Road, Islington, N1 8LN (7359 5361/ www.sandmcafe.co.uk). Angel tube. **Open** 7.30am-11pm Mon-Fri; 8.30am-11pm Sat; 8.30am-10.30pm Sun. **Main courses** £6-£8. **Credit** MC, V. **Map** p402 O2 **101 Sausage & mash café**

Racine. *See p218.*

INSIDE TRACK EAT TURKISH

Dalston Kingsland station up to Stoke Newington Church Street is the Turkish and Kurdish heart of Hackney, which means superb grills: **19 Numara Bos Cirrik** (34 Stoke Newington Road, N16 7XJ, 7249 0400) and **Mangal Ocakbasi** (10 Arcola Street, E8 2DJ, 7275 8981, www.mangal1.com) are favourites.

Although famously preserved by S&M founder Kevin Finch, the decor of the former Alfredo's café is a mix of periods, with panelling covering a probable multitude of building sins, blue Formica tables and tiny red leather chairs. It's cramped, but jovial. The all-day breakfasts are as popular as the eponymous sausage and mash.

Other locations 48 Brushfield Street, Spitalfields, E1 6AG (7247 2252); North Greenwich Centre, Peninsula Square, SE10 0DX (8305 1940); 268 Portobello Road, Ladbroke Grove, W10 5TY (8968 8898).

EAST LONDON

The steaks at **Hawksmoor** (*see p238*) are almost as notable as the cocktails. For options in Canary Wharf, *see p139* **Inside Track**.

Bistrotheque
23-27 Wadeson Street, Bethnal Green, E2 9DR (8983 7900/www.bistrotheque.com). Bethnal Green tube/rail/Cambridge Heath rail/55 bus. **Open** *Bar* 6pm-midnight Mon-Sat; 1pm-midnight Sun. *Restaurant* 6.30-10.30pm Mon-Thur; 6.30-11pm Fri; 11am-4pm, 6.30-11pm Sat; 11am-4pm, 6.30-10.30pm Sun. **Main courses** £10-£21. **Credit** AmEx, MC, V. **French**
An all-white warehouse space, with louche cabaret and a classily funky bar, Bistrotheque hits the area's new demographic on the head with its blend of sophistication and streetwise cool. Service is friendly and committed, the relaxed clientele happy with a menu crafted to their whims: cocktails, brunch, grazing, and a good prix fixe (even at weekends).

£ Brick Lane Beigel Bake
159 Brick Lane, E1 6SB (7729 0616). Liverpool Street tube/rail/8 bus. **Open** 24hrs daily. **No credit cards. Map** p403 **102** **Bagel bakery**
This charismatic little East End institution rolls out perfect bagels both plain and filled (egg, cream cheese, mountains of salt beef), superb bread and moreish cakes. Even at 3am, fresh baked goods are being pulled from the ovens at the back; no wonder the queue for bagels trails out the door when the innumerable local bars and clubs begin to close.

★ £ E Pellicci
332 Bethnal Green Road, Bethnal Green, E2 0AG (7739 4873). Bethnal Green tube/rail/8, 253 bus. **Open** 7am-4.45pm Mon-Sat. **Main courses** £5-£8. **No credit cards. Café**
Not just a caff, but a social club, taxi driver meeting room and unofficial matchmaking service, E Pellicci has been warmly welcoming customers since 1900. The heritage-listed marquetry-panelled interior is cramped and sharing tables to be expected, nay relished. The good-value cooking includes trad English and Italian dishes, sarnies and classic puds, and of course a roster of glistening fry-ups – everything from a set veggie breakfast to black pudding.

★ Eyre Brothers
70 Leonard Street, Shoreditch, EC2A 4QX (7613 5346/www.eyrebrothers.co.uk). Old Street tube/rail. **Open** noon-3pm, 6.30-10.45pm Mon-Fri; 6.30-10.45pm Sat. **Main courses** £13-£22. **Credit** AmEx, DC, MC, V. **Map** p403 Q4 **103** **Mediterranean**
The news has got around: Eyre Brothers does everything exceptionally well. Hence, it can be hard to reserve a table. Clean lines of chic leather furniture, designer lamps and divided dining areas create an aura of sophistication. It's a labour of love for brothers David and Robert, who evidently spend as much time crafting the frequently changing menu as fashioning the decor. Authentic Portuguese dishes reflect the brothers' upbringing in Mozambique, while Spanish and French flavours add range and luxury.

CONSUME

CONSUME

Gun

27 Coldharbour, Docklands, E14 9NS (7515 5222/
www.thegundocklands.com). Canary Wharf tube/
DLR/South Quay DLR. **Open** 11am-midnight
Mon-Fri; 11.30am-midnight Sat; 11.30am-11pm
Sun. **Main courses** £13-£19. **Credit** AmEx,
MC, V. **Gastropub**
The Gun takes its name from the cannon fired when
West India Dock opened in 1802. The whole build-
ing is full of history, even the toilets are labelled
Nelson and Emma in memory of Lady Hamilton and
her lover, who it is claimed used to rendezvous here.
There are two bars, two snugs and a waterside
terrace with a huge view of the O2 (*see p313*). The
separate menus for the pub and dining room are
both essentially British and steadfastly seasonal.

£ Kolapata

222 Whitechapel Road, Whitechapel, E1 1BJ
(7377 1200). Whitechapel tube. **Open** noon-
11.30pm daily. **Main courses** £4-£9. **No
credit cards. Bangladeshi**
In recent years Kolapata – 'banana leaf' in Bengali
– has been the leading destination to experience
Bangladeshi cooking in London. The restaurant
is modest, cheap and very popular with local
Bangladeshis. When the food is freshly cooked
and the full complement of chefs from Dhaka is
in the kitchen, the flavours and freshness sing; but
visit off-peak and you may find that the food is
rather less impressive.
▶ *For Pakistani dishes served canteen style, try
the nearby Lahore Kebab House (2 Umberston
Street, E1 1PY, 7488 2551, www.lahore-kebab
house.com) and Tayyabs (83 Fieldgate Street,
E1 1JU, 7247 9543, www.tayyabs.co.uk).*

£ Sông Quê

134 Kingsland Road, Shoreditch, E2 8DY
(7613 3222). Old Street tube/rail/26, 48, 55, 67,
149, 242, 243 bus. **Open** noon-3pm, 5.30-11pm
Mon-Sat; noon-11pm Sun. **Main courses** £5-£7.
Credit MC, V. **Map** p403 R3 ⓴ **Vietnamese**
North-east London retains its monopoly on the capital's most authentic Vietnamese restaurants. And
Sông Quê is still the benchmark. It's an efficient, can-
teen-like operation to which diners of all types are
attracted – be prepared to share tables at busy times.
See also p207 **Quality Fast Food.**

£ Story Deli

*3 Dray Walk, Old Truman Brewery, 91 Brick
Lane, E1 6QL (7247 3137). Liverpool Street
tube/rail.* **Open** noon-9pm daily. **Main courses**
£11. **Credit** AmEx, MC, V. **Map** p403 S5 ⓵⓪⓹
Pizza
A cosy little pizzeria that's ideal for a chat and a
chew, with its rough-hewn tables, little pod stools,
big wax church candles and ambient music, along
with a huge plate-glass window through which to
gaze at the hectic goings-on of Dray Walk.

£ Tea Smith

6 Lamb Street, Spitalfields, E1 6EA (7247 1333/
www.teasmith.co.uk). Liverpool Street tube/rail.
Open 11am-6pm daily. **Teas** from £3. **Credit**
MC, V. **Map** p403 R5 ⓵⓪⓺ **Teahouse**
For tea-drinkers after something special, this little
shop and tearoom on the edge of Old Spitalfields
Market is a godsend. The interior has a recognisably
Japanese aesthetic with simple, clean lines. The
owner is a self-confessed tea geek who researched
his teas in China and Japan and sources them direct
from the Far East – their quality is matched by select
accompanying nibbles.
▶ *For gourmet teas in central London, head
to Postcard Teas; see p257.*

Les Trois Garçons

1 Club Row, Shoreditch, E1 6JX (7613 1924/
www.lestroisgarcons.com). Liverpool Street tube/
rail/8, 388 bus. **Open** 7-10pm Mon-Thur; 7-
10.30pm Fri, Sat. **Set meals** £42.50 2 courses;
£49.50 3 courses. **Credit** AmEx, DC, MC, V.
Map p403 S4 ⓵⓪⓻ **French**
The decor is a happy, flamboyant collision between
a taxidermist's and an art installation, but the owners here have also made sure they get all the basics
right. Prices are a little overblown, though dishes are
mostly spot-on. A great place for a proper night out,
then, but not to count the pennies.

Wapping Food

*Wapping Hydraulic Power Station, Wapping
Wall, E1W 3ST (7680 2080/www.thewapping
project.com). Shadwell DLR.* **Open** noon-3.30pm,
6.30-11pm Mon-Fri; 10am-4pm, 7-11pm Sat; 1-
4pm Sun. **Main courses** £12-£21. **Credit**
AmEx, MC, V. **Modern European**
Housed in a spectacular Victorian pumping station,
often with a backdrop of stimulating contemporary
art, Wapping Food is an intriguing venue for a night
out. Some of the cooking is very good – interesting
combinations like a plum custard tart with lavender
ice-cream often come off – but the service isn't
always on the ball.

SOUTH-EAST LONDON

Greenwich lacks stand-out eateries. Aside from
some over-styled bistros and the high-street
chains, **Inside** (*see below*) is pretty much it.

Inside

*19 Greenwich South Street, SE10 8NW (8265
5060/www.insiderestaurant.co.uk). Greenwich
rail/DLR.* **Open** noon-2.30pm, 6.30-11pm Tue-Fri;
6.30-11pm Sat; noon-3pm Sun. **Main courses**
£11-£16. **Credit** AmEx, MC, V. **Modern
European**
That Inside is a local fine-dining fave is evident in
the polite familiarity between owners and patrons.
The interior is tasteful in white and dark brown,

Assaggi. *See p218.*

professionals still in their suits. We love the fact that Chez Bruce takes its food so seriously, but we'd prefer a less serious atmosphere. Book well ahead.

Glasshouse
14 Station Parade, Kew, Surrey TW9 3PZ (8940 6777/www.glasshouserestaurant.co.uk). Kew Gardens tube/rail. **Open** noon-2.15pm, 7-10.30pm Mon-Sat; 12.30-2.45pm, 7-10pm Sun. **Set meals** £21.50-£37.50. **Credit** AmEx, MC, V. **Modern European**
A cool sedate restaurant tucked away to one side of the forecourt at Kew's pretty mid-Victorian railway station, the Glasshouse is well worth the readies. Patrons of Chez Bruce (*see above*) will already be familiar with the subtle flavours and tasteful design.

WEST LONDON
Clarke's
124 Kensington Church Street, Kensington, W8 4BH (7221 9225/www.sallyclarke.com). Notting Hill Gate tube. **Open** 12.30-2pm Mon; 12.30-2pm, 7-10pm Tue-Fri; 11am-2pm, 7-10pm Sat. **Main courses** £14-£16. **Credit** AmEx, MC, V. **Map** p394 B7 ⑩ **Modern European**
It was the mid 1980s when Sally Clarke, inspired by her experiences dining at Chez Panisse in California, brought something fresh, light and sunny to a dour and grey London. A trailblazer she certainly was, but the road she travels today now seems familiar. Ingredients have always been at the heart of things here, and incidentals are spot-on, such as the fantastic bread: as you'd expect, as it comes from Clarke's own highly successful bakery.

with bleached tablecloths, wooden floors, framed photos and abstract art. But it's the food that's the real draw: based on classical Anglo-French traditions, dishes are cooked with flair and creativity, using the freshest ingredients. The set-price dinner is excellent value (£16.95 two courses; £20.95 three).

£ Pavilion Tea House
Greenwich Park, Blackheath Gate, SE10 8QY (8858 9695/www.capergreen.co.uk). Blackheath rail/Greenwich rail/DLR. **Open** *Summer* 9am-6pm daily. *Winter* 9am-4pm daily. **Main courses** £2-£8. **Credit** MC, V. **Café**
Bright, clean and busy – expect lengthy queues and marauding children at weekend lunchtimes – the Pavilion Tea House fields a menu that contains several hearty dishes: perfect for when you've scaled the heights of this hilly park.

SOUTH-WEST LONDON
Chez Bruce
2 Bellevue Road, Wandsworth, SW17 7EG (8672 0114/www.chezbruce.co.uk). Wandsworth Common rail. **Open** noon-2pm, 6.30-10.30pm Mon-Fri; 12.30-2.30pm, 6.30-10.30pm Sat; noon-3pm, 7-10pm Sun. **Set meals** £25.50-£40. **Credit** AmEx, DC, MC, V. **French**
This Wandsworth institution has an air of exclusivity, combining outstanding food with a mildly subdued, reverential feel. It was quietly enjoyed, when we visited, by an almost uniform crowd of young

★ Gate
51 Queen Caroline Street, Hammersmith, W6 9QL (8748 6932/www.thegate.tv). Hammersmith tube. **Open** noon-2.45pm, 6-10.45pm Mon-Fri; 6-10.45pm Sat. **Main courses** £8-£14. **Credit** AmEx, MC, V. **Vegetarian**
There are few dining rooms as immediately pleasing as the Gate's. Lush bamboo soars to the ceiling and there's a feeling of Zen-like calm. Much loved by sandal-wearers and meat-eaters alike, London's most famous vegetarian restaurant is a venue to which you would happily trek across town.

River Café
Thames Wharf, Rainville Road, Hammersmith, W6 9HA (7386 4200/www.rivercafe.co.uk). Hammersmith tube. **Open** 12.30-3pm, 7-9.30pm Mon-Sat; 12.30-3pm Sun. **Main courses** £23-£32. **Credit** AmEx, DC, MC, V. **Italian**
Following a kitchen fire, the legendary River Café added a private dining room-cum-cheese room, and now has an open kitchen and bar-counter dining. The produce-based menu still changes twice daily, while the wine list (try a chilled red) and riverside setting remain flawless. *See p209* **Eating Out.**

CONSUME

Pubs & Bars

Beautiful in the eye of the beer-holder.

Pubs in Britain have fallen on hard times recently, reeling from a combination of the smoking ban, the cheap booze on offer in supermarkets and ever-rising rents on the high street. Bad news for our local boozer, but good news for you: to fight back, many have adapted in considerable style, with new outdoor areas or smoking terraces (**Boisdale**), improving food and, perhaps most importantly of all, playing to their own unique and individual strengths (**Ye Old Mitre**, the **Nag's Head**). The sumptuously refurbished **Princess Louise**, for example, offers very reasonably priced beer, but it can now be enjoyed in particularly splendid surroundings. Four out of five pubs might be by-numbers, chain-affiliated and lacking in life, but with a careful eye and this guide to help, these can easily be avoided.

CONSUME

THE LOWDOWN

One of the most encouraging developments in recent years has been the increased availability of real ale (for more details and a pioneering London brewery, *see p232* **Profile**). Some pubs still embrace ales more thoroughly than others, but there has been a general move in the right direction. Gourmets will also be delighted to see two genres in particular – gastropubs and wine bars – are thriving. Even top-class cocktails, for many years available only in London's snootier hotel bars, are now easy to find (*see p237* **Good Mixers**), with many hotel bars responding to the competition by upping the quality and warming up the welcome.

THE SOUTH BANK & BANKSIDE

The **Anchor & Hope** (*see p197*) remains one of London's finest gastropubs.

★ Royal Oak

44 Tabard Street, Bankside, SE1 4JU (7357 7173). Borough tube. **Open** 11am-11pm Mon-Fri; noon-11pm Sat; noon-6pm Sun. **Credit** MC, V. **Map** p404 P9 ❶

About the reviews

This chapter was compiled from our Bars, Pubs & Clubs Guide *(£9.99), which is available from www.timeout.com.*

A pub for luvvies and lovers of Lewes brewery Harveys, the Royal Oak seems wonderfully trapped in time. Its ales from the Sussex stable – Mild, Pale, Old, Best and Armada – are all under £3, keg cider includes Thatcher's Heritage and Weston's Stowford Press, while a felt-tipped menu boasts classics such as game pie, rabbit casserole, Lancashire hotpot and braised lamb shank. Music hall stars Harry Ray and Flanagan & Allen, here celebrated in framed, hand-bill form, would have tucked into the same decades ago. These days there's wine too.

Skylon

Royal Festival Hall, Belvedere Road, South Bank, SE1 8XX (7654 7800/www.danddlondon.com). Waterloo tube/rail. **Open** *Bar* 11am-1am daily. *Brasserie* noon-11.45pm daily. *Restaurant* noon-2.30pm, 5.30-10.45pm daily. **Credit** MC, V. **Map** p401 M8 ❷

There can't be many better transport views than this in all London. Sit at the cocktail bar (in between the two restaurant areas), and gaze out at trains trundling out of Charing Cross station, cars and red buses whizzing across Waterloo bridge, and in between boats and cruisers pootling along the Thames. In spite of its aircraft-hangar proportions, the space feels particularly intimate: plenty of

---

❶ Green numbers given in this chapter correspond to the location of each pub or bar on the street maps. *See pp394-407.*

bronze, walnut and slate. The drinks menu includes ten bellinis, nine martinis and a list of 1950s classics (manhattans, sidecars, and so on), all at a price.

Wine Wharf
Stoney Street, Borough Market, SE1 9AD (7940 8335/www.winewharf.com). London Bridge tube/rail. **Open** noon-11pm Mon-Sat. **Credit** AmEx, DC, MC, V. **Map** p404 P8 ❸
There are many places to grab a drink while at Borough Market, but none has a better wine list than this temple to the grape. Leather sofas are stuffed in among wood beams, and wood tables provide surfaces on which to rest dishes such as potted salt beef while drinking. The sheer number of wines by the glass is commendable and, unlike many places, Wine Wharf gives the list a big going-over twice a year.
Other locations Brew Wharf, Stoney Street, Bankside, SE1 9AD (7378 6601/www.brew wharf.com).
▶ *Fancy a beer instead? The market's Utobeer stall ensures the nearby Rake (14 Winchester Walk, SE1 9AG, 7407 0557) is full of fine ales.*

THE CITY

Black Friar
174 Queen Victoria Street, EC4V 4EG (7236 5474). Mansion House tube/Blackfriars rail. **Open** 11am-11pm Mon-Wed, Sat; 11am-11.30pm Thur, Fri; noon-10.30pm Sun. **Credit** AmEx, MC, V. **Map** p404 O6 ❹
This curiously wedge-shaped pub at the north end of Blackfriars Bridge offers a handful of real ales, a dozen or so wines by the glass, the standard lagers, and pub nosh (from steak pie to goat's cheese tart) that's more than adequate. But, if you can manage to push your way inside, it's the extraordinary inte-

rior resplendent with wooden carvings of Dominican monks that delights the most. Loopy, but it works.

Vertigo 42
Tower 42, 25 Old Broad Street, EC2N 1HQ (7877 7842/www.vertigo42.co.uk). Bank tube/ DLR/Liverpool Street tube/rail. **Open** noon-3pm, 5-11pm Mon-Fri. **Credit** AmEx, DC, MC, V. **Map** p405 Q6 ❺
Short of introducing iris-recognition scanning, the process of going for a drink at Vertigo 42 (book in advance, then get X-rayed and metal-detected on arrival) could scarcely be more MI5. But it's worth it – the 42nd floor location delivers stupendous views and the champagne list ranges from an accessible £11.50 glass of Veuve Delaroy through to a cold-sweat inducing £795.50 magnum of 1990 Krug. Eight of the bottles are available by the flute.
▶ *Try frivolous bellinis and classic cocktails at nearby 1 Lombard Street (7929 6611, www. 1lombardstreet.com), a converted bank.*

HOLBORN & CLERKENWELL

Clerkenwell has a compelling claim to being the birthplace of the ubiquitous gastropub: the still wonderful **Eagle** (*see p202*) kicked things off. Other food pioneers that provide great drinking are **St John** (*see p202*) and **Cellar Gascon** (59 West Smithfield, EC1A 9DS, 7600 7561, 7796 0600, www.cellargascon.com; *see also p202*), while **Smiths of Smithfield** (*see p203*) works the 1990s warehouse aesthetic.

Café Kick
43 Exmouth Market, Clerkenwell, EC1R 4QL (7837 8077/www.cafekick.co.uk). Angel tube/ Farringdon tube/rail/19, 38 bus. **Open**

Champagne Bar at St Pancras. See p229.

CONSUME

noon-11pm Mon-Thur; noon-midnight Fri,
Sat; 4-10.30pm Sun (spring/summer only).
Credit MC, V. **Map** p402 N4 ❻
Clerkenwell's most likeable bar is this table-football
themed gem, now ten years old. The soccer paraphernalia is authentic, retro-cool and mainly Latin
(though you'll find a Zenit St Petersburg scarf amid
the St Etienne and Lusitanian gear); equally, bar
staff, beers and bites give the impression you could
easily be in Lisbon. A modest open kitchen ('we
don't microwave or deep-fry') dishes out tapas, sandwiches and charcuterie platters.
Other locations Bar Kick, 127 Shoreditch High
Street, Shoreditch (7739 8700).

★ Seven Stars

*53 Carey Street, Holborn, WC2A 2JB (7242
8521). Chancery Lane or Holborn tube.* **Open**
11am-11pm Mon-Fri; noon-11pm Sat; noon-
10.30pm Sun. **Credit** AmEx, MC, V. **Map**
p399 M6 ❼
Landlady Roxy Beaujolais' flagship pub goes from
strength to strength. It's a fantastic social hub
for London characters, from eccentric lawyers to
burlesque babes. If you can squeeze into the small
but perfectly proportioned interior, you'll get a slice
of low-rent, bohemian London: archive film posters,
checked tablecloths and an antique dumb waiter
bringing food down from the tiny kitchen upstairs.
It's one of the few London pubs where you're happy
to pay £6 for a large glass of burgundy because you
know you aren't being ripped off.

Three Kings of Clerkenwell

*7 Clerkenwell Close, Clerkenwell, EC1R 0DY
(7253 0483). Farringdon tube/rail.* **Open**
noon-11pm Mon-Fri; 5.30-11pm Sat. *Food
served* noon-3pm, 6.30-10pm Mon-Fri.
No credit cards. Map p402 N4 ❽
Rhino heads, Egyptian felines and Dennis
Bergkamp provide the decorative backdrop against
which a regular bunch of discerning bohos glug
Scrumpy Jack, Beck's Vier, Old Speckled Hen or
London Pride, and tap the well-worn tables to the
Cramps and other gems from an outstanding jukebox. Bottles of Tyskie and Lech point to a recent
invasion by jaw-droppingly gorgeous Poles.

Vinoteca

*7 St John Street, Clerkenwell, EC1M 4AA (7253
8786/www.vinoteca.co.uk). Farringdon tube/rail.*
Open noon-11pm Mon-Sat. **Credit** MC, V. **Map**
p402 O5 ❾
Inspired in name and approach by the Italian
enoteca (a blend of off-licence and wine bar, with bar
snacks thrown in for good measure), Vinoteca is
actually more of a gastropub in spirit. But even if
you're not in the mood for much more than a plate
of bread and olive oil, this place is worth heading to
for its impressive 200-bottle wine list, of which a
changing range of 19 are available by the glass.

★ Ye Old Mitre

*1 Ely Court, Ely Place, at the side of 8 Hatton
Gardens, Holborn, EC1N 6SJ (7405 4751).
Chancery Lane tube/Farringdon tube/rail.*
Open 11am-11pm Mon-Fri. **Credit** AmEx,
MC, V. **Map** p402 N5 ❿
The secluded location requires you to slink down an
alleyway just off Hatton Garden, and as you do so
you're transported to a parallel pub universe where
the clientele are disconcertingly friendly and the
staff (clad in pristine black and white uniforms)
briskly efficient. A Monday-to-Friday joint, it opens
for one weekend a year to coincide with the British
Beer Festival (*see p272*). Ales are certainly the speciality – Deuchars and Adnams are regulars, with
frequently changing guest beers beside them. It's a
pint-sized pub that's earned its top-notch reputation.
▶ *Close by, former coffee-house the Jerusalem
Tavern (55 Britton Street, 7490 4281, www.st
petersbrewery.co.uk) is now a fantastic little pub.
It's often packed, even though it's hard to find.*

BLOOMSBURY & FITZROVIA

For sheer style, try the bar at **Hakkasan** (*see
p205*). In King's Cross, **Camino** (*see p203*) has
a courtyard off the spacious bar, while the **Big
Chill House** (*see p321*) is for music fans.

★ All Star Lanes

*Victoria House, Bloomsbury Place, WC1B 4DA
(7025 2676/www.allstarlanes.co.uk). Holborn tube.*
Open 5-11.30pm Mon-Wed; 5pm-midnight Thur;
noon-2am Fri, Sat; noon-11pm Sun. *Bowling* (per
person per game) £7.50 before 5pm; £8.50 after
5pm. **Credit** AmEx, MC, V. **Map** p399 L5 ⓫
Of Bloomsbury's two subterranean bowling dens,
this is the one with aspirations. Walk past the lanes
and smart, diner-style seating, and you'll find yourself in a comfortable, subdued side bar with chilled
glasses, classy red furnishings, an unusual mix of
bottled lagers (try the delicious Anchor Steam) and
an impressive cocktail selection. A much bigger
location opened in late 2008 in Brick Lane.
Other locations Whiteleys, Bayswater,
W2 4YQ (7313 8363); Old Truman Brewery,
87 Brick Lane, E1 6QR (7422 8370).

CONSUME

▶ *Nearby, Bloomsbury Bowling Lanes (Tavistock Hotel basement, Bedford Way, 7183 1979, www. bloomsburybowling.com) offers a pints-and-worn-carpets take on the experience.*

Bradley's Spanish Bar

42-44 Hanway Street, Fitzrovia, W1T 1UT (7636 0359). Tottenham Court Road tube. **Open** noon-11pm Mon-Sat; 3-10.30pm Sun. **Credit** MC, V. **Map** p406 W1

Is it the jukebox? Is it the tatty velvet furniture and wobbly stools? Is it just habit? Whatever the reason, people love Bradley's. A hotchpotch of local workers, shoppers and amorous foreign exchange students fills the cramped two-floor space, enraging passing taxi drivers as they spill on to the narrow street outside. All that's changed since the 1990s is the staff – they're mainly Hungarian now.

Champagne Bar at St Pancras

St Pancras International Station, Pancras Road, Somers Town, NW1 2QP (3006 1550/www. searcystpancras.co.uk). King's Cross tube/rail/ St Pancras International rail. **Open** 8am-11pm daily. **Credit** AmEx, MC, V. **Map** p399 L3

Part of the impressive £800m refurb of St Pancras station is the 'longest champagne bar in Europe': 300ft of booth tables and ice buckets. Here you can ponder life's inessentials: is a glass of Pommery Brut Royal nicer than a Henriot Rosé? Is St Pancras as grand as New York's Grand Central? *Photo p227.*

★ Lamb

94 Lamb's Conduit Street, Bloomsbury, WC1N 3LZ (7405 0713/www.youngs.co.uk). Holborn or Russell Square tube. **Open** 11am-midnight Mon-Sat; noon-10.30pm Sun. **Credit** AmEx, MC, V. **Map** p399 M4

Founded in 1729, this Young's pub is the sort of place that makes you misty-eyed for a vanishing era. The Lamb found fame as a theatrical haunt when the A-list included Sir Henry Irving and sundry stars of music hall; they're commemorated in vintage photos, surrounded by well-worn seats, polished wood and vintage knick-knacks. Punters range from discerning students to Gray's Inn barristers.

Long Bar

Sanderson, 50 Berners Street, Fitzrovia, W1T 3NG (7300 1400/www.sandersonlondon.com). Oxford Circus or Tottenham Court Road tube. **Open** 11.30am-2am Mon-Wed; 11.30am-3am Fri, Sat; noon-10.30pm Sun. **Credit** AmEx, DC, MC, V. **Map** p398 J5

The Long Bar's early noughties glory days (the clientele is more civilian than celebrity in 2008) may be a faded memory, but there's still easy glamour for the taking. The long bar in question is a thin onyx affair, though nabbing one of the eyeball-backed stools is an unlikely prospect. A better bet is the lovely courtyard, where table service, candlelight and watery features make a much nicer setting for cocktails. And, really, it would be wrong to order

CONSUME

Vinoteca.

anything else, with a list of enticing flutes (£14), long drinks (£11) and martinis (£12) to choose from.

Shochu Lounge

Basement of Roka, 37 Charlotte Street, Fitzrovia, W1T 1RR (7580 9666/www.shochulounge.com). Goodge Street or Tottenham Court Road tube. **Open** 5pm-midnight Mon, Sat; noon-midnight Tue-Fri; 6pm-midnight Sun. **Credit** AmEx, DC, MC, V. **Map** p398 J5

Beneath a contemporary Japanese restaurant, slap-bang in media central, is this buzzy, evening-only basement whose decor is part classy 21st-century cosmopolitan, part feudal Japan. Shochu bases many of its cocktails on the titular vodka-like spirit, each of them an exercise in perfection, but quality sake is also served, both hot and cold. *See also p237* **Good Mixers**. *Photo p237.*

▶ *For chic sister-establishment Zuma, see p218.*

COVENT GARDEN & THE STRAND

★ Gordon's

47 Villiers Street, The Strand, WC2N 6NE (7930 1408/www.gordonswinebar.com). Embankment tube/Charing Cross tube/rail. **Open** 11am-11pm Mon-Sat; noon-10pm Sun. **Credit** AmEx, MC, V. **Map** p407 Y5

Gordon's is hardly à la mode. It's somewhere that's been serving drinks since 1890, and it looks like it – specialising in sweaty, yellowing, candle-lit alcoves. The wine list doesn't bear much scrutiny, and food is buffet-style, so focus on the assorted ports, sherries and Madeiras. Atmosphere is everything here: a place for assignations and furtive plans.

Lamb & Flag

33 Rose Street, Covent Garden, WC2E 9EB (7497 9504). Covent Garden tube. **Open** 11am-11pm Mon-Sat; noon-10.30pm Sun. **Credit** MC, V. **Map** p407 Y3

A pub for over 300 years and a fixture on Rose Street for longer, the unabashedly traditional Lamb & Flag is always a squeeze, but no one seems to mind. The afternoon-only bar upstairs is 'ye olde' to a fault, and pictures of passed-on regulars ('Barnsey', Corporal Bill West) give the place a great local feel. Character is in short supply around Covent Garden, and this place has bags of the stuff.

▶ *If it's impossibly busy, try the Benelux-themed Lowlander (36 Drury Lane, 7379 7446, www. lowlander.com), where efficient service brings a vast choice of beers to long tables.*

Lobby Bar

One Aldwych, the Strand, WC2B 4RH (7300 1070/www.onealdwych.com). Covent Garden or Temple tube. **Open** 8am-11.30pm Mon-Sat; 8am-10.30pm Sun. **Credit** AmEx, DC, MC, V. **Map** p407 Z3

Princess Louise

CONSUME

The signature bar of the upmarket urban hotel One Aldwych is known for the range and quality of its cocktails. From one of the elegantly high-backed chairs, select your own martini spirit from a range that includes Wyborowa (£9.40) and Kauffman Luxury Vintage 2003 (£20) – that is, if none of the 20 listed martinis (£9.95), such as a Gazpacho with lemon-infused Tanqueray, green pepper, Midori and elderflower cordial, grabs you.

Princess Louise
208-209 High Holborn, WC1V 7BW (7405 8816). Holborn tube. **Open** 11am-11pm Mon-Fri; noon-11pm Sat; noon-10.30pm Sun. *Food served* noon-2.30pm, 6-8.30pm Mon-Thur; noon-2.30pm Fri, Sat. **Credit** AmEx MC, V. **Map** p407 Z1 ⊕
Following an eight-month refurbishment, the Grade II-listed Princess Louise has scrubbed up something wonderful. Decorated tiles, stained-glass windows, finely cut mirrors and ornate plasterwork have all been given a polish, and Victorian wood partitions have been put back to create a pleasantly confusing warren of snugs and alcoves; the lavish lavs and Corinthian columns are especially impressive. The beer is all from Samuel Smith and sold for around £2 a pint: astonishing, given the fancy furnishings, but then it isn't the best pint in town.

SOHO & LEICESTER SQUARE

Amuse Bouche
21-22 Poland Street, Soho, W1F 8QG (7287 1661/www.abcb.co.uk). Tottenham Court Road or Oxford Circus tubes. **Open** noon-11.30pm Mon-Thur; noon-midnight Fri; 5pm-midnight Sat. **Credit** AmEx, DC, MV, V. **Map** p406 V2 ⊕
This Soho branch of the Parsons Green original carries on with the winning formula of quality champagne at low prices and has been shortlisted for the 2009 *Time Out* Eating & Drinking Awards for Best Bar. Once you've got used to the fact that this is a champagne bar without chandeliers, the appeal of Amuse Bouche to its young, up-for-it clientele becomes clear. We're talking champagne quaffing splendour at non-intimidating prices.
Other locations 51 Parsons Green Lane, Parsons Green, SW6 4JA (7371 8517).

Floridita
100 Wardour Street, Soho, W1F 0TN (7314 4000/www.floriditalondon.com). Tottenham Court Road tube. **Open** 5.30pm-2am Mon-Wed; (members or guest list, or doorman's discretion) 5.30pm-3am Thur-Sat. *Food served* 5.30pm-1am Mon-Wed; 5.30pm-1.30am Thur-Sat. **Admission** (after 7.30pm Thur-Sat) £15. **Credit** AmEx, DC, MC, V. **Map** p406 W2 ⊕
For a proper night out in the heart of Soho, take your beloved to Floridita. Named after the famous Hemingway haunt in Havana, this tastefully glitzy

THE BEST BOOZE HOLES

For British eccentricity
Nag's Head. *See p236.*

For living history
Ye Old Mitre. *See p228.*

For clandestine romance
Gordon's. *See p230.*

basement strives to get the drinks and entertainment just right. After your entrance and escorted sashay to table, you negotiate a cocktail menu categorised in Spanish. Most, priced at £8, involve Havana Club Anejo Blanco expertly shaken with fresh mint, fresh lime, sugars and various dashes. Live music comes courtesy of Salsa Unica every evening. *Photos p234.*

★ French House
49 Dean Street, Soho, W1D 5BG (bar 7437 2799/restaurant 7437 2477/www.frenchhouse soho.com). Leicester Square or Piccadilly Circus tube. **Open** noon-11pm Mon-Sat; noon-10.30pm Sun. *Restaurant* noon-3pm, 5.30-11pm Mon-Sat. **Credit** AmEx, DC, MC, V. **Map** p406 W3 ⊕
Through the door of this venerable Gallic establishment have passed many titanic drinkers of the pre- and post-war era, the Bacons and the Behans, with the venue's French heritage also enticing De Gaulle to run a Resistance operation from upstairs. His snozzle still fills the photograph behind the bar, beer is still served in half pints and litre bottles of Breton cider (£7) are still plonked on the famed back alcove table of this small but significant establishment.
▶ *Just up the road, corner boozer the Crown & Two Chairmen (no.31, 7437 8192) has a great array of global beers ('19 and counting').*

★ LAB
12 Old Compton Street, Soho, W1D 4TQ (7437 7820/www.lab-townhouse.com). Leicester Square or Tottenham Court Road tube. **Open** 4pm-midnight Mon-Sat; 4-10.30pm Sun. *Food served* 6-11pm Mon-Sat; 6-10.30pm Sun. **Credit** AmEx, MC, V. **Map** p407 X2 ⊕
LAB's two-floor space is invariably packed with Sohoites eager to be fuelled by London's freshest mixologists. Straight out of LAB school (LAB stands for the London Academy of Bartending), graduates are aided by colleagues of considerable global experience, and can fix some 30 original concoctions (most costing around £7) or 50 classics, using high-end spirits and fresh ingredients.

★ Player
8 Broadwick Street, Soho, W1F 8HN (7292 9945/ www.thplyr.com). Oxford Circus or Tottenham Court Road tube. **Open** 5.30pm-midnight Mon-*

CONSUME

Profile Real Ale

Once, London brewed many beers – Meantime wants us to taste them again.

Ale was first called 'real' in the 1970s by CAMRA, a campaign launched to save traditional beers from the rising tide of processed, yellow, super-fizzy keg lager made by the half-dozen megabreweries that then ran the British pub industry. Real ale matures and must be managed in its barrel or cask (hence it is also known as 'cask ale' or 'cask-conditioned ale'), giving it a rich complexity of flavour but making it more difficult to keep. Stored in the cool cellar of the pub, it must be served fresh on site, by hand pump (*pictured*), never electric tap. Hence, beer conglomerates prefer homogenous fizzy stuff.

Of the many different styles of real ale, the most widely available nowadays are various types of 'bitter'. It is a late Victorian derivative of Pale Ale (also India Pale Ale or IPA), first brewed for shipping out to the colonies during the period when London was the centre of the brewing world. Greenwich's **Meantime Brewery** aims to bring back more of these tipples we once exported – and, yes, drunk ourselves in considerable quantities. At the **Old Royal Naval College** (*see p147*), they are bringing the original brewery

block back into action (*below left*). It will initially produce Greenwich Porter, served to College pensioners in the 18th century, but Meantime's brew-master Alastair Hook (*below right*) is researching additional brews. While he labours, head to Meantime's sole pub, the **Greenwich Union** (*see p239*), or one of the following sturdy dispensers of proper Brit beer.

THREE TO TRY

Our favourite real ale pubs.

White Horse
See p240. A bit of a trek, but the esssential destination for beer fans.

Wenlock Arms
See p238. A local's local with well-kept ales.

Florence
See p239. Here they brew their own beer.

Meantime Brewery.

Wed; 5.30pm-1am Thur, Fri; 7pm-1am Sat. **Credit** AmEx, MC, V. **Map** p406 V2 ⓚ A drinks menu unchanged since 2005 and several head bartenders since the days of Dick Bradsell in 1999 (*see p237* **Good Mixers**), of late the Player hasn't been trying too hard to keep a buzz in this sexy basement space. Nonetheless, as the cocktail menu points out, 'don't fix what ain't broke'; the philosophy is ably demonstrated by the immaculately conceived drinks on offer.

▶ *Nearby jazz-tinged speakeasy Milk & Honey (61 Poland Street, W1F 7NU, 7292 9949, www.mlkhny.com) is open to non-members only with an advance booking.*

Two Floors
3 Kingly Street, Soho, W1B 5PD (7439 1007/ www.barworks.co.uk). Oxford Circus or Piccadilly Circus tube. **Open** noon-11.30pm Mon-Thur; noon-midnight Fri, Sat. **Credit** MC, V. **Map** p406 V3 ⓚ
Sparse, laid-back and bohemian, Two Floors is understated and quite wonderful. Beers here are mainly bottled, ales too, with draught Kirin and £6 caipirinhas, caipiroskas (plain, vanilla and cinnamon) and cosmopolitans thrown in. There are £4 lunchtime ciabattas too, though even the laziest daytime rendezvous might spark into a raging evening session along the new bar hub of Kingly Street.

OXFORD STREET & MARYLEBONE

Artesian
Langham, 1C Portland Place, Marylebone, W1B 1JA (7636 1000/www.artesian-bar.co.uk). Oxford Circus tube. **Open** 10am-2am Mon-Sat; 10am-midnight Sun. **Credit** AmEx, DC, MC, V. **Map** p398 H4 ⓚ
Even in this city of the three-quid pint and ten-quid cocktail, it's hard not to gasp at Artesian's list of cocktails: order any three and add service, and you won't get much change from a £50 note. At least you'll be drinking them in some style: David Collins has done a fine job regenerating this kidney-shaped, high-ceilinged room at the Langham, the back bar dramatically lit by huge hanging lamps. The drinks almost live up to the setting.

Duke of Wellington
94A Crawford Street, W1H 2HQ (7723 2790/ www.thedukew1.co.uk). Baker Street tube/ Marylebone tube/rail. **Open** noon-11pm Mon-Sat; noon-10.30pm Sun. **Credit** AmEx, MC, V. **Map** p395 F5 ⓚ
Since its makeover by the owners of the Brown Dog in Barnes, the Duke has attracted a moneyed clientele happy to splash out £30 on a decent Pouilly-Fumé or £55 on a better red from Pauillac. They're mostly here, though, for the food: for the roast guinea fowl with a puy lentil casserole or the lasagne

of ceps and jerusalem artichokes, for example. It's a Best Gastropub nominee for the 2009 *Time Out* Eating & Drinking Awards.

PADDINGTON & NOTTING HILL

Tom Conran's fine gastropub, the **Cow** (*see p218*), is often standing room only at the bar.

★ Lonsdale
44-48 Lonsdale Road, Notting Hill, W11 2DE (7727 4080/www.thelonsdale.co.uk). Ladbroke Grove or Notting Hill Gate tube. **Open** 6pm-midnight Mon-Thur; 6pm-1am Fri, Sat; 6-11.30pm Sun. **Credit** AmEx, MC, V. **Map** p394 A6 ⓚ
The beautifully over-designed main lounge (there are two more bars on different floors) is in 1970s sci-funk style, with brass 'bubble' walls and red leather seating. Dick Bradsell (*see p237* **Good Mixers**), king of London bartenders, no longer keeps bar here but his spirits live on. A whole chapter of the 18-page drinks menu pays homage to Bradsell classics, such as the Rose Petal martini (£8) or the Bramble (£7). The menu is a sweeping historical tour of England's love affair with the mixed drink, from claret cups to sangarees to sours.

▶ *Montgomery Place (31 Kensington Park Road, 7792 3921, www.montgomeryplace.co.uk) is also a slinky place, with glam staff and fine cocktails.*

Trailer Happiness
177 Portobello Road, Notting Hill, W11 2DY (7727 2700/www.trailerhappiness.com). Ladbroke Grove or Notting Hill Gate tube. **Open** 5-11.30pm Tue-Fri; 6-11.30pm Sat. **Credit** AmEx, MC, V. **Map** p394 A6 ⓚ
Tongue in cheek decor matched with a serious attitude to booze sums up the approach here. The basement is a riot of oranges and browns, with '60s furniture, huge smoked-glass mirrors and Tretchiko prints all over the walls. The bar takes pride of place and glows with a huge array of backlit bottles (many of them rum). Clued-up staff mix tikis and other rum

---

INSIDE TRACK
REGAL MOUSTACHES AND
ROYAL MEMORABILIA

Landlord Michael Tierney's obsession with British history and the royal family manifests itself in the absurd decor of **Windsor Castle** (29 Crawford Place, Marylebone, W1H 4LJ, 7723 4371), complete with a laughably bad portrait of Prince Charles, signed pictures of minor celebs, china sets and Toby jugs. Even better, the fantastic Handlebar Club has its moustachioed monthly meetings here.

cocktails, plus a number of house favourites such as the luscious grapefruit julep. This is one bar that's definitely worth spending some time in.

Westbourne House

65 Westbourne Grove, Westbourne Grove, W2 4UJ (7229 2233/ www.westbournehouse.net). Bayswater or Royal Oak tube. **Open** 11am-11.30pm Mon-Thur; 11am-midnight Fri, Sat; noon-10.30pm Sun. **Credit** AmEx, MC, V. **Map** p394 B6 ③

This big, handsome pub has swapped its nicotine stains and pint glasses for shiny surfaces, gilding on the mirrors and faux-French furniture, made all the more twinkly by low lighting and candles. The cocktail list is the work of drinks supremo Mat Perovetz. There are seven 'proper' martinis, spirits are premium, and the delivery is pristine. The food is no afterthought either. There's a bijou list of antipasti, mezedes, daily specials, sandwiches and salads. All in all, a fine bar.

PICCADILLY & MAYFAIR

★ Coburg Bar

Connaught, Carlos Place, Mayfair, W1K 2AL (7499 7070/www.the-connaught.co.uk). Bond Street or Green Park tube. **Open** noon-1am daily. **Credit** MC, V. **Map** p400 H7 ③

A Best Bar nominee for the 2009 *Time Out* Eating & Drinking Awards, the Coburg is everything you could hope for in a smart hotel bar: no velvet rope; no door-nazi attitude; and faultless service – formal, but not standoffish. In a room redesigned by Parisian designer India Mahdavi in a way that oozes

sophistication, the cocktail list is an amazing read, charting the drinks' history from Sours up to the modern day. Although most cost £12 a glass, they're worth it. Dress up.
▶ *Just across the lobby (but with its own external door), the hotel's modern, David Collins-designed Connaught bar feels like the inside of a deco cruise liner and is also superb.*

Galvin at Windows

28th floor, London Hilton, 22 Park Lane, Mayfair, W1K 1BE (7208 4021/www.galvin atwindows.com). Hyde Park Corner tube. **Open** 10am-1am Mon-Wed; 10am-3am Thur- Sat; 10am-10.30pm Sun. **Credit** AmEx, DC, MC, V. **Map** p400 G8 ③

There's no more remarkable site for a bar in London than Windows: 28 floors up, at the top of the Park Lane Hilton, with an extraordinary panoramic view of the capital. Add to that a sleek interior that mixes art deco glamour with a hint of '70s petrodollar kitsch, and you can't go wrong. Admittedly, it's not cheap – £11.95 for a cocktail – but the drinks are assembled with care, and service is attentive without being obsequious.

Only Running Footman

5 Charles Street, Mayfair, W1J 5DF (7499 2988/ www.therunningfootman.biz). Green Park tube. **Open** 7.30am-midnight daily. **Credit** AmEx, MC, V. **Map** p400 H7 ③

Recently reopened after a huge refurb, this place still looks as if it's been here forever. On the ground floor, jolly chaps prop up the mahogany bar, enjoying three decent ales on draught and an extensive menu:

Floridita. *See p231.*

anything from a bacon buttie takeaway to Welsh rarebit with watercress. A full English breakfast is served for only £7.50 – a third of the price you'd pay in nearby Claridge's. On the first floor there's a quieter, formal dining room, with a conservative and more expensive British menu. *Photo p239.*

WESTMINSTER & ST JAMES'S

The **Red Lion** (48 Parliament Street, SW1A 2NH, 7930 5826) is an old boozer distinguished by a division bell (there to call errant MPs in to vote) and TVs that tirelessly screen BBC Parliament, while the fine beer and traditional panelling of **St Stephen's Tavern** (10 Bridge Street, SW1A 2JR, 7925 2286), diagonally opposite the clock tower of Big Ben, almost distract you from the relentless crowds.

Albannach

66 Trafalgar Square, WC2N 5DS (7930 0066/ www.albannach.co.uk). Charing Cross tube/rail. **Open** noon-1am Mon-Sat; noon-3am Thur- Sun. **Credit** AmEx, DC, MC, V. **Map** p407 X5 ③⑤
Impressively located slap on Trafalgar Square, Albannach (as opposed to 'sassanach') specialises in Scotch whiskies and cocktails thereof. A map in the menu explains where these Highland and Island malts come from, the pages brimming with 17-year-old Glengoynes, 12-year-old Cragganmore and 29-year-old Auchentoshan. That said, kilted staff, illuminated reindeer and too many loud office groups detract from the quality on offer.

Boisdale

13-15 Eccleston Street, Belgravia, SW1W 9LX (7730 6922/www.boisdale.co.uk). Victoria tube/ rail. **Open/food served** noon-1am Mon-Fri; 7pm-1am Sat. **Admission** £12 (£4.50 before 10pm) after 10pm Mon-Sat. **Credit** AmEx, DC, MC, V. **Map** p400 H10 ③⑥
From the labyrinthine variety of bar and restaurant spaces to the overstated tartan accents, there's something faintly preposterous about this entire operation. Rest assured, though, that we write this with the utmost affection: there's nowhere quite like this posh, Scottish-themed enterprise, and that includes its sister branch in the City. If you're here to drink, you'll be drinking single malts, selected from a terrific range. Another very nice touch is the new heated cigar terrace. *Photo p240.*
Other locations Boisdale of Bishopsgate, Swedeland Court, 202 Bishopsgate, the City, EC2M 4NR (7283 1763).

★ Dukes Hotel

35 St James's Place, St James's, SW1A 1NY (7491 4840/www.dukeshotel.co.uk). Green Park tube. **Open** noon-11pm Mon-Sat; noon-10.30pm Sun. **Credit** AmEx, DC, MC, V. **Map** p400 J8 ③⑦

> ## INSIDE TRACK
> ## LOVING WINE
>
> Strange that the most traditional of London shops should have decided to import a flavour of the New World: its revamp has created a bar that wouldn't be out of place in Melbourne or San Francisco. **1707** (Fortnum & Mason, 181 Piccadilly, W1A 1ER, 7734 8040, www.fortnumandmason.com), designed in sleekly masculine style by David Collins and complete with a walk-in, temperature-controlled wine cellar, is a place to treat the wine-lover in your life.

This centenarian hotel was renovated top to bottom in 2007 by hotelier Campbell Gray (he of One Aldwych fame) and designer Mary Fox Linton, transforming its discreet, highly regarded but old-fashioned bar into a swish landmark destination. Ian Fleming was a regular and Dukes' dry martinis, flamboyantly made at guests' tables, may well have inspired Bond's favourite tipple. Though the bill at the end of the night may well be best approached with your eyes closed, the payload is probably the best martini in the world.

Speaker

46 Great Peter Street, SW1P 2HA (7222 1749/ www.pleisure.com). St James's Park tube. **Open** noon-11pm Mon-Fri. **Credit** MC, V. **Map** p401 K10 ③⑧
Friday lunch barflies – some suited, some in high-visibility vests – keep up an effortlessly cheery running commentary on all the comings and goings here. The Speaker does all the important things right – four real ales (Spitfire, Young's Bitter and excellent rare guests), racks of wine, jacket spuds or £2.50 sarnies – and defiantly ignores pretty much anything else. As they say themselves: this is a real pub.

CHELSEA

On the corner of Sloane Square, the **Botanist** (*see p216*) is a handsome venue for a drink.

Apartment 195

195 King's Road, SW3 5ED (7351 5195/www. apartment195.co.uk). Sloane Square tube then 11, 22 bus. **Open** 6-11pm Mon-Sat. **Credit** AmEx, MC, V. **Map** p397 E12 ③⑨
You need to press a buzzer to gain admittance here (a sure way to impress your mates). But a warm welcome awaits at the top of the stairs. There's a Vivienne Westwood meets laid-back gentlemen's club feel to the decor. The drinking is all about the cocktails, with legendary mojitos, though the star turn is the aptly named Crown Jewels: a glass of

CONSUME

honey-sweetened rare cognac topped with vintage champagne that'll set you back a staggering £350. Now that really would impress your friends.

Fox & Hounds
29 Passmore Street, SW1W 8HR (7730 6367). Sloane Square tube. **Open** 11am-11pm Mon-Sat; noon-10.30pm Sun. **Credit** MC, V. **Map** p400 G11 ④
This tiny piece of 'Little England' started life as one of the many front room pubs that flourished in the 19th century. Originally beer was served by the landlady through a hatch, but gradually the business overtook her living room and then kitchen – as the still-visible partitions reveal. Stepping into the diminutive bar still feels very much like entering someone's lounge, thanks to its compact cosiness, comfy old chesterfields, bookshelves, hunting-themed oil paintings and weatherworn regulars – many of whom are Chelsea Pensioners.

KNIGHTSBRIDGE & SOUTH KENSINGTON

Library
Lanesborough, 1 Lanesborough Place, Hyde Park Corner, SW1X 7TA (7259 5599/www. lanesborough.com). Hyde Park Corner tube. **Open** 11am-1am Mon-Sat; noon-10.30pm Sun. **Credit** AmEx, DC, MC, V. **Map** p400 G8 ④
Surprisingly, those books are real. But the whole place is otherwise a fabulous illusion: despite its olde worlde appearance, the Lanesborough hotel (*see p191*) was still a hospital until the 1980s. Whereas the bars at other nearby hotels – the Berkeley, say, or the Mandarin Oriental – are dressed to the eights and nines and draw a younger, more boisterous crowd, the Library remains gentle and mellow long into the night, in part thanks to a tinkling pianist and perpetually low lighting.

★ Nag's Head
53 Kinnerton Street, Belgravia, SW1X 8ED (7235 1135). Hyde Park Corner or Knightsbridge tube. **Open** 11am-11pm Mon-Sat; noon-10.30pm Sun. **Credit** MC, V. **Map** p400 G9 ④
It's unusual to see a landlord's name plastered on the front of a pub, but then there aren't many like Kevin Moran left in the trade. The Nag's Head reflects Moran's exuberant eccentricity, both by design (mobiles are banned; the walls are cluttered with everything from cartoons to baseball reports, garden tools to vintage penny-slots) and, most strikingly, by accident (the rooms could scarcely be wonkier, one stepped awkwardly above the other with a bar that somehow serves them both).

★ 190
Gore, 190 Queensgate, South Kensington, SW7 5EX (7584 6601/www.gorehotel.co.uk). Gloucester Road or South Kensington tube.

Open noon-1am Mon-Wed, Sun; noon-2am Thur-Sat. **Credit** AmEx, DC, MC, V. **Map** p397 D9 ④
Just around the corner from the Royal Albert Hall, the Gore hotel's heavy, mahogany-panelled walls and oil paintings of grand old dukes are a comical backdrop to the Euro-dance soundtrack, DJ nights and hip young bartenders showing off their knowledge of the 53-strong cocktail menu. Vodka lovers will be in heaven with 28 varieties; ditto whisky aficionados. A velvet-draped 'Cinderella's Carriage' alcove at the back can be hired by those seeking further inebriated pomp and circumstance.

NORTH LONDON

The **Lockside Lounge** (75-89 West Yard, Camden Lock Place, Camden, NW1 8AF, 7284 0007, www.locksidelounge.com) is an excellent Camden DJ bar, while the big terrace-cum-car park at Torquil's Bar at the **Roundhouse** (*see p313*) is typically north London urban. In Islington, the boisterous **King's Head** (*see p343*) is as good a pub as it is a theatre, and the **Duke of Cambridge** (*see p221*) might be a better pub than restaurant.

Albert & Pearl
181 Upper Street, Islington, N1 1RQ (7352 9993/www.albertandpearl.com). Highbury & Islington tube/rail. **Open** noon-midnight Mon-Wed, Sun; noon-1am Thur; noon-3am Fri, Sat. **Credit** MC, V. **Map** p402 O1 ④
This handsome bar is 1920s themed, which means chandeliers, objets d'art, velvet drapes and super-flattering lighting – but it also has a stonkingly good sound system and weekend DJs. Cocktails (including shared punches) and champagne are punters' tipples of choice, and bar snacks (courtesy of a nearby Tuscan restaurant) match claret with fine Italian cheese rather than fizzy lager with a packet of crisps.

Crown & Goose
100 Arlington Road, Camden, NW1 7HP (7485 8008). Camden Town tube. **Open** 11am-1am Mon-Thur, Sun; 11am-2am Fri, Sat. **Credit** MC, V. **Map** p398 J2 ④
Its popularity breeds contempt among some people, but the C&G remains an almost perfect local: far enough off the beaten track to elude the hordes and packed with Victorian charm, from the scrubbed furniture to the antique portraits and gilt-framed mirrors on its pea-green walls. Small and cosy – never more so than when evening comes and staff draw blinds and dim lights – the Crown also turns out simple but superb pub grub.

Gilgamesh
Stables Market, Chalk Farm Road, NW1 8AH (7482 5757/www.gilgameshbar.com). Camden Town tube. **Open** 6pm-2.30am Mon-Thur; noon-2.30am Fri-Sun. **Credit** AmEx, DC, MC, V.

CONSUME

A Babylonian theme bar and restaurant so screamingly over the top that it makes Kubla Khan's palace look like a bouncy castle. Every surface is embellished to a disorientating degree: bronze walls depict ancient battles, pillars are inlaid with polished stones, and ceilings shape-shift in the coloured spotlights. The restaurant's retractable glass roof and inspired pan-Asian cuisine is similarly unexpected, although by the time you've weaved a path to the lapis lazuli bar you'll probably be prepared for the cocktail menu.

▶ *Thinking that indie guitar mash-ups might be a bit more appropriate with your Camden cocktails? Time to head to Proud; see p323.*

★ Holly Bush
22 Holly Mount, Hampstead, NW3 6SG (7435 2892/www.hollybushpub.com). Hampstead tube/ Hampstead Heath rail. **Open** noon-11pm Mon-Sat; noon-10.30pm Sun. **Credit** MC, V.
Hampstead may have become part of London in 1888, but no one seems to have told the Holly Bush.

As the trend for gutting old pubs claims yet more NW3 boozers, this places's cachet increases. It's as picturesque as they come, tucked away on a quiet hilltop backstreet and delivering on all fronts: friendly staff, an ancient interior and fine, reasonably priced food – anything from a spruced-up sarnie to lamb shank in beer.

King Charles I
55-57 Northdown Street, King's Cross, N1 9BL (7837 7758). King's Cross tube/rail. **Open** noon-11pm Mon-Fri; 5-11pm Sat, Sun. **Credit** MC, V. **Map** p399 M2 ⑯
The King Charles is frequented by loyal (mainly male) regulars who are pleased as punch to partake of great beers in such a conspiratorial setting. Thwaites Original, Bishops Tipple, Deuchars IPA and a global range of bottled beers baffle the first-time visitor, as might the quirky decor touches: an old bar billiards table, unusual advertising for the Leu Family Tattoo Parlour, and a variety of ethnic figures and carnival masks.

Good Mixers

Bramble? Wibble? Snood Murdekin? London knows how to cocktail.

Just a decade ago, cocktail lovers ordering a martini or a manhattan in London took a major gamble. Outside a small collection of bars in the West End, cocktail bartending was terra incognita. Now even New Yorkers acknowledge the Brits know a thing or three. The inspiration came originally from the great bartenders working in the fancy hotels, almost all of them Italian. Peter Dorelli at the American Bar of the Savoy (due to reopen later this year), Gilberto Preti at Dukes Hotel and Salvatore Calabrese (originally at Dukes, then at the Lanesborough, now with his own members' club) set new standards.

Dick Bradsell is their equivalent for the current cocktail explosion. His creation of Dick's Bar at the Atlantic Bar & Grill (*see p219* **Profile**) signalled that cocktails could be, as Bradsell himself puts it, 'about fun'. Inventor of the Bramble (gin, creme de mure), Wibble (gin, sloe gin, grapefruit, creme de mure) and Snood Murdekin (vodka, Kahlua, Chambord) among many others, Bradsell trained bartenders who now work all over the world. Jonathan Downey's Match group began with Bradsell at the helm and is now, with three Match bars joined by **Player** (*see p231*) and **Milk & Honey** (*see p233*), a university of cocktail training. **LAB** (*see p231*) has continued the good work; the

Coburg (*see p234*) and **Dukes** (*see p235*) have honed their skills to perfection; and sophisticated operations like the **Shochu Lounge** (*see p230*), with its specialism in sake and shochu, continue to broaden Londoners' horizons.

Shochu Lounge.

★ Wenlock Arms

*26 Wenlock Road, Islington, N1 7TA (7608
3406/www.wenlock-arms.co.uk). Old Street
tube/rail.* **Open** noon-midnight Mon-Wed,
Sun; noon-1am Thur-Sat. **No credit cards.**
Map p402 P3 ⑰

God forbid this old boozer should ever tear out its
carpet or gastro-up its menu of doorstep sarnies: we
like it just fine as it is. The key is the unique mix of
people it attracts. On any given night, you might
find yourself sitting next to a table of beer-bellied
ale-hunters going through the excellent and ever-
changing range of beers, or a group of art students
on holiday from Hoxton, or, of course, the talkative
regulars. This is, first and foremost, a local pub for
local people and as such, perfect, more or less.

EAST LONDON

The **Gun** (*see p224*) in Docklands is a good
pub, as well as being a fine place to eat. And
late-night **Charlie Wright's** (*see p318*) is as
much about drinking as it is about live music.

Big Chill Bar

*Old Truman Brewery, off Brick Lane, E1 6QL
(7392 9180/www.bigchill.net). Aldgate East tube/
Liverpool Street tube/rail.* **Open** noon-midnight
Mon-Thur; noon-1am Fri, Sat; 11am-midnight
Sun. **Credit** MC, V. **Map** p403 S5 ㊽

The Big Chill dishes up drinks and dance music in
a setting relaxed enough to take in all-comers, from
straggly kids to grey-haired know-betters. A bull's
head with huge horns stares out the DJ across the
loungey front area, before the busy bar recedes into
a large main room and its overwhelmed chandelier.
Refinement isn't the point, but the £6.50 cocktails
are respectable and bottled beers include Duvel.
▶ *For the clubbier Big Chill House, see p321.*

★ Carpenter's Arms

*73 Cheshire Street, off Brick Lane, E2 6EG
(7739 6342/www.thecarpentersarmsfreehouse.
com). Liverpool Street tube/rail.* **Open** noon-
11.30pm Mon-Thur; noon-12.30am Fri, Sat; noon-
11.30pm Sun. **Credit** MC, V. **Map** p403 S4 ㊾

This was once a right naughty little boozer deep in
East End gangsterland. It was bought by the Kray
twins in 1967 for their dear old mum, Violet. It was
here that Ronnie tanked up on dutch courage before
murdering Jack 'The Hat' McVitie. Today, swathes
of dark wood and historic windows make for a cosy
place to plan a bank job, but the regulars are more
Thompson Twins than Kray Twins: Hoxtonites,
fashionistas, the odd ironic moustache and a few
ambitious hats.

Commercial Tavern

*142 Commercial Street, Spitalfields, E1 6NU
(7247 1888). Aldgate East tube/Liverpool Street
tube/rail.* **Open** 5-11pm Mon-Fri; noon-11pm Sat;

noon-10.30pm Sun. **Credit** AmEx, MC, V.
Map p403 R5 ㊿

The inspired chaos of retro-eccentric decor and
warm, inclusive atmosphere make this landmark
flatiron corner pub very likeable. It seems to have
escaped the attentions of the necking-it after-work
masses: perhaps because of the absence of wall-to-
wall lager pumps. The bar itself is made up of
colourful art deco tiles and there's a distinct decorative playfulness throughout: a great example of how
a historic pub can be quite lit up with new life.
▶ *Just down the street is the fabulous Golden
Heart (110 Commercial Street, 7247 2158), a
famous, crowded nursery for East End arty types.*

Dreambagsjaguarshoes

*34-36 Kingsland Road, Hoxton, E2 8DA
(7729 5830/www.dreambagsjaguarshoes.com).
Old Street tube/rail.* **Open** 5pm-midnight Mon;
noon-1am Tue-Fri; 5pm-1am Sat; noon-12.30am
Sun. **Credit** MC, V. **Map** p403 R3 ㉛

Still as trendy as the day it first opened, this bar
offers a fast-track education in what made (and continues to make) Shoreditch cool. Grungey but glam
scruffs lounge on the battered sofas, surrounded by
scrawled-on walls and lots of tatty art; bar staff look
like they have modelling contracts on the side; and
the background music is self-consciously edgy.

Grapes

*76 Narrow Street, Docklands, E14 8BP (7987
4396). Westferry DLR.* **Open** noon-3pm, 5.30-
11pm Mon-Thur; noon-11pm Fri, Sat; noon-
10.30pm Sun. **Credit** AmEx, MC, V.

As old school as they come, the Grapes ticks all the
right boxes with a creaky wood-panelled interior,
open fire and quirky memorabilia galore. Take
a pew at one of the wonky wooden tables after a
bracing Thames walk or join the blokey after-work
crowd for banter at the bar. There's no music to
distract you from the pint-supping task at hand,
though the Sunday roasts are rather diverting.
▶ *Along the way, the Narrow (44 Narrow Street,
7592 7950, www.gordonramsay.com), Gordon
Ramsay's first gastropub, does great bar snacks
and has plenty of space for actual drinking.*

★ Hawksmoor

*157 Commercial Street, Spitalfields, E1 6BJ
(7247 7392/www.thehawksmoor.com). Liverpool
Street tube/rail.* **Open** noon-midnight Mon-Fri;
6pm-midnight Sat. **Credit** MC, V.
Map p403 R5 ㉜

As a bar, Hawksmoor succeeds despite being stuck
at one side of a restaurant, with no dedicated
seating of its own beyond a few barstools. Those
stools are among London's finest ringside seats,
however, for Hawksmoor's laid-back bartenders are
cocktail intellectuals. The menu tracks historic
classics such as juleps and 'aromatic cocktails' from
their inception. Recommended.

CONSUME

Only Running Footman. See p234.

▶ *Nearby, the same team's Green & Red (51 Bethnal Green Road, 7749 9670, www.green ed.co.uk) is superb for high-end tequilas and Mexican snacks.*

Loungelover

1 Whitby Street, Shoreditch, E1 6JU (7012 1234/ www.loungelover.co.uk). Liverpool Street tube/rail. **Open** 6pm-midnight Mon-Thur, Sun; 6pm-1am Fri; 7pm-1am Sat. **Credit** AmEx, DC, MC, V. **Map** p403 S4 ⑤

Owned by the same concern as the feted Les Trois Garçons restaurant around the corner, this famously louche cocktail lounge parades tasteful, low-lit decadence in its decor, with distressed wooden armoires, hot-house plants, vintage palm-frond chandeliers, a stuffed hippo's head, man-sized Chinese urns, a giant disco ball and tea lights set on elegant, glass-topped tables. It may all be a little pretentious, but the staff are helpful to the cocktail-confused and if you're looking for somewhere that will impress, the place can hardly be bettered.

▶ *Looking a bit lived-in these days, nearby Sosho (2 Tabernacle Street, EC2A 4LU, 7920 0701, www.matchbar.com) is nonetheless still a fine cocktail bar – open to at least 3am all weekend.*

SOUTH-EAST LONDON

Bar du Musee

17 Nelson Road, Greenwich, SE10 9JB (8858 4710/www.bardumusee.com). Cutty Sark DLR. **Open** noon-1am Mon-Thur; noon-2am Fri, Sat; 11am-midnight Sun. **Credit** MC, V.

The BDM is now a serious operation with a huge dining area at the back and a more limited selection of the thing that makes it tick – wine. The front bar, with its French soldier's uniform, red walls, wrought-iron and candlelight, is a fine place to move seamlessly from chat to romance. Nibbles include platters of cured meats or French cheeses.

★ Florence

133 Dulwich Road, Dulwich, SE24 0NG (7326 4987/www.florencehernehill.com). Herne Hill rail. **Open** noon-12.30am Mon-Thur; noon-1.30am Fri; 11am-1.30am Sat; 11am-12.30am Sun. **Credit** MC, V.

At this light, airy pub, you can enjoy burgers from the open kitchen and interesting beers. It's a genuine free house, with tasting notes on every pump and an above-average bitter called Weasel brewed on the premises. Proximity to Brockwell Park and Brixton Beach – the Lido – means that the Florence has been colonised by families. But there's enough space amid its cowhide banquettes, conservatory and seemingly endless beer terrace for everyone to enjoy a visit.

Greenwich Union

56 Royal Hill, Greenwich, SE10 8RT (8692 6258/www.greenwichunion.com). Greenwich rail/DLR. **Open** noon-11pm Mon-Fri; 11am-11pm Sat; 11.30am-10.30pm Sun. **Credit** MC, V.

Alistair Hook's laudable Meantime Brewery flagship is based on the training and recipes he gleaned at age-old institutions in Germany. In-house Meantime produces London Stout, Pale Ale, Helles, Kölner, Union, Strawberry and Raspberry varieties, available on draught at reasonable prices. Throw in proper cheeses, steak and stout pies and it's no wonder the Union is reliably busy.

SOUTH-WEST LONDON

Also worth a look here are the **Dogstar** (*see p325*) on Brixton's Coldharbour Lane, and the **Windmill** (*see p317*) on Clapham Common.

Loft

67 Clapham High Street, SW4 7TG (7627 0792/www.theloft-clapham.co.uk). Clapham North tube. **Open** 6pm-midnight Mon-Thur; 6pm-1.30am Fri; noon-1.30am Sat; noon-midnight Sun. **Credit** MC, V.

A nominee for Best Bar in the *Time Out* Eating & Drinking Awards 2009, this glass-fronted space, courtesy of the good folk behind Brixton's Plan B, takes its music, and its food, seriously. And its

CONSUME

minimal breeze block walls, low-slung leather chairs and smoky glass windows make it just about possible to forget you're sitting above Tesco. There's a £5 'cocktail club' menu and reasonably priced bar snacks (chorizo and mash, pork belly sandwich) too. A huge DJ set-up is embedded into the high concrete bar.

Lost Society
697 Wandsworth Road, Battersea, SW8 3JF (7652 6526/www.lostsociety.co.uk). Clapham Common tube/Wandsworth Road rail/77, 77A bus. **Open** 5pm-midnight Tue, Wed; 5pm-1am Thur; 4pm-2am Fri; 11am-2am Sat; 11am-1am Sun. **Admission** £5 after 9pm Fri, Sat. **Credit** AmEx, MC, V.
Lost Society is one hell of a bar. Whichever of the six rooms you end up in, you'll find the same sense of stylish decadence. Like the fantasy country-house party of your dreams, Lost has a bit of a roaring '20s feel, with aristocratic opulence at every turn, art deco touches, high ceilings, chaises longues and a crystal-bead light shade above the main bar. Drink offerings have suitably glam appeal, the garden out back has a hidden, secret garden feel, and DJs spin a crowd-pleasingly eclectic mix.

Effra
38A Kellet Road, SW2 1EB (7274 4180). Brixton tube/rail. **Open** 3-11pm daily.
No credit cards.
This old-school boozer has more of an Afro-Caribbean community feel than many Brixton watering holes. The daily changing menu offers the likes of seaweed callaloo and jerk pork, and palm fronds tower over drinkers in the cosy patio

Boisdale. *See p235.*

garden (one of SW2's livelier outdoor drinking experiences). One look at the fading Victorian splendour of the gold-corniced ceiling and pretty domed glass lamps, and it's no wonder die-hard locals pack the place out each night.

★ White Horse
1-3 Parsons Green, Parsons Green, SW6 4UL (7736 2115/www.whitehorsesw6.com). Parsons Green tube. **Open** 9.30am-11.30pm Mon-Wed, Sun; 11am-midnight Thur-Sat. **Credit** AmEx, MC, V.
The White Horse's combination of Chesterfields and long chunky tables is equally welcome to drinker and diner – a rare feat for a food-led pub. The beer list is arguably the finest in London, with in excess of 80 bottled beauties and more than a dozen perfectly kept draught beers pulled through lines cleaner than a nun's conscience. Hush-seeking eaters head for the plush restaurant at the back, where every dish comes with suitable tipple recommended, and there's a terrific outside patio on which to scoff deluxe burgers. One of London's beer essentials.

WEST LONDON

Botanist on the Green
3-5 Kew Green, Kew, Surrey TW9 3AA (8948 4838/www.thebotanistkew.com). Kew Gardens tube/rail/65, 391 bus. **Open** noon-11pm Mon-Wed; noon-midnight Thur-Sat; noon-11pm Sun. **Credit** AmEx, DC, MC, V.
The name is a nod to its floral neighbour, the Royal Botanic Gardens (*see p156*), and this pub's position on the corner of Kew Green makes it a perfect place for a relaxing pint after a little mooch around the gardens. The substantial space has cosy nooks – one with a fabulous double-sided fireplace – and raised areas that give the place a more intimate feel. The outdoor space is as twinkly as a fairy grotto, and the food menu is impressive. On Sundays there's a clutch of roasts, and decent jazz.
▶ *Another smart option is the ambitious Inn at Kew Gardens (292 Sandycombe Road, Kew, 8940 2220, www.theinnatkewgardens.com), situated below the Kew Gardens Hotel.*

Ladbroke Arms
54 Ladbroke Road, Holland Park, W11 3NW (7727 6648/www.capitalpubcompany.com/ladbroke). Holland Park tube. **Open** 11am-11pm Mon-Sat; noon-10.30pm Sun. **Credit** AmEx, MC, V. **Map** p394 A7 ⑤
The Ladbroke is well known for its floral displays (the beer garden at the front is wildly colourful) and its food (with a smart dining section at the rear and a wine list to match) but it's still popular with low-key middle-aged locals who pop in for a pint and who appreciate the well-upholstered, carpeted interior and efficient air-conditioning. Real ales might include Sharp's Doom Bar or Adnams Broadside.

Shops & Services

Credit cards at the ready.

The recent relaunch of iconic British labels Biba and Ossie Clark signals the strength of the retro revival, but London retail exists in a constant state of fashionable flux. One of the world's most exciting and exhaustive retail centres, it's also one of the most eclectic, spanning multicultural street markets and deluxe department stores, mould-breaking fashion designers and trad tailors, flashy foodshops and dusty antiquarian dens. You'll also find some of the best places on the planet to buy books, records and second-hand clothes. There are bargains to be had, but pocket the plastic too.

CONSUME

THE LOWDOWN

We've only the space to cover a fraction of London's shopping here, so we concentrated on British brands and shops that are not only unique to the city, but also relatively central. For the key areas, *see p246* **Where to Shop**.

Most goods (except books, children's clothes and food) are subject to value added tax (VAT), usually included in marked prices. The usual rate of 17.5 per cent has been cut to 15 per cent until at least the end of 2009. If you're from outside the EC, you may be able to claim back VAT; *see p373*. Central London shops open late (7pm or 8pm) one night a week (Thur in the West End; Wed in Chelsea and Knightsbridge).

General

SHOPPING CENTRES & ARCADES

The **Royal Arcades** in the vicinity of Piccadilly are a throwback to shopping past – the Burlington Arcade (*see below*) is the largest.

★ Burlington Arcade
Piccadilly, St James's, W1 (7630 1411/www. burlington-arcade.co.uk). Green Park tube. **Open** 9.30am-5.30pm Mon-Fri; 10am-6pm Sat. **Credit** varies. **Map** p408 U4.

About the reviews
This chapter was compiled from the annual Time Out Shops & Services Guide (£9.99).

In 1819, Lord Cavendish commissioned Britain's very first shopping arcade and the Burlington is still London's most prestigious. It is also still patrolled by 'Beadles' decked out in top hats and tailcoats. Highlights include collections of classic watches, iconic British brands Mackintosh and Globe-Trotter (*see p255*); Luponde Tea is a new arrival.

Kingly Court
Carnaby Street, opposite Broadwick Street, Soho, W1B 5PW (7333 8118/www.carnaby.co.uk). Oxford Circus tube. **Open** 11am-7pm Mon-Sat; noon-6pm Sun. **Credit** varies. **Map** p408 U3.
Kingly Court has helped Carnaby Street reclaim some of its 1960s reputation as the heart of swinging London. The three-tiered complex boasts a funky mix of chains and independents.

Westfield London
Shepherd's Bush, W12 (www.westfield.com/ london). White City or Wood Lane tube/Shepherd's Bush tube/rail. **Open** 9am-10pm Mon-Fri; 9am-8pm Sat; noon-6pm Sun. **Credit** varies.

THE BEST BUDGET STYLE

For vintage at £10
Brick Lane Thrift Store. *See p253.*

For perfectly priced frocks
Beyond Retro. *See p253.*

For second-hand Savile Row
Old Hat. *See p253.*

Occupying 46 acres, and covering nine different postcodes, Westfield London took the crown of Europe's largest shopping centre when it opened in autumn 2008. The impressive site – which held the 1908 Olympics – cost around £1.6 billion to build and will house some 265 shops. Popular labels that have never had stand-alone stores in the UK, like Hollister and UGG, will have shops here, and you'll also find luxury fashion houses, including Louis Vuitton, Armani and Mulberry. Michelin-starred chefs Pascal Aussignac and Vincent Labeyrie can soothe away any shopping-induced stress with their gastronomic creations at Croque Gascon. If they don't manage to tempt your taste buds, then one of the other 50 eateries surely will.

DEPARTMENT STORES

High-street fave for undies and ready meals, **Marks & Spencer** (www.marksandspencer. co.uk) also offers several fashion ranges, including its designer Autograph collection for men and women, and the younger, trend-led Per Una line and Limited Collection.

★ Fortnum & Mason

181 Piccadilly, St James's, W1A 1ER (7734 8040/www.fortnumandmason.co.uk). Green Park or Piccadilly Circus tube. **Open** 10am-8pm Mon-Sat; noon-6pm Sun. **Credit** AmEx, DC, MC, V. **Map** p406 V4.

Diverse. *See p250*.

The revamped F&M is stunning: a sweeping spiral staircase soars through the four-storey building, while light floods down from a central glass dome. The iconic eau de nil blue and gold colour scheme with flashes of rose pink abound on both the store design and the packaging of the fabulous ground-floor treats, like the chocolates, biscuits, teas and preserves. The five restaurants, all redesigned by David Collins (of Wolseley fame), are every bit as beguiling. A new food hall in the basement has a huge range of fresh produce and more wines than ever before. The shop is redolent of a time when luxury meant the highest degree of comfort rather than ostentation, but that's not to say it's beyond the means of a modest budget. The famous hampers start from £40 and the blended teas from £2.75.
▶ *For more David Collins interiors, see pp40-42.*

Harrods

87-135 Brompton Road, Knightsbridge, SW1X 7XL (7730 1234/www.harrods.com). Knightsbridge tube. **Open** 10am-8pm Mon-Sat; noon-6pm Sun. **Credit** AmEx, DC, MC, V. **Map** p397 F9.

All the glitz and marble can be a bit much, but in the store that boasts of selling everything, it's hard not to leave with at least one thing you'll like. New additions to the legendary food halls and restaurants include the Andronicas world of coffee on the fourth floor, and the 5J ham and tapas bar from Sanchez Romero Carvajal, Spain's oldest Jabugo ham-producing company. It's on the fashion floors that Harrods really comes into its own, though, with well-edited collections from the heavyweights. New in 2008 was the eagerly awaited revival of Halston, the iconic 1970s design house, plus a boutique from Oscar de La Renta with opulent signature evening gowns and beautifully wearable day dresses.
▶ *Nearby Harvey Nichols (109-125 Knightsbridge, 7235 5000, www.harveynichols.com) feels like it's coasting a little these days, but you'll still find a worthy clutch of unique fashion brands.*

Liberty

Regent Street, Soho, W1B 5AH (7734 1234/ www.liberty.co.uk). Oxford Circus tube. **Open** 10am-9pm Mon-Sat; noon-6pm Sun. **Credit** AmEx, DC, MC, V. **Map** p406 U2.

Charmingly idiosyncratic, Liberty is housed in a 1920s mock Tudor structure. Walk in the main entrance on Great Marlborough Street, flanked by Paula Pryke's exuberant floral concession, and you'll find yourself in a room devoted to the store's own label, in the middle of a galleried atrium. Shopping here is about more than just spending money; artful and arresting window displays, exciting new collections and luxe labels make it an experience to savour for its own sake. And despite being fashion forward, Liberty still respects its dressmaking heritage with an extensive range of cottons in the third-floor haberdashery department. Stationery also pays court to

the traditional, with beautiful Liberty of London notebooks, address books, photo albums and diaries embossed with the art nouveau 'Ianthe' print.
▶ *Last year Liberty launched a stand-alone store (197 Sloane Street, 7573 9695), which sells a selection of their own-brand products.*

★ Selfridges
400 Oxford Street, Marylebone, W1A 1AB (0800 123 400/www.selfridges.com). Bond Street or Marble Arch tube. **Open** 9.30am-8pm Mon-Wed, Fri, Sat; 9.30am-9pm Thur; noon-6pm Sun. **Credit** AmEx, DC, MC, V. **Map** p398 G6.
It's no surprise Selfridges won our Shopping Award for Best Department Store in 2008: its concession boutiques, store-wide themed events and collections from the hottest new brands make it the first port-of-call for stylish one-stop shopping, while useful floor plans make navigating the store easy-peasy. It stocks a winning combination of new talent, hip and edgy labels, smarter high-street labels, and mid- and high-end brands. Last year, Sophie Hulme joined the hallowed second-floor womenswear halls with her dramatic first collection of luxury streetwear.
▶ *March 2009 is Selfridges's 100th anniversary. Celebration plans are still under wraps, but you can be sure they'll unveil something sensational.*

MARKETS

London's street markets are great places to sample street life while picking up bargains. Below is a selection of the best. For **Camden Market**, *see p126*; for **Borough**, *see p258*.

★ Columbia Road Market
Columbia Road, Bethnal Green, E2. Liverpool Street tube/rail, then 26, 48, bus/Old Street tube/rail then 55, 243 bus. **Open** 8am-2pm Sun. **Map** p403 S3.
On Sunday mornings, this unassuming East End street is transformed into a swathe of fabulous plant life and the air is fragrant with blooms. But it's not just about flora: alongside the market is a growing

number of shops selling everything from pottery and Mexican glassware to cupcakes and perfume. Get there early for the pick of the crop, or around 2pm for the bargains; refuel at Jones Dairy (23 Ezra Street, 7739 5372, www.jonesdairy.co.uk).

Portobello Road Market
Portobello Road, Notting Hill, W10 & W11 (www.rbkc.gov.uk/streettrading). Ladbroke Grove or Notting Hill Gate tube. **Open** *General* 8am-6.30pm Mon-Wed, Fri, Sat; 8am-1pm Thur. *Antiques* 4am-4pm Fri, Sat. **Map** p394 A6.
Best known for antiques and collectibles, this is actually several markets rolled into one: antiques start at the Notting Hill end; further up are food stalls; under the Westway and along the walkway to Ladbroke Grove are emerging designer and vintage clothes on Fridays (usually marginally less busy) and Saturdays (invariably manic).

Spitalfields Market
Commercial Street, between Lamb Street & Brushfield Street, E1 6AA (7247 8556/www. visitspitalfields.com). Liverpool Street tube/rail. **Open** *General* 9.30am-5pm Thur, Fri, Sun. *Antiques* 8.30am-4.30pm Thur. *Food* 10am-5pm Wed, Fri, Sun. *Fashion* 9.30am-5pm Fri. *Records & books* 10am-4pm 1st & 3rd Fri of the mth. **Map** p405 R5.
Recent redevelopment has given a new lease of life to this East End stalwart. The market now comprises the refurbished 1887 covered market and an adjacent modern shopping precinct. Around the edge of Old Spitalfields Market, stands sell grub from around the world. The busiest day is Sunday, when the nearby Brick Lane Market and Sunday (Up)Market in the Old Truman Brewery (strong on edgy designer and vintage fashion; *see above* **Inside Track**) create an *iD*-photo shoot-meets-Bangladeshi-bazaar vibe.

Specialist

BOOKS & MAGAZINES

Central branches of the big chains include **Borders** (203 Oxford Street, W1D 2LE, 7292 1600, www.bordersstores.co.uk) and the **Waterstone's** flagship (203-206 Piccadilly, SW1Y 6WW, 7851 2400, www.waterstones.co. uk), with its bar-café and Trailfinders branch.

General

Foyles
113-119 Charing Cross Road, Soho, WC2H 0EB (7437 5660/www.foyles.co.uk). Tottenham Court Road tube. **Open** 9.30am-9pm Mon-Sat; noon-6pm Sun. **Credit** AmEx, MC, V. **Map** p407 X2.
London's single most impressive independent bookshop, Foyles built its reputation on the sheer volume

Eastpak Store
1 Carnaby Street - LONDON.

EASTPAK

BUILT TO RESIST
www.eastpak.com

and breadth of its stock (there are no less than 56 specialist subjects in this flagship store). Its five storeys accommodate other shops too: Ray's Jazz (see p264) has recently moved up to the third floor, giving plenty more room to the first-floor café, which hosts low-key gigs and readings from the likes of John Gray, Billy Bragg and Sophie Dahl. In addition to those in Selfridges (see p243), the Southbank Centre (see p309), St Pancras International (see p79), a fifth branch is to open in Westfield London (see p241). See also p262 **Foyled Again**. Photo p262.

John Sandoe

10 Blacklands Terrace, Chelsea, SW3 2SR (7589 9473/www.johnsandoe.com). Sloane Square tube. **Open** 9.30am-5.30pm Mon, Tue, Thur-Sat; 9.30am-7.30pm Wed; noon-6pm Sun. **Credit** AmEx, DC, MC, V. **Map** p397 F11.
Tucked away on a Chelsea side street, this 50-year-old independent looks just as a bookshop should. The stock is literally packed to the rafters, and of the 25,000 books here, 24,000 are a single copy – so there's serious breadth.

★ London Review Bookshop

14 Bury Place, Bloomsbury, WC1A 2JL (7269 9030/www.lrbshop.co.uk). Holborn or Tottenham Court Road tube. **Open** 10am-6.30pm Mon-Sat; noon-6pm Sun. **Credit** AmEx, MC, V. **Map** p399 L5.
An inspiring bookshop, from the inviting and stimulating presentation to the quality of the books selected. Politics, current affairs and history are well represented on the ground floor, while downstairs, audio books lead on to exciting poetry and philosophy sections – everything you'd expect from a shop owned by the *London Review of Books*.

Specialist

Books for Cooks

4 Blenheim Crescent, Notting Hill, W11 1NN (7221 1992/www.booksforcooks.com). Ladbroke Grove tube. **Open** 10am-6pm Tue-Sat. **Credit** MC, V.
Books here cover hundreds of cuisines, chefs and techniques. Even better, the shop's kitchen-café tests different recipes daily, sold to customers from noon.

Magma

117-119 Clerkenwell Road, Holborn, EC1R 5BY (7242 9503/www.magmabooks.com). Chancery Lane tube/Farringdon tube/rail. **Open** 10am-7pm Mon-Sat. **Credit** AmEx, MC, V. **Map** p402 N4.
If you can visualise it, this art and design specialist has probably got a book on it. Magazines, DVDs, trendy toys, T-shirts and a series of commissioned limited-edition posters and cards are also sold.
Other locations 8 Earlham Street, Covent Garden, WC2H 9RY (7240 8498); 16 Earlham Street, Covent Garden, WC2H 9LN (7240 7571).

Stanfords

12-14 Long Acre, Cove... (7836 1321/www.stanfo... Garden or Leicester Squa... 7.30pm Mon, Wed, Fri; 9.30... 9am-8pm Thur; 10am-7pm Sa... **Credit** MC, V. **Map** p407 Y3.
Three floors of travel guides, trav... language guides, atlases and mag... ... ...se-ment houses the full range of Br... ...rdnance Survey maps, and you can plan your next trip over Fairtrade coffee in the ground-floor café.

Used & antiquarian

Biblion

1-7 Davies Mews, Mayfair, W1K 5AB (7629 1374/www.biblionmayfair.co.uk). Bond Street tube. **Open** 10am-6pm Mon-Fri. **Credit** MC, V. **Map** p398 H6.
Around 50 dealers display their various wares at these spacious premises in Grays Antique Market. The prices are as broad as the stock.

Simon Finch Rare Books

26 Brook Street, Mayfair, W1K 5DQ (7499 0974/www.simonfinch.com). Oxford Circus tube. **Open** 10am-6pm Mon-Fri. **Credit** AmEx, MC, V. **Map** p398 J6.
Housed in a narrow town house, this era-spanning, idiosyncratic collection has wonderful surprises, from one of the original copies of Hubert Selby Jr's *Last Exit to Brooklyn* to esoterica like *Mushrooms, Russia & History*. Prices start at around £20, so it's worth popping in even if you're not a collector.

Skoob

Unit 66, The Brunswick, Bloomsbury, WC1N 1AE (7278 8760/www.skoob.com). Russell Square tube. **Open** 10.30am-8pm Mon-Sat; 10.30am-6pm Sun. **Credit** MC, V. **Map** p399 L4.
A back-to-basics basement showcasing some 50,000 titles covering virtually every subject, from philosophy and biography to politics and the occult.

INSIDE TRACK BOOK ALLEY

Bookended by Charing Cross Road and St Martin's Lane, picturesque **Cecil Court** (www.cecilcourt.co.uk) is known for its antiquarian book, map and print dealers. Notable residents include children's specialist **Marchpane** (no.16, 7836 8661) and 40-year veteran **David Drummond at Pleasures of Past Times** (no.11, 7836 1142), who specialises in theatre and magic. A more recent arrival is **Red Snapper** (no.22, 7240 2075) for small-press fiction and counter-culture classics.

CONSUME

...EN

...nion

Try also baby superstore **Mamas & Papas** (256-258 Regent Street, W1B 3AF, 0870 850 2845, www.mamasandpapas.co.uk).

Caramel Baby & Child
291 Brompton Road, South Kensington, SW3 2DY (7589 7001/www.caramel-shop.co.uk).

South Kensington tube. **Open** 10am-6pm Mon-Sat; noon-5pm Sun. **Credit** AmEx, MC, V. **Map** p397 E10.

Tasteful togs for children from babies to 12-year-olds. The look is relaxed, but the clothes here are well finished in modern, muted colour schemes; while the styles have clearly been inspired by the sturdy clothes of the past, they never submit to full-blown nostalgia. Prices are commensurate with quality: around £40 for a boy's polo shirt, £50-£60 for knitwear and £60 or £70 for a dress.

Where to Shop
London's best shopping neighbourhoods in brief.

COVENT GARDEN & SOHO
The famous former flower market-turned-shopping precinct is choked with chains and crowds, but **Neal Street** and the streets radiating off **Seven Dials** rule for trainers and streetwise gear. Another urbanwear hotspot is Soho's **Carnaby Street**, which has traded tacky tourist shops for hip chains and independents. **Berwick Street** is still hanging on to some record shops, while **Charing Cross Road** (especially Cecil Court) is prime browsing territory for bookish types.

OXFORD STREET & MARYLEBONE
Oxford Street, London's commercial backbone, heaves with big chains and department stores, which spill over on to elegant, curving **Regent Street**. In contrast, **Marylebone** has a villagey

atmosphere and small shops that sell everything from designer jewellery to farmhouse cheeses. Venture further north to **Church Street** for antiques.

NOTTING HILL
Best known for its antiques market on **Portobello Road**, Notting Hill also has an impressive cache of posh boutiques around the intersection of **Westbourne Grove** and **Ledbury Road** – a laid-back alternative to the West End and Chelsea. The area is also good for rare vinyl and vintage clothes.

MAYFAIR & ST JAMES'S
The traditional home of tailors (**Savile Row**) and shirtmakers (**Jermyn Street**), this patch also retains venerable specialist hatters, cobblers and perfumers. **Bond**

Savile Row.

CONSUME

Other locations 77 Ledbury Road, Notting Hill, W11 2AG (7727 0906); 259 Pavillion Road, Brompton, SW1X 0BP (7730 2564); 82 Hill Rise, Richmond, Middx TW10 6UB (8940 6325).
▶ *Snack at nearby Hummingbird; see p217.*

Petit Aimé
34 Ledbury Road, Notting Hill, W11 2AB (7221 3123/www.aimelondon.com). Notting Hill Gate tube. **Open** 10.30am-6.30pm Mon-Sat. **Credit** AmEx, DC, MC, V. **Map** p394 A6.

Street glitters with posh jewellers and designer flagships.

CHELSEA & KNIGHTSBRIDGE
The legendary **King's Road** is pretty bland now, but punctuated with some interesting shops. Plush international designer salons line **Sloane Street** and mix with chains in **Knightsbridge**, which is anchored by deluxe department stores.

KENSINGTON
Once a hub of hip fashion, **Kensington High Street** has surrendered to the chains, but it's still worth exploring the backstreets leading up to Notting Hill Gate. Rarefied antiques shops gather on **Kensington Church Street**. In South Ken, **Brompton Cross** has glossy contemporary furniture showrooms and designer boutiques.

EAST LONDON
An unmissable destination for offbeat independent shops and some of the city's best markets. Head for **Brick Lane** and its offshoots for clothing, accessories and home goods made or adapted by idiosyncratic young designers, and for heaps of vintage fashion. **Shoreditch** and **Hoxton** have further hip boutiques, furniture stores and bookshops.

NORTH LONDON
The sprawling, grungy markets of **Camden** are best left to the under-25s, but nearby leafy **Primrose Hill** has an exquisite selection of small shops selling, among other things, quirky lingerie and vintage clothes. Antiques dealers are thinning out on Islington's **Camden Passage**, but there is a growing number of other indies, including a gourmet chocolatier and an ethical boutique.

Shoppers looking to bring a touch of Gallic chic to their child's wardrobe should head to this new boutique from French-Cambodian sisters Val and Vanda Heng-Vong. The shop stocks an adorable range of labels for children and babies.
▶ *Next door, the original Aimé store (no.32, 7221 7070, www.aimelondon.com) brings a cool 1970s sensibility to women's fashion.*

Their Nibs
214 Kensington Park Road, Notting Hill, W11 1NR (7221 4263/www.theirnibs.com). Ladbroke Grove or Notting Hill Gate tube. **Open** 10am-6pm Mon-Sat; noon-5pm Sun. **Credit** AmEx, MC, V. **Map** p394 A6.
A visit to this shop is a treat. There's a play corner with a blackboard, books and toys to occupy tinies while older ones browse, and the vintage-inspired gear encompasses quirky dungarees for crawling babes and demure summer frocks for preening girls.

Toys

Early Learning Centre (www.elc.co.uk) has many branches dedicated to imaginative play. **Their Nibs** (*see above*) has a great toy selection, while **Selfridges** (*see p243*) and **Harrods** (*see p242*) have dedicated toy departments.

Benjamin Pollock's Toyshop
44 The Market, Covent Garden, WC2E 8RF (7379 7866/www.pollocks-coventgarden.co.uk). Covent Garden tube. **Open** 10.30am-6pm Mon-Sat; 11am-4pm Sun. **Credit** AmEx, MC, V. **Map** p407 Z3.
Best-known for its toy theatres (from £2.95 for a tiny one in a matchbox to about £70 for elaborate models), Pollock's is also superb for traditional toys, such as knitted animals, china tea sets, masks, glove puppets, cards, spinning tops and fortune-telling fish.
▶ *For the associated toy museum, see p80.*

Honeyjam
267 Portobello Road, Notting Hill, W11 1LR (7243 0449/www.honeyjam.co.uk). Ladbroke Grove tube. **Open** 9.30am-5.30pm Mon-Sat; noon-4pm Sun. **Credit** AmEx, MC, V. **Map** p394 A6.
Despite the hype (the shop is co-owned by former model Jasmine Guinness), Honeyjam is full of fun, with a good selection of pocket money-priced trinkets.

★ Playlounge
19 Beak Street, Soho, W1F 9RP (7287 7073/ www.playlounge.co.uk). Oxford Circus or Piccadilly Circus tube. **Open** 10.30am-7pm Mon-Sat; noon-5pm Sun. **Credit** AmEx, MC, V. **Map** p406 V3.
Compact but full of fun, this groovy little shop has action figures, gadgets, books and comics, e boy posters, T-shirts and clothes that appeal to kids and adults alike. Those nostalgic for illustrated children's literature shouldn't miss the Dr Seuss PopUps and *Where the Wild Things Are* books.

CONSUME

ELECTRONICS & PHOTOGRAPHY

General

Ask

248 Tottenham Court Road, Fitzrovia, W1T 7QZ (7637 0353/www.askdirect.co.uk). Tottenham Court Road tube. **Open** 10am-7pm Mon-Wed, Fri, Sat; 10am-8pm Thur; noon-6pm Sun. **Credit** AmEx, DC, MC, V. **Map** p399 K5.
Some shops on Tottenham Court Road feel gloomy and claustrophobic, but Ask has four capacious, well-organised floors that give you space to browse. Stock – spanning digital cameras, MP3 players, radios, laptops as well as hi-fis and TVs and all the requisite accessories – concentrates on the major consumer brands. Prices are competitive.

Specialist

Behind its grand façade, the busy London **Apple Store** (235 Regent Street, 7153 9000, www.apple.com) offers all the services you'd expect, including the trademark 'Genius Bar' for technical support. Several shops on Tottenham Court Road offer laptop repairs, but we recommend **Einstein Computer Services** (07957 557065, www.einsteinpcs.co.uk), which operates on a call-out basis for £20 per hour. **Adam Phones** (2-3 Dolphin Square, Edensor Road, W4 2ST, 0800 123 000, www.adamphones. com) rent out mobile phone handsets for £1 a day with reasonable call charges. For film processing, try **Snappy Snaps** (www.snappy snaps.co.uk) and **Jessops** (www.jessops.com).

Calumet

93-103 Drummond Street, Somers Town, NW1 2HJ (7380 1144/www.calumetphoto.com). Euston tube/rail. **Open** 8.30am-5.30pm Mon-Fri; 9.30am-5.30pm Sat; 10am-4pm Sun. **Credit** AmEx, MC, V. **Map** p398 J3.
Caters mainly for professional snappers, students and darkroom workers. Lights, power packs, gels, tripods, printing and storage stock complement top-end digital gear. Also does repairs and rental.
Other locations 175 Wardour Street, Soho, W1F 8WU (7434 1848); 10 Heathmans Road, Parsons Green, SW6 4TJ (7384 3270).

FASHION

Designer

Key British designers with London flagships include **Vivienne Westwood** (44 Conduit Street, W1S 2YL, 7439 1109, www.vivienne westwood.com), **Paul Smith** (Westbourne House, 120 & 122 Kensington Park Road, W11 2EP, 7727 3553, www.paulsmith.co.uk),

Beyond Retro. *See p253.*

Alexander McQueen (4-5 Old Bond Street, W1S 4PD, 7355 0088, www.alexandermcqueen. com) and **Stella McCartney** (30 Bruton Street, W1J 6LG, 7518 3100, www.stellamccartney.com).

Albam

23 Beak Street, Soho, W1F 9RS (3157 7000/ www.albamclothing.com). Oxford Circus tube. **Open** noon-7pm Mon-Sat; noon-5pm Sun. **Credit** AmEx, DC, MC, V. **Map** p406 V3.
With its refined yet rather manly aesthetic, this menswear label dresses well-heeled gents, fashion editors and regular guys who like no-nonsense style. The focus is on classic, high-quality design with a subtle retro edge (Steve McQueen is an inspiration).

★ B store

24A Savile Row, Mayfair, W1S 3PR (7734 6846/ www.bstorelondon.com). Oxford Circus tube. **Open** 10.30am-6.30pm Mon-Fri; 10am-6pm Sat. **Credit** AmEx, MC, V. **Map** p406 U3.
A platform for cutting-edge designers, b store is holding its own among the trad tailors here. This is the place to preview the next big thing, such as Belgrade-born Roksanda Ilincic and Dane Camilla Staerk, alongside established iconoclasts such as Peter Jensen, Eley Kishimoto and Bï La Lï.

★ Browns

23-27 South Molton Street, Mayfair, W1K 5RD (7514 0000/www.brownsfashion.com). Bond

Street tube. **Open** 10am-6.30pm Mon-Wed, Fri, Sat; 10am-7pm Thur. **Credit** AmEx, MC, V. **Map** p398 H6.

Joan Burstein's venerable store has reigned supreme for nearly 40 years. Among the 100-odd designers jostling for attention in its five interconnecting shops (menswear is at no.23) are Chloé, Dries Van Noten and Balenciaga. New labels include cult legging label Les Chiffoniers, shoes by Charlotte Olympia and ethical denim by Shakrah Chakra, as well as exclusives from Balmain, Ossie Clark and Vince. Browns Focus is younger and more casual, while Labels for Less is loaded with last season's leftovers. **Other locations** 11-12 Hind Street, W1U 3BE (7514 0056); 6C Sloane Street, Chelsea, SW1X 9LE (7514 0040); Browns Focus, 38-39 South Molton Street, Mayfair, W1K 5RN (7514 0063); Browns Labels for Less, 50 South Molton Street, W1K 5RD (7514 0052).

Diverse

294 Upper Street, Islington, N1 2TU (7359 8877/www.diverseclothing.com). Angel tube. **Open** 10.30am-6.30pm Mon-Sat; noon-5.30pm Sun. **Credit** AmEx, DC, MC, V. **Map** p402 O1.

Islington stalwart Diverse does a fine job of keeping N1's style queens in fashion-forward mode. Despite the cool clobber, chic layout and striking window displays, this is the sort of place where you can rock up in jeans and scuzzy Converse and not feel uncomfortable trying on next season's See by Chloé. And while you're there, you might as well give that Marc by Marc Jacobs dress a try, and maybe those Repetto ballet slippers… You get the picture. *Photo p242.*
▶ *Also on Upper Street, Designer Francesca Forcolini's Labour of Love (no.193, 7354 9333, www.labour-of-love.co.uk) is crammed with hand-picked clothes and accessories.*

★ Dover Street Market

17-18 Dover Street, Mayfair, W1S 4LT (7518 0680/www.doverstreetmarket.com). Green Park tube. **Open** 11am-6pm Mon-Wed; 11am-7pm Thur-Sat. **Credit** AmEx, MC, V. **Map** p400 J7.

Comme des Garçons designer Rei Kawakubo's ground-breaking six-storey space combines the edgy energy of London's indoor markets – concrete floors, tills housed in corrugated-iron shacks, Portaloo dressing rooms – with rarefied labels. Recent additions include Oscar de la Renta and exclusive range by Stefano Pilati's Yves Saint Laurent Edition 24. All 14 of the Comme collections are here, alongside exclusive lines such as Azzedine Alaïa and Veronique Branquinho.

Koh Samui

65-67 Monmouth Street, Covent Garden, WC2H 9DG (7240 4280/www.kohsamui.co.uk). Covent Garden tube. **Open** 10.30am-6.30pm Mon-Wed, Fri, Sat; 10.30am-7pm Thur; noon-5.30pm Sun. **Credit** AmEx, DC, MC, V. **Map** p407 X3.

Vintage pieces sourced from around the world share rail space with a finely tuned selection of heavy-weight designers at Koh Samui, resulting in a delightfully eclectic mix of stock. Marc by Marc Jacobs, Balenciaga and Dries Van Noten are always well represented, alongside small independent labels. Vast glass cabinets glint with beads and baubles by a global array of independent designers; prices start at around £50 for a pair of earrings.

Luella

25 Brook Street, Mayfair, W1K 4HB (7518 1830/www.luella.com). Bond Street tube. **Open** 10am-6pm Mon-Wed, Fri, Sat; 10am-7pm Thur. **Credit** AmEx, MC, V. **Map** p398 H6.

The 1,400sq ft space – all wood panelling, old leather and pop culture references – houses Luella's ready-to-wear and accessories collections. She originally made her name with roomy, strappy, charm-laden bags, but her fun, sexy prom dresses have also been gaining momentum, with young London hipsters such as Alexa Chung and Lily Allen regularly snapped in them. A slew of covetable accessories include totes adorned with bells and ribbons. The trademark T-shirts (£79) are still strong. *Photo p252.*

Margaret Howell

34 Wigmore Street, Marylebone, W1U 2RS (7009 9009/www.margarethowell.co.uk). Bond Street tube. **Open** 10am-6pm Mon-Wed, Fri, Sat; 10am-7pm Thur. **Credit** AmEx, DC, MC, V. **Map** p398 H5.

Howell's wonderfully wearable clothes are made in Britain with an old-fashioned attitude to quality. These principles combine with her elegant designs to make for the best 'simple' clothes for sale in London. Her pared-down approach means prices seem steep, but unlike throwaway fashion these are clothes that get better with time – as will the new bags she's designed with Japanese label Porter.

★ No-one

1 Kingsland Road, Shoreditch, E2 8AA (7613 5314/www.no-one.co.uk). Old Street tube/rail. **Open** 11am-7pm Mon-Sat; noon-6pm Sun. **Credit** AmEx, DC, MC, V. **Map** p403 O1.

A favourite of Shoreditch locals and noncomformist style icons such as Róisín Murphy and Björk, this shop/café stocks a melange of cool merchandise: Bï La Lï womenswear, plus Mine, and YMC for men and women; shoes by Opening Ceremony and Bernhard Wilhelm; and quirky toys for grown-ups, vintage sunglasses and cult magazines and books.

Shop at Bluebird

350 King's Road, Chelsea, SW3 5UU (7351 3873/ www.theshopatbluebird.com). Sloane Square tube. **Open** 10am-7pm Mon-Sat; noon-6pm Sun. **Credit** AmEx, MC, V. **Map** p397 D12.

The Shop at Bluebird is part lifestyle boutique – DJs play at weekends – and part design gallery. The

CONSUME

Things Are What They Used to Be

The British emporiums that aren't ashamed to be backwar

A scattering of London shops, new and old, are doing a tidy trade in the sale of ultra-traditional British goods, sold to you in splendidly nostalgic settings and, of course, with good old-fashioned pleases and thankyous. One man in particular, in a corner of Covent Garden, is on a mission to revive the purveying of the frequently overlooked culinary riches of the British Isles in a civilised retail atmosphere. The **Albion Emporium** (*see p258*) – brainchild of former litigation solicitor Alex Betts (*pictured*), a passionate paganist who now prefers to be known as Albion – is the first shop in London to deal exclusively in fine traditional 'comestibles' and 'beverages' from the British Isles. On his shelves, you'll find such seemingly near-extinct British refreshments as nettle cordial, cider brandy and plum wine, as well as vintage treats along the lines of English rose chocolates, cinder toffee and clotted cream fudge. There's also a small café – sorry, refectory – at the back for a cream tea, a Ploughman's lunch made with punchy English cheddar or an honest-to-goodness meat pie.

With its handsome wooden counter, a pleasingly low-tech window display and – most unusually of all – a salesman decked out in Edwardian attire, Albion Emporium

is as much about nos celebrating English e about stocking the la

Just a few strides a of Victorian-style swe **Greenwood** (*see p258*) is peddling an even sweeter brand of nostalgia. This adorable 1950s-style, letterbox-red cornershop is the perfect place to find the sweets, sherbets, chews and chocolates that were once the focus of a proper British childhood. Tall glass jars filled with a wishlist of crunchy, chewy, suckable pleasures (parma violets, flying saucers, fizzy cola cubes and pink shrimps are all present and correct) line the back wall, and even the owners look the part: Miss Hope, beautifully turned out in her 1950s-style dress, will pop your sweets in a striped paper bag with a smile.

There is, however, nothing terribly retro about the prices in this fashionably old-fashioned outlet – a Gargantuan Tuckshop Jar of mixed delights will set you back £14.99, and Kitty Hope and John Greenwood 'splendid sweets' now grace the shelves of Harvey Nichols, Harrods and the Conran Shop. But the quality is scrupulously high and, let's face it, this is vintage shopping without the dust – unless you count the sherbet, that is.

CONSUME

...ce is a shifting showcase of clothing ...omen and children – think Ossie Clark, ...z and store-exclusive Andy & Deb), acces-...s, furniture, books and gadgets. An on-site spa ...ened last year and, for spring 2009, menswear will cover Marc Jacobs, Kitsune and PS by Paul Smith.

Discount

Scenes recalling the storming of the Bastille greeted the Oxford Street flagship of trend-led, cheap-as-chips retailer **Primark** (nos.499-517, 7495 0420, www.primark.co.uk) in 2007, and there are still plenty of bargains if you're happy to tussle with teens. Grown-ups might prefer **Browns Labels for Less** (see p249).

Burberry Factory Shop
29-53 Chatham Place, Hackney, E9 6LP (8328 4287). Hackney Central rail. **Open** 10am-6pm Mon-Sat; 11am-5pm Sun. **Credit** AmEx, DC, MC, V.
This warehouse space showcases seconds and excess stock reduced by 50% or more. Classic men's macs can be had for around £199 or less.

Paul Smith Sale Shop
23 Avery Row, Mayfair, W1X 9HB (7493 1287/ www.paulsmith.co.uk). Bond Street tube. **Open** 10.30am-6.30pm Mon-Wed, Fri, Sat; 10.30am-7pm Thur; 1-5.30pm Sun. **Credit** AmEx, DC, MC, V. **Map** p400 H7.
Samples and previous season's stock at a 30%-50% discount. Stock includes clothes for men, women and children, as well as a range of accessories.

General

The best of the high-street chains are young, designer-look **Reiss** (Kent House, 14-17 Market Place, Fitzrovia, W1H 7AJ, 7637 9112, www.reiss.co.uk) and H&M's upmarket sibling **COS** (222 Regent Street, W1B 5BD, 7478 0400, www.cosstores.com). **Topshop**'s massive, throbbing flagship (214 Oxford Street, W1W 8LG, 7636 7700, www.topshop.com) houses a boutique of high-fashion designer capsule ranges and vintage clothes, and a Hersheson (see p260).

Junky Styling
12 Dray Walk, Old Truman Brewery, 91-95 Brick Lane, Spitalfields, E1 6RF (7247 1883/ www.junkystyling.co.uk). Liverpool Street tube/rail. **Open** 11am-7pm daily. **Credit** AmEx, MC, V. **Map** p403 S5.
Junky offers an innovative take on second-hand clothes that fits in with our increased eco-awareness. Owners Kerry Seager and Anni Saunders take two or more formal garments (a pinstripe suit and a tweed jacket, say) and recycle them into an entirely new piece (skirts £50-£200, jackets £100-£350).

▶ *Also on Dray Walk, A Butcher of Distinction (no.11, 7770 6111, www.butcherofdistinction.com) is all understated cool with its denim and brogues.*

★ Three Threads
47-49 Charlotte Road, Shoreditch, EC2A 3QT (7749 0503/www.thethreethreads.com). Old Street tube/rail. **Open** 11am-7pm Mon-Sat; noon-5pm Sun. **Credit** MC, V. **Map** p403 R4.
Free beer, a jukebox well stocked with dad rock and conveniently placed bar stools around the till… the Three Threads tempts even the most shop-phobic male. While the threads themselves come in the form of exclusive, cult labels such as Japan's Tenderloin, Swedish outerwear by Fjall Raven, Danish label Won Hundred, and New York's Built by Wendy, the vibe is more like a pal's house. It now also stocks womenswear, from Carhartt, YMC, and bags from Mimi, as well as Pointers shoes for men and women.

Tailors

Chris Kerr
52 Berwick Street, Soho, W1F 8SL (7437 3727/ www.eddiekerr.co.uk). Oxford Circus tube. **Open** 8am-5.30pm Mon-Fri; 8.30am-1pm Sat. **Credit** MC, V. **Map** p406 V2.

Luella. *See p250.*

Chris Kerr, son of legendary 1960s tailor Eddie Kerr, is the man to see if Savile Row's prices or attitude aren't to your liking. The versatile Kerr has no house style; instead he makes every suit to each client's exact specifications – and those clients include Johnny Depp and David Walliams. The ideal place to commission your first bespoke suit.

Timothy Everest

35 Bruton Place, Mayfair, W1J 6NS (7629 6236/ www.timothyeverest.co.uk). Bond Street tube. **Open** 10am-6pm Mon-Fri; 11am-5pm alternate Sat. **Credit** AmEx, MC, V. **Map** p400 H7.

One-time apprentice to the legendary Tommy Nutter, Everest is a star of the latest generation of London tailors. He is well known for his relaxed 21st-century definition of style.

▶ *Finish off the outfit with bespoke shoes from Foster & Son (83 Jermyn Street, St James's, SW1Y 6JD, 7930 5385, www.wsfoster.com).*

Vintage & second-hand

Luna & Curious (*see p259*) has a reasonably priced selection of reconditioned pieces, while **Dover Street Market** (*see p250*) houses an outpost of LA store Decades.

★ Beyond Retro

112 Cheshire Street, Spitalfields, E2 6EJ (7613 3636/ www.beyondretro.com). Liverpool Street tube/rail. **Open** 10am-6pm Mon-Wed, Fri-Sun; 10am-8pm Thur. **Credit** MC, V. **Map** p405 S4.

This enormous bastion of second-hand clothing and accessories is the starting point for many an expert stylist, thrifter or fashion designer on the hunt for bargains and inspiration. The 10,000 items on the warehouse floor include '50s dresses, cowboy boots and denim hot pants, many under £20. *Photo p249.* **Other locations** 58-59 Great Marlborough Street, Soho, W1F 7JY (7434 1406).

Brick Lane Thrift Store

68 Sclater Street, off Brick Lane, Spitalfields, E1 6HR (7739 0242). Aldgate East tube/Liverpool Street tube/rail. **Open** noon-7pm daily. **Credit** AmEx, DC, MC, V. **Map** p403 S4.

At this new second-hand shop, almost everything is a magical £10 or less. Across two levels is a refined collection of best-sellers and popular lines from the East End warehouse, such as checked Western shirts. Men looking for the perfect trans-seasonal jacket should have a look at the rails of Harringtons. **Other locations** East End Thrift Store, Unit 1A, Watermans Building, Assembly Passage, Stepney, E1 4UT (7423 9700).

Girl Can't Help It

Alfie's Antique Market, 13-25 Church Street, Marylebone, NW8 8DT (7724 8984/www.thegirl canthelpit.com). Edgware Road tube/Marylebone

THE BEST OUT-THERE APPA[REL]

For established avant-g[arde]
B store. *See p249.*

For Shoreditch style
No-one. *See p250.*

For rising catwalk stars
Browns. *See p249.*

tube/rail. **Open** 10am-6pm Tue-Sat. **Credit** AmEx, MC, V. **Map** p395 E4.

Exuberant New Yorker Sparkle Moore and her Dutch partner Jasja Boelhouwer preside over the cache of vintage Hollywood kitsch. For ladies there are red-carpet gowns and 1950s circle skirts (£100-£350), plus glam accessories such as leopardprint shoes. The suave menswear encompasses Hawaiian shirts (from £50) and tiki-themed bar glasses.

Old Hat

66 Fulham High Street, Fulham, SW6 3LQ (7610 6558). Putney Bridge tube. **Open** 10.30am-6.30pm Mon-Sat. **Credit** MC, V.

A haunt of stylists and design teams from brands such as Burberry and Dunhill, David Saxby's menswear emporium is perfect for those with lord of the manor pretensions without the trust fund to match. Savile Row suits can be had for £100.

Rellik

8 Golborne Road, Ladbroke Grove, W10 5NW (8962 0089/www.relliklondon.co.uk). Westbourne Park tube. **Open** 10am-6pm Tue-Sat. **Credit** AmEx, DC, MC, V.

This celeb fave was set up in 2000 by three Portobello market stallholders: Fiona Stuart, Claire Stansfield and Steven Philip. The trio have different tastes, which means there's a mix of pieces by the likes of Halston, Vivienne Westwood, Bill Gibb, Christian Dior and the ever-popular Ossie Clark.

▶ *Oxfam's first 'boutique' second-hand store is over the Westway at 245 Westbourne Grove (7229 5000, www.oxfam.org.uk).*

FASHION ACCESSORIES & SERVICES

Clothing hire

Lipman & Sons

22 Charing Cross Road, Soho, WC2H 0HR (7240 2310/www.lipmanandsons.co.uk). Leicester Square tube. **Open** 9am-6pm Mon-Wed, Fri Sat; 9am-8pm Thur. **Credit** AmEx, DC, MC, V. **Map** p407 X4.

Reliable, long-standing formalwear specialist.

...ng & repairs

...ritish Invisible Mending Service

32 Thayer Street, Marylebone, W1U 2QT (7935 2487/www.invisible-mending.co.uk). Bond Street tube. **Open** 8.30am-5.30pm Mon-Fri; 10am-1pm Sat. **No credit cards. Map** p398 G5.
Family-run for over 50 years, with 24hr service.

Celebrity Cleaners

9 Greens Court, Soho, W1F 0HJ (7437 5324). Piccadilly Circus tube. **Open** 8.30am-6.30pm Mon-Fri. **No credit cards. Map** p406 W3.
Dry-cleaner to West End theatres and the ENO.
Other location Neville House, 27 Page Street, Pimlico, SW1P 4JJ (7821 1777).

Fifth Avenue Shoe Repairers

41 Goodge Street, Fitzrovia, W1T 2PY (7636 6705). Goodge Street tube. **Open** 8am-6.30pm Mon-Fri; 10am-6pm Sat. **Credit** (over £20) AmEx, MC, V. **Map** p398 J5.
High-calibre, speedy shoe repairs.

Hats

Bates the Hatter

21A Jermyn Street, St James's, SW1Y 6HP (7734 2722/www.bates-hats.co.uk). Piccadilly Circus tube. **Open** 9am-5.15pm Mon-Fri; 9.30am-4pm Sat. **Credit** AmEx, DC, MC, V. **Map** p400 J7.
With its topper-shaped sign and old-fashioned interior, Bates is a specialist gem. The traditional headwear spans panamas to tweed deerstalkers by way of dapper flat caps and, of course, classy top hats.

Philip Treacy

69 Elizabeth Street, Belgravia, SW1W 9PJ (7730 3992/www.philiptreacy.co.uk). Sloane Square tube. **Open** 10am-6pm Mon-Fri; 11am-5pm Sat. **Credit** AmEx, MC, V. **Map** p400 G10.
Hats by the king of couture headgear are not for the faint-hearted, although the ready-to-wear collection (think bold colours, graphic or animal prints, and oversized details) is tamer than the OTT catwalk creations. Men are catered for with sleek styles, and Treacy has branched out into bags.

Bags & luggage

Harrods (*see p242*) and **Selfridges** (*see p243*) have excellent selections of luggage and bags.

★ Ally Capellino

9 Calvert Avenue, Shoreditch, E2 7JP (7613 3073/www.allycapellino.co.uk). Liverpool Street tube/rail. **Open** noon-6pm Wed-Fri; 10am-6pm Sat; 11am-4pm Sun. **Credit** AmEx, MC, V. **Map** p403 R4.

The Rise of Mount Street

The stuffy Mayfair street that's in danger of becoming cool.

Mount Street, with its dignified Victorian terracotta façades and by-appointment art galleries, has seen a flurry of openings that have given it a surprisingly youthful twist. A street traditionally occupied by

the likes of master butcher **Allens of Mayfair** (no.117) and cigar shop **Sautter** (no.106), with its dusty collection of antique crocodile skin cigar cases, began to take on a new identity with the opening of Britain's first **Marc Jacobs** (no.24-25) boutique. It was the first of several shops to have been cherry-picked by real-estate consultants Wilson McHardy, who were charged with reinvigorating the area.

Another red-hot name to arrive is revered shoe-designer **Christian Louboutin** (no.17), whose storefront display features a woman prancing nonchalantly out of a giant gilded egg. Parisian perfumer **Annick Goutal** has opened shop at no.109, and contemporary jeweller **Fiona Knapp** will soon move in next door. A stand-alone **Marc by Marc Jacobs** is due to open at no.44 in spring 2009, while at no.12, near the refurbished Connaught (*see p183*), the **Balenciaga** (no.12) has set its super-chic clothing against a glowing sci-fi interior – really not very Mayfair at all.

The full range of Ally Capellino's stylishly understated unisex bags, wallets and purses. Prices start at £39 for a cute leather coin purse, rising to £300 for larger, more structured models, such as the large Bossy shoulder bag in lovely tanned brown leather.
► *For more sleek clutches and roomy satchels, head just off Brick Lane to Mimi (40 Cheshire Street, 7729 6699, www.mimiberry.co.uk).*

Globe-Trotter

54-55 Burlington Arcade, Mayfair, W1J 0LB (7529 5950/www.globe-trotterltd.com). Green Park tube. **Open** 10am-6pm Mon-Sat. **Credit** AmEx, MC, V. **Map** p400 J7.
Globe-Trotter's indestructible steamer-trunk-style luggage, available here in various sizes and colours, accompanied the Queen on honeymoon. Iconic Mackintosh coats share shop space.
► *After luggage that's a solution rather than an investment? The Marks & Spencer chain (www.marksandspencer.co.uk) does reliable basics.*

Lingerie & underwear

Agent Provocateur is now a glossy global chain but the original outpost of the shop that popularised high-class kink is still in Soho (6 Broadwick Street, W1V 1FH, 7439 0229, www.agentprovocateur.com). **Marks & Spencer** (www.marksandspencer.co.uk) is a reliable bet for men's and women's smalls. For serious bespoke service, try royal corsetière **Rigby & Peller** (22A Conduit Street, Mayfair, W1S 2XT, 7491 2200, www.rigbyandpeller.com).

Alice & Astrid

30 Artesian Road, Notting Hill, W2 5DD (7985 0888/www.aliceandastrid.com). Royal Oak tube. **Open** 10am-6pm Mon-Fri; 11am-6pm Sat. **Credit** AmEx, DC, MC, V. **Map** p394 A6.
The lingerie and loungewear displayed in this sweet little whitewashed shop is feminine and flirtatious rather than overtly sexy. Light cotton and silk dominate and seasonally changing prints include carrots, daisies and polka dots in tasteful pale shades, with items such as three-quarter-length bloomers, drawstring pyjama trousers and pretty camisoles.

Bordello

55 Great Eastern Street, Shoreditch, EC2A 3HP (7503 3334/www.bordello-london.com). Old Street tube/rail. **Open** 12.30-7.30pm Tue, Wed, Fri, Sat; 12.30- 9.30pm Thur. **Credit** MC, V. **Map** p403 R4.
Seductive yet welcoming, Bordello stocks luxurious lingerie by Damaris, Mimi Holliday, Myla, Buttress & Snatch and Pussy Glamore. Summer 2008 saw the introduction of Aussie swimwear label Jemma Jube, and Flamingo Sands bikinis will be added soon. The edgy vibe appeals to East End glamazons, first-daters and off-duty burlesque stars.

Jewellery

There are also some lovely pieces for sale in **Contemporary Applied Arts** (*see p259*).

Ec one

41 Exmouth Market, Clerkenwell, EC1R 4QL (7713 6185/www.econe.co.uk). Farringdon tube/rail. **Open** 10am-6pm Mon-Wed, Fri; 11am-7pm Thur; 10.30am-6pm Sat. **Credit** AmEx, MC, V. **Map** p402 N4.
Jos and Alison Skeates showcase jewellery from more than 50 designers, including serious statement pieces (with prices to match) by Jos. There's plenty of choice for those on tighter budgets, including Amanda Coleman's cupcake stud earrings (£27) and Alex Monroe's gorgeous fripperies for under £200. **Other locations** 56 Ledbury Road, Notting Hill, W11 2RH (7243 8811); 186 Chiswick High Road, Turnham Green, W4 1PP (8995 9515).

Garrard

24 Albemarle Street, Mayfair, W1S 4HT (0870 871 8888/www.garrard.com). Bond Street or Green Park tube. **Open** 10am-6pm Mon-Fri; 10am-5pm Sat, Sun. **Credit** AmEx, DC, MC, V. **Map** p406 U5.
Although Jade Jagger's contract as creative director ended a couple of years back, her impact is still felt: she managed to modernise the Crown Jeweller's diamond-studded designs in such a way as to appeal to a new generation of cash-heavy bling-seekers.

Kabiri

37 Marylebone High Street, Marylebone, W1U 4QE (7224 1808/www.kabiri.co.uk). Baker Street tube. **Open** 10am-6.30pm Mon-Sat; noon-5pm Sun. **Credit** AmEx, MC, V. **Map** p398 G5.
The work of more than 100 jewellery designers, from little-known talent to established names – is showcased in this small shop. Innovation and a sense of humour are linking themes. Cairo-based jeweller Dima has collaborated with fashion designer Giles Deacon to create a collection that fuses the modern and ancient (from £585 for a garnet snake ring). There's a Selfridges concession.

Shoes

Among the best footwear chains are **Office** (57 Neal Street, Covent Garden, WC2H 4NP, 7379 1896, www.office.co.uk), with fashion-forward, funky styles for guys and girls at palatable prices; **Kurt Geiger** (198 Regent Street, W1B 5TP, 3238 0044, www.kurtgeiger.com) and **Russell & Bromley** (24-25 New Bond Street, W1S 2PS, 7629 6903, www.russellandbromley.co.uk), both turning out classy takes on key trends for both sexes; and **Clarks** (476 Oxford Street, W1C 1LD, 7629 9609, www.clarks.co.uk), inventor of the iconic Desert Boot.

CONSUME

Georgina Goodman

44 Old Bond Street, Mayfair, W1F 4GD
(7493 7673/www.georginagoodman.com).
Green Park tube. **Open** 10am-6pm Mon-Wed,
Fri, Sat; 10am-7pm Thur. **Credit** AmEx, DC,
MC, V. **Map** p400 H8.

Goodman started her business crafting sculptural,
made-to-measure footwear from a single piece of
untreated vegetan leather, and a couture service is
still available at her airy, gallery-like shop (from
£750 for women, £1,200 for men). The ready-to-wear
range (from £165 for her popular slippers) brings
her individualistic approach to a wider customer
base; signature flourishes include hand-painted
materials and innovative heel shapes.

Jeffery-West

16 Piccadilly Arcade, St James's, SW1Y 6NH
(7499 3360/www.jeffery-west.co.uk). Green Park
or Piccadilly Circus tube. **Open** 10am-6pm Mon-
Wed, Fri, Sat; 10am-7pm Thur. **Credit** AmEx,
MC, V. **Map** p406 V5.

With its playboy vampire's apartment feel – red
walls, objets d'art, a skeleton in the window – this
shop is the perfect showcase for Marc Jeffery and
Guy West's rakish men's shoes, adored by modern
day dandies. Made to exacting traditional standards,
the stand-out Punched Gibson in polished burgundy
(£210) looks sharp and has a bewitching lustre.
Other locations 16 Cullum Street, the City,
EC3M 7JJ (7626 4699).

★ Sniff

1 Great Titchfield Street, Fitzrovia, W1W 8AU
(7299 3560/www.sniff.co.uk). Oxford Circus
tube. **Open** 10am-7pm Mon-Fri; 10am-6.30pm
Sat; noon-6pm Sun. **Credit** AmEx, MC, V.
Map p406 U1.

Sniff aims to provide an alternative to your average
high street shoe store, selling a range of shoes for
men and women that covers every eventuality from
sports to parties. There's a well-balanced mix of
brands, established – Paco Gil, Birkenstock, Ed
Hardy, French Sole – and up-and-coming – British
designer Miss L Fire whose eccentric collection
includes wedges covered in a strawberry motif.
Other locations 11 St Christopher's Place,
W1U 1NG (7935 0034); 115 Commercial Street,
Spitalfields, E1 6BG (7375 1580).

INSIDE TRACK EAT FASHION

For a quirky gift idea, T-Shirt Patisserie
takes some beating – order a plain T-
Shirt, decorated with the design of your
choice, at www.tshirtpatisserie.co.uk,
then pick it up from **Luna & Curious**
(*see p259*) in particularly sweet
packaging from £20.

Terra Plana

64 Neal Street, Covent Garden, WC2H 9P
(7379 5959/www.terraplana.com). Covent
Garden tube. **Open** 10am-7pm Mon-Thur, Sat;
10am-7.30pm Fri; noon-6pm Sun. **Credit** AmEx,
MC, V. **Map** p407 Y2.

Terra Plana is on a mission to revive artisan shoe-
making, producing eco-friendly shoes that are
stitched rather than glued and made from chrome-
free, vegetable-tanned leather and, often, recycled
materials. Better still, the utterly contemporary
styles are cool – no need to sacrifice fashion for ethics.
Other locations 124 Bermondsey Street,
Borough, SE1 3TX (7407 3758).

Tracey Neuls

29 Marylebone Lane, Marylebone, W1U 2NQ
(7935 0039/www.tn29.com). Bond Street tube.
Open 11am-6.30pm Mon-Fri; noon-5pm Sat.
Credit AmEx, MC, V. **Map** p398 G5.

Tracey Neuls challenges footwear conventions, right
down to the way her shoes are displayed – here they
dangle from the ceiling on ribbons. Her TN_29 label
(from £150) has gathered a global cult following, but
the Cordwainers-trained Canadian designer is based
in this small shop/studio. The new Tracey Neuls line
is handmade in Italy using luxurious materials.

FOOD & DRINK

Bakeries

Konditor & Cook

22 Cornwall Road, Waterloo, SE1 8TW (7261
0456/www.konditorandcook.com). Waterloo tube/
rail. **Open** 7.30am-6.30pm Mon-Fri; 8.30am-2.30pm
Sat. **Credit** AmEx, MC, V. **Map** p404 N10.

Gerhard Jenne caused a stir when he opened this
bakery in 1993, selling lavender-flavoured cakes
rudie gingerbread people for grown-ups. Success
continued with fashion-forward ideas such as Magic
Cakes, which spell out your name in individually
decorated squares. The brand is now a mini-chain,
also selling quality pre-packed salads and sarnies.
Other locations throughout the city.

Primrose Bakery

69 Gloucester Avenue, Primrose Hill, NW1 8LD
(7483 4222/www.primrosebakery.org.uk). Chalk
Farm tube. **Open** 8.30am-6pm Mon-Sat; 10am-
5.30pm Sun. **Credit** MC, V.

Catch a serious sugar high with Martha Swift's pretty, generously sized cupcakes in vanilla, coffee and
lemon flavours. The tiny, retro-styled shop also sells
peanut butter cookies and layer cakes.

Drinks

Algerian Coffee Stores

52 Old Compton Street, Soho, W1V 6PB (7437
2480/www.algcoffee.co.uk). **Open** 9am-7pm Mon-

Wed; 9am-9pm Thur, Fri; 9am-8pm Sat. **Credit** AmEx, DC, MC, V. **Map** p406 W3.

For 120 years, this unassuming little shop has been trading over this same wooden counter, from these same wooden shelves and display case. The range of coffees is broad, with house blends sold alongside single-origin beans, and serious teas and brewing hardware are also available.

▶ *Just passing? Take away a single or double espresso for 70p, a cappuccino or latte for 95p.*

Berry Bros & Rudd

3 St James's Street, St James's, SW1A 1EG (7396 9600/www.bbr.com). Green Park tube. **Open** 10am-6pm Mon-Fri; 10am-5pm Sat. **Credit** AmEx, DC, MC, V. **Map** p400 J8.

Britain's oldest wine merchant has been trading on the same premises since 1698 and its heritage is reflected in its panelled sales and tasting rooms. Burgundy- and claret-lovers will drool at the hundreds of wines, but there are also decent selections from elsewhere in Europe and the New World.

Cadenhead's Covent Garden Whisky Shop

26 Chiltern Street, Covent Garden, W1U 7QF (7935 6999). Baker Street tube. **Open** 10.30am-6.30pm Mon-Sat. **Credit** DC, MC, V. **Map** p407 Z3.

Cadenhead's is a survivor of a rare breed: the independent whisky bottler. And its shop is one of a kind – at least in London. Cadenhead's selects barrels from distilleries all over Scotland and bottles them without filtration or any other intervention.

▶ *For a wider range of spirits – by their own account, the widest in London – try Gerry's (74 Old Compton Street, Soho, W1D 4UW, 7734 4215, www.gerrys.uk.com).*

★ Postcard Teas

9 Dering Street, Mayfair, W1S 1AG (7629 3654/ www.postcardteas.com). Bond Street or Oxford Circus tube. **Open** 10.30am-6.30pm Tue-Sat. **Credit** AmEx, MC, V. **Map** p398 H6.

The range in this exquisite little shop is not huge, but it is selected with care: for instance, all its Darjeeling teas (£2.95-£4.75/50g) are currently sourced from the Goomtee estate, regarded as the best in the region. There's a central table for those who want to try a pot; downstairs is a selection of vintage postcards from the collection of art dealer Antony d'Offay, father of the shop's owner Timothy.

General

Sainsbury's (www.sainsburys.co.uk) and **Tesco** (www.tesco.com) supermarkets are everywhere, and superior-quality **Waitrose** has a central branch on Marylebone High Street (nos.98-101, 7935 4787, www.waitrose.com).

Whole Foods Market

63-97 Kensington High Street, Kensington, W8 5SE (7368 4500/www.wholefoodmarket. com). High Street Kensington tube. **Open** 8am-10pm Mon-Sat; 10am-6pm Sun. **Credit** AmEx, DC, MC, V.

Borough Market. See p258.

CONSUME

The London flagship of the American health-food supermarket chain occupies the handsome deco department store that was once Barkers. There are several eateries on the premises.

Markets

A resurgence of farmers' markets in the capital reflects growing concern over provenance and the environment. Two of the most central are in Marylebone (Cramer Street car park, corner of Moxton Street, off Marylebone High Street, 10am-2pm Sun) and Notting Hill (behind Waterstone's, access via Kensington Place, 9am-1pm Sat). For more, see **London Farmers' Markets** (7833 0338, www.lfm.org.uk).

★ Borough Market
Southwark Street, Borough, SE1 (7407 1002/ www.boroughmarket.org.uk). London Bridge tube/rail. **Open** 11am-5pm Thur; noon-6pm Fri; 9am-4pm Sat. **Map** p404 P8.
The foodie's favourite market occupies a sprawling site near London Bridge, but campaigners are currently battling a threat in the form of a rail viaduct planned for above the space. Gourmet goodies run the gamut from Flour Power City Bakery's organic loaves to chorizo and rocket rolls from Spanish specialist Brindisa, plus rare-breed meats, fruit and veg, cakes and all manner of preserves, oils and teas – head out hungry to take advantage of the numerous free samples. The market is now open on Thursdays, when it tends to be quieter than at always-mobbed weekends. *Photos p257.*

Specialist

A Gold
42 Brushfield Street, Spitalfields, E1 6AG (7247 2487). Liverpool Street tube/rail. **Open** 9.30am-5.30pm Mon-Fri; 11am-6pm Sat; 10am-6pm Sun. **Credit** AmEx, MC, V. **Map** p405 R5.
A Gold was flying the flag for British foods long before it became fashionable to do so. Opposite Spitalfields Market, it resembles a village shop from a bygone era. The baked goods alone take customers on a whistlestop tour of Britain: Cornish saffron

cakes, Dundee cakes, Welsh cakes, and (of course) Eccles cakes made in Lancashire. English mead, proper marmalade and teas, unusual chutneys and traditional sweets make great gifts.

Albion Emporium
38 Tavistock Street, Covent Garden, WC2E 7PB (7240 7222/www.thealbionemporium.co.uk). Covent Garden tube. **Open** 8.30am-7pm Mon-Fri; 10am-7pm Sat; 11am-6pm Sun. **Credit** MC, V. **Map** p407 Z3.
See p251 **Things Are What They Used to Be**.

Daylesford Organic
44B Pimlico Road, Belgravia, SW1W 8LP (7881 8060/www.daylesfordorganic.com). Sloane Square tube. **Open** 8am-8pm Mon-Sat; 10am-4pm Sun. **Credit** AmEx, MC, V. **Map** p400 G11.
Part of a wave of chic purveyors of health food, this excellent offshoot of Lady Carole Bamford's Cotswold-based farm shop is set over three floors, and includes a café. Expect to find a selection of ready-made dishes, store-cupboard staples such as pulses, pasta and sauces, cakes and breads, and fine charcuterie and cheeses.

Hope & Greenwood
1 Russell Street, Covent Garden, WC2B 5JD (7240 3314/www.hopeandgreenwood.co.uk). Covent Garden tube. **Open** 11am-7.30pm Mon-Wed; 11am-8pm Thur, Fri; 10.30am-7.30pm Sat 11.30am-5.30pm Sun. **Credit** MC, V. **Map** p407 Z3.
See p251 **Things Are What They Used to Be**.

★ Neal's Yard Dairy
17 Shorts Gardens, Covent Garden, WC2H 9UP (7240 5700/www.nealsyarddairy.co.uk). Covent Garden tube. **Open** 11am-7pm Mon-Thur; 10am-7pm Fri, Sat. **Credit** MC, V. **Map** p407 Y2.
Neal's Yard buys from small farms and creameries and matures the cheeses in its own cellars until ready to sell in peak condition. Names such as Stinking Bishop and Lincolnshire Poacher are as evocative as the aromas in the shop. It's best to walk in and ask what's good today – you'll be given various tasters by the well-trained staff.
Other locations 6 Park Street, Borough Market, SE1 9AB (7645 3554).

Paul A Young Fine Chocolates
33 Camden Passage, Islington, N1 8EA (7424 5750, www.payoung.net). Angel tube. **Open** 11am-6pm Wed, Thur, Sat; 11am-7pm Fri; noon-5pm Sun. **Credit** AmEx, MC, V. **Map** p402 O2.
A gorgeous boutique with almost everything – chocolates, cakes, ice-cream – made in the downstairs kitchen and finished in front of customers. Young is a respected pâtissier as well as chocolatier and has an astute chef's palate for flavour combinations: the white chocolate with rose masala is addictive.

THE BEST
TALKING-POINT SOUVENIRS

Limited-edition art
Shelf. *See p259.*

For exquisite hand-picked tea
Postcard Teas. *See p257.*

For London sauce
Coco de Mer. *See p259.*

▶ *England's oldest chocolatier Prestat (14 Princes Arcade, St James's, SW1Y 6DS, 7629 4838, www.prestat.co.uk) offers unusual and traditional flavours in brightly coloured gift boxes.*

GIFTS

★ Coco de Mer

23 Monmouth Street, WC2H 9DD (7836 8882/ www.coco-de-mer.co.uk). Covent Garden tube. **Open** 11am-7pm Mon-Wed, Fri, Sat; 11am-8pm Thur; noon-6pm Sun. **Credit** AmEx, MC, V. **Map** p407 Y2.

London's most glamorous erotic emporium sells a variety of tasteful books, toys and lingerie, from jewelled nipple clips via glass dildos that double as objets d'art to a Marie Antoinette costume of crotchless culottes and corset. Trying on items is fun as well: there are peepshow-style velvet changing rooms that allow your lover to watch you undress from a 'confession box' next door.

Contemporary Applied Arts

2 Percy Street, Fitzrovia, W1T 1DD (7436 2344/ www.caa.org.uk). Goodge Street or Tottenham Court Road tube. **Open** 10am-6pm Mon-Sat. **Credit** AmEx, MC, V. **Map** p399 K5.

This airy gallery, run by the charitable arts organisation, represents more than 300 makers. Work embraces functional pieces – textiles, tableware – as well as unique, purely decorative items, not least the jewellery. The ground floor hosts exhibitions by individual artists, or themed by craft, while in the basement shop are pieces for all pockets. Glass is always exceptional here.

★ James Smith & Sons

53 New Oxford Street, WC1A 1BL (7836 4731/ www.james-smith.co.uk). Holborn or Tottenham Court Road tube. **Open** 9.30am-5.15pm Mon-Fri; 10am-5.15pm Sat. **Credit** AmEx, MC, V. **Map** p407 Y1.

More than 175 years after it was established, this charming shop, with Victorian fittings still intact, is holding its own in the niche market of umbrellas and walking sticks. The stock here isn't the throwaway type of brollie that breaks at the first sign of bad weather. Lovingly crafted brollies, such as a classic City umbrella with a hickory crook at £110, are built to last and a repair service is offered.

Luna & Curious

198 Brick Lane, Spitalfields, E1 6SA (7033 4411/www.lunaandcurious.com). Aldgate East tube/Liverpool Street tube/rail. **Open** noon-6pm Thur-Sun. **Credit** MC, V. **Map** p405 S4.

The stock here, from vintage cocktail dresses to ultra-English teacups, is put together by a collective of young artisans. There's even jewellery made from ceramics, feathers and old embroidery from military jackets. Prices are surprisingly reasonable for products so lovingly put together.

★ Shelf

40 Cheshire Street, Spitalfields, E2 6EH (7739 9444/www.helpyourshelf.co.uk). Liverpool Street tube/rail. **Open** 1-6pm Fri, Sat; 11am-6pm Sun. **Credit** MC, V. **Map** p403 S4.

Artist Katy Hackney and costume designer Jane Petrie's gift shop-cum-gallery is a great place to pick up unique presents, such as Prague-based sculptor

CONSUME

Now You See Them

Pop-up shops have become an essential part of London's fashion scene.

Pop-up shops are the darlings of the fashion world: theatrical, unpredictable, unashamedly sought after. They are exactly how they sound, shops that 'pop-up' out of the blue, then disappear just as quickly – a day, a month, even a year later.

The concept came from Russ Miller, who in 2003 used a desolate warehouse in New York's trendy SoHo to display limited editions of the Vacant brand for a restricted time period. It was an instant success, so London wasn't slow to follow. Since then, brands as mainstream as Umbro (England football kit manufacturer, kids!) have showcased new collections in pop-up shops, no doubt hoping to give themselves a bit of edge. Oki-Ni, in collaboration with designers such as Alexander McQueen, had a short-term

shop in Little Portland Street, while Rei Kawakubo's **Dover Street Market** (*see p250*) has become a regular location for such ventures, with both Chanel and Comme des Garçons popping up there. Even **Selfridges** (*see p243*) got on-trend with a mini pop-up shop to showcase designs created for Graduate Fashion Week last year.

The ephemeral nature of pop-ups epitomises the rapid changes that characterise fashion itself. Marketing gimmick or not, they neatly blur the distinction between entertainment and retail. They are also, of course, impossible to predict: head to the Consume section of the weekly *Time Out* magazine or check www.timeout.com for news of the coolest new appearances this year.

Rough Trade East. See p264.

Pravoslav Rada's enigmatic ceramics, or one of the limited-edition collaborations with east London artist Rob Ryan, such as a recent series of 50 'polite notices' on vitreous enamel plaques (£250 each), produced by the supplier to London Underground.

HEALTH & BEAUTY
Complementary medicine

Hale Clinic
7 Park Crescent, Marylebone, W1B 1PF (7631 0156/www.haleclinic.com). Great Portland Street or Regent's Park tube. **Open** 9am-9pm Mon-Fri; 9am-5pm Sat. **Credit** (shop only) AmEx, MC, V. **Map** p398 H4.

Over 100 practitioners are affiliated to the Hale Clinic, which was founded with the aim of integrating complementary and conventional medicine and opened by the Prince of Wales in 1988. The treatment list is a veritable A-Z of alternative therapies, while the shop stocks supplements, skincare products and books.

Hairdressers & barbers

If the options we list below are out of your range, then try a branch of **Mr Topper's** (7631 3233; £6 men, £10-£12 women).

Daniel Hersheson
45 Conduit Street, Mayfair, W1F 2YN (7434 1747/www.danielhersheson.com). Oxford Circus tube. **Open** 9am-6pm Mon-Wed, Sat; 9am-8pm Thur, Fri. **Credit** AmEx, MC, V. **Map** p406 U3.

Despite its upmarket location, this modern two-storey salon isn't at all snooty, with a staff of very talented cutters and colourists. Prices start at £55 (£35 for men), though you'll pay £250 for a cut with Daniel. There's also a menu of therapies; the swish Harvey Nichols (*see p242*) branch has a dedicated spa.

Hersheson's Blow Dry Bar at Topshop (*see p252*; call 7927 7888 to book) offers catwalk looks for £21.
▶ *The undisputed queen of colour, with clientele including the Duchess of Cornwall and Liz Hurley, is fellow Mayfair hairdresser Jo Hansford (19 Mount Street, 7495 7774, www.johansford.com).*

F Flittner
86 Moorgate, the City, EC2M 6SE (7606 4750/ www.fflittner.com). Moorgate tube/rail. **Open** 8am-6pm Mon-Wed, Fri; 8am-6.30pm Thur. **Credit** AmEx, MC, V. **Map** p405 Q6.

In business since 1904, Flittner seems not to have noticed that the 21st century has begun. Behind beautifully frosted doors (marked 'Saloon') is a handsome room, done out with an array of classic barber's furniture that's older than your gran. Within these hushed confines, black-coated barbers deliver straightforward cuts (dry cuts £13.50-£15.50, wet cuts £18-£22) and shaves with skill and dignity.
▶ *For a modern take on the art of the wet shave, try Murdock (340 Old Street, Shoreditch, EC1V 9DS, 7729 2288, www.murdocklondon.com).*

Fish
30 D'Arblay Street, Soho, W1F 8ER (7494 2398/ www.fishweb.co.uk). Leicester Square tube. **Open** 10am-7pm Mon-Wed, Fri; 10am-8pm Thur; 10am-5pm Sat. **Credit** MC, V. **Map** p406 V2.

This relaxed and buzzing salon was a fishmonger's, hence the name. Staff are understatedly stylish and laid-back, offering a good mix of classic and fashion cuts for men and women, as well as own-brand hair products. Prices from £34 for men, £41 for women.

Opticians

Dollond & Aitchison (www.danda.co.uk) and **Specsavers** (www.specsavers.com) are chain opticians with branches on most high streets.

CONSUME

Cutler & Gross

16 Knightsbridge Green, Knightsbridge,
SW1X 7QL (7581 2250/www.cutlerandgross.
com). Knightsbridge tube. **Open** 9.30am-7pm
Mon-Sat; noon-4pm Sun. Credit AmEx, MC, V.
Map p397 F9.
Fashion is as important as focal length here. C&G's
stock of handmade frames runs from Andy Warhol-
inspired glasses to naturally light buffalo-horn
frames. Vintage eyewear from the likes of Ray-Ban
and Courrèges is at the sister shop down the road.
Other locations 7 Knightsbridge Green,
Knightsbridge, SW1X 7QL (7590 9995).

Michel Guillon Vision Clinic & Eye Boutique

35 Duke of York Square, King's Road, Chelsea,
SW3 4LY (7730 2142/www.michelguillon.com).
Sloane Square tube. **Open** 10am-7pm Mon-Thur,
Sat; 9.30am-7.30pm Fri. **Credit** AmEx, MC, V.
Map p397 F11.
Lined with striking blue cabinets, this ultra-modern
shop was designed by Ab (son of architect Richard)
Rogers. The changing range of designer frames –
Japanese Yellow Plus, Sama's retro-style two-tone
creations – is as edgy as the interior decor. Michel
Guillon is also a leading contact lens specialist.

Pharmacies

National chain **Boots** (www.boots.com) has
branches across the city, offering dispensing
pharmacies and photo processing. The store
on Piccadilly Circus (44-46 Regent Street, W1B
5RA, 7734 6126) is open until midnight (except
Sunday when it closes at 6pm).

DR Harris

29 St James's Street, St James's, SW1A 1HB
(7930 3915/www.drharris.co.uk). Green Park
or Piccadilly Circus tube. **Open** 8.30am-6pm
Mon-Fri; 9.30am-5pm Sat. **Credit** AmEx,
MC, V. **Map** p400 J8.
Founded in 1790, this venerable chemist has a royal
warrant. Wood-and-glass cabinets are filled with
bottles, jars and old-fashioned shaving brushes and
manicure kits. The smartly packaged own-brand
products such as the bright blue Crystal Eye Gel
have a cult following.

Shops

Eco pioneer **Neal's Yard Remedies** (15 Neal's
Yard, WC2H 9DP (7379 7222, www.ncalsyard
remedies.com) now has several central London
locations, each offering fine organic products, a
herbal dispensary and complementary therapies.
Ever-growing beauty chain **Space NK** (8-10
Broadwick Street, W1F 8HW, 7287 2667,
www.spacenk.com) is a great source of
niche skincare and make-up brands.

Liz Earle Naturally Active Skincare

53 Duke of York Square, King's Road, Chelsea,
SW3 4LY (7730 9191/www.lizearle.com). Sloane
Square tube. **Open** 10am-7pm Mon, Wed-Sat;
10.30pm-7pm Tue; 11am-5pm Sun. **Credit**
AmEx, MC, V. **Map** p397 F11.
Former beauty writer Liz Earle's hugely successful
botanical skincare range was previously only available from her HQ on the Isle of Wight. This London
flagship stocks the streamlined range of 23 products,
based on a simple, no-fuss regime of cleansing,
toning and moisturising. Superbalm is a calming
treatment for dry skin (£14.50). The 'minis' are a great
way to introduce yourself to the range (from £4).
► *On a corner of Sloane Square, Ortigia's sleek*
new flagship (no.55, 7730 2826, www.ortigia-
srl.com) sells divinely packaged smellies.

★ Lost in Beauty

117 Regent's Park Road, Primrose Hill, NW1
8UR (7586 4411/www.lostinbeauty.com). Chalk
Farm tube. **Open** 10.30am-7pm Mon-Fri;
10.30am-6.30pm Sat; noon-5.30pm Sun.
Credit AmEx, MC, V.
Kitted out with vintage shop fittings, this chic new
boutique stocks a well-edited array of beauty
brands, including Phyto, Australian brand Jurlique
(newly repackaged), Caudalie, Dr Hauschka Rodial,
REN, ZO1 sun-care products and Butter London nail
polish with supremely covetable colours.

Miller Harris

21 Bruton Street, Mayfair, W1J 6QD (7629
7750/www.millerharris.com). Bond Street or
Green Park tube. **Open** 10am-6pm Mon-Sat.
Credit AmEx, MC, V. **Map** p400 H7.
Grasse-trained British perfumer Lyn Harris's
distinctive, long-lasting scents, in their lovely
decorative packaging, are made with quality
natural extracts and oils. Perennial favourites
include Noix de Tubéreuse (£70/100ml), a lighter
and more palatable tuberose scent than many on
the market, and Citron Citron (£52/100ml), a
summery citrus-based fragrance.
Other locations 14 Needham Road, Notting
Hill, W11 2RP (7221 1545).

Spas & salons

Many luxury hotels – including the **Sanderson**
(*see p173*) and, when it reopens in spring, the
Dorchester (*see p184*) – make their spa
facilities available to the public.

Cowshed

119 Portland Road, Notting Hill, W11 4LN
(7078 1944/www.cowshedclarendoncross.com).
Holland Park tube. **Open** 9am-8pm Mon-Fri;
9am-7pm Sat; 10am-5pm Sun. **Credit** AmEx,
MC, V.

CONSUME

The London outpost of Babington House's Cowshed does its country cousin proud. The chic, white ground floor is buzzy, with a tiny café area across from a mani/pedi section, complete with retro mini-TVs. For facials, massages and waxing, head downstairs.

★ **Elemis Day Spa**
2-3 Lancashire Court, Mayfair, W1S 1EX
(7499 4995/www.elemis.com). Bond Street
tube. **Open** 9am-9pm Mon-Sat; 10am-6pm Sun.
Credit AmEx, MC, V. **Map** p398 H6.

This leading British spa brand's exotic, unisex retreat is tucked away down a cobbled lane off Bond Street. The elegantly ethnic treatment rooms are a lovely setting in which to relax and enjoy a spot of pampering, from wraps to results-driven facials.

Tattoos & piercings

Family Business
58 Exmouth Market, Clerkenwell, EC1R 4QE
(7278 9526/www.thefamilybusinesstattoo.com).

Foyled Again?

The paragon of eccentricity that became a successful bookshop.

Eccentric, iconic and fiercely independent, **Foyles** (*see p243*) is the grand dame of London's bookshops. Loved by an army of loyal customers (some have shopped here all their lives), it occupies a unique place in the capital's literary landscape. In March 2008, though, Christopher Foyle shocked staff by announcing his departure and appointing Sam Hussein, a businessman with no booktrade background, as CEO. Would this mean the end of a literary institution, a fixture since two brothers failed their civil service exams and decided to sell their textbooks in 1903?

Christopher inherited the business from his iron-willed aunt, Christina, who ran it from 1945 until six days before her death in 1999. By then, her refusal to modernise had begun to cause serious financial problems. Buying a book could take half an hour, because Christina refused to let assistants handle cash, creating a farcical situation where customers had to queue three times. 'Imagine if Kafka had gone into the book trade,' was one summation.

Christopher speaks passionately about the challenges he faced on inheriting the store. 'I had to decide whether to sell it, close it or turn it around. We had over £4 million in the bank, and so, partly for commercial and partly for sentimental reasons, I decided to try to save it.' This wasn't easy in an increasingly competitive market. 'The shop was in a state: ancient shelves, no computerisation (my aunt abhorred technology), handwritten signs. Our disorganisation was so notorious that one competitor advertised with the slogan "Foyled again? Try Dillons." Staff morale was awful: after workers went on strike in 1965, Christina refused to hire anyone for more than a year.'

Anyone walking into the freshly painted, well-lit, attractive shop that is Foyles today can see the fruits of Christopher's labours and even understand why he feels entitled to relax. But worries linger that the shop's individuality will disappear if the guardians of the brand are no longer there. Various spin-off stores have popped up, with Christopher's approval: the largest yet is to open in **Westfield London** (*see p241*). So, is Christopher's departure the end of an era? Not entirely: he hopes one of his daughters (both in their twenties) will step into their great-aunt's shoes. 'I'm certain there will still be a Foyles in a hundred years' time,' he says firmly. 'It's ready to face the future with its eccentricity and personality intact.'

CONSUME

Farringdon tube/rail. **Open** noon-7pm daily.
No credit cards. Map p402 N4.
This original, spacious studio is impressive, with decor that incorporates Catholic paraphernalia. Offering 'tasteful tattooing for first-timers, old-timers and serious collectors', it's large enough to accommodate six resident artists, including the celebrated Saira Hunjan.

Shangri-La Tattoo
52 Kingsland Road, Hoxton, E2 8DP (7739 3066).
Old Street tube/rail. **Open** 11am-6pm Mon-Sat.
No credit cards. Map p403 R3.
Run by former arts student Lesley Chan, this arty studio has its own exhibition space and sells prints and glossy books.

HOUSE & HOME

Antiques

Although boutiques have encroached on their territory, some quirky dealers remain on Islington's **Camden Passage** (off Upper Street, 7359 0190, www.camdenpassage antiques.com), especially in characterful Pierrepont Arcade. Marylebone's **Church Street** now the major area for shops, in a cluster around Alfie's Antique Market, but **Portobello Road** (*see p243*) remains the biggest, best-known market for antiques.

★ Alfie's Antique Market
13-25 Church Street, Marylebone, NW8 8DT
(7723 6066/www.alfiesantiques.com). Edgware Road tube/Marylebone tube/rail. **Open** 10am-6pm Tue-Sat. **Credit** varies. **Map** p395 E4.
Alfie's boasts over 100 dealers in vintage furniture and fashion, art, accessories, books, maps and more. Dodo Posters (on the first floor) do 1920s and '30s ads.

Antiquarius
131-141 King's Road, Chelsea, SW3 5PH (7823 3900/www.antiquarius.co.uk). Sloane Square tube, then 11, 19, 22, 319, 211 bus. **Open** 10am-6pm Mon-Sat. **Credit** varies. **Map** p397 E12.
Long-standing King's Road landmark houses around 60 dealers with specialisms from vintage trunks and jewellery to original film art.

Core One
The Gas Works, 2 Michael Road, Fulham, SW6 2AD. Fulham Broadway tube. **Open** 10am-6pm Mon-Fri; 11am-4pm Sat. **Credit** varies.
A group of antiques and 20th-century dealers has colonised this industrial building in Fulham, including Dean Antiques (7610 6997, www.deanantiques. co.uk) for dramatic pieces, Plinth (7371 7422) for quirky reconditioned vintage furniture and De Parma (7736 3384, www.deparma.com) for elegant mid-century design.

Grays Antique Market & Grays in the Mews
58 Davies Street, Mayfair, W1K 5LP & 1-7 Davies Mews, W1K 5AB (7629 7034/www.graysantiques. com). Bond Street tube. **Open** 10am-6pm Mon-Fri.
Credit varies. **Map** p398 H6.
Over 200 dealers have stalls in this smart covered market, selling anything from jewellery to rare books.

General

Habitat (121 Regent Street, W1B 4TB, 0844 499 1134, www.habitat.co.uk) is a good source of affordable modern design.

Conran Shop
Michelin House, 81 Fulham Road, Fulham, SW3 6RD (7589 7401/www.conran.co.uk). South Kensington tube. **Open** 10am-6pm Mon, Tue, Fri; 10am-7pm Wed, Thur; 10am-6.30pm Sat; noon-6pm Sun. **Credit** AmEx, MC, V. **Map** p397 E10.
Terence Conran's flagship store in the Fulham Road's beautiful 1909 Michelin Building showcases furniture and design for every room in the house as well as the garden; there are plenty of portable accessories, gadgets, books, stationery and toiletries that make great gifts or souvenirs.
Other locations 55 Marylebone High Street, Marylebone, W1U 5HS (7723 2223).

Labour & Wait
18 Cheshire Street, Spitalfields, E2 6EH (7729 6253/www.labourandwait.co.uk). Aldgate East tube/Liverpool Street tube/rail. **Open** by appointment Fri; 1-5pm Sat; 10am-5pm Sun. **Credit** MC, V. **Map** p403 S4.
This much-celebrated shop pays homage to timeless, unfaddy domestic goods that combine beauty with utility: think Victorian pantry crossed with 1950s kitchen. The quintessentially British homewares include traditional feather dusters (£8), tins of twine (£6.50), simple enamelware and sturdy canvas bags. Labour and Wait also has a space at concept store Dover Street Market (*see p250*).

Mint
70 Wigmore Street, Marylebone, W1U 2SF (7224 4406/www.mintshop.co.uk). Bond Street tube. **Open** 10.30am-6.30pm Mon-Wed, Fri, Sat; 10.30am-7.30pm Thur. **Credit** AmEx, DC, MC, V. **Map** p400 G6.

INSIDE TRACK
WAKE UP, SMELL THE TEA

Miller Harris (*see p261*) now serves a range of top-quality teas (sourced estimable **Postcard Teas**, see p2 cakes, to eat in or take away.

CONSUME

Surprising and inspirational, Mint is a compact two-level space full of globally sourced pieces from established designers and recent graduates alike. As well as statement furniture, there are more affordable items, such as Doris Banks's paper-thin ceramics glazed in gorgeous greens and oranges (pot with cover, £65) and Hella Jongerius's cushions (£150).

MUSIC & ENTERTAINMENT

CDs & records

HMV (www.hmv.co.uk) and **Zavvi** (www.zavvi.co.uk) are the big Oxford Street stores, but browsers head south: indie record stores cling on round Berwick and D'Arblay Streets.

Flashback
50 Essex Road, Islington, N1 8LR (7354 9356/www.flashback.co.uk). Angel tube then 38, 56, 73, 341 bus. **Open** 10am-7pm Mon-Sat; noon-6pm Sun. **Credit** AmEx, MC, V. **Map** p402 O1.
Stock is scrupulously organised at this second-hand treasure trove. The ground floor is dedicated to CDs, while the basement is vinyl-only: an ever-expanding jazz collection jostles for space with soul, hip hop and a carpal tunnel-compressing selection of library sounds. Rarities are pinned to the walls in plastic.

Honest Jon's
278 Portobello Road, Notting Hill, W10 5TE (8969 9822/www.honestjons.com). Ladbroke Grove tube. **Open** 10am-6pm Mon-Sat; 11am-5pm Sun. **Credit** AmEx, MC, V.
Honest Jon's found its way here in 1979, where it was reportedly the first place in London to employ a Rastafarian. The owner helped James Lavelle set up Mo'Wax records. You'll find jazz, hip hop, soul, broken beat, reggae and Brazilian music on the shelves.

INSIDE TRACK
LAMB'S CONDUIT STREET

Tucked away among residential back streets, Lamb's Conduit Street is perfect for browsing, whether you fancy a cool, custom-made suit from **Pokit** (no.53, 7430 9782, www.pokit.co.uk), cult menswear and cute women's knitwear from **Folk** (no.49, 7404 6458, www.folkclothing.com), a photographic book from

[...] 7405 8899,
[...]lassic vinyl
[...] (no.47, 7242
[...]b (*see p229*),
[...]in drag to peruse
[...]s at **French's**
[...]7404 7070,

★ Pure Groove Records
6-7 West Smithfield, Clerkenwell, EC1A 9JX (7778 9278/www.puregroove.co.uk). Farringdon tube/rail. **Open** 11am-7pm Mon-Fri. **Credit** MC, V. **Map** p402 O5.
Pure Groove is a stylish, multimedia treasure trove of vinyl, poster art and CD gems covering all things indie, alternative and cutting edge in guitar and electronic music. The rear, housing T-shirts, cotton bags and posters, doubles as a stage for the regular sets from bands and film screenings.
▶ *A stiff walk up Farringdon Road, Brill (27 Exmouth Market, 7833 9757, www.musiccoffee bagels.com) is a small CD shop-cum-café with an excellently curated selection.*

Ray's Jazz at Foyles
3rd floor, Foyles Bookshop, 113-119 Charing Cross Road, Soho, WC2H 0EB (7440 3205/www.foyles.co.uk). Tottenham Court Road tube. **Open** 9.30am-9pm Mon-Sat; 11.30am-6pm Sun. **Credit** AmEx, MC, V. **Map** p407 X2.
London's least beardy jazz shop has left its cramped first-floor quarters in Foyles (*see p243*) and ascended to the third. The predominantly CD-based stock remains as it was: expect blues, avant-garde, gospel, folk and world, with modern jazz the main draw.

Rough Trade East
Dray Walk, Old Truman Brewery, 91 Brick Lane, E1 6QL (7392 7788/www.roughtrade.com). Liverpool Street tube. **Open** 8am-9pm Mon-Thur; 8am-8pm Fri, Sat; 11am-7pm Sun. **Credit** AmEx, DC, MC, V. **Map** p403 S5.
In the midst of record shop closures across town, Rough Trade added this warehouse-style, 5,000sq ft store, café and gig space to the cluster of boutiques and bars off Brick Lane. It's a temple to things alternative, where staff happily blitz you with releases so new they've barely been recorded. *Photo p260.*
Other locations 130 Talbot Road, Notting Hill, W11 1JA (7229 8541).

Musical instruments

The site of legendary recording studio Regent Sounds in the 1960s, **Denmark Street**, off Charing Cross Road, remains a hub for music shops. This should be your first port of call if you're browsing for a new, second-hand or rare vintage guitar – or need repairs done.

Chappell of Bond Street
152-160 Wardour Street, Soho, W1F 8YA (7432 4400/www.chappellofbondstreet.co.uk). Tottenham Court Road tube. **Open** 9.30am-6pm Mon-Fri; 10am-5.30pm Sat. **Credit** AmEx, MC, V. **Map** p406 V2.
It has retained its old name, but a couple of years back Chappell moved from Bond Street, its home for practically 200 years. It now occupies this amazing

CONSUME

Freddy.

three-storey musical temple. Chappell is the leading Yamaha stockist in Britain, and the store's collection of sheet music (classical, pop and jazz) is said to be the largest in Europe.

SPORT & FITNESS

Harrods (*see p242*) has a good fitness department, including specialist concessions. For trainers, try **JD Sports** (www.jdsports. co.uk) or **NikeTown** (236 Oxford Street, W1W 8LG, 7612 0800, www.nike.com).

Freddy
30-32 Neal Street, Covent Garden, WC2H 9PS (7836 5291/www.freddy.it). Covent Garden tube. **Open** 10am-7pm Mon-Wed, Sat; 10am-8pm Thur; noon-6pm Sun. **Credit** AmEx, MC, V. **Map** p407 Y2.
Official outfitter to the Italian Olympic team and La fScala Ballet, Freddy has also been Italy's essential label for aerobics fans since the 1980s. Its first UK branch offers three floors of own-label sportswear. Think slouchy sweats, with simple jersey shirting, footless tights and cute legwarmers.

Run & Become
42 Palmer Street, Westminster, SW1H 0PH (7222 1314/www.runandbecome.com). St James's Park tube. **Open** 9am-6pm Mon-Wed, Fri, Sat; 9am-8pm Thur. **Credit** MC, V. **Map** p400 J9.
The experienced staff here, most of them enthusiastic runners, are determined to find the right pair of shoes for your particular physique and running style. The full gamut of running kit, from clothing to speed monitors, is also available.

TICKETS

For London performances, book ahead – even obscure acts sell out, and high-profile gigs and events can do so in seconds. It is almost always cheaper to bypass ticket agents and go direct to the box office – the former charge booking fees that could top 20 per cent. Should you have to use them, the agencies include **Ticketmaster** (0870 534 4444, www.ticketmaster.co.uk), **Stargreen** (7734 8932, www.stargreen.com), **Ticketweb** (0870 060 0100, www.ticketweb. co.uk), **SeeTickets** (0871 220 0260, www.see tickets.com) and **Keith Prowse** (0870 840 1111, www.keithprowse.com). For music tickets, *see p307* and *p311*; for theatre, *p336* and *p339*.

TRAVELLERS' NEEDS

Independent travel specialist **Trailfinders** (European travel 0845 050 5945, worldwide flights 0845 058 5858, www.trailfinders.com) has several branches in the capital, including one in the flagship **Waterstone's** (*see p243*).

Excess Baggage Company
4 Hannah Close, Great Central Way, Wembley, NW10 0UX (0800 783 1085/www.excess-baggage.com). **Credit** AmEx, MC, V.
This company ships goods to over 300 countries and territories worldwide, including the USA, Canada, Australia, New Zealand and South Africa, from a single suitcase to complete household removal. Prices are reasonable and include cartons and other packing materials. There are branches in the city's main rail stations, as well as Heathrow and Gatwick.

5 FLOORS OF THE WEIRD WACKY & WONDERFUL!

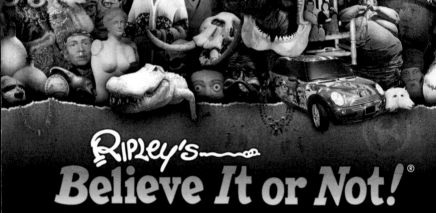

RIPLEY's
Believe It or Not!®

WELCOME TO THE WORLD OF RIPLEY'S BELIEVE IT OR NOT!

London's Biggest New Attraction. Situated in the heart of the West End at 1 Piccadilly Circus, the attraction features over 500 authentic, original and unbelievable exhibits, from a four-metre long model of Tower Bridge made out of matchsticks and an animated T-Rex to the world's tallest man and a Mini Cooper encrusted with 1,000,000 Swarovski crystals. Ripley's Believe It or Not! presents a unique mixture of entertainment, education and fun for the entire family - appealing to anyone with a basic sense of curiosity.

YOU WON'T BELIEVE YOUR EYES!

WWW.RIPLEYSLONDON.COM | 1 PICCADILLY CIRCUS | LONDON W1J 0DA | 020 3238 0022
OPEN UNTIL MIDNIGHT EVERYDAY!

Arts & Entertainment

Royal Opera House.
See p311.

Calendar **268**
  Standing on Ceremony **271**
  Christmas Markets **274**

Art Galleries **276**
  Festivals Art & Design **281**
  Art of the City **283**

Children **284**
  Festivals Children **287**

Comedy **290**
  Profile Comedy Store **291**

Dance **293**
  Hip Hop Steps Up **294**
  Festivals Dance **295**

Film **296**
  Festivals Film **297**
  Some Like It Short **298**

Gay & Lesbian **300**
  Festivals Gay & Lesbian **301**
  Reading Between the Lines **304**

Music **307**
  London Can Handel It **308**
  Festivals Classical **310**
  Festivals Rock, Pop & Roots **312**
  Out Come the Freaks **316**
  Festivals Jazz **318**

Nightlife **319**
  King's Cross… All Change! **320**
  What's the Matter? **326**

Sport & Fitness **327**
  A Twenty20 Vision? **328**
  The Sporting Year **332**

Theatre **335**
  In the Pound Seats **339**
  Profile Royal Shakespeare Company **340**
  Festivals Theatre **343**

Calendar

Stuff happens – we tell you where and when.

There's been an exponential growth in the number of seasonal events occurring in London each year, with a mind-boggling array taking place at any one time – we got quite dizzy just deciding which to list! Many of the most popular are based around Trafalgar Square or the revivified Southbank Centre, both of them brilliantly central locations that are easy to drop in on for a bit of free entertainment before you set about ticking something important off your sights itinerary. But there are also many specialist events – perhaps **Open House** or **Kew Spring Festival** – that can easily fill an entire day, as well as blockbusters such as the **Chinese New Year Festival** and **Notting Hill Carnival** that are well worth building an entire visit around.

THE LOWDOWN

We've packed in an eclectic haul of things to do, but there are plenty more in the **Festival** feature boxes that are dotted through the Arts & Entertainment chapters that follow. If you're already in town, *Time Out* magazine is invaluable for late announced events and up-to-date programme details of the major events; www.timeout.com is great for last-minute research before you leave. If you're planning your trip around a particular event – or going out of your way to attend one – be sure to confirm the details in advance: we've thoroughly checked the information here, but dates and programmes change, and events can be cancelled with little notice.

ALL YEAR

For the Changing of the Guard, *see p271* **Standing on Ceremony**.

Ceremony of the Keys
Tower of London, Tower Hill, the City, EC3N 4AB (0870 751 5177/www.hrp.org.uk). Tower Hill tube/Tower Gateway DLR. **Date** 9.30pm daily (advance bookings only). **Map** p405 R7.
Join the Yeoman Warders after hours at the Tower of London as they ritually lock the fortress's entrances in this 700-year-old ceremony. You enter the Tower at 9.30pm and it's all over just after 10pm, but places are hotly sought after – apply at least two months in advance; full details are on the website.

Gun Salutes
Green Park, Mayfair & St James's, W1, & Tower of London, the City, EC3. **Dates** 6 Feb (Accession Day); 21 Apr & 14 June (Queen's birthdays); 2 June (Coronation Day); 10 June (Duke of Edinburgh's birthday); 15 June (Trooping the Colour); State Opening of Parliament (*see p275*); 9 Nov (Lord Mayor's Show); 10 Nov (Remembrance Sunday); for state visits. **Map** p400 H8.
There are gun salutes on many state occasions. A cavalry charge features in the 41-gun salutes mounted by the Kings Troop Royal Horse Artillery in Hyde Park at noon (opposite the Dorchester, *see p184*), whereas, on the other side of town, the Honourable Artillery Company ditches the ponies and piles on the firepower with their 62-gun salutes (1pm at the Tower of London). If the dates happen to fall on a Sunday, the salute is held on Monday.

INSIDE TRACK
TRAFALGAR SQUARE

Among the former mayor's most popular initiatives was pedestrianising the north side of London's central square... and then programming almost weekly events there. Even under budget-slashing Mayor Boris, expect all kinds of entertainment here – music, film, theatre, dance – usually for free. For details, check www.london.gov.uk/trafalgarsquare.

JANUARY-MARCH

This is a good time of year for dance events, among them **Resolution!** and **Move It!**, *see p295*. For **National Storytelling Week** and the **Imagine** children's literature festival, *see p287*; for the **London Lesbian & Gay Film Festival**, *see p297*.

Russian Winter Festival

Trafalgar Square, WC2 (7183 2560/www. eventica.co.uk). Charing Cross tube/rail. **Date** mid Jan. **Map** p407 X5.

Out to show the impact of the New Russia on London, this celebration of Russian New Year begins with traditional music and dance and finishes with Russian rock and pop legends. Expect snow machines, choruses of 'Kalinka', blinis and plenty of borsch.

★ London International Mime Festival

7637 5661/www.mimefest.co.uk. **Date** 10-25 Jan.

This long-running festival will explode any prejudices you may have against mime. Expect innovative and visually stunning theatre from across the globe.
► *For more theatre events, see p343 Festivals.*

Joseph Grimaldi Memorial Service

Holy Trinity Church, Beechwood Road, Dalston, E8 3DY (www.clowns-international.co.uk). Dalston Kingsland tube/rail. **Date** 1 Feb.

Join hundreds of motley-clad 'Joeys' for their annual service commemorating the legendary British clown, Joseph Grimaldi (1778-1837).

★ Chinese New Year Festival

Around Gerrard Street, Chinatown, W1, Leicester Square, WC2, & Trafalgar Square, WC2 (7851 6686/www.chinatownchinese.co.uk). Leicester Square or Piccadilly Circus tube. **Date** 26 Jan. **Map** p406 W3.

Launch the Year of the Ox in style at celebrations that engulf Chinatown and Leicester Square. Dragon dancers writhe alongside a host of impressive acts in the grand parade to Trafalgar Square.
► *For sights around Chinatown, see p93.*

Pancake Day Races

Great Spitalfields *Dray Walk, Brick Lane, Spitalfields, E1 6QL (7375 0441/www. alternativearts.co.uk).* **Liverpool Street** tube/rail. **Poulters Annual** *Guildhall Yard, the City, EC2P 2EJ (www.poulters.org.uk). Bank tube/DLR/Moorgate tube/rail.* **Both Date** 24 Feb.

Shrove Tuesday brings out charity pancake racers across the capital. Don a silly costume and join in the fun at the Great Spitalfields Pancake Race (you'll need to register in advance) or watch City livery companies race in full regalia at the event organised by the Worshipful Company of Poulters.

Jewish Book Week

Royal National Hotel, Bedford Way, Bloomsbury, WC1 0DG (7446 8771/www.jewishbookweek. com). Russell Square tube. **Date** 21 Feb-1 Mar. **Map** p399 K4.

One of London's biggest literature festivals, it's renowned for its lively, authoritative debates and Q&A sessions with authors and intellectuals.

London International Mime Festival.

ARTS & ENTERTAINMENT

ARTS & ENTERTAINMENT

Who Do You Think You Are? Live
Olympia, Hammersmith Road, Kensington, W14 8UX (www.whodoyouthinkyouarelive.co.uk). Kensington Olympia tube. **Date** 27 Feb-1 Mar.
A spin-off from the hugely successful BBC TV series that keeps Brits glued to the box watching weepy celebs uncover their ancestry, this enormous family history event could help you trace yours.

National Science & Engineering Week
Various venues (0870 770 7101/www.the-ba.net). **Date** 6-15 Mar.
From the weirdly wacky to the profound, this annual series of events engages the public in celebrating science, engineering and technology.

St Patrick's Day Parade & Festival
Various venues (7983 4100/www.london.gov.uk). **Date** 15 Mar.
Join the London Irish out in force for this huge annual parade through central London followed by toe-tapping tunes in Trafalgar Square.

★ Kew Spring Festival
For listings, *see p156* **Royal Botanic Gardens**. **Date** 1 Mar-30 Apr.
Kew Gardens is at its most beautiful in spring, with five million flowers carpeting the grounds.

Oxford & Cambridge Boat Race
Thames, from Putney to Mortlake (01225 383483/www.theboatrace.org). Putney Bridge tube/Putney, Barnes Bridge or Mortlake rail. **Date** 29 Mar.
Blue-clad Oxbridge students race each other in a pair of rowing eights, watched by tens of millions worldwide. Experience the excitement from the riverbank (along with 250,000 other fans) for the 155th instalment of the historic race.

APRIL-JUNE

Early summer is, of course, terrific for outdoor events, among them excellent alfresco theatre at the **Greenwich & Docklands International Festival** and, on the South Bank, **Watch This Space** (for both, *see p343*). Sport fans can go racing (**Royal Ascot**, the **Epsom Derby**) or queue for **Wimbledon** tickets (for all, *see pp330-331*). For classical music at the **City of London Festival** and **Hampton Court Palace Festival**, or rockier fare at the **Camden Crawl**, **Wireless Festival** or **Summer Series** at Somerset House, *see p312*.

Spill – Edition 2
Various venues (7488 0800/www.spillfestival.com). **Date** 2-26 Apr.
This festival of international contemporary performance, live art and experimental theatre features world premieres and specially commissioned works.
▶ *For the capital's best art fairs, see p281.*

Shakespeare's Birthday
For listings, *see p51* **Shakespeare's Globe**. **Date** 25-26 Apr.
To celebrate the Bard's birthday, the Globe Theatre throws open its doors for a series of events.

Alternative Fashion Week
Spitalfields Traders Market, Crispin Place, Brushfield Street, Spitalfields, E1 6AA (7375 0441/www.alternativearts.co.uk). Liverpool Street tube/rail. **Date** 20-24 Apr. **Map** p403 R5.
Forget London Fashion Week, this is the place to discover the edgiest new designers – more than 60 took part in 2008.

★ Flora London Marathon
Greenwich Park to the Mall via the Isle of Dogs, Victoria Embankment & St James's Park (7902 0200/www.london-marathon.co.uk). Blackheath & Maze Hill rail/Charing Cross tube/rail. **Date** 26 Apr.
One of the world's elite long-distance races, the London Marathon is also one of the world's largest fund-raising events – nearly 80% of participants run for charity, so zany costumes abound among the 35,000 starters. If you haven't already applied to run, you're too late: just go along to watch. *Photo p272.*

Open Garden Squares Weekend.

Standing on Ceremony

Straight-faced and strait-laced, nowhere does pomp better than London.

London puts on military parades par excellence, every day throughout the year. On alternate days from 10.45am, one of the five Foot Guards regiments lines up in scarlet coats and tall bearskin hats in the forecourt of Wellington Barracks; at exactly 11.27am the soldiers march, accompanied by their regimental band, to Buckingham Palace (*see p114*) to relieve the sentries there in a 45-minute ceremony for the **Changing of the Guard** (subject to change: see www.changing-the-guard. com/sched.htm for updates). Not far away, at Horse Guards Parade in Whitehall, the Household Cavalry mount the guard daily at 11am (10am on Sunday). This is our preferred viewing, since the crowds aren't as thick as at the palace, and you aren't held far back from the action by railings. After the old and new guard have stared each other out in the centre of the parade ground, you can nip through to the Whitehall side to catch the departing old guard perform their hilarious dismount choreography – a synchronised, firm slap of approbation to the neck of each horse before the gloved troopers all swing off.

There are, however, less frequent parades on a far grander scale. Help the Queen celebrate her official birthday on 13 June (her real one's in April) at the **Trooping of the Colour** (7414 2479, www.trooping-the-colour.co.uk). At 10.45am she trots from Buckingham Palace to Horse Guards Parade to watch

the soldiers, then it's back to Buck House for a midday RAF flypast and the gun salute from Green Park.

Also at Horse Guards, on 3-4 June, a pageant of military music and precision marching begins at 7pm when the Queen (or another royal) takes the salute of the 300-strong drummers, pipers and musicians of the Massed Bands of the Household Division as part of **Beating the Retreat** (7414 2271, tickets 7839 5323).

Covent Garden May Fayre & Puppet Festival

Garden of St Paul's Covent Garden, Bedford Street, Covent Garden, WC2E 9ED (7375 0441/ www.alternativearts.co.uk). Covent Garden tube. **Date** 10 May. **Map** p407 Y4.
All-day puppet mayhem (10.30am-5.30pm) devoted to celebrating Mr Punch at the scene of his first recorded sighting in England in 1662. Mr P takes to the church's pulpit at 11.30am.

Coin Street Festival

Bernie Spain Gardens (next to Oxo Tower Wharf), South Bank, SE1 9PH (7021 1600/ www.coinstreet.org). Southwark tube/Waterloo tube/rail. **Date** June-Aug. **Map** p404 N8
Celebrating London's cultural diversity, this free summer-long Thameside festival features a series music-focused events; one of the best sessions is

Pulse in June, a wild mix of Eastern and Central European music from gypsy to new wave.

Open Garden Squares Weekend

Various venues (www.opensquares.org). **Date** 13-14 June.
Secret – and merely exclusive – gardens are thrown open to the public. You can visit roof gardens, prison gardens and children-only gardens, as well as a changing selection of those tempting oases railed off in the middle of the city's finest squares. Some charge an entrance fee.

Exhibition Road Music Day

Exhibition Road, SW7 (www.exhibitionroad musicday.org). South Kensington tube. **Date** 3rd Sat in June. **Map** p397 D9.
London's counterpart to France's midsummer Fête de la Musique ranges through institutions that

border Exhibition Road and spills into Hyde Park. With Imperial College and the Ismaili Centre among the participants you can expect anything from experimental music to Sufi chants.

JULY-SEPTEMBER

Summer sees some of the most important music festivals of the year – namely, the **BBC Sir Henry Wood Promenade Concerts** (the Proms to you and I), **Lovebox Weekender** and the **English Heritage Picnic Concerts** at Kenwood House (for all, *see p310*) – as well as the city's major gay event: **London Pride** (*see p301*). Teenagers love the **Underage** festival (*see p287*). There are also two cutting-edge dance events, the **Place Prize** and **Dance Umbrella** (for both, *see p295*).

Broadwalk Ballroom

Regent's Park, Marylebone, NW1 (www.dance alfresco.org). Regent's Park tube. **Date** July-Aug. **Map** p398 G3.
Regent's Park's Broadwalk transforms into a dance floor over two weekends in July and August from 2pm to 6pm. Ballroom is on Saturdays and tango on Sundays, with lessons for novices at 1pm.
▶ *For the city's excellent dance performance festivals, see p295 Festivals.*

Music Village

Hyde Park, W1 (7264 0000/www.cultural co-operation.org). **Date** mid July. **Map** p395 F7.

Europe's longest-running festival of world cultures is always inspirationally themed and magical, bringing global musicians together and showcasing London's own diaspora performers.

London Literature Festival

Southbank Centre, Belvedere Road, SE1 8XX (0871 663 2501/www.londonlitfest.com). Waterloo tube/rail. **Date** mid July. **Map** p401 M8.
Now in its third year, the programme usually combines superstar writers with stars from other fields: in 2008, there were architects, comedians, sculptors and cultural theorists examining anything from queer literature to migration.

★ Chap Olympiad

www.thechap.net. **Date** 12 July.
English eccentrics are in full cry at the annual event mounted by *The Chap* magazine, which starts with the lighting of the Olympic Pipe. 'Sports' include cucumber sandwich discus and hop, skip and G&T. Check the venue closer to the time: it was Hampstead Heath, appropriately enough, in 2008. *Photo p275.*

Great British Beer Festival

Earl's Court Exhibition Centre, Warwick Road, SW5 9TA (01727 867201/www.camra.org.uk). Earl's Court tube. **Date** 4-8 Aug. **Map** p396 A11.
Real ale is the star at this huge event devoted to British brews including cider and perry (a pear cider). Foreign beers and lagers get a look-in (tch!) at what's been called 'the biggest pub in the world'.
▶ *For our top three beer pubs, see p232 Profile.*

Flora London Marathon. *See p270.*

London Mela

Gunnersbury Park, Ealing, W3 (8469 1300/ www.londonmela.org). Acton Town or South Ealing tube. **Date** Aug.
Dubbed the Asian Glastonbury, thousands flock to west London for this exuberant celebration of Asian culture. You'll find urban, classical and experimental music, circus, dance, visual arts, comedy, children's events – and yummy grub.

Trafalgar Square Festival

Trafalgar Square, WC2 (www.london.gov.uk/ trafalgarsquare). Trafalgar Square tube. **Date** Aug. **Map** p407 X5.
Spectacular, specially commissioned street performances take over three weeks in August.

★ Notting Hill Carnival

Notting Hill, W10, W11 (7727 0072/www. lnhc.org.uk). Ladbroke Grove, Notting Hill Gate or Westbourne Park tube. **Date** 31 Aug. **Map** p394 A6.
Two million people stream in to Notting Hill to Europe's largest street party, full of the smells, colours and music of the Caribbean. Massive sound systems dominate with new dance tunes, but there's tradition too: calypso and a spectacular parade.
▶ *For sightseeing in Notting Hill, see p101.*

A Country Affair

Hampton Court Palace, East Molesey, Surrey KT8 9AU (8977 0705/www.hamptoncourt show.com). Hampton Court rail/riverboat from Westminster or Richmond to Hampton Court Pier. **Date** Aug.
The country comes to town (well, the suburbs) for a rural jamboree that the whole family will enjoy: hands-on activities, plus traditional fairground rides, Morris dancers, falconry displays, animal shows, a farmers' market and live music.

Great River Race

Thames, from Ham House, Richmond, Surrey TW10, to Island Gardens, Isle of Dogs, E14 (8398 6900/www.greatriverrace. co.uk). **Date** Sept.
The alternative Boat Race (*see p270*) – and much more fun, with an exotic array of around 300 traditional rowing boats from across the globe racing the

22 miles from Richmond to Greenwich. Hungerford Bridge, the Millennium Bridge and Tower Bridge all provide good viewpoints.

Thames Festival

Between Westminster Bridge & Tower Bridge (7928 8998/www.thamesfestival.org). Waterloo tube/rail/Blackfriars rail. **Date** 12-13 Sept. **Map** p404 N7.
A giant end-of-the-season party along the Thames. It's a spectacular and family-friendly mix of street arts, carnival, pyrotechnics, art installations, river events and live music alongside craft and food stalls. A highlight is the last-night lantern procession and firework finale.

Freewheel

www.londonfreewheel.com. **Date** 3rd Sun of Sept.
Begun in 2007, this cycling festival is very popular. Last year nearly 50,000 people rode the main traffic-free route from Buckingham Palace to the Tower and a number of subsidiary routes, enjoying music and the chance to meet Olympic cyclists on the way.
▶ *For cycle hire in London, see p365.*

★ Open House London

3006 7008/www.openhouse.org.uk. **Date** mid Sept.
Londoners' favourite opportunity to snoop round other people's houses: palaces, private homes, corporate skyscrapers, pumping stations, bomb-proof bunkers – you name it. Many are normally closed to the public. There's a programme of debates on architecture along with the 20-mile London Night Hike.
▶ *For more on architecture, see pp34-39.*

Great Gorilla Run

Mincing Lane, the City, EC3 (7916 4974/www. greatgorillas.org/london). Monument or Tower Hill tube/Fenchurch Street rail. **Date** last wk Sept. **Map** p405 R7.
Go ape with a 1,000-strong pack of gorilla-suited runners, who take on a 7km course through the City in aid of gorilla conservation.

OCTOBER-DECEMBER

Winter in London isn't just about Christmas: **Frieze** and **Zoo** (for both, *see p281*) are huge art fairs, the **London Film Festival** (*see p297*) takes place in October, and it's also the season for the **London Jazz Festival** (*see p318*) and the winter instalment of the **Spitalfields Festival** (*see p310*).

Pearly Kings & Queens Harvest Festival

St Martin-in-the-Fields, Trafalgar Square, Westminster, WC2N 4JJ (7766 1100/www.pearly society.co.uk). Leicester Square tube/Charing Cross tube/rail. **Date** 4 Oct. **Map** p407 Y4.

ARTS & ENTERTAINMENT

London's Pearlies assemble for their annual thanksgiving service dressed in spangly (and colossally heavy) Smother Suits covered in hundreds of pearl buttons. The sensational outfits evolved from Victorian costermongers' love of decorating their clothes with buttons.

Big Draw
Various venues (8351 1719/www.campaignfor drawing.org). **Date** Oct.
Engage with your inner artist at the tenth anniversary Big Draw, a nationwide frenzy of drawing using anything from pencils to vapour trails. The

British Library's Big Picture Party brings out heavy-hitters like Quentin Blake, a festival patron.

London to Brighton Veteran Car Run
Serpentine Road, Hyde Park, W2 2UH (01327 856024/www.lbvcr.com). Hyde Park Corner tube. **Date** 8 Nov. **Map** p395 E8.
A sedate procession of around 500 pre-1905 cars. The first pair trundles off at sunrise (7am-8.30am), but you can catch them a little later crossing Westminster Bridge or view them in repose on a closed-off Regent's Street the day before (11am-3pm).

Christmas Markets

Bored of the high-street frenzy? Mill instead where the fine wine mulls.

Christmas markets are becoming increasingly popular all over London, from Kingston to Carnaby Street. Mostly inspired by traditional German and East European markets, they're the perfect excuse to combine the shopping for stocking fillers with some festive cheer en plein air. Each market has its own style – activities range from mulled wine-tastings to ice skating under the stars – but all provide the chance to get into your winter woollies and the Christmas spirit.

On the **South Bank**, the German-style Christmas market is a particularly traditional affair. Several dozen wooden chalets are dotted along the river near the London Eye, selling a range of arts and crafts as well as various culinary delights. Christmas Deluxe (www.christmas-deluxe.com) in **Covent Garden** offers a similar range of stalls and luxury food market, but throws in a mix of live entertainment, a couture gift-wrapping service and even a decoration exchange point for last-year's baubles. Christmas Village (www.greenwichwhs.org) in **Greenwich** has its own Christmas currency – 'Mince Pounds' – which give you discounts on specific events when you spend over a certain amount in certain shops and stalls.

In **South Kensington**, the majestic Natural History Museum's Christmas fair (www.nhm.ac.uk) has a good choice of unusual gifts – everything from glassware to toys, ceramics and candles – alongside an ice rink, while just up the road the area between Hyde Park Corner and the Serpentine is transformed into a Winter Wonderland (www.hydepark winterwonderland.com) with markets, fairground rides, Santa's Grotto and the largest open-air ice rink in the city, as well as a giant observation wheel.

And, reviving an ancient London tradition, the annual Frost Fair (www.visit southwark.com) stretches between Tate Modern and the Globe. **Bankside** is covered with twinkly lights and enticing market stalls, and entertainment includes street parades and ice sculptures, carols and perhaps husky dog sledding. With a sausage in one hand and mulled wine in the other, who would want to be anywhere else?

Frost Fair.

Diwali

Trafalgar Square, WC2 (7983 4100/www. london.gov.uk). Charing Cross tube/rail.
Date Oct. **Map** p407 X5.
A vibrant celebration of the annual Festival of Light by London's Hindu, Jain and Sikh communities. There are fireworks, food, music and dancing.

Bonfire Night

Date 5 Nov or the closest weekend.
Diwali pyrotechnics segue seamlessly into Britain's best-loved excuse for setting off fireworks: the celebration of Guy Fawkes' failure to blow up the Houses of Parliament in 1605. Try Battersea Park, Alexandra Palace or Victoria Park, or pre-book a late ride on the London Eye (*see p47*).

★ Lord Mayor's Show

Through the City (7332 3456/www.lordmayors show.org). **Date** 14 Nov.
This big show marks the traditional presentation of the new Lord Mayor for approval by the monarch's justices. He leaves Mansion House in a fabulous gold coach at 11am, along with a colourful procession of floats and marchers, heading to the Royal Courts of Justice (*see p87*). There he makes his vows, and is back home easily in time for afternoon tea. At 5pm there's a fireworks display from a Thames barge.
▶ *The Lord Mayor is a City officer, elected each year by the livery companies; don't confuse him with the Mayor of London, Boris Johnson; see p31.*

Remembrance Sunday Ceremony

Cenotaph, Whitehall, Westminster, SW1. Charing Cross tube/rail. **Date** 8 Nov. **Map** p401 L8.
Held on the Sunday nearest to 11 November – the day World War I ended – this solemn comemmoration honours those who died fighting in the World Wars and later conflicts. The Queen, prime minister and other dignitaries lay poppy wreaths at the Cenotaph (*see p110*). A two-minute silence at 11am is followed by a service of remembrance.

State Opening of Parliament

House of Lords, Palace of Westminster, Westminster, SW1A 0PW (7219 4272/ www.parliament.uk). Westminster tube.
Date Nov. **Map** p401 L9.
Pomp and ceremony attend the Queen's official reopening of Parliament after its summer recess. She arrives and departs in the state coach, accompanied by troopers of the Household Cavalry.

Christmas Celebrations

Covent Garden (0870 780 5001/www.covent gardenmarket.co.uk); Bond Street (www.bond streetassociation.com); St Christopher's Place (7493 3294/www.stchristophersplace.com), Marylebone High St (www.marylebonevillage. com); Trafalgar Square (7983 4234/www. london.gov.uk). **Date** Nov-Dec.

Chap Olympiad. See *p272*.

Skip the commercialised lights on Oxford and Regent's Streets and head for smaller shopping areas like St Christopher's Place, Bond Street, Marylebone High Street and Covent Garden for real Christmas glitter. Unlike most big stores, Fortnum & Mason still create enchantingly old-fashioned Christmas windows and Harvey Nichols usually produces show-stopping displays (for both, *see p242*). It's traditional to sing carols beneath giant Christmas tree in Trafalgar Square (*see p107*) – an annual gift from Norway in gratitude for Britain's support during World War II – but you can also join in a mammoth singalong at the Albert Hall (*see p309*) or an evocative carol service at one of London's historic churches. Londoners have also taken to outdoor ice-skating in a big way, *see p327.*
Inside track. *See also p274* **Christmas Markets.**

New Year's Eve Celebrations

Date 31 Dec.
The focus of London's public celebrations has officially moved from the traditionally overcrowded Trafalgar Square (though it's still sure to be packed) to the full-on fireworks display launched from the London Eye and rafts on the Thames. The best view is from nearby bridges – but you'll have to get there early. Otherwise, overpriced festivities in clubs, hotels and restaurants take place across the capital. Those with stamina can take in the New Year's Day Parade next day.

alleries

't on: London's art scene remains in rude health.

nat's what you'll hear if
on gallerist whether the financial
as affected their trade. You might think
at a frothy market for contemporary art would
be susceptible to an economic downturn; indeed, in
private, art world insiders admit the likelihood of
casualties. But as yet, there's been no sign. Spaces
continue to open and the established galleries are
still going strong. For listings, check *Time Out*
magazine or www.timeout.com, or the free *New
Exhibitions of Contemporary Art*, available from
most galleries and at www.newexhibitions.com.

FINE ART

The rejuvenation of the West End art scene has
continued with the arrival in Fitzrovia of **Pilar
Corrias**'s new, Rem Koolhaas-designed space.
The area now offers excellent gallery-mooching,
with Corrias, **Stuart Shave/Modern Art**,
Alison Jacques and the **Approach** outpost
all just minutes from each other.

Alison Jacques Gallery
*16-18 Berners Street, Fitzrovia, W1T 3LN
(7631 4720/www.alisonjacquesgallery.com).
Goodge Street or Oxford Circus tube.* **Open**
10am-6pm Tue-Sat. **No credit cards.**
Map p398 J5.
At this swish gallery, Jacques shows emerging and
established names such as Jon Pylypchuk and
André Butzer, plus works from the estates of Robert
Mapplethorpe and Hannah Wilke. In 2009, expect
shows by Swedish ceramicist Klara Kristalova and
young US photographer Ryan McGinley.

★ Gagosian
*6-24 Britannia Street, King's Cross, WC1X 9JD
(7841 9960/www.gagosian.com). King's Cross
tube/rail.* **Open** 10am-6pm Tue-Sat. **No credit
cards. Map** p399 M3.
Visitors flock to this vast space, part of US super-
dealer Larry Gagosian's ever-expanding empire, to

see big names such as Cy Twombly, Jeff Koons,
Howard Hodgkin and Francesco Clemente, plus a
second tier of fashionable US and European artists
including Carsten Höller and Cecily Brown.
Other location 17-19 Davies Street, Mayfair,
W1K 3DE (7493 3020).

Gallery One One One
*111 Great Titchfield Street, Fitzrovia, W1W 6RY
(7637 0868/www.galleryoneoneone.com). Warren
Street tube.* **Open** 10am-6pm Tue-Fri; 11am-5pm
Sat. **No credit cards. Map** p398 J5.
David Roberts is the latest in a line of collectors of
contemporary art to start a charitable foundation
and open premises in which to show their acquisi-
tions. A second venue (37 Camden High Street, NW1
7JE) is due to open in spring 2009.
▶ *Gallery One One One is the newest of a
growing trend for non-profit venues; others
include the Parasol Unit (see p279), the Louise
T Blouin Institute (see p282) and 176 (see p279).*

Haunch of Venison
*6 Haunch of Venison Yard, off Brook Street,
Mayfair, W1K 5ES (7495 5050/www.haunch
ofvenison.com). Bond Street tube.* **Open** 10am-
6pm Mon-Wed, Fri; 10am-7pm Thur; 11am-5pm
Sat. **Credit** AmEx, MC, V. **Map** p398 H6.
Though Haunch of Venison is now owned by auc-
tion house Christie's, very little appears to have
changed in terms of its programme. In the eponymous yard, the splendid high-ceilinged converted
Georgian townhouse hosts large-scale installations
and shows by major names (Turner Prize winners
Keith Tyson and Richard Long) and mid-career
artists (Diana Thater, Zarina Bhimji).

About the author
Martin Coomer *writes about art for a number
of publications in London and abroad, including*
Modern Painters, Art Review, The Big Issue *and*
Time Out *magazine.*

Haunch of Venison.

ARTS & ENTERTAINMENT

★ Hauser & Wirth London

196A Piccadilly, Mayfair, W1J 9DY (7287 2300/www.hauserwirth.com). Piccadilly Circus tube. **Open** 10am-6pm Tue-Sat. **No credit cards. Map** p406 U5.
Founded in 1992 in Zurich, this Swiss-owned gallery opened in 2003 in a former bank, with intact basement vaults. H&W represents heavyweight artists including Louise Bourgeois and Paul McCarthy, international names such as Anri Sala and Pipilotti Rist, and home-grown talents such as Martin Creed. **Other location** Hauser & Wirth Colnaghi, 15 Old Bond Street, Mayfair, W1S 4AX (7287 2300).

Lisson

29 & 52-54 Bell Street, Marylebone, NW1 5DA (7724 2739/www.lissongallery.com). Edgware Road tube. **Open** 10am-6pm Mon-Fri; 11am-5pm Sat. **No credit cards. Map** p395 E5.
One of London's longer established contemporary galleries, the Lisson is a superb platform for major international names including the Lisson Sculptors: Anish Kapoor, Tony Cragg, Richard Wentworth and Richard Deacon. Work by Tatsuo Miyajima and Jonathan Monk is due for display in 2009. **Other location** 29 Bell Street, Marylebone, NW1 5BY (7535 7350).

Pilar Corrias

54 Eastcastle Street, Fitzrovia, W1W 8EF (7323 7000/www.pilarcorrias.com). Oxford Circus tube. **Open** 10am-6pm Mon-Fri; 11am-6pm Sat. **No credit cards. Map** p406 V1.
Formerly a director at the Lisson and Haunch of Venison, Corrias opened this Rem Koolhaas-designed art gallery in October 2008 with a giant aluminium Christmas tree by Philippe Parreno.

Look out for works by Tala Madani and Keren Cytter, as well as a large-scale project by Francis Alÿs in 2009.

Sadie Coles HQ

35 Heddon Street, Mayfair, W1B 4BP (7434 2227/www.sadiecoles.com). Oxford Circus or Piccadilly Circus tube. **Open** 10am-6pm Tue-Sat. **No credit cards. Map** p406 U3.

INSIDE TRACK
MAJOR MUSEUMS

In addition to the galleries in this chapter, there are many public spaces:

Barbican Art Gallery p63
British Museum p77
Courtauld Gallery p86
Design Museum p56
Dulwich Picture Gallery p144
Embankment Galleries p87
Hayward Gallery p49
ICA p115
National Gallery p107
National Portrait Gallery p109
Rivington Place p137
Royal Academy of Arts p106
Saatchi Gallery p118
Serpentine Gallery p124
Tate Britain p113
Tate Modern p52
V&A p122
V&A Museum of Childhood p138
Whitechapel Art Gallery p135

London's unmissable art experience

Art, buildings & culture
in two great galleries

TATE

Tate Modern
The world's favourite
gallery of modern art

Southwark · Bankside

Tate Britain
Home to five centuries
of British art

Pimlico · Millbank

Admission Free

To find out more, visit
www.tate.org.uk or call **020 7887 8888**

Coles represents some of the hippest artists from both sides of the Atlantic. The gallery opened a second, larger space in 2007 which shows the likes of John Currin, Sarah Lucas and Jim Lambie; a third space in nearby Balfour Mews has been used for installations by Urs Fischer and Gabriel Kuri. **Other location** 69 South Audley Street, Mayfair, W1K 2QZ (7434 2227).

Sprüth Magers London

7A Grafton Street, Mayfair, W1S 4EJ (7408 1613/www.spruethmagers.com). Green Park tube. **Open** 10am-6pm Tue-Sat. **No credit cards. Map** p400 H7.
Fischli & Weiss, Cindy Sherman and Robert Morris are just four of the major-league international artists that have shown in this handsome gallery housed in an 18th-century building just off Old Bond Street.

Stuart Shave/Modern Art

23-25 Eastcastle Street, Fitzrovia, W1W 8DF (7299 7950/www.modernart.net). Oxford Circus tube. **Open** 11am-6pm Tue-Sat. **No credit cards. Map** p406 V1.
In 2008, this always on-trend gallery relocated from the East End to Fitzrovia, more than doubling its exhibition space. Jonathan Meese, Matthew Monahan, Eva Rothschild and Barry McGee will show in 2009.

★ White Cube

25-26 Mason's Yard, St James's, SW1 6BU (7930 5373/www.whitecube.com). Green Park tube. **Open** 10am-6pm Tue-Sat. **Credit** AmEx, MC, V. **Map** p406 V5.
Jay Jopling's famous gallery reasserted its West End presence in 2006 with the opening of this purpose-built 5,000sq ft space. White Cube Hoxton Square still runs an excellent programme of shows by the gallery's ever-expanding stable, but this larger space seems designated for A-list Young British Artists, such as Damien Hirst, Tracey Emin, Jake and Dinos Chapman.
Other location 48 Hoxton Square, Shoreditch, N1 6PB (7930 5373).

North London

★ 176

176 Prince of Wales Road, Chalk Farm, NW5 3PT (7491 5720/www.projectspace176.com). Chalk Farm tube/Kentish Town West rail. **Open** 11am-3pm Thur, Fri; 11am-6pm Sat, Sun. **Credit** MC, V.
Launched in September 2007, this former Methodist chapel – a remarkable neoclassical building – holds three shows a year, enabling artists to create exper imental new work and curators to build exhibitions around the Zabludowicz Collection of global emerging art in all media. The first show of 2009 is by artist-in-residence Matt Stokes. *Photo p280.*

INSIDE TRACK
THURSDAYS

Many smaller galleries close during the early part of the week, so it's wise to focus visits on a Thursday, the most popular day for private previews. **Time Out First Thursdays** sees hundreds of East End galleries stay open for a few extra hours on the first Thursday of every month, with many holding special events. For details, including maps of East London art hotspots, see www.firstthursdays.co.uk.

Parasol Unit

14 Wharf Road, Islington, N1 7RW (7490 7373/www.parasol-unit.org). Angel tube/Old Street tube/rail. **Open** 10am-6pm Tue-Sat; noon-5pm Sun. **No credit cards. Map** p402 P3.
This former warehouse (adjacent to Victoria Miro, *see below*) has been beautifully converted by architect Claudio Silverstrin into exhibition spaces on two floors and a reading area. The Unit shows work by emerging and major-league figures: in 2009, expect works by Robert Mangold and a group show themed around parades and processions.

★ Victoria Miro

16 Wharf Road, Islington, N1 7RW (7336 8109/www.victoria-miro.com). Angel tube/Old Street tube/rail. **Open** 10am-6pm Tue-Sat; by appointment Mon. **Credit** MC, V. **Map** p402 P3.
A visit to this ex-Victorian furniture factory rarely disappoints. High-calibre artists on show include Chris Ofili, Peter Doig and Grayson Perry. In 2007, the gallery opened Victoria Miro 14, a sleek space next door to the original that's used for exhibitions and special projects. Christian Holstad, Tal R, Idris Khan and Doug Aitken will show in 2009.

East London

Hoxton Square, Cambridge Heath Road and **Vyner Street** are all good places to start an exploration of east London's galleries, but it's worth planning the timing of your visit carefully (*see p279* **Inside track**). For grass-roots alternatives, head east to Hackney Wick, where you'll find studios and galleries such as **Elevator** (www.elevatorgallery.co.uk) and **Decima** (www.decimagallery.com). Some have signed short leases while others stare demolition in the face (the area is in the shadow of the Olympics 2012 site), but the sense of impermanence breeds energy and the spirit of mischief that brought about the first **Hackney Wicked** (www.hackney wicked.com) festival in 2008.

176. *See p279.*

Approach E2

1st floor, 47 Approach Road, Bethnal Green,
E2 9LY (8983 3878/www.theapproach.co.uk).
Bethnal Green tube/Cambridge Heath rail.
Open noon-6pm Wed-Sun; or by appointment.
No credit cards.
Occupying a function room above a pub, the
Approach has a deserved reputation for showing
both emerging artists and more established names
such as painter Michael Raedecker and sculptor
Gary Webb.
Other location Approach W1, 74 Mortimer
Street, Fitzrovia, W1W 7RZ (7631 4210).

Carl Freedman Gallery

44A Charlotte Road, Shoreditch, EC2A 3PD
(7684 8888/www.carlfreedmangallery.com).
Old Street tube/rail. **Open** noon-6pm Wed-Sat.
Credit MC, V. **Map** p403 R4.
Responsible for seminal shows such as 1990's
Modern Medicine, Carl Freedman is an old hand at
promoting Young British Art. From this smart
gallery, he continues to focus his attention on
mainly home-grown talent and represents a small
stable of increasingly respected artists such as
Michael Fullerton, Peter Peri and Fergal Stapleton.

Chisenhale Gallery

64 Chisenhale Road, Bow, E3 5QZ (8981
4518/www.chisenhale.org.uk). Bethnal Green
or Mile End tube/8, 277, D6 bus. **Open** 1-6pm
Wed-Sun. **No credit cards**.
With a reputation for recognising new talent,
Chisenhale commissions up to five shows a year by
emerging artists. Rachel Whiteread's *Ghost*, the

concrete cast of a house, and Cornelia Parker's
exploded shed *Cold Dark Matter* were both
Chisenhale commissions. A new director, Polly
Staple, took over in late 2008.

Flowers East

82 Kingsland Road, Hoxton, E2 8DP (7920
7777/www.flowerseast.com). Old Street tube/rail.
Open 10am-6pm Tue-Sat. **Credit** AmEx, MC, V.
Map p403 E3.
Flowers East might not garner the press attention
of some of its neighbours, but it is an admired East
End institution. It represents more than 40 artists,
including Patrick Hughes, Derek Hirst and Nicola
Hicks, some of them since the gallery's inception in
Soho in 1970. The main gallery also houses Flowers
Graphics; there's a smaller West End space.
Other location Flowers Central, 21 Cork Street,
Mayfair, W1S 3LZ (7439 7766).

Hales Gallery

Tea Building, 7 Bethnal Green Road, Shoreditch,
E1 6LA (7033 1938/www.halesgallery.com).
Liverpool Street or Old Street tube/rail. **Open**
11am-6pm Wed-Sat. **Credit** AmEx, DC, MC, V.
Map p403 R4.
While the Tea Building never quite became the art
world epicentre some suggested it might, Hales oper-
ates successfully from a large ground-floor space,
showing emerging and mid-career artists such as
Turner Prize nominee Tomoko Takahashi.

Herald Street

2 Herald Street, Bethnal Green, E2 6JT (7168
2566/www.heraldst.com). Bethnal Green tube/rail.

Open 11am-6pm Tue-Fri; noon-6pm Sat, Sun.
No credit cards.
Herald Street has a reputation for showing work by
fashionable young things such as Oliver Payne and
Nick Relph, as well as that of a slightly older generation including Christina Mackie. The gallery
houses Donlon Books, selling rare and out-of-print
art, photography and fashion publications.

★ Matt's Gallery
42-44 Copperfield Road, Mile End, E3 4RR
(8983 1771/www.mattsgallery.org). Mile End
tube. Open 10am-6pm Wed-Sun; or by
appointment. No credit cards.
Few galleries in town are as well respected as Matt's,
named after founder/director Robin Klassnik's dog.
Since 1979, Klassnik has supported artists in their
often ambitious ideas for projects. Richard Wilson's
sump oil installation *20:50* (now in the Saatchi
Gallery, *see p118*) and Mike Nelson's *Coral Reef*
were both Matt's commissions. Lindsay Seers and
Richard Grayson will show during 2009.

★ Maureen Paley
21 Herald Street, Bethnal Green, E2 6JT (7729
4112/www.maureenpaley.com). Bethnal Green
tube/rail. Open 11am-6pm Wed-Sun; or by
appointment. No credit cards.

Maureen Paley opened her East End gallery long
before the area became the hip art mecca it is today.
The gallery represents high-profile artists such as
Turner Prize winners Wolfgang Tillmans and
Gillian Wearing, plus Paul Noble and sculptor
Rebecca Warren. Highlights of 2009 include photo-
graphic work by Londoner Anne Hardy and sculp-
ture and installation by LA artist Eric Wesley.

MOT International
54 Regents Studios, 8 Andrew's Road, Hackney,
E8 4QN (7923 9561/www.motinternational.org).
Bethnal Green tube/Cambridge Heath rail.
Open 11am-6pm Wed-Sat, 2-6pm Sun; or
by appointment. No credit cards.
Successfully making the transition from artist-run
space to commercial enterprise, Chris Hammond's
gallery shows rapidly emerging names including
Amanda Beech, Clunie Reid and Simon Bedwell in
a fifth-floor space overlooking Regent's Canal.

Vilma Gold
6 Minerva Street, Bethnal Green, E2 9EH
(7729 9888/www.vilmagold.com). Bethnal
Green tube/Cambridge Heath rail. Open
11am-6pm Wed-Sun. No credit cards.
Vilma Gold has made a smooth transition from
gallery-to-watch to East End staple. The cognoscenti

Festivals Art & Design

What not to miss this year.

The main event in London's art world
calendar is the **Frieze Art Fair** (15-18
Oct, www.friezeartfair.com), which sees
150 of the best galleries from around
the world descend on Regent's Park
(*see p99*) for four days of trading and
schmoozing. However, Frieze doesn't
have the town to itself. Held in the
same time-frame, the **Zoo Art Fair**
(www.zooartfair.com) is the original
and best Frieze satellite, showing
younger galleries, project spaces
and collectives at the Royal Academy
of Art (*see p106*). And then there's
Marylebone's cheeky **Free Art Fair**
(13-19 Oct, www.freeartfair.com),
an art festival that gives all the art
away for free on the last day.

Other London art festivals have a
tighter niche. The spring offers **Collect**
(15-17 May, www.craftscouncil.org.uk),
a contemporary applied arts fair held at
the new Saatchi Gallery (*see p118*) with
40 international galleries. Five months
later, **Origin** (8-20 Oct, ww.craftscouncil.
org.uk) sees 300 contemporary craft

makers of all disciplines bring their
wares to Somerset House (*see p87*).

Also not to be missed, the **London
Design Festival** (12-22 Sept, www.
londondesignfestival.com) is a monster
celebration of architecture and design
that includes exhibitions, fairs (100%
Design, www.100percentdesign.co.uk;
Tent London, www.tentlondon.co.uk),
tours and other events. Venues cover
museums such as the V&A (*see p122*),
public spaces including Trafalgar Square
(*see p107*) and countless smaller venues.

May and June offers a vast array of
degree shows from London's many art
schools. Among the best are the two
shows staged by the **Royal College of
Art** (www.rca.ac.uk): the first devoted
to painting and photography (29 May-7
June), the second dedicated to design
(26 June-5 July). And over at the Old
Truman Brewery off Brick Lane, **Free
Range** (29 May-21 July, www.free-
range.org.uk) is an eight-week degree
show bonanza featuring dozens of
London and regional colleges.

still flock here for such fashionable fare as the neo-expressionist paintings of Sophie von Hellermann and the anti-heroic assemblages of Brian Griffiths, as well as work by international newcomers such as LA installation artist Jennifer West.

Wilkinson Gallery
50-58 Vyner Street, Bethnal Green, E2 9DQ (8980 2662/www.wilkinsongallery.com). Bethnal Green tube/Cambridge Heath rail. **Open** 11am-6pm Wed-Sat; noon-6pm Sun; or by appointment. **No credit cards.**
Anthony and Amanda Wilkinson's gallery has raised its profile over the past few years by showcasing trendy German painters including Tilo Baumgartel, Matthias Weischer and Thoralf Knobloch. In 2007, they opened these larger premises, the first purpose-built gallery in E2.

★ Yvon Lambert
20 Hoxton Square, Hoxton, N1 6NT (7729 2687/www.yvon-lambert.com). Old Street tube/rail. **Open** 10am-6pm Mon-Sat. **No credit cards. Map** p403 R3.
Paris, New York, and now London. Veteran gallerist Lambert opened this gallery in October 2008 with animations and sculpture by the Mexican artist Carlos Amorales. The gallery occupies what was a municipal building once owned by the local church, and has exhibition spaces on both the ground and mezzanine levels.

South London

Albion
8 Hester Road, Battersea, SW11 4AX (7801 2480/www.albion-gallery.com). Sloane Square tube then 19 bus. **Open** 9am-5.30pm Mon-Fri; Sat during exhibitions. **No credit cards.**
Located since 2004 on the ground floor of this Foster & Partners-designed riverside apartment block, Albion hosts a broad range of exhibitions, including design by David Adjaye and the Campana Brothers, photography by Wang Qingsong, and film and installation by Mariko Mori and the Dutch group Atelier van Lieshout.

Jerwood Space
171 Union Street, Bankside, SE1 0LN (7654 0171/www.jerwoodspace.co.uk). Borough or Southwark tube. **Open** 10am-5pm Mon-Fri; 10am-3pm Sat; Sun during exhibitions; phone to check. **No credit cards. Map** p404 O8.
Part of a larger set-up of theatre and dance spaces (and a great café), the Jerwood had an erratic visual arts presence until recently. Now various awards, including the Jerwood Sculpture Prize (4 Mar-9 Apr 2009), the Jerwood Contemporary Painters (22 Apr-31 May 2009) and the Jerwood Contemporary Makers (10 Jun-19 Aug 2009), are grouped under the banner Jerwood Visual Arts.

INSIDE TRACK
CITY PLANNING

To see where London's building boom might be going, head to **New London Architecture** (Building Centre, 26 Store Street, Bloomsbury, WC1E 7BT, 7636 4044, www.newlondonarchitecture.org), where a permanent exhibition aims to provide an overview of the key developments in the city. The impressive centrepiece is a 39-foot scale model of London, a fascinating bird's-eye view of what the capital looks like now and what it might soon become.

★ South London Gallery
65 Peckham Road, Peckham, SE5 8UH (7703 9799/www.southlondongallery.org). Oval tube then 436 bus/Elephant & Castle tube/rail then 12, 171 bus. **Open** noon-6pm Tue-Sun. **No credit cards.**
On this site for over a century, the SLG became one of the main showcases for the emerging Young British Artists in the 1990s. Still one of the capital's foremost contemporary art venues, the gallery will show work by US artist Ellen Gallagher in 2009. It completes its expansion into an adjacent property this year, creating new exhibition areas and a café.

West London

Louise T Blouin Institute
3 Olaf Street, Shepherd's Bush, W11 4BE (7985 9600/www.ltbfoundation.org). Latimer Road tube. **Open** 10am-6pm Wed, Fri-Sun; 10am-9pm Thur. **Admission** £6; £3 reductions. **Credit** MC, V.
Head of the LTB Group of Companies, which publishes *Art+Auction* and *Modern Painters*, Louise T Blouin MacBain opened this non-profit space in 2006 over three storeys of a 1920s coachworks. The Institute has galleries, a conference centre, a cinema and a café. Experimentation, debate and learning are key principles, with crossovers between politics, science and art the subject of regular events. The 'political pop' of Chinese artist Wang Guangyi is the first show for 2009.

ARCHITECTURE & DESIGN
Architectural Association
36 Bedford Square, Fitzrovia, WC1B 3ES (7887 4000/www.aaschool.net). Tottenham Court Road tube. **Open** 10am-7pm Mon-Fri; 10am-3pm Sat. **Credit** MC, V. **Map** p399 K5.
Talks, events, exhibitions: three good reasons for visiting these elegant premises. The café makes that four. During the summer months, the gallery shows

work by students graduating from the AA School in a display that often spills into the square.

Royal Institute of British Architects

66 Portland Place, Marylebone, W1B 1AD (7580 5533/www.architecture.com). Great Portland Street tube. **Open** 10am-6pm Mon-Fri; 10am-5pm Sat. **Credit** MC, V. **Map** p398 H5.

Temporary exhibitions such as the annual Housing Design Awards are held in RIBA's Grade II-listed headquarters, which houses a bookshop, a first-floor café and one of the finest architectural libraries in the world. It also hosts an excellent lecture series.

Sebastian+Barquet London

19 Bruton Place, Mayfair, W1J 6LZ (7495 8988/www.sebastianbarquetlondon.com). Green Park tube. **Open** 9.30am-5.30pm Tue-Fri; 10am-1pm Sat. **Credit** AmEx, MC, V. **Map** p400 H7.

This design gallery, which specialises in curated shows of mid 20th-century international modernism, opened in October 2008 with the exhibition 'New Hope' featuring American designers such as Philip Lloyd Powell and Wendell Castle. Expect classic pieces by Isamu Noguchi and Jean Prouvé in 2009.

PHOTOGRAPHY

Michael Hoppen Gallery

3 Jubilee Place, Chelsea, SW3 3TD (7352 4499/ www.michaelhoppengallery.com). Sloane Square tube. **Open** noon-6pm Tue-Fri; 10.30am-5pm Sat; or by appointment. **Credit** MC, V. **Map** p397 E11.

This three-storey space shows a mixture of classic vintage photography by the likes of Weegee, Gary Winogrand and William Klein, and contemporary work, including Japanese photographer Nobuyoshi Araki. A 2008 highlight was a retrospective of mid 20th-century New York School street photography.

★ Photographers' Gallery

16-18 Ramillies Street, Soho, W1A 1AU (0845 262 1618/www.photonet.org.uk). Oxford Circus tube. **Open** 11am-6pm Tue-Wed, Sat, Sun; 11am-8pm Thur, Fri. **Credit** AmEx, DC, MC, V. **Map** p406 U2.

Home of the £30,000 Deutsche Börse Photography Prize (20 Feb-19 Apr 2009), this gallery hosts a diverse range of exhibitions and events. In late 2008, the gallery moved, along with its café and shop, to this transitional space. New six-storey premises will open on the same site, with a target date of 2011.

Art of the City

Dig out creative jewels in the ancient, money-mad Square Mile.

The focus of London's art world constantly shifts between east and west. But in the middle lies a small, vibrant scene that escapes the pendulum swing of the media's glare: the cash-happy City of London, packed with blue-chip treasures. It's worth exploring the area at any time, but it's particularly enticing at evenings and weekends when the suits have deserted the place.

A walk between Liverpool Street and Barbican stations, for instance, reveals a glut of luxurious lobby art in the offices of major financial institutions – a Hodgkin here, a Kapoor there. Tantalisingly, most of these well-stocked corporate collections are out of bounds, but there are exceptions. Insurer **Hiscox** (1 Great St Helen's, EC3A 6HX, 7448 6000, www. hiscoxartprojects.com, closed Sat & Sun) holds exhibitions in its arts café, making its collection – which includes pieces by Damien Hirst, Gregory Crewdson and Keith Coventry – accessible to the public as group shows or solo presentations.

A more project-based answer to corporate lobby art can be found at the **Bloomberg Space** (50 Finsbury Square,

EC2A 1HD, 7330 7959, www.bloomberg space.com, closed Sun). Rather than buying art for its European headquarters, the financial news and media provider has a dedicated gallery, running a programme that demonstrates more freedom and greater flexibility than those of both commercial outfits or publicly funded institutions. Each March, Bloomberg hosts ARTfutures (www.artfutures.org.uk), a sale of work by up-and-coming artists organised by the Contemporary Art Society (www.contempart.org.uk).

Moments north of the Barbican Centre, itself home to an excellent gallery and an additional free exhibition space (*see p63*), sits Whitecross Street, which has managed to resist wholesale gentrification. The best of its trio of small commercial spaces is **Ancient & Modern** (201 Whitecross Street, EC1Y 8QP, 7253 4550, www.ancient andmodern.org, closed Mon-Wed & Sun), a sliver of culture that puts on conceptually expansive shows that sometimes reflect the gallery's name with neat pairings of historical with contemporary work.

Children

When it comes to the little 'uns, the choice in London is large.

With so many parks, farms, museums and galleries clamouring for their attention, children will never get bored in London. Most of the key attractions (including the **British Museum** and the mighty South Ken triumvirate of the **Natural History Museum**, the **V&A** and the **Science Museum**) are free; even those that aren't (the **Tower of London**, **London's Transport Museum**) give you a lot of fun for your buck. Over-stimulation is more likely to be a problem: bustle the kids around too many landmarks and you risk teen sulks and toddler tantrums. This chapter will help you plan.

THE LOWDOWN

It pays to consult the experts before drawing up an itinerary. Check the Around Town pages in the weekly *Time Out* magazine. For useful tips, visit the Mayor's website at www.london.gov. uk/young-london, www.kidslovelondon.com or www.whatson4kids.com.

WHERE TO GO

South Bank & Bankside pp44-56

This is London's top stroll – there's so much to see and do for children – just tell them to watch out for joggers and cyclists. The expensive end is around the ever popular **London Eye** (*see p47*) and, across the way, the **London Aquarium** (*see p45*) and the **Movieum** (*see p47*). Moving east, visit the **Southbank Centre** (*see p309*) to see what's happening in the Festival Hall Foyer: free performances and workshops take place during holidays and weekends. Next, the **National Theatre** (*see p343*) offers free entertainment during summer. Keep going, past Gabriel's Wharf – a riverside cluster of arts and crafts shops intermingled with places to eat and drink – towards the Millennium Bridge, where **Tate Modern** (*see p52*) looms large. Try the trails

and games at the Family Zone or take part in an event at the Bloomberg Learning Zone on Level Five. (If you're up for more art, there's a boat service to **Tate Britain**, *see p113*.) Once you've emerged, pick up the Bankside Walk, ducking under the southern end of Southwark Bridge, past the old Anchor Tavern pub. Walk down cobbly Clink Street towards the **Golden Hinde** and **Southwark Cathedral**, having passed the **Clink Prison Museum** (*see p51*), a cheaper alternative to Tooley Street's twin horrors – the **London Dungeon** and its bête noir, the upstart **London Bridge Experience** (*see p53*). From Tooley Street, march through Hays Galleria to regain the riverside path, which takes you to the warship museum **HMS Belfast** (*see p56*) and on, past the dancing fountains to **City Hall** (*see p55*) and **Tower Bridge** (*see p55*).

About the author
Ronnie Haydon *has edited* Time Out London for Children *for eight years. She is also the editor of* Time Out's *Family Breaks in Britain and* 1,000 Things for Children to Do in the Holidays.

THE BEST LONDON LESSONS

For history
Tower of London. See *p71*.

For geography
Greenwich Meridian Line. See *p149*.

For literature
Shakespeare's Globe. See *p51*.

For modern, er, culture
Madame Tussauds. See *p97*.

The City pp57-71

It seems pricey, but the **Tower of London** (*see p71*) is a top day out for all ages; those Beefeaters make genial hosts. If it's free stuff you're after, though, look no further than the excellent **Museum of London**, undergoing a £20 million revamp. The London's Burning exhibition, which runs until winter 2009, often features workshops and storytelling sessions. The **Bank of England Museum** (*see p66*) is a surprising hit with bullion-obsessed youth.

Bloomsbury & Fitzrovia pp75-80

Children are captivated by the Egyptian mummies at the **British Museum** (*see p76* **Profile**). Be warned, it's a tad overwhelming, so children may prefer the short Eyeopener family tour to a meander around the galleries. Activity pack and tours for Young Friends of the Museum (see www.britishmuseum.org) also make the gargantuan collection more accessible. Central London's best playground, **Coram's Fields** (*see p289*), is close, and the **Foundling Museum** (*see p77*) next door should not be missed. The **Cartoon Museum** (*see p77*) holds children's workshops and family fun days every second Saturday of the month. **Pollock's Toy Museum** (*see p80*) is a nostalgia trip for parents, though kids will appreciate the shop. It stocks a great range of pop-up theatres as well as traditional wooden and handcrafted toys.

Covent Garden & the Strand pp81-87

London Transport Museum (*see p82*) is a joyful place with buses, trains and taxis that children can climb on. It has a programme of school-holiday events. For freestyle fun, the acts pulling in the crowds in front of **St Paul's Covent Garden** (*see p83*) are worth watching. On the south side of the Strand, **Somerset House** (*see p87*) allows kids to play outside among the dancing fountains in summer, skate on the winter ice rink or participate in regular arty workshops.

Trafalgar Square pp107-110

London's fantastic square (www.london.gov.uk/ trafalgarsquare) has been a free playground for children since time immemorial – those lions beg to be clambered on. Various festivals take place most weekends. Even if all is quiet in the Square, the **National Gallery** (*see p107*) has paper trails and audio tours, as well as regular kids' workshops and storytelling sessions for under-fives. For three- to 12-year-olds, the **National Portrait Gallery** (*see p109*) runs Small Faces art activities, storytelling sessions and can loan out free activity-filled rucksacks. Just nearby, the newly refurbished **St Martin-in-the-Fields** (*see p110*) has London's only brass-rubbing centre, an absorbing activity beloved by tweenies, as well as a fine café that does plenty of the type of food that goes down well with children.

ARTS & ENTERTAINMENT

Little Angel Theatre. *See p288.*

South Kensington pp121-123

Top on any Grand Day Out itinerary is this cultural goldmine. The **Science Museum** (*see p122*) offers plenty of excitement, with six play zones for all ages, from the Garden in the basement for under-6s to the relaunched Launchpad upstairs, where children can try some 50 experiments. Dinosaur fans won't rest until they've visited the **Natural History Museum** (*see p121*), but there's far more to this monster museum than prehistoric lizards. Though natural beasts may capture your attention, the real Beauty is the **Victoria & Albert Museum** (*see p122*). Its Sunday and school holiday Activity Cart are a great way to focus on the collection, and educational resources are available in the Sackler Centre studios and the Theatre & Performance Galleries (due to open in spring 2009).

Greenwich pp144-147

Magical Greenwich provides a lovely day out away from the mayhem of the West End. Arrive by boat to appreciate its riverside charms, then take time to get the latest on the restoration work to the **Cutty Sark** and to explore the very child-friendly **National Maritime Museum** (*see p145*). From here it's a pleasant leg-stretch in the Royal Park for views from the top of the hill, crowned by the spectacular **Royal Observatory & Planetarium** (*see p149*). When the stars come out, keep an eye out for the luminous green Meridian Line that cuts across the sky towards the city.

EATING & DRINKING

Of the places listed in the Restaurants & Cafés chapter, **Inn The Park** (*see p216*), **Masala Zone** (*see p221*) and **Wagamama** (*see p205*) are particularly child-friendly.

Frizzante@Hackney City Farm

1A Goldsmith's Row, Hackney, E2 8QA (7739 2266/www.frizzanteltd.co.uk). Bus 26, 48, 55. **Open** 10am-5.30pm Tue-Sun. **Main courses** £4.50-£7.50. **Credit** AmEx, DC, MC, V.
A family-run farmhouse kitchen in the heart of Hackney. Once you've trotted around visiting pigs, poultry and sheep you can settle down to eat their relatives (or stick to vegetarian options). The oilcloth-covered tables heave with families tucking into healthy nosh, including farm breakfasts.
▶ *Frizzante also runs the café at the Unicorn Theatre; see p289.*

Giraffe

Units 1&2, Riverside Level 1, Royal Festival Hall, SE1 8XX (7928 2004/www.giraffe.net). Waterloo tube/rail. **Open** 8am-11pm Mon-Fri; 9am-11pm Sat; 9am-10.30pm Sun. **Main courses** £6.95-£13.95. *Set meals (5-7pm)* £6.95 2 courses. **Credit** AmEx, MC, V. **Map** p401 M8.
This popular branch of the global mini-chain pulls families in with balloons and babycinos. Burgers are juicy and the brunch menu lists favourites such as pancakes and eggs and bacon. The kids' lunchtime deal (noon-3pm) includes a drink and dessert for £5.50. **Other locations** throughout the city.
▶ *Branches of noodle-bar Wagamama and pizzeria Strada are right next door.*

London Zoo. See *p288*.

Festivals Children

What not to miss this year.

London teems with events for toddlers, teens and everyone in between. **Imagine** is a childen's literature festival at the Southbank Centre (www.southbankcentre. co.uk) during the mid February half-term week. It entails not only stories, but jokes, stand-up, workshops, funny chairs and all sorts of frolics across the site. Children as young as five can have great fun here. In the summer, **Watch This Space** (*see p343*) makes the National Theatre's Theatre Square the jolliest piece of astroturf in town. Held in Hackney's Victoria Park in early August, the **Underage** festival (www.myspace.com/ underage_club), now in its third year, was the world's first under-17s music festival. In 2008, it attracted about 7,000 teens, who donned free T-shirts and grooved along to the Foals, the Maccabees and the Horrors, fuelled by soft drinks. But now even babies are getting into the groove, thanks to organisations like **Babygroove** (www.babygroove.co.uk), **Baby Loves Disco** (www.babylovesdisco.co.uk) and **Planet Angel** (www.planetangel.net), all of which run regular club nights and days for cool, cutting-edge or cutting-teeth

customers and their parents. Also in mid August, the **Free Time Festival** (www. somerset-house.org.uk) is a fresh-air festival offering arts, dance, music and storytelling among the fountains in Somerset House (*see p87*) and **Kids Week** (www.officiallondontheatre.co.uk) livens up London's Theatreland – for a fortnight in fact. Five- to 16-year-olds can see West End shows free, if accompanied by a full-paying adult. The cosy **Children's Book Week** (www.booktrust.org.uk) in early October gets libraries, schools and celebrated children's authors involved in encouraging children to read. In late November, the **Children's Film Festival** (www.londonchildrenfilm.org.uk) is based at the Barbican (*see p336*) for a week and includes the First Light Young Juries scheme, in which children aged between seven and 16 are invited to be film critics. **National Storytelling Week** (www.sfs. org.uk), in the first week of February, sees events for tellers and listeners of all ages all across town. In the dog days of winter, there's nothing better than curling up with your thumb in your mouth to listen to a good yarn really well told.

ARTS & ENTERTAINMENT

Mudchute Kitchen
Mudchute Park & Farm, Pier Street, Isle of Dogs, Docklands, E14 3HP (7515 5901/www. mudchute.org). Mudchute DLR. **Open** 9am-5pm Tue-Sun. **Main courses** £3-£8. **Credit** MC, V.
A farm fenced in by skyscrapers is an amusing place for anyone to eat lunch, but it's ideal for babies. Eat at farmhouse kitchen-tables, while your babies roll around on a big futon or in the toy corner. Other distractions include the irresistible cakes.
▶ *Older children love the pedestrian tunnel at Island Gardens; see p146 Inside Track.*

Rainforest Café
20 Shaftesbury Avenue, Piccadilly, W1D 7EU (7434 3111/www.therainforestcafe.co.uk). Piccadilly Circus tube. **Open** noon-10pm Mon-Thur, Sun; noon-7.30pm Fri, Sat. **Main courses** £10.25-£16. **Credit** AmEx, DC, MC, V. **Map** p401 K7.
The themed restaurant is designed to thrill children with animatronic wildlife, cascading waterfalls and jungle-sound effects. The menu has lots of family-friendly fare, from 'paradise pizza' and 'Bamba's bangers' to a host of amusing dishes for grown-ups. The children's menu costs £10.95 for two courses.

★ Tate Modern Café: Level 2
2nd floor, Tate Modern, Sumner Street, Bankside, SE1 9TG (7401 5014/www.tate. org.uk). St Paul's tube/Blackfriars tube/rail. **Open** 10am-5.30pm Mon-Thur, Sat, Sun; 10am-9.30pm Fri. **Main courses** £6.95-£10.50. **Credit** AmEx, MC, V. **Map** p404 O7.
In addition to views from the windows framing the busy Thames, there are literacy and art activities on the junior menu, handed out with a pot of crayons. Children can choose haddock fingers, pasta bolognese with parmesan or broccoli and spinach bake, with a choice of drink and an ice-cream or fruit pudding, all for £5.95. There is also a range of half-price mains from the adult menu, such as fish of the day.

TGI Friday's
6 Bedford Street, Covent Garden, WC2E 9HZ (7379 0585/www.tgifridays.co.uk). Covent Garden or Embankment tube/Charing Cross tube/rail. **Open** 11am-11.30pm Mon-Sat; noon-11pm Sun. **Main courses** £6.95-£17. **Credit** AmEx, MC, V. **Map** p401 L7.
The cheery staff, handing out balloons and crayons, are on a mission to make children welcome. The food is varied, but veers towards barbecues, Tex-Mex

dishes, burgers and chips. The children's menu has all the fried regulars, but also pasta dishes and fruity sundae for pudding – or dirt and worm pie for chocolate fiends.

That Place on the Corner
1-3 Green Lanes, Newington Green, N16 9BS (7704 0079/www.thatplaceonthecorner.co.uk). Highbury & Islington tube/Canonbury rail/21, 73, 141, 276, 341, 476 bus. **Open** 10.30-6pm Mon-Thur; 10.30-8pm Fri; 10.30am-2.30pm Sat, Sun. **Main courses** £4.85-£8.25. **Credit** MC, V.
London's only child-friendly café that won't let in unaccompanied grown-ups. There's a library, play shop and dressing-up corner, as well as baking, dance and music classes. The menu sticks to the trusted pasta/panini/big breakfast formula, with brasserie staples like fish cakes.

ENTERTAINMENT

City farms & zoos

There's always something new at **London Zoo** (*see p99*): this year it's the Children's Zoo as well as the wonderful Blackburn Pavilion for exotic birds. The admission charge seems high, but there's loads to do. Easier on the budget is the adorable **Battersea Park Children's Zoo** (www.batterseaparkzoo.co.uk), where Rocky the cheeky monkey, a community of house mice, inquisitive meerkats, playful otters

Diana, Princess of Wales Memorial Playground.

and kune kune pigs are among the inhabitants. City farms all over London charge nothing to get in. Try **Freightliners City Farm** (www.freightlinersfarm.org.uk) and **Kentish Town City Farm** (www.aapi.co.uk/cityfarm) or, in the east, **Mudchute City Farm** (www.mudchute.org) and **Hackney City Farm** (www.hackneycityfarm.co.uk), both of which have cafés (for both, *see pp286-287*).

Puppets

★ Little Angel Theatre
14 Dagmar Passage, off Cross Street, Islington, N1 2DN (7226 1787/www.littleangeltheatre.com). Angel tube/Highbury & Islington tube/rail. **Open** Box office 10am-6pm daily. **Tickets** £6-£12. **Credit** MC, V.
Established by John Wright in 1961, London's only permanent puppet theatre stages diverse productions, devised here or by visiting companies, that cover all aspects of puppetry. There's a Saturday Puppet Club and a Puppet Academy. *Photo p285.*

Puppet Theatre Barge
Opposite 35 Blomfield Road, Little Venice, W9 2PF (winter 7249 6876/summer 07836 202745 mobile/www.puppetbarge.com). Warwick Avenue tube. **Open** Box office 10am-8pm daily. **Tickets** £9.50; £8.50 reductions. **Credit** MC, V.
Moored at lovely Little Venice, this intimate waterborne stage is the setting for quality puppet shows that put a modern twist on traditional tales and kids' classics. The barge is here between December and June; regular performances are held at 3pm on Saturday and Sunday, daily during school holidays.
▶ *For boat trips here from Camden, see p126.*

Science & nature

FREE Camley Street Natural Park
12 Camley Street, King's Cross, NW1 0PW (7833 2311/www.wildlondon.org.uk). King's Cross tube/rail. **Open** 10am-5pm daily. **Admission** free. **Map** p399 L2.
A small but thriving green space on the site of a former coal yard, Camley Street is a lovely oasis at the heart of the renovated King's Cross. London Wildlife Trust's flagship reserve, it hosts pond-dipping and nature-watching for children and its wood-cabin visitor centre is used by the Wildlife Watch Club.

FREE Greenwich Peninsula Ecology Park
Thames Path, John Harrison Way, Greenwich, SE10 0QZ (8293 1904/www.urbanecology. org.uk). North Greenwich tube/108, 161, 422, 472, 486 bus. **Open** 10am-5pm (or dusk) Wed-Sun. **Admission** free.
This wetland haven on the Greenwich Peninsula is a pleasant riverside walk away from the the O2

(*see p313*). Family fun days, like Frog Day in March, and all-summer play activities are part of a busy calendar of events.

Theatre

Half Moon Young People's Theatre

43 White Horse Road, Stepney, E1 0ND (7709 8900/www.halfmoon.org.uk). Limehouse DLR/ rail. **Open** *Box office* 10am-6pm Mon-Fri; 10am-5pm Sat. **Tickets** £5. **Credit** MC, V.
The Half Moon's inclusive policy places particular emphasis on engaging those often excluded by ethnicity and disabilities. Two studios provide a calendar of performances for children aged from six months, and kids can join one of the seven youth theatre groups (for five- to 17-year-olds).

Unicorn Theatre

147 Tooley Street, Bankside, SE1 2HZ (7645 0560/www.unicorntheatre.com). London Bridge tube/rail/Tower Hill tube. **Open** *Box office* 9.30am-6pm Mon-Fri; 10am-6pm Sat; noon-5pm Sun. **Credit** MC, V. **Map** p405 Q8.
This light, bright building near More! London, with its huge white unicorn in the foyer has two performance spaces. Its ensemble company of six actors perform in all Unicorn shows and focus on an outreach programme for local children. Check the website for details of family workshops.

Theme parks

Three theme parks are within easy reach, west of London. **Legoland** (Winkfield Road, Windsor, Berks SL4 4AY, 0870 504 0404, www.legoland.co.uk) is always a hit with youngsters, with good rides, including the new wet 'n' wild Viking's River Splash, and the extraordinary Miniland London, made of 13 million Lego bricks and including a 1:50 scale model of One Canada Square. **Thorpe Park** (Staines Road, Chertsey, Surrey KT16 8PN, 0870 444 4466, www.thorpepark.com) has the fastest rollercoaster in Europe, called Stealth; it's best for older kids and teens. And **Chessington World of Adventures** (Leatherhead Road, Chessington, Surrey KT9 2NE, 0870 444 7777, www.chessington.co.uk) is a gentler option. This 77-year-old theme park is partly a zoo, and children can pay to be zoo keeper for a day. Always call or check the websites for opening times, which vary throughout the year. Only Thorpe Park is open all year; the others close in November until February or March. All cost about £33 per adult, with various different pricing schemes for families. Queues are often unavoidable; arrive early in the morning to make the best of it. Also note that height and health restrictions apply on some rides.

INSIDE TRACK ON THE BUS

Tours too expensive? An economical way of doing London as a family is by bus, since everyone under the age of 19 currently travels free (over-11s need identification; for details, *see p361*). Good routes for sightseeing are the 7, 8, 11 and 12 (all double-deckers). For a riverside route, take the RV1 (Tower Hill to South Bank). Routemasters 9 and 15 are Heritage Routes (*see p363*).

SPACES TO PLAY

London's parks are great escapes for little 'uns. **Hyde Park** (*see p124*) and lovely **St James's Park** (*see p114*) are in the centre of town, but it isn't far to **Regent's Park** (*see p99*) for ducks and boats or even **Hampstead Heath** (*see p127*) for a stroll and perhaps a swim.

FREE Coram's Fields

93 Guilford Street, Bloomsbury, WC1N 1DN (7837 6138/www.coramsfields.org). Russell Square tube. **Open** *Apr-Sept* 8am-8pm Mon-Fri; 9am-8am Sat, Sun. *Oct-Mar* 8am-dusk Mon-Fri; 9am-dusk Sat, Sun. **Admission** free (adults only admitted if accompanied by child under 16). **Map** p399 L4.
This historic site dates to 1747, when Thomas Coram established the Foundling Hospital, but only opened as a park in 1936. It has sandpits, a paddling pool, a football pitch and a zip wire.
▶ *For the Foundling Hospital museum, see p77.*

★ FREE Diana, Princess of Wales Memorial Playground

Near Black Lion Gate, Broad Walk, Kensington Gardens, W8 2UH (7313 9587/recorded information 7298 2141/www.royalparks.gov.uk). Bayswater or Queensway tube. **Open** *Summer* 10am-6.45pm daily. *Winter* 10am-dusk daily. **Admission** free; adults only admitted if accompanied by under-12s. **Map** p395 E8.
A firm favourite with young children who bring buckets and spades, as the pirate ship at its centre is moored in a sea of sand.

Discover

1 Bridge Terrace, Stratford, E15 4BG (8536 5555/www.discover.org.uk). Stratford tube/ rail/DLR. **Open** *Term-time* 10am-5pm Tue-Sun. *School holidays* 10am-5pm daily. **Admission** *Garden* free. *Story trail* £4; £3.50 reductions; free under-2s. **Credit** MC, V.
This is the UK's first creative learning centre for children. Outside, there's a Story Garden with a wooden play ship, a monster's tongue slide, and tunnels.

ARTS & ENTERTAINMENT

Comedy

London's laughing – with you, mostly.

With over 150 comedy clubs and an estimated 2,000 comedians, London is one of the world's greatest cities for stand-up. And it's not simply a matter of great venues and famous performers: most comics expect to be egged on by discerning audiences, in some places egged off. Bubbling away all through the year are plenty of terrific clubs with mixed bills – usually of three or four comics doing 20 minutes each. The venerable **Comedy Store** is the must-see: a key venue in the birth of 'alternative' comedy and of all its various children. For details of line-ups, see the weekly listings in *Time Out London* or at www.timeout.com.

CENTRAL

Amused Moose Soho

Moonlighting, 17 Greek Street, Soho, W1D 4DR (7287 3727/www.amusedmoose.com). Leicester Square or Tottenham Court Road tube. **Shows** 8.30pm Sat. **Admission** £9-£12.50. **Credit** (bookings only) MC, V. **Map** p406 W2.

The grande dame of the comedy world, Hils Jago runs her clubs with military precision. The bills are always strong. She also has a lot of special guests who can't be named – in other words really top names trying out some new material.

Comedy Camp

Barcode, 3-4 Archer Street, Soho, W1D 7AP (7483 2960/www.comedycamp.co.uk). Leicester Square or Piccadilly Circus tube. **Shows** 8.30pm Tue. **Admission** £10. **Credit** MC, V. **Map** p406 W3.

This intimate straight-friendly gay club, based in the heart of Soho, is one of the best nights out anywhere in town. The audiences are always up for a great evening, and resident host and promoter Simon Happily only books fabulous acts.

★ Comedy Store

1A Oxendon Street, Soho, SW1Y 4EE (Ticketmaster 0870 060 2340/www.thecomedy store.co.uk). Leicester Square or Piccadilly Circus tube. **Shows** 8pm Tue-Thur, Sun; 8pm & midnight Fri, Sat; Mon phone for details. **Admission** £15.25-£17.50; £8 reductions. **Credit** AmEx, MC, V. **Map** p406 W4. *See right* **Profile**.

Funny Side of Covent Garden

Corner Store, 33-35 Wellington Street, Covent Garden, WC2E 7BN (0870 446 0616/www. thefunnyside.info). Covent Garden tube. **Shows** 7pm Wed-Sun. **Admission** £12.50. **Credit** AmEx, MC, V. **Map** p407 Z3.

This award-winning medium-sized club in the basement of a cool bar hosts comedy five nights a week. It's one of the nicer rooms in which to watch comedians, and you can nearly always be certain of a cracking line-up of well-established acts.

Lowdown at the Albany

240 Great Portland Street, Marylebone, W1W 5QU (7387 5706/www.lowdownatthealbany.com). Great Portland Street tube. **Shows** 8pm. **Admission** £7-£10. **No credit cards**. **Map** p398 H4.

This rough-around-the-edges basement venue is a simple set-up that hosts stand-up, sketch shows and the odd play. Great for Edinburgh previews.
► *The Lowdown is programmed jointly with the estimable Hen & Chickens; see p292.*

★ Soho Theatre

21 Dean Street, Soho, W1D 3NE (7478 0100/box office 0870 429 6883/www.soho theatre.com). Tottenham Court Road tube. **Shows** 8pm. **Admission** £10-£17.50. **Credit** MC V. **Map** p397 K6.

Over the last few years the Soho Theatre has become one of the best places in London to see comics break out of their normal club sets to perform more substantial solo shows. There is always a good mix of homegrown and international talent on display.

ARTS & ENTERTAINMENT

Profile Comedy Store

After three decades, the Comedy Store remains London's must-see laugh centre.

Dubbed 'Comedy's Unofficial National Theatre', the **Comedy Store** (*see left*) was founded by Don Ward on 19 May 1979. A simple idea – to give would-be stand-ups a mic for as long as the audience would allow – became the legendary 'gong show', with comics being summarily dismissed from the stage by the sounding of a gong. During the 1980s, the Comedy Store made its name as the home of 'alternative comedy': Alexei Sayle, Rik Mayall, Jennifer Saunders, Dawn French, Keith Allen and Arnold Brown were among the radical young comics who cut their teeth here, with the likes of Clive Anderson, Chris Barrie, Paul Merton and Ben Elton hot on their heels. In 1985 the Comedy Store Players improv group was founded and, with a current line-up that includes Paul Merton, Josie Lawrence, Stephen Frost, Andy Smart and Neil Mullarkey, it still offers one of the funniest nights in town. It took the Store several moves around Leicester Square to find the current location, but in 1993

it was able to settle on Oxendon Street, a venue purpose-built for serious punters, with seats that are arranged in an almost gladiatorial semicircle.

Current up-and-comer Chris Mayo recalls his experience of facing those seats: 'One of my first London gigs was foolishly "The Gong Show" at the Comedy Store. Unfortunately, I knew nothing about its wild reputation. After watching act after act die horribly and the aggressive crowd slur and spew their heckles, I kicked off my set with some passing comment about the act before me, hoping to ingratiate myself with the crowd, not knowing he was actually a "Gong Show" legend. I muttered a few words, before the gong of destiny rang in my ears. I lasted 14 seconds.'

Just a quarter of a minute in the show's 30-year history? Chris: it could all have been much, much worse.

THREE TO SEE

Cutting Edge Team
Tuesdays. A deft swipe at current affairs.

Comedy Store Players
Wednesday & Sunday. The in-house improv team.

King Gong
Last Monday of the month. The night for just-a-minute Jennies and have-a-go Harries.

ARTS & ENTERTAINMENT

NORTH LONDON

Downstairs at the King's Head

2 Crouch End Hill, Crouch End, N8 8AA (8340 1028/office 01920 823265/www.downstairs atthekingshead.com). Finsbury Park tube/rail then W7 bus. **Shows** 8pm Tue, Thur, Sat, Sun. **Admission** £4, £3 reductions Tue, Thur; £9, £7 reductions Sat; £7, £5 reductions Sun. **No credit cards.**

Founded in 1981, this venue is still run with huge enthusiasm by the immensely knowledgeable promoter Pete Grahame. It's an easy-going place where comedians can experiment and play around with complete freedom.

★ Hen & Chickens

109 St Paul's Road, Highbury Corner, Islington, N1 2NA (7704 2001/www.henandchickens.com). Highbury & Islington tube/rail. **Shows** 7.30pm, 9.30pm. **Admission** £7-£10. **No credit cards.**

This dinky, black box theatre (seating only 54) above a cosy Victorian corner pub is well known as the place to see great solo shows, especially those warming up for a tour. Recent acts have included the likes of Jimmy Carr, Frankie Boyle and Rhona Cameron.

EAST LONDON

Comedy Café

66-68 Rivington Street, Shoreditch, EC2A 3AY (7739 5706/www.comedycafe.co.uk). Liverpool Street or Old Street tube/rail. **Shows** 9pm Wed, Thur, Sat; 8pm Fri. **Admission** free Wed; £8 Thur; £10 Fri; £15 Sat. **Credit** MC, V. **Map** p403 R4.

Comedy Café is another purpose-built club set up by a comedian. Noel Faulkner mainly keeps to the back room now but, with the emphasis on inviting bills and satisfied punters, his influence can still be felt. The atmosphere is fun and, as the name might suggest, food is an integral part of the experience.

INSIDE TRACK
FUNNY SEASON

There's an element of seasonality to London's comedy circuit. August is a quiet month, as many acts head up to Scotland hoping to make a splash at the Edinburgh Festival. Conversely, April to July is preview time, when big names try out material for the festival, often with reduced admission fees – try **Lowdown at the Albany** or the **Hen & Chickens**. From September to December comics show off Edinburgh successes in London, often at the **Soho Theatre** (*see p290*).

Theatre Royal Stratford East

For listings, *see p343* **Theatre Royal Stratford East**.

A gem of a comedy night is held every Monday inside the opulent surroundings of the Theatre Royal – and it's completely free. The gig, which takes place in the long bar upstairs, has great line-ups considering you're not paying a penny. A good night out.

SOUTH LONDON

Banana Cabaret

Bedford, 77 Bedford Hill, Balham, SW12 9HD (8682 8940/www.bananacabaret.co.uk). Balham tube/rail. **Shows** 9pm Fri, Sat. **Admission** £3 Tue; £13, £9 reductions Fri; £16, £13 reductions Sat. **Credit** (bookings only) MC, V.

Satisfaction is guaranteed every Friday and Saturday at this exciting club in a big roundhouse setting at the Bedford Arms in Balham. A safe bet.

Jongleurs Battersea

The Rise, 49 Lavender Gardens, SW11 1DJ (0844 844 0044/www.jongleurs.com). Clapham Junction rail. **Shows** 8.30pm Thur; 9pm Fri, Sat. **Admission** £9.50-£18.50. **Credit** AmEx, DC, MC, V.

Established back in 1983, this is the flagship of the Jongleurs chain, a chain with an unashamedly business-like approach to comedy. In other words, you get the biggest names on the circuit, but you also get boozed-up punters who would laugh at anything.

★ Up the Creek

302 Creek Road, Greenwich, SE10 9SW (8858 4581/www.up-the-creek.com). Greenwich DLR/rail. **Shows** 9pm Fri; 8.30pm Sat. **Admission** £10, £6 reductions Fri; £15, £12 reductions Sat. **Credit** MC, V.

Originally set up by the legendary Malcolm Hardee ('To say that he has no shame is to drastically exaggerate the amount of shame he has'), this extraordinary purpose-built club has been around since the 1990s, and is still one of the best places to see live comedy. It's renowned for its lively – some would say bear pit – atmosphere.

▶ *On a Sunday night there's a more chilled feel to the 'Sunday Special Club'.*

WEST LONDON

Headliners

George IV, 185 Chiswick High Road, Chiswick, W4 2DR (8566 4067/www.headlinerscomedy. com). Turnham Green tube. **Shows** 9pm Fri, Sat. **Admission** £12; £9 reductions (Fri only). **No credit cards.**

The only purpose-built club in west London (what is it that makes this side of the city such infertile ground for comedy?), with highly experienced Simon Randall at the helm. They're looking to open a second space.

Dance

London is alive with movement.

London's dance scene might initially seem limited in size and scope, but it takes little digging to discover the capital's multicultural, mixed-up vibe thrives across its contemporary dance scene, presenting a dazzling line-up of ethnic moves and truly original collaborations. From the world-renowned **Royal Opera House** to local, niche companies, the variety is rich and inviting. Public participation is encouraged too: when Wayne McGregor, the Royal Ballet's choreographer, hosted a festival to showcase the Royal Opera House, one of his main projects involved 50 young East Enders storming into Covent Garden's tourist hordes.

DANCE COMPANIES

At Sadler's Wells, look out in particular for Matthew Bourne's hugely popular **New Adventures** company (www.new-adventures.net), which reimagined everything from *The Picture of Dorian Gray* to *Edward Scissorhands*. The successful first season of Christopher Wheeldon's **Morphoses** company (www.morphoses.org) in both London and New York has been exciting news for contemporary dance fans, as is the ongoing work of **Russell Maliphant** (www.rmcompany.co.uk), **Sylvie Guillem** (www.sylvieguillem.com), the **Cholmondeleys** and **Featherstonehaughs** (pronounced 'Chumlees' and 'Fanshaws'; www.thechol mondeleys.org), and the **Michael Clark Dancers** (www.michaelclarkcompany.com).

But every year, a company seems to emerge that's ready to highlight and promote a forgotten dance tradition. The **Anwesha Dance Company**, for example, have brought the ancient Manipuri dance form to the capital, a tradition rooted in an isolated area of the Himalayas. The influence of Bollywood is considerable, and companies such as **CandoCo** (www.candoco.co.uk), a group of disabled and able-bodied dancers, have provided formidable inspiration – ballroom dance classes are now on offer for wheelchair users.

MAJOR VENUES

Barbican Centre

For listings, *see p307* **Barbican Centre**. Whenever you're in town, make sure you don't miss the dance elements of the year-round Barbican International Theatre Events (BITE; www.barbican.org.uk/theatre), or the chance to marvel at the vast brutalist architecture of the Barbican Centre itself, conceived in the 1960s and completed in 1982. The centre regularly attracts and nurtures experimental dance, and the Pit Theatre is a perfectly intimate space.

★ Place

17 Duke's Road, Bloomsbury, WC1H 9PY (7121 1000/www.theplace.org.uk). Euston tube/rail. **Box office** noon-6pm Mon-Sat; noon-8pm on performance days. **Tickets** £5-£15. **Credit** MC, V. **Map** p401 K3.
For genuinely emerging dance, look to the Place. This year's annual Place Prize features a season of performances by the shortlist, in addition to the Resolution! dance festival. The Robin Howard Dance Theatre has 300 seats raked to a stage 15m by 12m wide – it's truly electrifying.

INSIDE TRACK
BLUE ELEPHANT

Hidden off Camberwell Road, the **Blue Elephant Theatre** (59A Bethwin Road, Camberwell, SE5 0XT, 7701 0100, www. blueelephanttheatre.co.uk) is hard to find, but its accessible programme of high-class contemporary dance is a delight.

Hip Hop Steps Up

Street dance at Sadler's Wells? Not even choreographer Jonzi D was convinced.

One of the most exciting dance festivals in London, **Breakin' Convention** (May, www.breakinconvention.com) is also one of the most unusual – not least because this celebration of hip hop is hosted by the grand old dame of dance herself, Sadler's Wells (*see below*). Founded in 2004 by choreographer, dancer and

poet Jonzi D, Breakin' Convention is an international event that attracts not only the best in hip hop, but also everything from capoiera to tap.

So did Jonzi D ever imagine he'd find himself at Sadler's Wells? 'In truth, when I first went to Sadler's Wells [in 1987], I didn't think that hip hop would be there. Hip hop was something I enjoyed in the clubs, but theatre was a whole entity. I didn't take seriously the idea of marrying the two. It wasn't until I studied contemporary dance that I realised the possibility of [using all] movement rather than a specific style. I felt that the technique of hip hop dance gave us more on our palette of movement... In this way I always saw this as something that would be embraced by institutions like Sadler's Wells.'

Last year's programme saw a Danish hip hop reimagining of *The Nutcracker*, the disturbing work of Brazil's Membros and live DJ turntablist demonstrations from Tha En4cers, but there was also plenty of popping and b-boying. 'Hip hop going into the theatre will lose that raw, spontaneous, improvised quality that we see within the big nightclubs and the pub jams and the battles,' admits D. 'But ultimately, with theatre, we're doing something different. I think there's a lot more to gain, even though we do lose a little something.'

Breakin' Convention is a global event, but, for D, much of its success is down to the location. 'I've always lived in ondon and I think London thrives as a result of its diverse communities. That's the hip hop mentality: it's not where you're from, it's where you're at – and London is a great place to be at.'

Royal Albert Hall

For listings, *see p309* **Royal Albert Hall**. Perhaps better known for its wide variety of musical and comic performances, this huge venue is also a great place to see dance on a massive scale. It's worth a visit just to experience the imposing dimensions, although the English National Ballet performances are always breathtaking.

★ Royal Opera House

For listings, *see p311* **Royal Opera House**. For the fully elaborated ballet experience, nothing beats the Royal Opera House, home of the Royal Ballet. The current incarnation of the building is a monumentally appropriate venue to contain the onstage presence of legends such as Carlos Acosta. The Linbury Studio Theatre and the Clore Studio Upstairs are used for edgier fare; tours of the opera house sometimes take a peek at a ballet rehearsal.

★ Sadler's Wells

Rosebery Avenue, Finsbury, EC1R 4TN (box office 0870 737 7737/www.sadlerswells.com). Angel tube. **Box office** *In person* 9am-8.30pm Mon-Sat, times vary. *By phone* 24hrs daily. **Tickets** £10-£60. **Credit** AmEx, MC, V. **Map** p404 N3.

Purpose-built in 1998 on the site of the original 17th-century theatre of the same name, this dazzling complex is home to an impressive line-up of local and international performances. In addition to the main theatre, the smaller Lilian Baylis Studio offers smaller-scale new works and works-in-progress, while the Peacock Theatre (on Portugal Street in Holborn) operates as a satellite venue. A specially chartered bus departs after each performance to Farringdon, Victoria and Waterloo stations.

Siobhan Davies Dance Studios
85 St George's Road, Southwark, SE1 6ER (box office 7091 9650/www.siobhandavies.com). Elephant & Castle tube. **Box office** 9am-9pm Mon-Fri; 10am-2pm Sat, Sun. **Tickets** £3-£18. **Credit** AmEx, MC, V. **Map** p404 N10.

Opened in 2006, this award-winning studio was designed in consultation with dancers, ensuring that the building met their needs. Davies, who founded the company in 1988, often explores different spaces beyond this beautiful theatre, so be sure to check with the venue for her performances before setting out.

Southbank Centre
For listings, *see p309* **Southbank Centre**.

The refurbishment of the Royal Festival Hall has led to a revival in the dance programme of the cluster of venues collectively known as the Southbank Centre. In 2008, the Centre hosted the inaugural Dance Union, a celebration of European dance that drew works from 23 countries; Dance Umbrella also visits each year. And outside festival seasons, companies such as CandoCo often take over the mammoth Royal Festival Hall, the medium-sized Queen Elizabeth Hall, the intimate Purcell Room and the riverside terrace outside.

OTHER VENUES

Greenwich Dance Agency
Borough Hall, Royal Hill, Greenwich, SE10 8RE (8293 9741/www.greenwichdance.org.uk). Greenwich DLR/rail. **Box office** 9.30am-5.30pm Mon-Fri. **Classes** £8. **Tickets** £7-£15. **Credit** MC, V.

Home to resident artist Temujin Gill of the Temujin Dance Company and Noel Wallace, who made history as the English National Ballet's first black dancer, this fun art deco venue hosts classes and workshops, as well as the surely unique gDA cabaret – samples of dance performed among punters who are tucking into full table-service meals.

Laban Centre
Creekside, Deptford, SE8 3DZ (information 8691 8600/tickets from Greenwich Theatre 8469 9500/www.laban.org). Deptford DLR/Greenwich DLR/rail. **Open** 10am-6pm Mon-Sat; or until start of performance. **Tickets** £1-£15. **Credit** MC, V.

Festivals

What not to miss this

The biggest dance festival is the world-class **Dance Um** (Sept-Nov, www.danceumbrella founded in 1978 and just as strong ever. Held at venues across the capital it welcomes troupes and performers from home and abroad, working in a huge variety of styles.

Elsewhere, at Olympia, the four-day **Move It!** festival (5-8 Mar, www.dance -london.co.uk) hosts more than 100 performances in any number of styles – from classical ballet to ballroom to contemporary – alongside classes and seminars. And there's just as much variety at the **Big Dance** (July, www.londongov.uk/bigdance), a public celebration of dance that offers classes and shows in everything from capoeira to English folk dance. Last year, the festival included the Big Chair Dance, an event performed by 200 older Londoners in their own homes.

Lovers of modern dance should look into the **Deloitte Ignite Festival** at the Royal Opera House (Sept, www.royalopera.org), a mini-festival curated by Wayne McGregor that offers innovative dance performances, art installations and film screenings in and around the magnificent building. There's more contemporary dance at the Place: the lengthy **Resolution!** festival (6 Jan-14 Feb, www.theplace.org.uk) offers hundreds of performances by young dancers, while the prestigious **Place Prize** (Sept, www.theplaceprize.com) competition has become a mini-festival.

Other festivals take a particular niche, from the four-day, Thames-side **London International Tango Festival** (Sept, www.tangoinlondon.com) to the **Flamenco Festival** (Mar, www.sadlers wells.com) **and Breakin' Convention** (May; *see left* **Hip Hop Steps Up**).

The home of Transitions Dance Company, this beautiful independent conservatoire for dance training is renowned as the home of Rudolf Laban, founder and creator of a unique and enduring discipline for movement. The stunning premises, which cost £22m and were designed by Herzog & de Meuron, include a 300-seat auditorium.

▶ *Herzog & de Meuron were also responsible for the design of Tate Modern; see p52.*

...on-stop film scene.

(and indeed
n be found at
e art deco
s when you
s real cinema
... great quirky
independents like the **Curzon** and **Everyman** groups, the **Rio**, and the **Phoenix** are the best for a filmgoing treat. Next up are cinemas at art centres like the cutting-edge **ICA**, the mighty **Barbican** and the **Riverside Studios**. All these are likely to be screening programmes of first-run, low-budget independent and arthouse films, rare classics, mini-seasons and Sunday morning repertory screenings, as well as hosting the capital's multitudinous film festivals throughout the year.

WHERE TO GO

Queen of the repertories is **BFI Southbank**, Britain's national film theatre (its former name – it is still referred to by many Londoners as the NFT). It shows some first-run films, but the seasons delving into cinema and TV's more obscure byways are the real draw. It's become even more of a must for film lovers since its recent expansion and the opening of the fabulous Mediatheque, where you can view much of the BFI's film archives. After the BFI, London's best repertory cinema is the **Riverside Studios**, where you'll find special seasons and film events. Also worth checking out are the big museums and galleries, which frequently programme film seasons linked to their current exhibitions: check out the **British Museum** (*see p77*), **National Gallery** (*see p107*) and **Imperial War Museum** (*see p142*), or **Tate Modern** (*see p52*) for avant-garde art films. Several luxury hotels now have screening rooms open to the public: our favourites are those at the **Soho Hotel** and **One Aldwych** (for both, *see p177*).

Outdoor summertime screens have popped up across the capital. The most glamorous are the **Somerset House Summer Screen** (www.somersethouse.org.uk/film) for first-runs and old classics in its magnificent Georgian courtyard, and Park Nights at the **Serpentine Gallery** (*see p124*), where you can watch films in the latest of their annual summer pavilions.

Like a bit of mystery? Sign up for **Secret Cinema** (www.secretcinema.org) and five hours before their monthly screening you'll be emailed its secret location and the film's title. You could end up watching it on a rooftop.

The lowdown

Consult *Time Out* magazine's weekly listings or visit www.timeout.com/film for full details of what's on; programmes change on a Friday. Films released in the UK are classified under the following categories: **U** – suitable for all ages; **PG** – open to all, parental guidance is advised; **12A** – under-12s only admitted with an over-18; **15** – no one under 15 is admitted; **18** – no one under 18 is admitted.

FIRST-RUN CINEMAS

Central London

Barbican
Silk Street, the City, EC2Y 8DS (7382 7000/ www.barbican.org.uk). Barbican tube/Moorgate tube/rail. **Screens** 3. **Tickets** £8.50; £4.50-£6 reductions; £5.50 Mon. **Credit** AmEx, MC, V. **Map** p402 P5.
The three screens at the concrete behemoth (*see p307*) show new releases of world and independent cinema alongside an inventive range of seasons, such as the Bad Film Club.

Curzon
Chelsea *206 King's Road, Chelsea, SW3 5XP (7351 3742/www.curzoncinemas.com). Sloane Square tube then 11, 19, 22, 319 bus.* **Screens** 1. **Tickets** £7-£12; £5-£7 reductions. **Map** p397 E12.
Mayfair *38 Curzon Street, Mayfair, W1J 7TY (7495 0500/www.curzoncinemas.com). Green Park or Hyde Park Corner tube.* **Screens** 2. **Tickets** £8-£12; £5-£9 reductions. **Map** p400 H8.

Soho *99 Shaftesbury Avenue, Soho, W1D 5DY (information 7292 1686/box office 0870 756 4620/www.curzoncinemas.com). Leicester Square tube.* **Screens** 3. **Tickets** £8-£12; £5-£9 reductions. **Map** p407 X3.
All *www.curzoncinemas.com.* **Credit** MC, V.
Expect a superb range of shorts, rarities, double bills and seasons alongside new international releases at the Curzons. There's '70s splendour in Mayfair (it's sometimes used for premières) and comfort in Chelsea, which is perfect for a Sunday screening after a King's Road brunch. And coolest of the bunch, the Soho outpost has a buzzing café and surprisingly decent basement bar.

★ ICA Cinema
Nash House, the Mall, Westminster, SW1Y 5AH (information 7930 6393/box office 7930 3647/ www.ica.org.uk). Charing Cross tube/rail. **Screens** 2. **Tickets** £8; £7 reductions. **Credit** MC, V. **Map** p401 K8.
Hidden incongruously amid the white stucco of the Mall, London's leading contemporary arts centre (*see p115*) meets its brief not only by screening a hugely eclectic range of cinema, but distributing some of the most noteworthy films of recent years.

Odeon Leicester Square
Leicester Square, Soho, WC2H 7LQ (0871 224 4007/www.odeon.co.uk). Leicester Square tube.

Festivals Film

What not to miss this year.

Since the establishment of Film London, the capital's film development agency, in 2003, with a remit to bring new audiences to film with events reflecting the city's diversity, there's been an explosion in the number of film festivals in town. The **London Film Festival** (www.bfi.org.uk/lff, October) is far and away the capital's most prestigious. About 180 new British and international features are screened, mainly at BFI Southbank (*see p299*), the Odeon Leicester Square (*see above*) and other cinemas across town.

The **London Lesbian & Gay Film Festival** in late March is the UK's third largest film festival (7928 3232, www.llgff.org.uk). Earlier in the month comes the highly rated celebration of women filmmakers, **Birds Eye View** (www.birds-eye-view.co.uk). The **Human Rights Watch International Film Festival** (7713 2773, www.hrw.org/iff, 19-27 Mar) aims to put a human face on threats to individual freedom and dignity, while the **Palestine**

Film Festival (www.palestinefilm.org) in spring has grown from university society event to major fest. Closer to home, the **East End Film Festival** (www.eastend filmfestival.com, 23-30 Apr) explores cinema's great potential to cross cultural boundaries, reserving a special place for films starring London's East End.

Several thrusting young festivals now screen the output of up-and-coming regions. In May, the Ciné Lumière (*see p299*) joins in with its usually wonderful **Mosaiques** festival and, in the same month, among the best from Eastern Europe is the Polish Cultural Institute's **Kinoteka** (www.kinoteka.org.uk). In November, there are not one, but two Latin American film festivals: **Discovering Latin America** (www.discoveringlatin america.com) offers films, documentaries and shorts that rarely get distribution, and the **Latin American Film Festival** (www. latinamericanfilmfestival.com) showcases some of the latest commercial features.

ARTS & ENTERTAINMENT

Some Like It Short

David Jenkins, our online film editor, selects London's best short film events.

Short film nights in London are among the most laid-back and audience-friendly on the arts calendar, as well as often being quietly revelatory happenings.

Short and Sweet (www.shortand sweet.tv) is a weekly forum for catching short films, animation and music videos. They're usually based in the luxurious surroundings of Café 1001 (101 Brick Lane, corner of Dray Walk, 7247 9679). With a stern commitment to explore 'adventures in moving image', the trendy **OneDotZero** stable (www.onedotzero. com) offers more ambient, installation-type fare, with a particular interest in editing, shooting methods and technological innovation. Quality is assured from the excellent **Future Shorts** label (www.future shorts.com) who, at any one time, seem to be having a screening, launch or party in some far-flung global locale. In London, they usually put on at least two or three nights a month.

There's also a chance that you might end up in London during one of the many annual film festivals and celebrations. The big one is the **Times BFI London Film Festival** (www.bfi.org.uk/lff/) which usually runs for the last two weeks of October, with nine or ten themed programmes of short films screened at a variety of locations. Pipping the LFF to the post by a week or so is the innovative and always delightfully left-field **Raindance Festival** (www.raindance.co.uk), which offers some of the best shorts programmes on the cinematic calendar. If you're not around at the time, they also put out an annual 'Best of' DVD. Mid-to-late July there's the **Rushes Soho Shorts** festival (www.soho shorts.com) which features everything from documentaries, music promos and animation to all sorts of weird and quite wonderful esoterica. And if you want to ring in the year with a huge selection of shorts, then try the **London Short Film Festival** (www.shortfilms.org.uk) – until recently called the Halloween Film Festival – which boasts plenty of themed nights, guest speakers, newly soundtracked films and world premières. Ardent fans of animation will not want to miss the excellent annual **London International Animation Festival** (www.liaf.org.uk), which takes place in various central London locations and usually screens about 200 short works from all over the globe. And last but by no mean least is the annual **Portobello Film Festival** (www.portobellofilmfestival.com) where the screenings – aside from the admirable quality of its wide array of shorts – have the distinctly enticing advantage of being mostly free of charge.

Screens 1. **Tickets** £12.50-£17; £9-£14 reductions. **Credit** AmEx, MC, V. **Map** p407 X4. You'll often find the red carpets and crush barriers up outside this mighty art deco gem – it's London's classic site for star-studded premières. If you're lucky, you might catch one of its sporadic silent film screenings, with accompaniment on a 1937 organ that really does come up through the floor.

Outer London

Electric Cinema

191 Portobello Road, Notting Hill, W11 2ED (7908 9696/www.electriccinema.co.uk). Ladbroke Grove or Notting Hill Gate tube. **Screens** 1. **Tickets** £12.50-£14.50; £7.50-£10 Mon. **Credit** AmEx, MC, V.

A legend among London filmgoers, the Electric is one of the city's oldest. It's gone from past-it fleapit to luscious luxury destination with leather seats and sofas, footstools and a bar inside the auditorium. It also has a fashionable café restaurant.

Everyman & Screen Cinemas

Everyman *5 Hollybush Vale, Hampstead, NW3 6TX. Hampstead tube.* **Screens** 2. **Tickets** £12-£15; £7.50 reductions. **Credit** AmEx, MC, V. **Screen on the Green** *83 Upper Street, Islington, N1 0NP. Angel tube.* **Tickets** £8.50; £6-£6.50 reductions; £6 Mon. **Map** p402 O2. **All** *0870 066 4777/www.everymancinema.com.* **Credit** MC, V.

Is the Everyman the only cinema in town boasting a concierge station? Possibly London's most elegant cinema, the Everyman has a glamorous bar and two-seaters (£30) in its 'screening lounges', complete with foot stools and wine cooler. The Everyman recently bought London's three Screen cinemas, of which the Islington's Screen on the Green is our favourite.

★ Phoenix

52 High Road, East Finchley, N2 9PJ (8444 6789/www.phoenixcinema.co.uk). East Finchley tube. **Screens** 1. **Tickets** £8; £5 reductions. **Credit** MC, V.

Built in 1910, revamped in the 1930s, the Phoenix offers real old-fashioned glamour with its red and gold auditorium. Owned by a charitable trust enjoying strong community support, it runs a varied programme including a popular silent strand.

Rio Cinema
107 Kingsland High Street, Dalston, E8 2PB (7254 6677/www.riocinema.org.uk). Dalston Kingsland rail. **Screens** 1. **Tickets** £6-£8; £3.50-£6 reductions. **Credit** AmEx, MC, V.
Another great art deco survivor restored to its original sleek lines, the Rio is east London's finest independent. Alongside mainstream releases, the Rio is well-known for its Turkish and Kurdish film fests.

Vue O2 Multiplex
O2 Arena, Peninsula Square, North Greenwich, SE10 0AX (08712 240 240/www.myvue.com). North Greenwich tube. **Screens** 11. **Tickets** £6.80-£10; £5.50-£6 reductions. **Credit** MC, V.
The massive screen (apart from the IMAX cinemas, this is the largest in the UK) at the O2 (*see p313*) may make a trek out to the Dome worthwhile.

REPERTORY CINEMAS

Several first-run cinemas also offer rep-style fare – check *Time Out* magazine for locations.

★ BFI Southbank
South Bank, SE1 8XT (information 7928 3535/box office 7928 3232/www.bfi.org.uk). Embankment tube/Waterloo tube/rail. **Screens** 3. **Tickets** £8.60; £6.25 reductions; £5 Tue. **Credit** AmEx, MC, V. **Map** p401 M8.
London's National Film Theatre has had a name change foisted on it. That's all forgiven and forgotten now, thanks to expansion in 2007 and the opening of the Mediatheque, Studio and Gallery. And with a chic new café-bar, it's packing in crowds like never before.
► *The Mediatheque room gives free access to the BFI's huge archive of films and documentaries.*

Ciné Lumière
Institut Français, 17 Queensberry Place, South Kensington, SW7 2DT (7073 1350/www.institut-francais.org.uk). South Kensington tube. **Screens** 1. **Tickets** £9; £7 reductions. **Credit** MC, V. **Map** p397 D10.
This year should find Ciné Lumière all gussied up after the renovation of its swanky art deco interior. No longer for French films only, it's become a standard-bearer for world cinema in the capital.

Prince Charles
7 Leicester Place, Leicester Square, WC2H 7BY (box office 0870 811 2559/www.princecharles cinema.com). Leicester Square tube. **Screens** 1. **Tickets** £4-£5; £1.50-£3.50 reductions. **Credit** MC, V. **Map** p407 X3.

Cheap and cheerful Prince Charles sits just up an alley from the overpriced Leicester Square monsters. It's perfect for catching up on still-fresh films you missed first time round. And it's also famed for its riotous singalong screenings.

★ Riverside Studios
Crisp Road, Hammersmith, W6 9RL (8237 1111/www.riversidestudios.co.uk). Hammersmith tube. **Screens** 1. **Tickets** £7.50; £6.50 reductions. **Credit** MC, V.
Regular double-bills slot between special seasons, many spotlighting film from Eastern European countries. The café-bar and riverside terrace are usually packed with a voluble mix of film- and theatregoers.

IMAX

BFI IMAX
1 Charlie Chaplin Walk, South Bank, SE1 8XR (0870 787 2525/www.bfi.org.uk/imax). Waterloo tube/rail. **Screens** 1. **Tickets** £6.25-£12; £5-£9.75 reductions. **Credit** AmEx, MC, V. **Map** p401 M8.
Experience the biggest screen in the UK at the BFI's gigantic state-of-the-art IMAX. Mostly made-for-IMAX fare, you'll also find mainstream blockbusters like *Alien* or *300* – those of a sensitive disposition should stay away!
► *There's also an IMAX at the Science Museum, with an exhibition-themed programme; see p122.*

ARTS & ENTERTAINMENT

Gay & Lesbian

The inside scoop on where to be out.

Gay London can be a pleasing shock to visitors, thanks to its galloping vastness and diversity. Forget 'no sex, please, we're British': London is proud and sexy, as kinky and hard as you like, as playful and innocent as you fancy.

Although **G-A-Y** has gone south to **Heaven** (yes, we enjoyed typing that), Soho remains most visitors' first port of call, whether for drag nights, cocktails or a work-out. Over the river, Vauxhall is home to night-into-day house freaks. Alongside the City, Shoreditch is where to find the artiest, under-the-radar nightlife happenings, though the arrival in 2008 of the new **Ghetto** should shift things more mainstream. And all over town, you'll find the clubs more liberated than in Sydney and more numerous than in New York. In short, this is currently the best gay scene in the world.

GETTING OUT & ABOUT

The Soho scene centred on Old Compton Street continues to attract punters, with luvvies taking in a singalong at the **Green Carnation**, gAy-listers downing cocktails at the **Shadow Lounge**, fit-freaks working out at **Sweatbox** and lovers of drag heading to Trannyshack at the **Soho Revue Bar** (*see p321*). But check out London's other mini gay scenes: in Vauxhall you'll find the sparkling **Barcode Vauxhall**, leather bar the **Hoist**, a host of doof-doof clubs and the sensational **RVT**; and Shoreditch is the new home to **Ghetto**, plus a thriving network of small clubs whose nights aren't strictly gay but are always mixed (*see pp323-325*).

Chariots remains the sauna chain of choice, although **Vault 139** brings in new talent all the time. Most regular bars don't have backrooms, but club nights can get pretty raunchy, and the monthly **Hard On** event (www.hardonclub.co.uk) is the top pick on the calendar for lovers of fetish and leather.

For those who like dancing with their dudes, legendary **Heaven** – now owned by the people behind the almost equally famous G-A-Y night – still draws the crowds. However, your best bet is to seek out the themed nights at other venues that cater for individual tastes: Megawoof for muscle bears; Rudeboyz for chavs; and Starkers for, yes, naturists. If 'gay music' gives you a rash, seek out the ragga at **Club Caribana**, bhangra at **Club Kali** or salsa at **Exilio**

Latino. Fancy some live theatre or comedy? Top-drawer programmes are run at the **Drill Hall** (www.drillhall.co.uk) and **Soho Theatre** (*see p343*), and Barcode Soho's weekly stand-up gig, Comedy Camp, is a surefire hit.

The closure in autumn 2008 of Candy Bar, the capital's premier lesbian bar, leaves a major gap. However, the women-only **Glass Bar**, having survived a recent threat of closure, is back in vogue, and **First Out** is still jammed with lesbians on a Friday night. Code and Play at **Enclave** are popular monthly girls' nights.

CAFES & RESTAURANTS

Every café and restaurant in London welcomes gay custom, though some more than others. Among venues listed in this book, **J Sheekey** (*see p206*), the **Wolseley** (*see p215*), **Moro** (*see p202*), **Quo Vadis** (*see p211*), **Arbutus** (*see p208*) and **Wild Honey** (*see p215*) all have enthusiastic gay followings.

Balans

60 Old Compton Street, Soho, W1D 4UG (7439 2183/www.balans.co.uk). Leicester Square or Piccadilly Circus tube. **Open** 8am-5am Mon-Thur; 8am-6am Fri, Sat; 8am-2am Sun. **Admission** £5 after midnight Mon-Thur; £7 Fri, Sat. **Credit** AmEx, MC, V. **Map** p408 W3.

The gay café of choice for many years, Balans is all about location, location, location (and hot waiters, and pretty decent food). Across from Compton's bar

Horse Meat Disco at **Eagle London**. *See p302.*

and next door to Clone Zone, Balans is always busy and always flirty. The nearby Balans Café (No.34) serves a shorter version of the menu. Both are open almost all night: good for post-clubbers. *Photo p303.* **Other locations** 239 Old Brompton Road, Earl's Court, SW5 9HP (7244 8838); 187 Kensington High Street, Kensington, W8 6SH (7376 0115); 214 Chiswick High Road, Chiswick, W4 1BD (8742 1435).

First Out

52 St Giles High Street, Covent Garden, WC2H 8LH (7240 8042/www.firstoutcafebar.com). Tottenham Court Road tube. **Open** 10am-11pm Mon-Sat; 11am-10.30pm Sun. **Credit** MC, V. **Map** p409 X1/2.
This lesbian and gay café was London's first homosexual café (way back in 1986) and still packs in a mostly lesbian crowd. A busy noticeboard, friendly

service and a yummy vegetarian menu give the place a genuine community feel, while a licence for cocktails and beer make it a handy spot in which to enjoy pre-club drinks.

★ Randall & Aubin

16 Brewer Street, Soho, W1F 0SQ (7287 4447/www.randallandaubin.com). Piccadilly Circus tube. **Open** noon-11pm Mon-Sat; 4-10pm Sun. **Credit** AmEx, MC, V. **Map** p406 W3.
Established in 1906, this French seafood charcuterie and boucherie is an experience in itself, if you can bear the wait in the inevitable queue outside. A massive mirror ball and an exuberant, enthusiastic and camp waiting staff make it a well-known gay dining destination, although it attracts clients from everywhere. If the menu isn't always quite up to scratch, it makes up for it with its joyous ambience, smack in the heart of Soho.

Festivals Gay & Lesbian

What not to miss this year.

Summer is the key season. In June, **Pride London** (www.pridelondon.org) remains popular, perhaps more for the associated street party in a traffic-free Soho than for the long-standing parade from Oxford Street to Victoria Embankment. A two-week cultural festival precedes the big day. **Soho Pride** (www.sohopride.net) saw the same West End streets overrun for Sunday 17 August 2008, although

funding cuts may prevent it happening this year. In Regent's Park, **Black Pride** (www.ukblackpride.org.uk), a queer alternative to the Notting Hill Carnival (*see p273*) that continues to grow every year, celebrates its fourth birthday. In spring, there's the annual **London Lesbian & Gay Film Festival** (*see p297*), with an emphasis on edgier fare in the wake of *Brokeback Mountain*.

ARTS & ENTERTAINMENT

CLUB NIGHTS & VENUES

Themed nights at London's many clubs change frequently, but stalwart clubs such as **G-A-Y** and **Heaven** still draw crowds regardless.

Club Caribana

Factory, 65 Goding Street, SE11 5AW (0845 456 7686/mobile 07931 395 395/www.caribana club.com). Vauxhall tube. **Open** 11pm-6am 1st Sat of mth. **Admission** £5-£8 before midnight, then £10. **Credit** MC, V.
Held on the first Saturday of the month, this mixed gay Caribbean night features R&B, bashment ragga, reggaeton and soul. Look out for occasional theme nights and live PAs.

Club Kali

Dome, 1 Dartmouth Park Hill, Dartmouth Park, N19 5QQ (7272 8153/www.clubkali.com). Tufnell Park tube. **Open** 10pm-3am 3rd Fri of mth.
Admission £8; £5 reductions. **No credit cards.**
The world's largest LGBT Asian dance club offers Bollywood, bhangra, Arabic music, R&B and dance classics spun by DJs Ritu, Riz & Qurra, held every third Friday monthly.

Eagle London

349 Kennington Lane, Vauxhall, SE11 5QY (7793 0903/www.horsemeatdisco.co.uk). Vauxhall tube/rail. **Open** 8pm-3am Sun.
Admission £6. **No credit cards.**
Formerly known as South Central, this place has rapidly become a hub for those wishing to try a bit of leather without a strict dress code. It also hosts the deliciously mixed Sunday night Horse Meat Disco, where bears and fashionistas come together for an excellently random music mix, from dance, disco and soul to new wave and punk. *Photo p301.*

INSIDE TRACK
SUPER-LATE CLUBBING

Still craving shirts-off muscle boys going at some night-and-day techno? **Trade** (www.tradeuk.net), the original after-hours club, was made homeless when Turnmills closed last year, but still returns for special events. Otherwise, head to Vauxhall. At **Fire** (South Lambeth Road, SW8 1UQ, www.fireclub.co.uk), nights such as Gravity, Later, Orange and Open can keep you furnished with funky house from Friday morning through Tuesday. Seriously, our favourite night is the monthly Horizon, open 11pm-8am on second Saturdays. Other ideas are **Union** and neighbour **Area**, on the Albert Embankment (no.66 and no.67-68).

Exilio Latino

LSE, 3 Houghton Street, off Aldwych, Covent Garden, WC2E 2AS (mobile 07931 374391/ www.exilio.co.uk). Holborn tube. **Open** 10pm-3am Sat. **Admission** £5 before 11pm; £8 after 11pm.
No credit cards. Map p401 M6.
A gay club where you can actually salsa – a beacon of Latin music in a scene of gay pop, with DJs Chaci and Tet playing merengue, salsa, cumbia and Latin for a lesbian and gay crowd.

★ Ghetto

58 Old Street, the City, EC1V 9AJ (7287 3726/ www.ghetto-london.co.uk). Old Street tube/rail.
Open/admission/credit phone or check website for details. **Map** p402 P4.
This Soho institution has found a new location in the East End, where most of the arty and interesting elements of London's gay life now reside. The new venue has kept the red New York basement feel of its old home, but with better seating, lighting and sound. It also combines club and bar spaces, with Trash Palace resident upstairs. We reckon the currently homeless Popstarz night will be here for 2009; on other nights, expect to find the Cock (for indie), PYT (for R&B) and Miss Shapes (for women).

★ Heaven

Underneath the Arches, Villiers Street, WC2N 6NG (7930 2020/www.heaven-london.com). Embankment tube/Charing Cross tube/rail.
Open/admission/credit phone or check website for details. **Map** p409 Y5.
London's most famous gay club is a bit like *Les Misérables* – it's camp, it's full of history and tourists love it. Popcorn (Mon) has long been a good bet – the night recently celebrated its tenth birthday – but, with the club taken over by the massive G-A-Y night in autumn 2008, who knows what to expect? For years, divas with an album to flog (even broads as classy as Madonna) have turned up at G-A-Y on a Saturday. Expect big things to happen here.

★ RVT

Royal Vauxhall Tavern, 372 Kennington Lane, Vauxhall, SE11 5HY (7820 1222/www.rvt.org. uk). Vauxhall tube/rail. **Open** 7pm-midnight Mon-Fri; 9pm-2am Sat; 2pm-midnight Sun.
Admission £5-£7. **Credit** MC, V.
If you're seeking a very London gay experience, this is where to start. This pub-turned-legendary-gay-venue operates an anything-goes booking policy. The most famous fixture is Saturday's queer performance night Duckie (www.duckie.co.uk), with Amy Lamé hosting turns at midnight that range from strip cabaret to porn puppets; Sunday's Dame Edna Experience drag show, from 5pm, is also essential, drawing quasi-religious devotees. The aim is always to please the crowd of regulars, who are reliably vocal in their feedback. Punters verge on the bear – but the main dress code is 'no attitude'. *Photo p305.*

XXL

51/53 Southwark Street, Borough, SE1 1RU
(7403 4001/www.xxl-london.com). London
Bridge tube. **Open** 10pm-3am Wed; 9pm-6am
Sat. **Admission** £3-£12. **No credit cards.**
Map p404 P8.

The world's biggest club for bears and their admirers, XXL is nirvana for the chubbier, hairier and
blokier of London's gay men. True to its name the
venue is bigger than average, with two dance floors,
two bars and an outdoor beer garden. Also home to
muscle-bears and plenty of twinky admirers.

PUBS & BARS

Unless otherwise indicated, all the pubs and
bars listed here are open to both gay men and
lesbians. In the Shoreditch area, Trash Palace,
the bar section of **Ghetto** (*see left*), promises
to be a major draw.

Barcode Vauxhall

Arch 69, Goding Street, Vauxhall, SE11 4AD
(7582 4180/www.bar-code.co.uk). Vauxhall tube.
Open 4pm-1am Mon-Wed, Sun; 4pm-2am Thur;
4pm-3.30am Fri; 4pm-6am Sat. **Admission**
£4 after 10pm Fri, Sat. **Credit** AmEx, MC, V.
Map p408 W3.

This massive, lavish venue attracts a blokey-ish
crowd, despite its shiny surfaces, and it's a great
venue. Prior to the arrival of BCV, Vauxhall was
mostly for clubbing, with pre-dance drinks to be
enjoyed anywhere-else-but. Now those pre-dancing
punters are joined here by folks just after drink.
▶ *BCV's forerunner Barcode, off Shaftesbury*
Avenue, hosts the mostly gay and thoroughly
excellent Comedy Camp night (see p290).

Black Cap

171 Camden High Street, Camden, NW1 7JY
(7485 0538/www.theblackcap.com). Camden
Town tube. **Open** noon-2am Mon-Thur; noon-
3am Fri, Sat; noon-1am Sun. **Admission** £2-£5.
Credit AmEx, MC, V.

Drag central in the heart of north London – well
worth a visit for a taste of England's talented, foul-
mouthed, cross-dressing divas. It's the home venue
of Dave Lynn, who lovers of gay cinema might
remember as the drag queen who harassed the lovely boys in *Beautiful Thing.*

Box

Seven Dials, 32-34 Monmouth Street, Covent
Garden, WC2H 9HA (7240 5828/www.boxbar.
com). Leicester Square tube. **Open** 11am-11pm
Mon-Sat; noon-10.30pm Sun. **Credit** AmEx, MC,
V. **Map** p409 X/Y2.

Muscle boys and the gAy-listers love this place,
which is up the road from London's best show queen
music store and sits near the historic Seven Dials
monument, a popular perching point for Sunday

Balans. *See p300.*

afternoon tipplers. It's also opposite Dress Circle, a
music shop specialising in Broadway and West End
musicals. Just FYI.

Edge

11 Soho Square, Soho, W1D 3QE (7439 1313).
Tottenham Court Road tube. **Open** noon-1am
Mon-Sat; noon-11.30pm Sun. **Credit** MC, V.
Map p408 W2.

Just off the chaos of Oxford Street lies this tall monument to cocktails and a kind of glamour. Spread
over four floors, it's best patronised in summer,
when takeaway Pimm's and lemonades can be taken
to Soho Square opposite. It attracts a mixed crowd.

★ Enclave

25-27 Brewer Street, Soho, W1F 0RR (7434
2911/www.enclavesoho.com). Piccadilly Circus
tube. **Open** 5pm-1am Mon-Thur; 5pm-3am Fri,
Sat. **Credit** MC, V. **Map** p406 W3.

A gorgeous new addition to the Soho scene, this stylish cocktail bar has a downstairs dance floor and a
bizarre 'enclave' room in the back, where B-listers
can lounge on beanbags against designer wallpaper.
It's a popular venue with lesbians, especially for
Code (first and third Fri) and Play (second Sat).

Freedom Bar

66 Wardour Street, Soho, W1F 0TA (7734
0071/www.freedombarsoho.com). Piccadilly
Circus tube. **Open** 5pm-3am Mon-Sat; 5-11.30pm
Sun. **Credit** MC, V. **Map** p406 W3.

ARTS & ENTERTAINMENT

Shaun Given, who gave the Edge an edge back in 2005, began to work his magic on Freedom in early 2008. Once the favourite haunt of the gay glitterati, it now has softer lighting and friendlier staff. The huge basement, a ballroom with pink vinyl seating and the obligatory poles, hosts varied entertainment (*see below* **Reading Between the Lines**).
▶ *In winter, the cosy, padded alcoves of nearby retro-styled basement bar Friendly Society (no.79, 7434 3805) are great for cocktails.*

G-A-Y Bar

30 Old Compton Street, Soho, W1D 4UR (7494 2756/www.g-a-y.co.uk). Leicester Square tube. **Open** noon-midnight daily. **Credit** MC, V. **Map** p408 W3.

The G-A-Y night at Heaven (*see p302*) gets the celebrity cameos, but this popular bar is still a shrine to queer pop idols, with nightly cheap drink specials based on how quickly players pick up on pop anthems. There's also a women's bar in the basement, called (delightfully) Girls Go Down.

★ Glass Bar

West Lodge, 190 Euston Road, NW1 2EF (7388 9555/www.theglassbar.org.uk). Euston tube/rail. **Open** 4-11pm Mon, Tue; 4pm-midnight Wed-Fri. **No credit cards. Map** p399 K3.
Reopened in 2007 after threat of closure, this is London's sole women-only bar, located down a spiral staircase in one of Euston Station's original stone-faced lodges, its cornerstones inscribed with

---

Reading Between the Lines

Time Out's Paul Burston on his part in London's gay literary boom.

ARTS & ENTERTAINMENT

I'd like to say that it all started with my gay salon night Polari, but that wouldn't be true. There were gay salon events happening in London long before I had the idea to combine authors, drinking and general merriment in 'an evening of gay words and music'. The **House of Homosexual Culture** (www.myspace.com/homoculture) have been hosting events of all kinds, including gay literary soirées, for the past three years. Then there's the women-only salon night, **Tart** (www.tartsalon.co.uk/home.php), with its mission statement: 'Where Intelligent Discussion is Expected and Encouraged'. And lest we forget, shops like **Gay's The Word** (66 Marchmont Street, WC1N 1AB, 7278 7654, www.gaystheword.co.uk) and **Prowler Soho** (5-7 Brewer Street, W1R 3FN, 7734 4031) have hosted readings for as long as they've been in business. But since **Polari** (www.myspace.com/polarigaysalon) arrived in late 2007, the gay salon scene seems to have exploded.

I decided to call the night Polari after the so-called 'lost language of gay men', a dialect spoken in the dark days before decriminalisation, when code words were a necessary way of communicating if you wanted to avoid arrest. Polari (the gay language) was made famous in the 1960s by Hugh Paddick and Kenneth Williams in the classic BBC radio comedy series *Round the Horne*, although its origins may date back to the 1800s. But it wasn't until the 1950s that it flourished in Britain, at a time when homosexual witch-hunts were at their most intense.

Polari (the gay salon) takes place at 7pm every second Wednesday at **Freedom Bar** (*see p303*), and it's free to get in. In the first year, we hosted big-name authors from Neil Bartlett to Charlotte Mendelson. Will Self addressed the audience in polari and cheerfully introduced himself as 'a gay author who happens to be a practising heterosexual'. In Febuary 2008, to mark LGBT History Month, Polari joined forces with the House of Homosexual Culture for a one-off event in the basement at Freedom that drew 150 people through the door on a Tuesday. Neil Bartlett was moved. Maureen Duffy was declared a national treasure. And **Foyles** (*see p243*) sold lots of books. Everyone was happy.

Everyone, that is, except myself and Rupert Smith, head honcho at the House of Homosexual Culture. Bringing gay literature to the gay scene was all very well, but what about the wider world? Shortly afterwards, we were approached by the Southbank Centre and invited to programme a series of gay literary events for the **London Literature Festival** (*see p272*) in July. We did three in all, bringing together authors, performers, singers and even male strippers. Rupert and I take great pride in saying that we were the people who put the cock in the Royal Festival Hall. They've asked us back.

So the gay literary salon scene is no longer confined to the gay scene. It's now mainstream, with regular events planned at what is one of London's leading arts institutions. What would Julian and Sandy say about that? 'Bona', most likely.

Duckie at **RVT**. *See p302.*

the enticing destinations once served by the railway. Knock at the large wooden door to be let in. Weekdays tend to be quiet and civilised.

Green Carnation
4-5 Greek Street, Soho, W1D 4DD (7434 3323/ www.greencarnationsoho.co.uk). Tottenham Court Road tube. **Open** 4pm-12.30am Sun. **Admission** £5 Mon-Thur; £7 after 11pm Fri, Sat. **Credit** AmEx, MC, V. **Map** p408 W2.
Formerly Element (itself formerly Sanctuary), the Green Carnation has had a major refit to spectacular effect. Head upstairs for cocktails in posh surroundings, with chandeliers and piano music to heighten the senses and raise the tone. There's a bar and dance floor downstairs. A haven for West End Wendies, always on hand to belt out a minor Sondheim in the wee hours.

Hoist
Arches 47B & 47C South Lambeth Road, Vauxhall Cross, Vauxhall, SW8 1RH (7735 9972/www.thehoist.co.uk). Vauxhall tube/rail. **Open** 8pm-midnight 3rd Thur of mth; 10pm-3am Fri; 10pm-4am Sat; 2-8pm, 10pm-2am Sun. **Admission** £6 Fri, Sun; £10-£12 Sat; varies Thur. **No credit cards**.
One of two genuine leather bars in town, this club sits under the arches and makes the most of its underground and industrial setting. Wear leather, uniform, rubber, skinhead or boots only – trainers will see you shunned at the door. A weekly Sunday afternoon naked event called SBN (Stark Bollock Naked) is popular with those whose leather wardrobe consists only of boots.

KW4
77 Hampstead High Street, Hampstead, NW3 1RE (7435 5747/www.kw4.co.uk). Hampstead tube/Hampstead Heath rail. **Open** 11am-11pm Mon-Thur; 11am-midnight Thur- Sun. **Credit** AmEx, MC, V.
The perfect evening ending (or beginning!) to time spent on the Heath, this fab old local – the King William IV or even King Willy to those with longer memories – attracts a very Hampstead crowd (read: well-off and ready for fun). Summer cruisers can also enjoy the beer garden.

★ Profile
56 Frith Street, Soho, W1D 3JG (7734 8300/ www.profilesoho.com). Tottenham Court Road tube. **Open** noon-1am Mon-Sat; 1-11.30pm Sun. **Credit** AmEx, MC, V. **Map** p406 W2.
A bar for fans of www.gaydar.com, this fabulous and brand-spanking-new nightspot is spread over three floors and offers free internet access and an 'interactive text screen service'. The friendly middle bar is a classic example of '80s TV sci-fi chic and is hugely popular. Outsider Tart, a tremendous American bakery, serves delectable cakes here from noon to 5pm daily.
▶ *Sister dance-club Lo-Profile (84-86 Wardour Street, 7734 1053, www.profilesoho.com) is a massively popular newcomer to the Soho scene.*

Retro Bar
2 George Court, off the Strand, Covent Garden, WC2N 6HH (7839 8760). Charing Cross tube/ rail. **Open** noon-11pm Mon-Fri; 5-11pm Sat; 5-10.30pm Sun. **Credit** AmEx, MC, V. **Map** p409 Y4.

Imagine a gay bar with pictures of Iggy Pop and Kate Bush on the walls, and nights dedicated to indie rock and Eurovision hits and you have the Retro Bar. The crowd is mixed in every sense: gay/straight, gay/lesbian and scene queen/true eccentric. Quiz nights are popular, and the bar on occasion lets punters be the DJ – bring your iPod!

Rupert Street
50 Rupert Street, Soho, W1V 6DR (7494 3059/ www.rupertstreet.com). Leicester Square or Piccadilly Circus tube. **Open** noon-11pm Mon-Sat; noon-10.30pm Sun. **Credit** AmEx, MC, V. **Map** p408 W3.
It has a great location and is popular with besuited professionals, but Rupert Street lacks the warmth of other bars in the area. A perennial favourite as a 'first meeting spot' for a busy Friday/Saturday itinerary. The dress code, by no means enforced, is collared shirts and a pout.

Shadow Lounge
5 Brewer Street, Soho, W1F 0RF (7287 7988/www.theshadowlounge.co.uk). Piccadilly Circus tube. **Open** 10pm-3am Mon-Wed; 9pm-3am Thur-Sat. **Admission** £3 after 11pm Mon; £3-£5 Tue; £5 Wed, Thur; £5-£10 Fri, Sat. **Credit** AmEx, MC, V. **Map** p408 W3.
For professional cocktail waiters, celebrity sightings, suits, cutes and fancy boots this is your venue. Expect a hefty cover charge and a queue on the weekend, but sublime atmosphere once inside.

Two Brewers
114 Clapham High Street, Clapham, SW4 7UJ (7836 7395/www.the2brewers.com). Clapham Common tube. **Open** 5pm-2am Mon-Thur, Sun; 5pm-4am Fri, Sat. **Admission** free-£5. **Credit** AmEx, MC, V.

INSIDE TRACK
CAB LORE

'**Vauxhall** has a big one-way system,' says Angela, a taxi-driver for three years. 'After a club, make your way to the bridge, on the south side of the railway, for a ride to the northern side of the river. You'll catch cabs that have gone south and are coming back.' If you're in **Soho**, meanwhile, the trick is to leave: 'Try and get on to Shaftesbury Avenue, Charing Cross Road or Oxford Street', says Peter, another cabbie. 'The Soho side-streets become very congested at night so not many drivers go there.' Still stuck? **Addison Lee** (7387 8888, www. addisonlee.com) dispatches drivers swiftly and texts you when they arrive.

Clapham's high street is yet another gay village, and visitors should make this their first stop if they make it to this part of town. It's busy at weekends with locals who are happy to keep the fun south of the river (even south of Vauxhall).

Yard
57 Rupert Street, Soho, W1V 7BJ (7437 2652/www.yardbar.co.uk). Piccadilly Circus tube. **Open** 2-11.30pm Tue-Sat; 2pm-midnight Fri, Sat. **Credit** AmEx, MC, V. **Map** p408 W3.
Come for the courtyard in summer, stay for the Loft Bar in winter. This unpretentious bar offers a great open-air courtyard in a great location, which attracts pretty boys, blokes and lesbians in equal measure.

SEX CLUBS & SAUNAS

Chariots
1 Fairchild Street, Shoreditch, EC2A 3NS (7247 5333/www.gaysauna.co.uk). Liverpool Street tube/rail. **Open** noon-9am daily. **Admission** £14; £12 reductions. **Credit** AmEx, MC, V. **Map** p405 R4.
Chariots is a sauna chain with outlets all over town. The original is this one in Shoreditch, the biggest and busiest, although not necessarily the best. That accolade probably goes to the newest member of the team on the Albert Embankment at Vauxhall (nos.63-64, 7735 6709). The Waterloo branch (101 Lower Marsh, 7247 5333) has the biggest sauna in the UK – enough steam for 50 guys.
Other locations throughout the city.

★ Sweatbox
Ramillies House, 1-2 Ramillies Street, Soho, W1F 7LN (3214 6014/www.sweatboxsoho.com). Oxford Circus tube. **Open** 2pm-midnight daily. **Admission** £20/day; £10/day reductions. *Spa only* £15/day. *Massage* £40-£95 (plus free entry). **Credit** MC, V. **Map** p406 U2.
Sweatbox Soho looks more like a nightclub than a typical gymnasium, with the intimidatingly sleek red-and-black design offset by extremely friendly staff. Though small, the space is well laid out, with a multigym (complete with four state-of-the-art Body Shaker machines) and a free weights room. Qualified masseurs offer treatments from Deep Tissue Massage to the Full Body LA Stone Special. If that doesn't do the trick – or you've only come here to do a trick yourself – there's a sauna downstairs.

Vault 139
139 Whitfield Street, Fitzrovia, W1T 5EN (7388 5500/www.vault139.com). Warren Street tube. **Open** 4pm-1am Mon-Sat; 2pm-midnight Sunday. **Admission** £4-£7; £3-£6 reductions. **No credit cards. Map** p398 J4.
Located in the heart of central London, this new venue takes over from Southwark's Manbar, which closed last year.

Music

London is filled with the food of love.

London is the dominant force in the British music scene. Other UK cities have their own lively and distinctive musical personalities (often livelier and more distinctive than the capital), but musicians have to make a conscious decision not to come here. In every genre, London still rules the roost. The acid test of the capital's vitality is its off-the-beaten-path venues. Acts big enough to fill major halls elsewhere are often delighted to play the tiny backroom of a London pub; these places are also where to find all manner of next big things. Check out *Time Out* magazine for the weekly picture.

Classical & Opera

It's been all change for London's classical music world of late. The **Royal Festival Hall** and the **Barbican Centre**, the capital's two major arts centres, have both been given expensive refurbishments; the **Wigmore Hall** and the **Coliseum** have gone through sometimes controversial management changes; and, best of all, the excellent **Kings Place** has joined venues like **Cadogan Hall** and **LSO St Luke's** that are hardly in their dotage. The capital's music schools also stage regular concerts by pupils and visiting professionals, most of which are free; check the websites of the **Royal Academy of Music** (7873 7300, www.ram.ac.uk), the **Royal College of Music** (7589 3643, www.rcm.ac.uk), the **Guildhall School of Music & Drama** (7628 2571, www.gsmd.ac.uk) and **Trinity College of Music** (8305 4444, www.tcm.ac.uk).

Tickets & information

Tickets for most classical and opera events are available direct from the venues, online or by phone. Always book ahead, especially at small venues such as the Wigmore Hall. Several venues, such as the Barbican and Southbank, operate standby schemes, offering unsold tickets at cut-rate prices just before the show.

About the author

John Lewis was a Time Out *magazine music critic for eight years and deputy editor of our 1,000 Songs to Change Your Life. He writes for Uncut,* The Times *and the* Guardian, *among others.*

CLASSICAL VENUES

★ Barbican Centre

Silk Street, the City, EC2Y 8DS (7638 4141/ box office 0845 020 7550/www.barbican.org.uk). Barbican or Moorgate tube/rail. **Box office** 9am-8pm daily. **Tickets** £6.50-£45. **Credit** AmEx, MC, V. **Map** p402 P5.

The Barbican's labyrinthine array of spaces aren't easy to navigate, but a recent renovation improved the FreeStage area in front of the main hall and the acoustics in the main hall. At the core of the music roster, performing 90 concerts a year, is the London Symphony Orchestra (LSO), currently looking to consolidate its reputation as one of the world's best orchestras, under principal conductor Valery Gergiev.
▶ *For the Barbican's theatre, see p336; for its cinema, see p297.*

Cadogan Hall

5 Sloane Terrace, Chelsea, SW1X 9DQ (7730 4500/www.cadoganhall.com). Sloane Square tube. **Box office** 10am-8pm Mon-Sat; 4-8pm Sun (performance days only). **Tickets** £10-£65. **Credit** MC, V. **Map** p400 G10.

INSIDE TRACK
LUNCHEON MUSIC

On Fleet Street, **St Bride's** (*see p59*) hosts atmospheric classical concerts at 1.15pm most Tuesdays and Fridays. For other City church concerts, check www.cityevents.co.uk.

Built a century ago as a Christian Science church, this austere building was transformed into a light and airy auditorium in 2004. It's hard to imagine how the renovations could have been bettered: the 905-capacity hall is comfortable and the acoustics excellent.

★ Kings Place

90 York Way, King's Cross, N1 9AG (0844 264 0321/www.kingsplace.co.uk). Kings Cross tube/rail. **Box office** 10am-8pm Mon-Sat; noon-8pm Sun. **Tickets** £6.50-£34.50. **Credit** MC, V. **Map** p399 L2.

Part of a complex that includes galleries and office space that will house, among others, the *Guardian* and *Observer* newspapers, the main 420-seat auditorium opened in autumn 2008 with a wide-ranging series of concerts. Although Kings Place will be the permanent home of both the London Sinfonietta and the Orchestra of the Age of Enlightenment, there's

also jazz, folk, leftfield rock and spoken word on the menu – some performances using a more flexible, subsidiary 220-seater room. Decent catering too.

★ LSO St Luke's

161 Old Street, the City, EC1V 9NG (information 7490 3939/Barbican box office 7638 8891/www. lso.co.uk/lsostlukes). Old Street tube/rail. **Box office** 9am-8pm daily. **Tickets** £6.50-£45. **Credit** AmEx, MC, V. **Map** p402 P4.

The London Symphony Orchestra's conversion of this decaying Hawksmoor-designed church into a rehearsal room, music education centre and 370-seat concert hall cost around £20m, but it was worth every penny. The programme takes in lunchtime recitals (some free), evening chamber concerts, and even some jazz and rock shows.
► *Hawksmoor also designed Christ Church Spitalfields; see p133.*

London Can Handel It

The capital celebrates three musical anniversaries this year.

George Frideric Handel has always held a special place in the heart of Londoners, with his works featured constantly in the concert calendar. But this year, the 250th anniversary of his death, will be something else. Alongside the inevitable concerts (including a *Messiah* in Westminster Abbey on 14 April), the **Handel House Museum** (*see p105*) will host an exhibition curated by his biographer. A new oratorio that follows a dialogue between an aging, half-blind Handel and his younger self will be premiered at St George's Church, Hanover Square, on 1 March. The anniversary will also be celebrated by the **Royal Festival Hall** (a concert performance of *Agrippina* in May), the Orchestra of the Age of Enlightenment (now based at **Kings Place**, *see above*), countertenor Iestyn Davies (touring *Ode to St Cecilia*, *Samson* and *Agrippina*) and tenor Ian Bostridge (touring a programme of Handel songs).

Handel is often regarded as London's first great composer, but he was preceded by one of the founding fathers of baroque. Henry Purcell was born in Westminster in 1659 (he died aged just 36, allegedly of chocolate poisoning) and his 350th anniversary is being marked by a series of concerts. *Dido & Aeneas*, the first great English opera, will be staged at the **Royal Opera House** (*see p311*) in April and May, and at the English Bach Festival (www. ebf.org.uk) in February; the Academy of Ancient Music will feature Purcell all year

Handel House Museum.

at the **Wigmore Hall** (*see right*); and in March there will be a *Choral Evensong* at **Westminster Abbey** (*see p112*), where Purcell was buried.

What's more, the anniversaries of both Handel and Purcell – along with the 200th anniversary of the death of Haydn, another composer with connections to the capital – will anchor the classical output at the **Barbican** (*see p307*) in 2009.

Royal Albert Hall

Kensington Gore, South Kensington, SW7 2AP (information 7589 3203/box office 7589 8212/ www.royalalberthall.com). South Kensington tube/ 9, 10, 52, 452 bus. **Box office** 9am-9pm daily. **Tickets** £4-£150. **Credit** AmEx, MC, V. **Map** p397 D9.

Built as a memorial to Queen Victoria's husband, this vast rotunda is best approached for the annual BBC Proms (*see p310* **Festivals**), despite acoustics that do orchestras few favours. Occasional classical concerts are held throughout the year – look out for recitals on the Willis pipe organ.

▶ *Albert is also commemorated opposite the hall in Hyde Park with the Albert Memorial; see p121.*

St James's Piccadilly

197 Piccadilly, St James's, W1J 9LL (7381 0441/ www.sjpconcerts.org). Piccadilly Circus tube. **Open** 8am-6.30pm daily. **Admission** free-£20; tickets available at the door 30mins before performances. **No credit cards. Map** p406 V4.

The only Wren church outside the City to hold free lunchtime recitals (Mon, Wed, Fri at 1.10pm) also offers regular evening concerts. The church has a café attached.

St John's, Smith Square

Smith Square, Westminster, SW1P 3HA (7222 1061/www.sjss.org.uk). Westminster tube. **Box office** 10am-5pm Mon-Fri, or up to 30mins after start of performance; from 1hr before performance Sat, Sun. **Tickets** £5-£45. **Credit** MC, V. **Map** p401 K10.

This elegant 18th-century church hosts more or less nightly orchestral and chamber concerts, with occasional vibrant recitals on its magnificent Klais organ. There's a secluded restaurant in the crypt, open whether or not there's a concert that night.

St Martin-in-the-Fields

Trafalgar Square, Westminster, WC2N 4JJ (information 7766 1100/www.stmartin-in-the-fields.org). Charing Cross tube/rail. **Box office** 10am-5pm Mon-Fri, or until start of performance. **Admission** *Lunchtime concerts* free; donations requested. *Evening concerts* £6-£18. **Credit** MC, V. **Map** p407 X4.

As befits the church's location in the heart of tourist London, the evening concert programme at the atmospheric St Martin's is packed with crowd-pleasers: expect lashings of Mozart and Vivaldi by candlelight. The thrice-weekly lunchtime recitals (Mon, Tue, Fri) offer less predictable fare.

▶ *For more on the church, see p110.*

★ Southbank Centre

Belvedere Road, South Bank, SE1 8XX (switchboard 0871 663 2501/bookings 0871 663 2500/www.rfh.org.uk). Embankment tube/ Waterloo tube/rail. **Box office** *In person*

Wigmore Hall.

11am-8pm daily. *By phone* 9.30am-8pm daily. **Tickets** £5-£75. **Credit** AmEx, MC, V. **Map** p401 M8.

The 3,000-capacity Royal Festival Hall reopened in 2007 after a £90m renovation. Access has been made easier, but the real meat of the project is the acoustic refurbishment of the main hall itself. Showcase events include summer's Meltdown (*see p312* **Festivals**), and the Shell Classic International Season, which continues into 2009 with the Zurich Opera and the Chamber Orchestra of Europe.

Next door is the 900-seat Queen Elizabeth Hall, a rather uninviting space that also houses pop and jazz gigs, and the 250-capacity Purcell Room, which hosts everything from chamber concerts to plays and poetry readings.

★ Wigmore Hall

36 Wigmore Street, Marylebone, W1U 2BP (7935 2141/www.wigmore-hall.org.uk). Bond Street tube. **Box office** *In person* 10am-8.30pm daily. *By phone* 10am-7pm daily. **Tickets** £8-£60. **Credit** AmEx, DC, MC, V. **Map** p398 G6.

INSIDE TRACK
CAB LORE

For classical music fans leaving the **Royal Albert Hall** (*see above*), there's a very useful taxi rank outside Boujis nightclub, which runs at all hours of the night. Head south down Exhibition Road, past the museums, to 43 Thurloe Street.

Royal Opera House.

Built in 1901 as the display hall for Bechstein Pianos, but now boasting perfect acoustics, art nouveau decor and an excellent basement restaurant, the Wiggy is one of the world's top chamber-music venues. Programming leans on the classical and Romantic periods. The Monday-lunchtime recitals, broadcast live on BBC Radio 3, are excellent value, as are the Sunday morning coffee concerts.

OPERA VENUES
Coliseum
St Martin's Lane, Covent Garden, WC2N 4ES (box office 0871 911 0200/www.eno.org). Leicester Square tube/Charing Cross tube/rail. **Box office** *By phone 10am-8pm Mon-Sat. In person from 10am on day of performance.*

Festivals Classical

What not to miss this year.

The daddy of all the classical festivals is the **Proms** – or, as they're officially known, the BBC Sir Henry Wood Promenade Concerts (www.bbc.co.uk/proms), held mainly at the Royal Albert Hall (*see p309*) from mid July until mid September. The event features around 70 concerts that take in a huge variety of the classical repertoire. You can buy seats in advance, but many prefer to queue on the day for £5 tickets for the seatless area in front of the stage (or for the gallery at the top of the auditorium, where the sound is far better).

Cadogan Hall, which hosts around a dozen lunchtime Proms each year, is the focal point of June's **Chelsea Festival** (www.chelseafestival.org.uk), which offers a range of international events. At around the same time, for three weeks in June and July, the **City of London Festival** (7583 3585, www.colf.org) offers an adventurous programme with a focus on

chamber music staged in churches and in the halls of ancient livery companies. Nearby is the **Spitalfields Festival** (7377 1362, www.spitalfieldsfestival.org.uk), based around the lovely Christ Church Spitalfields (*see p133*). For several weeks in June and December, it fields a strong line-up of early music and baroque works coupled with more modern music.

In summer, music moves outdoors. June's **Hampton Court Palace Festival** (www.hamptoncourtfestival.com) is one of a series of 'picnic-concert' festivals staged in the grounds of beautiful stately homes. Another excellent outdoor event is **Opera Holland Park** (0845 230 9769, www.opera hollandpark.com), which sees a canopied theatre host a season of opera. You'll also find a few big classical or opera names at the **English Heritage Picnic Concerts** at Kenwood House (www.picnicconcerts. com; *see p130*) in July and August.

Tickets £10-£85. **Credit** AmEx, MC, V.
Map p407 X4.

The Coliseum's 2,350-seat auditorium, built as a grand music hall in 1904 by the renowned architect Frank Matcham, was restored to its former glory in 2004 as part of an £80m restoration. All the resident English National Opera (ENO) needs is for new artistic director Edward Gardner to develop an impressive programme to match it. Productions for 2009 include a revival of Anthony Minghella's *Madam Butterfly* in June. Unlike at the Royal Opera House (*see below*), all works are performed in English.
▶ *The English National Ballet (www.ballet. org.uk) also make their home here.*

★ Royal Opera House

Covent Garden, WC2E 9DD (7304 4000/www. roh.org.uk). Covent Garden tube. **Box office** 10am-8pm Mon-Sat. **Tickets** £4-£195, restricted view seats from £7. **Credit** AmEx, MC, V. **Map** p407 Z3.

Having secured its position as one of the world's great opera houses following a turn-of-the-century refurbishment, the ROH has been able to conduct something of a PR campaign: in a bold move to woo new audiences, the opening performance of 2008's *Don Giovanni* was made exclusive to *Sun* readers at knockdown rates and beamed live to a chain of cinemas, and the Ignite Festival drew punters in with a terrific range of art installations, films and performances. Book ahead for a behind-the-scenes tour.
▶ *For the resident Royal Ballet, see p294.*

Rock, Pop & Roots

Meat-and-potatoes indie sludge remains the bedrock of London's rock circuit, but variety is the spice of the scene's life. On any given night, you may find Scandinavian death metallers, Celtic folk troubadours and Malian griots taking to the capital's various stages.

The buoyancy of the music scene itself can foster complacency among the businesses that showcase it. Many major venues get away with wretched sound, surly staff, overpriced drinks and expensive tickets. Happily, some smaller venues are keener to impress – the likes of the **Luminaire**, **Bush Hall**, the **Union Chapel** and the **Scala** are showing the big boys how it should be done.

Tickets & information

Your first stop should be *Time Out* magazine, which lists hundreds of gigs a week. Most venues' websites detail their future shows.

Always check ticket availability before setting out: venues, large and small, can sell out weeks in advance. The main exceptions are small pub venues, which only sell tickets on the day. Prices vary wildly: one night, you could pay £150 to see Madonna at Earl's Court or see a superb singer-songwriter for free.

Many venues offer tickets online via their websites, but beware: most online box offices are operated by ticket agencies, which add booking fees that can raise the ticket price by as much as 30 per cent. Try and pay cash in person if possible, but for details of the ticket agencies, *see p265*.

There's often a huge disparity between door times and stage times; the Jazz Café opens at 7pm, for instance, but the gigs often don't start until after 9pm. Some venues run club nights after the gigs, which means the show has to be wrapped up by 10.30pm; but at other venues, the main act won't even start until nearer 11pm.

MAJOR VENUES

In addition to the venues below, the **Barbican** (*see p307*), the **Southbank Centre** (*see p309*) and the **Royal Albert Hall** (*see p309*) stage regular gigs, and Fabric seem to be holding to their promise of programming live music in their fabulous new club **Matter** (*see p325*).

★ Carling Academy Brixton

211 Stockwell Road, Brixton, SW9 9SL (information 7771 3000/box office 0870 771 2000/www.brixton-academy.co.uk). Brixton tube/rail. **Box office** *By phone* 24hrs daily. **Tickets** £10-£40. **Credit** MC, V.

Built in the 1920s as a cinema, the Academy is London's most credible major rock venue. Although it's echo-ey when half-full, the 5,000-capacity space is popular because of the sloping standing area gives good sightlines. Pop acts such as Goldfrapp feature, but programming favours metal, indie and alt-rock.

Carling Academy Islington

N1 Centre, 16 Parkfield Street, Islington, N1 0PS (information 7288 4400/box office 0870 771 2000/www.islington-academy.co.uk). Angel tube. **Box office** *In person* noon-4pm Mon-Sat. *By phone* 24hrs daily. **Tickets** £3-£20. **Credit** MC, V. **Map** p402 N2.

IndigO2.

Located in a mall, this 800-capacity room was never going to be London's most atmospheric venue. Still, the gigs are decent – fast-rising indie bands and cultured singer-songwriters, mostly – and the solid sound system ensures the acts get their message across. The adjacent Bar Academy hosts new bands, including *Time Out*'s popular 'On The Up' nights.

Forum

9-17 Highgate Road, Kentish Town, NW5 1JY (information 7428 4099/box office 0871 230 1093/www.kentishtownforum.com). Kentish Town tube/rail. **Box office** *In person* 4-5pm on show days or from the Jazz Café (*see p315*). *By phone* 24hrs daily. **Tickets** £10-£30. **Credit** MC, V. Dormant for a while, this grand old 2,000-capacity art deco hall (built as a cinema in 1934) is back hosting club nights (such as the Church and School Disco) alongside a mix of alt-rock and pop acts (Vampire Weekend, Kaiser Chiefs, the Roots).
▶ *The time-honoured choice for a pre-gig pint is the Bull & Gate; see p315.*

Festivals Rock, Pop & Roots

What not to miss this year.

You can't really pitch a tent and camp at any of London's music festivals, but it feels like every square inch of the city hosts some kind of wingding between April and October. First up is April's two-day **Camden Crawl** (www.thecamdencrawl. com), which sees 100-plus indie acts spreadeagled across every music venue in Camden. Its youth-oriented programme is a far cry from the zeitgeist-capturing Summer Series of open-air shows at **Somerset House** (*see p87*) between June and August, or the idiosyncratic **Meltdown** at the Southbank Centre (*see p309*) – a fortnight of gigs, films and other events at the end of June, curated each year by a guest musician (in previous years Jarvis Cocker, Patti Smith and Massive Attack).

For something more focused, try the Southbank's increasingly popular **London African Music Festival** (7328 9613, www.londonafricanmusicfestival. com, late Sept) or the fortnight of contemporary Latin American music that is **La Linea** (8693 1042, www. comono.co.uk, from mid Apr). London's parks also offer an array of festivals. Hyde Park's **Wireless Festival** (www.o2wirelessfestival.co.uk) in mid June offers big-name acts – New Order, Daft Punk, Kaiser Chiefs – headlining over three nights; the same stage is usually used again for another big event the following week. Out east, Victoria Park hosts Groove Armada's upbeat **Lovebox Weekender** (www.lovebox.net) in mid July.

Hammersmith Apollo

Queen Caroline Street, Hammersmith, W6 9QH (information 8748 8660/box office 0844 844 4248/www.getlive.co.uk). Hammersmith tube. **Box office** *In person* 4pm-event starts on performance days only. *By phone* 24hrs daily. **Tickets** £10-£40. **Credit** MC, V.
This 1930s cinema had a big refit in 2002 – it now doubles as a 3,600-capacity all-seater theatre (popular with big comedy acts and children's shows) and a 5,000-capacity standing-room-only gig space, hosting everyone from Kenny Rogers to Slipknot.

IndigO2

For listings, *see below* **O2 Arena**.
The little brother of the vast O2 Arena isn't really all that little. In fact, with a capacity of 2,350 – part standing room, part amphitheatre seating, sometimes part table seating – IndigO2 is one of the city's bigger venues. It attracts big soul, funk and pop-jazz acts (Roy Ayers, Stacey Kent), knackered old pop stars (Howard Jones, Gary Numan) and all points in-between.

KOKO

1A Camden High Street, Camden, NW1 7JE (information 0870 432 5527/box office 0870 145 1115/www.koko.uk.com). Mornington Crescent tube. **Box office** *In person* 12.30-4.30pm Mon-Fri. *By phone* 24hrs daily. **Tickets** £3-£25. **Credit** AmEx MC, V.
Opened in 1900 as a music hall, the former Camden Palace scrubbed up nicely during a 2004 refit and has built up a roster of events to match. The 1,500-capacity auditorium stages a fair few club nights alongside an indie-heavy gig programme.

INSIDE TRACK
BOAT TO THE O2

You can get to the **O2 Arena**, **IndigO2** and **Matter** by tube, but it's far more fun to take the 20-minute river ride on **Thames Clipper** (*see p363*) from London Bridge or Waterloo. The boats even have a little bar on board.

★ O2 Arena

Millennium Way, North Greenwich, SE10 0BB (8463 2000/box office 0871 984 0002/www. theo2.co.uk). North Greenwich tube. **Box office** *In person* noon-7pm daily. *By phone* 24hrs daily. **Tickets** £10-£100. **Credit** AmEx, MC, V.
Since its launch in July 2007, this conversion of the former Millennium Dome has been a huge success. It's now a state-of-the-art, 23,000-capacity enormo-dome with good acoustics and sightlines, hosting big acts (Prince, Stevie Wonder, Justin Timberlake). ▶ *There are two other substantial venues on the site: IndigO2 (see above) and Matter (see p325).*

★ Roundhouse

Chalk Farm Road, Camden Town, NW1 8EH (information 7424 9991/box office 0844 482 8008 /www.roundhouse.org.uk). Chalk Farm tube. **Box office** *In person* 11am-6pm Mon-Sat. *By phone* 9am-7pm Mon-Sat; 9am-4pm Sun. **Tickets** £8-£35, standing tickets available for some gigs from £4. **Credit** MC, V.
A one-time railway turntable shed, the Roundhouse was used for experimental theatre and hippie

Roundhouse.

happenings in the 1960s before becoming a rock venue in the '70s. After years of dormancy, the venue reopened a few years ago, and now mixes arty rock gigs with dance, theatre and multimedia events. Sightlines can be poor, but acoustics are good.
▶ *There are pubs galore nearby, but Gilgamesh offers a classier pre-show drink; see p236.*

Scala
275 Pentonville Road, King's Cross, N1 9NL (7833 2022/www.scala-london.co.uk). King's Cross tube/rail. **Box office** 10am-6pm Mon-Fri. **Tickets** (cash only) £8-£15. **Map** p399 L3.
Built as a cinema shortly after World War I, this surprisingly capacious building now stages a laudably broad range of indie, electronica, avant hip hop and folk. And the staff are extremely personable.

Shepherd's Bush Empire
Shepherd's Bush Green, W12 8TT (8354 3300/ box office 0870 771 2000/www.shepherds-bush-empire.co.uk). Shepherd's Bush Market tube/ Shepherd's Bush tube/rail. **Box office** *In person* 4-6pm, 6.30-9.30pm show nights only. *By phone* 24hrs daily. **Tickets** £8-£40. **Credit** MC, V.
This former BBC theatre is a great mid-sized venue, holding 2,000 standing or 1,300 seated. The sound is decent (with the exception of the alcove behind the stalls bar) and the staff are lovely. Bookings range from Steve Winwood to the Ting Tings.

Wembley Arena
Arena Square, Engineers Way, Wembley, Middx HA9 0DH (8782 5566/box office 0870 060 0870/www.livenation.co.uk/wembley). Wembley Park tube. **Box office** *In person* 10am-4pm Mon-Fri; noon-start of performance Sat, Sun. *By phone* 24hrs daily. **Tickets** £5-£100. **Credit**, MC, V.
A £30m refurbishment has improved this much-derided 12,500-capacity venue no end, with comfy seating, better acoustics and decent sightlines. The food and drink could be cheaper and better though.

CLUB & PUB VENUES

London's smaller music venues come in clusters. There are several in Soho, a fair few in Camden

and a growing number out in Shoreditch, plus smatterings around Islington, Shepherd's Bush, Brixton and New Cross.

In addition to the venues below, a handful of nightclubs stage gigs. Try the **Notting Hill Arts Club** (*see p326*), **Madame Jo Jo's** (*see p321*) and the all-encompassing **ICA** (*see p115*). Fans of garage rock should check out the Dirty Water Club on Fridays at the **Boston Arms** (178 Junction Road, Tufnell Park, N19 5QQ, 7272 8153, www.dirtywaterclub.com); those into mellower fare may enjoy the **Enterprise** (2 Haverstock Hill, Camden, NW3 2BL, 7485 2659).

Amersham Arms
388 New Cross Road, New Cross, SE14 6TY (8469 1499/www.amersham-arms.co.uk). New Cross or New Cross Gate rail/buses 453, 436, 36, 177, 171, 21, 136, 225, 321, N21, N36. **Open** noon-midnight Mon-Wed, Sun; noon-2am Thur; noon-3am Fri, Sat. **Tickets** vary.
The nexus of south-east London's live music scene, the Amersham Arms brings together the character (and prices) of a trad pub with a souped-up sound-system and 3am licence, an upstairs arts space and a walled garden for smokers. The roster is dominated by young and fashionable up-and-comers.

Bardens Boudoir
36-44 Stoke Newington Road, N16 7XJ (7249 9557/07767 428415 (mobile)/www.bardensbar. co.uk). Dalston Kingsland rail/67, 76, 149, 243 bus. **Box office** phone for details. **Shows** 8pm Tue-Sun. **Tickets** £4-£6. **No credit cards**.
Located in the heart of Turkish Dalston below a disused furniture store, the 300-capacity Boudoir is something of a shambles – the room is at least three times wider than it is deep, and the stage isn't really a stage at all. None of this bothers the often out-there line-ups nor the hipsters that love them.
▶ *Next door is 19 Numara Bos Cirrik (34 Stoke Newington Road, 7249 0400), one of the best Turkish restaurants in the city.*

★ Barfly
49 Chalk Farm Road, Chalk Farm, NW1 8AN (0844 8472 424/box office 0870 907 0999/ www.barflyclub.com). Chalk Farm tube. **Open** 5.30pm-1am Mon-Thur; 5.30pm-3am Fri, Sat; noon-12am Sun. *Shows* from 7pm daily. **Admission** £5-£8. **No credit cards**.
This pokey, 200-capacity upstairs venue is a big part of the reason why guitar-meets-electro parties have been doing so well of late. Kill Em All Let God Sort It Out, held every other Saturday, stages bands guaranteed to get the crowd going; Adventures Close to Home (monthly) also packs out the dancefloor.
▶ *The same people run Fly (36-38 New Oxford Street, Bloomsbury, WC1A 1EP, 7636 9475).*

Amersham Arms.

Bloomsbury Bowling Lanes

Basement, Tavistock Hotel, Bedford Way, WC1H 9EU (7183 1979/www.bloomsbury bowling.com). Russell Square tube. **Open** noon-2am Mon-Thur; noon-3am Fri/Sat; 1pm-midnight Sun. **Admission** varies. **Credit** AmEx, MC, V. **Map** p399 K4.

Already a hip destination for University of London students and those wanting a late drink away from Soho, BBL have started putting on live bands and DJs on Mondays, Fridays and Saturdays, sometimes with a 1950s theme. If you get bored of the bands or the bowling, hole up in one of the karaoke booths.

▶ *For more bowling alleys, see p334.*

Bull & Gate

389 Kentish Town Road, Kentish Town, NW5 2TJ (8826 5000/www.bullandgate.co.uk). Kentish Town tube/rail. **Shows** 8-11pm daily. **Tickets** £5-£12. **No credit cards.**

Nirvana played their first London gig at this old boozer, still perhaps the best place to see unsigned guitar bands. Expect to find groups with names such as Two Bear Mambo and Dancing with Henry.

▶ *Camden has lots more of this sort of thing: try also the Dublin Castle (94 Parkway, NW1 7AN, 7700 0550, www.bugbearbookings.com).*

Corsica Studios

Units 4/5, Elephant Road, Newington, SE17 1LB (7703 4760/www.corsicastudios.com). Elephant & Castle tube. **Box office** 10am-6am daily. **Shows** vary. **Tickets** £5-£12. **No credit cards.**

This flexible performance space is increasingly being used as one of London's most adventurous live music venues and clubs, featuring acts such as Silver Apples, Acoustic Ladyland and Lydia Lunch. It's open until midnight or 1am for gigs, and until 6am for some club nights.

★ Jazz Café

5 Parkway, Camden, NW1 7PG (box office 7485 6834/0870 060 3777/www.jazzcafe.co.uk). Camden Town tube. **Box office** *In person* 10am-2pm, 3-6pm Mon-Sat. *By phone* 24hrs daily. **Tickets** £10-£30. **Credit** MC, V.

There's some jazz on the schedule here, but this two-floor club deals more in soul, R&B and hip hop these days, and has become the first port of call for soon-to-be-huge US acts (Mary J Blige, John Legend and the Roots all played their first European dates here).

★ Luminaire

311 Kilburn High Road, Kilburn, NW6 7JR (7372 8668/www.theluminaire.co.uk). Kilburn tube/Brondesbury rail. **Open** 6pm-2am daily. **Tickets** (cash only) £3-£20. **Credit** (bar) MC, V.

The booking policy here is fantastically broad, taking in everything from the Young Gods to Scritti Politti via Acoustic Ladyland. The sound system is up to scratch, the decor is stylish, the drinks are fairly priced and the staff are approachable.

93 Feet East

150 Brick Lane, Spitalfields, E1 6QL (7247 3293/www.93feeteast.co.uk). Aldgate East tube

Out Come the Freaks

London's music scene goes far beyond the pop charts.

Londoners often grumble that the city's music venues are becoming a faceless chain of aircraft hangars run by corporate monsters, an endless series of Academies and Apollos and Arenas with the same fast-food franchises, the same beer sponsors and the same excessive booking fees.

There's truth in such complaints, but there's also a whole world of music away from this mainstream. Sitting near the intersection of improvised jazz, post-punk and avant-garde classical music are a series of out-there events that can be hilarious, ridiculous, terrifying, puzzling, breathtaking and terrible – often all at once.

The king of London's freak scene is the **Klinker** (www.iotacism.com/klinkerizer/index.shtml), founded and still run by heroically eccentric Hackneyite Hugh Metcalfe. Having jumped from venue to venue throughout its history, it's now held at two separate venues: every Tuesday at 8pm in **Maggie's Bar** (98-100 Stoke Newington Church Street, N16 0AP, 8964 0657), and every other Thursday at 8.30pm at the **Cross Kings** (126 York Way, N1 0AX, 7278 8318, www.thecross kings.co.uk). On an average evening, you might find performance artists,

sound poets, avant-garde dancers, experimental films and a large helping of freely improvised jazz.

Other pockets of resistance to the banal are dotted all over London, particularly in Dalston at the long-established **Vortex** (*see p318*) and the newer **Café Oto** (*see p318*). The calendar on the London Musicians Collective website (www.l-m-c.org.uk) reveals a slew of other oddball nights, among them **Boat-Ting**, a sporadic improv session on a moored Thameside boat (Yacht Club, Temple Pier, Victoria Embankment, WC2R 2PN, 7836 1566).

Classical music isn't immune to such invention. Held at the Macbeth (70 Hoxton Street, N1 6LP), **Nonclassical** (www.nonclassical.co.uk) is run by Gabriel Prokofiev – classical composer, leader of the punk-funk collective Spektrum, producer for grime starlet Lady Sovereign and grandson of Sergei. Expect a mash of electronics, DJ culture and and the more experimental end of classical composition. And check out the **Kings Place** (*see p308*) programme: the venue announced its arrival with a number of appealingly off-beat classical offerings, such as those curated as This Isn't For You.

Music

or *Liverpool Street tube/rail.* **Open** 5-11pm
Mon-Thur; 5pm-1am Fri; noon-1am Sat; noon-
10.30pm Sun. *Shows* vary. **Admission** free-£5.
No credit cards. Map p403 S5.
With three rooms, a balcony and a wrap-around
courtyard that's made for summer barbecues, 93
Feet East manages to overcome the otherwise crip-
pling lack of a proper late licence. There are plenty
of good nights: Big Bang and Hoxtonlab are student
house parties without the puke on the carpet; Unruly
Screenings mixes short films with local bands.

★ 100 Club
*100 Oxford Street, Soho, W1D 1LL (7636
0933/www.the100club.co.uk). Oxford Circus or
Tottenham Court Road tube.* **Shows** 7.30pm-
midnight Mon; 7.30-11.30pm Tue-Thur; 7.30pm-
12.30am Fri; 7.30pm-1am Sat; 7.30-11pm Sun.
Tickets £6-£20. **Credit** MC, V. **Map** p397 K6.
Perhaps the most adaptable venue in London, this
wide, 350-capacity basement room has provided a
home for trad jazz, pub blues, northern soul and
punk – the venue staged a historic show in 1976 that
featured the Sex Pistols, the Clash and the Damned.
These days, it offers jazz, indie acts and ageing rockers such as Nine Below Zero and the Blockheads.

Pigalle Club
*215 Piccadilly, St James's, W1J 9HN (office 7734
8142/box office 0845 345 6053/www.vpmg.net/
pigalle). Piccadilly Circus tube.* **Open** 7pm-2am
Mon-Wed; 7pm-3am Thur-Sat. **Tickets** free-£65.
Credit AmEx, MC, V. **Map** p406 V4.
The Pigalle is Vince Power's upmarket Jazz Café, an
old-fashioned, 400-capacity supper club where
prices imply a certain measure of sophistication.
Acts are generally jazzy, with the occasional big-
name soul or pop singer thrown in for added appeal.
▶ *Power also owns the similarly slick Bloomsbury
Ballroom (Bloomsbury Square, WC1B 4DA,
7404 7612, www.bloomsburyballroom.co.uk).*

12 Bar Club
*22-23 Denmark Place, Soho, WC2H 8NL (office
7240 2120/box office 7240 2622/www.12bar
club.com). Tottenham Court Road tube.* **Open**
Café 11am-9pm Mon-Sat. *Bar* 11am-3am Mon-
Sat; 6pm-midnight Sun. *Shows* from 7.30pm;
nights vary. **Admission** £5-£15. **No credit
cards. Map** p406 W4.
This cherished hole-in-the-wall – if smoking were
still allowed, this is the kind of place that would be
full of it – books a grab-bag of stuff. The size (capacity of 100, a stage that barely accommodates a trio)
dictates a predominance of singer-songwriters.

Underworld
*174 Camden High Street, Camden, NW1 0NE
(7482 1932/box office 7734 8932/www.the
underworldcamden.co.uk). Camden Town tube.*
Box office *In person* 11am-11pm daily. *By*

phone 24hrs daily. **Shows** 7-11pm; nights vary.
Admission £5-£20. **No credit cards.**
A dingy maze of pillars and bars below Camden, this
subterranean oddity is an essential for metal and
hardcore fans. The somewhat insalubrious interior
is enlivened by youthful, friendly audiences and a
community feel. If you can keep a straight face when
telling friends you're off to see Ghengis Tron and
Bonded By Blood, you'll fit in just fine.

Union Chapel
*Compton Terrace, Islington, N1 2XD (7226
1686/www.unionchapel.org.uk). Highbury &
Islington tube/rail.* **Open** varies. **Tickets**
free-£40. **No credit cards.**
This 500-capacity Victorian Gothic church still holds
regular services each Sunday, but it's also been one
of London's best gig venues for the past decade. The
acoustics are pretty poor for full-band rock, but great
for unamplified world music acts and low-key solo
performers such as Juan Martin, Baby Dee, Michelle
Shocked and José Gonzaléz.

Windmill
*22 Blenheim Gardens, Brixton, SW2 5BZ
(8671 0700/www.windmillbrixton.co.uk).
Brixton tube/rail.* **Shows** 8-11pm Mon-Thur;
8pm-1am Fri, Sat; 5-11pm Sun. **Admission**
free-£6. **No credit cards.**
If you can live with the iffy sound system and amus-
ingly taciturn barflies, you might think this pokey
little L-shaped pub is one of the city's best venues.
Mark it down to the adventurous bookings (punk,
country, techno, folk, metal) and cheap admission.

Jazz

In addition to the venues below, the **100 Club**
(*see above*) hosts trad groups, the **Spice of
Life** at Cambridge Circus (6 Moor Street, W1,
7739 3025) has excellent mainstream jazz, and
the **Oh! Bar** in Camden (111 Camden High
Street, NW1 7JN, 7383 0330) has an expanding
jazz programme. The **Jazz Café** (*see p315*)
lives up to its name from time to time, and both
the **Barbican** (*see p307*) and the **Southbank
Centre** (*see p309*) host dozens of big names
every year, including the bulk of the **London
Jazz Festival** (*see p318* Festivals). For left-
field jazz, *see p316* **Out Come the Freaks**.
For more, see www.jazzinlondon.net.

Bull's Head
*373 Lonsdale Road, Barnes, SW13 9PY (8876
5241/www.thebullshead.com). Barnes Bridge rail.*
Open 11am-11pm Mon-Sat; noon-11pm Sun.
Shows 8.30pm Mon-Sat; 1-3.30pm, 8.30-11pm Sun.
Admission £5-£12. **Credit** AmEx, DC, MC, V.
This venerable riverside pub underwent a refurbish-
ment of sound and lighting a few years ago, leaving

the rechristened Yamaha Jazz Room in better shape than ever. The venue specialises in mainstream British jazz and swing: regular guests include ace veteran pianist Stan Tracey and sax maestro Peter King, with Mondays given over to blues.

★ Café Oto
18-22 Ashwin Street, Dalston, E8 3DL (7923 1231/www.cafeoto.co.uk). Dalston Kingsland rail/30, 38, N38, 67, 76, 149, N149, 56, 277, 242 bus. **Open** 9.30am-1am Mon-Fri; 10am-midnight Sat, Sun. *Shows* from 8pm. **Admission** £3-£8. **No credit cards**.
This excellent new café and 150-capacity venue is most certainly not a jazz club. However, its 'new music' remit takes in plenty of free improvising noiseniks – Eddie Prévost, Evan Parker – alongside Japanese noise rockers and artists from the stranger ends of the rock, folk and classical scenes.

Charlie Wright's International Bar
45 Pitfield Street, Hoxton, N1 6DA (7490 8345/www.myspace.com/charliewrights). Old Street/Liverpool Street tube/rail. **Open** noon-1am Sun-Wed; noon-2am Thur; noon-3am Fri/Sat. *Shows* 8-10pm daily. **Admission** free-£10. **Credit** AmEx, MC, V. **Map** p403 Q3
A ramshackle Hoxton pub, Charlie Wright's has hosted occasional gigs for years, but it's recently started staging an excellent regular jazz programme on all nights except Saturdays. Expect to see US, African and Brazilian names alongside British players from the Jazz Warriors, Jazz Jamaica and the

---

Festivals Jazz
What not to miss this year.

The big event on London's jazz calendar each year is November's **London Jazz Festival** (7324 1880, www.serious.org.uk, www.londonjazz festival.org.uk), a creatively curated ten-day event that spans many genres and venues, from Kings Place (see *p308*) to the Wigmore Hall (see *p309*). July sees two free events: **Jazz on the Streets** (www.jazzonthestreets.co.uk), a week of low-key music in Soho cafés and bars, and the westerly **Ealing Jazz Festival** (8825 6064, www.ealing. gov.uk), which stages mainstream acts over five late July evenings in Walpole Park. And in late September, Greenwich's **Riverfront Jazz Festival** (8921 4456, www.riverfrontjazz.co.uk) dishes up a spread of small-scale shows; the same organisers run a mini-festival in mid May.

F-IRE Collective. Gigs don't usually start until 10pm but continue late on Thursdays and Fridays.

★ Pizza Express Jazz Club
10 Dean Street, Soho, W1D 3RW (7439 8722/www.pizzaexpress.co.uk). Tottenham Court Road tube. **Open** 7.30-11.15pm daily. *Shows* 9-11.15pm daily. **Admission** £15-£25. **Credit** AmEx, DC, MC, V. **Map** p406 W2.
The upstairs restaurant (7437 9595) is jazz-free, but the 120-capacity basement venue is one of Europe's best modern mainstream jazz venues. Big-name American guests are slightly rarer than they were a few years ago, but you can still find excellent residencies from the likes of Mose Allison, Scott Hamilton, Kenny Garrett and Lea DeLaria.

Ronnie Scott's
47 Frith Street, Soho, W1D 4HT (7439 0747/www.ronniescotts.co.uk). Leicester Square or Tottenham Court Road tube. **Open** 6pm-3am Mon-Sat; 6pm-midnight Sun. *Shows* 7pm daily. **Admission** (non-members) £25-£100. **Credit** AmEx, DC, MC, V. **Map** p406 W2.
Opened by the British saxophonist Ronnie Scott in 1959, this legendary institution was completely refurbished in 2006. Capacity has been expanded to 250, and the food is better – but the improvements have come at a cost. The bookings have declined in quality, with decent jazz heavyweights (Roy Haynes, Bill Charlap, Mark Murphy) now outnumbered by some distinctly average pop and funk artists.

606 Club
90 Lots Road, Chelsea, SW10 0QD (7352 5953/www.606club.co.uk). Earl's Court or Fulham Broadway tube/11, 211 bus. **Shows** 9-11.45pm Mon; 7.30pm-12.30am Tue, Wed; 8pm-midnight Thur; 9.30pm-1.30am Fri, Sat; 8.30pm-1am Sun. **Admission** £8-£12. **Credit** AmEx, MC, V. **Map** p396 C13.
The stage at this Chelsea club is limited to British jazz musicians. The policy sounds like a recipe for commercial suicide, but manager Steve Rubie has guided this charmingly furnished, 150-capacity club into its fourth decade. There's no stand-alone entry fee: instead, the bands are funded from a music charge that's added to your bill at the end of the night. Alcohol can only be served with food.

★ Vortex Jazz Club
Dalston Culture House, 11 Gillet Street, Dalston, N16 8JN (7254 4097/www.vortexjazz.co.uk). Dalston Kingsland rail. **Shows** 8.30-11.15pm daily. **Admission** free-£12. **Credit** MC, V.
Formerly based in Stoke Newington, the Vortex reopened in 2005 on the first floor of a handsome new Dalston building (there's a restaurant on the ground floor). The space can feel a bit sterile but the line-ups are as good as ever, packed with left-field talent from Britain, Europe and the US. *Photo p316.*

Nightlife

The old map of London clubs has been redrawn – here

Always volatile at the fringes, London's nightlife has over the last couple of years seen dramatic changes right at its core: destination clubs in the West End, Clerkenwell and King's Cross have all closed. The still fabulous **Fabric** – which has recently extended its empire to north Greenwich with **Matter** – and **Ministry of Sound** fly the tattered flag for the superclubs, but for the edgiest and most creative nights, the advice remains as it has been for the last several years: get yourself to the little out-of-centre clubs. Shoreditch still has a virtual monopoly on London's indie-electro nights, with venues such as **Catch** and **Cargo** joined by newcomers the **Star of Bethnal Green** and **East Village**. It's also the heartland of the thriving alt-cabaret scene. And King's Cross is still keepin' things cheerful with the **Big Chill House** and EGG.

THE LOWDOWN

So, 2007 was cheerio to mighty King's Cross triumvirate Cross, the Key and Canvas. Then Turnmills waved goodbye – after two decades of hands in the air by the speaker stack – in March last year, to be followed by the End, a steadfast, unarguable electronic institution, sold and due to go dark in early 2009. With transport redevelopment closing Ghetto, SIN and Astoria 2, the evisceration of West End clubbing is complete. The 2007 smoking ban has been another kick in the nethers. While it hardly affected some clubs (**EGG** has a large smoking garden; the **Big Chill House** and **Dex** have spacious terraces), others have found it an enduring headache.

But wait…! A smattering of excellent venues have opened their doors to roadblocks every night. You'll find a fine selection of them in Shoreditch: refurbished watering hole **Star of Bethnal Green** and sparkling new venue **East Village** among them. Messy yet dressy 'Ditchsters swing into **Catch** for gin-soaked, rockin' affairs, and lovers of urban head to **Cargo**. The cream on the clubbing cake, however, is brand-new superclub **Matter**

About the author
Kate Hutchinson is a Time Out staff writer. She also reviews nightlife for publications such as Clash, Big Cheese and Loud & Quiet.

(*see p326* **What's the Matter?**). In the West End, we've high hopes that the rejuvenated **Bar Rumba** will take up some of the slack created by all the closures.

Meanwhile, the cabaret juggernaut rolls on, smashing through into mainstream clubland. To see the best, head to **Volupté**, which hosts opulent burlesque nights (including, of late, a number of wacky new European acts), and the always innovative **Bethnal Green Working Men's Club**. Whatever you do, go with an open mind.

London rewards those who are willing to chance something new, but not all risks are worth taking. Find out which night bus gets you home and where you get it from before you head out (the tube doesn't start until around 7am on Sundays), but if it still proves too mind-boggling at stupid o'clock then check out our guide to catching that elusive cab (*see p306, p314 & p325* **Inside Track**). Whatever you do, though, make sure your cab is an official one (to find out how to tell, *see p364*).

CENTRAL

Bar Rumba
36 Shaftesbury Avenue, Soho, W1D 7EP (7287 6933/www.barrumba.co.uk). Piccadilly Circus tube. **Open** 9pm-3am Mon; 6pm-3am Tue; 7pm-3am Wed; 8pm-3.30am Thur; 6pm-3.30am Fri; 9pm-4am Sat; 9pm-2.30am Sun. **Admission** £3-£10;

ARTS & ENTERTAINMENT

Big Chill House.

King's Cross... All Change!

Neighbourhood regeneration has brought an intriguing new nightlife scene.

New Year's Day 2008 marked a raucous last hurrah for an enclave of legendary King's Cross clubs: the Cross, the Key and Canvas. The area they inhabited was just workaday industrial buildings in the badlands north of King's Cross, but a lowly goods yard off York Way had contrived to become the location of some of London's best nightlife.

Despite the success of these clubs over some 15 years, the largest urban regeneration project in Europe has finally swept them away. The whole quarter has been taken over by University of the Arts London. The plan is to create up to fifty – yes, fifty! – new arts and music venues within the historic buildings around the site, including pubs, bars, new theatres, independent cinemas and exhibition spaces, transforming the area into an entirely new cultural quarter. If nearby **Kings Place** (*see p308*) is a sign of things to come, we're already excited. The arts quarter is due to throw open its doors in late 2010.

Pacha London's owner Billy Reilly, who ran the nightlife triad at the yard, sees the new quarter as a fusion of Shoreditch and Covent Garden – smarter than the former, trendier than the latter. For the time being, though, his efforts are focused on a stylish venture up the road, at the junction of Caledonian and Wharfdale Roads, with the acquisition of a boozer called the Driver. Likely to be renamed **Pacha Terrace**, it will boast a classy members' club feel, a New York loft-style interior and an electronic music policy straight out of Hoxton. A measure of Reilly's ambition is his decision to commission a French landscape artist to construct a vertical hanging garden over the whole façade.

Reilly's plan isn't so outlandish. The **Big Chill House** (*see opposite*) has been going from strength to strength over the last few years, thanks to diverse, urban and world-flavoured programming, a stellar soundsystem and a generous terrace. You can get in for free on most nights too. And even a rave-chasing hedonist can still get a sniff of all-night party action hereabouts: just head to **EGG** (*see p323*) and its fabulous new sister cabaret club, the Apothecary. On any given night you might find a bizarre mix of slack-jawed drag queens, neon-splattered fashion kidz and jaded City boys, but on a Friday the cool, hip hop-flavoured electro, dubstep, grime and techno should get you bouncing around, while Ibiza-themed and funky house nights pepper Saturday nights.

free before 10pm Mon, Sat; free before 9pm Tue-Fri. **Credit** AmEx, MC, V. **Map** p408 W4.

Smack bang in the middle of the West End, Bar Rumba's small basement club was already known for its deep urban flavours and surprisingly un-West End crowd, but a relaunch late last year saw it take on a more underground, techno and electro twist. Movement is the fortnightly Thursday junglist and drum 'n' bass session, while salsa fans love Barrio Latino on Tuesday. Weekends are for over-21s only.

★ Fabric

77A Charterhouse Street, Clerkenwell, EC1M 3HN (7336 8898/advance tickets 0870 902 0001/www.fabriclondon.com). Farringdon tube/rail. **Open** 10pm-6am Fri; 11pm-8am Sat. **Admission** £13-£16. **Credit** AmEx, MC, V. **Map** p402 O5.

Fabric is the club that most party people come to see in London, with good reason. Fridays belong to the bass: guaranteed highlights include DJ Hype, who takes over all three rooms once a month for his drum 'n' bass and dubstep night Playaz, and Switch and Sinden's electro bass-tastic Get Familiar party, which is a sell-out every other month. Saturdays descend into techy, minimal, deep house territory, with plenty of live artists you just can't hear anywhere else.

▶ *For Fabric's ambitious new venture, see p326.*

Madame JoJo's

8-10 Brewer Street, Soho, W1F 0SE (7734 3040/www.madamejojos.com). Leicester Square or Piccadilly Circus tube. **Open** 8pm-3am Tue; 9pm-3am Thur; 10pm-3am Fri, Sun; 7pm-3am Sat.* **Admission** £4-£10. **Credit** AmEx, MC, V. **Map** p408 W3.

JoJo's is a beacon for those seeking to escape post-work chain pubs. The basement space is very red and slightly shabby. Treasured nights include variety (the all new London Burlesque Social Club, first Thursdays; Kitsch Cabaret, every Saturday), Keb Darge's long-running Deep Funk and Tuesday's indie racket White Heat.

Pacha London

Terminus Place, Victoria, SW1V 1JR (0845 371 4489/www.pachalondon.com). Victoria tube/rail. **Open** 10pm-5am Fri, Sat. **Admission** £15-£20. **Map** p400 H10.

One of the great unanswered clubland questions is why this outpost of the über-glamorous Ibizan superclub had to be located in... a bus depot. Attracting the suited, booted and minted with a range of sassy house parties, it's a swanky, stylish place for clubbers who have money to burn.

▶ *For more on owner Billy Reilly's plans for a new Pacha, see opposite.*

Social

5 Little Portland Street, Marylebone, W1W 7JD (7636 4992/www.thesocial.com). Oxford Circus

tube. **Open** noon-m... Thur, Fri; 1pm-1am ... website for details. A... **Credit** AmEx, MC, V...

A discreet, opaque fro... and DJ bar of suprem... Heavenly Records near... drinks upstairs, its cliente... ers, alt-rock nonebrities and ... ble downstairs to an intimate ... ace rocked by DJs six nights a week. ... monthly Hip Hop Karaoke night (www.hiphopkaraokelondon.co.uk) is a giggle.

Soho Revue Bar

11-12 Walker's Court, off Brewer Street, Soho, W1F 0ED (7734 0377/www.sohorevuebar.com). Leicester Square or Piccadilly Circus tube. **Open** 7.30pm-3am Mon-Sat; 7.30pm-midnight Sun. **Performances** 8pm. **Admission** £10; £5 reductions. **Credit** AmEx, MC, V. **Map** p408 W3.

Two grand rooms here host the weekly ladies 'n' drag queens only Trannyshack, as well as cabaret most Saturdays, presented in supper-club style and followed by their house party, er, 'House Party'. Jodie Harsh, drag queen du jour, hosts Friday's electro-rock celeb hangout Circus.

★ Volupté

7-9 Norwich Street, Holborn, EC4A 1EJ (7831 1622/1677/www.volupte-lounge.com). Chancery Lane tube. **Open** from 11.30am Tue-Fri; from 7.30pm Sat. **Admission** £8-£12. **Credit** MC, V. **Map** p406 N5.

Expect to suffer extreme wallpaper envy as you enter the ground-floor bar then descend to the club proper. Punters enjoy some of the best cabaret talent in town from tables set beneath absinthe-inspired vines. Wednesday nights are Cabaret Salon and once a month the Black Cotton Club turns back the clock to the 1920s.

NORTH LONDON

Better known as gig venues, **KOKO** (*see p313*) and **Barfly** (*see p314*) also have a good reputation for feisty club nights.

★ Big Chill House

257-259 Pentonville Road, King's Cross, N1 9NL (7427 2540/www.bigchill.net). King's Cross tube/rail. **Open** noon-midnight Mon-Wed, Sun; noon-1am Thur; noon-3am Fri, Sat. **Admission** £5 after 10pm Fri, Sat. **Credit** MC, V. **Map** p399 M3.

A festival, a record label, a bar (*see p236*) and now also a house, the Big Chill empire rolls on. A good thing too, if it keeps offering such interesting things as this three-floor space. The likes of A Skillz and owner Pete Lawrence regularly handle deck duties, and there's great terrace.

EGG

200 York Way, King's Cross, N7 9AP (7609 8364/www.egglondon.net). King's Cross tube/rail then free shuttle from York Way. **Open** 10pm-6am Fri; 10pm-2am Sat. **Admission** £6-£15. **Credit** (bar) MC, V. **Map** p399 L2.

With its Mediterranean-styled three floors, garden and enormous terrace (complete with a small pool), EGG is big enough to lose yourself in but manages to retain an intimate atmosphere. The upstairs bar in red ostrich leather is rather elegant, but the main dancefloor downstairs has a warehouse rave feel.

▶ *Looking for some kinky fun? New cabaret club Apothecary (3 Vale Royal, N7 9AP, 7609 8364, www.apothecarybar.co.uk) is just next door.*

★ Proud

Horse Hospital, Stables Market, Chalk Farm Road, Camden, NW1 8AH (7482 3867/www. proudcamden.com). Chalk Farm tube. **Open** 7.30pm-1am Mon-Wed; 7.30pm-2am Thur, Fri, Sat; 7.30pm-midnight Sun. **Admission** free-£10. **Credit** AmEx, MC, V.

North London guitar slingers do rockstar debauchery at this former Horse Hospital, whether draping themselves – cocktail in hand – over the luxurious textiles in the individual stable-style booths, sinking into deck chairs on the outdoor terrace, or spinning around in the main band room to trendonista electro, indie and alternative sounds.

Scala

For listings, *see p314* **Music**.

One of London's best-loved gig venues, this multi-floored monolith is the frequent destination for one-off superparties now that many of London's superclubs have bitten the dust. Drum & Bass Arena can often be found piling in as many succulent basslines as they can, and funky, electro and tech house bash Smartie Partie has relocated here from Turnmills with a monthly residency. A venue to get very lost in on nights that get very messy.

EAST LONDON

Aquarium

256 & 260 Old Street, Shoreditch, EC1V 9DD (7251 6136/www.clubaquarium.co.uk). Old Street tube/rail. **Open** 10pm-11am Fri, Sat; 10pm-4am Sun. **Admission** £7-£15. **Credit** MC, V. **Map** p403 Q4.

There's not much cool about this ever-popular club – except the wildly dressed clientele at trendy Sunday night minimal rave-up Wet Yourself! Otherwise, the queues of out-of-town girls know to pack bikinis for long-running Saturday night disco Carwash – Club Aquarium boasts a swimming pool *and* jacuzzi.

Old Blue Last

38 Great Eastern Street, Shoreditch, EC2A 3ES (7739 7033/www.theoldbluelast.com). Liverpool

Proud.

Street or Old Street tube/rail. **Open** noon-midnight Mon-Wed; noon-12.30am Thur, Sun; noon-1.30am Fri, Sat. **Admission** free-£5. **Credit** AmEx, MC, V. **Map** p403 R4.

This shabby two-floor Victorian boozer was transformed by hipster handbook *Vice* in 2004. Klaxons, Amy Winehouse, Arctic Monkeys and Lily Allen have all played secret shows in the sauna-like upper room, but its high-fashion rock 'n' rollers also dig regular club nights from girlie indie DJ troupe My Ex Boyfriend's Records and Sean McLusky's scuzzy electro rock nights.

★ Bethnal Green Working Men's Club

42-44 Pollard Row, Bethnal Green, E2 6NB (7739 2727/www.workersplaytime.net). Bethnal Green tube. **Open** check website for details. **Admission** £5-£12 after 8pm Fri, Sat.

The sticky red carpet and broken lampshades perfectly suit the programme of quirky lounge, retro rock 'n' roll and fancy-dress burlesque parties from spandex-lovin' dance husband-and-wife Duotard or Grind a Go Go, for which burlesque starlets get a hip 1960s dancefloor. The mood is friendly, the playlist upbeat and the air always full of artful, playful mischief.

Cargo

Kingsland Viaduct, 83 Rivington Street, Shoreditch, EC2A 3AY (7739 3440/www.cargo-london.com). Old Street tube/rail. **Open** 11am-

ARTS & ENTERTAINMENT

East Village.

Local lad Stuart Patterson, one of the Faith crew of DJ/promoters of all-day house-music parties across London since 1999, took over the Medicine Bar last year, transforming it into this two-floor, 'real house' bar-club. The top-notch, eclectic programme of DJs should suit any sophisticated clubber. The bi-monthly residency of funky techno heads DDD is storming, as indeed is the NYC-styled disco punk night Sweatshop.

Herbal
10-14 Kingsland Road, Hoxton, E2 8DA (7613 4462/www.herbaluk.com). Old Street tube/rail. **Open** 9pm-3am Fri, Sat; 9pm-2am Sun. **Admission** free-£10. **Credit** (bar only) AmEx, MC, V. **Map** p403 R3.
After spending summer 2007 running a reduced programme, this loved but under-the-weather two-floor venue is now back at full bore. Make space in your schedule for all-girl monthly bass sesh Feline, intimate parties from vocal disco-house funksters Bobby&Steve Presents, after-party Sunday sessions that run all day into Monday morning, and a veritable plethora of underground junglist nights.

On the Rocks
25 Kingsland Road, Hoxton, E2 8AA (no phone). Old Street tube/rail. **Open** from 10.30pm Fri; 9pm-2am Sat. **Admission** £5, £3 reductions; £3 before 11pm. **Map** p403 R3.
There are run-down, after-the-after-party clubs… and then there's On the Rocks. Dark, small and full of UV light, it's a haven for Shoreditch's dedicated

1am Mon-Thur; 11am-3am Fri; 6pm-3am Sat; 1pm-midnight Sun. **Admission** free-£12. **Credit** AmEx, MC, V. **Map** p403 R4.
Located down a side street and under a bridge, the bricks 'n' arches of Cargo keeps Shoreditch music fans in a blissful state of whatever-next-ness. It's increasingly about live music here, but seminal nights such as Go!Zilla, Karen P's Broad Casting and the all new Wonky Pop have also made this place home. Check out the great street-food café and the Shephard Fairey-styled street art in the garden.

Catch
22 Kingsland Road, Hoxton, E2 8DA (7729 6097/www.thecatchbar.com). Old Street tube/rail. **Open** 6pm-midnight Mon, Tue, Wed; 6pm-2am Thur-Sat; 6pm-1am Sun. **Credit** AmEx, MC, V. **Map** p403 R3.
Catch isn't anything special – it doesn't look like much, and staff can be somewhat surly – but the small upstairs room attracts a great mix of adventurous young promoters. Get Rude is a bass-heavy tropical and electro outing run by international DJ duo Zombie Disco Squad (second Saturdays).
▶ *Just up the road is louche drinking hole Dreambagsjaguarshoes; see p238.*

★ East Village
89 Great Eastern Street, Shoreditch, EC2A 3HX (7739 5173/www.eastvillageclub.com). Old Street tube/rail. **Open** 5pm-1am Mon, Tue; 5pm-3am Wed-Sun. **Admissions** £8. **Credit** AmEx, MC, V. **Map** p403 Q4.

Dex.

party people. Hannah Holland, a cracking local-turned-superstar mash-up DJ, is resident at the mainly gay and totally twisted electro party Trailer Trash each week.

Plastic People

147-149 Curtain Road, Shoreditch, EC2A 3QE (7739 6471/www.plasticpeople.co.uk). Old Street tube/rail. **Open** 9pm-2am 2nd Thur of mth; 10pm-4am Fri, Sat; 8-11.30pm Sun. **Admission** £5-£10. **Credit** MC, V. **Map** p405 R4.
Plastic People subscribes to the old-school line that all you need for a kicking party is a dark basement and a sound system (the rig embarrasses those in many larger clubs). Some of London's most progressive club nights here range from underground techno at Lost presents Spacebase to dubstep and grime at Sunday's pioneering night FWD.

Star of Bethnal Green

359 Bethnal Green Road, Bethnal Green, E2 6LG (07932 869705/www.starofbethnalgreen.com). Bethnal Green tube. **Open** 5pm-midnight Mon-Thur, Sun; 4pm-2am Fri, Sat. **Admission** free-£5. **Credit** MC, V.
Here's one star that's shining brightly in Bethnal Green, having been taken over and brilliantly refurbished by house and electro promoter Rob Star. A bold red and silver star stamps the wall behind the stage in this intimate boozer, and there are low-key gigs from big bands and an eclectic yet funky fresh line-up of disco to house to indie nights. Watch out for madcap, booty house bash Bastard Batty Bass on monthly Thursdays, led by DJ Hannah Holland.

333

333 Old Street, Hoxton, EC1V 9LE (7739 5949/www.333mother.com). Old Street tube/rail. **Open** 10pm-2.30am Fri; 10pm-5am Sat. **Bar** 8pm-2.30am daily. **Admission** *Club* £5-£10. **Credit** MC, V. **Map** p405 Q4.
While no longer the be-all and end-all of East End clubbing, this three-floored clubbing institution still draws queues for indie-rave mash-ups at the weekends. The basement's dark and intense, which works well for the dubstep talent. Upstairs is just like a house party, complete with broken loos and random strangers falling over your shoes.

SOUTH LONDON

Dex

467-469 Brixton Road, Brixton, SW9 8HH (7326 4455/www.dexclub.co.uk). Brixton tube/rail. **Open** 10pm-6am Fri, Sat. **Admission** £10. **Credit** AmEx, MC, V.
Opened in 2007, this plush members' club and boutique hotel is a beacon for Brixton's new young professional media crowd looking for somewhere sexy for post-work and late-night drinks. Its USP? The two-tiered rooftop bar with its hot tub and panoram-

ic views over Brixton where techno (Kerfuffle), hip hop (Mind Yuh Business) and even Balkan (raucous rompers Stranger Than Paradise) DJs blast the beats. Opening times vary – phone ahead to check.

Dogstar

389 Coldharbour Lane, Brixton, SW9 8LQ (7733 7515/www.antic-ltd.com/dogstar). Brixton tube/rail. **Open** 4pm-2am Mon-Thur; noon-4am Fri, Sat; noon-2am Sun. **Admission** £5 after 10pm Fri, Sat. **Credit** MC, V.
A Brixton institution from back when Coldharbour Lane was somewhere people feared to go, Dogstar is a big street-corner pub exuding the urban authenticity loved by clubbers. The atmosphere can be intense, but it's never less than vibrant. The music varies from night to night but quality generally stays high.

★ Matter

O2 Arena, Peninsula Square, SE10 0DY (7549 6686/Ticketweb 0870 0600 100/www.matter london.com). North Greenwich tube. **Box office**

INSIDE TRACK CAB LORE

You're out, you've had your fun and now you want your bed... where's the sodding cab? If you're in **Shoreditch**, according to Dimi, who's been working behind the wheel for 14 years, 'you'll always catch a cab where Bethnal Green Road meets Shoreditch High Street, by the members' club Shoreditch House. Many cabbies will have stopped at Beigel Bake (*see p223*) for a quick munch, so there are a lot around there. You can also find them at the other end, at the junction of Hackney Road and Kingsland Road, where the Browns bar and the church is.' The advice for **Notting Hill** is straightforward: 'Don't stand where WH Smith is on the corner,' Peter points out. 'Walk towards Kensington Park Road, where the small roundabout is, where cabs return to Notting Hill Gate.' Getting back from **Brixton**, however, isn't easy: 'It can be tough to get a cab here, so pick a night when there's a big gig on at the Brixton Academy (*see p311*),' says another driver. 'Try outside the Fridge nightclub on Brixton Hill, because there's a taxi rank there too.'

If none of these suggestions work and you've got your phone, ring spot-on private hire company **Addison Lee** (7387 8888, www.addisonlee.com) who can dispatch drivers swiftly and text you when they've arrived.

ARTS & ENTERTAINMENT

By phone 9am-8pm daily. **Tickets** £10-£30.
Credit AmEx, MC, V.
Meet superclub Fabric's dream venue, a 2,600-capacity venue built under the former Millennium Dome.
Expect the same stellar programming as at its legendary older brother, with state-of-the-art 3D mapped audiovisuals on interlocking screens. It sounds all very sci-fi – not to mention far from central London at 6am, but Thames Clipper boats operate half hourly to Waterloo Bridge and Thames Pier.
A mind-blowing experience for the adventurous clubber. *See also below* **What's the Matter?**
▶ *For IndigO2 and the O2 Arena, see p313.*

Ministry of Sound
103 Gaunt Street, off Newington Causeway, Newington, SE1 6DP (0870 060 0010/www. ministryofsound.com). Elephant & Castle tube/ rail. **Open** 10.30pm-late Fri; 11pm-7am Sat.
Admission £12-£17. **Credit** AmEx, MC, V.
Map p404 O10.
Cool it ain't (there's little more naff in all London than the VIP rooms here), but home to a killer sound system the Ministry most certainly is. Post-Turnmills, long-running trance night the Gallery has made its home here on Fridays (expect large sets from Paul Oakenfold and Sander van Doorn), while

the Saturday Sessions chop and change between deep techno, fidget house, electro and much more.

Plan B
418 Brixton Road, Brixton, SW9 7AY (0870 116 5421/www.plan-brixton.co.uk). Brixton tube/rail. **Open** 7pm-3am Thur; 9pm-5am Fri, Sat; 9pm-3am Sun. **Admission** £5-£10. **Credit** AmEx, MC, V.
It may be small, but Plan B punches well above its weight thanks to a constant flow of hip hop and funk stars at Fidgit on Fridays, and plenty of soulful house and international hip hop on Saturdays.

WEST LONDON
Notting Hill Arts Club
21 Notting Hill Gate, Notting Hill, W11 3JQ (7460 4459/www.nottinghillartsclub.com). Notting Hill Gate tube. **Open** 6pm-2am Mon-Fri; 4pm-2am Sat; 4pm-1am Sun. **Admission** £5-£8; free before 8pm. **Credit** MC, V. **Map** p394 A7.
Cool west London folk are grateful for this small, basement club. It isn't much to look at, but almost single-handedly keeps this side of town on the radar thanks to nights like Thursday's YoYo – for fans of eclectic crate-digging, from funk to 1980s boogie.

What's the Matter?

It's here and it's hot: London's biggest club-gig space opens its doors.

Not everyone agrees with the conservative Christian views of Philip Anschutz, the billionaire behind one of the world's biggest entertainment companies. However, few people disagree with one basic point: his Anschutz Entertainment Group know how to run a big venue.

Under AEG's watch, the white elephant that was the Millennium Dome has been transformed from a national joke into a sleek, well-catered, 20,000-capacity temple of entertainment called the **O2 Arena** (*see p313*). This follows the group's transformations of the London Arena in Docklands, Manchester's MEN Arena and dozens of American sports teams. But the group's latest venue is a little different: the opening of **Matter** (*see p325*) sees AEG move confidently into the domain of the counterculture, specifically underground dance music. In this case, quite literally underground: Matter is located beneath the Millennium Dome.

The venue has been formed through a partnership between AEG and **Fabric** (*see p321*), one of London's most successful dance music venues. However, Fabric and

Matter are very different spaces. Whereas the 1,500-capacity Fabric is dedicated to dance music, the larger Matter has been designed by architect William Russell to operate as a concert venue, a club, a performing arts space or a VIP club. Sightlines are great and the sound is amazing – Matter's 'BodyKinetic' floor is a step forward from Fabric's famous 'BodySonic' dancefloor, designed to vibrate to the frequencies of the bass speakers built directly below it.

With big names such as Sasha and Armand van Helden featuring in the early days, Matter looks set to build on Fabric's already strong reputation among the dance music cognoscenti. But beyond Saturday nights you can also expect a forward-thinking accommodation with live rock music. The venue is hoping to pioneer a series of themed nights, where artists like Hot Chip and UNKLE will curate evenings of live music, DJs and audio-visual events. 'The only policy that we're really subscribing to,' says the venue's lead programmer Will Harold, 'is that if it's good, it goes on.'

Sport & Fitness

London's already limbering up for the Games of a lifetime.

It's still three years away, but Britain's success in Beijing during 2008 has got London even more excited about the 2012 Olympics. Nervousness about construction cost overruns was temporarily shoved from the headlines, as the country basked in the afterglow of its 47 medals (the most since the London Olympics of 1908).

But even during the countdown to 2012, there's plenty of sport to enjoy. London has numerous professional teams in a variety of sports, and a little advance planning should land you tickets to a big game. There are also lots of opportunities to get active, whether at hotel gyms or on a jogging loop around one of the city's magnificent parks. Check the Sport & Fitness section of *Time Out* magazine for a round-up of the best of the coming week's action.

MAJOR STADIUMS

There's a mass of building work at the Olympic site near Stratford, east London. In 2012, the **Olympic Park** will include a £600-million, 80,000-capacity stadium (due to be remodelled after the event), an aquatic centre, a velopark, a hockey centre and the Olympic village. See www.london2012.com for more.

The **O2 Arena** (*see p313*) hosts sporadic events, including ice-hockey and basketball; the refurbished **Wembley Arena** (*see p314*) offers boxing, snooker, basketball and show jumping.

Crystal Palace National Sports Centre

Ledrington Road, Crystal Palace, SE19 2BB (8778 0131/www.gll.org). Crystal Palace rail.
Until the Olympic stadium in Stratford is completed, this Grade II-listed building and leisure centre remains the major athletics venue in the country, and hosts popular summer Grand Prix events.

★ Wembley Stadium

Stadium Way, Wembley, Middx HA9 0WS (0844 980 8001/www.wembleystadium.com). Wembley Park tube/Wembley Stadium rail.
Britain's most famous sports venue finally reopened in early 2007 after an expensive redevelopment. Designed by Sir Norman Foster, the 90,000-capacity stadium is some sight, its futuristic steel arch now an imposing feature of the skyline. All England football internationals and cup finals are played here, as are a number of one-off sporting events and concerts. There has been criticism of the high percentage of spaces set aside for corporate guests at big matches; guided tours offer alternative access. *Photo p329.*

SPECTATOR SPORTS

Basketball

London Capital are currently the city's sole representatives in the pro British Basketball League (www.bbl.org.uk); perhaps regular pre-season NBA games at the **O2** (*see p313*) will generate more enthusiasm. Contact the **English Basketball Association** (0114 223 5693, www.englandbasketball.co.uk) for more details.

INSIDE TRACK
SEASONAL SKATING

There are permanent skating rinks at **Broadgate Circle** in the City (outdoors) and **Queen's Ice & Bowl** (indoors). But Christmas visitors should note that a variety of temporary rinks spring up all over town during the festive season. **Somerset House** (*see p87*) set the trend; It's since been followed by **Hampton Court Palace** (*see p157*) and **Kew Gardens** (*see p155*). Check the weekly *Time Out* magazine for a full list.

London Capital *Capital City Academy, Doyle Gardens, NW10 3ST (8838 8700/www.london capital.org). Kensal Green tube.*

Cricket

Typically, the English national team hosts Test and one-day series against two international sides each summer. Tickets will be hard to come by in 2009, when England host old rivals Australia; your best chance of seeing some action is on the last day of a five-day Test, for which tickets are not normally sold in advance (matches are often completed before the five days are up). In 2009, England will also host the world Twenty20 championship (*see below*); ticket demand will also be huge.

Seats are easier to come by for domestic county games, both four-day and one-day matches. The season runs from April to September. Surrey play at the Oval, and

Middlesex play at Lord's; both grounds also host international matches.

Brit Oval *Kennington Oval, Kennington, SE11 5SS (7582 6660/7764/www.surreycricket.com). Oval tube.* **Tickets** *International £15-£103. County £12-£20.*
★ **Lord's** *St John's Wood Road, St John's Wood, NW8 8QN (MCC 7289 1611/tickets 7432 1000/www.lords.org). St John's Wood tube.* **Tickets** *International Call for details. County £14-£16.*

Cycling

After Mark Cavendish won four individual stages in the 2008 Tour de France, and the British cycling team brought home eight gold medals from the Beijing Olympics (including two for London's Bradley Wiggins), cycling looks set for a resurgence in popularity.

A Twenty20 Vision?

The sport for snoozing old men wakes up to the 21st century.

With its arcane rules, impenetrable language and meandering five-day matches, the quintessentially English sport of cricket often confuses uninitiated visitors. But the rapid rise of Twenty20, a shortened form of the game that debuted in 2003, has provided many outsiders with a handy way in to the game.

Twenty20 was invented by the England & Wales Cricket Board in 2003, as the cash-strapped domestic county teams sought new audiences for poorly attended county matches. The reasoning was simple: unlike all other forms of the game, Twenty20 can be played in the early evening, with an average game taking about three-and-a-half hours. And the short form puts the emphasis on big hitting, daredevil shot-making and acrobatic fielding, all of which are crowd-pleasers.

So it proved. Traditionalists grumbled that Twenty20 bore little relation to the episodic subtleties and intricacies of four- or five-day cricket, but crowds flooded to the action. Indeed, the game developed subtleties of its own. Twenty20 quickly became an established part of the English game, and is comfortably the biggest money-spinner on the domestic circuit.

It didn't take long for the rest of the cricketing world to catch on. In 2007, South Africa staged the first Twenty20 international competition, which was

won in style by India. The ramifications of their victory have been huge. Within a year, two lucrative but controversial Twenty20 leagues were set up in India, followed in late 2008 by a Twenty20 Champions League that featured the leading domestic sides from the major cricketing nations. Most bizarrely of all, American billionaire Sir Allen Stanford organised a series of five Twenty20 matches between an England XI and a 'Stanford Super Stars' side in the Caribbean, its $20m winner-takes-all prize provoking a keen scramble for places in the squads.

For evidence that Twenty20 is now the game's leading financial motor, look to the World Twenty20 championship, held across England in June. **Lord's** and the **Oval** (for both, *see above*) will host a number of matches, with Lord's staging the final; crowds should be huge.

If (as seems distinctly likely) you can't get tickets to the big matches, the domestic Twenty20 Cup is a good bet. Both Middlesex (Lord's) and Surrey (the Oval) will host regional group games against other counties, and a game should offer excitement and atmosphere without taking too much time out of your schedule. And who knows? Perhaps it could kindle an enthusiasm for the longer form of this most compelling of sports.

Each September, the city hosts a stage of the annual **Tour of Britain**, a road race that follows a different course around Britain every year. Of quirkier interest is the **Smithfield Nocturne** (www.smithfieldnocturne.co.uk): held in June each year around the famous market, it features elite, schools and even folding bike races, attracting more than 200 participants. And it's free.

Riders should try the **Herne Hill Velodrome** (Burbage Road, Herne Hill, SE24, www.vcl.org.uk), the world's oldest cycle circuit, or the newly opened **Redbridge Cycle Centre** (Forest Road, Hainault, Essex, IG6, 8500 9359), which boasts a road circuit, a mountain bike track and seven different circuit combinations.

Football

Playing in the lucrative, glamorous Barclays Premier League, **Arsenal** and **Chelsea** are the capital's major players. Arsenal moved in 2006 to a new 60,000-capacity stadium, which the club hope will boost their revenues; Chelsea, meanwhile, depend heavily on the largesse of Russian oil tycoon Roman Abramovich. Other Premier League clubs in London include resolute **Fulham**, troubled **West Ham** and underachieving **Tottenham**, who suffered their worst ever start to a season in 2008. The Chelsea Centenary Museum has recently joined similar exhibitions at West Ham and Arsenal.

Tickets for Premier League games can be hard to obtain, but a visit to Fulham is a treat: a superb setting by the river, a historic ground and seats in the 'neutral' section often available on the day. For London clubs in the lower leagues (the Coca-Cola Championship, Coca-Cola Football League 1 and Coca-Cola Football League 2), tickets are cheaper and easier to obtain. Prices given are for adult non-members.

The English national team plays its home fixtures at **Wembley Stadium** (*see p327*). Tickets can be hard to come by.

Arsenal *Emirates Stadium, Ashburton Grove, N7 7AF (7704 4040/tickets 0844 277 3625/www.arsenal.com). Arsenal tube.* **Tickets** £33-£66. Premier League
Chelsea *Stamford Bridge, Fulham Road, Chelsea, SW6 1HS (0871 984 1905/www.chelseafc.com). Fulham Broadway tube.* **Tickets** £40-£65. Premier League
Crystal Palace *Selhurst Park, Whitehorse Lane, Selhurst, SE25 6PU (0871 200 0071/ www.cpfc.co.uk). Selhurst rail/168 bus* **Tickets** £25-£35. Championship
Fulham *Craven Cottage, Stevenage Road, Fulham, SW6 6HH (0870 442 1234/ www.fulhamfc.com). Putney Bridge tube.* **Tickets** £25-£55. Premier League

Wembley Stadium. *See p327*.

Leyton Orient *Matchroom Stadium, Brisbane Road, Leyton, E10 5NF (8926 1111/www. leytonorient.com). Leyton tube/Leyton Midland Road rail.* **Tickets** £20-£22. League 1
Queens Park Rangers *Loftus Road Stadium, South Africa Road, Shepherd's Bush, W12 7PA (0870 112 1967/www.qpr.co.uk). White City tube.* **Tickets** £20-£35. Championship
Tottenham Hotspur *White Hart Lane Stadium, 748 High Road, Tottenham, N17 0AP (0844 844 0102/www.tottenhamhotspur. com). White Hart Lane rail.* **Tickets** £37-£49. Premier League
West Ham United *Upton Park, Green Street, West Ham, E13 9AZ (0870 112 2700/ www.whufc.com). Upton Park tube.* **Tickets** £35-£63. Premier League

Greyhound racing

For a cheap night out that could end up paying for itself, head to one of London's greyhound tracks. Walthamstow Stadium was sold for housing development in 2008 (the campaign to rescue it continues at http://saveourstow.word press.com); in its absence, the most accessible track is at **Wimbledon** (Plough Lane, 8946 8000, www.lovethedogs.co.uk). Further afield, you can also take in the chirpy charms of **Romford** (London Road, 01708 762345, www.romfordgreyhoundstadium.co.uk) or the relaxed atmosphere at **Crayford** (Stadium Way, 01322 557836, www.crayford.com). For more information, visit www.thedogs.co.uk.

Tour of Britain. *See p329.*

Horse racing

The racing year is divided into the flat-racing season, from April to September, and the National Hunt season over jumps, from October to April. For more information about the 'sport of kings', visit www.discover-racing.com. The Home Counties around London are liberally sprinkled with a fine variety of courses, each of which offers an enjoyable day out from the city.

Impressive **Epsom** hosts the Derby in June, while cultured **Royal Ascot** offers the famous Royal Meeting in June and the King George Day in July; you may need to book ahead for them all. **Sandown Park**, which pushes horses to the limit with a hill finish, hosts the Whitbread Gold Cup in April and the Coral Eclipse Stakes in July. There's also racing at unglamorous but popular **Kempton Park**; delightful, Thameside **Windsor**; and **Great Leighs**, which became the first new racing venue in Britain for 80 years when it opened in 2008.

Epsom *Epsom Downs, Epsom, Surrey KT18 5LQ (01372 726311/tickets 0844 579 3004/ www.epsomdowns.co.uk). Epsom Downs or Tattenham Corner rail.* **Open** *Box office 9 am-5pm Mon-Fri.* **Admission** *Grandstand* £40-£50 (The Derby).
Great Leighs *Moulsham Hall Lane, Great Leighs, Chelmsford, Essex CM3 1QP (01245 362412/www.greatleighs.com). Braintree/*

Braintree Freeport/Chelmsford rail. **Open** *Box office 9am-5pm Mon-Fri.* **Admission** £13.50-£20.
Kempton Park *Staines Road East, Sunbury-on-Thames, Middx TW16 5AQ (01932 782 292/tickets 0844 579 3004/www.kempton.co.uk). Kempton Park rail.* **Open** *Box office 9am-5pm Mon-Fri.* **Admission** from £16.
★ **Royal Ascot** *Ascot Racecourse, Ascot, Berks SL5 7JX (0870 722 7227/www.ascot.co.uk). Ascot rail.* **Open** *9am-5pm Mon-Fri.* **Admission** *Phone for details.*
Sandown Park *Portsmouth Road, Esher, Surrey KT10 9AJ (01372 463 072/tickets 0844 579 3004/www.sandown.co.uk). Esher rail.* **Open** *Box office 9am-5pm Mon-Fri.* **Admission** £15-£22.
Windsor *Maidenhead Road, Windsor, Berks SL4 5JJ (01753 498400/www.windsor-race course.co.uk). Windsor & Eton Riverside rail.* **Open** *Box office 9am-5.30pm Mon-Fri.* **Admission** £13-£28.

Motorsport

Wimbledon Stadium (8946 8000, 01252 322920, www.spedeworth.co.uk) is the place to come for pedal-to-the-metal action: every other Sunday bangers, hot rods and stock cars come together for family-oriented mayhem.
Rye House Stadium (01992 440400) in Hoddesdon, on the northern edges of London

near the M25 motorway, also hosts speedway, providing a home for the Rye House Rockets (www.ryehouse.com). Matches usually take place on Saturday evenings.

Rugby

For more than a century, there have been two rival rugby 'codes', each with their own rules and traditions: rugby union and rugby league.

Rugby union dominates in the south of England. The Guinness Premiership runs from early September to May; most games are played on Saturday and Sunday afternoons. Look out, too, for matches in the Heineken Cup, the pan-European competition for the continent's best clubs. Local Premiership teams – including Wasps, the current champions – are listed below; for a full list of clubs, contact the Rugby Football Union (8892 2000, www.rfu.com).

The English national team's home games in the Six Nations Championship (Jan-Mar) are held at **Twickenham** (Rugby Road, Twickenham, Middx, 8892 2000, www.rfu.com; *see also p158*), the home of English rugby union, tickets are almost impossible to get hold of, but other matches are more accessible. There are also internationals in October and November.

Rugby league's heartland is in the north of England – London's sole Super League club is **Harlequins RL**. However, in late summer, Wembley Stadium hosts the sport's Challenge Cup final, which has been won by St Helens for the past three seasons.

Harlequins *Stoop Memorial Ground, Langhorn Drive, Twickenham, Middx TW2 7SX (0871 527 1315/www.quins.co.uk). Twickenham rail.* **Tickets** £17-£40.
Harlequins Rugby League *Stoop Memorial Ground, Langhorn Drive, Twickenham, Middx TW2 7SX (0871 527 1351/www.quins.co.uk). Twickenham rail.* **Tickets** £10-£35.
London Irish *Madejski Stadium, Shooters Way, Reading, Berks RG2 0FL (0870 999 1871/www.london-irish.com). Reading rail then £2 shuttle bus.* **Tickets** £20-£35.

INSIDE TRACK
CIRCUS SKILLS

If you've ever wanted an honours degree in circus arts, head to **Circus Space** in Hoxton (Coronet Street, 7729 9522, www.thecircusspace.co.uk). The former power station offers a range of classes spread over a number of performance spaces, among them the staggering, cavernous Combustion Chamber.

London Wasps *Adams Park, Hillbottom Road, High Wycombe, Bucks HP12 4HJ (8993 8298/ tickets 0870 414 1515/www.wasps.co.uk). High Wycombe rail.* **Tickets** £15-£45.
Saracens *Vicarage Road Stadium, Watford, Herts WD18 0EP (01923 475222/www.saracens.com). Watford High Street rail.* **Tickets** £15-£40.

Tennis

Getting into the **Wimbledon Championships** at the All England Lawn Tennis Club (22 June-5 July 2009) requires forethought. Seats on Centre and Number One courts are distributed by ballot the previous year, although enthusiasts who queue on the day may gain entry to the outer courts. You can also turn up later in the day and pay a reasonable rate for seats vacated by spectators who have left early. Wimbledon is preceded by another grass-court tournament at **Queen's Club** (8-14 June 2009), where stars from the men's circuit can be seen warming up for the main event.

★ **All England Lawn Tennis Club** *Church Road, Wimbledon, SW19 5AE (8944 1066/ tickets 8971 2700/www.wimbledon.org). Southfields tube.*
Queen's Club *Palliser Road, West Kensington, W14 9EQ (7385 3421/www.queensclub.co.uk). Barons Court tube.*

PARTICIPATION & FITNESS

Golf

You don't have to be a member to tee off at the many public courses in the London area, but you will need to book in advance. There's a list of clubs at www.englishgolfunion.org, but two accessible beauties are the lovely **Dulwich & Sydenham Hill Golf Club** in Dulwich (8693 8491, www.dulwichgolf.co.uk, £40, members only Sat & Sun) and the testing **North Middlesex Golf Club** near Arnos Grove (8445 3060, www.northmiddlesexgc.co.uk, £15-£30, members only before 1pm Sat & Sun).

Health clubs & sports centres

Many health clubs and sports centres admit non-members and even allow them to join classes. Some of the main contenders are listed below; for a list of all venues in Westminster, call 7641 1846, or for Camden, call 7974 4456. Note that last entry is normally 45-60 minutes before the listed closing times. For more independent spirits, Hyde Park, Kensington Gardens and Battersea Park have particularly good jogging trails.

ARTS & ENTERTAINMENT

Central YMCA

112 Great Russell Street, Bloomsbury, WC1B 3NQ (7343 1700/www.centralymca.org.uk). Tottenham Court Road tube. **Open** 6.30am-10pm Mon-Fri; 10am-8pm Sat; 10am-7pm Sun. **Map** p399 K5.

Conveniently located and user-friendly, the Y has a good range of cardiovascular and weight-training equipment, a pool and a squash court, as well as a full timetable of excellently taught classes.

Jubilee Hall Leisure Centre

30 The Piazza, Covent Garden, WC2E 8BE (7836 4835/www.jubileehallclubs.co.uk). Covent Garden tube. **Open** 6.45am-10pm Mon-Fri; 9am-9pm Sat; 10am-5pm Sun. **Map** p407 Z3.

A reliable and central venue that provides calm surroundings for cardiovascular workouts. They also offer a selection of therapies and treatments. There are other Jubilee Hall centres in Southwark, Westminster and Hampstead.

The Sporting Year

What not to miss this year.

Rugby Union: Six Nations

Twickenham (see p158). **Date** 7 Feb, 15 Mar, 21 Mar.
England take on Italy, France, Wales, Ireland and Scotland.

Football: Carling Cup Final

Wembley Stadium (see p327). **Date** 1 Mar.
The League Cup is seen as the lesser of the country's domestic tournaments, though victory ensures a place in the UEFA Cup.

Rowing: Boat Race

Date 29 Mar. *See p270.*

Rugby Union: EDF Energy Cup Final

Twickenham (see p158). **Date** 18 or 19 Apr.
The showpiece domestic knockout competition reaches its climax.

Athletics: Flora London Marathon

Date 26 Apr. *See p270.*

Cricket: Internationals

Lord's (see p328). **Date** *Test matches* 16-20 July v Australia. *One-day internationals* 6 & 12 Sept v Australia.
Brit Oval (see p328). **Date** *Test matches* 20-24 Aug v Australia. *One-day internationals* 4 Sept v Australia.
England take on their fiercest and longest-standing international rivals in a series of Tests (five-day fixtures) and one-dayers (limited to 50 overs per side).

Football: Play-off Finals

Wembley Stadium (see p327). **Date** 23-25 May.
A promotion place is up for grabs for the winners of these often-enthralling end-of-season games between teams from the Championship and Leagues 1 and 2.

Football: FA Cup Final

Wembley Stadium (see p327). **Date** 30 May.
The climax of the historic tournament. Portsmouth, who beat Championship side Cardiff City in 2008, showed that smaller clubs can still win big trophies.

Horse Racing: Epsom Derby

Epsom Racecourse (see p330). **Date** 5-6 June.
One of Britain's best-known flat races.

Cricket: World Twenty20 Title

Lord's & Brit Oval (see p328). **Date** 5-21 June.
After winning the inaugural tournament in South Africa in 2007, holders India defend their trophy in the shortest form of the game (*see p328* **A Twenty20 Vision?**).

Horse Racing: Royal Ascot

Ascot Racecourse (see p330). **Date** 16-20 June.
Major races include the Ascot Gold Cup on the Thursday, which is Ladies' Day. Expect sartorial extravagance and fancy hats.

Tennis: Wimbledon

All England Club (see p331). **Date** 22 June-5 July.
Following two weeks after the British Tennis Championships at nearby Queen's Club (8-14 June), this Grand Slam tournament draws packed houses.

Rowing: Henley Royal Regatta

Henley Reach, Henley-on-Thames, Oxon RG9 2LY (01491 572153/www.hrr.co.uk). Henley-on-Thames rail. **Date** 1-5 July.
First held in 1839, and under royal patronage since 1851, Henley is a posh, five-day affair.

ARTS & ENTERTAINMENT

Westway Sports Centre
*1 Crowthorne Road, Ladbroke Grove,
W10 6RP (8969 0992/www.westwaysport
scentre.org). Ladbroke Grove or Latimer Road
tube.* **Open** 8am-10pm Mon-Fri; 8am-8pm Sat;
10am-10pm Sun.
A smart sports centre with a diverse range of activities on offer, including all-weather pitches, tennis courts, a swim centre and gym, plus the largest indoor climbing facility in the country.

Athletics: Norwich Union London Grand Prix
*Crystal Palace National Sports Centre
(see p327).* **Date** 24-25 July (provisional).
Big names turn out for this annual track and field event.

Rugby Union: Middlesex Sevens
Twickenham (see p158). **Date** mid-Aug.
A curtain raiser to the season, featuring short, fast seven-a-side matches.

Rugby League: Challenge Cup FInal
Wembley Stadium (see p327). **Date** Aug.
The north's big day out, drawing boisterous, convivial crowds.

Cycling: Tour of Britain
Around London. **Date** 19 Sept.
Join thousands on the streets for the finale of British cycling's biggest outdoor event.

American Football: NFL
Wembley Stadium (see p327). **Date** Oct.
The NFL took a regular-season fixture out of North America for the first time in 2007. The experiment was repeated in October 2008 and may also recur this year.

Darts: Ladbrokes PDC World Championshop
*Alexandra Palace (www.pdcworld
championship.co.uk).* **Date** Dec-Jan.
Widely regarded as of greater stature than the rival BDO tournament at Frimley Green (www.bdodarts.com) in January. Raucous, good-humoured and growing in popularity.

Horse Racing: Stan James Christmas Festival
Kempton Park (see p330). **Date** Dec.
The King George VI three-mile chase on Boxing Day is the highlight of this festival.

Riding

There are various stables in and around the city; for a list of all those that have been approved by the British Horse Society, see www.bhs.org.uk. The following run classes for all ages and abilities.

Hyde Park & Kensington Stables
*63 Bathurst Mews, Lancaster Gate, W2 2SB
(7723 2813/www.hydeparkstables.com). Lancaster
Gate tube.* **Open** *Summer* 7.15am-5pm daily.
Winter 7.15am-3pm daily. **Fees** *Group lessons*
£50-£59/hr. *Private lessons* £74-£95/hr.
Map p395 D6.

Wimbledon Village Stables *24 High Street,
Wimbledon, SW19 5DX (8946 8579/www.wv
stables.com). Wimbledon tube/rail.* **Open** 9am-
5pm Tue-Sun. **Fees** *Group lessons* £50-£55/hr.
Private lessons £70-£75/hr.

Street sports

Under the Westway in Acklam Road, W10,
Baysixty6 Skate Park (www.baysixty6.com)
has a large street course and four halfpipes, all wooden and covered. **Stockwell Skate Park**
(Stockwell Park Road, SW9, www.stockwell
skatepark.com) is the city's most popular outdoor park, but it's now rivalled by
Cantelowes Skatepark (Cantelowes Gardens, Camden Road, NW1, www.cantelowesskate
park.co.uk), which opened in April 2007. Many skateboarders prefer unofficial street spots. such as the **South Bank** under the Royal Festival Hall. Look out for the **Sprite Urban Games** held on Clapham Common every July. Inliners should keep an eye on www.londonskaters.com.

Swimming

There are indoor pools scattered all over London, with the **Ironmonger Row Baths** and the **Oasis Sports Centre** both worth a visit. To find your nearest pool, check the *Yellow Pages*. For pools well suited to children, check www.britishswimming.co.uk.
　　If alfresco swimming is more your thing, there are open-air lidos at **Parliament Hill Fields**, the **Serpentine, Tooting Bec, Brockwell Park** and **London Fields**.
The survival of such pools is testament to the tireless work of the London Pools Campaign (www.londonpoolscampaign.com).

Ironmonger Row Baths *1-11 Ironmonger
Row, Finsbury, EC1V 3QF (7253 4011/
www.aquaterra.org). Old Street tube/rail.*
Open 6.30am-9pm Mon-Fri; 9am-6pm Sat;
10am-6pm Sun. **Admission** £3.70; £1.70 reductions; free under-3s.

Oasis Sports Centre *32 Endell Street, Covent Garden, WC2H 9AG (7831 1804/ www.gll.org). Holborn tube.* **Open** *Indoor* 6.30am-9pm Mon; 6.30am-5.30pm Tue; 6.30am-7.30pm Wed; 6.30am-7pm Thur; 6.30am-4pm Fri; 9.30am-5pm Sat, Sun. *Outdoor* 7.30am-9pm Mon-Fri; 9.30am-5.30pm Sat, Sun. **Admission** £3.75; £1.05-£1.40 reductions.

Tennis

Many parks around the city have council-run courts that cost little or nothing to use; keener players should try the **Islington Tennis Centre**, though non-members can only book up to five days ahead. For grass courts, phone the Lawn Tennis Association's Information Department (8487 7000, www.lta.org.uk).

Islington Tennis Centre *Market Road, Islington, N7 9PL (7700 1370/www.aqua terra.org). Caledonian Road tube/Caledonian Road & Barnsbury rail.* **Open** 7am-10pm Mon-Thur; 7am-9pm Fri; 8am-9pm Sat, Sun. **Court hire** *Indoor* £19; £17.50 reductions. *Outdoor* £9; £7.70 reductions.

Ten-pin bowling

A useful first stop when looking for lanes is the **British Ten-pin Bowling Association** (8478 1745, www.btba.org.uk). Less serious-minded bowlers will do well to check out the more nightlife-focused **All-Star Lanes** or its less swanky counterpart **Bloomsbury Bowling Lanes** (for both, *see pp228-229*).

Rowans Bowl *10 Stroud Green Road, Finsbury Park, N4 2DF (8800 1950/www. rowans.co.uk). Finsbury Park tube/rail.* **Open** 10.30am-12.30am Mon-Thur, Sun; 10.30am-2.30am Fri, Sat. **Admission** £1-£3. *Bowling* £2.70-£3.90 per game + £1 shoe hire. **Lanes** 24.

Queens Ice & Bowl *17 Queensway, Bayswater, W2 4QP (7229 0172/www.queensiceandbowl. co.uk). Bayswater tube.* **Open** 10am-11.30pm daily. *Bowling* £6.50 per game. **Lanes** 12. **Map** p394 C7.

Yoga & Pilates

For something more substantial than just a quick stretch in your hotel room, check out the yoga activities and classes (and fully equipped Pilates studio) at Triyoga. You may also want to consult the **British Wheel of Yoga** (www.bwy.org.uk).

Triyoga *6 Erskine Road, Primrose Hill, NW3 3DJ (7483 3344/www.triyoga.co.uk). Chalk Farm tube.* **Open** 6am-10pm Mon-Fri; 8am-8.30pm Sat; 9am-9pm Sun. **Cost** £12-£16/session. **Other location** 2nd floor, Kingly Court, Carnaby Street, W1B 5PW (7483 3344).

Cantelowes Skatepark. *See p333.*

Theatre

The lights go up left, right and centre stage all over London.

For lovers of theatre, London is truly a choice destination. Pots of commercial and subsidised cash, plenty of cosmopolitan influences and increasing numbers of bums on seats keep things buoyant at all levels, from fringe to full-scale productions. The capital's huge regional pull means that most good British productions end up here eventually, and London's theatres cater for all tastes – straight, gay, intellectual, in-yer-face or risibly sentimental. Ever popular with punters are the musicals – vibrant or tacky, depending on your point of view – that illuminate Shaftesbury Avenue

and surrounding streets. Musicals have ruled the commercial roost for decades, but there are also signs of a long-awaited return of serious theatre to the non-subsidised West End.

STAGE NOTES

Knight of the West End, the multimillionaire composer Sir Andrew Lloyd Webber, still has several long-running shows (including 1980s classic **Phantom of the Opera**), but the best of last year's new crop – jukebox musical **Jersey Boys** – began on Broadway. Instead, the biggest local news was Michael Grandage, artistic director of the **Donmar Warehouse** (one of London's smallest and classiest theatres), supervising the ongoing one-off Donmar West End season at the lovingly refurbished **Wyndham's Theatre** – Jude Law's *Hamlet* will be the big summer box office draw, but the smart money's on Judi Dench in *Madame de Sade*, directed by Grandage and running from March to May.

London thesps are traditionally a left-wing lot and, under the artistic directorship of Dominic Cooke, the **Royal Court** has looked to young British, old European and liberal American writers for polemic and socially articulate drama. The Court is also at the vanguard of excellent new European and American work. If your tastes are international, the **Barbican Centre** has an intriguing, high-quality programme: look for outward-looking companies Cheek by Jowl and Complicite.

About the author
Caroline McGinn *is deputy theatre editor for* Time Out *magazine.*

Indeed, the Olivier for Best Play in 2007/8 wasn't won by a writer but by Complicite for its devised piece, *A Disappearing Number*. Other departures from the British tradition of dominance by theatre writers (in contrast to European physical theatre and auteur-directors) were Rupert Goold – a post-modern director with the gift of making ideas sexy – sweeping the awards board with his *Macbeth*, and the phenomenal success of Punchdrunk's *The Masque of the Red Death*. The latter immersed theatre-goers in a masked revel, with Gothic scenes, fights, magic and dancers cavorting over five floors of the **BAC**. Yes, experimental theatre – where 'found' spaces like warehouses are transformed into theatrical labyrinths and the audience walks around in search of the action – is no longer underground, although it remains popular with the hippest theatre-goers.

Check the weekly theatre section of *Time Out London* magazine to see what's on now: it offers a brief but pertinent critique of every West End show running, as well as fuller reviews of the most intriguing Fringe and Off-West End work.

WHERE TO GO

In theatrical terms, the 'West End' is not strictly limited to the traditional theatre district, a bustling area bounded by Shaftesbury Avenue (home of the blockbuster) in the north, historic Drury Lane in the east, Haymarket in the west, and the Strand in the south. Most of London's musicals, big-money productions and transfers of successful smaller-scale shows end up here, though some of the city's best theatre is at innovative subsidised venues like the South Bank's **National Theatre** and the Royal Court in Chelsea and the Barbican in the City.

'Off-West End' denotes smaller budgets and smaller capacity. These theatres – many of which are sponsored or subsidised – push the creative envelope with new, experimental writing, often brought to life by the best acting and directing talent. The **Soho Theatre** and the **Bush** are good for up-and-coming young playwrights, while the **Almeida** and **Donmar Warehouse** are safe bets for very elegantly produced shows, sometimes with big stars.

TICKETS AND INFORMATION

The first rule when buying tickets for London performances is to book ahead. The second rule is to bypass agents and, whenever possible, go direct to the theatre's own box office. Booking agencies such as **Ticketmaster** (0870 534 4444, www.ticketmaster.co.uk) and **Keith Prowse** (0870 840 1111, www.keithprowse. com) sell tickets to many shows, but hit you with booking fees that could top 20 per cent. In a late bid to fill their venues, many West End theatres offer reduced-price tickets for shows that have not sold out on the night, known as **standby** tickets. Some standby deals are limited to those with student ID, and when tickets go on sale varies. The **tkts** cut-price booths are also worth a shot; for cheap theatre, *see p339* **In the Pound Seats**.

WEST END

Barbican Centre

Silk Street, the City, EC2Y 8DS (0845 120 7550/www.barbican.org.uk). Barbican tube/ Moorgate tube/rail. **Box office** 9am-8pm daily. **Tickets** *Barbican £7-£50. Pit £15.* **Credit** AmEx, MC, V. **Map** p402 P5.

The annual BITE season (Barbican International Theatre Events) continues to cherry-pick exciting and eclectic theatre companies from around the globe: chic shorts at the tiny Pit theatre, while the likes of Robert Lepage man the main stage. It will look east over the coming seasons – to east London, with the 2012 Olympics, and to the eastern hemisphere. Watch out for Complicite's new show *Shun-Kin*, performed by an all-Japanese cast; Shochiku Grand Kabuki's *Twelfth Night* directed by the great Yukio Ninagawa; a trilogy by Romeo Castellucci inspired by Dante's *Divine Comedy* and the excellent Cheek by Jowl's *Andromaque*.
▶ *For music at the Barbican; see p307.*

★ National Theatre

South Bank, SE1 9PX (information 7452 3400/ box office 7452 3000/www.nationaltheatre.org.uk). Embankment or Southwark tube/Waterloo tube/rail. **Box office** 9.30am-8pm Mon-Sat. **Tickets** *Olivier & Lyttelton £10-£41. Cottesloe £10-£29.* **Credit** AmEx, DC, MC, V. **Map** p401 M8.

She's the concrete-clad, 1960s modernist grandmother of them all: no theatrical tour of London is complete without a visit to the National, whose three auditoriums and rolling repertory programme offer a choice of several productions in a single week. After a very British year last year (with successful

Royal Court Theatre.

George Bernard Shaw revivals and less successful new writing from old-guard playwrights) artistic director Nicholas Hytner is looking to the mainstream European classical repertoire. He's picked some fine directors for the task: Buchner's *Danton's Death* will be directed by Michael Grandage; Racine's *Phèdre* by himself; and Brecht's *Mother Courage* by Deborah Warner. Man-of-the-moment Rupert Goold is directing JB Pristley's *Time & the Conways*, while the National's smallest stage, the Cottesloe, will see Marlowe's *Dido Queen of Carthage*, directed by James Macdonald.

▶ *In summer, check out the free outdoor stage called Watch This Space; see p343 Festivals.*

Old Vic

The Cut, Waterloo, SE1 8NB (0870 060 6628/ www.oldvictheatre.com). Waterloo tube/rail. **Box office** 9am-9pm Mon-Sat. **Tickets** £12-£45. **Credit** AmEx, MC, V. **Map** p404 N9.

The combination of double-Oscar winner Kevin Spacey and top producer David Liddiment at this 200-year-old theatre continues to be a commercial success, and sometimes a critical one too, especially when Spacey himself takes to the stage. Late spring 2009 heralds the first of Sam Mendes's Bridge Projects, an Anglo-American collaboration between Mendes, Spacey's Old Vic and Joseph V Melillo's Brooklyn Academy of Music. Expect Simon Russell Beale in *The Winter's Tale* and Tom Stoppard's adaptation of *The Cherry Orchard*, alongside Sinead Cusack, Josh Hamilton and Ethan Hawke.

Open Air Theatre

Regent's Park, NW1 4NR (7935 5756/box office 0870 060 1811/www.openairtheatre.org). Baker Street tube. **Tickets** £10-£35. **Credit** AmEx, MC, V. **Map** p398 G3.

The verdant setting of this alfresco theatre lends itself perfectly to summery Shakespeare romps in a season that runs from June to September. Standards are well above village green dramatics, and this year's season will include a Shakespeare for adults, one for children, and a musical. Book well ahead and take an extra layer to fight chills during Act Three. If you don't want to bring a picnic, good-value, tasty grub can be bought at the funkily refurbed Garden Café – or plump for traditional tea or Pimms on the lawn.

★ Royal Court Theatre

Sloane Square, Chelsea, SW1W 8AS (7565 5000/www.royalcourttheatre.com). Sloane Square tube. **Box office** 10am-6pm Mon-Sat. **Tickets** 10p-£25; all tickets £10 Mon. **Credit** AmEx, MC, V. **Map** p400 G11.

A hard-hitting theatre in a well heeled location, the emphasis here has always been on new voices in British theatre – from John Osborne's *Look Back in Anger* in the inaugural year, 1956, to numerous discoveries over the past decade: Sarah Kane, Joe Penhall and Conor McPherson among them. Artistic

INSIDE TRACK FRINGE VENUES

Lurking under the Fringe moniker are dozens of smaller theatres, not always guaranteed to deliver quality, but supplied by a limitless number of hopefuls looking for their London stage debut. The area around and in the vaults underneath London Bridge Station is home to some of the coolest. **Shunt Vaults** (7378 7776, www.shunt.co.uk), a members' club beneath the station, is a DJ-bar with live art and theatre installations; the 'day membership' scheme effectively means entry on the night for £5. The **Southwark Playhouse** (Shipwright Yard, corner of Tooley Street & Bermondsey Street, 0844 847 1656, www.southwarkplayhouse. co.uk) recently relocated to refurbished vaults nearby. Above ground, the **Menier Chocolate Factory** (51-53 Southwark Street, 7907 7060, www.menierchocolate factory.com) is perhaps the classiest of them all, and is great for a glass of wine and food post-play. Out in north-east London, the **Arcola Theatre** (27 Arcola Street, Dalston, 7503 1646) is also often well worth the trek up from Shoreditch for smart new writing.

director Dominic Cooke has injected plenty of politics into the programme, and successfully decreased the age of his audiences too. This is where you'll find rude, lyrical new work set on the London streets by first-time playwrights like Bola Agbaje and the more established but no less cool Debbie Tucker Green. US and European writers with a message also feature. Look out for quality shorts programmed at 6pm and 9pm, and more of the usual vividly produced British and international work by young writers.

Royal Shakespeare Company

01789 403444/box office 0844 800 1110/www. rsc.org.uk. **Box office** *By phone* 9am-8pm Mon-Sat. **Tickets** £10-£48. **Credit** AmEx, MC, V.

The RSC is currently doing massive reconstruction works on its main theatres in Stratford-upon-Avon. Bad news for them, but good news for London, as the capital continues to welcome RSC shows to the Novello. *See also p340* **Profile.**

★ Shakespeare's Globe

21 New Globe Walk, Bankside, SE1 9DT (7401 9919/www.shakespeares-globe.org). Southwark tube/London Bridge tube/rail. **Box office** *Off season* 10am-5pm Mon-Fri. *Theatre* 10am-5pm daily. **Tickets** £5-£32. **Credit** AmEx, MC, V. **Map** p404 O7.

ARTS & ENTERTAINMENT

hairspray

'**THE ULTIMATE FEEL-GOOD SHOW**'

GUARDIAN

'**A HIT JUST GO!**'

MAGIC

'**THE MUSICAL WITH EVERYTHING A TRIUMPH!**'

OBSERVER

Sam Wanamaker's dream – to recreate the theatre where Shakespeare first staged many of his plays – has become a successful reality, underpinned in part by outreach work (you can drop in for free Q&As with cast and director twice a week). The open-air, free-standing Pit tickets are excellent value, if a little marred by low-flying aircraft. This year, Dominic Dromgoole opens 'The Season of Young Love' on Shakepeare's birthday (23 April) with *Romeo & Juliet*.

Wyndham's Theatre
Charing Cross Road, WC2H 0DA (0844 482 5120/www.donmarwarehouse.com). Leicester Square tube. **Box office** 10am-7.45pm Tue-Sat; 11am-3.30pm Sun. **Tickets** £10-£32.50. **Credit** MC, V. **Map** p407 X3.

The Donmar West End Season continues at Wyndham's until August 2009, with the excellent little Off-West End theatre programming work which includes Derek Jacobi in *Twelfth Night*, Judi Dench in *Madame de Sade* and Jude Law in *Hamlet*, all three directed by Donmar supremo Michael Grandage.

LONG-RUNNERS & MUSICALS

★ Billy Elliot the Musical
Victoria Palace Theatre, Victoria Street, Victoria, SW1E 5EA (0870 895 5577/www.victoriapalace theatre.co.uk). Victoria tube/rail. **Box office** 10am-8.30pm Mon-Sat. **Tickets** £17.50-£60. **Credit** AmEx, MC, V. **Map** p400 H10.

During the 1984 miners' strike, a skinny, northern, working-class lad realises he loves ballet – to the great consternation of his father. Scored by Elton John and directed by Stephen Daldry.

Chicago
Cambridge Theatre, Earlham Street, Covent Garden, WC2H 9HU (0870 890 1102/www. cambridgetheatre.co.uk). Covent Garden or Leicester Square tube. **Box office** *Seetickets* 24hrs daily. **Tickets** £17.50-£55. **Credit** MC, V. **Map** p407 Y2.

The jailbird roles are passed at regular intervals from one blonde TV star to the next, but this production still razzle-dazzles 'em with high spirits.

Hairspray
Shaftesbury Theatre, 210 Shaftesbury Avenue, WC2H 8DP (0870 040 0046/www.keithprowse. com). Holborn or Tottenham Court Road tube. **Box office** 10am-6pm daily. **Tickets** £20-£60. **Credit** MC, V. **Map** p407 Y2.

So, chubby heroine Tracy Turnblad (victim of high school anti-fat bimbos) teams up with the black kids from Special Ed to overthrow '60s American racial prejudice and fulfil her dreams by busting their non-white dance moves on TV. Preposterous? Yes. Insanely uplifting? Hell yes. Bouffant for the spirits.

★ Jersey Boys
Prince Edward Theatre, 28 Old Compton Street, W1D 4HS (0844 482 5151/www.delfont mackintosh.co.uk). Leicester Square or Piccadilly Circus tube. **Box office** 10am-8pm Mon-Sat. *Seetickets* 24hrs daily. **Tickets** £20-£60. **Credit** AmEx, MC, V. **Map** p406 W2.

In the Pound Seats
Getting the most out of the box office.

If you want to see a West End musical from the stalls you could end up booking months in advance and spending £60 per head. There is another way: **tkts** (Clocktower Building, Leicester Square, Soho, WC2H 7NA, www.officiallondon theatre.co.uk) is a last-minute gem. The two branches (the other is between platforms 4 and 5 of the Canary Wharf DLR) offer tickets for as little as half-price on the day of performance. Their first-come, first-served policy rewards early birds – the Leicester Square branch opens at 10am daily, or noon on Sundays – and, unlike many ticket sellers, the booths are thoroughly legitimate; they're run by the Society Of London Theatre.

Subsidised theatre often offers better value than commercial theatre: at the **National Theatre** (*see p336*), for the

Travelex sponsored season, two-thirds of the seats go for £10. However, the Donmar at **Wyndham's** (*see p339*) is an exception to the commercial rule, with top-price tickets only £32.50 and all seats in the top two circles costing a tenner.

Some of the best offers – and the best fun – is to be had at the **Royal Court Theatre** (*see p337*), where productions can be seen for as little as 10p: that's if you're willing to stand in the slips. They also have 'Cheap Mondays', with all tickets at £10.

Southwark Playhouse (*see p337* **Inside Track**) has an 'airline style' pricing scheme: the earlier you book, the cheaper the ticket. The first third of their 150 seats go for £7, then the price rises to £13. If a play does well, tickets for the end of the run go up to £20.

Profile Royal Shakespeare Company

The country's flagship theatre company has never been in better shape.

The **Royal Shakespeare Company** turns 50 in 2011 and, despite being mostly homeless, it's in fine trim. Back in the '60s it was the radical directorship of Peter Brook that took the company from an annual theatre festival to a publicly funded permanent insititution second only to the National Theatre – and then only in a bad year. But before Michael Boyd took over in 2003, there had been a few of those. The company's main theatre in Stratford-upon-Avon was in dire need of serious improvement, its long London residency at the Barbican had been abandoned but not replaced, and its future direction was uncertain. Happily, Boyd's reign has brought rejuvenation. The Complete Works Season in 2007/8 was a defining moment for the Company, which brought in exciting new work from abroad to help stage the full canon and widen its own horizons. North London's **Roundhouse** (*see p313*), previously an acoustic challenge, was tremendously improved when the RSC's technicians clad its echoing interior (in the shape of the Courtyard Theatre in Stratford,

with its thrust stage) for Boyd's pacy and acrobatic drama-marathon of the eight plays in the History Cycle. It was a resounding success.

The Company still lacks a London home – although the **Novello** (Aldwych, WC2B 4LD, 0844 482 5135, www.delfont mackintosh.co.uk) is again receiving its winter transfers – but Boyd's emphasis on new writing has placed RSC-commissioned (and even devised) new works in several of London's most interesting Off-West End theatres. These include the **Soho** (*see p343*), the beautifully dilapidated **Wilton's Music Hall** (www.wiltons.org. uk) and the hard-hitting **Tricycle** (*see p344*). Back in Stratford-upon-Avon, the old Royal Shakespeare Theatre will reopen in 2010 after a multi-million pound reconstruction. In the same year, the 'Other Russia' season will bring new writing from the former Soviet Union, featuring a Ukrainian famine epic and putting a war play about Chechnya on the thrust stage at the Courtyard. Until then, it's a case of watch this space – or indeed all of these spaces.

WATCH OUT FOR As You Like It Michael Boyd heads into the Forest of Arden.

The Winter's Tale David Farr sets sail for Bohemia.

Romeo & Juliet In 2010, director Rupert Goold tackles the celebrated doomed young romance.

Best of the jukebox musicals, this Broadway import had the critics singing the praises of Ryan Molloy who hits the high notes (quite literally) in Frankie Valli and the Four Seasons' doo-wop standards. This standard tale of early struggle, success and break-up is elevated by a smart book and pacy direction.

Les Misérables

Queen's Theatre, Shaftesbury Avenue, Soho, W1D 6BA (7494 5040/www.lesmis.com/www. delfontmackintosh.co.uk). Leicester Square or Piccadilly Circus tube. **Box office** *In person* 10am-8pm Mon-Sat. *Seetickets* 24hrs daily. **Tickets** £15-£55. **Credit** AmEx, MC, V. **Map** p406 W3.
It's more than two decades since the RSC's version of Boublil and Schönberg's musical came to the London stage. When you've been singing these songs since your first audition, it's easy to take it that half-inch too far. Still, the voices are lush, the revolutionary sets are film-fabulous, and the lyrics and score (based on Victor Hugo's novel) will be considerably less chirpy than whatever's on next door.

Mousetrap

St Martin's Theatre, West Street, Cambridge Circus, Covent Garden, WC2H 9NZ (0870 162 8787/www.the-mousetrap.co.uk). Leicester Square tube. **Box office** 10am-8pm Mon-Sat. **Tickets** £13.50-£37.50. **Credit** AmEx, MC, V. **Map** p407 X3.
This is the longest long-runner of them all: Agatha Christie's drawing-room whodunnit is a murder mystery Methuselah, and will probably still be booking when the last trump sounds.

Phantom of the Opera

Her Majesty's Theatre, corner of Haymarket & Charles II Street, St James's, SW1Y 4QR (0870 534 4444/www.reallyuseful.com). Piccadilly Circus tube. **Box office** *By phone* 24hrs daily. **Tickets** £25-£55. **Credit** AmEx, MC, V. **Map** p406 W5.
Once upon a time, if you threw a stone on Shaftesbury Avenue you'd hit an Andrew Lloyd Webber musical. *Phantom* remains a beacon to those in search of madness, Gothic tragedy, lavish sets and great love songs with loads of vibrato.

Spamalot

Palace Theatre, Cambridge Circus, Soho, W1D 5AY (0870 895 5579/www.monty pythonsspamalot.com). Leicester Square tube. **Box office** *In person* 10am-8pm Mon-Sat. *By phone* 24hrs daily. **Tickets** £17.50-£60. **Credit** AmEx, MC, V. **Map** p407 X3.
The Tony Award-winning musical based on the lunacy that is *Monty Python & the Holy Grail.* All together now: 'We're knights of the Round Table/We dance whene'er we're able/We do routines and chorus scenes/With footwork impecc-able…'.

★ Zorro

Garrick Theatre, Charing Cross Road, Covent Garden, WC2H 0HH (0870 890 1104/www. zorrothemusical.com). Leicester Square tube. **Box office** *In person* 10am-8pm Mon-Sat. *Seetickets* 24hrs daily. **Tickets** £15-£60. **Credit** AmEx, MC, V. **Map** p407 X4.
Propelled by a rumba and flamenco score by the Gipsy Kings, *Zorro* squeezes in a lot of magnificent swash, buckle and swinging from the rafters. The choreography is raw and visceral, the script dashing and full of self-deprecatingly camp bravado.

OFF-WEST END

★ Almeida

Almeida Street, Islington, N1 1TA (7359 4404/ www.almeida.co.uk). Angel tube. **Box office** *In person* 10am-6pm Mon-Sat. *By phone* 24hrs daily. **Tickets** £6-£29.50. **Credit** AmEx, MC, V. **Map** p402 O1.
Well groomed and with a rather funky bar, the Almeida turns out thoughtfully crafted theatre for grown-ups. Under artistic director Michael Attenborough it has drawn top directors like Howard Davies and Richard Eyre, and premières from the likes of Stephen Adly Guirgis.

BAC (Battersea Arts Centre)

Lavender Hill, Battersea, SW11 5TN (7223 2223/www.bac.org.uk). Clapham Common tube/ Clapham Junction rail/77, 77A, 345 bus. **Box office** 10am-6pm Mon-Fri; 2-6pm Sat. **Tickets** £5-£10; 'pay what you can' Tue (phone ahead). **Credit** MC, V.
The forward-thinking BAC, which inhabits the old Battersea Town Hall, plays alma mater to new writers and theatre companies – expect the very latest in quirky, fun and physical theatre. Artistic director David Jubb started up the famous Scratch programme, which shows a work in progress to larger and larger audiences until it's finished and polished, and he aims to transform the BAC into a promenade performance space – perhaps inspired by last year's successful run by Punchdrunk. *Photos p344.*

Bush

Shepherd's Bush Green, Shepherd's Bush, W12 8QD (8743 5050/www.bushtheatre.co.uk). Goldhawk Road tube/Shepherd's Bush tube/rail. **Box office** *In person* 5-8pm Mon-Sat (nights of performances only). *By phone* 10am-7pm Mon-Sat. **Tickets** £10-£15. **Credit** AmEx, MC, V.
A small, cash-poor champion of new writers and performers, the Bush has over 30 years' experience under its belt. It may not be big but it's certainly determined – not even a leaky roof killing the lights stopped the programme in autumn 2008 – and it has a great record in comedy, satire and West End transfers. Alumni include Stephen Poliakoff, Mike Leigh and Jim Broadbent.

The best guides to enjoying London life

(but don't just take our word for it)

'More than 700 places where you can eat out for less than £20 a head... a mass of useful information in a genuinely pocket–sized guide'

Mail on Sunday

'Armed with a tube map and this guide there is no excuse to find yourself in a duff bar again'

Evening Standard

'I'm always asked how I keep up to date with shopping and services in a city as big as London. This guide is the answer'

Red Magazine

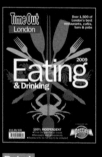

'Get the inside track on the capital's neighbourhoods'

Independent on Sunday

'A treasure trove of treats that lists the best the capital has to offer'

The People

Rated 'Best Restaurant Guide'

Sunday Times

TIME OUT GUIDES
WRITTEN BY
LOCAL EXPERTS
timeout.com/shop

★ Donmar Warehouse

*41 Earlham Street, Covent Garden, WC2H 9LX
(0870 060 6624/www.donmarwarehouse.com).
Covent Garden or Leicester Square tube.* **Box
office** *In person* 10am-7.30pm Mon-Sat. *By
phone* 9am-9pm Mon-Sat; 10am-6pm Sun.
Tickets £12-£30. **Credit** AmEx, MC, V.
Map p407 Y2.

The Donmar is less a warehouse than an intimate
chamber. Artistic director Michael Grandage has
kept the venue on a fresh, intelligent path, despite
also running a dual season at Wyndham's (*see p339*)
since 2008. The combination of artistic integrity and
intimate space is hard to resist, which is perhaps
why so many high-profile film actors have returned
to their roots on stage here: among them former-*X
Files* star Gillian Anderson in Ibsen's *A Doll's House*
from May to July.

Gate Theatre

*Above the Prince Albert, 11 Pembridge Road,
Notting Hill, W11 3HQ (7229 0706/www.
gatetheatre.co.uk). Notting Hill Gate tube.*
Box office *By phone* 10am-6pm Mon-Fri.
Tickets £16; £11 reductions. **Credit** MC, V.
Map p394 A7.

A doll's house of a theatre, with rickety wooden
chairs as seats, the Gate devotes itself almost exclusively to foreign drama, often in specially commissioned new translations.

King's Head Theatre

*115 Upper Street, Islington, N1 1QN (7226
1916/www.kingsheadtheatre.org). Angel tube.*
Box office 10am-7.30pm daily. **Tickets** £10-
£20. **Credit** MC, V. **Map** p402 N2.

Started in the 1970s on a spectacularly lean budget,
London's first pub theatre is a tiny space tucked
away at the back of a charming, if somewhat ramshackle, Victorian boozer. In the past, it's launched
a raft of stars, among them Hugh Grant. It's also a
favourite crossover spot for television actors to exercise their comedy muscles.

Lyric Hammersmith

*Lyric Square, King Street, Hammersmith,
W6 0QL (0871 221 1722/www.lyric.co.uk).
Hammersmith tube.* **Box office** 10am-6pm
Mon-Sat; 9.30am-8pm performance nights.
Tickets £10-£27. **Credit** MC, V.

The Lyric has a knack for vibrant, offbeat schedul-
ing. Outgoing artistic director David Farr enjoys
experimenting and last year's programme ranged
from a gala performance of Pinter's *The Birthday
Party* to celebrate its 50th anniversary, to head-
phone-assisted voyeuristic theatre which invited
audience-members to spy on an *s&m*-style murder
in the tower block across the square. In 2009, innovative theatrical adaptations of classic texts – such
as Tamasha's Bollywood *Wuthering Heights* – are
the order of the day.

Soho Theatre

*21 Dean Street, Soho, W1D 3NE (7478 0100/
box office 0870 429 6883/www.sohotheatre.com).
Tottenham Court Road tube.* **Box office** *In
person* 10am-6pm Mon-Sat; 10am-7.30pm
performance nights. **Tickets** £5-£20. **Credit**
MC, V. **Map** p397 K6.

Its cool blue neon lights, front-of-house café and
occasional late-night shows may blend it into the
Soho landscape, but since taking up residence on
Dean Street in 2000 this theatre has made quite a
name for itself. It attracts a younger, hipper crowd
than most theatres, and brings on aspiring writers
with a free script-reading service and workshops.
▶ *For comedy at the Soho, see p290.*

Theatre Royal Stratford East

*Gerry Raffles Square, Stratford, E15 1BN (8534
0310/www.stratfordeast.com). Stratford tube/
rail/DLR.* **Box office** 10am-7pm Mon-Sat.
Tickets £10-£20. **Credit** MC, V.

A community theatre with many shows written,
directed and performed by black or Asian artists.
Musicals are big here – whether about hip hop

Festivals Theatre

What not to miss this year.

Last year in June the **Greenwich &
Docklands International Festival**
(www.festival.org) let a 60ft French
caterpillar and abseiling acrobats loose
on Canary Wharf. This year, the slick
corporate skyline will be transformed
by another free public spectacle. From
July to September, **Watch This Space**
takes place on a square of astroturf
in front of the National Theatre (www.
nationaltheatre.org.uk). Largely free and
all alfresco, the programme presents
riverside theatre, dance, circus and,
erm, drag bingo. Like so many things
in the run-up to the 2012 Olympics,
August's lively international **Lift Festival**
(www.liftfest.org.uk) has shifted east,
with its international events taking
place in Stratford as well as on the
South Bank. Also in August, an eclectic
bunch of new, experimental and short
performances sprint through the
Camden Fringe (www.camdenfringe.
org). And then there's the **London
International Mime Festival** (www.
mimefest.co.uk) in January, a treat
for adults and kids, with an exciting
programme of challenging and often
acclaimed physical theatre from
around the world.

culture or the Windrush generation of immigrants. Ex-Kinks frontman Ray Davies penned *Come Dancing*, which may well follow homegrown success *The Harder They Come* to the West End.
► *There's a great comedy night upstairs on Mondays; see p292.*

★ Tricycle

269 Kilburn High Road, Kilburn, NW6 7JR (7328 1000/www.tricycle.co.uk). Kilburn tube. **Box office** 10am-9pm Mon-Sat; 2-9pm Sun. **Tickets** £8.50-£23. **Credit** MC, V.
Passionate and political, the Tricycle consistently finds original ways into difficult subjects. In the last few years it has pioneered 'tribunal' docu-dramas – transcript-based theatre that investigates subjects such as the murder of black teenager Stephen Lawrence, and Guantanamo Bay. 'Pay What You Can' every Tuesday at 8pm and Saturday at 4pm.

★ Young Vic

66 The Cut, Waterloo, SE1 8LZ (7922 2922/ www.youngvic.org). Waterloo tube/rail. **Box office** 10am-6pm Mon-Sat. **Tickets** £10-£24.50. **Credit** MC, V. **Map** p404 N8.
The Young Vic finally returned to its refurbished home in the Cut in 2007 with acclaimed community-based show *Tobias & the Angel*. As you would expect, it's got more verve and youthful nerve than its grown-up sibling across the road (*see p337*), and has also fared better critically. Director David Lan's eclectic programming of rediscovered European classics has proved popular with the critics, and we expect Pete Postlethwaite's *King Lear* (until 28 March) will be a big success. There's a popular bar and restaurant, with an open-air balcony terrace for smokers – which come with a young, discerning crowd attached; the volume of chat in the upstairs bar can often be deafening.

BAC. *See p341.*

Escapes & Excursions

**Thames skiff,
Walton-on-
Thames**.
See p357.

Getting Around **346**
   Map Escapes & Excursions **347**

Brighton **348**

Canterbury **351**

Dungeness, Romney & Rye **354**

Woodstock & Blenheim **356**
   Dreamy Father Thames **357**

Escapes & Excursions

Rolling hills, seaside walks and ancient cities are all within your grasp.

We love London, OK? Just not *all* the time. So, for those moments when you start to feel everything about the Big Smoke is giving you a tickly throat, we've selected four outstanding excursions – and one idyllic Thames-borne escape. Two of the excursions are by the sea, but otherwise could hardly be more different: **Brighton** with its breezy boho credentials and full-on nightlife; **Dungeness, Rye & Romney** with their other-worldly atmosphere, cranky charm and weird light. Inland and nestling happily in the lee of the North Downs, **Canterbury** is a buzzy medieval city, its cathedral and ruined abbey of such historical significance they were listed as a UNESCO World Heritage Site. **Woodstock**, a charming town set on the edge of the pretty Cotswolds, is right by stately Blenheim Palace.

GETTING THERE

All the destinations that have been included in this chapter are within easy reach of London, perfect for either a day trip or an overnight stay. **Brighton** is the easiest of the four to reach by train, although **Canterbury** is also a simple train ride from London. **Woodstock**, on the other hand, can be easily reached by bus after getting off the London train at Oxford. **Dungeness**, **Romney** and **Rye** amply reward the effort required to reach them – and are, in any case, a relatively easy journey by road should you wish to hire a car.

For the main attractions, we've included details of opening times, admission prices and transport details, but be aware that these can change without notice: always phone to check. Major sights are open all through the year, but many of the minor ones close out of season, often from November to March. Before setting out, drop in on the **Britain & London Visitor Centre** (*see p375*) for additional information.

About the chapter

This section was adapted from Time Out's Weekend Breaks in Great Britain & Ireland *(£14.99), available from www.timeout.com.*

By train

For information on train times and ticket prices, call **National Rail Enquiries** on 0845 748 4950. Ask about the cheapest ticket for the journey you're planning; be aware that for long journeys, tickets may be considerably cheaper the earlier you book. The website **www.nationalrail.co.uk** gives timetable information for any British train company, as does **www.virgintrains.co.uk** . You can buy your tickets online for any UK train operator at **www.thetrainline.com**.

If you need extra help, there are rail travel centres in London's main-line stations, as well as at Heathrow and Gatwick airports. These can give you guidance for things like timetables and booking. We specify the departure station(s) in the 'Getting there' section for each destination; the journey times cited there are the fastest available.

By coach

Coaches run by **National Express** (0870 580 8080, www.nationalexpress.com) travel throughout the country and depart from Victoria Coach Station (*see p348*), ten minutes'

Escapes & Excursions

© Copyright Time Out Group 2009

walk from Victoria rail and tube stations.
Green Line Travel (0870 608 7261,
www.greenline.co.uk) also runs coaches.

Victoria Coach Station

*164 Buckingham Palace Road, Victoria, SW1W
9TP (7730 3466/www.tfl.gov.uk). Victoria
tube/rail.* **Map** p400 G11.
Britain's most comprehensive coach company,
National Express (*see above*), is based at Victoria
Coach Station, as are many other companies that
operate to Europe (some depart from Marble Arch).

By car

If you're in a group of three or four, it may
be cheaper to hire a car (*see p365*), especially
if you plan to take in several sights within an
area. The road directions given in the listings
below should be used in conjunction with a
proper map.

By bicycle

Capital Sport (01296 631671, www.capital-
sport.co.uk) offers gentle cycling tours along
the Thames from London. Leisurely itineraries
include plenty of time to explore royal palaces,
parks and historic attractions; the website
contains full details of all the tours available.
Alternatively, you could try **Country Lanes**
(www.countrylanes.co.uk), which leads cycling
tours all over the beautiful New Forest in
Hampshire (01590 622627).

Salty Nightlife

BRIGHTON

Britain's youngest city, England's most popular
tourist destination after London, and the host to
the nation's biggest annual arts festival outside
Edinburgh – Brighton is thriving. A welter of
exciting new projects are reaching fruition, but
novelty is nothing new to Brighton, which has
evolved throughout its existence.

Brighton began life as Brighthelmstone, a
small fishing village; it remained so until 1783,
when the future George IV transformed it into
a fashionable retreat. George kept the architect
John Nash busy converting a modest abode into
a faux-oriental pleasure palace; it's now the
Royal Pavilion (*see right*), and remains an
ostentatious sight. Next door, the **Brighton
Museum & Art Gallery** (Royal Pavilion
Gardens, 01273 292882) has entertaining
displays and a good permanent art collection.

Only two of Brighton waterfront's three
Victorian piers are still standing. Lacy, delicate
Brighton Pier is a clutter of hot-dog stands,
karaoke and fairground rides, filled with
customers in the summertime. Still, with
seven miles of coastline, Brighton retains all
the traditional seaside resort trappings. Look
out for the free **Brighton Fishing Museum**
(201 King's Road Arches, on the lower prom
between the piers, 01273 723064) and the **Sea-
Life Centre** (*see right*), the world's oldest
functioning aquarium.

A gay hub, a major student town and a child-friendly hub, Brighton still welcomes weekend gaggles of hen parties, ravers, nudists, discerning vegetarians, surfers, sunseekers and all-round wastrels. Many are satisfied to tumble from station to seafront, calling in at a couple of bars down the hill – and, perhaps, visiting the huge number of independent shops in and around **North Laine**, and in the charming network of narrow cobbled streets known as the **Lanes** – before plunging on to the pier or the pebbles. But to get the best out of Brighton, seek out its unusual little pockets: the busy gay quarter of **Kemp Town**, the savage drinking culture of **Hanover**, the airy terraces of **Montpelier**. Although hilly, all of the city is readily accessible by an award-winning bus network, with an all-night service on main lines.

★ Royal Pavilion

Brighton, BN1 1EE (01273 292820/www.royal pavilion.org.uk). **Open** *Apr-Sept* 9.30am-5.45pm daily. *Oct-Mar* 10am-5.15pm daily. *Tours* by appointment. Last entry 45mins before closing. **Admission** £8.50; £6.50 reductions; £5.10 under-15s; free under-5s. **Credit** AmEx, MC, V.

Sea-Life Centre

Marine Parade, BN2 1TB (01273 604234/ www.sealifeeurope.com). **Open** *Mar-Sept* 10am-6pm daily (last admission 5pm). *Oct-Feb* 10am-5pm daily (last admission 4pm). **Admission** £12.95; £9.50-£11 reductions; free under-3s. **Credit** AmEx, MC, V.

Where to eat & drink

Brighton offers a ridiculous amount of dining possibilities for a town of its size. A handful would hold their head up in any city in the UK. **Gingerman** (21A Norfolk Square, 01273 326688, www.gingermanrestaurants.com) offers top-quality continental (mainly French) cuisine at accessible prices. Located in a former bank, **Seven Dials** (1 Buckingham Place, 01273 885555, www.sevendialsrestaurant.co.uk) does two- and three-course deals. **Terre à Terre** (71 East Street, 01273 729051, www.terreaterre. co.uk) is Brighton's reliably inventive flagship vegetarian restaurant. **La Capannina** (15 Madeira Place, 01273 680839) is hands down the best Italian in town. **Riddle & Finns** (12B Meeting House Lane, 01273 323008, www.riddleandfinns.co.uk) is an accomplished champagne and oyster bar. And stylish tapas bar **Pintxo People** (95-99 Western Road, 01273 732323, www.pintxopeople.co.uk) lives up to its good reputation.

Of the city's countless drinking holes, **Brighton Rocks** (6 Rock Place, 01273 601139, www.brighton-rocks.com) is Kemp Town's most talked-up small bar, with a heated terrace, sparkling cocktails and superb organic cuisine. Of the pubs, the **Hand in Hand** (33 Upper St James Street, 01273 699595), is neither a throbbing gay den of iniquity nor an indie student haunt but a small, traditional boozer that attracts an older, discerning clientele thanks to its outstanding range of ales. The

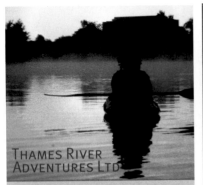

THAMES RIVER ADVENTURES LTD

If you fancy doing something a bit more adventurous while on holiday or on your day off, then give kayaking on the River Thames or Canal Network through London a try. It's fun, it's active, and it's also a great way to see the sights of London leaving no carbon footprint using paddle powered crafts. A British Canoe Union instructor guides all our tours. We offer exclusive sunrise and sunset tours which at premium rates are ideal for gifts.

www.thamesriveradventures.co.uk
Danny Gillard
Mobile 07773720860
E-mail: info@thamesriveradventures.co.uk

THE ROALD DAHL MUSEUM AND STORY CENTRE

Enter the chocolate doors of this great little museum and

- delve into Roald Dahl's archive on our touch-screen monitors
- create your own gobblefunk words and stories
- pick up writing tips from Roald Dahl and other top writers

Great Missenden   HP16 0AL
www.roalddahlmuseum.org
www.roalddahlstore.com
01494 892192

40 minutes by train direct
from London Marylebone

enjoyEngland
Awards for
Excellence 2008
GOLD WINNER

Airline flights are one of the biggest producers of the global warming gas CO_2. But with **The CarbonNeutral Company** you can make your travel a little greener.

Go to **www.carbonneutral.com** to calculate your flight emissions then 'neutralise' them through international projects which save exactly the same amount of carbon dioxide.

CarbonNeutral®flights

Contact us at
shop@carbonneutral.com
or call into the office on
0870 199 99 88
for more details.

Lion & Lobster (24 Sillwood Street, 01273 327299) is a wonderful little pub with a fine vibe, cool and communal. The Sidewinder (65 Upper St James Street, 01273 679927) is a pre-club bar with DJs. Of the gay bars, the most fun is to be had at the Amsterdam Hotel (11-12 Marine Parade, 01273 688826, www.amsterdam.uk.com). Doctor Brighton's (16-17 King's Road, 01273 328765), on the seafront, is also worth a punt, with regular DJs playing house and techno.

Where to stay

Given Brighton's popularity with tourists, it's not surprising that hotel prices can be on the high side. Drakes (43-44 Marine Parade, 01273 696934, www.drakesofbrighton.com, doubles £125-£325) is one of Brighton's high-end designer hotels. The in-house restaurant is run by the best chef in town, Ben McKellar of Gingerman fame (see p349). Another is the typically chic myhotel Brighton (17 Jubilee Street, 01273 900300, www.myhotels.com, doubles £140-£600), which has a penthouse suite containing a 400-year-old carousel horse.

On the recently developed Brighton Marina, the Alias Hotel Seattle (Brighton Marina, 01273 679799, www.aliashotels.com, doubles £125-£180) feels much like a state-of-the-art liner. Blanch House (17 Atlingworth Street, 01273 603504, www.blanchhouse.co.uk, doubles £130-£230) is an unassuming Georgian terrace house with a dozen rooms themed after snow-storms, plus roses, rococo decor and a 1970s disco. The pampering Nineteen (19 Broad Street, 01273 675529, www.hotelnineteen.co.uk, doubles £80-£250) has just seven rooms in a stylish townhouse.

Another good quality stop is Hotel du Vin (2-6 Ship Street, 01273 718588, www.hoteldu vin.com, doubles £180-£480), which also has an estimable restaurant. The Amherst (2 Lower Rock Gardens, 01273 670131, www.amherst hotel.co.uk, doubles £90-£150) is one of the best bargains among Brighton's contemporary hotels, while the George IV (34 Regency Square, 01273 321196, www.georgeiv.hotel.co.uk, doubles £80-£150) is surely the best bargain, offering sea views from the city.

Getting there

By train Trains for Brighton leave from Victoria (50mins; map p400 H10) or King's Cross/London Bridge (1hr 10mins; map p399 L2/3).
By coach National Express coaches for Brighton leave from Victoria Coach Station (1hr 50mins).
By car Take A23, the M23, then the A23 again to Brighton (approx 1hr 20mins).

Tourist information

Tourist Information Centre
10 Bartholomew Square, Brighton, East Sussex, BN1 1JS (0906 711 2255/www.visitbrighton. com). Open *Summer* 10am-5pm Mon-Sat; 10am-4pm Sun. *Winter* 10am-5pm Mon-Sat.

Ancient History
CANTERBURY

The home of the Church of England since St Augustine was based here in 597, the ancient city of Canterbury is rich in atmosphere. Gaze up at its soaring spires, or around you at the enchanting medieval streets, and you'll soon feel blessed, even if you're not an Anglican.

The town's busy tourist trade and large university provide a colourful counterweight to the brooding mass of history present in its old buildings. And, of course, to the glorious Canterbury Cathedral (see p352); it's at its most inspirational just before dusk, especially if there's music going on within and the coach parties are long gone. Inside, you'll find superb stained glass, stone vaulting and a vast Norman crypt. A plaque near the altar marks what is believed to be the exact spot where Archbishop Thomas à Becket was murdered; the Trinity Chapel contains the site of the original shrine, plus the tombs of Henry IV and the Black Prince. Be prepared to shell out for entry, but it's well worth it.

A pilgrimage to Becket's tomb was the focus of one of the earliest and finest long poems in all English literature: Geoffrey Chaucer's *Canterbury Tales*, written in the 14th century. At the exhibition named after the poem (see p352), visitors are given a device that they point at tableaux inspired by Chaucer's tales of a knight, a miller, a Wife of Bath, and others, enabling them to hear the stories.

Just down the road from Christ Church Gate, the Royal Museum & Art Gallery (High Street, 01227 452747) is a monument to high Victorian values. Permanent exhibitions include

Canterbury Cathedral.

Oct-Easter 9am-4.30pm Mon-Sat; 12.30-2pm
Sun. Admission restricted during services and
special events. **Admission** £7; £5.50 reductions;
free under-5s. **Credit** MC, V.

Canterbury Tales

*St Margaret's Street, CT1 2TG (01227
454888/479227/www.canterburytales.org.uk).*
Open *Mid Feb-June, Sept, Oct* 10am-5pm daily.
July, Aug 9.30am-5pm daily. *Nov-mid Feb* 10am-
4.30pm daily. **Admission** £7.75; £5.75-£6.75
reductions; free under-4s. **Credit** MC, V.

Roman Museum

*Butchery Lane, CT1 2JR (01227 785575/
www.canterbury-museums.co.uk).* **Open** *Nov-May*
10am-5pm Mon-Sat. *June-Oct* 10am-5pm Mon-Sat;
1.30-5pm Sun. Last entry 1hr before closing.
Admission £3; £2 reductions; free under-5s.
Credit MC, V.

Where to eat & drink

Michael Caines has brought a touch of Michelin
glamour to the Canterbury eating scene. As well
as his fine dining restaurant and champagne
bar at his hotel **ABode** (*see p353*), there's also
his **Old Brewery Tavern** (High Street, 01227
826682, www.michaelcaines.com), where huge
prints of grizzled coopers rolling barrels hang
on the walls. The MC OB doesn't look like
a traditional boozer, but it also shies away
from gastropub cliché. The food is solid and
comforting – leek and potato soup, fish and
chips – but there are lighter numbers.

Elsewhere, the **Goods Shed** (Station Road
West, 01227 459153, main courses £10-£18)
occupies a lofty Victorian building, formerly
a railway freight store. On a raised wooden
platform, diners sit at scrubbed tables and
choose from the specials chalked on the board.
Only ingredients on sale in the farmers' market
below them are used in the restaurant. For
people who care about their food and its
provenance, this is heaven.

Pub wise, Canterbury is in thrall to its
students, who take over the West Gate Inn
Wetherspoons when they're tired of drinking
on campus. Most of the better pubs are owned
by Shepherd Neame (the local brewery up the
road in Faversham), and the best both happen
to be in St Dunstan's Street: the **Unicorn**
(no.61, 01227 463187) has a kitsch garden and
real ales, while the **Bishop's Finger** (no.13,
01227 768915) unsurprisingly serves Bishops
Finger, and attracts both students and more
mature clientele. Built in 1370, the **Parrot** (1-9
Church Lane, St Radigands, 01227 762355) is
the oldest pub in Canterbury and also one of the
oldest buildings. A good choice of ales and cider
is served in a truly charming setting.

the national collection of the art of cattle painter
Thomas Sidney Cooper, as well as work by Van
Dyck, Sickert and Epstein. Admission is free.

Founded to provide shelter for pilgrims,
Eastbridge Hospital (25 High Street, 01227
471688) retains the smell of ages past. Visitors
can tour the hospital and admire the undercroft
with its Gothic arches, the Chantry Chapel, the
Pilgrims' Chapel and the refectory with an
enchanting early 13th-century mural showing
Christ in Majesty (there's only one other like
this, and it's in France).

The **Roman Museum** (*see below*) has
the remains of a townhouse and mosaic
floor among its treasures, augmented with
computer reconstructions and time tunnels.
From here, you also get a super view of the
cathedral tower. After the Romans comes
St Augustine, or at least the ruins of the
abbey he had built (Longport, 01227 767345,
www.english-heritage.org.uk); it's now in the
capable hands of English Heritage, which has
attached a small museum and shop to the site.

Everything you want to see, do or buy in
Canterbury is within walking distance. And
that includes the seaside – at least, it does if you
fancy a long (seven-mile) walk or cycle along
the Crab and Winkle Way, a disused railway
line to pretty Whitstable.

★ Canterbury Cathedral

*The Precincts, CT1 2EH (01227 762862/
www.canterbury-cathedral.org).* **Open** *Easter-
Sept* 9am-5pm Mon-Sat; 12.30-2pm Sun.

Canterbury.

Where to stay

The third in a small chain of smart hotels created by Andrew Brownsword, **ABode** (30-33 High Street, 01227 766266, www.abode hotels.co.uk, doubles £130-£325) has brought a welcome breath of chic into Canterbury's somewhat chintzy accommodation options. The 72 rooms are a treat, ordered by price and size ranging from 'comfortable', through 'desirable' and 'enviable' to 'fabulous' (a penthouse with superior views and a tennis court-sized bed). **Michael Caines Fine Dining Restaurant** (01227 826684, www.michaelcaines.com, main courses £17.50-£24.95) has a young, two Michelin-starred chef at the helm. The restaurant's looks and the elaborate menu are all you would expect, though the most satisfying part of a meal here might prove to be the selection of British cheeses.

Elsewhere, **Canterbury Cathedral Lodge** (The Precincts, 01227 865350, www.canterbury cathedrallodge.org, doubles £89-£109) is right inside the cathedral precincts. The hotel is hardly historic (it's only five years old) but the views certainly are, with bright and comfortable accommodation in a private courtyard. Nearby, the **Cathedral Gate Hotel** (36 Burgate, 01227 464381, www.cgate.co.uk, doubles £60-£135) is a splendid old hotel built in 1438 and pre-dates the Christ Church Gate it sits alongside. Its 25 rooms with sloping floors and ceilings are reached via dark narrow corridors and low doorways.

Greyfriars (6 Stour Street, 01227 456255, www.greyfriars-house.co.uk, doubles £55-£100) is a ancient but comfortable city-centre hotel with free parking for its guests; but, like all the others it's booked up at graduation time and in high season. **Magnolia House** (36 St Dunstan's Terrace, 01227 765121, www. magnoliahousecanterbury.co.uk, doubles £65-£125) is compact but recommended; the breakfast is delicious and well worth lingering over. The walk to and from town takes you through peaceful Westgate Gardens. Further out, the **Ebury Hotel** (65-67 New Dover Road, 01227 768433, www.ebury-hotel.co.uk, doubles £75-£145) is really quite grand-looking, with a sweeping drive and a Gothic exterior. The best bedrooms have views of the garden, but most of them are large, light and comfortable.

INSIDE TRACK
RIVER RIDES

Get off the streets and on to the water for an unusual perspective on Canterbury. The rower is your loquacious guide for the 40-minute **Canterbury Historic River Tour** (www.canterburyrivertours.co.uk), departing from the King's Bridge. Or grab a picnic and be punted through the city by the **Canterbury River Navigation Company** (www.crnc.co.uk), leaving from the Westgate Gardens.

Getting there

By train From Victoria to Canterbury East (1hr 20mins; map p400 H10), or from Charing Cross (map p401 L7) to Canterbury West (1hr 30mins).
By coach National Express from Victoria Coach Station (1hr 50mins).
By car Take the A2, the M2, then the A2 again (approx 2hrs).

Tourist information

Tourist Information Centre *12-13 Sun Street, Buttermarket, Canterbury, Kent, CT1 2HX (01227 378100/www.canterbury.co.uk).* **Open** *Mar-June; Sept, Oct* 9.30am-5pm Mon-Sat; 10am-4pm Sun. *July, August* 9.30am-6pm Mon-Sat; 10am-4pm Sun. *Nov-Feb* 10am-4pm Mon-Sat.

Wild Horizons

DUNGENESS, ROMNEY & RYE

Perhaps because it's difficult to reach from London (though there are rail links to Rye and Hastings), Romney Marsh is other-worldly in a way that conjures up science fiction scenarios in Tarkovsky movies; you half expect to see Steed and Mrs Peel in *The Avengers* supping ale in the eerily unchanged villages. It's a strange but appealing mix of olde-worlde cobbled streets and ancient inns, sandy beaches, the world's largest expanse of shingle and event-horizoned marshland, criss-crossed by canals and studded with tiny medieval churches and strange concrete defence constructions dating back to post-World War I. So long as the transport links remain as poor as they are, we suspect (and rather hope) that there won't be any real changes here for decades to come. Hastings is the ideal starting point for a circular tour (by car) that takes in Winchelsea and Rye, Romney Marsh and Dungeness.

Winchelsea was built on a never-completed medieval grid pattern (first laid out by King Edward I) when the 'old' settlement was swept into the sea in the storms of 1287. The place is proud of its status as England's smallest town, but really it's a sleepy village of 400 residents. It's almost too quaint to be true – like **Rye**, which is a photogenic jumble of Norman, Tudor and Georgian architecture perched on one of the area's few hills. It's worth taking a look at the medieval Landgate gateway and the **Castle Museum** and 13th-century **Ypres Tower** (*see below*). The **Rye Art Gallery** (107 High Street, 01797 222433, www.ryeartgallery.co.uk) offers a changing series of excellent exhibitions, mostly by local artists.

East from Rye lies **Romney Marsh**, flat as a pancake and laced with cycle paths. Bikes can be hired from **Rye Hire** (1 Cyprus Place, Rye, 01797 223033) – it's an ideal way to explore the lonely medieval churches that dot the level marsh. Heading out of Rye along the coast road takes you to the ever-popular **Camber Sands**, a vast and glittering sandy beach that's a great spot for kite-flying, riding, sand-yachting and invigorating walking.

Beyond is **Dungeness Point**, a huge beach of flint shingle, stretching miles out into the sea. Clustered on this strange promontory are a lighthouse that offers wonderful views and a good café. The light on this remote, gloriously bleak patch of land is odd, reflected from the sea on both sides, and the oddness of the landscape is enhanced by the presence of the massive Dungeness nuclear power station that dominates the horizon; such man-made wonders are set against a magnificent natural backdrop.

When the miniature **Romney, Hythe & Dymchurch Railway** train barrels by, you know you're in an episode of *The Prisoner*. Proudly proclaiming to be the 'world's smallest public railway', it is fully functioning but one-third of the standard size. The diminutive train, built by the millionaire racing driver Captain Howey in 1927, even includes a buffet car. Sitting in one of the tiny carriages is a delightfully surreal experience, as you meander from the wide-open shingle of the Point behind back gardens and caravan parks, through woodland and fields to arrive at **Hythe**, 13.5 miles away.

Rye Castle Museum & Ypres Tower

3 East Street, TN31 7JY (01797 226728/www.ryemuseum.co.uk). **Open** *Museum* Easter-Oct 2-5pm Mon, Thur, Fri; 10.30am-5pm Sat, Sun. Closed Oct-Easter. *Tower* Easter-Oct 10.30am-5pm Mon, Thur-Sun. Oct-Easter 10.30am-3.30pm Sat, Sun. **Admission** *Museum* £2.50; £2 reductions. *Tower* £2.95; £2 reductions. *Both* £5; £4 reductions. **No credit cards.**

INSIDE TRACK
SEA FISHING

Charter a sea fishing trip with local skipper **Eric Whenday**; novices welcome. His Sussex coble – or open beach boat – can be hired for £150 plus bait for a weekday (£180 at weekends) from the Point Tackle Shop (Allendale, Dungeness, Romney Marsh, TN29 9ND, 01797 320049). Eric is Operations Manager for the local lifeboat, so you're in safe hands.

Rye.

Where to eat & drink

You'll find some of the finest food on the south-east coast here. In Rye, the **Landgate Bistro** (5-6 Landgate, Rye, 01797 222829, www.land gatebistro.co.uk, mains £13.20-£16.60) once ruled the roost with its attractive, inventive and pleasingly unfussy dishes, but now faces real competition from the **George in Rye** (98 High Street, 01797 222114, www.thegeorgein rye.com, mains £12-£16.95), where the food is also scrumptious without being overpriced. The chef is Rod Grossmann, previously at London's Moro. It's also a hotel – luxurious, stylish, welcoming and absolutely top of the range.

The light and informal **Fish Café** (17 Tower Street, 01797 222210, www.thefishcafe. com) serves some of the best seafood in town. If fancy isn't your thing, Rye has plenty of simpler eateries: authentic pasta at **Simply Italian** (The Strand, 01797 226024, www. simplyitalian.co.uk) or sound pub grub at any number of lovely boozers in town.

The finest option on the seaside is still the **Place** (New Lydd Road, Camber, 01797 225057, www.theplacecambersands.co.uk, mains £10.25-£17.95) at Camber Sands, which prides itself on its use of locally sourced and eco-friendly produce. Further east, the **Pilot** (Battery Road, Lydd, 01797 320314, www.the pilot.uk.com, mains £6.95-£12.95) has long been a Dungeness institution serving some of the best fish and chips in Kent. For a dinner with a difference, try the Sunday Fly 'n' Dine at **Lydd Airport** (Lydd, Romney Marsh, reservations 01797 322207, www.lyddair.com/flyanddine. html), which consists of a low-level 20-minute flight over the Kent coast and a three-course carvery meal – for £49.95.

Of the many pubs, the **Woolpack Inn** (Beacon Lane, nr Brookland, 01797 344321, mains £4.75-£23.95) is one of the best, with low ceilings and original 15th-century beams, sourced, enterprisingly, from local shipwrecks. The tiny, multi-award-winning **Red Lion** (Snargate, Romney Marsh, 01797 344648) is something of a Romney Marsh institution, famed for the fact that its interior hasn't been touched since World War II. It doesn't do food, but you're welcome to bring your own.

Where to stay

Even in the winter months, accommodation in Rye needs to be booked as far in advance as possible. If the tweeness of many of Rye's B&Bs is overly intimate for your tastes but you still want a place with character and also some individuality, the **Hope Anchor Hotel** (Watchbell Street, 01797 222216, www.thehopeanchor.co.uk, doubles £85-£120) is a reliable bet. It's set in a lovely location in the heart of town, at the end of a pretty, cobbled street. The **White Vine House** (24 High Street, 01797 224748, www.whitevinehouse.co.uk, doubles £125-£165) has seven individual and tastefully decorated bedrooms.

Wonderfully located on Rye's quaintest cobbled street, the atmospheric 17th-century **Jeake's House** (Mermaid Street, 01797 222828, www.jeakeshouse.com) has 11 individually decorated rooms; the gold room features an impressive inglenook fireplace in which a lovely wood stove nestles. The 16th-century **Mermaid Inn** (Mermaid Street, 01797 223065, www.mermaidinn.com) offers olde-worlde tradition at its finest (including an accomplished restaurant), complete with wood panelling and stone fireplaces, four posters, wonky floors and secret passages.

Winchelsea's **Strand House** (Tanyard's Lane, 01797 226276, www.thestrandhouse.co.uk, doubles £70-£120) is a 15th-century house with ten rooms and a delightful garden. The **Romney Bay House Hotel** (Coast Road, Littlestone-on-Sea, New Romney, 01797 364747, doubles £90-£160) is a ten-bedroom 1920s mansion designed for Hollywood gossip columnist Hedda Hopper by Sir Clough Williams-Ellis of Portmeirion fame. It's perched on the seafront, right at the end of the bumpy coastal road, with welcoming, individually styled rooms (two with four-posters). And if you're looking for lovingly prepared food with an emphasis on locally sourced ingredients, you'd be hard pushed to find a better place to eat on the peninsula. In Hastings, the **Zanzibar International Hotel** (9 Eversfield Place, 01424 460109, www.zanzibarhotel.co.uk, doubles £99-£215) is a tall, thin seafront house that feels like a private house rather than a boutique hotel.

Getting there

By train From London Bridge or Cannon Street to Rye via Ashford International (approx 1hr 45mins; map p404 P7). From Charing Cross, Waterloo East or London Bridge to Hastings (approx 1hr 30mins; map p401 L7).
By car Take the A20, the M20, then the A259 (approx 2hrs 30mins).

Tourist information

Hastings Tourist Information *Queen Square, Hastings, East Sussex TN34 1TL (0845 274 1001/www.visit1066country.com).* **Open** 8.30am-6.15pm Mon, Tue, Thur, Fri; 10am-6.15pm Wed; 9am-5pm Sat; 10.30am-4.30pm Sun.
Folkestone Tourist Office *103 Sandgate Road, Folkestone, East Sussex, CT20 2BQ (01303 258 594/www.discoverfolkestone.co.uk).* **Open** 9am-5pm Mon-Fri.
Rye Tourist Information *Rye Heritage Centre, Strand Quay, Rye, East Sussex TN31 7AY (01797 226696/www.visitrye.co.uk).* **Open** *Easter-Oct* 10am-5pm daily. *Oct-Easter* 10am-4pm daily.

Country Classic

WOODSTOCK & BLENHEIM

The triangle of countryside between Oxford, Chipping Norton and Cirencester is one of the prettiest, most photogenic parts of England. The historic market town of Woodstock lies eight miles north of Oxford, perfectly placed for those wishing to visit the twin monuments to extravagance, **Blenheim Palace** (*see p358*) and Bicester Village. Blenheim is the only non-royal home in the country grand enough to call itself a palace, with its grounds offering delightful walks to a variety of viewpoints. The country seat of the Duke of Marlborough and the birthplace of Sir Winston Churchill, Blenheim is a splendid edifice designed by Sir John Vanbrugh, and its sheer size stops first-time visitors in their tracks. The same could be said of **Bicester Village** (50 Pingle Drive, 01869 323200, www.bicester-village.co.uk), a massive outdoor shopping mall that sells name brands at large discounts. The crowds at both are daunting; visit early in the day or later.

Woodstock itself is best known for two trades – glove-making and decorative steel work. You can find out more about the area's heritage at the wide-ranging **Oxfordshire Museum** (*see p358*), but you won't see many

---

INSIDE TRACK
FUNGAL INJECTION

The **Blenheim Estate** and **Woodstock** area are ideal mushroom-hunting turf, with acres of sheep-cropped grass and dense deciduous and coniferous woodlands. For more on forays and fungi generally, contact **Mycologue** (7490 3396, www.mycologue.co.uk).

Dreamy Father Thames

Sick of the city? Drift along the Thames in Edwardian langour.

An escape that begins in sweat, pain and embarrassment may not be pencilled in at the top of your holiday must-dos. Still, that's how this escape begins... and near the top of your to-do list it should be.

Affable Tom Balm of **Thames Skiff Hire** (64 Carlton Road, Walton-On-Thames, KT12 2DG, 01932 232433, www.skiffhire. com) rents out double-skulling Thames skiffs, the tent-cum-rowboat in which Jerome K Jerome holidayed for his classic comic novel *Three Men in A Boat* (1889). And Tom has decided to set us loose in *Edward* – a long, elegant 130-year-old veteran of the river. Its smart green canvas is ready to be stretched over metal hoops when it's time for bed; a neatly stowed kitbag contains padded mats to take the bumps out of sleeping on the wooden deck. It all looks splendidly neat, compact and functional. Unlike us.

Having launched *Edward* from the public slip at Walton-on-Thames, Tom gets in to demonstrate the rudiments of rowing, rivercraft and erecting a boat tent as we glide among the swans. But then, Tom's gone and we're on our own. And that's when our problems begin.

Against Tom's advice, we leave the covering furled on its hoops, thinking it will save time and trouble later. Out from the slipway, a couple of strokes upriver and... the wind and current take us racing towards a bridge. We dock (OK, crash into a bush) and gather our breath. After a couple of hours, we haven't made it back to the slipway. We resolve to just camp where we are, but Tom reappears and again suggests taking down the canopy. The second we do so, the wind drops, the sun comes out and the Edwardian idyll suddenly establishes itself. In minutes, we're smoothly slicing through the water.

Skiffing is a steep learning curve for precisely one day. Tying up, manoeuvring the skulls (not oars), steering, locks – it's a challenge. But after that day, even city-dwelling neophytes will feel like they've been rowing all their life. The quiet rhythm of the skulls is seductive; within hours you're buried in a strange subculture, a way of life that couldn't be more remote from the urban hustle of London. We awoke next morning, a little stiff in the shoulders, to brew a morning cuppa under the gaze of a neon blue kingfisher.

signs of artisan life in the streets, which are filled with cars bringing custom to the classy pubs and restaurants.

Garden-lovers should take a detour north to **Rousham House** (01869 347110, www.rousham.org), near Steeple Aston. The imposing – if rather gloomy – Jacobean mansion was remodelled in Tudor Gothic style by William Kent, an important predecessor of 'Capability' Brown, in the 18th century. But the real highlight here is his outstanding garden, inspired by Italian landscape painting. Rousham is determinedly and delightfully uncommercialised, with no shop or tearoom; you're encouraged to bring a picnic and wander the grounds.

★ Blenheim Palace

Woodstock, Oxon, OX20 1PX (01993 811091/ recorded information 08700 602080/www. blenheimpalace.com). **Open** *Feb-Oct* 10.30am-5.30pm daily. *Nov-Dec* 10.30am-5.30pm Wed-Sun. **Admission** £16.50; £10-£13.50 reductions; £44 family ticket. **Credit** MC, V.

FREE Oxfordshire Museum

Park Street, Woodstock, Oxon, OX20 1SN (01993 811456/www.oxfordshire.gov.uk). **Open** 10am-5pm Tue-Sat; 2-5pm Sun. **Admission** free.

Where to eat & drink

Attractive country pubs and restaurants abound, but this is well moneyed land – while standards are high, so are prices, and tastes tend towards the conservative. Don't be surprised to see guests sporting black tie in your hotel dining room.

The **Feathers Hotel** (*see below*) offers an intimate fine dining experience in its antique, oak-panelled dining room where a modern-leaning European menu is beautifully cooked and presented. The lunchtime 'market menu' is a gourmet steal at £19, offering hearty fare such as rump of lamb or roast mackerel. There's also a less formal bistro here. Elsewhere in town, there's the well-regarded Chinese **Chef Imperial** (22 High Street, 01993 813593, mains £6.50-£8.95), **Brothertons Brasserie** (1 High Street, 01993 811114), and **Hampers** deli and café (31-33 Oxford Street, 01993 811535).

Further afield, but worth the trek, the **Red Lion** (South Side, Steeple Aston, 01869 340225, mains £8-£14.50) is a small, attractive country pub boasting a paved garden, low-ceilinged bar (complete with resident spaniel), separate lounge with squashy leather sofas, and wood-beamed conservatory dining room (children are permitted). Food is fairly traditional, but the ham is absolutely top-rate; game pie goes down a treat with a pint of Old Hooky.

Where to stay

Woodstock's finest accommodation remains the **Feathers Hotel** (16-20 Market Street, Woodstock, 01993 812291, www.feathers. co.uk, doubles £165-£275) made up of seven interconnected 17th-century houses, and named by a stuffed bird-collecting former hotelier. It's a cosy maze of corridors and elegantly furnished bedrooms, the best of which is equipped with its own private steam room. The garden is pleasant on balmy afternoons; in winter, the wood-panelled lounge with huge fireplace is perfect for relaxed drinks. There's also a beauty salon, Preen (treatments must be pre-booked).

One step down is the **Bear Hotel** (Park Street, 0870 400 8202, www.bear hotelwoodstock.co.uk, doubles £184-£230). Woodstock's largest hotel comprises an impressive 13th-century coaching inn and an adjoining glove factory, converted into guest rooms and conference facilities in the 1960s. Happily, the corporate aspects don't detract from the main building's grandeur and appeal – there are still plenty of winding corridors, creaky wooden floors, oak beams and fireplaces for atmosphere, and a snug little bar if you want a quiet drink. Richard Burton and Elizabeth Taylor once famously holed up here.

The **King's Arms Hotel** (19 Market Street, 01993 813636, www.kings-hotel-woodstock.co.uk, doubles £140-£150) is a comfortable, contemporary hotel, just across the road from the Feathers. The listed Georgian building has been painstakingly renovated to retain its character, but is carefully balanced with neutral tones and modern furnishings; the only dark furniture you'll find here are the leather chairs in the restaurant, a converted billiards room. There's decent bistro fare (with appealing vegetarian options) in the restaurant, while the bar is popular with Woodstock's youth.

Getting there

By train & coach From Paddington to Oxford (1hr; map p395 D5), then bus no.20 to Woodstock (approx 40mins).
By car Take the A40(M), the M40, then the A34.

Tourist information

Woodstock Tourist Informaton

Oxfordshire Museum, Park Street, Woodstock, Oxon OX20 1SN (01993 813276/www.oxford shirecotswolds.org). **Open** *Mar-Oct* 9.30am-5.30pm Mon-Sat; 2-5pm Sun. *Nov-Feb* 10am-5pm Mon-Sat; 2-5pm Sun.

Directory

London Transport Museum.
See p82.

Getting Around **360**

Resources A-Z **366**
   Travel Advice **366**
   The Local Climate **376**

Further Reference **377**

Index **379**

Advertisers' Index **388**

Getting Around

ARRIVING & LEAVING

For London's domestic rail and coach stations, *see p346.*

By air

Recent security measures have resulted in limits to carry-on baggage. Check www.baa.com for updates at the time of travel.

Gatwick Airport *0870 000 2468/www.baa.co.uk/gatwick. About 30 miles south of central London, off the M23.*
Of the three rail services that link Gatwick to London, the quickest is the **Gatwick Express** (0845 850 1530, www.gatwickexpress.co.uk) to Victoria station, which takes 30mins and runs 3.30am-12.30am daily. Tickets cost £15.90 single, £16.30 for a day return (after 9.30am) and £26.80 for an open return (valid for 30 days). Under-15s pay £6.50 for a single and half-price for returns; under-5s go free.
Southern (0845 748 4950, www.southernrailway.com) also runs a rail service between Gatwick and Victoria, with trains every 5-10mins (every 25mins between 1am and 4am). It takes about 35 mins, and costs £8.90 for a single, £9.20 for a day return (after 9.30am) and £17.80 for an open period return (valid for one month). Under-16s get half-price tickets; under-5s go free.
If you're staying in King's Cross or Bloomsbury, consider trains run by **Thameslink** (0845 748 4950, www.firstcapitalconnect.co.uk) to St Pancras. Tickets cost £8.90 single, £9.50 day return (after 9.32am) or £17 for a 30-day open return.
By road, **National Express dot2dot** (08453 682 368, www.dot 2dot.com) offers a coach service at £20 each way (£24 online). A **taxi** costs about £100 and takes ages.

Heathrow Airport *0870 000 0123/www.baa.co.uk/heathrow. About 15 miles west of central London, off the M4.*
The **Heathrow Express** train (0845 600 1515, www.heathrow express.co.uk) runs to Paddington every 15mins (5.10am-11.25pm daily), and takes 15-20mins. The train can be boarded at the tube station that serves Terminals 1, 2

and 3 (aka Heathrow Central), or the separate station serving the new Terminal 5; passengers travelling to or from Terminal 4 can connect with a shuttle train at Heathrow Central. Tickets cost £15.50 single or £29 return (£1 less online, £2 more if you buy on board); under-16s go half-price. Many airlines have check-in desks at Paddington.
The journey by tube into central London is longer but cheaper. The 50-60min **Piccadilly Line** ride into central London costs £4 one way (£2 under-16s). Trains run every few minutes from about 5am to 11.57pm daily (6am-11pm Sun).
The **Heathrow Connect** (0845 678 6975, www.heathrowconnect. com) rail service offers direct access to Hayes, Southall, Hanwell, West Ealing, Ealing Broadway and Paddington stations in west and north-west London. The trains run every half-hour, with stops at two stations at Heathrow: one serving Terminals 1, 2 and 3, and the other serving Terminal 4; there's a shuttle from the T4 station to Terminal 5. A single from Paddington is £6.90; an open return is £12.90.
National Express (0870 580 8080, www.nationalexpress.com) runs daily coach services to London Victoria (90mins, 5am-9.35pm daily), leaving Heathrow Central bus terminal every 20-30mins. It's £4 for a single (£2 under-16s) or £8 (£4 under-16s) for a return.
By road, **National Express dot2dot** (*see above*) offers an airport-to-hotel coach service for £19 each way. A **taxi** into town will cost roughly £100 and take an hour or more, depending on traffic.

London City Airport *7646 0000/ www.londoncityairport.com. About 9 miles east of central London.*
The **Docklands Light Railway (DLR)** now includes a stop for London City Airport. The journey to Bank station in the City takes around 20mins, and trains run 5.30am-12.30am Mon-Sat or 7am-11.30pm Sun. By road, a **taxi** runs around £30 to central London; less to the City or to Canary Wharf.

Luton Airport *01582 405100/ www.london-luton.com. About 30 miles north of central London, J10 off the M1.*

It's a short bus ride from the airport to Luton Airport Parkway station. From here, the **Thameslink** rail service (*see above*) calls at many stations (St Pancras International and City among them); journey time is 35-45mins. Trains leave every 15mins or so and cost £11.90 single one-way and £21.50 return, or £11 for a cheap day return (after 9.30am Mon-Fri, all day weekends). Trains between Luton and King's Cross run at least hourly all night.
By coach, the Luton to Victoria journey takes 60-90mins. **Green Line** (0870 608 7261, www.green line.co.uk) runs a 24-hour service. A single is £11 and returns cost £16; under-16s go half-price. A **taxi** into London will cost upwards of £50.

Stansted Airport *0870 000 0303/www.stansedairport.com/ www.baa.co.uk/stansted. About 35 miles north-east of central London, J8 off the M11.*
The quickest way to get to London from Stansted is on the **Stansted Express** train (0845 748 4950) to Liverpool Street station; the journey time is 40-45mins. Trains leave every 15-45mins, and tickets cost £15 single, £25 return; under-16s travel half-price, under-5s free.
The **Airbus** (0870 580 8080, www.nationalexpress.com) coach service from Stansted to Victoria takes at least 80mins. Coaches run roughly every 30mins (24hrs daily), more frequently at peak times. A single is £10 (£5 for under-16s), return is £17 (£8.50 for under-16s). A taxi to London is about £80.

By coach

Coaches run by **National Express** (0870 580 8080, www. nationalexpress.com), the biggest coach company in the UK, arrive at **Victoria Coach Station** (164 Buckingham Palace Road, SW1W 9TP, 7730 3466, www.tfl.gov.uk) near Victoria tube. This is also where companies such as Eurolines (01582 404511, www.eurolines.com) dock their European services.

By rail

Trains from mainland Europe run by Eurostar (0870 518 6186, www. eurostar.com) arrive at **St Pancras**

International station (Pancras Road, King's Cross, NW1 2QP, 0870 518 6186, www.stpancras.com). In 2009, services should also begin to Stratford station in east London.

PUBLIC TRANSPORT

Compared to some other European cities, getting around London on public transport is relatively easy but really quite expensive.

Information

Details on timetables and other travel information are provided by **Transport for London** (7222 1234, www.tfl.gov.uk/journey planner). Complaints or comments on most forms of public transport can also be taken up with **London TravelWatch** (7505 9000).

Travel Information Centres
TfL's Travel Information Centres provide information about the tube, buses and Docklands Light Railway (DLR; *see p363*). You can find them in **Camden Town Hall**, opposite St Pancras station (9am-5pm Mon-Fri), and in the stations below. Call 7222 1234 for more information.

Euston mainline rail station 7.15am-9.15pm Mon-Fri; 7.15am-6.15pm Sat; 8.15am-6.15pm Sun.
Heathrow Terminals 1, 2 & 3 tube station 6.30am-10pm daily.
Liverpool Street tube station, Piccadilly Circus tube station, Victoria mainline rail station 7.15am-9.15pm Mon-Sat; 8.15am-8pm Sun.

Fares & tickets

Tube and DLR fares are based on a system of six zones, stretching 12 miles out from the centre of London. A flat cash fare of £4 per journey applies across zones 1-6 on the tube; customers save up to £2.50 per journey with a pre-pay Oyster card (*see below*). Anyone caught without a ticket or Oyster card is subject to a £50 on-the-spot fine (reduced to £25 if you pay within three weeks).

Oyster cards A pre-paid smart-card, Oyster is the cheapest way of getting around on buses, tubes and the DLR. You can charge up standard Oyster cards at tube stations, Travel Information Centres (*see above*), some rail stations and newsagents. There is a £3 refundable deposit payable on each card; to collect your deposit, call 0845 330 9876.

In addition to standard Oyster cards, new **Visitor Oyster** cards are available from Gatwick Express outlets, National Express coaches, Superbreak, visitlondon.com, visitbritaindirect.com, Oxford Tube and on Eurostar services. The only difference between Visitor Oysters and 'normal' Oysters is that they come pre-loaded with money.

A tube journey in zone 1 using Oyster pay-as-you-go costs £1.50 (50p for under-16s), compared to the cash fare of £4. A single tube ride within zones 2, 3, 4, 5 or 6 costs £1 (50p for under-16s); single journeys from zones 1-6 using Oyster are £3.50 (7am-7pm Mon-Fri) or £2 (all other times), or £1 for children.

If you make a number of journeys using Oyster pay-as-you-go on a given day, the total fare deducted will always be capped at 50p less than the price of an equivalent Day Travelcard. However, if you only make one journey using Oyster pay-as-you-go, you will only be charged a single Oyster fare.

Day Travelcards If you're only using the tube, DLR, buses and trams, using Oyster to pay as you go will always be 50p cheaper than the equivalent Day Travelcard. However, if you're also using National Rail services, Oyster may not be accepted: opt, instead, for a Day Travelcard, a standard ticket with a coded stripe that allows travel across all networks.

Anytime Day Travelcards can be used all day. They cost from £6.80 for zones 1-2 (£3.40 child), up to £13.80 for zones 1-6 (£6.90 child). Tickets are valid for journeys started by 4.30am the next day. The cheaper **Off-Peak Day Travelcard** allows travel after 9.30am Mon-Fri and all day at weekends and public holidays. It costs from £5.30 for zones 1-2 up to £7 for zones 1-6. Up to four children pay £1 each when accompanied by an adult with a Travelcard.

3-Day Travelcards You can also buy three-day versions of the regular Travelcard. The **Anytime 3-Day Travelcard** costs £17.40 (zones 1-2) or £40 (zones 1-6), while the **Off-Peak 3-Day Travelcard** costs £20 for zones 1-6. The time restrictions are the same as for the one-day versions mentioned above.

Children Under-14s travel free on buses and trams without the need to provide any proof of identity. 14- and 15-year-olds can also travel free, but need to obtain an Under-16

Oyster photocard. For details, visit www.tfl.gov.uk/fares or call 0845 330 9876. Under-11s travel free on the tube and DLR as well.

An 11-15 Oyster photocard is needed by 11- to 15-year-olds to pay as they go on the tube/DLR and to buy 7-Day, monthly or longer period Travelcards, and by 11- to 15-year-olds if using the tram to/from Wimbledon.

Photocards Photocards are not required for 7-Day Travelcards or Bus Passes, adult-rate Travelcards or Bus Passes charged on an Oyster card. For details of how to obtain under-14, 14-15 or 16-17 Oyster photocards, see www.tfl.gov.uk/fares or call 0845 330 9876.

London Underground

Delays are common. Some lines close at weekends for engineering. The trains are hot and crowded in rush hour (8-9.30am and 4.30-7pm Mon-Fri). Even so, the 12 colour-coded lines that together comprise the underground rail system – also known as 'the tube' – is still the quickest way to get around London. Comments or complaints are dealt with by **LU Customer Services** on 0845 330 9880 (8am-8pm daily); for lost property, *see p371*.

Using the system You can get Oyster cards from www.tfl.gov.uk/oyster, by calling 0870 849 9999, at tube stations, Travel Information Centres, some rail stations and newsagents. Single or day tickets can be bought from ticket offices or machines. You can buy most tickets and top up Oyster cards at self-service machines. Some ticket offices close early (around 7.30pm); carry a charged-up Oyster card to avoid being stranded.

To enter and exit the tube using an Oyster card, simply touch it to the yellow reader, which will open the gates. Make sure you also touch the card to the reader when you exit the tube, or you'll be charged a higher fare when you next use your card to enter a station.

To enter using a paper ticket, place it in the slot with the black magnetic strip facing down, then pull it out of the top to open the gates. Exiting is done in much the same way; however, if you have a single journey ticket, it will be retained by the gate as you leave.

Timetables Tube trains run daily from around 5am (except Sunday, when they start an hour or so later

DIRECTORY

THE SHORTLIST

WHAT'S NEW | WHAT'S ON | WHAT'S BEST

- Pocket-sized guides
- What's on, month by month
- Full colour fold-out maps

depending on the line, and Christmas Day, when there's no service). You shouldn't have to wait more than ten minutes for a train; during peak times, services should run every two or three minutes. Times of last trains vary; they're usually around 12.30am daily (11.30pm on Sun). The tubes run all night only on New Year's Eve; otherwise, you're limited to night buses (see below).

Fares The single fare for adults across the network is £4. Using Oyster pay-as-you-go, the fare varies by zone: zone 1 costs £1.50; zones 1-2 costs £1.50 or £2, depending on the time of day; zones 1-6 is £2 or £3.50. The single fare for children aged 11-15 is £2 for any journey that includes zone-1 travel and £1.50 for others. Under-11s travel free (see also p361).

National Rail & London Overground services

Independently run commuter services coordinated by **National Rail** (0845 748 4950, www.national rail.co.uk) leave from the city's main rail stations. Visitors heading to south London, or to more remote London destinations such as Hampton Court Palace, will need to use these overground services. Travelcards are valid on these services within the right zones, but not all routes accept Oyster pay-as-you-go; check before you travel.

Operated by Transport for London, meaning it does accept Oyster, the **London Overground** rail line runs a loop through north London from Stratford in the east to Richmond in the south-west. New spurs connect Willesden Junction in the north-west to Clapham Junction in the south-west, and Gospel Oak in the north to Barking in the east, as well as heading north-west from Euston. Trains run about every 20mins (every 30mins on Sun).

For lost property, see p371.

Docklands Light Railway (DLR)

DLR trains (7363 9700, www.tfl. gov.uk/dlr) run from Bank (where they connect with the tube sytem's Central and Waterloo & City lines) or Tower Gateway, close to Tower Hill tube (Circle and District lines). At Westferry station, the line splits east and south via Island Gardens to Greenwich and Lewisham; a change at Poplar can take you north to Stratford. The easterly branch forks after Canning Town to either

Beckton or London City Airport; the latter is due to extend across the river to Woolwich Arsenal this year. Trains run 5.30am-12.30am daily. For lost property, see p371.

Fares Adult single fares on the DLR are the same as for the tube (see p361) except for DLR-only journeys in zones 2-3, which cost £1.50 (£1 with Oyster pay-as-you-go) or 70p for 11-15s, 70p (50p with Oyster pay-as-you-go).

The DLR also offers one-day Rail & River Rover tickets, which add one day's DLR travel to hop-on, hop-off travel on **City Cruises** riverboats (10am-6pm, see p365) between Westminster, Waterloo, Tower and Greenwich piers.

Starting at Tower Gateway (due to reopen in spring), trains leave hourly from 10am for a special tour, with a guide adding commentary. It costs £11 for adults or £5.50 for kids; a family pass (two adults and up to three under-16s), which must be bought in person from the piers, costs £27. Under-5s go free.

Buses

You must have a ticket or valid pass before boarding any bus in zone 1, and before boarding any articulated, single-decker bus (aka 'bendy buses'; the name is self-explanatory) anywhere in the city. You can buy a ticket (or a 1-Day Bus Pass) from machines at bus stops, although they're often not working; better to travel with an Oyster card or some other pass (see p361). Inspectors patrol buses at random; if you don't have a ticket or pass, you may be fined £50.

All buses are now low-floor vehicles that are accessible to wheelchair-users and passengers with buggies. The only exceptions are Heritage routes 9 and 15, which are served by the world-famous open-platform Routemaster buses.

For lost property, see p371.

Fares Using Oyster pay-as-you-go costs £1 a trip; your total daily payment, regardless of how many journeys you take, will be capped at £3. Paying with cash at the time of travel costs £2 for a single trip. Under-16s travel for free (using an Under-14 or 14-15 Oyster photocard as appropriate; see p361). A 1-Day Bus Pass gives unlimited bus and tram travel for £3.50.

Night buses Many bus routes operate 24 hours a day, seven days a week. There are also some special

night buses with an 'N' prefix, which run from about 11pm to 6am. Most night services run every 15-30mins, but busier routes run a service around every 10mins. Fares are the same as for daytime buses; Bus Passes and Travelcards can be used at no extra fare until 4.30am of the morning after they expire.

Green Line buses Green Line buses (0870 608 7261, www.green line.co.uk) serve the suburbs within 40 miles of London. Its office is opposite **Victoria Coach Station** (see p360); services run 24 hours.

Tramlink

In south London, trams run between Beckenham, Croydon, Addington and Wimbledon. Travelcards that cover zones 3, 4, 5 or 6 are valid, as are Bus Passes. Cash fares are £2 (£1 with Oyster pay-as-you-go; 50p for 16-17 Oyster photocard holders ineligible for free bus travel).

For lost property, see p371.

Water transport

Most river services operate every 20-60mins between 10.30am and 5pm, and may run more often and later in summer. For commuters, **Thames Clippers** (0870 781 5049, www.thamesclippers.com) runs a regular, reliable service between Embankment Pier and Royal Arsenal Woolwich Pier; stops include Blackfriars, Bankside, London Bridge, Canary Wharf and Greenwich. A standard day roamer ticket (valid 10am-5pm) costs £8, while a single from Embankment to Greenwich is £4, but Oyster travelcard holders get a third off. **Thames Executive Charters** (www.thamesexecutivecharters.com) also offers travelcard discounts on its River Taxi between Putney and Blackfriars, calling at Wandsworth, Chelsea Harbour, Cadogan Pier and Embankment, meaning a £3.75 standard single becomes £2.10.

Westminster Passenger Service Assocation (7930 2062, www.wpsa.co.uk) runs a scheduled daily service from Westminster Pier to Kew, Richmond and Hampton Court from April to October. At £12 for a single, it's not cheap, but it is a lovely – and leisurely – way to see the city, and there are discounts of 30-50% for Travelcard holders.

Thames River Services (www.westminsterpier.co.uk) operates from the same pier, offering trips to Greenwich, Tower

DIRECTORY

Pier and the Thames Barrier. A trip to Greenwich costs £7.50, though £10 buys you a Rivercard, which allows you to hop on and off at will. Travelcard holders travel for 30% off.

For commuter service timetables, plus a full list of leisure operators and services, see www.tfl.gov.uk.

For lost property, see p371.

TAXIS

Black cabs

The licensed London taxi, aka 'black cab' (although, since on-car advertising, they've come in many colours), is a much-loved feature of London life. Drivers must pass a test called 'the Knowledge' to prove they know every street in central London, and the shortest route to it.

If a taxi's orange 'For Hire' sign is lit, it can be hailed. If a taxi stops, the cabbie must take you to your destination if it's within seven miles. It can be hard to find an empty cab, especially just after the pubs close. Fares rise after 8pm on weekdays and at weekends.

You can book black cabs from the 24hr **Taxi One-Number** (0871 871 8710, a £2 booking fee applies, plus 12.5% if you pay by credit card), **Radio Taxis** (7272 0272) and **Dial-a-Cab** (7253 5000; credit cards only, with a booking fee of £2). Comments or complaints about black cabs should be made to the **Public Carriage Office** (0845 602 7000, www.tfl.gov.uk/pco). Note the cab's badge number, which should be displayed in the rear of the cab and on its back bumper.

For lost property, see p371.

Minicabs

Minicabs (saloon cars) are generally cheaper than black cabs, but can be less reliable. Only use licensed firms (look for a disc in the front and rear windows), and avoid those who illegally tout for business in the street: drivers may be unlicensed, uninsured and dangerous.

Trustworthy and fully licensed firms include **Addison Lee** (7387 8888), which will text you when the car arrives, and **Lady Cabs** (7272 3300), **Ladybirds** (8295 0101) and **Ladycars** (8981 7111), which employ only women drivers. Otherwise, text HOME to 60835 ('60tfl'). Transport for London will then text you the numbers of the two nearest licensed minicab operators and the number for Taxi One-Number, which provides licensed black taxis in London.

The service costs 35p plus standard call rate. No matter who you choose, always ask the price when you book and confirm it with the driver.

Motorbike taxis

For speedy journeys or airport dashes, weave through traffic on the back of a motorbike. Both **Passenger Bikes** (0700 596 3292, www.passengerbikes.com) and **Taxybikes** (7255 4269, www. addisonlee.com/services/taxybikes) have a minimum £25 charge, and offer fixed airport rates; the bikes are equipped with panniers, and can carry a small to medium suitcase. You pay a premium for the thrill: central London to Gatwick currently costs £110-£120.

DRIVING

London's roads are often clogged with traffic and roadworks, and parking (see below) is a nightmare. Walking or using public transport are better options. But if you do hire a car, you can use any valid licence from outside the EU for up to a year after arrival. Speed limits in the city are generally 20 or 30mph on most roads. Don't use a mobile phone (unless it's hands-free) while driving or you risk a £1,000 fine.

Congestion charge

Drivers coming into central London between 7am and 6pm Monday to Friday have to pay £8, a fee known as the congestion charge. The congestion charge zone is bordered by King's Cross (N), the Old Street roundabout (NE), Tower Bridge (E), Elephant & Castle (S), Vauxhall, Chelsea, Kensington (SW), Holland Park, Bayswater, Paddington (W), Marylebone and Euston (N); see the map on pp392-393. You'll know when you're about to drive into the charging zone from the red 'C' signs on the road.

The thoroughfare formed by Vauxhall Bridge Road, Grosvenor Place and Park Lane is the sole toll-free route through the zone. If you stick to this road alone while crossing central London, you won't have to pay. There's currently a debate on whether to lift the charge in the zone's western extension (essentially, west of Park Lane); however, this wouldn't happen until the end of this year at the earliest.

There are no tollbooths – the scheme is enforced by numberplate recognition from CCTV cameras. Passes can be bought from some

newsagents, garages and NCP car parks; you can also pay online at www.cclondon.com, by phone on 0845 900 1234 or by SMS (you'll need to pre-register at the website for the latter option). You can pay any time during the day; payments are also accepted until midnight on the next charging day, although the fee is £10 if you pay then. Expect a fine of £50 if you fail to pay, rising to £100 if you delay payment.

Breakdown services

If you're a member of a motoring organisation in another country, check if it has a reciprocal agreement with a British one. The AA and the RAC offer schemes that cover Europe in addition to the UK.

AA (Automobile Association)
Information 0870 550 0600/ breakdown 08457 887766/ www.theaa.com.
ETA (Environmental Transport Association)
0845 389 1010/www.eta.co.uk.
RAC (Royal Automobile Club)
Information 0870 572 2722/ breakdown 0800 828282/ www.rac.co.uk.

Parking

Central London is scattered with parking meters, but free spots are rare. Meters cost up to £1 for 15mins, and are limited to two hours. Parking on a single or double yellow line, a red line or in residents' parking areas during the day is illegal, and you may end up being fined, clamped or towed.

However, in the evening (from 6pm or 7pm in much of central London) and at various times at weekends, parking on single yellow lines is legal and free. If you find a clear spot on a single yellow line during the evening, look for a sign giving the local regulations. Meters also become free at certain times during evenings and weekends. Parking on double yellow lines and red routes is illegal at all times.

NCP 24-hour car parks (0845 050 7080, www.ncp.co.uk) are numerous but pricey (£2-£7.20 for two hours). Central ones include Arlington House, Arlington Street, St James's, W1; Snowsfields, Southwark, SE1; and 4-5 Denman Street, Soho, W1.

Clamping & vehicle removal
The immobilising of illegally parked vehicles with a clamp is commonplace in London. There will be a label on the car telling you

which payment centre to phone or visit. You'll have to stump up an £80 release fee and show a valid licence. The payment centre will de-clamp your car within four hours. If you don't remove your car at once, it might get clamped again, so wait by your vehicle.

If your car has disappeared, it's either been stolen or, if it was parked illegally, towed to a car pound for the local authorities. A release fee of £200 is levied for removal, plus £40 per day from the first midnight after removal. To add insult to injury, you'll also probably get a parking ticket of £60-£100 when you collect the car (reduced by a 50% discount if paid within 14 days). To find out how to retrieve your car, call the **Trace Service** hotline (7747 4747).

Vehicle hire

To hire a car, you must have at least one year's driving experience with a full driving licence. If you're an overseas visitor, your licence is valid in Britain for a year.

Alamo *0870 400 4508/ www.alamo.com.*
Avis *0844 581 0147/ www.avis.co.uk.*
Budget *0844 581 9999/ www.budget.co.uk.*
Easycar *www.easycar.com.*
Enterprise *0870 607 7757/ www.enterprise.com.*
Europcar *0870 607 5000/ www.europcar.co.uk.*
Hertz *0870 599 6699/ www.hertz.co.uk.*

CYCLING

London isn't the friendliest of towns for cyclists, but the **London Cycle Network** (www.londoncyclenetwork.org.uk) and **London Cycling Campaign** (7234 9310, www.lcc.org.uk) help make it better. **Transport for London** (7222 1234) offers a printable route-finder for cyclists, along with 14 free cycling area maps.

Cycle hire

London Bicycle Tour Company *1A Gabriel's Wharf, 56 Upper Ground, South Bank, SE1 9PP (7928 6838/www.london bicycle.com). Southwark tube.* **Open** 10am-6pm daily. **Hire** £3/hr; £19/1st day; £9/day thereafter. *Deposit* £180 cash or £1 by credit card. **Credit** AmEx, MC, V. **Map** p404 N7. Bikes, tandems and

rickshaw hire. Lights are included, but helmets and panniers are extra.
OY Bike *0845 226 5751/www.oy bike.com.* **Open** 24hrs daily. **Hire** £2/hr, £8/day. *Deposit* £10. To rent a bike 24/7 from OY Bike's 40 pick-up points, pre-register with £10 credit, then call to electronically release the lock. At the end of your ride, return the bike to a stand; trips of less than 30mins are free.
Velorution *18 Great Titchfield Street, Fitzrovia, W1W 8BD (7637 4004/www.velorution.biz). Oxford Circus tube.* **Open** 9am-7pm Mon-Fri; 10.30am-6.30pm Sat. **Hire** £15/day. **Map** p406 U1. Choose between a Brompton or Dahon Vitesse with the 'Rent-a-Folder' scheme: for £20, with local delivery.

WALKING

The best way to see London is on foot, but the city's street layout is very complicated – even locals often carry maps. We've included street maps of central London in the back of this book (starting on p394), and essential locations clearly marked; the standard Geographers' *London A-Z* and Collins' *London Street Atlas* are useful supplements. There's also route advice at www.tfl.gov.uk/tfl/gettingaround.

GUIDED TOURS

By bicycle

The **London Bicycle Tour Company** (*see above*) runs a range of tours in central London.

By boat

City Cruises: Rail River Rover *7740 0400/www.citycruises. com.* **Rates** £11; £5.50 reductions. Combines hop-on, hop-off travel on any regular City Cruise route (pick-ups at Westminster, Waterloo, Tower and Greenwich piers) with free travel on the DLR.
Jason's Trip Canal Boats *7286 3428/www.jasons.co.uk.* **Rates** £7.50-£8.50; £6.50-£7.50 reductions. These 90min narrowboat tours between Little Venice and Camden are unremittingly popular.
London RIB Voyages *7928 8933/www.londonribvoyages.com.* **Rates** £26.50-£39.
Flying Fish Tours *0844 991 5050/www.flyingfishtours.co.uk.* **Rates** £29-£36. Both London RIB and Flying Fish offer Thames tours in a speedy RIB (rigid inflatable boat). You'll need to book in advance.

By bus

Big Bus Company *7233 9533/ www.bigbustours.com.* **Rates** £24; £10 reductions; free under-5s. These open-top buses (8.30am-6pm, or until 4.30pm in winter) cover more than 70 stops in town, among them Haymarket, Green Park (near the Ritz) and Marble Arch. There's live commentary in English, and recorded commentary in eight other languages. Passengers can hop on and hop off as many times as they like. Tickets include a river cruise.
Original London Sightseeing Tour *8877 1722/www.theoriginal tour.com.* **Rates** £22; £12 reductions; £65 family; free under-5s. OLS's hop-on, hop-off bus tours cover 90 stops in central London, including Marble Arch and Trafalgar Square. Commentary comes in seven languages. Tickets include a free river cruise.
London Duck *7928 3132/ www.londonducktours.co.uk.* **Rates** £19; £13-£15 reductions; £57.50 family. Tours of Westminster in an amphibious vehicle. The 75min road/river trip starts on Chicheley Street (behind the London Eye) and enters the Thames at Vauxhall.

By helicopter

Cabair *8953 4411/www.cabair helicopters.com.* **Rates** £170/person. Cabair runs half-hour tours (Sun, some Sat) that depart from Elstree Aerodrome in north London and follow the Thames.

By taxi

Black Taxi Tours of London *7935 9363/www.blacktaxitours. co.uk.* **Rates** £90-£100. Tailored two-hour tours for up to five people.

On foot

Good choices for group tours on a variety of subjects, both mainstream and arcane, include **And Did Those Feet** (8806 4325, www.chr.org.uk), **Performing London** (01234 404774, www.performinglondon. co.uk), **Silver Cane Tours** (07720 715295, www.silvercanetours.com) and **Urban Gentry** (8149 6253, www.urbangentry.com).

Original London Walks *7624 3978, www.walks.com.* **Rates** £7; £5 reductions. An astonishing 140 different walks on a variety of themes, the most popular being Jack the Ripper.

DIRECTORY

Resources A-Z

TRAVEL ADVICE

For up-to-date information on travel to a specific country – including the latest on safety and security, health issues, local laws and customs – contact your home country government's department of foreign affairs. Most have websites with useful advice for would-be travellers.

AUSTRALIA
www.smartraveller.gov.au

CANADA
www.voyage.gc.ca

NEW ZEALAND
www.safetravel.govt.nz

REPUBLIC OF IRELAND
foreignaffairs.gov.ie

UK
www.fco.gov.uk/travel

USA
www.state.gov/travel

ADDRESSES

London postcodes are less helpful than they could be for locating addresses. The first element starts with a compass point – out of N, E, SE, SW, W and NW, plus the smaller EC (East Central) and WC (West Central) – which at least gives you a basic idea. However, the number that follows relates not to geography (unless it's a 1, which indicates that the address is central) but to alphabetical order. So N2 is way out in the boondocks (East Finchley), while W2 covers the very central Bayswater.

AGE RESTRICTIONS

Buying/drinking alcohol 18
Driving 17
Sex 16
Smoking 18

ATTITUDE & ETIQUETTE

Don't mistake reserve for rudeness or indifference; strangers striking up a conversation are likely to be foreign, drunk, mad or in some kind of shared adversity. The weather is a safe subject on which to broach a conversation. Avoid personal questions or excessive personal contact beyond a handshake. First names should never automatically be shortened on first acquaintance. If you want to rile a Londoner in the underground, stand blocking the escalator during rush hour (the code is simple and works very well: stand on the right, walk on the left). While use of a map doesn't mark you out as a tourist in this sometimes bewildering city, trying to flag down a black cab with its orange light off surely does, as this means it's occupied (*see p364*).

BUSINESS

As the financial centre of Europe, London is well equipped to meet the needs of business travellers. The financial action is increasingly centred on Canary Wharf. Marketing, advertising and entertainment companies have a strong presence in the West End.

Conventions & conferences

Visit London *7234 5800/ www.visitlondon.com.*
A venue enquiry service for conventions and exhibitions.
Queen Elizabeth II Conference Centre *Broad Sanctuary, Westminster, SW1P 3EE (7222 5000/www.qeiicc.co.uk). Westminster tube.* **Open** *8am-6pm Mon-Fri. Conference facilities* 24hrs daily. **Map** p401 K9.
Some of the best conference facilities in the capital.

Couriers & shippers

DHL *08701 100 300/ www.dhl.co.uk.*
FedEx *0845 607 0809/ www.fedex.com.*

Office services

ABC Business Machines *115 Freston Road, W11 4BD (7486 5634/www.abcbusiness.co.uk). Latimer Road tube.* **Open** 9am-5pm Mon-Fri; Sat phone for details. **Credit** MC, V. **Map** p398 G5.
British Monomarks *27 Old Gloucester Street, Holborn, WC1N 3XX (7419 5000/www.british monomarks.co.uk). Holborn tube.* **Open** *Mail forwarding* 9.30am-5.30pm Mon-Fri. *Phone answering* 9am-6pm Mon-Fri. **Credit** AmEx, MC, V. **Map** p399 L5.

CONSUMER

Consumer Direct *0845 4040 506/www.consumerdirect.gov.uk.* Funded by the government's Office of Fair Trading, this is a good place to start for consumer advice on all goods and services.

CUSTOMS

See also www.hmrc.gov.uk. For details on how to claim back VAT on purchases, *see p373*.

From inside the EU

You may bring in the following quantities of tax-paid goods, as long as they are for your own consumption: 3,200 cigarettes or 400 cigarillos or 200 cigars or 3kg (6.6lb) tobacco; 90 litres of wine and 110 litres of beer plus either 10 litres of spirits or liqueurs (more than 22% alcohol by volume, or ABV) or 20 litres of fortified wine (under 22% ABV), sparkling wine or other liqueurs.

From outside the EU

You are allowed to bring in 200 cigarettes or 100 cigarillos or 50 cigars or 250g of tobacco; 2 litres of still table wine plus either 1 litre of spirits or strong liqueurs over 22% volume or 2 litres of fortified wine, sparkling wine or other liqueurs; £145 worth of all other goods including gifts and souvenirs.

DISABLED

As a city that evolved long before the needs of disabled people were considered, London is a difficult place for disabled visitors, though legislation is slowly improving access and general facilities. In

DIRECTORY

2004, anyone who provides a service to the public was required to make 'reasonable adjustments' to their properties. The capital's bus fleet is now low-floor for easier wheelchair access, there are no steps for any of the city's trams, and all DLR stations have either lifts or ramp access. The tube and overland trains, however, often have steps and escalators and so are of only limited use to wheelchair users. A blue symbol on the tube map (*see p416*) indicates stations with step-free access. The *Tube Access Guide* booklet is free; call the Travel Information line (7222 1234) for more details.

Most major attractions and hotels offer good accessibility, though provisions for the hearing- and sight-disabled are patchier. Enquire about facilities in advance. *Access in London* is an invaluable reference book for disabled travellers, available for a £10 donation (sterling cheque, cash US dollars or online via PayPal to gordon.couch@virgin.net) from **Access Project** (39 Bradley Gardens, West Ealing, W13 8HE, www.accessproject-phsp.org).

Artsline *21 Pine Court, Wood Lodge Gardens, Bromley, Kent BR1 2WA (7388 2227/www.artsline. org.uk).* **Open** 9.30am-5.30pm Mon-Fri. **Map** p399 K3. Handy information on disabled access to arts and culture events.
Can Be Done *11 Woodcock Hill, Harrow, Middx HA3 0XP (8907 2400/www.canbedone.co.uk).* *Kenton tube/rail.* **Open** 9.30am-5pm Mon-Fri. Disabled-adapted holidays and tours in London, around the UK and worldwide.
Royal Association for Disability & Rehabilitation *12 City Forum, 250 City Road, Islington, EC1V 8AF (7250 3222/ textphone 7250 4119/www.radar. org.uk).* *Old Street tube/rail.* **Open** 9am-5pm Mon-Fri. **Map** p402 P3. A national organisation for disabled voluntary groups that also publishes books and the bimonthly magazine New Bulletin (£35/yr).
Tourism for All *0845 124 9971/www.tourismforall.org.uk.* **Open** *Helpline* 9am-5pm Mon-Fri. Information for older people and people with disabilities in relation to accessible accommodation and other tourism services.
Wheelchair Travel & Access Mini Buses *1 Johnston Green, Guildford, Surrey GU2 9XS (01483 233640/www.wheelchair- travel.co.uk).* **Open** 9am-5.30pm

Mon-Fri; 9am-noon Sat. Hires out converted vehicles (driver optional), plus cars with hand controls and wheelchair-adapted vehicles.

DRUGS

Illegal drug use remains higher in London than the UK as a whole, though is becoming less visible on the streets and in clubs, due to stricter police 'stop and search' policies. Despite fierce debate, cannabis remains a Class C drug, meaning that possession may only result in a warning and confiscation. More serious Class B and A drugs (ecstasy, LSD, heroin, cocaine and the like) carry stiffer penalties, with a maximum of seven years in prison for possession.

ELECTRICITY

The UK uses the standard European 220-240V, 50-cycle AC voltage. British plugs use three pins, so travellers with two-pin European appliances should bring an adaptor, as should anyone using US appliances, which run off 110-120V, 60-cycle.

EMBASSIES & CONSULATES

American Embassy *24 Grosvenor Square, Mayfair, W1A 1AE (7499 9000/http://london.us embassy.gov).* *Bond Street or Marble Arch tube.* **Open** 8.30am-5.30pm Mon-Fri. **Map** p400 G7.
Australian High Commission *Australia House, Strand, Holborn, WC2B 4LA (7379 4334/www.uk.embassy.gov.au).* *Holborn or Temple tube.* **Open** 9am-5pm Mon-Fri. **Map** p401 M6.
Canadian High Commission *38 Grosvenor Street, Mayfair, W1K 4AA (7258 6600/www. canada.org.uk).* *Bond Street or Oxford Circus tube.* **Open** 8am-4pm Mon-Fri. **Map** p400 H7.
Embassy of Ireland *17 Grosvenor Place, Belgravia, SW1X 7HR (7235 2171/passports & visas 7225 7700/www.inis.ie).* *Hyde Park Corner tube.* **Open** 9.30am-1pm, 2.30-5pm Mon-Fri. **Map** p400 G9.
New Zealand High Commission *New Zealand House, 80 Haymarket, St James's, SW1Y 4TQ (7930 8422/www.nz embassy.com).* *Piccadilly Circus tube.* **Open** 9am-5pm Mon-Fri. **Map** p406 W4.
South African High Commission *South Africa House, Trafalgar Square, St James's,*

WC2N 5DP (7451 7299/www. southafricahouse.com). *Charing Cross tube/rail.* **Open** 9.45am-12.45pm (by appoinment), 3-4pm (collections) Mon-Fri. **Map** p407 X5.

EMERGENCIES

In the event of a serious accident, fire or other incident, call **999** – free from any phone, including payphones – and ask for an ambulance, the fire service or police. For hospital Accident & Emergency departments, *see below*; for helplines, *see p370*; for police stations, *see p373*.

GAY & LESBIAN

The *Time Out Gay & Lesbian London Guide* (£12.99) is the ultimate handbook to the capital. The phonelines below offer help and information; for information on HIV and AIDS, *see p369*.

London Friend *7837 3337/ www.londonfriend.org.uk.* **Open** 7.30-10pm daily.
London Lesbian & Gay Switchboard *7837 7324/www. llgs.org.uk.* **Open** 10am-11pm daily.

HEALTH

British citizens or those working in the UK can go to any general practitioner (GP). People ordinarily resident in the UK, including overseas students, are also permitted to register with a National Health Service (NHS) doctor. If you fall outside these categories, you will have to pay to see a GP. Your hotel concierge should be able to recommend one.

A pharmacist will dispense medicines on receipt of a prescription from a GP. NHS prescriptions cost £6.85; under-16s and over-60s are exempt from charges. Contraception is free for all. If you're not eligible to see an NHS doctor, you'll be charged cost price for any medicines prescribed.

Free emergency medical treatment under the NHS is available to the following:
● European Union nationals, plus those of Iceland, Norway and Liechtenstein. They may also be entitled to treatment for a non-emergency condition on production of a European Health Insurance Card (EHIC). The EHIC is normally valid for three to five years and covers any medical treatment that becomes necessary during your

DIRECTORY

trip, because of either illness or an accident. The card gives access to state-provided medical treatment only, and you'll be treated on the same basis as an 'insured' person living in the country you're visiting.

● Nationals of New Zealand, Russia, most former USSR states and the former Yugoslavia.

● Residents, irrespective of nationality, of Anguilla, Australia, Barbados, the British Virgin Islands, the Channel Islands, the Falkland Islands, Iceland, the Isle of Man, Montserrat, Poland, Romania, St Helena and the Turks & Caicos Islands.

● Anyone who has been in the UK for the previous 12 months.

● Anyone who has come to the UK to take up permanent residence.

● Students and trainees whose courses require more than 12 weeks in employment in the first year.

● Refugees and others who have sought refuge in the UK.

● People with HIV/AIDS at a special clinic for the treatment of STDs. The treatment covered is limited to a diagnostic test and counselling associated with the test.

There are no NHS charges for services including:

● Treatment in hospital Accident & Emergency departments.

● Emergency ambulance transport to a hospital.

● Diagnosis and treatment of certain communicable diseases, including STDs.

● Family planning services.

● Compulsory psychiatric treatment.

Accident & emergency

Listed below are most of the central London hospitals that have 24-hour Accident & Emergency departments.

Charing Cross Hospital
Fulham Palace Road, Hammersmith, W6 8RF (8846 1234). Barons Court or Hammersmith tube.

Chelsea & Westminster Hospital *369 Fulham Road, Chelsea, SW10 9NH (8746 8000). South Kensington tube.* Map p396 C12.

Royal Free Hospital *Pond Street, Hampstead, NW3 2QG (7794 0500). Belsize Park tube/Hampstead Heath rail.*

Royal London Hospital *Whitechapel Road, Whitechapel, E1 1BB (7377 7000). Whitechapel tube.*

St Mary's Hospital *Praed Street, Paddington, W2 1NY (7886 6666). Paddington tube/rail.* Map p395 D5.

St Thomas' Hospital *Lambeth Palace Road, Lambeth, SE1 7EH (7188 7188). Westminster tube/Waterloo tube/rail.* Map p401 L9.

University College Hospital *235 Grafton Road, NW1 2BU (0845 155 5000). Euston Square/Warren Street tube.* Map p398 J4.

Complementary medicine

British Homeopathic Association *0870 444 3950/ www.trusthomeopathy.org.* **Open** *Phone enquiries* 9am-5pm Mon-Fri. Referrals to your nearest homeopathic chemist/doctor.

Contraception & abortion

Family planning advice, contraceptive supplies and abortions are free to British citizens on the NHS, and also to EU residents and foreign nationals living in Britain. Phone the **Contraception Helpline** on 0845 310 1334 or visit www.fpa.org.uk for your local **Family Planning Association**. The 'morning after' pill (around £25), effective up to 72 hours after intercourse, is available over the counter at pharmacies.

British Pregnancy Advisory Service *0845 730 4030/ www.bpas.org.* **Open** *Helpline* 8am-9pm Mon-Fri; 8.30am-6pm Sat; 9.30am-2.30pm Sun. Callers are referred to their nearest clinic for treatment. Contraceptives and pregnancy testing are offered.

Brook Advisory Centre *7284 6040/helpline 0800 018 5023/www.brook.org.uk.* **Open** *Helpline* 9am-5pm Mon-Fri. Information on sexual health, contraception and abortion, plus free pregnancy tests for under-25s. Call for your nearest clinic.

Marie Stopes House *Family Planning Clinic/Well Woman Centre, 108 Whitfield Street, Fitzrovia, W1P 6BE (0845 300 8090/www.mariestopes.org.uk).* *Warren Street tube.* **Open** *Clinic* 8.30am-4.30pm Mon-Fri. *Helpline* 24hrs daily. Map p398 J4. For contraceptive advice, emergency contraception, pregnancy testing, an abortion service, cervical and health screening or gynaecological services. Fees may apply.

Dentists

Dental care is free for resident students, under-18s and people on benefits. All others must pay. To find an NHS dentist, contact the local Health Authority or a Citizens' Advice Bureau (*see p370*).

Dental Emergency Care Service *Guy's Hospital, St Thomas Street, Borough, SE1 9RT (7188 0511). London Bridge tube/rail.* **Open** 9am-5pm Mon-Fri. Map p404 Q8. Queues start forming at 8am; arrive by 10am if you're to be seen at all.

Hospitals

For a list of hospitals with Accident & Emergency departments, *see above*; for other hospitals, consult the Yellow Pages directory.

Opticians

See p260.

Pharmacies

Also called 'chemists' in the UK. Branches of Boots and larger supermarkets have a pharmacy, and there are independents on the high street (*see p261*). Staff can advise on over-the-counter medicines. Most pharmacies keep shop hours (9am-6pm Mon-Sat).

STDs, HIV & AIDS

NHS Genito-Urinary Clinics (such as the Centre for Sexual Health) are affiliated to major hospitals. They provide free, confidential treatment of STDs and other problems, such as thrush and cystitis; offer counselling about HIV and other STDs; and can conduct blood tests.

The 24-hour **Sexual Healthline** (0800 567 123, www.playingsafely. co.uk) is free and confidential. Visit the website to find your nearest clinic. For other helplines, *see below*; for abortion and contraception, *see above*.

Ambrose King Centre *Royal London Hospital, Whitechapel Road, Whitechapel, E1 1BB (7377 7306/www.bartsandthelondon.nhs. uk). Whitechapel tube.* **Open** 9am-6pm Mon; 9am-3pm Tue, Fri; 9am-4pm Thur; noon-4pm Wed. Screening for and treatment of STDs, HIV testing and counselling. Services are provided on a walk-in basis. Doors open 30mins before clinic hours.

DIRECTORY

Mortimer Market Centre for Sexual Health *Mortimer Market, off Capper Street, Bloomsbury, WC1E 6JB (7530 5050). Goodge Street or Warren Street tube.* **Open** 9am-6pm Mon, Thur; 9am-7pm Tue; 1-6pm Wed; 8.30am-3pm Fri. **Map** p398 J4.

Terrence Higgins Trust Lighthouse *314-320 Gray's Inn Road, Holborn, WC1X 8DP (office 7812 1600/helpline 0845 122 1200/www.tht.org.uk). King's Cross tube/rail.* **Open** *Office* 9.30am-5.30pm Mon-Fri. *Helpline* 10am-10pm Mon-Fri; noon-6pm Sat, Sun. **Map** p399 M5. Advice for those with HIV/AIDS, their relatives, lovers and friends. It also offers free leaflets about AIDS and safer sex.

HELPLINES

Helplines dealing with sexual health issues are listed under **STDs, HIV & AIDS** (*see above*).

Alcoholics Anonymous *0845 769 7555/www.alcoholics-anonymous.org.uk.* **Open** 10am-10pm daily.

Citizens' Advice Bureaux *www.citizensadvice.org.uk.* The council-run CABs offer free legal, financial and personal advice. Check the phone book or see the website for your nearest office.

NHS Direct *0845 4647/www.nhsdirect.nhs.uk.* **Open** 24hrs daily. A free, first-stop service for medical advice on all subjects.

Missing People *0500 700 700/www.missingpeople.org.uk.* **Open** 24hrs daily. This volunteer-run organisation publicises information on anyone reported missing, and helps to find missing persons. Its 'Message Home' freephone service (0800 700 740) allows runaways to reassure friends or family of their well-being without revealing their location.

Rape & Sexual Abuse Support Centre *8683 3300/www.rapecrisis.org.uk.* **Open** *Helpline* noon-2.30pm, 7-9.30pm Mon-Fri; 2.30-5pm Sat, Sun. Provides support and information for victims and families.

Samaritans *0845 790 9090/www.samaritans.org.uk.* **Open** 24hrs daily. The Samaritans listen to anyone with emotional problems. Lines can be busy.

Victim Support *7268 0200/www.victimsupport.org.uk).* **Open** *Support line* 9am-9pm Mon-Fri; 9am-7pm Sat, Sun. **Map** p398 H5.

Emotional and practical support to victims of crime, including advice on legal procedures. Interpreters can be arranged where necessary.

ID

Unless you look young for your age, you're unlikely to be asked for ID in London when buying alcohol or tobacco, although many supermarkets and some bars follow a policy of checking anyone who looks 21 or under. Passports and photographic driver's licences are acceptable forms of ID.

INSURANCE

Insuring personal belongings can be difficult to arrange once you have arrived in London, so do so before you leave home.

Medical insurance is usually included in travel insurance packages. Unless your country has a reciprocal medical treatment arrangement with Britain (*see p367*), it's very important to ensure you have adequate health cover.

INTERNET

Most hotels have at least a modem plug-in point (dataport) in each room, if not broadband or wireless access. Those that don't have either usually offer some other form of surfing. There are plenty of cybercafés dotted around town, but we prefer cafés with wireless access to the 'worker cube' discomfort of most cybercaffs; we've listed some handy ones below. You'll also find terminals in public libraries (*see p371*). For further wireless locations, visit the occasionally erratic www.wi-fihotspotlist.com.

Apostrophe *9 Tottenham Court Road, Bloomsbury, W1T 7PT (7436 6688/www.apostrophe uk.com). Goodge Street tube.* **Open** 7.30am-6pm Mon-Fri; 9.30am-5pm Sat.

Benugo Bar & Kitchen *BFI Southbank, Belvedere Road, South Bank, SE1 8XT (7401 9000/www.benugo.com). Waterloo tube/rail.* **Open** 9.45am-11pm Mon-Fri; 11am-11pm Sat; 11am-10.30pm Sun.

Hummus Brothers *88 Wardour Street, Soho, W1F 0TJ (7734 1311/www.hbros.co.uk). Oxford Circus tube.* **Open** 11am-10pm Mon-Wed; 11am-11pm Thur, Fri; noon-11pm Sat; noon-10pm Sun.

Peyton & Byrne *Wellcome Collection, 183 Euston Road,*

Bloomsbury, NW1 2BE (7611 2138/www.peytonandbyrne.com). Euston tube/rail. **Open** 10am-6pm Tue, Wed, Fri, Sat; 10am-10pm Thur; 11am-6pm Sun.

LEFT LUGGAGE

Airports

Gatwick Airport *South Terminal 01293 502014/North Terminal 01293 502013.*

Heathrow Airport *Terminal 1 8745 5301/Terminals 2-3 8759 3344/Terminal 4 8897 6874/Terminal 5 8283 5073.*

London City Airport *7646 0162.*

Stansted Airport *01279 663213.*

Rail & bus stations

Security precautions mean that London stations tend to have left-luggage desks rather than lockers; to find out whether a station offers this facility, call 0845 748 4950.

Charing Cross *7930 5444.* **Open** 7am-11pm daily.
Euston *7387 8699.* **Open** 7am-11pm daily.
King's Cross *7837 4334.* **Open** 7am-11pm daily.
Paddington *7313 1514.* **Open** 7am-11pm daily.
Victoria *7963 0957.* **Open** 7am-midnight daily.

LEGAL HELP

Those in difficulties can visit a Citizens' Advice Bureau (*see above*) or contact the groups below. Try the **Legal Services Commission** (7759 0000, www.legalservices.gov.uk) for information. If you're arrested, your first call should be to your embassy (*see p367*).

Community Legal Services Directory *0845 345 4345/www.clsdirect.org.uk.* **Open** 9am-6.30pm Mon-Fri. Service providing free information for those with legal problems.

Joint Council for the Welfare of Immigrants *115 Old Street, Hoxton, EC1V 9RT (7251 8708/www.jcwi.org.uk).* **Open** *Enquiries* 2-5pm Tue, Thur. JCWI's telephone-only legal advice line offers guidance and referrals.

Law Centres Federation *7839 2998/www.lawcentres.org.uk. Piccadilly Circus tube.* **Open** *Enquiries* 10am-5.30pm Mon-Fri.

Local law centres offer free legal help for people who can't afford a lawyer and are living or working in the immediate area; this central office connects you with the nearest.

LIBRARIES

Unless you're a London resident, you won't be able to join a lending library. At the **British Library** (*see p78*), only exhibition areas are open to non-members, but the libraries listed here can be used for reference by anyone.

Barbican Library *Barbican Centre, Silk Street, the City, EC2Y 8DS (7638 0569/www.cityoflondon. gov.uk/barbicanlibrary). Barbican tube/Moorgate tube/rail.* **Open** 9.30am-5.30pm Mon, Wed; 9.30am-7.30pm Tue, Thur; 9.30am-2pm Fri; 9.30am-4pm Sat. **Map** p402 P5.
Holborn Library *32-38 Theobald's Road, Bloomsbury, WC1X 8PA (7974 6345). Chancery Lane tube.* **Open** 10am-7pm Mon, Thur; 10am-6pm Tue, Wed, Fri; 10am-5pm Sat. **Map** p399 M5.
Kensington Central Library *12 Philimore Walk, Kensington, W8 7RX (7937 2542/www.rbkc. gov.uk/libraries). High Street Kensington tube.* **Open** 9.30am-8pm Mon, Tue, Thur; 9.30am-5pm Wed, Fri, Sat.
Marylebone Library *109-117 Marylebone Road, Marylebone, NW1 5PS (7641 1300/www. westminster.gov.uk/libraries). Baker Street tube/Marylebone tube/rail.* **Open** 9.30am-8pm Mon, Tue, Thur, Fri; 10am-8pm Wed; 9.30am-5pm Sat; 1.30-5pm Sun. **Map** p395 F4.
Victoria Library *160 Buckingham Palace Road, Belgravia, SW1W 9UD (7641 4258/www.westminster.gov.uk/ libraries). Victoria tube/rail.* **Open** 9.30am-8pm Mon; 9.30am-7pm Tue, Thur, Fri; 10am-7pm Wed; 9.30am-5pm Sat. *Music library* 11am-7pm Mon-Fri; 10am-5pm Sat. **Map** p400 H10.
Westminster Reference Library *35 St Martin's Street, Westminster, WC2H 7HP (7641 4636/www.westminster.gov.uk/ libraries). Leicester Square tube.* **Open** 10am-8pm Mon-Fri; 10am-5pm Sat. **Map** p407 X4.
Women's Library *25 Old Castle Street, Whitechapel, E1 7NT (7320 ????/www.thewomens library.ac.uk). Aldgate or Aldgate East tube.* **Open** *Reading room* 9.30am-5pm Tue, Wed, Fri; 9.30am-8pm Thur; 10am-4pm Sat. **Map** p405 S6.

LOST PROPERTY

Always inform the police if you lose anything, if only to validate insurance claims; *see p373* or the *Yellow Pages* for police station locations. Only dial 999 if violence has occurred; use 0300 1231212 for non-emergencies. Report lost passports both to the police and to your embassy (*see p367*).

Airports

For items left on the plane, contact the relevant airline; Otherwise, phone the following:

Gatwick Airport *01293 503162.*
Heathrow Airport *8745 7727.*
London City Airport *7646 0000.*
Luton Airport *01582 395219.*
Stansted Airport *01279 663293.*

Public transport

If you've lost property in an overground station or on a train, call 0870 000 5151, and give the operator the details.

Transport for London *Lost Property Office, 200 Baker Street, Marylebone, NW1 5RZ (7918 2000/www.tfl.gov.uk).* *Baker Street tube.* **Open** 8.30am-4pm Mon-Fri. **Map** p398 G4.
Allow three working days from the time of loss. If you lose something on a bus, call 7222 1234 and ask for the phone numbers of the depots at either end of the route. If you lose something on a tube, pick up a lost property form from any station.

Taxis

The **Transport for London** office (*see above*) deals with property found in registered black cabs. You are advised to allow seven days from the time of loss. For items lost in a minicab, you must contact the office of the relevant company.

MEDIA

Magazines

Time Out remains London's only quality listings magazine. Widely available in central London every Tuesday, it gives listings for the week from Wednesday. If you want to know what's going on and whether it's going to be any good, this is where to look.

Nationally, *Loaded*, *FHM* and *Maxim* are big men's titles, while women read handbag-sized *Glamour* and glossy weekly *Grazia*, alongside *Vogue*, *Marie Claire* and *Elle*. The appetite for celebrity magazines like *Heat*, *Closer* and *OK* doesn't seem to have abated, while style mags such as *i-D* and *Dazed & Confused* have found a profitable niche.

The *Spectator*, *Prospect*, the *Economist* and the *New Statesman* are at the serious, political end of the market, with the satirical *Private Eye* bringing some levity to the subject. The *London Review of Books* ponders life and letters in considerable depth. The laudable *Big Issue* is sold across the capital by registered homeless vendors.

For the best London webzines, *see p378.*

Newspapers

London's main daily paper is the sensationalist, right-wing *Evening Standard*, published Monday to Friday. *Metro*, an *Evening Standard* spin-off, led what in 2006 became a deluge of free dailies: *London Lite* (the *Standard* again) and *thelondonpaper* are overpriced at gratis – pick up one of the copies discarded on the tube or a bus to see what we mean.

Quality national dailies include, from right to left, the *Daily Telegraph* and *The Times* (which is best for sport), the *Independent* and the *Guardian* (best for arts). All go into overdrive on Saturdays and have bulging Sunday equivalents bar the *Guardian*, which has a sister Sunday paper, the *Observer*. The pink *Financial Times* (daily except Sunday) is the best for business.

In the middle market, the leader is the right-wing *Daily Mail* (and *Mail on Sunday*); the *Daily Express* (and *Sunday Express*) tries to compete. Tabloid leader is the right-wing *Sun* and Sunday's *News of the World* (The). The *Daily Star* and left-wing *Mirror* are the main lowbrow contenders.

Radio

The stations listed below are broadcast on standard wavebands as well as digital, where they are joined by some interesting new channels, particularly from the BBC. The format is not yet widespread, but you might be lucky enough to have digital in your hotel room or hire car.

DIRECTORY

BBC Radio 1 *97-99 FM.*
Standard mix of youth-oriented
pop, indie, metal and dance.
BBC Radio 2 *88-91 FM.* Bland
during the day, but good after dark.
BBC Radio 3 *90-93 FM.*
Classical music dominates,
but there's also discussion,
world music and arts.
BBC Radio 4 *92-95 FM,
198 LW.* The BBC's main speech
station. News agenda-setter *Today*
(6-9am Mon-Fri, 7-9am Sat) exudes
self-importance.
BBC Radio 5 Live *693, 909
AM.* Rolling news and sport. Avoid
the morning phone-ins, but *Up All
Night* (1-5am nightly) is terrific.
BBC London *94.9 FM.*
Danny Baker (3-5pm Mon-Fri)
is brilliant.
BBC World Service *648 AM.*
A distillation of the best of all the
other BBC stations; transmitted
worldwide.
Capital FM *95.8 FM.* London's
best-known station: chat and music.
Classic FM *100-102 FM.*
Easy-listening classical.
Heart FM *106.2 FM.* Capital
for grown-ups.
Smooth *102.2 FM.* Aural
wallpaper.
LBC *97.3 FM.* Phone-ins and
features. The cabbies' favourite.
Resonance *104.4 FM.* Arts radio
– an inventively oddball mix.
Xfm *104.9 FM.* Alternative rock.

Television

With a multiplicity of formats,
there are plenty of pay-TV options.
However, the relative quality of free
TV (most notably the BBC's digital
channels) keeps subscriptions from
attaining US levels.

The five main free-to-air networks
are as follows:
BBC1 The Corporation's mass-
market station. Relies too much on
soaps, game shows and lifestyle
TV, but has quality offerings too,
notably in nature and drama. As
with all BBC stations, there are no
commercials.
BBC2 A reasonably intelligent
cultural cross-section and plenty of
documentaries, but upstaged by the
BBC's digital arts channel, BBC4
(*see below*).
ITV1 ITV London provides
monotonous weekday mass-appeal
shows. ITV2 does much the same
on digital.
Channel 4 C4's output includes a
variety of extremely successful US
imports (the likes of *Ugly Betty* and
ER, many of which get previewed

on digital counterpart E4), but it
still comes up with gems of its own,
particularly documentaries.
Five Sex-oriented programmes,
TV movies, rubbish comedy,
US sport and the occasional
good documentary.

Satellite, digital and cable channels
include the following:
BBC3 *EastEnders* reruns and
other light fare, plus comedy.
BBC4 Highbrow stuff, including
earnest documentaries and dramas.
BBC News Rolling 24hr news.
BBC Parliament Live debates
and highlights from Parliament.
Discovery Channel Science and
nature documentaries.
E4/Film4 C4's entertainment and
movie channels.
Five US US sport, drama and
documentaries.
ITV4 'Challenging' drama,
comedy and film.
Sky News Rolling news.
Sky One Sky's version of ITV.
Sky Sports Screens Premiership
football and cricket live. There are
also Sky Sports 2 and 3.

MONEY

Britain's currency is the pound
sterling (£). One pound equals 100
pence (p). Coins are copper (1p, 2p),
silver (round: 5p, 10p; seven-sided:
20p, 50p), yellowy-gold (£1) or
silver in the centre with a yellowy-
gold edge (£2). Paper notes are blue
(£5), orange (£10), purple (£20) or
red (£50). You can exchange foreign
currency at banks, bureaux de
change and post offices; there's no
commission charge at the last of
these (for addresses of the most
central, *see below*). Many large
stores also accept euros (€).

Western Union *0800
833833/www.westernunion.co.uk.*
The old standby for bailing
out cash-challenged travellers.
Chequepoint (*see below*) also
offers this service.

Banks & ATMs

As well as inside and outside
banks, cash machines can be
found in some supermarkets and
in larger tube and rail stations.
Some commercial premises have
'pay-ATMs', which charge for
withdrawals (usually £1.50 per
transaction). If you are visiting
from outside the UK, your cash card
should work via one of the debit
networks, but check charges in
advance. ATMs also allow you to

make withdrawals on your credit
card if you know your PIN number;
you will be charged interest plus,
usually, a currency exchange
fee. Generally, getting cash with
a card is the cheapest form of
currency exchange but increasingly
there are hidden charges, so
do your research. Bank of America
customers can use Barclays
Bank ATMs free.
 Credit cards, especially
MasterCard and Visa, are accepted
in pretty much every shop (except
small corner shops) and restaurant
(except caffs) in the capital.
However, American Express and
Diners Club tend to be accepted
at more expensive outlets.
 You will usually not be allowed
to make a purchase with your
card without your PIN number.
For more information, see
www.chipandpin.co.uk.
 No commission is charged
for cashing sterling travellers'
cheques if you go to one of the
banks affiliated with the issuing
company. You do have to pay to
cash travellers' cheques in foreign
currencies, and to change cash.
You will always need to produce
ID to cash travellers' cheques.

Bureaux de change

You'll be charged for cashing
travellers' cheques or buying
and selling foreign currency
at bureaux de change. The
commission varies. Major rail
and tube stations have bureaux,
and there are many in tourist areas
and on major shopping streets.
Most open 8am-10pm.

Chequepoint *550 Oxford Street,
Marlyebone, W1C 1LY (7724
6127/www.chequepoint.com).
Marble Arch tube.* **Open** 8am-10pm
Mon-Sat; 10am-10pm Sun.
Map p398 G6. **Other locations**
throughout the city.
Garden Bureau *30A Jubilee
Market Hall, Covent Garden,
WC2E 8BE (7240 9921). Covent
Garden tube.* **Open** 9.30am-6pm
daily. **Map** p407 Z3.
Thomas Exchange
*13 Maddox Street, Mayfair, W1S
2QG (7493 1300/www.thomas
exchange.co.uk). Oxford Circus tube.*
Open 8.45am-5.30pm Mon-Fri.
Map p406 U3.

Lost/stolen credit cards

Report lost or stolen credit cards
immediately to both the police and
the services below.

American Express
01273 696933.
Diners Club *01252 513500.*
MasterCard/Eurocard
0800 964767.
Switch *0870 600 0459.*
Visa/Connect *0800 895082.*

Tax

With the exception of food, books, newspapers and a few other items, purchases in the UK are subject to VAT: Value Added Tax, aka sales tax. It's usually 17.5%, but will be 15% until at least the end of 2009. VAT is included in prices quoted by mainstream shops, but may not be included in hotel room rates.

You may be able to take advantage of a scheme allowing you to claim back the VAT you have been charged on most of the goods you take out of the EC (European Community). The scheme is typically advertised in UK shops as 'Tax Free Shopping'. To be able to claim a refund you must be an eligible traveller who is a non-EC visitor to the UK, or a UK resident emigrating from the European Community. When you buy the goods the retailer will ask to see your passport. They will then ask you to fill in a simple refund form. You need to have one of these forms to make your claim; till receipts alone will not do.

If you're leaving the UK direct for a destination outside the EC, you must show your goods and refund form to UK Customs at the airport/port from which you're leaving. If you're leaving the EC via another EC country, you must show your goods and refund form to Customs staff of that country.

After Customs have certified your form, you can get your refund by posting the form to the retailer from whom you bought the goods, posting the form to a commercial refund company or handing your form in at a refund booth to get immediate payment. Customs are not responsible for making the refund: when you buy the goods, ask the retailer how the refund is paid.

OPENING HOURS

The following are general guidelines. Government offices all close on every bank (public) holiday (*see p376*); shops are increasingly remaining open, with only Christmas Day seeming sacrosanct. Most attractions remain open on the other public holidays, but always call first.

Banks 9am-4.30pm (some close at 3.30pm, some 5.30pm) Mon-Fri; sometimes also Saturday mornings.
Businesses 9am-5pm Mon-Fri.
Post offices 9am-5.30pm Mon-Fri; 9am-noon Sat.
Pubs & bars 11am-11pm Mon-Sat; noon-10.30pm Sun.
Shops 10am-6pm Mon-Sat; some to 8pm. Many are also open on Sunday, usually 11am-5pm or noon-6pm.

POLICE STATIONS

The police are a good source of information about the area and are used to helping visitors. If you've been robbed, assaulted or involved in an infringement of the law, go to your nearest police station. (We've listed a handful in central London; look under 'Police' in Directory Enquiries or call 118 118, 118 500 or 118 888 for more.)

If you have a complaint, ensure that you take the offending officer's identifying number (it should be displayed on his or her epaulette). You can then register a complaint with the **Independent Police Complaints Commission** (90 High Holborn, WC1V 6BH, 0845 300 2002). In non-emergency situations, call 0300 1231212; for emergencies, *see p367.*

Belgravia Police Station
202-206 Buckingham Palace Road, Pimlico, SW1W 9SX (7730 1212). Victoria tube/rail. **Map** p400 H10.
Camden Police Station
60 Albany Street, Fitzrovia, NW1 4EE (7404 1212). Great Portland Street tube. **Map** p398 H4.
Charing Cross Police Station
Agar Street, Covent Garden, WC2N 4JP (7240 1212). Charing Cross tube/rail. **Map** p407 Y4.
Chelsea Police Station
2 Lucan Place, Chelsea, SW3 3PB (7589 1212). South Kensington tube. **Map** p397 E10.
Islington Police Station
2 Tolpuddle Street, Islington, N1 0YY (7704 1212). Angel tube. **Map** p402 N2.
Kensington Police Station
72-74 Earl's Court Road, Kensington, W8 6EQ (7376 1212). Earl's Court tube. **Map** p396 B11.
Marylebone Police Station *1-9 Seymour Street, Marylebone, W1H 7BA (7486 1212). Marble Arch tube.* **Map** p395 F6.
West End Central Police Station *27 Savile Row, Mayfair, W1X 2DU (7437 1212). Piccadilly Circus tube.* **Map** p406 U3.

POSTAL SERVICES

You can buy stamps at all post offices and many newsagents and supermarkets. Current prices are 34p for first-class and 24p for second-class letters and small items weighing less than 100g, or 48p for letters to the EU and 78p to the United States. Rates for other letters and parcels vary by weight, size and destination. *See also p366* **Business: Couriers & shippers**.

Post offices

Post offices are usually open 9am-6pm Mon-Fri and 9am-noon Sat, with the exception of **Trafalgar Square Post Office** (24-28 William IV Street, WC2N 4DL, 0845 722 3344), which opens 8.30am-6.30pm Mon-Fri and 9am-5.30pm Sat. Listed below are the other main central London offices. For general enquiries, call 0845 722 3344 or consult www.postoffice.co.uk.

Albemarle Street *nos.43-44, Mayfair, W1S 4DS. Green Park tube.* **Map** p406 U5.
Baker Street *no.111, Marylebone, W1U 6SG. Baker Street tube.* **Map** p398 G5.
Great Portland Street *nos.54-56, Fitzrovia, W1W 7NE. Oxford Circus tube.* **Map** p398 H4.
High Holborn *no.181, Holborn, WC1V 7RL. Holborn tube.* **Map** p407 Y1.

Poste restante

If you want to receive mail while you're away, you can have it sent to Trafalgar Square Post Office (*see above*), where it will be kept for a month. Your name and 'Poste Restante' must be clearly marked on the letter. You'll need ID to collect it.

RELIGION

Times may vary; always phone to check.

Anglican & Baptist

Bloomsbury Central Baptist Church *235 Shaftesbury Avenue, Covent Garden, WC2H 8EP (7240 0544/www.bloomsbury.org.uk). Tottenham Court Road tube.* **Open** 10am-4pm Mon-Fri. *Friendship Centre* Oct-June 10am-4pm Tue. **Services & meetings** 11am, 6.30pm Sun. **Classical concerts** phone for details. **Map** p399 Y1.

St Paul's Cathedral
For listings, see p61. **Services** 7.30am, 8am, 12.30pm, 5pm Mon-Sat; 8am, 10.15am, 11.30am, 3.15pm, 6pm Sun. **Map** p404 O6.

Westminster Abbey
For listings, see p112. **Services** 7.30am, 8am, 12.30pm, 5pm Mon-Fri; 8am, 9am, 12.30pm, 3pm Sat; 8am, 10am, 11.15am, 3pm, 5.45pm Sun. **Map** p401 K9.

Buddhist

Buddhapadipa Thai Temple
14 Calonne Road, Wimbledon, SW19 5HJ (8946 1357/www. buddhapadipa.org). Wimbledon tube/rail then 93 bus. **Open** *Temple* 9-6pm Sat, Sun. *Meditation retreat* 7-9pm Tue, Thur; 4-6pm Sat, Sun. *See also p156.*

London Buddhist Centre
51 Roman Road, Bethnal Green, E2 0HU (0845 458 4716/www.lbc. org.uk). Bethnal Green tube. **Open** see website.

Catholic

Brompton Oratory
For listings, see p120. **Services** 7am, 8am (Latin mass), 10am, 12.30am, 6pm Mon-Fri; 7am, 8.30am, 10am, 6pm Sat; 7am, 8.30am, 10am (tridentine), 11am (sung Latin), 12.30pm, 3.30pm, 4.30pm, 7pm Sun. **Map** p397 E10.

Westminster Cathedral
For listings, see p114. **Services** 7am, 8am, 9am, 10.30am, 12.30pm, 5pm Mon-Fri; 8am, 9am, 12.30pm, 6pm Sat; 7am, 8am, 9am, 10.30am, noon, 5.30pm, 7pm Sun. **Map** p400 J10.

Islamic

Islamic Cultural Centre & London Central Mosque
146 Park Road, Marylebone, NW8 7RG (7724 3363/www.iccuk.org). Baker Street tube/74 bus. **Open** dawn-dusk daily. **Services** vary; phone 7725 2213 for details.

East London Mosque
82-92 Whitechapel Road, Whitechapel, E1 1JQ (7650 3000/www.eastlondon mosque.org.uk). Aldgate East or Whitechapel tube. **Open** 10am-10pm daily. **Services** *Friday prayer* 1.30pm (1.15pm in winter). **Map** p405 S6.

Jewish

Liberal Jewish Synagogue
28 St John's Wood Road, St John's Wood, NW8 7HA (7286 5181/ www.ljs.org). St John's Wood tube.

Open 9am-5pm Mon-Thur; 9am-1pm Fri. **Services** 6.45pm Fri; 11am Sat.

West Central Liberal Synagogue
21 Maple Street, Fitzrovia, W1T 4BE (7636 7627/ www.wcls.org.uk). Warren Street tube. **Services** 3pm Sat. **Map** p398 J4.

Methodist & Quaker

Methodist Central Hall
Central Hall, Storey's Gate, Westminster, SW1H 9NH (7222 8010/www.c-h-w.co.uk). St James's Park tube. **Open** *Chapel* 8am-6pm daily. **Services** 12.45pm Wed; 11am, 6.30pm Sun. **Map** p401 K9.

Religious Society of Friends (Quakers)
173-177 Euston Road, Bloomsbury, NW1 2BJ (7663 1000/www.quaker.org.uk). Euston tube/rail. **Open** 8.30am-9.30pm Mon-Fri; 8.30am-4.30pm Sat. **Meetings** 6.30pm Mon; 11am Sun. **Map** p399 K3.

SAFETY & SECURITY

There are no real 'no-go' areas in London as such, and despite endless media coverage of teenage stabbings you're much more likely to get hurt in a car accident than as a result of criminal activity, but thieves haunt busy shopping areas and transport nodes as they do in all cities.

Use common sense and follow some basic rules. Keep wallets and purses out of sight, and handbags securely closed. Never leave briefcases, bags or coats unattended, beside, under or on the back of a chair – even if they aren't stolen, they are likely to trigger a bomb alert. Don't put bags on the floor near the door of a public toilet. Don't take short cuts through dark alleys and car parks. Keep your passport, cash, and credit cards in separate places. Don't carry a wallet in your back pocket. Always be aware of your surroundings.

SMOKING

July 2007 saw the introduction of a ban on smoking in all enclosed public spaces, including pubs, bars, clubs, restaurants, hotel foyers and shops, as well as on public transport. Smokers now face a penalty fee of £50 or a maximum fee of £200 if they are prosecuted for smoking in a smoke-free area. Many bars and clubs offer smoking gardens or terraces.

TELEPHONES

Dialling & codes

London's dialling code is 020; standard landlines have eight digits after that. You don't need to dial the 020 from within the area, so we have not given it in this book.

If you're calling from outside the UK, dial your international access code, then the UK code, 44, then the full London number, omitting the first 0 from the code. For example, to make a call to 020 7813 3000 from the US, dial 011 44 20 7813 3000. To dial abroad from the UK, first dial 00, then the relevant country code from the list below. For more international dialling codes, check the phone book or see www.kropla.com/dialcode.htm.

Australia 61
Canada 1
New Zealand 64
Republic of Ireland 353
South Africa 27
USA 1

Mobile phones

Mobile phones in the UK work on either the 900 or 1800 GSM system. If you're a US traveller, your home service provider will use the GSM system, and your phone probably runs on the 800 or 1900 MHz band, so you'll need to acquire a tri- or quad-band handset.

The simplest option may be to buy a 'pay-as-you-go' phone (about £50-£200); there's no monthly fee, you top up talk time using a card. Check before buying whether it can make and receive international calls. **Phones4u** (www.phones4u.co.uk) and **Carphone Warehouse** (www.carphonewarehouse.com), which both have stores throughout the city, offer a wide range of options. For phone rental, *see also p249.*

Operator services

Call **100** for the operator if you have difficulty in dialling; for an alarm call; to make a credit card call; for information about the cost of a call; and for help with international person-to-person calls. Dial **155** for the international operator if you need to reverse the charges (call collect) or if you can't dial direct, but be warned that this service is very expensive.

Directory enquiries

This service is now provided by various six-digit 118 numbers. They're pretty pricey to call: dial (free) 0800 953 0720 for a rundown of options and prices. The best known is **118 118**, which charges 49p per call, then 14p per minute thereafter; **118 888** charges 49p per call, then 9p per minute; **118 180** charges 25p per call, then 30p per minute. Online, use the free www.ukphonebook.com.

Yellow Pages This 24-hour service lists the phone numbers of thousands of businesses in the UK. Dial **118 247** (49p/min) and identify the type of business you require, and in which area of London.

Public phones

Public payphones take coins or credit cards (sometimes both). The minimum cost is 40p, which buys a 110-second local call. Some payphones, such as the counter-top ones found in many pubs, require more. International calling cards, offering bargain minutes via a freephone number, are widely available.

Telephone directories

There are several telephone directories for London, divided by area, which contain private and commercial numbers. Available at post offices and libraries, these hefty tomes are also issued free to all residents, as is the invaluable Yellow Pages directory (also online at www.yell.com), which lists businesses and services.

TIME

London operates on Greenwich Mean Time (GMT), which is five hours ahead of the US's Eastern Standard Time. In spring (29 March 2009) the UK puts its clocks forward by one hour to British Summer Time. In autumn (25 October 2009), the clocks go back to GMT.

TIPPING

In Britain it's accepted that you tip in taxis, minicabs, restaurants (some waiting staff rely heavily on tips), hotels, hairdressers and some bars (not pubs). Ten per cent is normal, with some restaurants adding as much as 15%. Always

check whether service has been included in your bill: some restaurants include an automatic service charge, but also leave space for a gratuity on your credit card slip.

TOILETS

Pubs and restaurants generally reserve the use of their toilets for customers only. However, all mainline rail stations and a few tube stations – Piccadilly Circus, for one – have public toilets (you will often be charged a small fee). Department stores usually have loos that you can use free of charge, and museums (most of which no longer charge an entry fee) generally have good facilities. At night, options are worse. The scattering of coin-operated toilet booths around the city may be your only option.

TOURIST INFORMATION

Visit London (7234 5800, www.visitlondon.com) is the city's official tourist information company. In addition to the tourist offices below, there is a brand-new centre by **St Paul's** (*see p57*).

Britain & London Visitor Centre *1 Lower Regent Street, Piccadilly Circus, SW1Y 4XT (7808 3800/www.visitbritain.com). Piccadilly Circus tube.* **Open** 9.30am-6.30pm Mon; 9am-6.30pm Tue-Fri; 10am-4pm Sat, Sun. **Map** p406 W4.

Greenwich Tourist Information Centre *Pepys House, 2 Cutty Sark Gardens, SE10 9LW (0870 608 2000/ www.greenwich.gov.uk/tourism). Cutty Sark DLR.* **Open** 10am-5pm daily.

London Information Centre *Leicester Square, WC2H 7BP (7292 2333/www.londontown.com). Leicester Square tube.* **Open** 8am-6pm Mon-Fri; 10am-6pm Sat, Sun. *Helpline* 8am-midnight Mon-Fri; 9am-10pm Sat, Sun.

Richmond Tourist Information Centre *Old Town Hall, Whittaker Avenue, Richmond, Surrey TW9 1TP (8940 9125/ www.visitrichmond.co.uk). Richmond tube/rail.* **Open** 10am-5pm Mon-Sat.

Southwark Tourist Information Centre *Tate Modern: Level 2, Bankside, SE1 9TG (7401 5266/www.visitsouth wark.com). St Paul's or Southwark tube.* **Open** 10am-6pm daily.

VISAS & IMMIGRATION

EU citizens do not require a visa to visit the UK; citizens of the USA, Canada, Australia, South Africa and New Zealand can also enter with only a passport for tourist visits of up to six months as long as they can show they are able to support themselves during their visit and plan to return home afterwards. Use www.ukvisas.gov.uk to check your visa status well before you travel, or contact the British embassy, consulate or high commission in your own country. You can arrange visas online at www.fco.gov.uk. For work permits, *see p376*.

Home Office *Border & Immigration Agency, Lunar House, 40 Wellesley Road, Croydon, Surrey CR9 2BY (immigration information 0870 606 7766/nationality information 0845 010 5200/www.ind.home office.gov.uk).* **Open** *Phone enquiries* 9am-4.45pm Mon-Thur; 9am-4.30pm Fri.

WEIGHTS & MEASURES

It has taken a considerable amount of time, and the intervention of the European authorities, but the UK is slowly moving towards full metrication. Distances are still measured in miles but all goods are officially sold in metric quantities, with no legal requirement for the imperial equivalent to be given. We've used the still more common imperial measurements throughout this guide.

Below are listed some useful conversions, first into metric figures and then from metric back to imperial:

1 inch (in) = 2.54 centimetres (cm)
1 yard (yd) = 0.91 metres (m)
1 mile = 1.6 kilometres (km)
1 ounce (oz) = 28.35 grammes (g)
1 pound (lb) = 0.45 kilogrammes (kg)
1 UK pint = 0.57 litres (l)
1 US pint = 0.8 UK pints or 0.46 litres

1 centimetre (cm) = 0.39 inches (in)
1 metre (m) = 1.094 yards (yd)
1 kilometre (km) = 0.62 miles
1 gramme (g) = 0.035 ounces (oz)
1 kilogramme (kg) = 2.2 pounds (lb)
1 litre (l) = 1.76 UK pints or 2.2 US pints

WHEN TO GO

Climate

The British climate is famously unpredictable, but Weathercall on 0906 850 0401 (60p/min) can offer some guidance. *See also below* **The Local Climate**. The best websites for weather news and features include **www.metoffice.gov.uk**, **www.weather.com** and **www.bbc.co.uk/london/ weather**, which all offer good detailed long-term forecasts and are easily searchable.

Spring extends from March to May, though frosts can last into April. March winds and April showers may be a month early or a month late, but May is often very pleasant.

Summer (June, July and August) can be very unpredictable, with searing heat one day followed by sultry greyness and violent thunderstorms the next. There are usually pleasant sunny days, though they vary greatly in number from year to year. High temperatures, humidity and pollution can create problems for those with hay fever or breathing difficulties, and temperatures down in the tube can be uncomfortably hot in rush hour. Do as the locals do and carry a bottle of water.

Autumn starts in September, although the weather can still have a mild, summery feel. Real autumn comes with October, when the leaves start to fall – on sunny days the red and gold leaves can be breathtaking. When the November cold, grey and wet sets in, though, you'll be reminded that London is situated on a northerly latitude.

Winter can have some delightful crisp, cold days, but don't bank on them. The usual scenario is for a disappointingly grey, wet Christmas, followed by a cold snap in January and February, when London may even see a sprinkling of snow – and immediate public transport chaos.

Public holidays

On public holidays (bank holidays), many shops remain open, but public transport services generally run to a Sunday timetable. On Christmas Day, almost everything, including public transport, closes down.

Good Friday Fri 10 Apr
Easter Monday Mon 13 Apr
May Day Holiday Mon 4 May
Spring Bank Holiday
　Mon 25 May
Summer Bank Holiday
　Mon 31 Aug
Christmas Day Fri 25 Dec
Boxing Day Sat 26 Dec
New Year's Day Fri 1 Jan

WOMEN

London is home to dozens of women's groups and networks, from day centres to rights campaigners; www.gn.apc.org and www.wrc.org.uk provide information and many links. It also has Europe's largest women's studies archive, the **Women's Library** (*see p371*).

For helplines, *see pp369*; for health issues, *see pp367-369*.

WORKING IN LONDON

Finding temporary work in London can be a full-time job. Ideas can be found in *Summer Jobs in Britain*, published by Vacation Work, 9 Park End Street, Oxford OX1 1HJ (£10.99 plus £1.75 p&p); its website is www.vacationwork. co.uk.

Work permits

With few exceptions, citizens of non-European Economic Area (EEA) countries have to have a work permit before they can legally work in the United Kingdom. Permits are issued only for high-level jobs.

Au Pair Scheme Citizens aged 17 to 27 from the following non-EEA countries (along, of course, with EEA nationals) are permitted to make an application to become au pairs: Andorra, Bosnia-Herzegovina, Bulgaria, Croatia, the Faroe Islands, Greenland, Macedonia, Monaco, Romania, San Marino, Turkey. See the various pages of www.workingintheuk. gov.uk for details, or contact the **Border & Immigration Agency** (*see below* **Home Office**).

Working holidaymakers
Citizens of Commonwealth countries aged from 17 to 27 are allowed to apply to come to the UK as a working holidaymaker. Start by contacting your nearest British diplomatic post in advance. You are then allowed to take part-time work without a DfEE permit. Contact the **Border & Immigration Agency** (*see below* **Home Office**) for more information.

Useful addresses

BUNAC *16 Bowling Green Lane, Clerkenwell, EC1R 0QH (7251 3472/www.bunac.org.uk). Farringdon tube/rail.* **Open** 9.30am-5.30pm Mon-Thur; 9.30am-5pm Fri. **Map** p402 N4.
Council on International Educational Exchange *300 Fore Street, Portland, ME 04101, USA (001-20 7553 4000/www.ciee. org).* **Open** 9am-5pm Mon-Fri. The CIEE helps young people to study, work and travel abroad.
Home Office *Border & Immigration Agency, Lunar House, 40 Wellesley Road, Croydon, Surrey CR9 2BY (0870 606 7766/www. ind.homeoffice.gov.uk).* **Open** *Phone enquiries* 9am-4.45pm Mon-Fri; 9am-4.30pm Fri. Advice on whether or not a work permit is required; application forms can be downloaded from the website.

THE LOCAL CLIMATE

Average temperatures and monthly rainfall in London.

	High (°C/°F)	Low (°C/°F)	Rainfall (mm/in)
Jan	6 / 43	2 / 36	54 / 2.1
Feb	7 / 44	2 / 36	40 / 1.6
Mar	10 / 50	3 / 37	37 / 1.5
Apr	13 / 55	6 / 43	37 / 1.5
May	17 / 63	8 / 46	46 / 1.8
June	20 / 68	12 / 54	45 / 1.8
July	22 / 72	14 / 57	57 / 2.2
Aug	21 / 70	13 / 55	59 / 2.3
Sept	19 / 66	11 / 52	49 / 1.9
Oct	14 / 57	8 / 46	57 / 2.2
Nov	10 / 50	5 / 41	64 / 2.5
Dec	7 / 44	4 / 39	48 / 1.9

Further Reference

BOOKS

Fiction & poetry

Peter Ackroyd *Hawksmoor; The House of Doctor Dee; Great Fire of London; The Lambs of London* Intricate studies of arcane London.
Monica Ali *Brick Lane* Arranged marriage in Tower Hamlets.
Martin Amis *London Fields* Darts and drinking way out east.
Jonathan Coe *The Dwarves of Death* Mystery, music, mirth, male violence and the like.
Norman Collins *London Belongs to Me* Witty saga of 1930s Kennington.
Sir Arthur Conan Doyle *The Complete Sherlock Holmes* Reassuring sleuthing shenanigans.
Joseph Conrad *The Secret Agent* Anarchism in seedy Soho.
Charles Dickens *Oliver Twist; David Copperfield; Bleak House; Our Mutual Friend* Four of the Victorian master's most London-centric novels.
Maureen Duffy *Capital* The bones beneath us and the stories they tell.
Christopher Fowler *Soho Black* Walking dead in Soho.
Anthony Frewin *London Blues* Kubrick assistant explores the 1960s Soho porn movie industry.
Graham Greene *The End of the Affair* Adultery and Catholicism during the Blitz.
Neil Hanson *The Dreadful Judgement* The embers of the Great Fire raked over.
Patrick Hamilton *Twenty Thousand Streets Under the Sky* Dashed dreams at the bar of the Midnight Bell in 1950s Fitzrovia.
Alan Hollinghurst *The Swimming Pool Library; The Line of Beauty* Gay life around Russell Square; beautiful, ruthless look at metropolitan debauchery – won the 2004 Booker.
Hanif Kureishi *The Buddha of Suburbia; Something to Tell You* Sexual confusion and identity crisis in the 1970s; psychoanalyst looks back at his experiences of the same.
Doris Lessing *The Golden Notebook; The Good Terrorist* Nobel winner's best London books.
Colin MacInnes *City of Spades; Absolute Beginners* Coffee 'n' jazz, Soho 'n' Notting Hill.

Derek Marlowe *A Dandy in Aspic* A capital-set Cold War classic.
Michael Moorcock *Mother London* A roomful of psychiatric patients kiss a love letter to London.
Alan Moore *From Hell* Amazing, dark graphic novel on the Ripper.
Daljit Nagra *Look We Have Coming to Dover!* Zesty poems of the British Indian experience.
George Orwell *Keep the Aspidistra Flying; Nineteen Eighty-Four* Saga of a struggling writer; bleak vision of totalitarianism.
Jonathan Raban *Soft City* Part autobiographical urban classic.
Derek Raymond *I Was Dora Suarez* The blackest London noir.
Nicholas Royle *The Matter of the Heart; The Director's Cut* Abandoned buildings and secrets.
Iain Sinclair *Downriver; Radon Daughters; White Chappell/Scarlet Tracings* The Thames's *Heart of Darkness*; East London Gothic novelists; the Ripper murders and shady book dealers.
Sarah Waters *Affinity; Nightwatch* Millbank's Octagon prison; World War II Home Front.
HG Wells *War of the Worlds* SF classic with Primrose Hill finale.
Virginia Woolf *Mrs Dalloway* A kind of London *Ulysses*.

Non-fiction

Peter Ackroyd *London: The Biography; Thames: Sacred River* Loving but wilfully obscurantist histories of the city and its river.
Nicholas Barton *The Lost Rivers of London* Fascinating studies of old watercourses and their legacy.
James Boswell *Boswell's London Journal 1762-1763* Rich account of a ribald literary life.
Ed Glinert *A Literary Guide to London; The London Compendium* Essential London minutiae.
Sarah Guy (ed) *Time Out Book of London Walks volumes 1 & 2* Writers, cartoonists, comedians and historians walk the capital.
Richard Hamblyn *The Invention of Clouds* London's 1800s science craze and the naming of the clouds.
Sarah Hartley *Mrs P's Journey* Biography of Phyllis Pearsall, the woman who created the *A–Z*.
Edward Jones & Christopher Woodward *A Guide to the*

Architecture of London A brilliant exploration of the subject.
Jack London *The People of the Abyss* Poverty in the East End.
Daniel Miller *The Comfort of Things* Anthropologist interviews residents of shabby London street.
Tim Moore *Do Not Pass Go* Monopoly addict's London.
Charles Nicholl *The Reckoning: The Murder of Christopher Marlowe; The Lodger: Shakespeare on Silver Street* Forensic studies of the great Elizabethan playwrights, with captivating period detail.
George Orwell *Down & Out in Paris & London* Waitering, begging and starving.
Samuel Pepys *Diaries* Plagues, fires and bordellos. (An entry a day is posted at www.pepysdiary.com.)
Liza Picard *Dr Johnson's London; Restoration London* London past, engagingly revisited.
Patricia Pierce *Old London Bridge* The story of the world's longest inhabited bridge.
Roy Porter *London: A Social History* An all-encompassing work.
Sukhdev Sandhu *Night Haunts* A night with London's helicopter police, Samaritans and exorcists.
Iain Sinclair *Lights Out for the Territory; London Orbital* Time-warp visionary crosses London; time-warp visionary prowls round London on the M25.
Iain Sinclair (ed) *London: City of Disappearances* Scraps, clippings and scribbled post-it notes from contemporary city mythologisers.
Stephen Smith *Underground London: Travels Beneath the City Streets* Absorbing writing on the subterranean city.
Richard Tames *Feeding London; East End Past* Eating history from coffee houses onwards; a close look at the East End.
Adrian Tinniswood *His Invention So Fertile* Illuminating biography of Sir Christopher Wren.
Richard Trench & Ellis Hillman *London Under London: A Subterranean Guide* Tunnels, lost rivers, disused tube stations, military bunkers – fascinating.
Ben Weinreb & Christopher Hibbert (eds) *The London Encyclopaedia* Brilliant, thorough, indispensable reference guide, thoroughly updated in 2008 by historians John and Julia Keay.

Jerry White *London in the 19th Century: 'A Human Awful Wonder of God'*; *London in the 20th Century: A City & Its People.* How London became a global city.

FILMS

A Clockwork Orange (Stanley Kubrick, 1971) Kubrick's vision still shocks – but so does Thamesmead, location for many Orange scenes.
Alfie (Lewis Gilbert, 1966) What's it all about, Michael?
Blow-Up (Michelangelo Antonioni, 1966) Swinging London caught in unintentionally hysterical fashion.
Bourne Ultimatum (Paul Greengrass, 2007) Pacy thriller with brilliantly staged CCTV scene in Waterloo station.
Breaking & Entering (Anthony Minghella, 2006) Star-studded thievery in Kings Cross.
Da Vinci Code (Ron Howard, 2006) Film version of Dan Brown's blockbuster novel, partly filmed in London (including Inner Temple).
Death Line (Gary Sherman, 1972) The last of a Victorian cannibal race is found in a lost tube station.
Dirty Pretty Things (Stephen Frears, 2002) Body organ smuggling among immigrants.
Eastern Promises (David Cronenberg, 2007) London-set Russian mafia flick, with brutal knife fight in the Finsbury Baths.
Harry Potter & the Order of the Phoenix (David Yates, 2007) Overlong, but with stunning aerial shots of London.
Jump London (Mike Christie, 2003) Insane traceurs hop all over the city's landmarks.
The Krays (Peter Medak, 1990) The life and times of the most notorious East End gangsters.
Life is Sweet; **Naked**; **Secrets & Lies**; **Vera Drake**; **Happy-Go-Lucky** (Mike Leigh, 1990-2008) Metroland; urban misanthropy; familial tensions; sympathy for post-war abortionist; day and night with a North London optimist.
Lock, Stock & Two Smoking Barrels; **Snatch**; **RocknRolla** (Guy Ritchie, 1998-2008) Former Mr Madonna's cheeky London faux-gangster flicks.
London; **Robinson in Space** (Patrick Keiller, 1994-1997) Quality arthouse fiction meets documentary.
The Long Good Friday (John MacKenzie, 1989) Bob Hoskins in the classic London gangster flick.
Mona Lisa; **The Crying Game** (Neil Jordan, 1986-1992) Prostitutes, terrorists, transvestites.

Notting Hill (Roger Michell, 1999) Hugh Grant and Julia Roberts get it on in west London.
Peeping Tom (Michael Powell, 1960) Powell's creepy murder flick: a young man films his dying victims.
Performance (Nicolas Roeg & Donald Cammell, 1970) This cult movie to end all cult movies made west London cool for life.
Somers Town (Shane Meadows, 2008) Sweet, slight tale of unlikely friends in love with the same girl.
28 Days Later (Danny Boyle, 2002) Post-apocalyptic London, with bravura opening sequence of the deserted streets.
Wonderland (Michael Winterbottom, 1999) Love, loss and deprivation in Soho.

MUSIC

Lily Allen *Alright, Still* Feisty, urban reggae-pop, still perfect for summer fun.
Babyshambles *Down in Albion* Pete Doherty's odd vision of an idealised England.
Blur *Modern Life is Rubbish*; *Parklife* Modern classics by the Essex exiles.
Billy Bragg *Must I Paint You a Picture? The Essential Billy Bragg* The bard of Barking's greatest hits.
The Bug *London Zoo* Boomtastic thrills amid the electronic gloom.
Burial *Untrue* Beautiful, menacing dubstep ode to the brooding city.
Chas & Dave *Don't Give a Monkey's* Cockney singalong revivalists hit the old joanna.
The Clash *London Calling* Epoch-making punk classic.
Dizzee Rascal *Maths + English* Rough-cut sounds and street-smart lyrics from grime's crossover king.
Ian Dury *New Boots & Panties* Cheekily essential listening from the Essex pub maestro.
Hot Chip *The Warning* Wonky electro-pop from the indie geeks.
The Jam *This is the Modern World* Weller at his splenetic finest.
The Kinks *Something Else* Classic album, 'Waterloo Sunset' and all.
Linton Kwesi Johnson *Dread, Beat an' Blood*; *Forces of Victory*; *Bass Culture* Angry reggae from the man Brixton calls 'the Poet'.
Madness *Rise & Fall* The nutty boys at their lyrical best.
The Real Tuesday Weld *The London Book of the Dead* Noir soundtrack stylings and literate lyrics of chiselled melancholy.
The Rolling Stones *December's Children (& Everybody's)* Moodily cool evocation of the city.

Saint Etienne *Tales from Turnpike House* Kitchen-sink opera by London-loving indie dance band.
Small Faces *Ogdens' Nut Gone Flake* Concept album by band fronted by East End-born Steve Marriott.
Squeeze *Greatest Hits* Lovable south London geezer pop.
The Streets *Original Pirate Material* Pirate radio urban meets Madness on Mike Skinner's finest geezer pop record.

WEBSITES

www.alwaystouchout.com The city's proposed and ongoing transport projects.
www.bbc.co.uk/london News, travel, weather, sport.
www.classiccafes.co.uk The city's finest 1950s and '60s caffs.
www.crockattandpowell. blogspot.com Independent bookstore holds forth.
http://diamondgeezer.blogspot. com Interesting and creative blogger on all things London.
www.filmlondon.org.uk
www.getlondonreading.co.uk/ Books-in-London Fun interactive map of London books by district.
www.gumtree.com Very useful online community noticeboard.
www.hidden-london.com The city's undiscovered gems.
http://londoncabby.blogspot. com Musings of a black cab driver.
www.london-footprints.co.uk Free walks to print out.
www.london.gov.uk The Greater London Assembly's official website.
www.londonremembers.com Excellent plaques and statues.
www.london2012.com/blog/ Official London Olympics site.
http://london-underground. blogspot.com Daily Tube blog.
www.pubs.com Trad boozers.
www.smokers-london. typepad.com Reviews and amenities identified for drinkers who haven't quit.
www.storyoflondon.com Superb historical resource.
www.streetsensation.co.uk Shopping streets navigable as a sequence of photos.
www.3ammagazine.com/3am/ buzzwords Literary blog.
www.timeout.com A vital source: our most recent eating and drinking reviews, features and events listings.
www.tfl.gov.uk/tfl Transport for London journey planners and maps.
www.victorianlondon.org
www.walklondon.org.uk
http://wildweb.london.gov.uk Wildlife in the city.

DIRECTORY

Index

Note: Page numbers in **bold** indicate section(s) giving key information on a topic; *italics* indicate photographs.

A

Abbey Road Studios 127
Abney Park Cemetery 132
abortion 369
accident & emergency services 367, 369
accommodation 166-196
apartment rental 195-196
by price: cheap 175-177, 179, 180-181, 183, 189, 192, 193, 195; deluxe 169, 171-173, 177-179, 181, 183-187, 189, 190-192; expensive 169, 170-171, 173-175, 179-180, 181, 187, 189-190, 192-193; moderate 167, 169-170, 171-173, 175, 180, 181-183, 187-189, 192, 193-194, 194-195
camping & caravanning 196
hostels 176
university residences 196
youth hostels 196
see also p386 Accommodation index
addresses 366
Adjaye, David 41
age restrictions 366
AIDS 369
airlines & airports 360
left luggage 370
lost property 371
Albert Memorial 121

Aldwych 86-87
Alexander Fleming Laboratory Museum 100
Alfred the Great 17
All Hallows by the Tower **68, 70**
All Saints 80
Almeida Theatre 132, 341
Alternative Fashion Week 270
apartment rental 195-196
Apsley House 106
aquarium 46
architecture 34-39, 41-42
Arsenal Football Club 132
art galleries 276-283
see also museums & galleries
ATMs 372

B

backpackers 176
bag shops 254
bakeries 256
Banglatown 134
Bank 64
Bank of England Museum **64, 66**
banks 372
Bankside 51-53
Bankside Gallery 51
Banqueting House **110, 111**
barbers 260
Barbican Art Gallery 63
Barbican Centre 63, **293, 307, 336**
Barnes 153
bars *see* pubs & bars
basketball 327
Battersea 153
Battersea Park 153
BBC 27
BBC Television Centre 161
Beating the Retreat 271

beer 232, 272
Belgravia 120
Benjamin Franklin House 86
Berwick Street 91
Bethnal Green 137-138
BFI Southbank **296, 299**
bicycles *see* cycling
Big Ben 112
Big Draw 274
Black Death 21
Blenheim 356-358
Blitz, the 27
Bloomsbury & Fitzrovia 75-80
accommodation 171-177
for children 285
pubs & bars 228-230
restaurants & cafés 203-206
boat services 363-364
tours 365
Bonfire Night 275
Bonnington Square 151
books & literature 377-378
shops 243-245
Borough 53
Borough Market 53, **258**
Bow Street Runners 24
breakdown services 364
Breakin' Convention 294
Brick Lane 134, *135*
restaurants & cafés 221
Brighton 348-351
Brit Oval 142, **328**
British Library 78, *79*
British Museum **76, 76, 77**
Brixton 151-153
Brixton Art Gallery 151
Broadcasting House 95
Broadwalk Ballroom 272

Brompton Oratory 120
Brunel Engine House & Tunnel Exhibition 145
BT Tower 80
Buckingham Palace & Royal Mews **106, 114, 115**
bureaux de change 372
Burston, Paul 304
bus services 108, **363**
Routemaster 108
tours 365
business services 366

C

Cabbages & Frocks market 99
Cabinet War Rooms & Churchill Museum 111
cafés *see* restaurants & cafés
Camberwell 143
Camden 125-127
Camden Market **125, 126, *126***
Camden Passage antiques market 131
Camley Street Natural Park 288
camping 196
Canterbury 351-354
Canute 17
caravanning 196
Carlyle's House 118, 119
cars & driving 364-365
Cartoon Museum 77
Cenotaph **110**, 275
Centre of the Cell 135
Ceremony of the Keys 268
Changing of the Guard 271
Chap Olympiad 272
Charing Cross Station 85
Charles Dickens Museum **75, 77**

INDEX

Charles I 23
Chelsea 117-119
  accommodation
    189-190
  pubs & bars 235-236
  restaurants & cafés
    216-217
  shops 247
Chelsea Embankment
  118-119
Chelsea Old Church
  118, **119**
Chelsea Physic
  Garden **117**, **119**
Chessington World
  of Adventures 289
Cheyne walk 118-119
children 284-289
  areas 284-286
  eating & drinking
    286-288
  entertainment
    288-289
  festivals 287
  play spaces 289
  shops & services
    246-247
Chinatown 93
  restaurants & cafés
    206
Chinese New Year
  Festival 269
Chislehurst 150
Chiswick 161-163
Chiswick House **161**,
  162
Christ Church
  Spitalfields 133
Christmas
  Celebrations 275
Christmas markets
  274
Churchill, Winston 53
cinemas 297-299
City, the 57-71
  accommodation
    169-170
  for children 285
  pubs & bars 227
  restaurants & cafés
    199-201
City Hall 37, 55, *56*
City of London
  Information
  Centre 57
Clapham 153
Clapham Common
  153
Clarence House 116
Clerkenwell 74
climate 376

Clink Prison Museum
  51
Clissold Park 132
Clockmakers'
  Museum & Library
  65, **66**
clothes shops 249-253
Cnut 17
coach services 360
cocktails 228, 237
Coin Street Festival
  271
College of Arms 61
comedy 290-292
Comedy Store 290,
  291
complementary
  medicine 369
Conan Doyle, Sir
  Arthur 95, 99
conference centres 366
congestion charge 364
Conran, Terence 186
Constable, John 129
consulates 367
consumer advice 366
contraception 369
convention centres
  366
Coram's Fields 289
Country Affair, A 273
County Hall 44
courier services 366
Courtauld Gallery 86
**Covent Garden &
  the Strand** 81-87
  accommodation 177
  for children 285
  pubs & bars 230-231
  restaurants & cafés
    206-208
  shops 246
Covent Garden May
  Fayre & Puppet
  Festival 271
cricket 328
Cromwell, Oliver 23
Crown Jewels 71
Crystal Palace 25,
  144
customs 366
Cutty Sark 146
cycling 328, 365

D

Daily Express
  building 39, 58
Dali Universe **44**, **45**
Dalston 132

dance 293-295
Darwin, Charles 148
Dennis Severs' House
  133, **134**
dentists 369
Design Museum 56,
  186
dialling codes 374
Diana, Princess of
  Wales Memorial
  Playground 124,
  288, 289
disabled access
  366-367
Discover 289
Diwali 275
Docklands 138-140
Docklands Light
  Railway (DLR) 363
Dr Johnson's House
  59
Down House **148**,
  148, **150**
driving *see* cars
  & driving
drugs 367
Dulwich 143-145
Dulwich Picture
  Gallery 144, *144*
Dungeness 354-356

E

Earl's Court 160-161
East London
  133-141
  accommodation
    193-194
  nightlife 323-326
  pubs & bars 238
  restaurants & cafés
    223-224
  shops 247
East London Mosque
  135
Edgware Road 100
  restaurants & cafés
    216
Edward the Confessor
  17
Electric Avenue 153,
  155
electricity 367
electronics shops 249
Elephant & Castle 142
Elizabeth I 21
Eltham Palace 150
Embankment 83-86
Embankment
  Galleries 87

embassies 367
emergency services
  367, **369**
Emirates Stadium
  132, 329
Estorick Collection
  of Modern Italian
  Art 132
events *see* festivals
  & events
excursions
  346-358
Exhibition Road
  Music Day 271

F

Fan Museum 146
Faraday Museum
  104, *104*, **105**
farms, city 288
Farringdon 74
fashion 41, 249-256
  accessories &
    services 253-256
fast food 207
Fawkes, Guy 21
Fenton House **127**,
  129
festivals & events
  268-275
  art & design 281
  classical music 310
  dance 295
  film 297, 298
  for children 287
  gay & lesbian 301
  jazz music 318
  rock, pop & roots
    music 312
  sports 332-333
  theatre 343
Fielding, Henry 24
film 296-299
  cinemas 297-299
  set in London 378
Fire of 1666 *see*
  Great Fire
Firepower 149
Fitzrovia 79-80
Fleet River 74
Fleet Street 57-59
Fleming, Alexander
  100
Flora London
  Marathon 270, *272*
Florence Nightingale
  Museum 45
food & drink shops
  256-259

football 329
Fortnum & Mason
 105, **242**
Foster, Lord Norman
 39
Foundling Museum
 77
Foyles **243**, **262**
Franklin, Benjamin 86
Freewheel 273
Freud Museum 129
Fulham 160-161
Fulham Palace &
 Museum **160**,
 160, **161**
Fuller's Brewery
 161, **162**

G

Gabriel's Wharf 49
Garden Museum 45
Gatwick Airport 360
gay & lesbian
 300-306
 clubs 302-303
 help & information
 367
 pubs & bars 303-306
 restaurants & cafés
 300-301
 sex clubs & saunas
 306
Geffrye Museum 137
General Strike of 1926
 27
'Gherkin', the 68, *69*
gift shops 259
gin 24
Gog and Magog 67
Golden Hinde 51
golf 331
Great British Beer
 Festival 272
Great Fire 23, 35, 66
Great Gorilla Run 273
Great River Race 273
Greater London
 Council (GLC) 28
Green Chain Walk
 150
Green Park 105-106
Greenfield, Baroness
 Susan 104
Greenwich 146
 for children 286
Greenwich Peninsula
 Ecology Park 146,
 288
Greyhound racing 329

Groucho Club 89
Guards Museum
 114, **115**
Guildhall **65**, **67**
Guildhall Art Gallery
 65, **67**
Gun Salutes 268
Gunpowder Plot, the
 21
Gurdwara Sri Guru
 Singh Sabha
 Southall 164

H

Hackney 140
hairdressers 260
Half Moon Young
 People's Theatre
 289
Ham House 156
Hammersmith 161
Hampstead 127-131
Hampstead Heath
 127, **128**, *130*
 walk 128-129
Hampton Court
 Palace **156**, **157**
Handel House
 Museum **103**,
 103, **105**
Handel, George
 Frideric 77,
 105, 308
Harley Street 95
Harriot, Thomas 164
Harrods 120, **242**
Harvey Nichols 120
hat shops 254
Hayward 48, 49
health & beauty
 shops 260-263
health clubs 331
health services
 291-293
Heathrow Airport 360
helicopter tours 365
helplines 370
Henry VIII 21, 71
Highbury Fields 132
Highgate 131
Highgate Cemetery
 131
Hippodrome, 93
history 16-30
 key events 30
HIV 369
HMS Belfast **55**, **56**
Hogarth's House **161**,
 162

Holborn &
 Clerkenwell
 72-74
 accommodation
 170-171
 pubs & bars 227-228
 restaurants & cafés
 201-203
Holland Park
 159-160
Horniman Museum
 144, *145*
Horse Guards Parade
 271
horse racing 330
horse riding 333
hospitals 369
hostels 176
hotels *see*
 accommodation
house & home shops
 263-264
House of Commons 19
House of Lords 19
Household Cavalry
 Museum **114**, **115**
Houses of Parliament
 110, **111**
Hoxton 137
Hunter, John 73
Hunterian Museum
 72, **73**
Hyde Park 124, *124*

I

ICA **114**, **115**
ID 370
immigration 375
Imperial College 121
Imperial War
 Museum 142, *143*
insurance 370
internet
 access 370
 useful websites 378
Isle of Dogs 139-140
Islington Museum
 131, **132**
Iveagh Bequest **129**,
 130

J

Jack the Ripper 135
James II 23
jazz 317-318
Jewel Tower 111
jewellery shops 255

Jewish Book Week
 269
John Wesley's House
 & Museum of
 Methodism **63**, **64**
Johnson, Boris 108
Jones, Inigo 35
Joseph Grimaldi
 Memorial Service
 269

K

Keats House **129**,
 130
Kennington 142-143
Kensal Green
 Cemetery 101
Kensington 159-160
Kensington Gardens
 124
Kensington Palace
 124
Kenwood
 House/Iveagh
 Bequest **129**, **130**
Kew 155-156
Kew Bridge Steam
 Museum **161**,
 162, **163**, *163*
Kew Spring Festival
 270
King's Cross 78
 nightlife 320-321
King's Head 132, 343
King's Road 117
Klinker 316
Knightsbridge
 & South
 Kensington
 120-124
 accommodation
 190-192
 pubs & bars 236
 restaurants & cafés
 217-218
 shops 247

L

Lamb's Conduit Street
 265
Lambeth Palace 45
left luggage 370
legal assistance 370
Leicester Square **91**,
 91, **93**
libraries 371
Limehouse 139

INDEX

Limehouse Basin **132, 139**
Lincoln's Inn Fields 72
lingerie & underwear shops 255
Linley Sambourne House 160
Little Angel Theatre *285*, 288
Little Portugal 151
Livingstone, Ken 28, 29,108
Lloyd George, David 27
London Aquarium **44, 46**
London Bridge 55
London Bridge Experience **53, 55**
London Canal Museum **78, 79**
London County Council (LCC) 27
London Dungeon 53
London Eye **44**, *45*, **46**
London Fashion & Textile Museum 56
London International Mime Festival 269
London Literature Festival 272
London Mela 273
London Stone 65
London to Brighton Veteran Car Run 274
London Transport Museum 82, *82*
London Underground 25, **361**
London Zoo 39, **99**, 126, **288**
Lord Mayor's Show 275
Lord's cricket ground 127
lost property 371
luggage shops 254

M

MacDonald, Ramsay 27
Madame Tussauds **95, 97**
magazines 371
Magna Carta 19
major museums 277

Mansion House 65
marathon 270, *272*
Marble Arch **94, 95**
Marble Hill House **156, 158**
markets 243, 258
Marylebone 95-97
shops 246
Marylebone Cricket Club (MCC) Museum 127
Matthews, Jessie 89
Mayfair 103-105
shops 246
media 371-372
Merrick, Joseph 'the Elephant Man' 135
Metroland 27
military parades 271
Millbank 112-113
Millennium Bridge 51, 61, *62*
Millennium Dome *see* O2
money 372
Monument **66**, *66*, **67**
motorsport 330
Mount Street 254
Movieum **44, 46**
Mudchute Park & Farm 139
Museum & Library of the Order of St John 74
Museum of Brands, Packaging & Advertising 101
Museum of Childhood 137
Museum of London 63
Museum of London Docklands **139**, **140**, *141*
Museum of Methodism **63, 64**
Museum of St Bartholomew's Hospital 63
museums & galleries
archeology: British Museum **76**, *76*, **77**; Petrie Museum of Egyptian Archaeology 78
art: Bankside Gallery 51; Barbican Art Gallery 63; Cartoon Museum 77; Courtauld

Gallery 86; Dali Universe **44, 45**; Dulwich Picture Gallery 144, *144*; Embankment Galleries 87; Estorick Collection of Modern Italian Art 132; Guildhall Art Gallery **65**, **67**; Hayward 48, 49; Hogarth's House **161, 162**; ICA **114, 115**; Kenwood House/Iveagh Bequest **129**, **130**; National Gallery 107, *109*; National Portrait Gallery 109; Orleans House Gallery **156, 158**; Royal Academy of Arts 105, 106; Saatchi Gallery 118; Victoria & Albert Museum **121, 122**
canals: London Canal Museum **78, 79**
childhood: Foundling Museum 77; Pollock's Toy Museum 80; Ragged School Museum 138; V&A Museum of Childhood 138
clocks: Clockmakers' Museum & Library **65, 66**
design: Design Museum 56, **186**; Geffrye Museum 137
fans: Fan Museum 146
fashion: London Fashion & Textile Museum 56
finance: Bank of England Museum **64, 66**
gardens: Garden Museum 45
general interest: British Museum **76**, *76*, **77**;

Horniman Museum 144, *145*
historic buildings: Apsley House 106; Banqueting House **110, 111**; Buckingham Palace & Royal Mews **106, 114**, *115*; Chiswick House **161, 162**; Clarence House 116; Dennis Severs' House **133, 134**; Eltham Palace 150; Fenton House **127, 129**; Fulham Palace & Museum **160**, *160*, **161**; Guildhall **65, 67**; Ham House 156; Hampton Court Palace **156, 157**; Hogarth's House **161, 162**; Kensington Palace 124; Kenwood House/Iveagh Bequest **129**, **130**; Linley Sambourne House 160; Marble Hill House **156, 158**; Old Royal Naval College *38*; Queen's House 147; Red House 150; Spencer House 116; Sutton House 140; Syon House **162,163**; Tower of London **68**, *70*, 71
horror: London Dungeon 53
literary: Carlyle's House 118, 119; Charles Dickens Museum **75, 77**; Dr Johnson's House 59; Freud Museum 129; Keats House **129**, **130**; Sherlock Holmes Museum 99
local history: Museum of London 63;

INDEX

Museum of London Docklands **139**, **140**, *141*; North Woolwich Old Station Museum 149
maritime: Cutty Sark 146; Golden Hinde 51; HMS Belfast **55**, **56**; National Maritime Museum 147
medical: Alexander Fleming Laboratory Museum 100; Faraday Museum **104**, *104*, **105**; Florence Nightingale Museum 45; Freud Museum 129; Old Operating Theatre, Museum & Herb Garret 53; Museum of St Bartholomew's Hospital 63
music: Fenton House **127**, **129**; Musical Museum **161**, **163**
natural history: Natural History Museum **121**, **123**
prisons: Clink Prison Museum 51
religions: John Wesley's House & Museum of Methodism **63**, **64**; Museum & Library of the Order of St John 74
science: Planetarium *147*, 149; Science Museum **121**, **122**
sport: Marylebone Cricket Club (MCC) Museum 127; Wimbledon Lawn Tennis Museum 156, *157*; World Rugby Museum/Twickenham Stadium **156**, **158**

technology: Kew Bridge Steam Museum **161**, **162**, **163**, *163*; Three Mills Island 141; Tower Bridge Exhibition 56, 71
transport: London Transport Museum 82, *82*
war: Cabinet War Rooms & Churchill Museum 111; Firepower 149; Guards Museum **114**, **115**; Imperial War Museum 142, *143*; National Army Museum **118**, **119**; Winston Churchill's Britain at War Experience 53
waxworks: Madame Tussauds **95**, **97**
wine: Vinopolis **51**, **52**
music 307-318 classical & opera 307-311 jazz 317-318 local artists 378 rock, pop & roots 311-317 shops 264 Music Village 272 musical instruments shops 265 musicals 339-341 Musical Museum **161**, **163**

N

Nash, John 37
National Army Museum **118**, **119**
National Gallery 107, *109*
National Maritime Museum 147
National Portrait Gallery 109
National Science & Engineering Week 270
National Sports Centre 144, 327

National Theatre 336
Natural History Museum **121**, **123**
Nelson's Column 107, *108*
New Year's Eve Celebrations 275
newspapers 371
nightlife 319-326
North London 125-132 accommodation 192-193 nightlife 321-323 pubs & bars 236-238 restaurants & cafés 221-223 shops 247
North Woolwich Old Station Museum 149
Notting Hill 101 shops 246
Notting Hill Carnival 273
Nunhead 143

O

Odeon Leicester Square 93
office services 366
Old Bailey 61
Old Compton Street 89-91
Old Curiosity Shop 72
Old Operating Theatre, Museum & Herb Garret 53
Old Royal Naval College *38*
Old Vic 51, **337**
One Canada Square 139
Open Garden Squares Weekend 271
Open House London 273
opening hours 373
opera 307-311
opticians 260
Orleans House Gallery **156**, **158**
Orton, Joe 131
O2 **146**, **313**
Oxford & Cambridge Boat Race 270
Oxford Circus 94

Oxford Street & Marylebone 94-99 accommodation 179-181 pubs & bars 233-234 restaurants & cafés 212-213 shops 246 walk 96-97
Oxo Tower Wharf 49

P

Paddington & Notting Hill 100-101 accommodation 181-183 restaurants & cafés 218-221
Pancake Day Races 269
parking 364
parliament 19
Parliament Square 110
Pearly Kings & Queens Harvest Festival 273
Peckham 143
Petrie Museum of Egyptian Archaeology 78
Peyton, Oliver 219, *219*
pharmacies **261**, **369**
photography galleries 283 shops 249
Piccadilly 105-106
Piccadilly Circus & Mayfair 102-106 accommodation 183-187 pubs & bars 234-235 restaurants & cafés 213-215
pilates 334
plague 21, 23
Planetarium *147*, 149
police stations 373
Pollock's Toy Museum 80
Portland Place 95
Portobello Green Market 101
Portobello Road 101

INDEX

INDEX

postal services 373
Princess Diana
Memorial Fountain
124
Proms, the 310
public holidays 376
public transport
361-364
lost property 371
pubs & bars
226-240
best, the 231
in hotels 191
*see also p387 Pubs
& Bars index*
Puppet Theatre Barge
288
Putney 153-155

Q

Queen Victoria 24, 26
Queen's House 147

R

radio 371
Ragged School
Museum 138
rail *see* train services
Red House 150
Regent Street 102
Regent's Canal 126
Regent's Park 99, *99*
religion 373-374
Remembrance
Sunday Ceremony
275
Rennie, Sir John 55
**restaurants &
cafés** 197-225
*see also p386
Restaurants &
Cafés index*
Richmond 155-156
Richmond Park 156
Ritz, the 106
river services *see*
boat services
Rivington Place 41,
137
Romans 17, 19
Romney 354-356
Ronnie Scott's 318
Roof Gardens 159
Rose, the 51
Rotherhithe 145-146
Roundhouse 313
Routemaster 108

Royal Academy of
Arts 105, 106
Royal Academy of
Music 95
Royal Albert Hall 121,
294, **309**
Royal Botanic
Gardens, Kew 132,
155
Royal College of Art
121
Royal College of
Music 121
Royal Courts of
Justice **86**, **87**
Royal Exchange 65
Royal Festival Hall 47
Royal Hospital
Chelsea **118**,
119, *119*
Royal Institution &
Faraday Museum
104, *104*, **105**
Royal National
Theatre 49
Royal Observatory
146, *147*, **149**
Royal Opera House
83, 294, **311**
Royal Shakespeare
Company **337**, **340**
Royal Vauxhall
Tavern 151, *158*
rugby 331
Russell, John (first
Earl of Bedford) 81
Russian Winter
Festival 269
Rye 354-356

S

Saatchi Gallery 118
Sadler's Wells 294
safety 374
St Bartholomew-the-
Great (St Bart's)
62, **63**, *64*
St Botolph's without
Aldgate **68**, **70**
St Bride's Church **57**,
58, **59**
St Ethelburga Centre
for Reconciliation
& Peace 70
St Etheldreda **72**, **73**
St George's
Bloomsbury 78
St Helen's
Bishopsgate **68**, **70**

St James's 116
shops 246
St James's Palace 116
St James's Park 114
St James's Piccadilly
106
St John's, Smith
Square 112
St John's Wood 127
St Magnus the Martyr
67
St Margaret's Church
112
St Martin-in-the-
Fields 85, **107**,
110, *110*
St Pancras Gardens
79
St Pancras
International 38,
78, **79**, *80*
St Pancras Old
Church 79
St Patrick's Day
Parade & Festival
270
St Paul's Cathedral
36, **59**, **61**, *62*
St Paul's Covent
Garden **81**, **83**, **85**
Savile Row 103
Savoy **85**, **86**
Science Museum
121, **122**
Scott, Sir George
Gilbert 38
Scottee 42, *42*
Screen on the Green
cinema 132, 298
Selfridges 94, **243**
Serpentine Gallery
124
Shaftesbury Avenue
102
Shaftesbury Memorial
102
Shakespeare's
Birthday 270
Shakespeare's Globe
51, **337**
Shepherd Market 105
Shepherd's Bush 161
Sherlock Holmes
Museum 99
shoe shops 255
shops & services
241-265
best areas 246-247
department stores
242-243
markets 243, 258

shopping centres &
arcades 241-242
see also specific
products
Shoreditch 137
Shri Swaminarayan
Mandir 164
Sir John Soane's
Museum **72**, **73**
skateboarding 333
Sloane Square 117
Smithfield Market
62, 74
smoking 374
Soane, Sir John 37,
144
**Soho & Leicester
Square** 88-93
accommodation
177-179
pubs & bars 231-233
restaurants & cafés
208-212
shops 246
walk 92-93
Soho Square 88-89, *89*
Somerset House &
the Embankment
Galleries **85**,
87, *87*
see also Courtauld
Gallery
**South Bank &
Bankside** 44-56
accommodation 167
for children 284
pubs & bars 226-227
restaurants & cafés
197-199
South-east London
142-150
accommodation 194
pubs & bars 239
restaurants & cafés
224-225
South Kensington
121-123
for children 286
shops 247
South London Gallery
143, 282
**South-west
London** 151-158
accommodation 194
pubs & bars 239-240
restaurants & cafés
225
Southall 163-164
Southall Market 163
Southbank Centre **47**,
295, 309

Southwark Cathedral 53
souvenir shops 258
spas & salons 261
Speakers' Corner 124
Spencer House 116
Spill – Edition 2 270
Spitalfields 133-134
Spitalfields Market **133**, *134*, **243**
sport & fitness 327-334
  events 332-333
  participation & fitness 331-334
  shops 265
  spectator sports 327-331
sports centres 331
Square Mile 57
Stamford Bridge 160
Stansted Airport 360
State Opening of Parliament 275
STDs 369
Stockwell 151-153
Stoke Newington 132
Strand, the 83-86
Stratford 141
Stuarts 25
Sutton House 140
Sweeney Todd 59
swimming 333
Syon House **162,163**

T

Tate Britain **112, 113**
Tate Modern **51, 52**, *52*, 61
tattoos & piercings 262-263
tax 373
taxis 364
  lost property 371
  tours 365
telephones & dialling codes 374-375
television 372
Temple Church *58*, 59
tennis 331, 334
ten pin bowling 334
Thames 357
Thames Barrier 149
Thames Barrier Information & Learning Centre 149

Thames Festival 273
Thatcher, Margaret 28
theatre 335-344
  for children 289
  long-runners & musicals 339-341
  off-West End 341-344
  West End 336-339
theme parks 289
30 St Mary Axe 'the Gherkin' 68, *69*
Thorpe Park 289
Three Mills 141
Three Mills Island 141
time 375
tipping 375
toilets 375
Topolski Century 46
tourist information 375
tours 365
Tower Bridge 55, **68, 71**
Tower Bridge Exhibition 56, 71
Tower of London **68, 70**, 71
toy shops 247
Trafalgar Square 107-110, 268
  for children 285
Trafalgar Square Festival 273
train services 360-361, 363
  left luggage 370
Tramlink 363
transport *see* public transport
travel advice 366
Trocadero 102
Trooping of the Colour 271
tube *see* London Underground
Tudors 21
Twickenham Stadium **156, 158**
2 Willow Road **129, 131**
Tyler, Wat 21

U

Unicorn Theatre 289
university residences 196

V

V&A *see* Victoria & Albert Museum
V&A Museum of Childhood 138
Vauxhall 151-153
Victoria & Albert Museum **121, 122**
Victoria 113-114
  see also Queen Victoria
Vikings 17
Vinopolis **51, 52**
visas 375
Vortex Jazz Club 132, *318*

W

walking 365
  Green Chain Walk 150
  tours 365
walks (self-guided)
  Hampstead Heath 128-129
  Oxford Street 96-97
  Soho 92-93
Wallace Collection 97
Walpole, Sir Robert 23
Walthamstow Village **140, 141**
Wandsworth 153
Wapping 139
Waterloo 49
Waterloo Bridge 49
weather 376
weights & measures 375
Wellcome Collection 78
Wellington Arch 106
Wellington, Duke of 106
Wembley Stadium 327, *329*
West End Theatres 336-339
West London 159-164
  accommodation 194-195
  nightlife 326
  pubs & bars 240
  restaurants & cafés 225

West Soho 91-93
Westminster & St James's 107-116
  accommodation 187-189
  pubs & bars 235
  restaurants & cafés 216
Westminster Abbey **111, 112**
Westminster Cathedral 113
Whispering Gallery 62
Whitechapel 134-136
Whitechapel Art Gallery **135, 136**, *136*
Whitechapel Bell Foundry 135
Whitehall 110
Whittington, Richard 'Dick' 65, 131
Who Do You Think You Are? Live 270
Wibbley Wobbly barge 145
Wigmore Hall 97, 309
William Morris Gallery 141
William, Duke of Normandy 17
Wimbledon 156
Wimbledon Championships 331
Wimbledon Lawn Tennis Museum 156, *157*
Winston Churchill's Britain at War Experience 53
women 376
Woodstock 356-358
Woolwich Arsenal 149
working in London 376
World Rugby Museum/ Twickenham Stadium **156, 158**
World War I 27
World War II 27
Wren, Sir Christopher 23, 35, 36, 61, 66
WWT Wetland Centre 155

INDEX

Y

yoga 334
youth hostels 196

Z

zeppelin raids 27
zoos 39, **99**, 126, **288**

ACCOMMODATION INDEX

Academy Hotel 173
Andaz Liverpool
  Street 169, *169*
Apex City of London
  Hotel 169
Arosfa 175
Ashlee House 175
Aster House 192
B+B Belgravia 187,
  189
Baglioni 190
Base2Stay 194
Bentley 190
Blakes 191
Brown's 183
Cadogan 189
Charlotte Street Hotel
  171
Church Street Hotel
  194
City Inn Westminster
  187
Claridge's 183
Clink Hostel 175, *176*
Colonnade 193
Connaught 184,
  184-185
Covent Garden Hotel
  177
Cumberland 179
Dorchester 184
EasyHotel 195
Fox & Anchor 171,
  173
Garden Court Hotel
  183
Gore 191
Guesthouse West 181
Halkin 191
Hampstead Village
  Guesthouse 193
Harlingford Hotel 175
Haymarket Hotel 185
Hazlitt's 179
Hempel 181
High Road House 194

Hotel 55 195
Hoxton Hotel 193
Jenkins Hotel 175
Lanesborough 191
Malmaison 170
Mayflower Hotel 195
Meininger 192
Metropolitan 185
Milestone Hotel &
  Apartments 192
Miller's Residence 181
Montagu Place 179
Morgan 177
Morgan House 189
Myhotel Bloomsbury
  173
Myhotel Chelsea 189,
  190
New Linden 181
No.5 Maddox Street
  185
Number Sixteen 192
One Aldwych 177
Park Plaza County
  Hall 167
Pavilion 183
Piccadilly
  Backpackers 179
Portobello Hotel *180*,
  181
Premier Inn London
  County Hall 167
Ritz 187
Rockwell 195
Rookery 170
Sanderson 173
Sherlock Holmes
  Hotel 179
Soho Hotel 177
Southwark Rose 167
St James's Hotel &
  Club 187
St Martins Lane Hotel
  177
Stylotel 183
Sumner 180
Threadneedles 169
Trafalgar 187
Twenty Nevern
  Square 195
22 York Street 180
Vancouver Studios
  183
Vicarage Hotel 192
Weardowney
  Guesthouse 180
Windermere Hotel 189
Windmill on the
  Common 194
York & Albany 192
Zetter 170

RESTAURANTS & CAFES INDEX

Abeno Too 206
Amaya 217
Anchor & Hope 197
Arbutus 208
Assaggi 218, *225*
Atelier de Joël
  Robuchon, L' 206
Autre Pied, L' 212
Balans 300
Baltic 199
Baozi Inn 208
Bar Shu 208
Bentley's Oyster Bar
  & Grill 213
Bincho 199, *201*
Bistrotheque 223
Bluebird 216
Bodean's 199
Botanist 216
Brick Lane Beigel
  Bake 223
Busaba Eathai 209
Café Anglais, Le 218,
  220
Camino 203
Cha Cha Moon *207*,
  209
Chez Bruce 225
Chutney Mary 217
Cinnamon Club 216
Clarke's 225
Clerkenwell Kitchen
  201
Comptoir Gascon, Le
  202
Cow 218
Dehesa 209, *211*
Duke of Cambridge
  221
E Pellicci 223
Eagle 202
Eyre Brothers 223
Fairuz 212
Fernandez & Wells
  211
First Out 301
Fish Central 201, *203*
Food for Thought 206
Frizzante@Hackney
  City Farm 286
Fromagerie, La 213
Galvin Bistrot de
  Luxe 213
Gate 225
Gaucho Piccadilly 214
Geales 218
Giaconda Dining
  Room 203

Giraffe 286
Glasshouse 225
Golden Hind 213
Great Queen Street
  206
Gun 224
Haché 221
Hakkasan 205
Hereford Road 218
Hibiscus 214
Hix Oyster & Chop
  House 202
Hummingbird Bakery
  217
Hummus Bros 211
Inn The Park 216
Inside 224
J Sheekey 206
Kiasu 220
Kolapata 224
Konstam at the Prince
  Albert 205
Landau 205
Ledbury 220
Little Lamb 211
M Manze 199
Magdalen 199
Maison Bertaux 211
Manna 221
Masala Zone 221
Maze 214
Meals 205
Modern Pantry 202
Momo 214
Morgan M 222
Moro 202
Mudchute Kitchen
  287
Nahm 217
National Dining
  Rooms 216
Nordic Bakery 211
Northbank 201
Olivomare 218
Ooze 205
Osteria Stecca 222
Ottolenghi 222
Parlour 214
Pavilion Tea House
  225
Petite Maison, La 215
Providores & Tapa
  Room 213, *214*
Quo Vadis 211
Racine 218, *222-223*
Rainforest Café 287
Randall & Aubin 301
Red Fort 211
Rhodes W1 213
River Café 225
Roast 199

Rock & Sole Plaice 207
Royal China Club 213
S&M Café 222
Sake No Hana 216
Salt Yard 205
Sauterelle 201
Scoop 207
Scott's 215, *217*
Sketch 215
Snazz Sichuan 205
Sông Quê 224
Spiga 212
St John 202
St John 203
Story Deli 224
Sweetings 201
Tamarind 215
Taqueria 221
Tate Modern Café: Level 2 287
Tea Smith 224
TGI Friday's 287
That Place on the Corner 288
Tom's Kitchen 217
Trois Garçons, Les 224
Tsuru 199
Urban Turban 221
Wagamama 205
Wahaca 208
Wapping Food 224
Wild Honey 215
Wolseley 215
Yauatcha 212, *213*
Yoshino 215
Zuma 218

PUBS & BARS INDEX

Albannach 235
Albert & Pearl 236
All Star Lanes 228
Amuse Bouche 231
Apartment 195 235
Artesian 233
Bar du Musee 239
Barcode Vauxhall 303
Big Chill Bar 238
Black Cap 303
Black Friar 227
Boisdale 235, *240*
Botanist on the Green 240
Box 303
Bradley's Spanish Bar 229
Café Kick 227

Carpenter's Arms 238
Champagne Bar at St Pancras *227*, 229
Coburg Bar 234
Commercial Tavern 238
Crown & Goose 236
Dreambags-jaguarshoes 238
Duke of Wellington 233
Dukes Hotel 235
Edge 303
Effra 240
Enclave 303
Florence 239
Floridita 231, *234*
Fox & Hounds 236
Freedom Bar 303
French House 231
Galvin at Windows 234
G-A-Y Bar 304
Gilgamesh 236
Glass Bar 304
Gordon's 230
Grapes 238
Green Carnation 305
Greenwich Union 239
Hawksmoor 238
Hoist 305
Holly Bush 237
King Charles I 237
KW4 305
LAB 231
Ladbroke Arms 240
Lamb & Flag 230
Lamb 229
Library 236
Lobby Bar 230
Loft 239
Long Bar 229
Lonsdale 233
Lost Society 240
Loungelover 239
Nag's Head 236
190 236
Only Running Footman 234, *239*
Player 231
Princess Louise *230*, 231
Profile 305
Retro Bar 305
Royal Oak 226
Rupert Street 306
Seven Stars 228
Shadow Lounge 306
Shochu Lounge 230, *237*
Skylon 226

Speaker 235
Three Kings of Clerkenwell 228
Trailer Happiness 233
Two Brewers 306
Two Floors 233
Vertigo 42 227
Vinoteca 228, *229*
Wenlock Arms 238
Westbourne House 234
White Horse 240
Wine Wharf 227
Yard 306
Ye Old Mitre 228

Advertisers' Index

Please refer to the relevant pages for contact details

Lion King	**IFC**

In Context

Beatles Store	**14**
Bistro 1	**14**
It's only Rock 'n' Roll	**14**
National Maritime Museum	**18**
Queens House	**18**
Royal Observatory	**18**
Cass Art	**22**

Sights

London Eye	**46**
Science Museum	**46**
London Aquarium	**50**
Geffrye Museum	**54**
Keats House	**54**
Shakespeare's Globe	**54**
Museum of London	**60**
Museum of London Docklands	**60**
Museum of the Order of St John	**84**
Freud Museum London	**84**
HMS Belfast	**84**
Imperial War Museum London	**84**
Churchill Museum and Cabinet War Rooms	**84**
Charles Dickens Museum	**90**
Ragged School Museum	**90**
Wallace Collection	**90**
Spencer House	**98**
Wellcome Collection	**98**
British Library	**98**
V&A	**154**
London Canal Museum	**154**

Consume

Hotels

londontown.com	**168**
Lincoln House Hotel	**172**
Abbey Court	**172**
Clink Hostel	**172**
Ashlee House	**172**
LSE	**174**
Hampstead Village Guesthouse	**174**
Hart House Hotel	**174**
Stylotel	**178**
Cardiff Hotel	**178**
Garden Court Hotel	**182**
Falcon Hotel	**182**
Barry House	**182**
Vandon House	**182**
Strand Palace Hotel	**188**
Sagar	**188**

Restaurants

Sagar	**198**
Hard Rock Cafe	**200**
Wagamama	**204**
Ekin	**210**
Modhubon	**210**
Sông Quê Café	**210**

Shops

Eastpak	**244**
Milroy's of Soho	**248**
Natural Shoe Store	**248**
Intoxica!	**248**
Bang Bang Menswear	**248**

Arts & Entertainment

Ripley's Believe It or Not!	**266**

Art Galleries

Tate	**278**

Nightlife

Late Night London	**322**

Theatre

Hairspray	**338**

Escapes & Excursions

Thames River Adventures	**350**
Roald Dahl Museum and Story Centre	**350**

londontown.com	**IBC**

INDEX

Maps

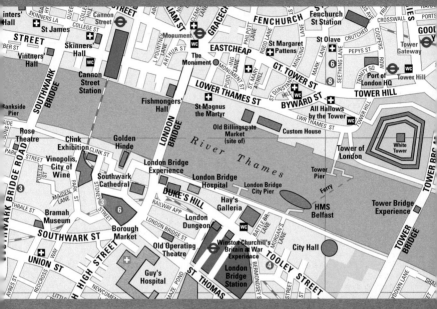

Major sight or landmark	
Railway or coach station	
Underground station	⊖
Park	
Hospital or place of learning	
Casualty unit	✚
Church	✚
Synagogue	✡
Congestion Zone	⊙
District . . . . MAYFAIR
Theatre	●

Street Maps 390
London Overview **390**
Central London by Area **392**
Street Maps **394**
West End **406**
Street Index **408**

Transport Maps 416
London Underground **416**

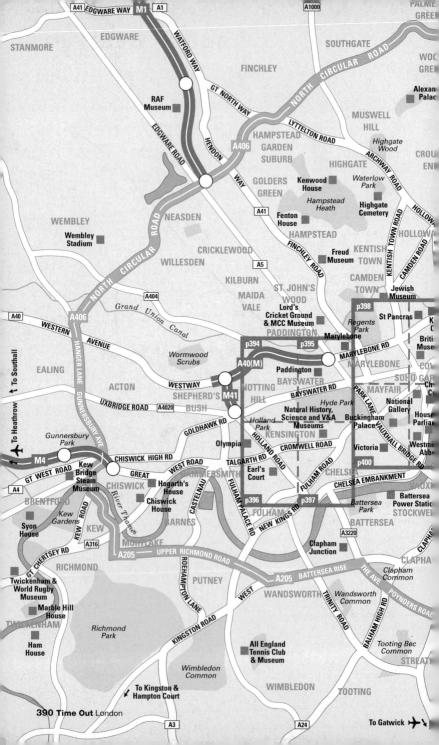

London Overview

Central London
by Area

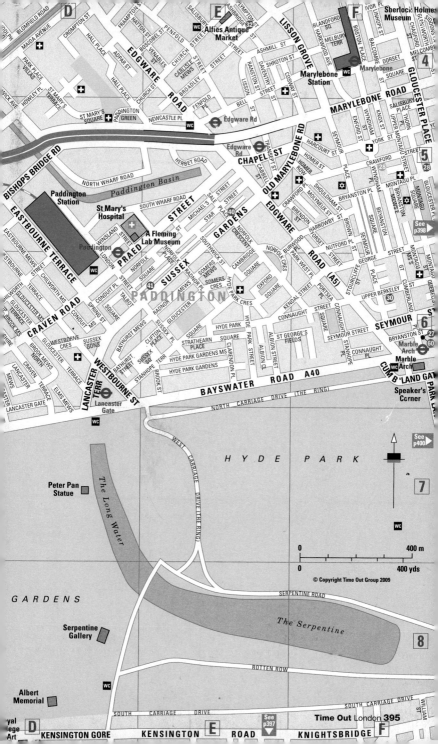

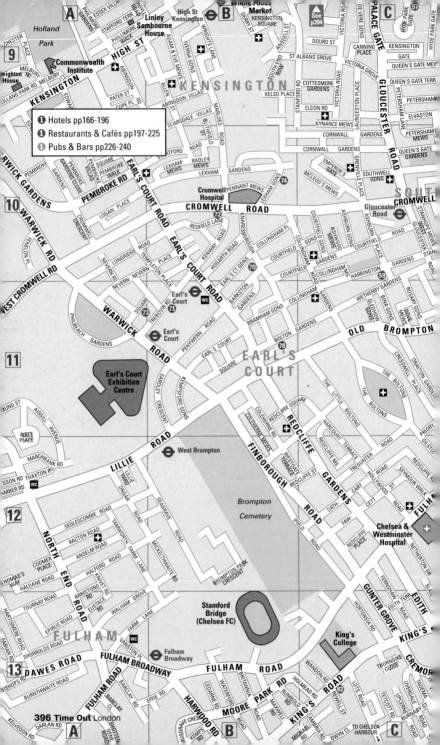

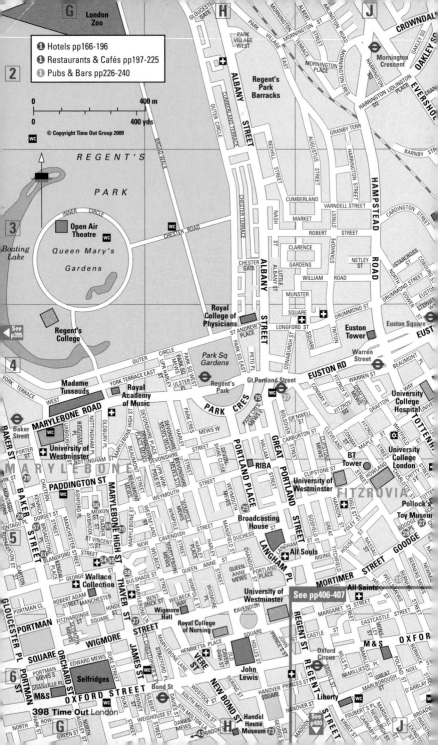

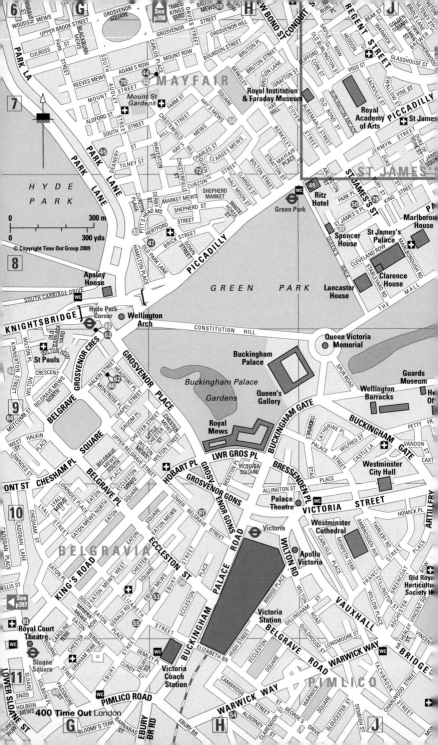

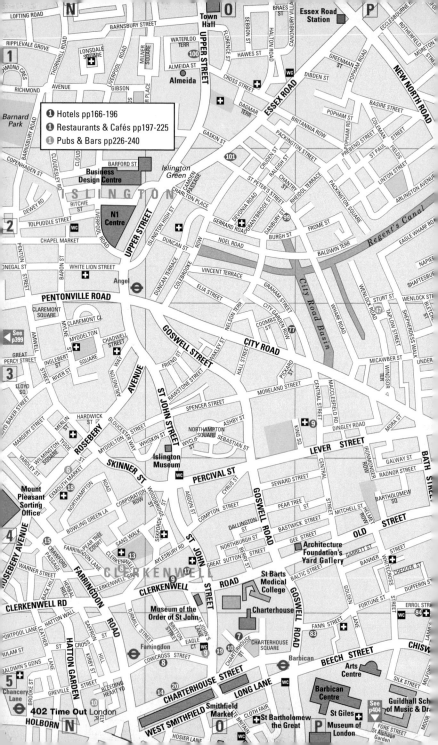

Time Out London **403**

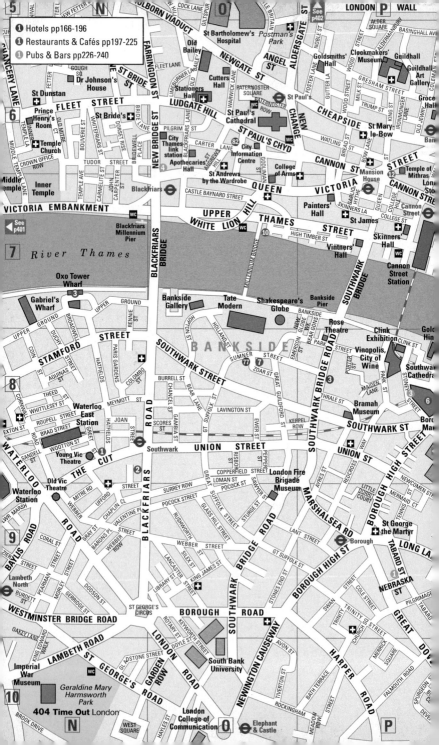

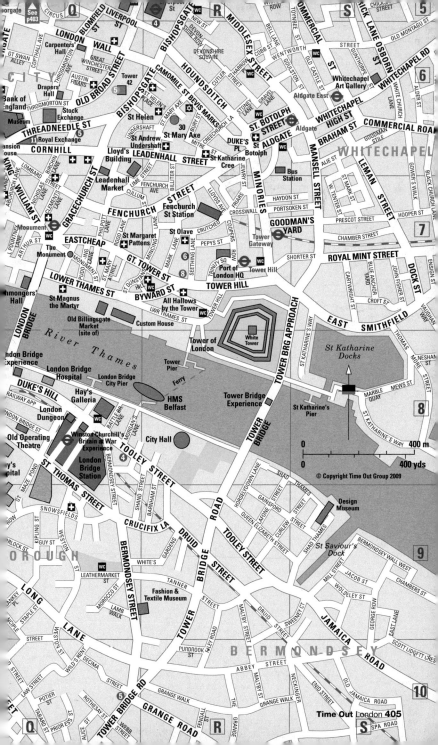

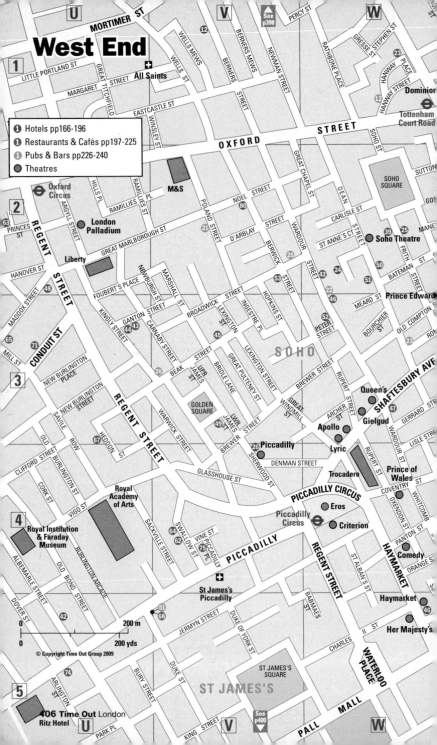

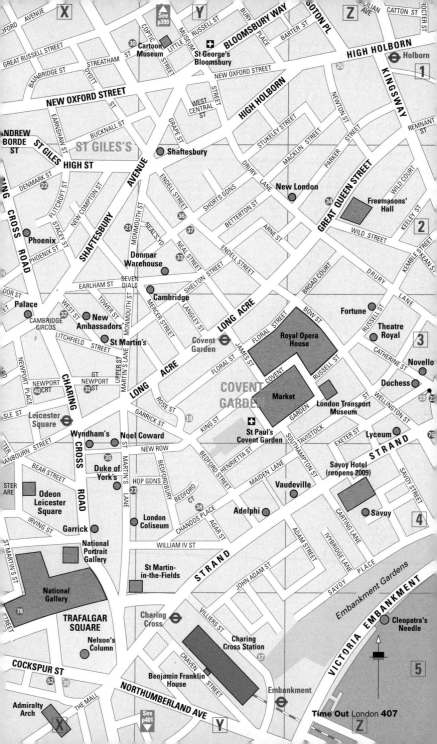

Street Index

**Abbey Orchard Street -
p401 K9**
Abbey Street - p405 R10/S10
Abchurch Lane - p405 Q7
Abingdon Road - p396 A9/B10
Abingdon Street - p401 L9
Abingdon Villas - p396 A9/B9
Acton Mews - p403 R1
Acton Street - p399 M3
Adam & Eve Mews - p396 B9
Adam Street - p401 L7,
p407 Z4
Adam's Row - p400 G7
Agar Street - p401 L7, p407 Y4
Agdon Street - p402 O4
Aisgill Avenue - p396 A11/12
Albany Street - p398 H2/3
Albemarle Street - p400 H7/J7,
p406 U4/5
Albert Bridge - p397 E13
Albert Bridge Road - p397 E13
Albert Court - p397 D9
Albert Embankment -
p401 L10/11
Albert Street - p398 J2
Albion Close - p395 E6
Albion Drive - p403 S1
Albion Square - p403 S1
Albion Street - p395 E6
Aldenham Street - p399 K2
Alder Square - p404 P6
Alder Street - p405 S6
Aldermanbury - p404 P6
Alderney Street - p400 H11
Aldersgate Street -
p404 O6/P5/6
Aldford Street - p400 G7
Aldgate - p405 R6
Aldridge Road Villas - p394 A5
Aldwych - p399 M6
Alexander Square - p397 E10
Alexander Street - p394 B5
Alfred Place - p399 K5
Alfred Road - p394 B4
Alice Street - p405 Q10
Alie Street - p405 S6
All Saints Street - p399 M2
Allen Street - p396 B9/10
Allington Street - p400 H10
Almeida Street - p402 O1
Almorah Road - p403 Q1
Amberley Road - p394 B4
Ambrosden Avenue - p400 J10
Ampton Street - p399 M3
Amwell Street - p402 N3
Andrew Borde Street - p399 K6,
p407 X1/2
Angel Street - p404 O6
Anhalt Road - p397 E13
Ann Lane - p397 D13
Ansdell Street - p396 B9
Anselm Road - p396 A12
Appleby Street - p403 S2
Appold Street - p403 Q5/R5
Aquinas Street - p404 N8
Archer Street - p401 K7,
p406 W3
Argyle Square - p399 L3
Argyle Street - p399 L3
Argyll Road - p394 A9,
p396 A9/B9
Arlington Avenue - p402 P2
Arlington Road - p398 J2
Arlington Street - p400 J8,
p406 U5
Armstong Road - p396 A12
Arne Street - p399 L6, p407 Y2
Arnold Circus - p403 R4/S4
Artesian Road - p394 A6
Arthur Street - p405 Q7
Artillery Lane - p403 R5
Artington Way - p402 N3
Arundel Street - p401 M6/7

Aryll Street - p398 J6
Ashbridge Street - p395 E4
Ashburn Gardens - p396 C10
Ashburn Place - p396 C10
Ashburnham Road - p396 C13,
p397 D13
Ashby Street - p402 O3
Ashmill Street - p395 E4
Ashwood Mews - p396 C10
Astell Street - p397 E11
Atterbury Street - p401 K11
Aubrey Road - p394 A7/8
Aubrey Walk - p394 A7/8
Augustus Street - p398 J2/3
Austin Friars - p405 Q6
Avery Row - p400 H6
Aybrook Street - p398 G5
Ayers Street - p404 P8/9
Aylesbury Road - p402 O4

**Babmaes Street - p401 K7,
p406 W5**
Baches Street - p403 Q3
Back Church Lane - p405 S6/7
Back Hill - p402 N4
Bacon Street - p403 S4
Bainbridge Street - p399 K5,
p407 X1
Baker Street - p398 G4/5
Balcombe Street - p395 F4
Balderton Street - p398 G6
Baldwin Terrace - p402 P2
Baldwin's Gardens - p402 N5
Balfe Street - p399 L2
Balmes Road - p403 Q1
Baltic Street - p402 P4
Bankside - p404 P7
Banner Street - p402 P4
Barclay Close - p396 A13
Barclay Road - p396 A13
Barford Street - p402 N2
Baring Street - p403 Q1/2
Bark Place - p394 B6/7
Barkston Gardens - p396 B11
Barnabas Street - p400 G11
Barnby Street - p398 J3
Barnham Street - p405 Q9
Barnsbury Road - p402 N1/2
Barnsbury Street - p402 N1/O1
Baron Street - p402 N2
Barons Place - p404 N9
Barter Street - p399 L5,
p407 Y1/Z1
Bartholomew Square - p402 P4
Basil Street - p397 F9
Basinghall Avenue - p404 P6
Basinghall Street - p404 P6
Basire Street - p402 P1
Bastwick Street - p402 O4/4
Bateman Street - p399 K6,
p406 W2
Bateman's Row - p403 R4
Bath Street - p402 P3/4
Bath Terrace - p404 P10
Bathurst Mews - p395 D6
Bathurst Street - p395 D6
Battersea Bridge - p397 E13
Battersea Bridge Road -
p397 E13
Battersea Church Road -
p397 E13
Battle Bridge Lane - p405 Q8
Battle Bridge Road - p399 L2
Bayley Street - p399 K5
Baylis Road - p404 N9
Bayswater Road - p394 B7/C7,
p395 E6/F6
Beak Street - p400 J6, p406 V3
Bear Gardens - p404 P7/8
Bear Lane - p404 O8
Bear Street - p401 K7, p407 X4
Beauchamp Place - p397 F9/10
Beaufort Street - p397 D12

Beaumont Mews - p398 G5
Beaumont Place - p398 J4
Beaumont Street - p398 G5
Bedford Avenue - p399 K5,
p407 X1
Bedford Court - p401 L7,
p407 Y4
Bedford Gardens - p394 A8/B8
Bedford Place - p399 L5
Bedford Row - p399 M5
Bedford Square - p399 K5
Bedford Street - p401 L7,
p407 Y4
Bedford Way - p399 K4
Bedfordbury - p401 L7,
p407 Y4
Beech Street - p402 P5
Beeston Place - p400 H9
Belgrave Mews North -
p400 G9
Belgrave Mews South -
p400 G9
Belgrave Place - p400 G10
Belgrave Road - p400 H10/J11
Belgrave Square - p400 G9
Belgrave Street - p399 L3
Bell Lane - p405 R6
Bell Street - p395 E4/5
Bell Yard - p399 M6
Belvedere Road - p401 M8/9
Bentinck Street - p398 H5
Berkeley Square - p400 H7
Berkeley Street - p400 H7
Bermondsey Place - p405
Q8/9/10
Bermondsey Wall West -
p405 S9
Bernard Street - p399 L4
Berners Mews - p398 J5,
p406 V1
Berners Street - p398 J5/6,
p406 V1
Berry Street - p402 O4
Berwick Street - p398 J6,
p399 K6, p406 V2
Bethnal Green Road -
p403 R4/S4
Betterton Street - p399 L6,
p407 Y2
Bevenden Street - p403 Q3
Bevis Marks - p405 R6
Bickenhall Street - p395 F5
Bidborough Street - p399 L3
Billiter Street - p405 R6/7
Bina Gardens - p396 C11
Bingham Place - p398 G4
Binney Street - p398 G6
Birchin Lane - p405 Q6
Birdcage Walk - p401 K9
Birkenhead Street - p399 L3
Bishops Bridge Road - p394
C5, p395 D5
Bishops Road - p396 A13
Bishopsgate - p405 Q6/R5/6
Black Prince Street - p401
L11/M11
Blackburn Mews - p400 G7
Blackfriars Bridge - p404 O7
Blackfriars Lane - p404 O6
Blackfriars Road - p404 N8,
p405 O8
Blackland Terrace - p397 F11
Blandford Square - p395 F4
Blandford Street - p398 G5
Blantyre Street - p397 D13
Bleeding Heart Yard - p402 N5
Bletchley Street - p402 P3
Blithfield Street - p396 B10
Blomfield Road - p394 C4,
p395 D4
Blomfield Street - p405 Q5/6
Blomfield Villas - p394 C5
Bloomfield Terrace - p400 G11

Bloomsbury Square - p399 L5
Bloomsbury Street - p399 K5
Bloomsbury Way - p399 L5,
p407 Y1
Blossom Street - p403 R5
Blue Anchor Yard - p405 S7
Bolsover Street - p398 H4/J5
Bolton Gardens - p396
B11/C11
Bolton Street - p400 H7/8
Bonhill Street - p403 Q4
Borough High Street -
p404 P8/9
Borough Road - p404 O9
Boscobel Street - p395 E4
Boston Place - p395 F4
Boswell Street - p399 L5
Boundary Street - p403 R4
Bourchier Street - p399 K6,
p406 W3
Bourdon Street - p400 H7
Bourne Street - p400 G11
Bourne Terrace - p394 B5/C5
Bouverie Street - p404 N6
Bow Lane - p404 P6
Bow Street - p399 L6, p407 Z3
Bowling Green Lane - p402 N4
Brad Street - p404 N8
Braes Street - p402 O1
Braham Street - p405 S6
Bramber Road - p396 A12
Bramerton Street - p397 E12
Bramham Gardens - p396 B11
Bray Place - p397 F11
Bread Street - p404 P6
Bream's Building - p404 N6
Brendon Street - p395 F5
Bressenden Place -
p400 H9/J10
Brewer Street - p400 J7, p401
K6, p406 V3/4
Brick Lane - p403 S4/5,
p405 S5/6
Brick Street - p400 H8
Bride Lane - p404 N6
Bridewell Place - p404 N6
Bridge Place - p400 H11
Bridge Street - p401 L9
Bridgeway Street - p399 K2
Bridle Lane - p400 J6/7,
p406 V3
Bridstow Place - p394 B5
Brill Place - p399 K2
Bristol Gardens - p394 C4
Britannia Road - p396 B13
Britannia Row - p402 P1
Britannia Street - p399 M3
Britten Street - p397 E11
Britton Street - p402 O4/5
Broad Street - p395 E4
Broad Walk - p398 H2/3
Broadley Street - p395 E4
Broadstone Place - p398 G5
Broadway - p401 K9
Broadwell - p404 N7/8
Broadwick Street - p398 J6,
p406 V2/3
Brompton Gardens - p397 F9
Brompton Park Crescent -
p396 B12
Brompton Place - p397 F9
Brompton Road - p397
E9/10/F9
Brompton Square - p397 E9
Brook Drive - p404 N10
Brook Mews North - p395 D6
Brook Street W1 - p398 H6,
p400 H6
Brook Street W2 - p395 E6
Brooke Street - p402 N5
Brook's Mews - p400 H6
Brown Hart Gardens - p398 G6
Brown Street - p395 F5

Brownlow Mews - p399 M4
Brownlow Road - p403 S1
Brownlow Street - p399 M5
Brunswick Gardens - p394 B7/8
Brunswick Place - p403 Q3/4
Brunswick Square - p399 L4
Brushfield Street - p403 R5
Bruton Lane - p400 H7
Bruton Place - p400 H7
Bruton Street - p400 H7
Bryanston Mews East - p395 F5
Bryanston Place - p395 F5
Bryanston Square - p395 F5
Bryanston Street - p395 F6
Buckingham Gate - p400 H9/J9
Buckingham Palace Road - p400 H10
Buckland Street - p403 Q2
Bucknall Street - p399 K6/L6, p407 X1
Bulmer Place - p394 A7
Bunhill Row - p402 P4, p403 Q4
Burbage Close - p404 P10
Burdett Street - p404 N9
Burgh Street - p402 O2
Burlington Arcade - p400 J7, p406 U4/5
Burnaby Street - p396 C13
Burnthwaite Road - p396 A13
Burrell Street - p404 O8
Burton Street - p399 K3/4
Burwood Place - p395 E5
Bury Place - p399 L5, p407 Y1
Bury Street EC3 - p405 R6
Bury Street SW1 - p400 J7/8, p406 U5/V5
Bury Walk - p397 E11
Bute Street - p397 D10
Buttesland Street - p403 Q3
Buxton Street - p403 S5
Byward Street - p405 Q7/R7
Bywater Street - p397 F11

Cabbell Street - p395 E5
Cadell Close - p403 S3
Cadogan Gardens - p397 F10/11
Cadogan Lane - p400 G10
Cadogan Place - p400 G10
Cadogan Square - p397 F10
Cadogan Street - p397 F10/11
Cale Street - p397 E11
Caledonia Street - p399 L2
Caledonian Road - p399 L2/M2
Callendar Road - p397 D9
Callow Street - p397 D12
Calshot Street - p399 M2
Calthorpe Street - p399 M4
Calvert Avenue - p403 R4
Calvin Street - p403 R5/S5
Cambria Road - p396 C13
Cambridge Circus - p399 K6, p407 X3
Cambridge Square - p395 E6
Cambridge Street - p400 H11
Camden Passage - p402 O2
Camley Street - p399 K2/L2
Camomile Street - p405 R6
Campden Grove - p394 B8
Campden Hill Gardens - p394 A7
Campden Hill Road - p394 A8/B9
Campden Hill Square - p394 A7
Campden Street - p394 A8/B7
Canning Place - p396 C9
Cannon Street - p404 P6/7
Canonbury Villas - p402 O1
Capper Street - p398 J4, p399 K4
Carburton Street - p398 H4/J4
Cardington Street - p398 J3
Carey Street - p399 M6
Carlisle Lane - p401 M9/10
Carlisle Mews - p395 E4
Carlisle Place - p400 J10
Carlisle Street - p399 K6, p406 W2
Carlton Gardens - p401 K8
Carlton House Terrace - p401 K8
Carlyle Square - p397 E12

Carmelite Street - p404 N7
Carnaby Street - p398 J6, p406 U3/V3
Carnegie Street - p399 M2
Caroline Terrace - p400 G10
Carriage Drive North - p397 F13
Carriage Drive West - p397 F13
Carter Lane - p404 O6
Carting Lane - p401 L7, p407 Z4
Carton Street - p398 G5
Cartwright Gardens - p399 L3
Cartwright Street - p405 S7
Castle Baynard Street - p404 O7
Castle Lane - p400 J9
Cathcart Road - p396 C12
Catherine Place - p400 J9
Catherine Street - p401 M6, p407 Z3
Catton Street - p399 L5/M5, p407 Z1
Causton Street - p401 K11
Cavendish Square - p398 H5/6
Caversham Street - p397 F12
Caxton Street - p400 J9, p401 K9
Cedarne Road - p396 B13
Centaur Street - p401 M9
Central Avenue - p397 F13
Central Street - p402 P3/4
Chadwell Street - p402 N3
Chagford Street - p395 F4
Chalton Street - p399 K2/3
Chamber Street - p405 S7
Chambers Street - p405 S9
Chancel Street - p404 O8
Chancery Lane - p399 M5, p404 N6
Chandos Place - p401 L7, p407 Y4
Chandos Street - p398 H5
Chantry Street - p402 O2
Chapel Market - p402 N2
Chapel Side - p394 B6/7
Chapel Street NW1 - p395 E5
Chapel Street SW1 - p400 G9
Chaplin Close - p404 N9
Chapter Street - p401 K11
Charing Cross Road - p399 K6, p401 K7, p407 X2/3/4
Charles II Street - p401 K7, p406 W5
Charles Square - p403 Q3/4
Charles Street - p400 H7
Charlotte Road - p403 R4
Charlotte Street - p398 J5, p399 K5
Charlotte Terrace - p399 M2
Charlton Place - p402 O2
Charlwood Street - p400 J11
Charrington Street - p399 K2
Chart Street - p403 Q3
Charterhouse Square - p402 O5
Charterhouse Street - p402 O5
Cheapside - p404 P6
Chelsea Embankment - p397 F12
Chelsea Manor Street - p397 E11/12
Chelsea Park Gardens - p397 D12
Chelsea Square - p397 D11/E11
Cheltenham Terrace - p397 F11
Cheney Road - p399 L2
Chenies Mews - p399 K4
Chenies Street - p399 K5
Chepstow Crescent - p394 A6
Chepstow Place - p394 B6
Chepstow Road - p394 A5/B6
Chepstow Villas - p394 A6
Chequer Street - p402 P4
Cherbury Street - p403 Q2
Chesham Place - p400 G9
Chesham Street - p400 G10
Cheshire Street - p403 S4
Chesson Road - p396 A12
Chester Gate - p398 H3
Chester Mews - p400 H9
Chester Road - p398 H3
Chester Row - p400 G10/11

Chester Square - p400 G10
Chester Street - p400 G9/H9
Chester Terrace - p398 H3
Chesterfield Hill - p400 H7
Chesterfield Street - p400 H7/8
Cheval Place - p397 E9
Cheyne Mews - p397 E12
Cheyne Row - p397 E12
Cheyne Walk - p397 D13/E12/13
Chicheley Street - p401 M8
Chichester Road - p394 B5
Chicksand Street - p405 S5
Chiltern Street - p398 G5
Chilton Street - p403 S4
Chilworth Mews - p395 D6
Chilworth Street - p395 D6
Chippenham Mews - p394 A4/5
Chiswell Street - p402 P5, p403 Q5
Chitty Street - p398 J5
Christchurch Street - p397 F12
Christopher Street - p403 Q5
Church Square - p404 P9
Church Street - p395 D5/E4
Churchway - p399 K3
Cirencester Street - p394 B4
City Garden Row - p402 O3
City Road - p402 O3/3, p403 Q4/5
Clabon Mews - p397 F10
Clanricarde Gardens - p394 B7
Claremont Square - p402 N3
Clarence Gardens - p398 H3/J3
Clarendon Place - p395 E6
Clarendon Street - p400 H11
Clareville Grove - p397 D10
Clareville Street - p397 D10
Clarges Mews - p400 H7/8
Clarges Street - p400 H7/8
Clarissa Street - p403 S1
Clement's Inn - p399 M6
Clements Lane - p405 Q7
Clerkenwell Close - p402 N4
Clerkenwell Green - p402 N4
Clerkenwell Road - p402 N4/O4
Cleveland Road - p403 Q1
Cleveland Row - p400 J8
Cleveland Square - p394 C6
Cleveland Street - p398 J4/5
Cleveland Terrace - p394 C5/6, p395 D5
Clifford Street - p400 J7, p406 U4
Clifton Gardens - p394 C4
Clifton Place - p395 E6
Clifton Street - p403 Q5
Clifton Villas - p394 C4
Clink Street - p404 P8
Clipstone Mews - p398 J4
Clipstone Street - p398 J5
Cloth Fair - p402 O5
Cloudesley Road - p402 N1/2
Cloudesley Square - p402 N1/2
Cloudesley Street - p402 N1/2
Club Row - p403 S4
Cobb Street - p405 R6
Cobourg Street - p398 J3
Cock Lane - p404 O5
Cockspur Street - p401 K7, p407 X5
Code Street - p403 S4/5
Coin Street - p404 N8
Cole Street - p404 P9
Colebrook Row - p402 O2
Coleherne Mews - p396 B11/12
Coleherne Road - p396 B11/12
Coleman Fields - p402 P1/2
Coleman Street - p404 P6
College Hill - p404 P7
College Street - p404 P7
Collier Street - p399 M2
Collingham Mews - p396 C10
Collingham Place - p396 B10
Collingham Road - p396 C10/11
Colombo Street - p404 N8
Colonnade - p399 L4
Columbia Road - p403 S3
Colville Road - p394 A6
Colville Terrace - p394 A6
Commercial Road - p405 S6

Commercial Street - p403 R5/S5, p405 S5/6
Compton Street - p402 O4
Concert Hall Approach - p401 M8
Conduit Mews - p395 D6
Conduit Place - p395 D6
Conduit Street - p400 H7/J6, p406 U3
Connaught Place - p395 F6
Connaught Square - p395 F6
Connaught Street - p395 E6/F6
Constitution Hill - p400 H8/9
Conway Street - p398 J4
Coombs Street - p402 O3
Coomer Place - p396 A12
Coopers Lane - p399 K2
Coopers Row - p405 R7
Cope Place - p396 A9
Copenhagen Street - p402 N2
Copperfield Street - p404 O8
Copthall Avenue - p405 Q6
Coptic Street - p399 L5, p407 Y1
Coral Street - p404 N9
Coram Street - p399 L4
Cork Street - p400 J7, p406 U4
Cornhill - p405 Q6
Cornwall Gardens - p396 C10
Cornwall Road - p404 N8
Corporation Row - p402 N4
Corsham Street - p403 Q3
Cosser Street - p401 M10
Cosway Street - p395 E4/F5
Cottesmore Gardens - p396 C9
Coulson Street - p397 F11
Courtfield Gardens - p396 B10/11
Courtfield Road - p396 C10
Courtnell Street - p394 A5/6
Covent Garden - p401 L6/7, p407 Y3/Z3
Coventry Street - p401 K7, p406 W4
Cowcross Street - p402 O5
Cowper Street - p403 Q4
Cramer Street - p398 G5
Cranbourn Street - p401 K7, p407 X3/4
Cranleigh Street - p398 J2
Cranley Gardens - p397 D11
Cranley Mews - p397 D11
Cranley Place - p397 D11
Cranwood Street - p403 Q4
Craven Hill - p394 C6
Craven Hill Gardens - p394 C6
Craven Road - p395 D6
Craven Street - p401 L7, p407 Y5
Craven Terrace - p395 D6
Crawford Passage - p402 N4
Crawford Place - p395 E5/F5
Crawford Street - p395 F5
Creechurch Lane - p405 R6
Cremer Street - p403 R3
Cremorne Road - p396 C13, p397 D13
Cresswell Place - p396 C11
Crestfield Street - p399 L3
Crinian Street - p399 L2
Croft Street - p405 S7
Cromer Street - p399 L3
Crompton Street - p395 D4
Cromwell Mews - p397 D10
Cromwell Place - p397 D10
Cromwell Road - p396 B10/C10/D10
Crondall Street - p403 Q3/R3
Cropley Street - p403 Q2
Crosby Row - p405 Q9
Cross Street - p402 O1
Crosswall - p405 R7
Crown Office Row - p404 N6
Crowndale Road - p398 J2, p399 K2
Crucifix Lane - p405 Q9/R9
Cruden Street - p402 O1/2
Crutched Friars - p405 R7
Cubbitt Street - p399 M3
Culford Gardens - p397 F11
Cullum Street - p405 Q7/R7
Culross Street - p400 G7

STREET INDEX

Cumberland Gate - p395 F6
Cumberland Market -
p398 H3/J3
Cumberland Terrace -
p398 H2/3
Cumming Street - p399 M2
Cundy Street - p400 G11
Cure Street - p401 K11
Curlew Street - p405 R9/S9
Cursitor Street - p404 N6
Curtain Road - p403 R4
Curzon Place - p400 G8
Curzon Street - p400 H7/8
Cutler Street - p405 R6
Cynthia Street - p399 M2
Cyrus Street - p402 O4

Dacre Street - p401 K9
Dagmar Terrace - p402 O1
Dallington Street - p402 O4
Danbury Street - p402 O2
Danube Street - p397 E11
Danvers Street - p397 D12/E12
D'Arblay Street - p398 J6,
p406 V2
Darlan Road - p396 A13
Dartmouth Close - p394 A5
Daventry Street - p395 E4/5
Davies Mews - p398 H6
Davies Street - p398 H6,
p400 H6/7
Dawes Road - p396 A13
Dawson Place - p394 B6
De Beauvoir Crescent -
p403 Q1
De Beauvoir Road - p403 R1
De Beauvoir Square - p403 R1
De Vere Gardens - p394 C9,
p396 C9
Deal Street - p403 S5
Dean Bradley Street -
p401 K10/L10
Dean Ryle Street -
p401 K10/L10
Dean Stanley Street - p401 L10
Dean Street - p399 K6,
p406 W2/3
Deanery Street - p400 G7
Dean's Yard - p401 K9
Decima Street - p405 Q10
Delamere Terrace - p394 C4
Denbigh Road - p394 A6
Denbigh Street - p400 J11
Denbigh Terrace - p394 A6
Denman Street - p400 J7,
p406 V4/W4
Denmark Street - p399 K6,
p407 X2
Denyer Street - p397 F10
Derby Street - p400 H8
Dering Street - p398 H6
Derry Street - p396 B9
Deverell Street - p404 P10
Devonia Road - p402 O2
Devonshire Close - p398 H4/5
Devonshire Mews South -
p398 H5
Devonshire Mews West -
p398 H4
Devonshire Place - p398 G4/H4
Devonshire Place Mews -
p398 G4
Devonshire Row - p405 R6
Devonshire Square - p405 R6
Devonshire Street - p398 H4
Devonshire Terrace - p395 D6
Dewey Road - p402 N2
Dibden Street - p402 P1
Dilke Street - p397 F12
Dingley Road - p402 P3
Dock Street - p405 S7
Dodson Street - p404 N9
Dombey Street - p399 M5
Donegal Street - p399 M2,
p402 N2
Doric Way - p399 K3
Dorset Rise - p404 N6
Dorset Square - p395 F4
Dorset Street - p398 G5
Doughty Mews - p399 M4
Doughty Street - p399 M4
Douglas Street - p401 K11

Douro Street - p396 C9
Dove Mews - p396 C11
Dovehouse Street -
p397 E11/12
Dover Street - p400 H7/J7,
p406 U5
Down Street - p400 G8/H8
Downham Road - p403 Q1
Downing Street - p401 K8/L8
Doyle Street - p404 O10
Drake Street - p399 M5
Draycott Avenue - p397
E10/F12
Draycott Place - p397 F11
Draycott Terrace - p397 F10
Drayton Gardens - p396 C11,
p397 D11/12
Drayton Mews - p394 B8
Druid Street - p405 R9/S10
Drummond Crescent - p399 K3
Drummond Street - p398 J3/4
Drury Lane - p399 L6/M6,
p407 Y2/Z2/3
Drysdale Street - p403 R3
Duchess of Bedford's Walk
p394 A8
Duchess Street - p398 H5
Duchy Street - p404 N8
Dufferin Street - p402 P4
Duke of York Street - p400 J7,
p406 V5
Duke Street - p398 G6
Duke Street, St James's -
p400 J7/8, p406 V5
Duke's Hill - p405 Q8
Dukes Lane - p394 B8
Duke's Place - p405 R6
Duke's Road - p399 K3
Duncan Street - p402 O2
Duncan Terrace - p402 O2
Dunloe Street - p403 S3
Dunraven Street - p400 G6
Dunston Road - p403 R2/S2
Durham Street - p394 B5
Dyott Street - p399 L6, p407 X1
Dysart Street - p403 Q5

Eagle Court - p402 O4/5
Eagle Street - p399 M5
Eagle Wharf Road - p402 P2,
p403 Q2
Eardley Crescent - p396 B11
Earl Street - p403 Q5
Earlham Street - p399 K6/L6,
p407 X2
Earl's Court Square - p396 B11
Earl's Court Gardens -
p396 B10
Earl's Court Road - p396
A9/10/B10/11
Earls Walk - p396 E10
Earnshaw Street - p399 K6,
p407 X1/2
East Lane - p405 S9
East Road - p403 Q3
East Smithfield - p405 S7
Eastbourne Mews - p395 D5/6
Eastbourne Terrace - p395 D5/6
Eastcastle Street - p398 J5/6,
p406 U1/V1
Eastcheap - p405 Q7
Eaton Mews - p400 H10
Eaton Place - p400 G9/10
Eaton Square - p400 G10/H10
Eaton Terrace - p400 G10/12
Ebury Bridge - p400 H11
Ebury Bridge Road - p400 G11
Ebury Mews - p400 H10
Ebury Square - p400 G11
Ebury Street - p400
G10/11/H10
Ecclesbourne Road - p402 P1
Eccleston Mews - p400 G9
Eccleston Place - p400 H10
Eccleston Square - p400 H11
Eccleston Street - p400
G10/H10
Edge Street - p394 A7
Edgware Road - p395 D4/E4/5
Edith Grove - p396 C12/13
Edith Terrace - p396 C13
Edward Mews - p398 G6

Edwardes Square - p396 A9/10
Effie Road - p396 A13/B13
Egerton Crescent - p397 E10
Egerton Gardens - p397 E10
Egerton Terrace - p397 E10
Elcho Street - p397 E13
Elder Street - p403 R5
Eldon Road - p396 C9
Eldon Street - p403 Q5
Elia Street - p402 O2
Elizabeth Avenue - p402 P1,
p403 Q1
Elizabeth Bridge - p400 H11
Elizabeth Street - p400
G10/H10
Elkstone Road - p394 A4
Elliot's Row - p404 O10
Elm Park Gardens -
p397 D11/12
Elm Park Lane - p397 D12
Elm Park Road - p397 D12
Elm Place - p397 D11
Elm Street - p399 M4
Elms Mews - p395 D6
Elvaston Place - p396 C9,
p397 D9
Elverton Street - p401 K10
Ely Place - p402 N5
Elystan Place - p397 F11
Elystan Street - p397 E11
Emerald Street - p399 M5
Emerson Street - p404 O8
Emperor's Gate - p396 C10
Endell Street - p399 L6,
p407 Y2
Endsleigh Gardens - p399 K3/4
Endsleigh Street - p399 K4
Enford Street - p395 F5
Enid Street - p405 S10
Ennismore Gardens - p397 E9
Ennismore Mews - p397 E9
Ensign Street - p405 S7
Epirus Road - p396 A13
Epworth Street - p403 Q4
Erasmus Street - p401 K11
Errol Street - p402 P4
Essex Road - p402 O1/P1
Essex Street - p401 M6
Essex Villas - p396 A9
Eustace Road - p396 A13
Euston Road - p398 J4,
p399 K3/4/L3/4
Euston Street - p398 J3
Evelyn Gardens - p397 D11
Evershott Street - p398 J2,
p399 K3
Ewer Street - p404 O8
Exeter Street - p401 L7,
p407 Z3
Exhibition Road - p397 D9/10
Exmouth Market - p402 N4
Exton Street - p404 N8

Fabian Road - p396 A13
Falkirk Street - p403 R3
Falmouth Road - p404 P10
Fann Street - p402 P5
Fanshaw Street - p403 R3
Farm Lane - p396 A13/B13
Farm Street - p400 H7
Farringdon Lane - p402 N4
Farringdon Road - p402 N4/5
Farringdon Street - p404 N6/O6
Fashion Street - p405 S5
Fawcett Street - p396 C12
Featherstone Street - p403 Q4
Fenchurch Avenue - p405 R7
Fenchurch Street - p405 Q7/R7
Fendall Street - p405 R10
Fenelon Place - p396 A10
Fernshaw Road - p396 C12/13
Fetter Lane - p404 N6
Finborough Road - p396
B12/C12
Finsbury Circus - p403 Q5,
p405 Q5
Finsbury Pavement - p403 Q5
Finsbury Square - p403 Q5
First Street - p397 E10
Fisher Street - p399 L5
Fitzalan Street - p401 M10
Fitzhardinge Street - p398 G6

Fitzroy Square - p398 J4
Fitzroy Street - p398 J4
Flaxman Terrace - p399 K3
Fleet Lane - p404 O6
Fleet Street - p404 N6
Fleur de Lis Street - p403 R5
Flitcroft Street - p399 K6,
p407 X2
Flood Street - p397 E12/F12
Flood Walk - p397 E12
Floral Street - p399 L6, p401
L6, p407 Y3
Florence Street - p402 O1
Foley Street - p398 J5
Folgate Street - p403 R5
Fore Street - p402 P5
Formosa Street - p394 C4
Forset Street - p395 F5/6
Fortune Street - p402 P4
Foster Lane - p404 P6
Foubert's Place - p398 J6,
p406 U2
Foulis Terrace - p397 D11
Fournier Street - p403 S5
Frampton Street - p395 D4
Francis Street - p400 J10
Franklin's Row - p397 F11
Frazier Street - p404 N9
Frederick Street - p399 M3
Friend Street - p402 O3
Frith Street - p399 K6,
p406 W2/3
Frome Street - p402 P2
Fulham Broadway -
p396 A13/B13
Fulham Road - p396 A13/
B13/C12/13/D12,
p397 D11/12/E11
Furnival Street - p404 N5

Gainsford Street - p405 R9/S9
Galway Street - p402 P3/4
Gambia Street - p404 O8
Garden Row - p404 O10
Garlichythe - p404 P7
Garrick Street - p401 L7
Garway Road - p394 B6
Gaskin Street - p402 O1
Gate Place - p397 D10
Gaunt Street - p404 O10
Gee Street - p402 O4/4
Geffrye Street - p403 R2
George Row - p405 S9
George Street - p395 F5/6,
p398 G5
Gerald Road - p400 G10
Gerrard Road - p402 O2
Gerrard Street - p401 K6/7,
p406 W3
Gerridge Street - p404 N9
Gertrude Street - p397 D12
Gibson Road - p401 M11
Gibson Street - p402 N1
Gilbert Place - p399 L5
Gilbert Street - p398 H6
Gillingham Street - p400
H10/J10
Gilston Road - p396 C12
Giltspur Street - p404 O5
Gladstone Street - p404
N10/O10
Glasshill Street - p404 O9
Glasshouse Street - p400 J7,
p406 V4
Glebe Place - p397 E12
Gledhow Gardens - p396 C11
Glendower Place - p397 D10
Glentworth Street - p395 F4
Gloucester Gate - p398 H2
Gloucester Mews - p395 D6
Gloucester Place - p395 F5,
p398 G5/6
Gloucester Place Mews -
p395 F5
Gloucester Road - p396 C9/10
Gloucester Square - p395 E6
Gloucester Street - p400 J11
Gloucester Terrace - p394 C5,
p395 D6
Gloucester Walk - p394 B8
Gloucester Way - p402 N3
Godfrey Street - p397 E11

Godliman Street - p404 O6
Golden Lane - p402 P4/5
Golden Square - p400 J7,
  p406 V3
Goldington Crescent - p399 K2
Goldington Street - p399 K2
Goodge Place - p398 J5
Goodge Street - p398 J5,
  p399 K5
Goodman's Yard - p405 R7/S7
Goods Way - p399 L2
Gordon Place - p394 B8
Gordon Square - p399 K4
Gordon Street - p399 K4
Gore Street - p397 D9
Gosfield Street - p398 J5
Goslett Yard - p399 K6,
  p406 W2
Gosset Street - p403 S3
Goswell Road - p402 O3/4/5/P5
Gough Square - p404 N6
Gough Street - p399 M4
Goulston Street - p405 R6/S6
Gower Mews - p399 K5
Gower Place - p399 K4
Gower Street - p399 K4/5
Gower's Walk - p405 S6/7
Gracechurch Street -
  p405 Q6/7
Grafton Mews - p398 J4
Grafton Place - p399 K3
Grafton Street - p400 H7
Grafton Way - p398 J4
Graham Street - p402 O2/3
Graham Terrace - p400 G11
Granby Street - p403 S4
Granby Terrace - p398 J2
Grange Court - p399 M6
Grange Road - p405 R10
Grange Walk - p405 R10
Grantbridge Street - p402 O2
Granville Place - p398 G6
Granville Square - p399 M3
Gravel Lane - p405 R6
Gray Street - p404 N9
Gray's Inn Road -
  p399 L3/M3/4/5
Great Castle Street - p398 J6,
  p406 U1
Great Chapel Street - p399 K6,
  p406 V2/W2
Great College Street -
  p401 K9/10
Great Cumberland Place -
  p395 F6
Great Dover Street - p404
  P9/10, p405 Q10
Great Eastern Street -
  p403 Q4/R4
Great George Street - p401 K9
Great Guildford Street -
  p404 O8
Great James Street - p399 M5
Great Marlborough Street -
  p398 J6, p406 U2/V2
Great Maze Pond -
  p405 Q8/9
Great Newport Street - p401
  K6, p407 X3
Great Ormond Street -
  p399 L5/M4
Great Percy Street - p399 M3,
  p402 N3
Great Peter Street - p401 K10
Great Portland Street -
  p398 H5/J5
Great Pulteney Street - p400 J6,
  p406 V3
Great Queen Street - p399 L6,
  p407 Z2
Great Russell Street -
  p399 K5/L5, p407 X1
Great Smith Street -
  p401 K9/10
Great Suffolk Street -
  p404 O8/9
Great Sutton Street -
  p402 O4
Great Titchfield Street - p398
  J5/6, p406 U1
Great Tower Street - p405
  Q7/R7

Great Western Road -
  p394 A4/5
Great Winchester Street -
  p405 Q6
Great Windmill Street - p401
  K7, p406 V3
Greek Street - p399 K6,
  p406 W2
Green Street - p398 G6
Greencoat Place - p400 J10
Greenman Street - p402 P1
Greenwell Street - p398 H4/J4
Greet Street - p404 N8
Grenville Place - p396 C10
Grenville Street - p399 L4
Gresham Street - p404 P6
Gresse Street - p399 K5,
  p406 W1
Greville Street - p402 N5
Grey Eagle Street - p403 S5
Greycoat Street - p400 J10,
  p401 K10
Groom Place - p400 G9
Grosvenor Crescent - p400 G9
Grosvenor Gardens - p400
  H9/10
Grosvenor Hill - p400 H7
Grosvenor Place - p400 G9/H9
Grosvenor Square - p400 G6/7
Grosvenor Street - p400 H6/7
Great Swan Alley - p405 Q6
Guildhouse Street - p400
  J10/11
Guilford Street - p399 L4/M4
Gun Street - p403 R5
Gunter Grove - p396 C13
Gunthorpe Street - p405 S6
Gutter Lane - p404 P6
Guy Street - p405 Q9
Gwyn Close - p396 C13

Haberdasher Street - p403 Q3
Hackney Road - p403 R3/S3
Haggerston Road - p403 R1/S1
Haldane Road - p396 A12
Half Moon Street - p400 H8
Halford Road - p396 A12
Halkin Place - p400 G9
Halkin Street - p400 G9
Hall Place - p395 D4/5
Hall Street - p402 O3
Hallam Street - p398 H4/5
Halliford Street - p402 P1,
  p403 Q1
Halsey Street - p397 F10
Halton Road - p402 O1
Hamilton Park Road - p402 O1
Hamilton Place - p400 G8
Hampstead Road - p398 J3
Hanbury Street - p403 S5
Handel Street - p399 L4
Hankey Place - p405 Q9
Hanover Square - p398 H6
Hanover Street - p398 H6/J6,
  p406 U2
Hans Crescent - p397 F9
Hans Place - p397 F9
Hans Road - p397 F9
Hans Street - p397 F9
Hanson Street - p398 J5
Hanway Place - p399 K5,
  p406 W1
Hanway Street - p399 K5,
  p406 W1
Harbet Road - p395 E5
Harcourt Street - p395 F5
Harcourt Terrace - p396 C11/12
Hardwick Street - p402 N3
Harewood Avenue - p395 F4
Harley Place - p398 H5
Harley Street - p398 H4/5
Harper Street - p404 P10
Harpur Street - p399 M5
Harriet Walk - p397 F9
Harrington Gardens - p396 C10
Harrington Road - p397 D10
Harrington Square - p398 J2
Harrington Street - p398 J2/3
Harrison Street - p399 L3
Harrow Place - p405 R6
Harrow Road - p394 A4/B4/5
Harrowby Street - p395 F5

Hartismere Road - p396 A13
Harwood Road - p396 B13
Hasker Street - p397 F10
Hastings Street - p399 L3
Hatfields - p404 N8
Hatherley Grove - p394 B5/6
Hatherley Street - p400 J10
Hatton Garden - p402 N5
Hatton Street - p395 D4/E4
Hatton Wall - p402 N5
Hawes Street - p402 O1
Hay Hill - p400 H7
Haydon Street - p405 R7/S7
Hayles Street - p404 O10
Haymarket - p401 K7,
  p406 W4/5
Hay's Mews - p400 H7
Headfort Place - p400 G9
Hearn Street - p403 R4
Heathcote Street - p399 M4
Heddon Street - p400 J7,
  p406 U3/4
Helmet Row - p402 P4
Hemsworth Street - p403 R2
Heneage Street - p403 S5
Henrietta Place - p398 H6
Henrietta Street - p401 L7,
  p407 Y4
Herbal Hill - p402 N4
Herbrand Street - p399 L4
Hercules Road - p401 M9/10
Hereford Road - p394 B5/6
Herrick Street - p401 K11
Hertford Road - p403 R1
Hertford Street - p400 H8
Hester Road - p397 E13
Hide Place - p401 K11
High Holborn - p399 L5/6/M5,
  p407 Y1/Z1
High Timber Street - p404
  O7/P7
Hill Street - p400 H7
Hillgate Place - p394 A7
Hillgate Street - p394 A7
Hills Place - p398 J6, p406 U2
Hillsleigh Road - p394 A7
Hobart Place - p400 H9
Hobury Street - p397 D12
Hogarth Road - p396 B10
Holbein Mews - p400 G11
Holbein Place - p400 G11
Holborn - p402 N5
Holborn Viaduct - p404
  N5/O5/6
Holland Park Road - p396 A9
Holland Street SE1 - p404 O7/8
Holland Street W8 - p394 B8
Holland Walk - p394 A8
Holles Street - p398 H6
Holly Street - p403 S1
Hollywood Road - p396 C12
Holmead Road - p396 C13
Holywell Lane - p403 R4
Holywell Row - p403 Q4/R4
Homer Row - p395 F5
Homer Street - p395 F5
Hooper Street - p405 S7
Hop Gardens - p401 L7,
  p407 Y4
Hopkins Street - p398 J6,
  p406 V3
Hopton Street - p404 O7/8
Horatio Street - p403 S3
Hornton Street - p394 B8
Horseferry Road - p401 K10
Horseguards Avenue - p401 L8
Horseguards Parade - p401 K8
Horseguards Road - p401 K8
Horselydown Lane - p405 R8/9
Hortensia Road - p396 C13
Hosier Lane - p402 O5
Hotspur Street - p401 M11
Houndsditch - p405 R6
Howick Place - p400 J10
Howie Street - p397 E13
Howland Street - p398 J4/5
Howley Place - p395 D4/5
Hows Street - p403 R2/S2
Hoxton Square - p403 R3
Hoxton Street - p403 R2
Hudson's Place - p400 H10
Hugh Street - p400 H10/11

Hungerford Bridge - p401
  L8/M8, p407 Z5
Hunter Street - p399 L4
Huntley Street - p399 K4/5
Hunton Street - p403 S5
Hyde Park Crescent - p395 E6
Hyde Park Gardens - p395 E6
Hyde Park Gardens Mews -
  p395 E6
Hyde Park Gate - p396 C9
Hyde Park Square - p395 E6
Hyde Park Street - p395 E6
Hyde Road - p403 Q2

Ifield Road - p396 B12/C12
Ilchester Gardens - p394 B6
Ilchester Place - p396 A9
Imperial College Road -
  p397 D9
Ingestre Place - p398 J6,
  p406 V3
Inglebert Street - p402 N3
Inner Circle - p398 G3
Inner Temple Lane - p404 N6
Inverness Terrace - p394 C6/7
Ironmonger Lane - p404 P6
Ironmonger Row - p402 P3/4
Irving Street - p401 K7, p407 X4
Islington Green - p402 O2
Islington High Street - p402 O2
Istarcross Street - p398 J3
Ivatt Place - p396 A11/12
Iverna Gardens - p396 B9
Ives Street - p397 E10
Ivor Place - p395 F4
Ivy Street - p403 R2
Ivybridge Lane - p401 L7,
  p407 Z4
Ixworth Place - p397 E11

Jacob Street - p405 S9
Jamaica Road - p405 S9/10
James Street W1 - p398 G6
James Street WC2 - p401 L6,
  p407 Y3
Jay Mews - p397 D9
Jermyn Street - p400 J7,
  p406 U5/V4/5
Jewry Street - p405 R6/7
Joan Street - p404 N8
Jockey's Field - p399 M5
John Adam Street - p401 L7,
  p407 Y4/5
John Carpenter Street -
  p404 N7
John Fisher Street - p405 S7
John Islip Street - p401 K10/11
John Prince's Street - p398 H6
John Street - p399 M4/5
John's Mews - p399 M4/5
Jonathan Street - p401
  L11/M11
Jubilee Place - p397 E11
Judd Street - p399 L3
Juer Street - p397 E13
Juxon Street - p401 M10

Kean Street - p399 M6,
  p407 Z2
Keeley Street - p399 M6,
  p407 Z2
Kelso Place - p396 B9
Kelvedon Road - p396 A13
Kemble Street - p399 L6/M6,
  p407 Z2
Kemps Road - p396 B13
Kempsford Gardens - p396 B11
Kendal Street - p395 E6/F6
Kendall Place - p398 G5
Kennington Road - p404 N9/10
Kenrick Place - p398 G5
Kensington Church Street -
  p394 B7/8
Kensington Court - p394 B9,
  p396 B9
Kensington Gardens Square -
  p394 B6
Kensington Gate - p396 C9
Kensington Gore - p395 D9
Kensington High Street -
  p396 A9/B9
Kensington Mall - p394 B7

STREET INDEX

Kensington Palace Gardens
p394 B7/8
Kensington Park Gardens -
p394 A6
Kensington Park Road -
p394 A6/7
Kensington Place - p394 A7
Kensington Road - p394 B9/C9,
p395 E9/F9
Kensington Square - p396 B9
Kent Street - p403 S2
Kenton Street - p399 L4
Kenway Road - p396 B10
Keppel Row - p404 O8/P8
Keppel Street - p399 K5
Keystone Crescent - p399 M2
Keyworth Street - p404 O9/10
Kildare Terrace - p394 B5
Killick Street - p399 M2
King Charles Street -
p401 K9/L9
King Edward Walk - p404 N10
King James Street - p404 O9
King Street EC2 - p404 P6
King Street SW1 - p400 J8
King Street WC2 - p401 L7,
p406 V5, p407 Y3
Kingly Street - p398 J6,
p406 U3
King's Cross Road - p399 M3
King's Mews - p399 M4
King's Road - p396 C13, p397
D12/13/E11/12/F11
King's Road - p400 G10
Kingsland Road - p403 R1/2/3
Kingsway - p399 M6, p407 Z1/2
Kinnerton Street - p400 G9
Kipling Street - p405 Q9
Kirby Street - p402 N5
Knightsbridge - p400 G8
Knivet Road - p396 A12
Knox Street - p395 F5
Kynance Mews - p396 C9

Laburnum Road - p403 R2/S2
Lackington Street - p403 Q5
Ladbroke Road - p394 A7
Ladbroke Square - p394 A7
Ladbroke Terrace - p394 A7
Ladbroke Walk - p394 A7
Lafone Street - p405 R9
Lamb Street - p403 R5
Lamb Walk - p405 Q9
Lambeth Bridge - p401 L10
Lambeth High Street - p401 L10
Lambeth Palace Road -
p401 L10/M9
Lambeth Road - p401 M10,
p404 N10
Lambeth Walk - p401 M10/11
Lamb's Conduit Street -
p399 M4/5
Lamb's Pass - p402 P5
Lamont Road - p397 D12
Lancaster Gate - p394 C6/7,
p395 D6/7
Lancaster Mews - p395 D6
Lancaster Place - p401 M7
Lancaster Street - p404 O9
Lancaster Terrace - p395 D6
Langham Place - p398 H5
Langham Street - p398 H5/J5
Langley Street - p399 L6,
p407 Y3
Langton Street - p396 C12/13
Lansdowne Terrace - p399 L4
Lant Street - p404 O9/P9
Launceston Place - p396 C9/10
Laurence Pountney Lane -
p405 Q7
Lavender Grove - p403 S1
Lavington Street - p404 O8
Law Street - p405 Q10
Lawford Road - p403 R1
Lawrence Street - p397 E12
Leadenhall Street - p405 Q6/R6
Leake Street - p401 M9
Leamington Road Villas -
p394 A5
Leather Lane - p402 N5/11 N5
Leathermarket Street - p405 Q9

Ledbury Road - p394 A6
Lee Street - p403 R1/S1
Leeke Street - p399 M3
Lees Place - p400 G6
Leicester Place - p401 K7,
p407 X3/4
Leicester Square - p401 K7,
p407 X4
Leigh Street - p399 L3
Leinster Gardens - p394 C6
Leinster Square - p394 B6
Leinster Terrace - p394 C6/7
Leman Street - p405 S6/7
Lennox Gardens - p397 F10
Lennox Gardens Mews -
p397 F10
Leonard Street - p403 Q4
Lever Street - p402 P3
Lexham Gardens - p396 B10
Lexham Mews - p396 B10
Lexington Street - p398 J6,
p400 J6, p406 V3
Lidlington Place - p398 J2
Lillie Road - p396 A12/B11
Lillie Yard - p396 A12
Lime Street - p405 Q7/R6
Limerston Street - p397 D12
Lincoln Street - p397 F11
Lincoln's Inn Fields -
p399 M5/6
Linden Gardens - p394 B7
Linhope Street - p395 F4
Linton Street - p402 P2
Lisle Street - p401 K7, p406
W3/4, p407 X3
Lisson Grove - p395 E4/F4
Lisson Street - p395 E4/5
Litchfield Street - p401 K6,
p407 X3
Little Albany Street - p398 H3
Little Britain - p402 O5,
p404 O5
Little Chester Street - p400 H9
Little Dorrit Court - p404 P9
Little Portland Street - p398 J5,
p406 U1
Little Russell Street - p399 L5,
p407 Y1
Livermore Road - p403 S1
Liverpool Road - p402 N1/2
Liverpool Street - p405 Q5/6
Lloyd Baker Street - p402 N3
Lloyd Square - p402 N3
Lloyds Avenue - p405 R7
Lofting Road - p402 N1
Logan Place - p396 A10
Lollard Street - p401 M10/11
Loman Street - p404 O8
Lombard Street - p405 Q6/7
London Bridge - p405 Q7/8
London Bridge Street - p405 Q8
London Road - p404 O10
London Street - p395 D5/6
London Wall - p404 P5/Q6
Long Acre - p399 L6, p401
L6/7, p407 Y3
Long Lane EC1 - p402 O5
Long Lane SE1 - p404 P9/Q9
Long Street - p403 R3
Longford Street - p398 H4/J4
Longmoore Street - p400
J10/11
Longridge Road - p396 A10
Lonsdale Road - p394 A6
Lonsdale Square - p402 N1
Lord Hills Road - p394 C4
Lorenzo Street - p399 M3
Lots Road - p396 C13,
p397 D13
Love Lane - p404 P6
Lower Belgrave Street -
p400 H10
Lower Grosvenor Place -
p400 H9
Lower James Street - p400 J7,
p406 V3
Lower Marsh - p401 M9
Lower Sloane Street -
p400 G11
Lower Thames Street -
p405 Q7/R7
Lowndes Square - p397 F9

Lowndes Street - p400 G9
Lucan Place - p397 E10/11
Ludgate Hill - p404 O6
Luke Street - p403 Q4/R4
Lumley Street - p398 G6
Luxbough Street - p398 G4/5
Lyall Mews - p400 G10
Lyall Street - p400 G10

Macclesfield Road - p402 P3
Macklin Street - p399 L6,
p407 Z1/2
Maddox Street - p398 J6,
p406 U2/3
Maguire Street - p405 S9
Maida Avenue - p395 D4
Maiden Lane WC2 - p401 L7,
p407 Y4
Maiden Lane SE1 - p404 P8
Malet Street - p399 K4/5
Mallow Street - p403 Q4
Maltby Street - p405 R9/10
Malvern Road - p403 S1
Manchester Square -
p398 G5/6
Manchester Street - p398 G5
Manciple Street - p405 Q9
Manette Street - p399 K6,
p406 W2
Manresa Road - p397 E11/12
Mansell Street - p405 S6/7
Mansfield Street - p398 H5
Manson Mews - p397 D10
Manson Place - p397 D10
Maple Street - p398 J4
Mapledene Road - p403 S1
Marble Quay - p405 S8
Marchbank Road - p396 A12
Marchmont Street - p399 L4
Margaret Street - p398 J5/6
Margaretta Terrace - p397 E12
Margery Street - p402 N3
Mark Lane - p405 R7
Market Mews - p400 H8
Markham Square - p397 F11
Markham Street - p397 F11
Marlborough Road - p400 J8
Marloes Road - p396 B9/10
Marshall Street - p398 J6,
p406 V2/3
Marshalsea Road - p404 P9
Marsham Street - p401 K10/11
Marylands Road - p394 B4
Marylebone High Street -
p398 G4/5
Marylebone Lane - p398 G5/H6
Marylebone Mews - p398 H5
Marylebone Road - p395 F4/5,
p398 G4
Marylebone Street - p398 G5
Marylee Way - p401 M11
Maunsel Street - p401 K10
Maxwell Road - p396 B13
Mayfair Place - p400 H7
Mcleod's Mews - p396 C10
Meadow Row - p404 P10
Meard Street - p399 K6,
p406 W3
Mecklenburgh Square -
p399 M4
Medburn Street - p399 K2
Medway Street - p401 K10
Melbury Court - p396 A9
Melbury Road - p396 A9
Melbury Terrace - p395 F4
Melcombe Street - p395 F4
Melton Court - p397 D10
Melton Street - p399 K3
Mepham Street - p401 M8
Mercer Street - p399 L6,
p407 Y3
Merlin Street - p402 N3
Mermaid Court - p404 P9
Merrick Square - p404 P10
Mews Street - p405 S8
Meymott Street - p404 N8
Micawber Street - p402 P3
Michael Road - p396 B13/C13
Mickelthwaite Road - p396 B12
Middle Temple Lane -
p404 N6/7
Middlesex Street - p405 R5/6

Middleton Road - p403 S1
Midland Road - p399 L2/3
Milford Lane - p401 M6/7
Milford Street - p402 P5
Milk Street - p404 P6
Mill Street W1 - p400 H6/J6,
p406 U3
Mill Street SE1 - p405 S9
Millbank - p401 L10/11
Millman Street - p399 M4
Milman's Street -
p397 D12/13
Milner Place - p402 N1/O1
Milner Square - p402 N1/O1
Milner Street - p397 F10
Mincing Lane - p405 R7
Minera Mews - p400 G10
Minories - p405 R6/7
Mintern Street - p403 Q2
Mitchell Street - p402 P4
Mitre Road - p404 N9
Molyneux Street - p395 F5
Monck Street - p401 K10
Monmouth Street - p399 L6,
p407 X2/3
Montagu Mansions - p398 G5
Montagu Mews South -
p395 F6
Montagu Place - p395 F5
Montagu Square - p395 F5
Montagu Street - p395 F6
Montague Place - p399 K5
Montague Street - p399 L5
Montpelier Place - p397 E9
Montpelier Street - p397 E9
Montpelier Terrace - p397 E9
Montpelier Walk - p397 E9
Montrose Place - p400 G9
Monument Street - p405 Q7
Moor Lane - p402 P5
Moor Street - p399 K6,
p407 X2/3
Moore Park Road - p396 B13
Moore Street - p397 F10
Moorfields - p403 Q5
Moorgate - p403 Q5,
p405 Q5/6
Moorhouse Road - p394 A5/6
Mora Street - p402 P3
Moreland Street - p402 O3/3
Moreton Road - p402 P1
Moreton Street - p400 J11
Morgan's Lane - p405 Q8
Morley Street - p404 N9
Mornington Crescent - p398 J2
Mornington Place - p398 J2
Mornington Street - p398 H2/J2
Mornington Terrace -
p398 H2/J2
Morocco Street - p405 Q9
Morpeth Terrace - p400 J10
Mortimer Road - p403 R1
Mortimer Street - p398 J5,
p406 U1
Morwell Street - p399 K5,
p406 W1
Moscow Road - p394 B6
Mossop Street - p397 E10
Motcomb Street - p400 G9
Mount Pleasant - p399 M4
Mount Row - p400 H7
Mount Street - p400 G7
Moxon Street - p398 G5
Mund Street - p396 A11
Munster Square -
p398 H3/4/J3/4
Muriel Street - p399 M2
Murray Grove - p402 P3,
p403 Q3
Museum Street - p399 L5/6,
p407 Y1
Musgrave Crescent - p396 B13
Myddelton Square - p402 N3
Myddelton Street - p402 N3/O3
Mylne Street - p402 N3

Napier Grove - p402 P2
Nash Street - p398 H3
Nassau Street - p398 J5
Nazral Street - p403 R3
Neal Street - p399 L6, p407 Y2
Neal's Yard - p407 Y2

STREET INDEX

Nebraska Street - p404 P9
Neckinger - p405 S10
Nelson Terrace - p402 O3
Nesham Street - p405 S8
Netherton Grove - p396 C12
Netley Street - p398 J3
Nevern Place - p396 A10/B10
Nevern Square - p396 A11
Neville Street - p397 D11
New Bond Street - p398 H6,
p400 H6/7
New Bridge Street - p404 O6
New Burlington Place - p400
J6, p406 U3
New Cavendish Street -
p398 G5/H5/J5
New Change - p404 O6
New Compton Street - p399
K6, p407 X2
New Fetter Lane - p404 N5
New Globe Walk - p404 O8/P7
New Inn Yard - p403 R4
New North Road - p402 P1,
p403 Q2/3
New North Street - p399 L5
New Oxford Street - p399
K6/L5, p407 X1/Y1
New Quebec Street - p395 F6
New Row - p401 L7, p407 Y4
New Square - p399 M6
New Street - p404 N5/6,
p405 R5/6
New Wharf Road - p399 M2
Newburgh Street - p398 J6,
p406 U2/V2
Newcastle Place - p395 E5
Newcomen Street - p404 P9/Q9
Newgate Street - p404 O6
Newington Causeway -
p404 O9/10
Newman Street - p398 J5,
p406 V1
Newnham Terrace - p401 M9
Newport Place - p401 K6/7,
p407 X3
Newport Street -
p401 L11/M10/11
Newton Road - p394 B6
Newton Street - p399 L5/6,
p407 Z1
Nicholas Lane - p405 Q7
Nile Street - p402 P3, p403 Q3
Noble Street - p404 P5/6
Noel Road - p402 O2
Noel Street - p398 J6, p406 V2
Norfolk Crescent - p395 E5
Norfolk Place - p395 E5/6
Norfolk Square - p395 D6/E6
North Audley Street - p398 G6
North Carriage Drive -
p395 E6/F6
North Crescent - p399 K5
North End Road - p396 A12/13
North Gower Street - p398 J3/4
North Mews - p399 M4
North Row - p398 G6
North Wharf Road - p395 D5
Northampton Road - p402 N4
Northampton Square - p402 O3
Northburgh Street - p402 O4
Northchurch Road - p403 Q1
Northdown Street - p399 M2
Northington Street - p399 M4
Northumberland Avenue - p401
L8, p407 X5/Y1
Northumberland Place -
p394 A5/6
Notting Hill Gate - p394 A7
Nottingham Place - p398 G4
Nottingham Street - p398 G4/5
Nutford Place - p395 F5
Nuttal Street - p403 R2

Oakey Lane - p404 N9/10
Oakley Gardens - p397 E12
Oakley Square - p398 J2
Oakley Street - p397 E12
Ogle Street - p398 J5
Old Bailey - p404 O6
Old Barrack Yard - p400 G9
Old Bond Street - p400 J7,
p406 U4/5

Old Broad Street - p405 Q6
Old Brompton Road - p396
C11, p397 D11
Old Burlington Street - p400 J7,
p406 U3/4
Old Castle Street - p405 S6
Old Cavendish Street -
p398 H6
Old Church Street -
p397 D11/12/E12
Old Compton Street -
p399 K6, p406 W3
Old Court Place - p394 B8
Old Gloucester Street - p399 L5
Old Jamaica Road - p405 S10
Old Jewry - p404 P6
Old Marylebone Road -
p395 E5/F5
Old Mitre Court - p404 N6
Old Montagu Street - p405 S5/6
Old Nichol Street - p403 R4/S4
Old Paradise Street - p401 M10
Old Park Lane - p400 G8
Old Pye Street - p401 K10
Old Quebec Street - p398 G6
Old Queen Street - p401 K9
Old Street - p402 P4, p403
Q4/R4
Oldbury Place - p398 G4
Ongar Road - p396 A12/B12
Onslow Gardens - p397 D11
Onslow Square - p397
D10/11/E10/11
Orange Street - p401 K7,
p406 W4
Orchard Street - p398 G6
Orde Hall Street - p399 M5
Orme Court - p394 B7
Orme Lane - p394 B7
Ormonde West Road -
p397 F12
Ormsby Street - p403 R2
Orsett Terrace - p394 C5
Osborn Street - p405 S6
Osnaburgh Street - p398 H4
Ossington Street - p394 B7
Ossulston Street - p399 K3
Outer Circle - p398 G4/H2/3/4
Ovington Gardens - p397 E9/10
Ovington Street - p397 F10
Oxendon Street - p401 K7,
p406 W4
Oxford Square - p395 E6
Oxford Street - p398 G6/H6/J6,
p399 K6

Packington Square - p402 P2
Packington Street - p402 O1/P1
Paddington Green - p395 D5
Paddington Street - p398 G5
Page Street - p401 K10
Pakenham Street - p399 M4
Palace Avenue - p394 B8/C8
Palace Court - p394 B6/7
Palace Garden Mews - p394 B7
Palace Gardens Terrace -
p394 B7/8
Palace Gate - p396 C9
Pall Mall - p400 J8, p401 K8,
p406 W5
Palmer Street - p400 J9
Panton Street - p401 K7,
p406 W4
Paradise Walk - p397 F12
Paris Garden - p404 N8
Park Crescent - p398 H4
Park Crescent Mews East -
p398 H4
Park Crescent Mews West -
p398 H4
Park Lane - p395 F6, p400 G7/8
Park Place - p400 J8, p406 U5
Park Place Villas - p395 D4
Park Square East - p398 H4
Park Square Mews - p398 H4
Park Square West - p398 H4
Park Street SE1 - p404 P8
Park Street W1 - p400 G7
Park Village East - p398 H2
Park Village West - p398 H2
Park Walk - p397 D12
Park West Place - p395 F6

Parker Street - p399 L6,
p407 Z1/2
Parkfield Street - p402 N2
Parkgate Road - p397 E13
Parliament Square - p401 K9
Passmore Street - p400 G11
Pater Street - p396 A9
Paternoster Row - p404 O6
Paternoster Square - p404 O6
Paul Street - p403 Q4
Paultons Square - p397 D12
Paultons Street - p397 E12
Pavilion Road - p397 F9/10
Pear Tree Court - p402 N4
Pear Tree Street - p402 O4/4
Pearman Street - p404 N9
Pearson Street - p403 R2
Pedley Street - p403 S4
Peel Street - p394 A7/8
Pelham Crescent - p397 E10
Pelham Place - p397 E10
Pelham Street - p397 E10
Pembridge Crescent - p394 A6
Pembridge Gardens - p394 A7
Pembridge Mews - p394 A6
Pembridge Place - p394 A6
Pembridge Road - p394 A7
Pembridge Square - p394
A5/B6
Pembridge Villas - p394 A6
Pembroke Gardens - p396 A10
Pembroke Gardens Close -
p396 A10
Pembroke Road - p396 A10
Pembroke Villas - p396 A10
Pembroke Walk - p396 A10
Penfold Place - p395 E4/5
Penfold Street - p395 E4
Penn Street - p403 Q2
Pennant Mews - p396 B10
Penton Rise - p399 M3
Penton Street - p402 N2
Pentonville Road - p399 L3/M3,
p402 N2
Penywern Road - p396 B11
Pepper Street - p404 O8
Pepys Street - p405 R7
Percey Circus - p399 M3
Percival Street - p402 O4
Percy Street - p399 K5,
p406 V1/W1
Peter Street - p399 K6,
p406 W3
Petersham Lane - p396 C9
Petersham Place - p396 C9
Peto Place - p398 H4
Petty France - p400 J9
Phene Street - p397 E12
Philbeach Gardens - p396 A11
Phillimore Gardens - p394 A8/9,
p396 A9
Phillimore Walk - p394 B9,
p396 A9
Phillimore Place - p394 A9
Phillip Street - p403 R2
Philpott Lane - p405 Q7
Phoenix Place - p399 M4
Phoenix Road - p399 K2/3
Phoenix Street - p399 K6,
p407 X2
Piccadilly - p400 H8/J7,
p406 U5/V4
Piccadilly Circus - p401 K7,
p406 W4
Pickard Street - p402 O3
Pickering Mews - p394 C5/6
Pilgrim Street - p404 O6
Pilgrimage Street - p404 P9/Q9
Pimlico Road - p400 G11
Pindar Street - p403 Q5
Pinder Street - p403 Q5/R5
Pitfield Street - p403 Q2/3/4/R2
Pitt Street - p394 B8
Platt Street - p399 K2
Plough Yard - p403 R4
Plumbers Row - p405 S6
Plympton Street - p395 E4
Pocock Street - p404 O8/9
Poland Street - p398 J6,
p406 V2
Polygon Road - p399 K2
Pond Place - p397 E11

Ponsonby Place - p401 K11
Pont Street - p397 F10,
p400 G10
Poole Street - p403 Q2
Popham Road - p402 P1
Popham Street - p402 P1
Poplar Place - p394 B6/C6
Porchester Gardens -
p394 B6/C6
Porchester Road - p394 C5
Porchester Square - p394 C5
Porchester Terrace - p394 C6/7
Porchester Terrace North -
p394 C5
Porlock Street - p405 Q9
Porter Street SE1 - p404 P8
Porter Street W1 - p398 G4
Portland Place - p398 H4/5
Portman Close - p398 G5
Portman Mews South -
p398 G6
Portman Square - p398 G6
Portman Street - p398 G6
Portobello Road - p394 A6
Portpool Lane - p402 N5
Portsea Place - p395 F6
Portsoken Street - p405 R7/S7
Portugal Street - p399 M6
Potier Street - p405 Q10
Powis Gardens - p394 A5
Powis Square - p394 A6
Powis Terrace - p394 A5
Pownall Row - p403 S2
Praed Street - p395 D6/E5
Pratt Walk - p401 M10
Prebend Street - p402 P1/2
Prescot Street - p405 S7
Primrose Street - p403 Q5/R5
Prince Consort Road - p397 D9
Princelet Street - p403 S5
Princes Gardens - p397 D9/E9
Prince's Square - p394 B6
Princes Street EC2 - p404
P6/Q6
Princes Street W1 - p398 H6,
p406 U2
Princeton Street - p399 M5
Prioress Street - p405 Q10
Priory Green - p399 M2
Priory Walk - p396 C11
Procter Street - p399 M5,
p407 Z1
Provost Street - p403 Q3
Pudding Lane - p405 Q7
Purbrook Street - p405 R10
Purcell Street - p403 R2
Purchese Street - p399 K2

Quaker Street - p403 S5
Queen Anne Mews - p398 H5
Queen Anne Street - p398 H5
Queen Anne's Gate - p401 K9
Queen Elizabeth Street -
p405 R9
Queen Square - p399 L4
Queen Street EC4 - p404 P6/7
Queen Street W1 - p400 H7
Queen Victoria Street -
p404 O7/P6/7
Queen's Gardens - p394 C6
Queens Gate - p397 D9/10
Queen's Gate Gardens -
p396 C10
Queen's Gate Mews - p396 C9
Queen's Gate Place Mews -
p397 D10
Queen's Gate Terrace - p396
C9, p397 D9
Queen's Walk - p400 J8
Queensborough Terrace -
p394 C6/7
Queensbridge Road -
p403 S1/2
Queensbury Place - p397 D10
Queensway - p394 B5/6/C6/7
Quilter Street - p403 S3

Racton Road - p396 A12
Radley Mews - p396 B10
Radnor Mews - p395 E6
Radnor Place - p395 E6
Radnor Street - p402 P4

Street Index

Radnor Walk - p397 F11/12
Railway Approach - p405 Q8
Railway Street - p399 L2
Raleigh Street - p402 O2
Ramillies Place - p398 J6, p406 U2
Ramillies Street - p398 J6, p406 U2
Rampayne Street - p401 K11
Randall Road - p401 L11
Randall Row - p401 L11
Randolph Road - p394 C4, p395 D4
Ranelagh Grove - p400 G11
Ranston Street - p395 E4
Raphael Street - p397 F9
Rathbone Place - p399 K5, p406 W1
Rathbone Street - p398 J5
Ravenscroft Street - p403 S3
Ravent Road - p401 M10/11
Rawlings Street - p397 F10
Rawstone Street - p402 O3
Raymond Buildings - p399 M5
Red Lion Square - p399 M5
Red Lion Street - p399 M5
Redan Place - p394 B6
Redburn Street - p397 F12
Redchurch Street - p403 R4/S4
Redcliffe Gardens - p396 B11/C12
Redcliffe Mews - p396 C12
Redcliffe Place - p396 C12
Redcliffe Road - p396 C12
Redcliffe Square - p396 B11/C11
Redcliffe Street - p396 C12
Redcross Way - p404 P8/9
Redesdale Street - p397 F12
Redfield Lane - p396 B10
Redhill Street - p398 H2/3
Reece Mews - p397 D10
Reeves Mews - p400 G7
Regan Way - p403 R2/3
Regency Street - p401 K10/11
Regent Square - p399 L3
Regent Street - p398 J6, p400 J6/7, p401 K7, p406 U1/2/3/V4/W4/5
Remnant Street - p399 M6, p407 Z1
Rennie Street - p404 N7
Rewell Street - p396 C13
Rheidol Terrace - p402 P2
Richmond Avenue - p402 N1
Richmond Crescent - p402 N1
Richmond Terrace - p401 L8
Ridgmount Gardens - p399 K4/5
Ridgmount Street - p399 K5
Riding House Street - p398 J5
Riley Road - p405 R9/10
Riley Street - p397 D13
Ripplevale Grove - p402 N1
Risbor Street - p404 O8
Ritchie Street - p402 N2
River Street - p402 N3
Rivington Street - p403 R4
Robert Adam Street - p398 G5
Robert Street - p398 H3/J3
Rochester Row - p400 J10
Rockingham Street - p404 O10/P10
Rodmarton Street - p398 G5
Rodney Street - p399 M2
Roger Street - p399 M4
Roland Gardens - p396 C11, p397 D11
Romilly Street - p399 K6, p406 W3, p407 X3
Romney Street - p401 K10
Rood Lane - p405 Q7
Ropemaker Street - p403 Q5
Ropley Street - p403 S3
Rosary Gardens - p396 C11
Rose Street - p401 L7, p407 Y3
Rosebery Avenue - p402 N3/4
Rosemoor Street - p397 F10
Rotary Street - p404 O9

Rotherfield Street - p402 P1, p403 Q1
Rothesay Street - p405 Q10
Rotten Row - p395 E8/F8
Roupell Street - p404 N8
Royal Avenue - p397 F11
Royal Hospital Road - p397 F11/12
Royal Mint Street - p405 S7
Royal Street - p401 M9
Rugby Street - p399 M4
Rumbold Road - p396 B13
Rupert Street - p401 K6/7, p406 W3/4
Rushworth Street - p404 O9
Russell Square - p399 L4/5
Russell Street - p399 L6, p401 L6, p407 Z3
Russia Row - p404 P6
Rutherford Street - p401 K10
Rutland Gate - p397 E9
Rutland Street - p397 E9

Sackville Street - p400 J7, p406 U4/V4
Saffron Hill - p402 N5
Sail Street - p401 M10
St Alban's Street - p401 K7, p406 W4
St Alphage Gardens - p402 P9
St Andrews Hill - p404 O6
St Andrew's Place - p398 H4
St Anne's Court - p399 K6, p406 W2
St Anne's Street - p401 K9/10
St Botolph Street - p405 R6
St Bride Street - p404 N6
St Chad's Place - p399 L3/M3
St Chad's Street - p399 L3
St Christopher's Place - p398 H6
St Clement's Lane - p399 M6
St Cross Street - p402 N5
St Dunstens Hill - p405 Q7
St George Street - p398 H6, p400 H6
St George's Circus - p404 N9
St George's Drive - p400 H11/J11
St George's Fields - p395 E6/F6
St George's Road - p404 N10/O10
St Giles High Street - p399 K6, p407 X2
St Helen's Place - p405 R6
St James's Place - p400 J8
St James's Square - p400 J7/8, p406 V5
St James's Street - p400 J8
St John Street - p402 O3/4/5
St John's Lane - p402 O4/5
St Katherine's Way - p405 S8
St Leonard's Terrace - p397 F11
St Loo Avenue - p397 F12
St Luke's Road - p394 A5
St Luke's Street - p397 E11
St Mark Street - p405 S7
St Martin's Lane - p401 L7, p407 X4
St Mary At Hill - p405 Q7
St Mary Axe - p405 R6
St Mary's Square - p395 D5
St Mary's Terrace - p395 D4
St Matthews Row - p403 S4
St Michael's Street - p395 E5
St Pancras Road - p399 K2
St Paul Street - p402 P1/2
St Paul's Churchyard - p404 O6
St Peters Street - p402 O2
St Petersburgh Mews - p394 B6/7
St Petersburgh Place - p394 B6/7
St Swithins Lane - p405 Q6/7
St Thomas Street - p405 Q8/9
St Vincent Street - p398 G5
Salamanca Street - p401 L11
Sale Place - p395 E5
Salem Road - p394 B6
Sandell Street - p404 N8

Sandland Street - p399 M5
Sandwich Street - p399 L3
Sans Walk - p402 N4
Savile Row - p400 J7, p406 U3/4
Savoy Place - p401 L7/M7, p407 Z4
Savoy Street - p401 M7, p407 Z4
Sawyer Street - p404 O8/9
Scala Street - p398 J5
Scarsdale Villas - p396 A10/B9
Sclater Street - p403 S4
Scores Street - p404 O8
Scott Lidgett Crescent - p405 S10
Scriven Street - p403 S1
Scrutton Street - p403 Q4/R4
Seacoal Lane - p404 O6
Seaford Street - p399 L3
Seagrave Road - p396 B12
Searles Close - p397 E13
Sebastian Street - p402 O3
Sebbon Street - p402 O1
Sedlescombe Road - p396 A12
Seething Lane - p405 R7
Sekforde Street - p402 O4
Selwood Terrace - p397 D11
Semley Place - p400 G11/H11
Senior Street - p394 B4
Serle Street - p399 M6
Serpentine Road - p395 E8/F8
Seven Dials - p399 L6, p407 X2
Seward Street - p402 O4/4
Seymour Place - p395 F5/6
Seymour Street - p395 F6
Seymour Walk - p396 C12
Shad Thames - p405 R8/S9
Shaftesbury Avenue - p401 K6/7/L6, p406 W3, p407 X2/Y1/2
Shaftesbury Street - p402 P2
Shalcomb Street - p397 D12
Shand Street - p405 Q9/R8
Shawfield Street - p397 E11/F12
Sheffield Terrace - p394 A8/B8
Sheldrake Place - p394 A8
Shelton Street - p399 L6, p407 Y2/3
Shenfield Street - p403 R3
Shepherd Street - p400 H8
Shepherdess Walk - p402 P2/3
Shepherds Market - p400 H8
Shepperton Road - p402 P1, p403 Q1
Sherbourne Street - p403 Q1
Sherwood Street - p400 J7, p406 V4
Shipton Street - p403 S3
Shoe Lane - p404 N5/6
Shoreditch High Street - p403 R4/5
Shorter Street - p405 R7/S7
Shorts Gardens - p399 L6, p407 Y2
Shottendene Road - p396 A13
Shouldham Street - p395 F5
Shrewsbury Road - p394 A5
Shroton Street - p395 E4
Shrubland Road - p403 S1
Sicilian Avenue - p399 L5, p407 Z1
Siddons Lane - p395 F4
Sidford Place - p401 M10
Sidmouth Street - p399 L3/M3
Silex Street - p404 O9
Silk Street - p402 P5
Skinner Street - p402 N4/O4
Skinners Lane - p404 P7
Slaidburn Street - p396 C12/13
Sloane Avenue - p397 E10/F11
Sloane Gardens - p400 G11
Sloane Street - p397 F9/10
Smith Square - p401 K10/L10
Smith Street - p397 F11/12
Smith Terrace - p397 F11
Snowden Street - p403 R5
Snowsfields - p405 Q9
Soho Square - p399 K6, p406 W2

Soho Street - p399 K6, p406 W1/2
Somers Crescent - p395 E6
Soton Place - p399 L5
South Audley Street - p400 G7
South Carriage Drive - p395 E8/F8/G8
South Crescent - p399 K5
South Eaton Place - p400 G10
South End Row - p396 B9
South Molton Lane - p398 H6
South Molton Street - p398 H6
South Parade - p397 D11
South Place - p403 Q5
South Street - p400 G7
South Terrace - p397 E10
South Wharf Road - p395 D5/E5
Southampton Row - p399 L5
Southampton Street - p401 L7, p407 Z3/4
Southgate Grove - p403 Q1
Southgate Road - p403 Q1
Southwark Bridge - p404 P7
Southwark Bridge Road - p404 O9/10/P7/8
Southwark Street - p404 O8/P8
Southwick Street - p395 E5/6
Spa Road - p405 S10
Spencer Street - p402 O3
Spital Square - p403 R5
Spital Street - p403 S5
Sprimont Place - p397 F11
Spring Street - p395 D6
Spur Road - p400 J9
Spurgeon Street - p404 P10
Stableyard Road - p400 J8
Stacey Street - p399 K6, p407 X2
Stafford Place - p400 J9
Stafford Terrace - p396 A9
Stag Place - p400 J9
Stamford Street - p404 N8
Stanford Road - p396 B9
Stanford Street - p400 J11
Stanhope Gardens - p396 C10, p397 D10
Stanhope Mews East - p397 D10
Stanhope Mews West - p396 C10
Stanhope Place - p395 F6
Stanhope Street - p398 J3
Stanhope Terrace - p395 E6
Stanway Street - p403 R2/3
Staple Street - p405 Q9
Star Street - p395 E5
Station Road - p401 M9
Stean Street - p403 R1
Stephen Street - p399 K5, p406 W1
Stephenson Way - p398 J3/4
Steward Street - p403 R5
Stillington Street - p400 J10
Stone Buildings - p399 M6
Stone Street - p404 N6
Stones End Street - p404 O9
Stoney Lane - p405 R6
Stoney Street - p404 P8
Store Street - p399 K5
Storey's Gate - p401 K9
Stourcliffe Street - p395 F6
Strand - p401 L7/M6/7, p407 Y4/5
Stratford Place - p398 H6
Stratford Road - p396 B10
Strathearn Place - p395 E6
Stratton Street - p400 H7/8
Streatham Street - p399 K5/L5, p407 X1/Y1
Stukeley Street - p399 L6, p407 Y1/2/Z1
Sturge Street - p404 O9
Sturt Street - p402 P2
Suffolk Street - p401 K7, p406 W4/5
Sumner Place - p397 D10/11
Sumner Street - p404 O8/P8
Sun Street - p403 Q5
Surrey Row - p404 O8/9
Surrey Street - p401 M6/7
Sussex Gardens - p395 E5/6

STREET INDEX

Sussex Place - p395 E6
Sussex Square - p395 D6/E6
Sutherland Avenue - p394 B4
Sutherland Place - p394 A5/6
Sutton Row - p399 K6, p406 W2
Swallow Street - p400 J7, p406 V4
Swan Street - p404 P9
Swan Walk - p397 F12
Swanfield Street - p403 S4
Sweeney Court - p405 S10
Swinton Street - p399 M3
Sydney Close - p397 E11
Sydney Place - p397 E11
Sydney Street - p397 E11
Symons Street - p397 F11

Tabard Street - p404 P9/Q10
Tabernacle Street - p403 Q4
Tachbrook Street - p400 J11
Tadema Road - p396 C13
Talbot Road - p394 A5/B5
Talbot Square - p395 D6
Tamworth Farm Lane - p396 A12
Tanner Street - p405 R9
Taplow Street - p402 P3
Tavistock Crescent - p394 A5
Tavistock Place - p399 L4
Tavistock Road - p394 A5
Tavistock Square - p399 K4
Tavistock Street - p401 L6/7, p407 Z3
Taviton Street - p399 K4
Tedworth Square - p397 F12
Temple Avenue - p404 N7
Temple Place - p401 M7
Tennis Street - p404 P9
Tetcott Road - p396 C11
Thanet Street - p399 L3
Thaxton Road - p396 A12
Thayer Street - p398 G5
The Boltons - p396 C11
The Broad Walk - p394 C7/8
The Cut - p404 N8
The Grange - p405 R10
The Little Boltons - p396 C11
The Mall - p401 J8/K8
The Vale - p397 D12
Theberton Street - p402 N1/O1
Theed Street - p404 N8
Theobald's Road - p399 L5/M5
Thirleby Road - p400 J10
Thomas More Street - p405 S8
Thorn Place - p395 F5
Thorndike Close - p396 C13
Thorney Crescent - p397 E13
Thorney Street - p401 L10
Thornhill Road - p402 N1
Thrale Street - p404 P8
Threadneedle Street - p405 Q6
Three Kings Yard - p400 H6
Throgmorton Avenue - p405 Q6
Throgmorton Street - p405 Q6
Thurloe Place - p397 E10
Thurloe Square - p397 E10
Thurtle Road - p403 S2
Tilney Street - p400 G7
Tinworth Street - p401 L11
Tite Street - p397 F12
Tiverton Street - p404 O10
Tolpuddle Street - p402 N2
Tonbridge Street - p399 L3
Tooley Street - p405 Q8/R8/9
Tor Gardens - p394 A8
Torrington Place - p399 K4
Torrington Square - p399 K4
Tothill Street - p401 K9
Tottenham Court Road - p398 J4, p399 K5
Tottenham Street - p398 J5
Tower Bridge - p405 R8
Tower Bridge Approach - p405 R8/S7
Tower Bridge Road - p405 Q10/R8/9/10
Tower Hill - p405 R7
Tower Street - p399 K6, p407 X3
Toynbee Street - p405 S5/6

Trafalgar Square - p401 K7, p407 X5
Transept Street - p395 E5
Trebovir Road - p396 B11
Tregunter Road - p396 C12
Trevor Place - p397 E9
Trinity Square - p405 R7
Trinity Street - p404 P9/10
Triton Square - p398 J4
Trump Street - p404 P6
Tryon Street - p397 F11
Tudor Street - p404 N6
Tufton Street - p401 K10
Turks Row - p397 F11, p400 G11
Turnmill Street - p402 N5/O5
Tyers Street - p401 M10
Tysoe Street - p402 N3

Ufford Street - p404 N9
Ufton Road - p403 Q1
Ulster Place - p398 H4
Undershaft - p405 Q6/R6
Underwood Street - p402 P3
Union Street - p404 O8/P8
Union Walk - p403 R3
University Street - p398 J4, p399 K4
Upcerne Road - p396 C13
Upper Belgrave Street - p400 G9
Upper Berkeley Street - p395 F6
Upper Brook Street - p400 G7
Upper Cheyne Row - p397 E12
Upper Ground - p404 N7/8
Upper Harley Street - p398 H4
Upper James Street - p400 J6, p406 V3
Upper Marsh - p401 M9
Upper Montagu Street - p395 F5
Upper Phillimore Gardens - p394 A8/9
Upper St Martin's Lane - p401 L6, p407 X3
Upper Street - p402 N2/O1/2
Upper Thames Street - p404 O7/P7
Upper Wimpole Street - p398 H5
Upper Woburn Place - p399 K3/4
Uverdale Road - p396 C13
Uxbridge Street - p394 A7

Valentine Place - p404 N9
Vandon Street - p400 J9
Vanston Place - p396 A13
Varndell Street - p398 J3
Vaughan Way - p405 S7
Vauxhall Bridge - p400 J10/11, p401 K11
Vauxhall Street - p401 M11
Vauxhall Walk - p401 L11/M11
Venables Street - p395 E4
Vere Street - p398 H6
Vernon Rise - p399 M3
Verulam Street - p402 N5
Vicarage Gate - p394 B8
Victoria Embankment - p401 L7/8/M7, p404 N7, p407 Z4
Victoria Garden Mews - p394 B7
Victoria Grove - p396 C9
Victoria Road - p394 C9/3 C9
Victoria Square - p400 H9
Victoria Street - p400 H10/J10/K9/8
Vigo Street - p400 J7, p406 U4
Villiers Street - p401 L7/8, p407 Y5
Vincent Square - p400 J10/11, p401 K10/11
Vincent Street - p401 K10
Vincent Terrace - p402 O2
Vine Street - p400 J7, p406 V4
Virgil Street - p401 M10
Virginia Road - p403 R4/S3/4

Wakefield Street - p399 L3/4
Wakley Street - p402 O3

Walbrook - p404 P6/7
Walham Grove - p396 A13/B12
Walnut Tree Walk - p401 M10
Walpole Street - p397 F11
Walton Street - p397 E10/F10
Wandon Road - p396 C13
Wardour Street - p398 J6, p399 K6, p401 K7, p406 V2/W2/3/4
Warner Street - p402 N4
Warren Street - p398 J4
Warwick Avenue - p394 C4, p395 D4/5
Warwick Crescent - p394 C5
Warwick Gardens - p396 A10
Warwick Lane - p404 O6
Warwick Place - p394 C4
Warwick Road - p396 A10/11/B11
Warwick Square - p400 J11
Warwick Street - p400 J7, p406 V3/4
Warwick Way - p400 H11/J11
Waterford Road - p396 B13
Waterloo Bridge - p401 M7
Waterloo Place - p401 K7, p406 W5
Waterloo Road - p401 M8, p404 N8/9
Waterloo Terrace - p402 O1
Watling Street - p404 P6
Watton Place - p397 F9
Waverton Street - p400 H7
Webb Street - p405 Q10
Webber Row - p404 N9
Webber Street - p404 N9/O9
Weighhouse Street - p398 G6/H6
Welbeck Street - p398 H5
Welbeck Way - p398 H5
Wellington Row - p403 S3
Wellington Square - p397 F11
Wellington Street - p401 L6/7, p407 Z3
Wells Mews - p398 J5, p406 V1
Wells Street - p398 J5/6, p406 V1
Wenlock Road - p402 P2/3
Wenlock Street - p402 P2, p403 Q2
Wentworth Street - p405 R6/S6
Werrington Street - p399 K2/3
West Carriage Drive - p395 E7
West Central Street - p399 L6, p407 Y1
West Cromwell Road - p396 A11
West Halkin Street - p400 G9
West Smithfield - p402 O5
West Square - p404 N10
West Street - p399 K6, p407 X3
West Tenter Street - p405 S7
Westbourne Crescent - p395 D6
Westbourne Park Road - p394 A5/B5
Westbourne Gardens - p394 B5
Westbourne Grove - p394 A6/B6
Westbourne Park Villas - p394 B5
Westbourne Street - p395 D6
Westbourne Terrace - p394 C5, p395 D6
Westgate Terrace - p396 B12
Westminster Bridge - p401 L9
Westminster Bridge Road - p401 M9, p404 N9
Westmoreland Street - p398 H5
Weston Rise - p399 M3
Weston Street - p405 Q9/10
Weston Street - p405 Q9
Westway Ap40 (M) - p394 A4/B5/C5
Wetherby Gardens - p396 C11
Weymouth Mews - p398 H5
Weymouth Street - p398 G5/H5
Weymouth Terrace - p403 S2/3
Wharf Road - p402 P2/3
Wharfedale Road - p399 L2/M2
Wharton Street - p399 M3
Wheeler Street - p403 R4/5

Whetstone Park - p399 M5
Whidborne Street - p399 L3
Whiskin Street - p402 O3
Whistlers Avenue - p397 D13/E13
Whiston Road - p403 R2/S2
Whitcomb Street - p401 K7, p406 W4, p407 X4/5
White Church Lane - p405 S6
White Horse Street - p400 H8
White Lion Hill - p404 O7
White Lion Street - p402 N2
Whitechapel High Street - p405 S6
Whitechapel Road - p405 S6
Whitecross Street - p402 P4/5
Whitefriars Street - p404 N6
Whitehall - p401 L8/9
Whitehall Place - p401 L8
Whiteheads Grove - p397 F11
White's Gardens - p405 Q9/R9
White's Row - p405 R5
Whitfield Street - p398 J4/5, p399 K5
Whitgift Street - p401 L11/M11
Whitmore Road - p403 R2
Whittlesey Street - p404 N8
Wicklow Street - p399 M3
Wigmore Place - p398 H5
Wigmore Street - p398 G6
Wild Court - p399 L6, p407 Z2
Wild Street - p399 L6, p407 Z2
Wild's Rent - p405 Q10
Wilfred Street - p400 J9
Wilkes Street - p403 S5
William IV Street - p401 L7, p407 Y4
William Mews - p400 G9
William Road - p398 J3
William Street - p395 F8/9
Willow Place - p400 J10
Willow Street - p403 Q4
Wilmington Square - p402 N3/4
Wilson Street - p403 Q5
Wilton Crescent - p400 G9
Wilton Mews - p400 G9
Wilton Place - p400 G9
Wilton Road - p400 H10/J10
Wilton Row - p400 G9
Wilton Square - p403 Q1
Wilton Street - p400 H9
Wimbourne Street - p403 Q2
Wimpole Mews - p398 H5
Wimpole Street - p398 H5
Winchester Street - p400 H11
Windmill Street - p399 K5
Windsor Terrace - p402 P3
Winsland Street - p395 D5
Winsley Street - p398 J6, p406 V1
Woburn Place - p399 L4
Woburn Square - p399 K4
Woburn Walk - p399 K3
Wolseley Street - p405 S9
Wood Street - p404 P6
Woodbridge Street - p402 O4
Woodfall Street - p397 F11
Woods Mews - p400 G6/7
Woodseer Street - p403 S5
Woodstock Street - p398 H6
Wootton Street - p404 N8
Worfield Street - p397 E13
Worship Street - p403 Q4/5/R5
Wren Street - p399 M4
Wrights Lane - p396 B9
Wyclif Street - p402 O3
Wyndham Place - p395 F5
Wyndham Street - p395 F5
Wynford Road - p399 M2

Yardley Street - p402 N4
Yeoman's Row - p397 E10
York House Place - p394 B8
York Road - p401 M8/9
York Street - p395 F5, p398 G5
York Way - p399 L2
Young Street - p394 B9, p396 B9

Zoar Street - p404 O8

London Underground